Though the business corporation has played a central role in our economy, its evolution has received little attention. The history of the very early corporations and the histories of certain corporations have been written, but few scholars have set themselves to the task of presenting an aggregate picture that covers both a wide area and a long span of time. This study fills in some of the gap; it supplies a portion of the story of corporation development since 1800.

Many state series were compiled that deal with the number of incorporations and their authorized capital stock. Some series are for long periods; for example, one extends for approximately a century and a third. The incorporations of the pre-Civil War period are treated in combination, while an index of incorporations under general laws was constructed to describe the course of charters granted since 1860.

Analysis of the data has, among other things, produced a corporate life table, revealed patterns in the chartering of corporations of different size, and shown the relation between different states as chartering agencies. Through a detailed classification of incorporations according to their industrial objectives, the United States at work and at play is observed. This classification permits also an examination of the nature of the long cycles present in some of the data. For the shorter cycles in incorporations the peaks and troughs are related to those of business.

The extensive appendix gives by states the basic (usually monthly) data on the number of incorporations, on the total by size and by industrial objective, and on authorized capital stock. Information is thus made available for the further exploration of hypotheses concerning the incorporation of business enterprises.

The author, G. Heberton Evans, Jr., is Professor of Political Economy and Chairman of the Department of Political Economy at The Johns Hopkins University. He was a research associate of the National Bureau of Economic Research in 1939-40, at which time this study was begun.

Publications of the

National Bureau of Economic Research, Inc.

Number 49

BUSINESS INCORPORATIONS
IN THE UNITED STATES
1800–1943

Business Incorporations
in the
United States
1800-1943

GEORGE HEBERTON EVANS, JR.

Professor of Political Economy

The Johns Hopkins University

NATIONAL BUREAU OF ECONOMIC RESEARCH, INC.

PREFACE

Incorporation should be a matter of concern not merely to persons interested in an enterprise that uses the corporate form of business organization. A community in which the corporation is utilized is likely to be very different from one in which it is not utilized. The corporation may be regarded as a catalytic agent. Introduce it into a community and many things occur outside the particular business units incorporated. The investments of individuals, for example, would be rearranged to take advantage of new opportunities to diversify holdings. Enterprises could be launched that formerly could not have been started because of the large amounts of capital required. In turn, enterprises dependent upon the existence of such large undertakings could be started after the large ones had begun to function.

Despite the potent and conspicuous role of the corporation in the development of the economy of the United States, published data on corporations seem remarkably meager. For only about two years have we had a regular publication of the number of charters granted by each state. Dun & Bradstreet collects and publishes this information monthly. Previously an index based upon the experience of four states recorded the variations in the number of incorporations, but the individual state figures upon which the index was constructed were not readily obtainable. The index, moreover, covered only a short period. The Census and the Statistics of Income data on corporations supply other basic information. Of course, much can be learned about the large corporations of the country from the financial manuals, and a few governmental and private studies have contributed to our knowledge of corporations. But the information on our population of artificial persons—our corporations—is at best small when compared with that concerning the population of natural persons. When it is said that a certain number of natural persons were born in the United States during any recent year, the statement carries a rather definite meaning. A continuation of the sex ratio, a high degree of constancy in the relationship between white and colored births, etc. are, with reason, assumed. But even when the number of incorporations in a year is known, much additional material is needed in order to under-

stand the nature and the significance of the newly chartered units. This volume tries to describe in some detail the size and the nature of the additions to the population of artificial persons.

The corporation, in contrast to most other forms of business organization, must leave some public records of its existence. These records are not adequate for individual histories, but in the aggregate they reveal much about the general outlines of a large segment of business enterprise. The task of putting together the pieces of public record left by the separate corporations is enormous. A portion of the task is attempted here; much more can be done.

A complete set of time series dealing with the number of charters granted by all states in the United States and a definitive analysis of each series is not presented here. Some of the state incorporation series could have been extended; a few more states could have been covered for at least brief periods; and the various state incorporation series that have been compiled could have been examined more intensively. But I have reached that point of diminishing returns at which I feel it desirable to set forth what I have done. If it is found interesting, others can use it, add to it, or correct it. To facilitate addition and correction, I have tried to give in the numerous appendices my sources and methods. Despite careful checking of the compilations and calculations, errors have doubtless been made, but it is hoped that they are not many.

My indebtedness to others in connection with this research is large. A grant from the Carnegie Corporation made it possible for me to spend a year at the National Bureau of Economic Research. Upon my return to Johns Hopkins University, the Rockefeller Foundation provided funds that enabled me to continue the collection and analysis of data. Without these two grants I could not have assembled the basic data that appear in this volume. The Lessing Rosenthal Fund for Economic Research, established some years ago at Johns Hopkins University to assist economic inquiry, has contributed liberally toward the cost of publishing the study. The three grants are gratefully acknowledged.

Professor Joseph S. Davis and Dean Homer B. Vanderblue allowed me to use their unpublished data on New York incorporations, which are embodied in Table 9. Their kindness is deeply appreciated.

The National Bureau of Economic Research and its staff have contributed greatly to my study. Much was accomplished on my book during the year I spent at the Bureau; discussions with my colleagues were most helpful, and my assistants gave excellent service. My year there is to me a memorable one. The Committee of the National Bureau Directors that examined my manuscript—Arthur H. Cole, G. A. Elliot, and George Soule —made criticisms that led to a number of improvements. The 'map' of the study, which appears in the first chapter, and other smaller passages are the direct result of a pleasant conference with Professor Cole. Wesley C. Mitchell, Arthur F. Burns, Leo Wolman, William J. Carson, Moses Abramovitz, Geoffrey H. Moore, and David Durand have helped me at many stages of my efforts. Some have encouraged me and made valuable criticisms; some have carefully read the manuscript and made helpful suggestions. Martha Anderson has painstakingly edited the manuscript. H. Irving Forman prepared the charts for publication. To all I am very much indebted, and I gratefully acknowledge their assistance.

G. H. E., Jr.

The Johns Hopkins University
April 1948

Contents

PREFACE   V

CHAPTER

1 The Nature of the Study   1
2 The Significance of an Incorporation   4
3 The Period of the Special Charter   10
4 Trends in Business Incorporations, 1875–1943   31
5 The Number of Incorporations and Their Authorized Capital Stock   36
6 Large, Medium, and Small Business Corporations   42
7 An Industrial Classification of Incorporations   50
8 Fields of Corporate Enterprise   66
9 Incorporations and Business Cycles   75

APPENDIX

1 Private Nonbusiness Incorporations   89
2 Maryland Business Incorporations Classified According to Authorized Capital Stock   91
3 Business Incorporations and Their Authorized Capital Stock   95
4 Industrial Classification of Business Incorporations   153
5 Two Tests: Capital Stock as an Index of the Size of a Corporation; The Charter as a Source of Information on Corporate Purposes   171
6 Total Incorporations Used in Constructing the Monthly Aggregate Index of Incorporations and in Analyzing Cyclical Movements   177

INDEX   180

TABLES AND CHARTS

TABLE

1 Business Incorporation Series Compiled for this Study Unless Otherwise Specified   2
2 Previous Status of Maryland Companies Incorporated in 1934 and 1935 that had Predecessors and Remained in Business more than One Year after Incorporation   5
3 All Maryland Business Corporations Chartered in 1925, 1926, and 1927 and the Number of those Companies on the Maryland Forfeiture List of February 22, 1931 (classified by authorized capital stock)   6
4 Maryland Corporation Life Table   8
5 Chronology of Initial State Constitutional Provisions that Necessitated Incorporation under General Laws   11
6 Business Incorporations, Eight States, 1800–1875   12
7 Maryland Business Incorporations by Special Acts, 1800–1852   14
8 New Jersey Business Incorporations: By Special Acts, 1800–1875; Under General Laws, 1864–1899   15
9 New York Business Incorporations Under Special and General Laws, 1800–1845   17
10 Ohio Business Incorporations: By Special Acts, 1803–1851; Under General Laws, 1856–1899   18
11 Incorporations Classified Industrially, Four States; Percentage Distribution by Decades, 1790–99 to 1890–99   20
12 States in the Annual Median Index of Incorporations with the Periods of Their Inclusion   34
13 Annual Aggregate and Median Indexes of Incorporations, 1860–1943   34
14 Incorporations, United Kingdom, 1863–1937   35
15 Ohio Incorporations, Total Authorized Capital Stock, Annual Averages, 1872–1918   40

16 New Jersey Corporations with Authorized Capital Stock of $20,000,000 or more Chartered under General Laws, 1881–1902   48
17 Number of New Jersey Corporations with Authorized Capital Stock of $20,000,000 or more Chartered under General Laws, 1880–1918   49
18 Number of Delaware Corporations with Authorized Capital Stock of $20,000,000 or more Chartered under General Laws, 1916–1943   49
19 Industrial Categories used in Classifying Incorporations   51
20 A Sample of Pennsylvania Corporations Chartered in 1902 Classified on Basis of Bradstreet and Charter Descriptions   54
21 Title Guarantee and Trust Incorporations, Pennsylvania, December 1899–November 1904   58
22 Corporations Reporting for Income Taxation: Percentage Distribution by Major Industrial Categories; New Jersey, Ohio, and Pennsylvania, 1916–1918 and 1921–1930   59
23 Incorporations under General Laws: Percentage Distribution by Major Industrial Categories; New Jersey, Ohio, and Pennsylvania, 1872–1930   60
24 Number and Percentage of Basic Categories of Table 19 Used in Classifying Industrially the Incorporations of Each Year, 1800–1930: New Jersey, Ohio, and Pennsylvania   63
25 Business Incorporations: Percentage Distribution by One-Letter Industrial Categories; New Jersey, Ohio, and Pennsylvania   66
26 Mining and Quarrying Incorporations: Percentage Distribution by Two-Letter Industrial Categories; New Jersey, Ohio, and Pennsylvania   67

27 Percentages of Total Manufacturing Incorporations that Fitted into Certain Two-Letter Industrial Categories: New Jersey, Ohio, and Pennsylvania   68
28 Years in which Annual Incorporations in Certain Manufacturing Industries First Equaled or Exceeded 7½ Percent of the Total Annual Manufacturing Incorporations: New Jersey, Ohio, and Pennsylvania   68
29 Public Utility Incorporations: Percentage Distribution by Two-Letter Industrial Categories; New Jersey, Ohio, and Pennsylvania   68
30 Incorporations of Companies Supplying Services: Percentage Distribution by Two-Letter Industrial Categories; New Jersey, Ohio, and Pennsylvania   69
31 Percentages of Total Incorporations of Financial Enterprises that Fitted into Certain Two-Letter Industrial Categories: New Jersey, Ohio, and Pennsylvania   69
32 Oil Incorporations as a Percentage of Total Business Incorporations, Texas, 1901   73
33 Gas Incorporations, Ohio and Pennsylvania, 1880–1893   73
34 Mining and Total Business Incorporations, Colorado, 1891–1897   73
35 Indexes of Seasonal Variation in Business Incorporations: Maine, Ohio, and Texas   76
36 States in the Monthly Aggregate Index of Incorporations with the Periods of Their Inclusion   79
37 Seasonal Indexes Used in Computing the Monthly Aggregate Index of Incorporations   80
38 Monthly Aggregate Index of Incorporations, 1860–1941   80
39 States in the Monthly Median Index of Incorporations with the Periods of Their Inclusion   81
40 Monthly Median Index of Incorporations, 1860–1943   83
41 Timing of Cycles in Total Incorporations   85
42 Timing of Cycles in the Monthly Median Index of Incorporations   85
43 Specific-Cycle Patterns in Total Incorporations   86
44 Reference-Cycle Patterns in Total Incorporations   88

CHART
1 Business Incorporations, Eight States, 1800–1875   13
2 Turnpike Incorporations, Five States, 1800–1877   22
3 Manufacturing Incorporations, Four States, 1800–1877   23

4 Railroad Incorporations, Four States, 1800–1876   25
5 Maryland Business Incorporations (excluding Turnpike and Manufacturing) by Special Acts, 1800–1852   26
6 New Jersey Business Incorporations (excluding Turnpike and Manufacturing): By Special Acts, 1800–1845; Under Special and General Laws, 1846–1875   27
7 New York Business Incorporations (excluding Turnpike and Manufacturing) under Special and General Laws, 1800–1845   28
8 Ohio Business Incorporations (excluding Turnpike and Manufacturing): By Special Acts, 1803–1851; Under General Laws, 1856–1875   29
9 Business Incorporations, Sixteen States, Annually, 1860–1943   32
10 Delaware Business Incorporations, Number and Authorized Capital Stock, 1916–1943   37
11 Texas Business Incorporations, Number and Authorized Capital Stock, 1872–1920   38
12 Ohio Business Incorporations, Number and Authorized Capital Stock, 1872–1918   39
13 Illinois Business Incorporations, Number and Authorized Capital Stock, 1897–1918   40
14 Colorado Business Incorporations by Size Groups, 1891–1908   43
15 Delaware Business Incorporations by Size Groups, 1916–1943   43
16 Illinois Business Incorporations by Size Groups, 1897–1918   44
17 Maryland Business Incorporations by Size Groups, 1870–1939   45
18 New Jersey Business Incorporations by Size Groups, 1875–1918   46
19 Ohio Business Incorporations by Size Groups, 1872–1918   46
20 Incorporations under General Laws and Corporations Reporting for Income Taxation: Percentage Distribution by Major Industrial Categories   62
21 Long Cycles in Incorporations, New Jersey, Ohio, and Pennsylvania, 1872–1930: Communication, Transportation, Other Public Utilities, Building and Loan Associations   70
22 Business Incorporations, Four States, 1881–1907   77
23 Public Utility Incorporations, New Jersey, Ohio, and Pennsylvania, 1875–1930   78
24 Manufacturing Incorporations, New Jersey, Ohio, and Pennsylvania, 1875–1930   78
25 Monthly Aggregate and Median Indexes of Business Incorporations, 1860–1943   82
26 Average Cyclical Patterns of Monthly Aggregate Incorporations   87

CHAPTER 1

The Nature of the Study

This study of business incorporations was undertaken with several aims. An examination of incorporations, it was believed, would reveal new information about the plans of entrepreneurs, whose activities center largely in the organization of business units, substantial expansions of established units, and strenuous efforts to adapt them to a changing environment. Some of these terms obviously lack precision, but they are designed to confine entrepreneurial activity to the dynamic operations of business men. The private individual entrepreneurs are conceived to be the business executives who stimulate and introduce new ideas and alter the rate at which the wheels of enterprise turn.[1] Of course, not all of the plans of these entrepreneurs are reflected in incorporations, but some appear in applications for charters. In the data on corporations the dynamic individuals behind large ventures are represented more completely than small business men; and the entrepreneurs of recent years are more completely covered than those of an earlier date, since formerly the corporation was less common. Despite the limitations imposed by these considerations, it was felt that data on newly chartered companies would afford a vantage ground from which to review the development of the economy.

To the degree that entrepreneurs' ideas about business opportunities are reflected in the number and character of incorporations, a study of charters should add to our knowledge about business cycles and to our understanding of the larger movements of economic growth. Since new information would be available concerning state competition in granting charters, the corporation itself could be comprehended better. State rivalry for the chartering business has been a powerful factor in molding the corporation to the changing needs of the economy. Such adaptation might—or might not —have been brought about as efficiently by some other device; but that is a problem in itself. This study supplies some basic data for exploring the desirability of continuing state chartering or of adopting an alternative such as federal chartering. Finally, in examining the changing kinds of enterprise for which charters were taken out, the opportunities to invest that were open to capital from time to time should become apparent.

Most of the data for the tables and charts were compiled from published state documents. The other figures were built up from official records of certain state incorporating agencies. The published documents list by name the companies chartered—often with the authorized capital stock and less frequently with a statement of the industrial purposes for which each company was chartered. To get even a sketchy picture of the incorporation of business units throughout the United States would be impossible for an individual research worker—or even a small group—without such published data. Though far from complete, they are adequate for an examination of the questions explored here.

The size and perhaps some of the utility of the task may be gathered from a few brief comments upon the Ohio data, one of the most extensive series compiled, covering 129,796 incorporations. Factual material was published on the business corporations chartered by Ohio from 1803, the year of statehood, until 1937, with the exception of approximately four years, January 1852 through November 1855. Thus, for a century and a third the name of each corporation and the date on which it was chartered are listed. For most of the period, the authorized capital stock of each company and the primary industrial purposes for which it was organized are also given. Information on charters granted by other states is not available for as long a period, but there are other incorporation series of great interest. For example, New Jersey reports cover incorporations from 1800 through 1918. Table 1 lists the business incorporation series given in this volume. With the few exceptions indicated, the series were compiled for this study.

An arbitrary, but simple and perhaps acceptable, definition of a *business* corporation has been used whenever the sources indicated the presence and absence of capital stock: a corporation with authorized capital stock was classified as a business enterprise, while companies without capital stock were considered nonbusiness enterprises. Of course, some corporations that do not operate with a view to profits are chartered with capital stock, but that is not usual. They were few, and their classification as business concerns certainly does not appreciably distort the general picture. The above

---

[1] The adjective 'private' is used because entrepreneurs in the government might be referred to as 'public entrepreneurs'. The adjective 'individual' is used because in certain circumstances it would be appropriate to refer to a firm as an entrepreneur. For discussions of the concept 'entrepreneur' see G. H. Evans, Jr., A Theory of Entrepreneurship, *Journal of Economic History*, Supplemental Issue (The Tasks of Economic History), Dec. 1942, pp. 142–6; A. H. Cole, An Approach to the Study of Entrepreneurship, *ibid*., Supplement VI, 1946, pp. 1–15; J. H. Stauss, The Entrepreneur: The Firm, *Journal of Political Economy*, June 1944, pp. 112–27; and J. A. Schumpeter, *Business Cycles* (McGraw-Hill, 1939), I, 102 ff., and *The Theory of Economic Development* (Harvard University Press, 1934), Ch. II and IV.

definition of a business corporation also led to the exclusion of some enterprises that ought properly to be regarded as business units—mutual insurance companies, for example. Despite their business aspect, there was definite advantage in excluding them: whenever a series on the number of corporations chartered in a state is paralleled by a series on the capital stock authorized for newly created companies, the two series can be examined with the assurance that they were constructed from identical corporations. Again, it is felt that the descrip-

TABLE 1
Business Incorporation Series
Compiled for this Study Unless Otherwise Specified

STATE	BASED ON CHARTERS GRANTED BY SPECIAL ACTS (ANNUAL DATA)	BASED ON CHARTERS ISSUED UNDER GENERAL LAWS (MONTHLY DATA UNLESS OTHERWISE SPECIFIED)	
	No. of Incorporations	No. of Incorporations	Authorized Capital Stock
Arizona		1912–1924	
Colorado		1890–1908	1890–1908
Connecticut		1837–1870	
"		1880–1932	
Delaware		1899–1915[d, h]	
"		1916–1943	1916–1943
Florida		1901–1922	1901–1922
Illinois		1896–1918	1896–1918
		1925–1943[e]	
Louisiana		1937–1943[f]	
Maine	1820–1891	1870–1943	
Maryland	1800–1852[a]	1870–1939	1870–1939
Massachusetts		1851–1921	1851–1921
New Jersey	1800–1875	1846–1918	1846–1918
New York	1800–1845[b]	1800–1845[b, h]	
" "		1901–1923[g, h]	
" "		1924–1943[g]	
Ohio	1803–1851	1855–1936	1871–1919
Pennsylvania	1800–1860[c]	1875–1887[h]	
"		1887–1921	1887–1921
Texas		1872–1920	1872–1920
Virginia		1903–1941	1903–1918

For data and full description of each state series, see Appendix 3.
[a] J. G. Blandi's figures.
[b] Figures of J. S. Davis and H. B. Vanderblue.
[c] William Miller's figures.
[d] R. C. Larcom's figures.
[e] Corporation Trust Company's figures.
[f] *Louisiana Business Review* figures.
[g] Figures from a New York State document.
[h] Data are merely annual.

tion and analysis of the course of business incorporations have not been distorted by adhering to the above definition of a business corporation, which excludes the relatively few nonstock business enterprises chartered. This definition did not have to be used for some states, for example, Maine, because the companies chartered were called 'business corporations' in the state documents. In other words, whenever the documents called an enterprise a business corporation, the state's designation was accepted regardless of the presence or absence of capital stock figures.

To identify nonbusiness concerns was more difficult

when states either did not segregate their business from their nonbusiness incorporations or did not give authorized capital stock figures. Business and nonbusiness incorporations, however, had to be separated since there were *a priori* no grounds for believing that the direction and extent of variations in their chartering would be similar. When the state documents listed corporations with similar objectives together, it was easier to separate the business from the nonbusiness units. For example, corporations listed as churches or Masonic organizations could be put into the nonbusiness group after very brief study. As a last resort business or nonbusiness objectives were determined by the name of the corporation. Groupings and names as bases of classification are obviously crude devices, but fortunately they did not have to be used as often as might be imagined.[2] The incorporation series of this study certainly consist more exclusively of business enterprises than if various concerns considered to be nonbusiness had not been eliminated; but they doubtless still contain some nonbusiness enterprises.[3]

Neither the renewal of a charter nor the rechartering of a company was counted as an incorporation. On the other hand, reorganizations were counted. The charter renewal was considered a mere extension of legal life without economic significance, whereas when a company

[2] The name alone was used to separate the nonbusiness from the business units in only two state series for two periods: Arizona, 1912–24; and New Jersey, 1871–75. In New Jersey, 1800–70, and in Ohio, 1803–51 and Nov. 16, 1855–Nov. 15, 1871, the industrial groupings of incorporations, appearing in the documents, were used with the names as the means for identifying business and nonbusiness units.

[3] Types of corporation excluded as nonbusiness:
a) Boards of trade, including chambers of commerce
b) Charitable organizations, including benevolent societies, community chests, foundations, welfare leagues
c) Clubs, including Masonic organizations. (Of course, some clubs are organized with a view to profits, but to draw the line between profit-seeking and nonprofit-seeking clubs was impossible. Exclusion of all seemed the best procedure.)
d) Ecclesiastical institutions, including churches, mission societies, Y.M.C.A.'s
e) Educational institutions, including alumni associations, foundations, libraries, universities. (Because of the large number of business colleges and private schools, all colleges and schools were treated as business corporations.)
f) Farm bureaus
g) Fire companies and fire departments, including hook and ladder companies
h) Hospitals and health associations except sanatoriums and sanitariums
i) Local government units
j) Mutual insurance companies
k) Professional associations, including bar associations
l) Taxpayers' leagues
m) Trade associations
n) Travelers' aid associations. (Tourist bureaus were treated as business corporations.)

was reorganized so many adjustments probably had to be made that a new business unit could be said to have come into existence. In these decisions and elsewhere, the question arose: What is the significance of an incorporation? This question is dealt with in Chapter 2, and through an examination of some Maryland material an answer is attempted.

The data for the early years studied pertain to corporations created under both special and general laws, particularly under the former. The special charter was, of course, the original method of incorporation, and it held primacy until nearly 1875. Discussion of the number and kinds of incorporations in eight states during the period when the special charter dominated serves as a background for the material of subsequent chapters. Specially chartered companies were excluded from the tabulations for the later years because of their dwindling numbers and because charters under general law, granted by administrative agencies operating continuously on a routine basis, can reflect more promptly entrepreneurial activities and desires than a series containing special incorporations, which are subject to the meeting times and whims of legislatures.

At the outset of the study it became necessary to decide whether the data on the number of incorporations or their authorized capital stock, or both, should be used in examining the course of incorporations. The large companies are dwarfed when incorporations are merely counted; on the other hand, series on capital stock become very erratic when the largest companies are included. Chapter 5 shows why most of the study relates merely to the number of charters granted.

Capital stock figures, however, were useful in classifying incorporations by size. Separation of incorporations into three size groups—large, medium, and small—adds to an understanding of the nature of an incorporation series. For example, whenever small incorporations form a large percentage of the total incorporations of a state, one can confidently predict that a series on the number of incorporations will have cyclical movements that are less pronounced than similar series for states that create primarily the medium-sized or large corporation.

Since some of the sources from which information was gathered on the number of charters contained also data on the corporations' industrial objectives, it seemed desirable to see what such material could reveal about incorporation movements. Through these purpose data, for example, long waves of incorporation in some broad industrial fields are shown to be mere combinations of more or less unrelated chartering episodes. Other long waves, such as those of incorporations in the construction field, parallel recognized industrial movements. Moreover, incorporations in some fields, such as public utilities, are more closely related to business cycles than incorporations in other industries.

In exploring the relation between incorporations and business cycles two indexes of incorporations were constructed. These extend from 1860 until the early 1940's and were built upon the incorporations of sixteen states (Tables 12 and 39). As is shown in Chapter 9, an upturn in business incorporations has generally preceded an upturn in business; peaks in incorporations likewise have led peaks in business, but by a smaller time interval and somewhat less regularly.

The indexes of incorporations as well as the separate state series have a rising trend in the number of business incorporations in the United States until the closing months of 1919 or the early part of 1920. The rate of growth is by no means uniform, nor do all states follow precisely the same pattern. All state series, however, have a rising trend from about 1875 until the early 1890's. Growth was arrested during the middle 'nineties but was resumed in the last years of the nineteenth century. From that point until about 1920 most state incorporation series showed growth but at a less rapid rate than in the pre-1890 period. After 1920 the trend is downward in many states. New York and Delaware are among the few states that chartered more companies in 1929 than in 1920.

CHAPTER 2

The Significance of an Incorporation

In recent years enterprises have on occasion been chartered in the morning, accomplished their purposes in the early afternoon, and filed dissolution papers before the close of business on the same day. The knowledge that such a short-lived 'legal person' has sometimes been used to facilitate a single transaction and the suspicion that the process is often a mere matter of manipulation challenge the economic significance of an incorporation. Each incorporation certainly does not carry the same import. Some reflect the situation just mentioned; the vast majority have more enduring implications.

D. H. Macgregor, discussing the meaning of an incorporation, states: "But it is assumed that in general the assumption of the company form means an expansion of enterprise."[1] This position is perhaps justifiable, but it may be more appropriate to contend merely that many incorporations in an industrial field are evidence of activity on the part of entrepreneurs. The activity may be associated with either the organization of new producing units or the enlargement of old ones. It may be associated also with the mere adoption of the corporate form, without any expansion of facilities, by enterprises previously operating under some other form of organization. For the public, these conversions, even when they do not need substantial additional capital, create possibilities that may eventuate in investment opportunities; these potentialities could not exist when the enterprises operated as unincorporated units. Hence from the investor's point of view, an increase in incorporations may open new investment opportunities even though there is no "expansion of enterprise". Whenever incorporations in any one industrial field are numerous, it seems reasonable to infer that movements of economic significance are in process: enterprise is restive and seeking an object for its energy; opportunities to invest are being multiplied either through the creation of entirely new outlets or the opening of existing outlets to more people.

To assert or assume that an increase in incorporations indicates a big expansion of enterprise or the opening of old investment outlets to a larger number of capitalists is not to substantiate the proposition. Proof is hard to obtain. The nature and significance of a Maryland incorporation, however, is revealed, to some extent, in its first tax assessment return. When a company files its first report, it is required to state whether it is a new company, a partnership converted into a corporation, or a combination of several corporations, etc. These data may be supplemented by information, discussed below, concerning the extent to which incorporators failed to utilize their charters—indicating the force of the impact of an incorporation upon the economy. But it must be borne in mind that the problem of measuring the impact of an incorporation is different from the problem of using incorporations as an indicator of entrepreneurial plans. Many charters taken out at one time might indicate that entrepreneurs desired to develop certain plans. If the charters were forfeited without being put to use, the repercussions upon the community might be negligible. While the emphasis of this study is upon incorporations as a reflection of entrepreneurs' hopes and beliefs, this chapter contains some data that are not strictly relevant but are helpful.

The tax assessment returns of Maryland corporations reporting for the first time revealed that many companies subject to the requirement of filing had not done so, and that of those that had filed some failed to answer the question concerning pre-incorporation status. The incompleteness of the returns is to be attributed partly to the fact that a fairly large portion of the charters were never exercised and incorporators who did not complete their promotions did not file tax returns. Why some of the reporting concerns were not compelled to give the required information is not as easily explained.

The tax returns for the companies chartered in 1934 and 1935 were selected for a study of pre-incorporation history because the State Tax Commission could make them accessible without much difficulty. About 60 percent of the companies that were supposed to give their pre-incorporation history did so. If, however, the companies that may be assumed to have operated less than one year[2]—hereafter called abortive—are deducted from those that were supposed to report, and the difference is taken as the number that might be expected to report,[3] then about 51 percent reported no previous

---

[1] *Enterprise, Purpose & Profit* (Oxford University Press, 1934), p. 78.

[2] For the purposes of this study, companies that forfeited their charters for nonpayment of taxes at the first opportunity after incorporation, called abortive companies, were treated as though they had remained in business less than one year. Some of these corporations doubtless lived longer, but others never operated at all. The size of the abortive group is discussed below.

[3] The number of those that might be expected to report was computed as follows:

	1935	1934
1) Maryland charters granted	771	816
2) Corporations not required by law to report previous status	14[a]	31[b]

business history (that is, they considered themselves new enterprises), about 24 percent failed to give the pre-incorporation information, and about 25 percent reported a previous existence.[4] Since more than half of the incorporations that functioned through the first year were new ventures, variations in total incorporations would seem to reflect fairly well "expansion of enterprise" in its narrow sense—the opening of entirely new outlets for capital. It is difficult to guess whether few or many of the companies that failed to disclose their pre-incorporation history were new enterprises. One could argue with some plausibility that many had a previous existence and were trying to hide it from the State Tax Commission in an effort to get an assessment unbiased by the record; the assessors are aware of such efforts. It would nevertheless probably be safe to guess that among the nonreporting 24 percent there were more reconstituted old enterprises than new business ventures.

Maryland corporations of 1934 and 1935 that both had a previous business existence and operated for at least one year after their incorporation were studied further (Table 2). A large proportion—about 32 percent—answered the tax return question concerning pre-incorporation history vaguely. It would not be unreasonable to distribute those in this category among the other groups—except two, to which the vagueness in phraseology never seemed to apply—in proportion to the numbers that clearly belong in each group. The two categories that would not receive any of this uncertain class are those containing incorporations: (1) that took place when corporations of other states procured Maryland charters; (2) that represented consolidations. If the 'uncertain' group is distributed and the percentages of the total in the different categories are averaged for the two years, the following becomes the picture of the pre-incorporation status of these companies: 49 percent had been individual proprietorships; 26 percent had been

3) Subtotal	757	785
4) Abortive corporations not included in line 2	294	280
5) Those that might be expected to report	463	505

[a] Includes 1 abortive company.
[b] Includes 4 abortive companies.
[4] The 51 percent, which can probably be increased because of the unknown 24 percent, may be compared with percentages calculated from the Dun & Bradstreet figures on 'completely-new' incorporated and unincorporated business enterprises in the United States for 1936–39—58.0 to 61.0 percent of all new firms (see *Dun's Review*, Aug. 1941, p. 23). Alfred R. Oxenfeldt has questioned the Dun & Bradstreet figures and estimated that completely new firms, excluding what he terms 'extensions', constituted annually about 37 percent of all new business formations (see his *New Firms and Free Enterprise*, American Council on Public Affairs, 1943, pp. 40–2).

partnerships; 18 percent were reincorporations of single Maryland companies; 4 percent had been single out-of-state corporations; and 3 percent resulted from combinations of two or more corporations.

The 4 percent for out-of-state corporations is probably not a fair index of the extent to which an American company switches its state of incorporation during any given year. Since Maryland has a 'liberal' chartering policy, its experience cannot be expected to be typical. A few figures for Pennsylvania may be given as evidence. For three two-year periods (June 1, 1909 to May 31, 1911; June 1, 1913 to May 31, 1915; and June 1, 1915 to May 31, 1917) the documents that list incorporations in Pennsylvania contain the names of 13, 6, and

TABLE 2

Previous Status of Maryland Companies Incorporated in 1934 and 1935 that had Predecessors and Remained in Business more than One Year after Incorporation

| PREVIOUS STATUS | 1935 | | 1934 | |
	No.	% of Total	No.	% of Total
1 An individual proprietorship	38	29.7	41	35.7
2 A partnership	18	14.1	23	20.0
3 A corporation	23	18.0	16	13.9
a) Maryland	15	11.7	14	12.2
b) Foreign	8	6.2	2	1.7
4 Several corporations	4	3.1	3	2.6
5 Companies with statements too vague to permit definite assignment	45	35.2	32	27.8
Total	128	100.1	115	100.0

Constructed from corporate tax returns filed with the State Tax Commission of Maryland.

10 "Foreign corporations made domestic".[5] As total incorporations numbered 3,191, 2,808, and 3,416, three-tenths of 1 percent of business charters granted were on the average issued to enterprises that switched their domiciles from another state to Pennsylvania.

Pre-incorporation histories reveal information about the nature of entrepreneurial activity and by implication about possible demands for capital. In contrast, the extent to which charters were exercised reflects primarily the initial success of entrepreneurs in carrying out their projects. Incorporations tell something about what entrepreneurs wanted to do; incorporations less abortive enterprises tell something about what entrepreneurs were able to do. It must be admitted, however, that in some, perhaps many, of the abortive corporations the promoting groups did something. The something may have involved raising capital, but the entire effort must in each case have soon come to an end and must have resulted in little or no production.

An abortive corporation was defined as one that

[5] For a description of these documents, see the Pennsylvania section of Appendix 3.

forfeited its charter in consequence of having paid no state taxes except at the time of its incorporation. Such corporations forfeited their charters at the earliest possible date. Until 1939 a Maryland company that was chartered in the year X was first assessed and billed for property taxes in the year X+1. If taxes remained unpaid for the years X+1, X+2, and X+3, the company forfeited its charter in the spring of the year X+4. There is little doubt that some of these companies operated though they did not pay taxes, but the State Tax Commission staff is of the opinion that few remained in business for a full year. A large portion of the first tax bills, which were based on arbitrary assessments and mailed to these companies in the year X+1, regularly returned unclaimed. Successive assessments were raised arbitrarily when taxes were not paid or assessments were disputed, but in only rare cases did such procedure bring forth a response. It seems likely that the economic significance of the corporations that forfeited at the first opportunity has been negligible.

Since the law concerning charter forfeiture was changed in 1939, the definition of an abortive corporation had to be modified. A company chartered in the year X forfeited its charter in the fall of the year X+2 if it had not paid taxes for the year X+1. The consequent modification in the definition must be borne in mind when examining the following percentages of Maryland incorporations that were abortive: 1927, 35.8; 1928, 35.9; 1929, 36.3; 1930, 43.6; 1931, 46.3; 1932, 42.8; 1933, 38.3; 1934, 34.8; 1935, 38.3; 1936, 45.7; 1937, 34.5; and 1938, 31.3. Except for the transitional period the effect of the change is not great. The 1927–35 data were computed in a comparable way; the 1936 figure is in a class by itself since the change in the Maryland forfeiture law affected the calculation for that year;[6] the annual figures for 1937 and 1938 are based on the new definition. On the average about 39 percent of Maryland incorporations were abortive; the variations in the figures making up the average suggest a relation between business conditions and the proportion of abortive companies.[7] In examining the annual data the reader must not jump to the conclusion that the low

[6] Two forfeiture lists were issued in 1939, the first in February under the old law and the second in October under the new law. No company chartered in 1936 appeared on the February 1939 list. The October list, however, included an unduly large number of companies created in 1936, since it contained 1936 companies that would have appeared on the February 1940 and February 1941 forfeiture lists, had the old law remained in effect.

[7] Compare English abortive company figures of about 30, 27, and 25 percent for 1893–1902, 1902–13, and 'recent years', respectively, in Macgregor, *op. cit.*, pp. 101–2; also data on first-year failures among retailers in Oxenfeldt, *op. cit.*, pp. 174 and 179. The latter data do not pertain to any particular form of business organization.

values for the years since 1936 indicate an error in the procedure used for the years before. Voluntary dissolution was an unusual way of terminating a Maryland corporation's existence until a simplified procedure was introduced by a statute enacted in 1935.[8] As voluntary dissolutions increased, forfeitures for nonpayment of taxes decreased. Thus the 1927–35 figures record almost all corporate 'deaths'; the 1937 and 1938 rates have a smaller coverage.

TABLE 3

All Maryland Business Corporations Chartered in 1925, 1926, and 1927 and the Number of those Companies on the Maryland Forfeiture List of February 22, 1931

(classified by authorized capital stock)

AUTHORIZED CAPITAL STOCK	COMPANIES CHARTERED		FORFEITURES IN 1931		% NO. OF FORFEITURES IS OF NO. CHARTERED
	No.	% of Total	No.	% of Total	
1927 Corporations					
Under $25,000	354	33.9	135	36.1	38.1
$25,000– 50,000	102	9.8	34	9.1	33.3
$50,000– 100,000	148	14.2	64	17.1	43.2
$100,000–1,000,000	373	35.7	126	33.7	33.8
$1,000,000 & over	68	6.5	15	4.0	22.1
All size groups	1,045	100.1	374	100.0	35.8
1926 Corporations					
Under $25,000	283	27.0	35	25.7	12.4
$25,000– 50,000	127	12.1	16	11.8	12.6
$50,000– 100,000	160	15.3	21	15.4	13.1
$100,000–1,000,000	405	38.6	61	44.9	15.1
$1,000,000 & over	74	7.1	3	2.2	4.1
All size groups	1,049	100.1	136	100.0	13.0
1925 Corporations					
Under $25,000	291	28.2	24	28.6	8.2
$25,000– 50,000	116	11.2	6	7.1	5.2
$50,000– 100,000	161	15.6	11	13.1	6.8
$100,000–1,000,000	398	38.6	36	42.9	9.0
$1,000,000 & over	66	6.4	7	8.3	10.6
All size groups	1,032	100.0	84	100.0	8.1

Constructed from the forfeiture list of February 22, 1931 and other records in the office of the State Tax Commission of Maryland.

Abortive corporations are not confined to any particular size (using authorized capital stock as a measure of size), nor are the companies that live from one to two years and those that live from two to three years.[9] These points are brought out in Table 3. In Appendix 2, other tables are presented for those who care to explore the matter further. Since the 1931 forfeiture list is the first on which companies incorporated in 1927 could have appeared, they are considered to be abortive, that is, to have lived less than one year. Similarly, the companies on that forfeiture list that were chartered in 1926 and 1925 are said to have lived between one and two years

[8] *Maryland Laws, 1935*, Ch. 551.

[9] See Chapter 6 for a justification of the use of capital stock as an indicator of size.

and two and three years, respectively. Comparison of the percentage-of-total figures bears out the contention that, as far at least as the first three years of life are concerned, the corporations of any given size are no more or less likely to survive than corporations of any other size.[10] Of the abortive group, 36.1 percent had an authorized capital stock of less than $25,000, while 33.9 percent of all incorporations were in this size group. In the higher size groups the figures for the abortive companies are 9.1, 17.1, 33.7, and 4.0 percent; the figures for all business incorporations are 9.8, 14.2, 35.7, and 6.5 percent. Examination of the ratios in the last column of Table 3 confirms the lack of correlation between size and a short life-span. Some observers may think they can see in the figures of this table (and the tables in Appendix 2) a slight tendency for the small company to succumb in infancy to misfortune more easily than the large concern. The Maryland figures, however, certainly do not seem to justify the fairly widespread belief that the small company is a 'fly-by-night' affair.[11] This generalization is doubtless due to the impressively large absolute number of forfeitures among small concerns.

The Maryland forfeiture lists were used also to construct a corporation life table. The companies on each list were classified by the year of their incorporation, and the number for each year was expressed as a percentage of the total incorporations of that year. The procedure will be easier to follow if the reader studies the accompanying tabulation. For example, of the total number of companies on the February 22, 1931 forfeiture list (815), 374 were chartered in 1927 and 136 in 1926. Those corporations of 1927 constituted 35.8 percent of all companies chartered by Maryland in that year, and those of 1926 constituted 13.0 percent of all Maryland corporations of 1926.

To put these data into the life table, the years of incorporation in column 1 were replaced by figures on the estimated life span. That is, a 1927 corporation that forfeited at the first opportunity—namely, February 22, 1931—was considered to have lived not more than one year; and 1926 corporations on that same forfeiture list were considered to have lived more than one but less than two years. The resulting table and similar ones

built upon subsequent forfeiture lists were combined to form Table 4, hereafter referred to as the Maryland Corporation Life Table.[12] The procedure may have produced a slight bias toward a short life, but it seems justifiable in the light of what has been said above about the tax assessment and billing of corporations by the State Tax Commission. The figures of Table 4 can be

Year of Incorporation of Business Corporations on the Maryland Forfeiture List of February 22, 1931

YEAR OF INCORPORATION	NO. OF CORPORATIONS ON 2/22/31 FORFEITURE LIST	NO. OF INCORPORATIONS IN GIVEN YEAR	% (2) IS OF (3)
(1)	(2)	(3)	(4)
1927	374	1,045	35.8
1926	136	1,049	13.0
1925	84	1,032	8.1
1924	43	934	4.6
1923	29	903	3.2
1922	39	881	4.4
1921	17	852	2.0
1920	18	946	1.9
1919	14	864	1.6
1918	7	403	1.7
1917	2	563	.4
1916	7	580	1.2
1915	4	562	.7
1914	5	521	1.0
1913	3	541	.6
1912	1	566	.2
1911	1	531	.2
Prior to 1911	28		
Unknown	3		
Total	815		

Column 2 was built up through the use of the forfeiture list and the corporate records in the office of the State Tax Commission of Maryland. For the source of column 3, see the Maryland section of Appendix 3.

tied to the above figures by observing the diagonal of data that appears in Table 4 in the first line under 1927, the second line under 1926, the third line under 1925, etc. The diagonal that should have been constructed from the forfeiture list of 1939 (and would appear in Table 4 in the first line under 1936, in the second line under 1935, etc.) was not calculated because of the two forfeiture lists in 1939 (see note 6). As explained above,

---

[10] The percentages of the total in Table 3 and in the last table of Appendix 2 should be used to supplement the data on the size distribution of incorporations in Chapter 6.

[11] See, for example, the comment by the Secretary of State of New York: ". . . they [recently incorporated companies] have a substantial capitalization and are not of the fly by night sort that spring up like mushrooms and vanish almost as quickly" (Press Release on Incorporations, Oct. 1927). See also a Press Release dated July 1928 issued by the same office: ". . . the greater number of companies are substantially capitalized and there are few of the so-called fly-by-night concerns which incorporate at low capitalization and sooner or later vanish from sight."

[12] Several studies provide comparative data on the life spans of business enterprises. Usually figures are for all firms in a few industries; sometimes data on corporations are given. In comparing figures on corporations, one must note whether the mortality tables are built upon all incorporations or merely corporations that have opened for business. Compare Ruth G. Hutchinson, A. R. Hutchinson, and Mabel Newcomer, A Study in Business Mortality: Length of Life of Business Enterprises in Poughkeepsie, New York, 1843–1936, *American Economic Review*, XXVIII, 3 (Sept. 1938), pp. 497 ff.; A. E. Heilman, *Mortality of Business Firms in Minneapolis, St. Paul, and Duluth, 1926–1930*, Bulletins of the University of Minnesota Employment Stabilization Research Institute, II, 1 (May 1933); E. D. McGarry, *Mortality in Retail Trade* (University of Buffalo Studies in Business, No. 4, 1930); and A. E. Boer, Mortality Costs in Retail Trades, *Journal of Marketing*, II, 1 (July 1937), pp. 52 ff.

TABLE 4
Maryland Corporation Life Table

PERCENTAGE OF THE TOTAL NUMBER OF CORPORATIONS CHARTERED IN THE SPECIFIED YEAR THAT HAD THE INDICATED LENGTH OF LIFE

(percentages)

EST. LIFE IN YEARS	1938	1937	1936	1935	1934	1933	1932	1931	1930	1929	1928	1927	1926	1925	1924	1923	1922	1921	1920	1919	1918	1917	1916	1915	1914	1913	1912	1911	MAXIMUM[a]	MINIMUM[a]	SIMPLE AV.[a]	CUM. SIMPLE AV.[a]	CHAINED AV.[a]	CUM. CHAINED AV.[a]
0-1	31.3	34.5	45.7	38.3	34.8	38.3	42.8	46.3	43.8	36.3	35.9	35.8																	46.3	34.8	39.1	39.1	39.1	39.1
1-2		6.2	4.4	13.4	10.5	7.3	8.0	8.8	10.4	9.9	11.1	7.8	13.0																13.0	7.3	9.6	48.7	9.2	48.3
2-3				2.6	6.4	5.8	4.5	3.6	2.7	5.2	5.7	6.6	5.0	8.1															8.1	3.6	5.6	54.3	5.1	53.4
3-4					2.1	4.9	3.6	3.0	1.7	2.2	6.3	5.0	4.1	5.3	4.6														6.3	1.7	4.1	58.4	3.7	57.1
4-5						1.5	4.7	3.6	1.9	1.8	2.0	1.9	2.7	2.9	3.6	3.2													5.0	1.6	3.1	61.5	2.7	59.8
5-6							1.9	1.4	2.5	1.8	1.6	1.5	3.0	3.1	2.9	3.3	4.4												4.4	1.6	2.6	64.1	2.1	61.9
6-7									.3	2.0	1.7	1.0	1.1	3.6	2.8	3.9	2.8	2.0											3.9	1.5	2.6	66.7	2.1	64.0
7-8								3.6		.4	2.2	1.0	1.2	1.2	2.2	1.9	2.3	.5	1.9										2.8	.5	1.7	68.4	1.3	65.3
8-9								1.4			2.0	1.5	1.8	1.0	2.1	3.2	1.8	1.6	1.0	1.6	1.7								3.2	1.0	1.6	70.0	1.3	66.6
9-10											.9	.4	.5	.8	2.8	2.1	1.4	1.1	.8	.9	1.0	.4							2.1	.4	1.3	71.3	.9	67.5
10-11														.9	1.4	1.7	1.8	1.3	1.2	1.4	1.2	.9	1.2						1.8	.7	1.0	72.3	.8	68.2
11-12													1.8	1.5	.6	1.0	.7	1.1	2.1	.7	1.0	.7	1.0	.7					2.1	.0	1.1	73.4	.8	69.0
12-13													.5	.6	1.4	.7	.0	1.3	1.3	1.6	1.2	.5	.9	1.1	1.0				1.3	.7	.9	74.3	.7	69.7
13-14															1.8	1.0	.9	.9	.1	.8	1.0	1.6	.9	1.2	1.2	.6			1.6	.1	.9	75.2	.7	70.4
14-15															.1	1.1	1.0	.2	.8	.6	.5	1.1	.7	.5	.8	.0	.2		1.6	.2	.9	76.1	.7	71.1
15-16																.3		.8	.1	.7	.5	1.1	.3	.3	.6	.7	.0	.2	1.1	.0	.6	76.7	.5	71.6
16-17																	.9	.9	.4	.5	.7	.2	.3	.2	.6	.6	.5	.4	1.1	.0	.5	77.2	.5	72.1
17-18																	.2	.0			.9	.9	.3	.7	1.8	.6	.7	.6	1.2	.2	.5	77.7	.5	72.6
18-19																			.5	.7		.9		.5	.2	.6	.9	.0	.7	.3	.6	78.3	.3	73.2
19-20																			.3	.5	1.0			.3	.4	.6	.0	.4	.7	.2	.5	78.7	.4	73.6
20-21																		.9			.2	2.9	.3	.2		2.0	.2	.4	.7	.2	.4	79.2	.5	74.1
21-22																		.0				.0	.0	.7		.4	.4	.4	.7	.0	.4	79.6	.4	74.5
22-23																										.0			.2	.0	.1	79.7	.1	74.6
23-24																								.0	.0			.4	.4	.2	.4	80.0	.3	74.9
24-25																								.4		1.1	.7	.4	.4	.4	.4	80.4	.3	75.2
25-26																										.2	.5	.2						
26-27																												.4						
27-28																												.2						
Total incorp. of each year[b]	643	748	757	771	816	1012	890	870	904	1141	1058	1045	1049	1032	934	903	881	852	946	864	403	563	580	562	521	541	566	531						

For the construction of this table, see the text.

[a] In calculating each figure in this column the first two percentages at the left of each line were excluded because the effects of the change in the law relating to forfeiture had probably not subsided.

[b] These figures were taken from the Maryland section of Appendix 3.

1936 was the year chiefly affected by the change in the Maryland law with respect to forfeitures. In the final columns of Table 4, the maximum, minimum, simple average, and 'chained' average percentages for each line are given, together with the cumulations of the average percentages. In calculating each average figure the two percentages at the left of each line were not used, because they were rather seriously affected by the change in the law relating to forfeiture. The 'chained' average needs some further explanation. The figure for 0–1 year of estimated life is the same as that obtained for the simple average. Succeeding 'chained' figures were procured by computing average percentages for each two adjacent life spans for identical sets of years, computing the percentage the second of each pair was of the first, and chaining the results together on 39.1 percent, the figure for 0–1 year of estimated life. These 'chained' figures are given as an alternate series to those obtained by the simple average, because the latter are built on the incorporations of different sets of years.

According to the Maryland Corporation Life Table, almost half of the corporations lived less than 2 years, about 70 percent less than 10 years, while 75–80 percent did not survive their twenty-fifth year. Of course, total incorporations are not fully accounted for except by the inference that 20–25 percent survived more than a quarter of a century. Table 4 indicates a slightly longer life-span for Maryland corporations than the facts warrant, because it is made up only of terminations that were brought about by nonpayment of taxes. (This bias is perhaps partly counteracted by the possible bias referred to above.) The omission of other causes of 'death' is not especially important for the period covered since the voluntary dissolutions and the involuntary dissolutions under court decrees were relatively few.[13]

The extent to which the Maryland Corporation Life Table may be a basis for generalizations about the life span of American corporations cannot be stated precisely. Since Maryland is one of the so-called 'liberal' states, the mortality rates of the first year or two may be somewhat higher than those of the average state. This hypothesis was partly confirmed by a life table constructed from Virginia forfeiture lists. The table is not reproduced here, because it does not reflect corporate mortality as completely as the table built on Maryland forfeitures; voluntary dissolutions and surrenders have been important methods of terminating Virginia corporations, and it was not feasible to dig out the figures to combine with those from the forfeiture lists.[14] In attempting to generalize about a life table for all American corporations from the Maryland figures, it must also be realized that we know little or nothing about trends in the life span of corporations. Life expectancy of individuals has been lengthening in recent years; it would not be rash to predict that studies of corporate life would reveal similar changes.

[13] For example, during 1932–35 there was roughly one voluntary dissolution for every 11 forfeitures. (Dissolution figures are published in the biennial reports of the State Tax Commission of Maryland; the data on forfeitures can be calculated from Table 4, but care must be taken to get the sets of diagonal figures that pertain to the forfeiture lists for the years under discussion.)

[14] Voluntary dissolutions and surrenders of Virginia charters have averaged about 320 annually during the last 27 years; charters revoked and annulled have averaged about 570.

CHAPTER 3

The Period of the Special Charter

As the work of Joseph S. Davis on the earliest American corporations covered their development through 1800, this study begins with that year.[1] The first three-quarters of the 19th century are a unit in that most incorporations were by special charter. General incorporation laws were, of course, enacted in several states, but not until about 1875 had constitutional provisions requiring incorporation under general laws become so numerous that special charters might be considered a thing of the past for most fields of enterprise in most states of the Union (see Table 5).

Since the data for the pre-1875 period come largely from special acts of legislatures, only annual figures can be presented in this chapter. In some respects the calendar year is not a very appropriate period for a compilation of corporate charters granted by special acts. The legislative session is to be preferred for many purposes, but it would lack regularity for a given state and would not be uniform in date or length from state to state. The calendar year is therefore selected for want of a better period; but, as will appear later, it is at times well to work with a moving average of annual data. Some series are built upon charters issued in accordance with special acts alone, others on charters issued solely under general law, and still others on charters issued under both. This lack of uniformity is not a handicap when merely broad tendencies are to be observed, though it must be remembered when attention is directed to details.

Table 6 gives for 1800–75 some data on incorporations by eight states—Connecticut, Maine, Maryland, Massachusetts, New Jersey, New York, Ohio, and Pennsylvania.[2] Two-item centered moving averages were computed for incorporations under both special and general laws, whenever the two sets of figures were available; otherwise, the moving averages were built upon charters issued under the one or the other (see Chart 1). If figures on incorporations granted under general law in the first year that a charter could have been procured under it were for less than twelve months,

they had to be omitted from the moving averages based upon charters issued solely under general law. To have included them would have given an erroneous impression of the incorporation movement. On the other hand, when moving averages were made for charters granted under both special and general laws, figures for the former that covered only part of a year had to be added to those for the latter, since then they merely complemented the special charter picture.

Only one series of Table 6, that for New Jersey, covers the entire period studied, but an examination of all series makes possible several observations. Apparently there were three long waves of incorporation: 1800–21, 1821–43, and 1843–61 (Chart 1). A fourth long wave may perhaps be said to begin with 1861, but its terminal date cannot be marked off. The Ohio annual series, after the recessions of 1867 and 1870 and a high peak in 1872, reaches a deep trough in 1878.[3] The New Jersey annual series seems to have a trough about 1875.[4] The Maine incorporation series, based upon charters issued under both general and special laws, has a trough in 1876 (see the tables of Maine data in App. 3). Unfortunately, no chart shows for the post-1875 period the number of charters issued under both general and special laws. The Massachusetts annual series falls from a peak in 1864 into several minor wave-like movements which fluctuate about a horizontal trend and end with a rise in 1879 (see Chart 9). The four series thus suggest the late 'seventies as the terminal date for the fourth

[1] *Essays in the Earlier History of American Corporations* (Harvard Economic Studies, XVI, No. I–IV, 1917).

[2] See Appendix 3 for the sources of these data and for comments upon them. Figures for more states could have been added by the laborious process of examining state statutes. The states in which incorporations were numerous in this period are included and the coverage seems sufficient to warrant the general statements that follow.

[3] See Chart 9. From 1862 to 1875 in Ohio there were three intense periods of chartering in three industrial fields: (1) In mining the number of charters granted reached a peak in 1865 (the 2-item centered moving average for mining incorporations shows a peak in the same year). (2) In railroads a peak in chartering was reached in 1871 (the 2-item centered moving average of railroad incorporations, plotted on Chart 4, shows a peak in the same year). (3) In manufacturing a peak in chartering was reached in 1873 (the 5-item moving average of manufacturing incorporations, plotted on Chart 3, shows a peak in 1872).

The incorporation of building and loan associations under general law began in 1867. Many associations were soon chartered, 86 being incorporated in 1868 alone. The addition of building and loan incorporations raised the total number of charters granted by Ohio substantially.

[4] For New Jersey incorporations, reference cannot be made to Chart 9 as in the case of the Ohio series; the New Jersey series on Chart 1 covers incorporations under both special and general laws while the New Jersey series on Chart 9 is based solely on charters granted under general laws.

TABLE 5

Chronology of Initial State Constitutional Provisions that Necessitated Incorporation under General Laws

STATE[a]	DATE ADOPTED	DATE EFFECTIVE	SOURCE[b] Document	SOURCE[b] Constitution
Louisiana	11/ 5/1845	11/ 5/1845	A, III, 1392 n. *a*, 1405	1845: Title VI, Art. 123
Iowa	8/ 3/1846	12/28/1846[c]	A, II, 1132 (for dates: B, III, 499 n. 1)	1846: VIII, 2
New York	11/ 3/1846	1/ 1/1847	A, V, 2669 (for dates: B, III, 1096 n. 1)	1846: VIII, 1
Illinois	3/ 5/1848	3/ 5/1848	A, II, 985 n. *b*, 1005	1848: X, 1
Wisconsin	3/13/1848	5/29/1848[c]	B, III, 1688 n. 1, 1693–4, 1701	1848: IV, 31, 32; XI, 1
California	11/13/1849	12/20/1849[d]	A, I, 396 (for dates: B, III, 138 n. 1)	1849: IV, 31
Michigan	11/ 5/1850	11/ 5/1850	*Mich. Laws, 1851*, pp. xxvii–ix	1850: XV, 1
Maryland	6/ 4/1851	6/ 4/1851	A, III, 1712 n. *a*, 1726–7	1851: III, 47
Ohio	6/17/1851	9/ 1/1851	A, V, 2931 (for dates: B, III, 1192 n. 1)	1851: XIII, 1 & 2
Indiana	8/ 4/1851	11/ 1/1851	B, III, 482 n. 1, 495	1851: XI, 13
Minnesota	10/13/1857	5/11/1858[c]	B, III, 828 n. 1, 846	1857: X, 2
Oregon	11/ 9/1857	2/14/1859[c]	B, III, 1298 n. 1, 1312–3	1859: XI, 2
Kansas	10/ 4/1859	1/29/1861[c]	B, III, 516 n. 1, 528	1859 [or 1861]: XII, 1 [cf.: 1855, XIII, 1 (A, II, 1191); 1857, XII, 1 (*ibid.*, 1213); 1858, XIV, 1 (*ibid.*, 1235)]
West Virginia	4/ 3/1862	6/19/1863[c]	A, VII, 4012–3, 4013 n. *a*, 4031	1861–63: XI, 5
Nevada	9/ 7/1864	10/31/1864[c]	B, III, 1007 n. 1, 1020	1864: VIII, 1
Missouri	1/ 6/1865	1/ 6/1865	A, IV, 2191 n. *a*, 2212	1865: VIII, 4
Nebraska	6/21/1866	3/ 1/1867[c]	A, IV, 2359 (for dates: B, III, 982 n. 1)	1866–67: II, Corporations, 1 & 2
Alabama	12/ 6/1867	7/20/1868	A, I, 132 n. *a*, 150	1867: XIII, 1
North Carolina	1868	1868	A, V, 2800 n. *b*, 2816	1868: VIII, 1
Arkansas	3 /1868	3 /1868	A, I, 314 (for dates: B, III, 98 n. 1)	1868: V, 48
Tennessee	3/26/1870	3/26/1870	B, III, 1472 n. 1, 1486	1870: XI, 8
Pennsylvania	12/16/1873	1/ 1/1874	B, III, 1325 n. 1, 1329	1873 [or 1874]: III, 7
New Jersey	9/ 7/1875	9/ 7/1875	B, III, 1056, 1056 n. 9	1844 as amended Sept. 7, 1875
Maine	9/13/1875	9/13/1875	A, III, 1646 n. *a*, 1656	1819 as amended Sept. 13, 1875: IV, 14
Texas	2/17/1876	2/17/1876	B, III, 1489 n. 1, 1526	1876: XII, 1 & 2
Colorado	7/ 1/1876	8/ 1/1876[c]	B, III, 234 n. 1, 267	1876: XV, 2
Georgia	12/ 5/1877	12/ 5/1877	A, II, 851–2 (for dates: B, III, 357 n. 1)	1877: III, 7, ¶xviii [Cf. Const. of March 11, 1868 (A, II, 822 n. *a*, 830)]
North Dakota	10/ 1/1889	11/ 2/1889[c]	B, III, 1155 n. 1, 1170	1889: VII, 131
South Dakota	10/ 1/1889	11/ 2/1889[c]	B, III, 1432 n. 1, 1435, 1457–8	1889: III, 23, item 9; XVII, 1
Montana	10/ 1/1889	11/ 8/1889[c]	B, III, 944 n. 1, 968	1889: XV, 2
Washington	10/ 1/1889	11/11/1889[c]	B, III, 1626 n. 1, 1646	1889: XII, 1
Idaho	11/ 5/1889	7/ 3/1890[c]	B, III, 425 n. 1, 442	1890: XI, 2
Wyoming	11/ 5/1889	7/10/1890[c]	B, III, 1710 n. 1, 1715, 1728	1889: III, 27; X, 1
Mississippi	11/ 1/1890	11/ 1/1890	B, III, 860 n. 1, 877	1890: VII, 178
Kentucky	9/28/1891	9/28/1891	B, III, 533 n. 1, 539	1890 [or 1891]: Sec. 59, 17th
Utah	11/ 5/1895	1/ 4/1896[c]	B, III, 1538 n. 1, 1555	1895: XII, 1
South Carolina	12/ 4/1895	12/31/1895	B, III, 1369 n. 1, 1378, 1404–5	1895: III, 34, item III; IX, 2 [Cf. 1868, XII, 1 (A, VI, 3302)]
Delaware	6/ 4/1897	6/10/1897	A, I, 627 (for dates: B, III, 298 n. 1)	1897: IX, 1
Florida	1900	1900	*General Statutes of Florida, 1906*, p. 41. Joint Res. #2, Acts of 1899, adopted at general election of 1900	
Virginia	6/26/1902	7/10/1902	B, III, 1578 n. 1, 1588–9, 1605	1902: IV, 63, 64; XII, 154
Oklahoma	11/16/1907	11/16/1907[c]	B, III, 1224 n. 1, 1258	1907: IX, 38
New Mexico	1/21/1911	1/ 6/1912[c]	B, III, 1064 n. 1, 1084	1912: XI, 13
Arizona	2/ 9/1911	2/14/1912[c]	B, III, 65 n. 1, 86	1912: XIV, 2
Vermont	3/ 4/1913	3/13/1913	B, III, 1576 n. 28, 1577	1793: Ch. II, Sec. 65, added by 1913 amendment

[a] Four states—Connecticut, Massachusetts, New Hampshire, and Rhode Island—do not have constitutional provisions requiring incorporation under general laws. On this point, however, see the Rhode Island constitution of 1843 in *Reports of the Constitutional Convention Committee*, III, *Constitutions of the States and United States*, New York State Constitutional Convention Committee (Albany, 1938), 1361.

[b] This table was constructed from two sources: *The Federal and State Constitutions, Colonial Charters, and Other Organic Laws of the States, Territories, and Colonies Now or Heretofore Forming the United States of America*, compiled and edited by Francis Newton Thorpe (House Doc. 357, 59th Cong., 2d Sess.); and *Reports of the Constitutional Convention Committee*, III.

To minimize the space devoted to citations, those sources are referred to as A and B. In the 'Document' column the letter A or B is followed by a Roman numeral indicating the volume, then by page references in Arabic numerals. In the 'Constitution' column the date of the constitution involved is followed by the article in Roman numerals and the section in Arabic numerals. Departures from the above arrangements are clearly indicated.

[c] Date of statehood.

[d] The constitution was proclaimed by the Governor on December 20, 1849; California was admitted to the Union on September 9, 1850.

TABLE 6
Business Incorporations, Eight States, 1800–1875

Year	CONN. Under General Law	MAINE Under General Law	MAINE By Special Act	MAINE Total	MD. By Special Act	MASS. Under General Law	NEW JERSEY Under General Law	NEW JERSEY By Special Act	NEW JERSEY Total	NEW YORK Under General Law	NEW YORK By Special Act	NEW YORK Total	OHIO Under General Law	OHIO By Special Act	OHIO Total	PA. By Special Act
1800					0			2	2		5	5				0
1801					2			3	3		13	13				2
1802					0			3	3		14	14				0
1803					0			0	0		9	9		2	2	6
1804					1			12	12		12	12		0	0	14
1805					10			0	0		28	28		0	0	4
1806					2			9	9		25	25		0	0	6
1807					0			4	4		12	12		0	0	9
1808					5			5	5		36	36		2	2	2
1809					0			5	5		25	25		3	3	13
1810					11			0	0		44	44		1	1	15
1811					0			11	11	12ᵇ	43	55		1	1	17
1812					9			9	9	12	31	43		2	2	12
1813					0			4	4	29	25	54		1	1	11
1814					11			9	9	40	28	68		3	3	69
1815					10			13	13	19	19	38		1	1	15
1816					23			9	9	10	23	33		18	18	22
1817					10			2	2	5	27	32		18	18	23
1818					12			3	3	4	26	30		3	3	11
1819					10			3	3	1	28	29		2	2	24
1820			3	3	2			2	2	1	9	10		2	2	9
1821			13	13	1			1	1	3	7	10		0	0	4
1822			10	10	3			5	5	3	18	21		1	1	5
1823			13	13	8			5	5	6	32	38		0	0	11
1824			10	10	4			13	13	2	40	42		2	2	4
1825			17	17	4			13	13	10	56	66		3	3	12
1826			18	18	7			5	5	10	25	35		8	8	30
1827			19	19	6			0	0	8	24	32		7	7	16
1828			12	12	16			25	25	10	44	54		8	8	22
1829			17	17	21			5	5	9	37	46		12	12	18
1830			13	13	6			10	10	2	32	34		17	17	22
1831			20	20	5			14	14	8	40	48		8	8	37
1832			21	21	22			11	11	3	70	73		37	37	39
1833			25	25	27			13	13	6	48	54		14	14	38
1834			47	47	13			14	14	10	47	57		31	31	35
1835			24	24	9			13	13	12	26	38		38	38	30
1836			131	131	36			35	35	20	116	136		71	71	70
1837	12ᵃ		104	104	12			45	45	17	44	61		92	92	31
1838	23		34	34	13			9	9	4	28	32		55	55	64
1839	9		14	14	35			14	14	4	36	40		67	67	43
1840	4		3	3	10			6	6	5	15	20		10	10	33
1841	10		18	18	6			6	6	12	17	29		9	9	31
1842	4		11	11	4			6	6	3	8	11		11	11	23
1843	8		10	10	3			1	1	0	6	6		10	10	31
1844	9		17	17	8			7	7	14	17	31		29	29	40
1845	20		30	30	12			18	18	13	17	30		53	53	25
1846	18		44	44	22		4ᵇ	21	25					49	49	25
1847	26		32	32	24		5	20	25					22	22	17
1848	14		27	27	34		5	28	33					80	80	51
1849	29		34	34	0		1	31	32					103	103	90
1850	38		27	27	71		7	20	27					*192	192	98
1851	44		8	8	0	8ᵃ	18	36	54					170	170	131
1852	85		52	52	18	20	13	44	57							74
1853	133		61	61		21	19	46	65							147
1854	106		63	63		13	21	51	72							126
1855	48		33	33		31	16	66	82				7ᵃ			90
1856	26		38	38		26	8	41	49					64	64	91
1857	28		39	39		20	11	43	54					47	47	117
1858	18		14	14		11	20	27	47					49	49	49
1859	22		29	29		20	5	49	54					97	97	122
1860	26		31	31		21	7	43	50					36	36	94
1861	14		16	16		16	2	37	39					25	25	
1862	18		19	19		20	11	22	33					26	26	
1863	27		16	16		56	7	30	37					51	51	
1864	76		33	33		174	12	60	72					91	91	
1865	93		38	38		136	8	69	77					358	358	
1866	123		61	61		103	25	123	148					281	281	
1867	66		55	55		87	25	140	165					266	266	
1868	72		50	50		89	13	148	161					295	295	
1869	68		65	65		56	14	128	142					333	333	
1870	62	11	68	79		65	19	135	154					304	304	
1871		19	54	73		84	27	122	149					336	336	
1872		6	58	64		81	23	119	142					401	401	
1873		23	68	91		88	35	133	168					360	360	
1874		20	93	113		80	38	83	121					298	298	
1875		12	66	78		86	51	44	95					333	333	

Source: Appendix 3
ᵃ Not a full year. Not included in moving averages plotted on Chart 1.
ᵇ Not a full year. Included in moving averages plotted on Chart 1.

wave, if there was one.[5] A different interpretation may be put upon the 1861–78 period, as is done in the next chapter, though for the present a fourth wave in these early data is assumed.

To aid understanding of these long waves and the nature of the other movements, the total incorporations by four states (Maryland, New Jersey, New York, and Ohio) were arranged according to a uniform industrial classification scheme (see Tables 7–10).

Table 7 is a revision of some data originally compiled by Joseph G. Blandi from Maryland laws.[6] For each business corporation chartered prior to the spring of 1852 a special statute was passed. Though a constitutional provision requiring business charters to be procured under general laws was ratified in June 1851, no general incorporating statutes were enacted in compliance with it until a year later.[7] Mutual insurance companies were removed from the Blandi figures since that type of company is not included in the business incorporation series of this study (see Ch. 1). The charters of the corporations in Blandi's Miscellaneous group were reclassified according to their stated purposes.[8] The Canal and River Improvement figures of Table 7 are combinations of Blandi's two groups— Canals and Navigation. His category, Wharf Companies, forms part of the Miscellaneous Transportation group of Table 7.

The New Jersey material in Table 8A was compiled from a document published by John Hood when he was Secretary of State for New Jersey,[9] and from the New

[5] Little can be said about a possible long wave in the Connecticut series for the Civil War and post-Civil War period, since the incorporation series for that state is broken. Connecticut data for 1871–80 have not been published.
[6] Maryland Business Corporations, 1783–1852 (Johns Hopkins University Studies in Historical and Political Science, LII, 2, 1934), pp. 14, 93–111.
[7] Maryland Laws, 1852, Ch. 322, 338, 369.
[8] Two were added to the Mining group—1 in 1836, 1 in 1850; 4 were added to the Manufacturing group—1 in 1832, 1 in 1835, 1 in 1837, 1 in 1847; 11 were added to Miscellaneous Transportation (which includes also Blandi's 3 Wharf companies)—1 in 1829, 1 in 1830, 2 in 1832, 2 in 1840, 1 in 1845, 1 in 1847, 2 in 1850, 1 in 1852; 1 was added to the Commercial Banking figure for 1850; 2 were added to the Real Estate figures—1 in 1817, 1 in 1838; and 39 Steamboat companies, 2 Telegraph companies, 1 Gas company, 2 Trading companies, 4 Amusement companies, and 2 Agricultural companies were set up in six separate groups.
[9] Index of Titles of Corporations chartered under general and special laws by the legislature of New Jersey, between the years 1693–1870, inclusive . . . (Trenton, 1871). Because the data in that volume, together with the adjustments made in working up the material, are described fully in the New Jersey section of Appendix 3, only the various decisions that had to be made with respect to the grouping of the corporations by the purposes for which they were organized are commented on here.

CHART 1

Business Incorporations, Eight States, 1800-1875

2-item Centered Moving Averages of Annual Data

Number of incorporations

Connecticut
Maine
Maryland
Massachusetts
New Jersey
New York
Ohio
Pennsylvania

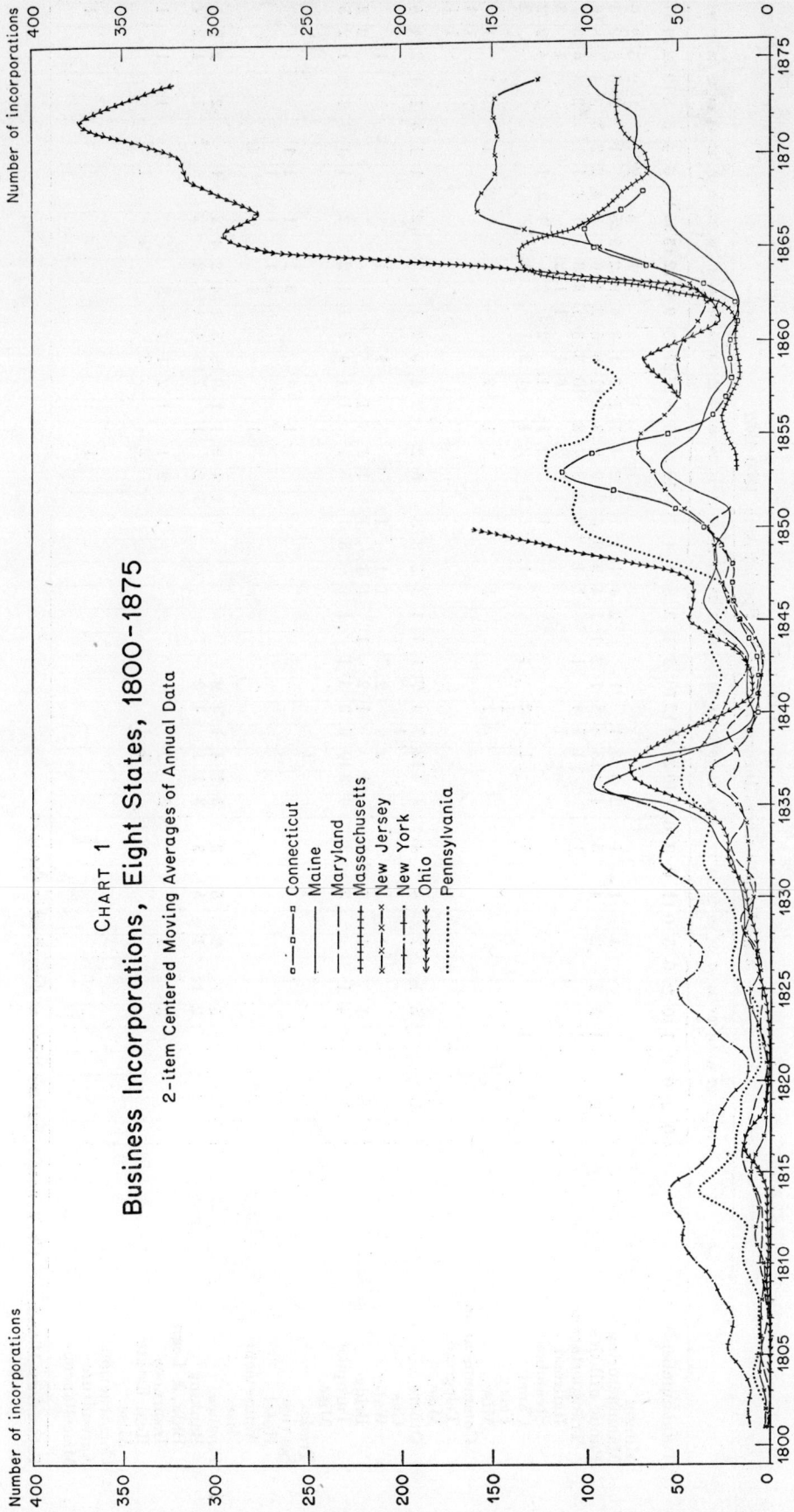

Source of annual data: Table 6.

TABLE 7

Maryland Business Incorporations by Special Acts, 1800–1852

	'00	'01	'02	'03	'04	'05	'06	'07	'08	'09	'10	'11	'12	'13	'14	'15	'16	'17	'18	'19	'20	'21	'22	'23	'24	'25	'26	'27	'28	'29	'30	'31	'32	'33	'34	'35	'36	'37	'38	'39	'40	'41	'42	'43	'44	'45	'46	'47	'48	'49	'50	'51	'52
Total number	0	2	0	0	1	10	0	2	5	0	11	0	9	0	0	11	10	23	10	12	10	2	1	3	8	4	4	7	6	16	21	6	5	22	27	13	9	36	12	13	35	10	6	4	3	8	12	22	24	34	71	0	18
Mining																																																					
Manufacturing																																																					
Public utilities																																																					
Transportation																																																					
Railroad																																																					
Steamboat																																																					
Canal																																																					
Ferry																																																					
Misc.																																																					
Communication																																																					
Telegraph																																																					
Misc.																																																					
Others																																																					
Gas																																																					
Water																																																					
Bridge																																																					
Turnpike																																																					
Misc.																																																					
Trade																																																					
Service																																																					
Hotel																																																					
Amusement																																																					
Misc.																																																					
Finance																																																					
Banking																																																					
Bldg. & Loan																																																					
Insurance																																																					
Real Estate																																																					
Misc.																																																					
Construction																																																					
Agriculture																																																					
Miscellaneous																																																					

Taken from Blandi (see Ch. 3, note 6) but modified as described in the text.

14

TABLE 8

New Jersey Business Incorporations

A By Special Acts, 1800–1875

Row categories (left to right columns are years 1800, '01, '02, '03, '04, '05, '06, '07, '08, '09, '10, '11, '12, '13, '14, '15, '16, '17, '18, '19, '20, '21, '22, '23, '24, '25, '26, '27, '28, '29, '30, '31, '32, '33, '34, '35, '36, '37, '38, '39, '40, '41, '42, '43, '44, '45, '46, '47, '48, '49, '50, '51, '52, '53, '54, '55, '56, '57, '58, '59, '60, '61, '62, '63, '64, '65, '66, '67, '68, '69, '70, '71, '72, '73, '74, '75):

- Total number
- Mining
- Manufacturing
- Public utilities
- Transportation
  - Railroad
  - Steamboat
  - Canal
  - Ferry
  - Misc.
- Communication
  - Telegraph
  - Misc.
- Others
  - Gas
  - Water
  - Bridge
  - Turnpike
  - Misc.
- Trade
- Service
  - Hotel
  - Amusement
  - Misc.
- Finance
  - Banking
  - Bldg. & Loan
  - Insurance
  - Real Estate
  - Misc.
- Construction
- Agriculture
- Miscellaneous

Compiled from Hood volume cited in Ch. 3, note 9, and from New Jersey statutes for 1871–75. For complete data, see Appendix 4.

B Under General Laws, 1846–1899

Row categories (columns are years 1846, '47, '48, '49, '50, '51, '52, '53, '54, '55, '56, '57, '58, '59, '60, '61, '62, '63, '64, '65, '66, '67, '68, '69, '70, '71, '72, '73, '74, '75, '76, '77, '78, '79, '80, '81, '82, '83, '84, '85, '86, '87, '88, '89, '90, '91, '92, '93, '94, '95, '96, '97, '98, '99):

- Total number
- Mining
- Manufacturing
- Public utilities
- Transportation
  - Railroad
  - Steamboat
  - Canal
  - Ferry
  - Misc.
- Communication
  - Telegraph
  - Misc.
- Others
  - Gas
  - Water
  - Bridge
  - Turnpike
  - Misc.
- Trade
- Service
  - Hotel
  - Amusement
  - Misc.
- Finance
  - Banking
  - Bldg. & Loan
  - Insurance
  - Real Estate
  - Misc.
- Construction
- Agriculture
- Miscellaneous

Compiled from sources cited in the New Jersey section of Appendix 3. For complete data, see Appendix 1

15

Jersey statutes for 1871–75.[10] While the companies listed in the first source are grouped into several industrial categories useful in constructing Table 8A, the name of a company was in some cases more helpful in indicating the primary corporate objective.[11] This was particularly true of companies that are duplicated in the Hood volume and appear in two or more of his industrial categories. When corporate objectives could not be surmised, the companies were placed in the Miscellaneous group of Table 8A.

Table 8B was compiled from New Jersey reports that list each newly chartered company by name, give its authorized capital stock, and describe briefly its corporate objectives.[12] For the charts of this chapter that

show New Jersey incorpoations, the data of the two sections of Table 8 are combined for the period of incorporation under both general and special laws, that is, 1846–75. Figures for 1875–99 are given in this chapter in order that the trends shown in Table 11 may be visualized for the post-1875 period.

Table 9 is a rearrangment of an unpublished table constructed by Jospeh S. Davis from data for New York compiled by Homer B. Vanderblue from original sources.[13] As elsewhere in this study, mutual insurance companies were excluded from the data on business incorporations. In contrast to the New Jersey tables, which present incorporations under general and special laws separately, the New York table applies to charters procured under both types of law.

The Ohio purpose data of Table 10A were compiled from the *Annual Report of the Secretary of State, to the Governor of the State of Ohio, for the Year 1885,*[14] where incorporations are grouped by industry. On the whole, the names of the companies—the only information by which the industrial groupings by the office of the Secretary of State could be checked—did not give much ground for suggesting reallocation.[15] In 1851 Ohio

[10] Nonbusiness corporations were excluded from the count for 1871–75 on the basis of the company name; the same criterion was used in deciding the industrial allocation of each corporation.

[11] Hood's classification of companies was modified in the following manner, in addition to the changes necessitated by the elimination of duplications too numerous to note here:

1) A building and loan company of 1870 was transferred from the Banking to the Building and Loan group.

2) Docks and Wharves, and Express companies were added to Miscellaneous Transportation companies.

3) Ice companies were added to Manufacturing.

4) Most Improvement companies were classified as Real Estate companies; but on the basis of the company names some were put into other groups such as Agriculture, Construction, Building and Loan, Trade, Miscellaneous Other Public Utilities, and Miscellaneous Finance.

5) Hood's Manufacturing group includes mining companies. Only entries that had 'mining' in the title or for some other reason were clearly mining concerns were treated as mining corporations. Consequently, the Mining group of Table 8A is probably somewhat smaller than it should be, and the Manufacturing group correspondingly inflated.

6) The Market group was divided on the basis of the company names among the Real Estate, Trade, and Miscellaneous Transportation groups of Table 8A.

7) The Miscellaneous group, allocated entirely on the basis of name, fell largely into the Mining group—many companies being oil or marl producing enterprises.

8) Some companies were transferred from the Railroad group to Miscellaneous Transportation—horse car companies, horse railroads, street railroads, and tramways.

9) Some entries under Hood's Steamboat classification were added to the Canal group.

10) Water companies were divided between the Water group (which has to do only with the supply of water for domestic purposes) and Miscellaneous Other Public Utilities (which includes the supply of water power).

11) Except for the elimination of duplications noted above and the two exclusions noted here, modifications were not necessary in the following Hood classes: Bridge, Canal, Gas Light, Hall (after nonbusiness had been excluded), Hotel, Insurance (after mutuals had been excluded), Navigation, Telegraph, and Turnpike companies.

[12] These documents are listed in the New Jersey section of Appendix 3. In Chapters 7 and 8 the information on the industrial objectives of New Jersey corporations chartered under general laws 1846–1907 is described fully.

[1] [13] Professor Davis and Dean Vanderblue have kindly permitted use of their material. Less comprehensive data on New York incorporations, namely, figures on incorporations under the New York 1811 general incorporation act for manufacturing enterprises, were published by W. C. Kessler in *The Journal of Political Economy*, XLVIII, 6 (Dec., 1940), pp. 877–82. The portion of the Davis-Vanderblue figures that applies to incorporation under the general law of 1811 differs slightly, but not significantly, from the Kessler data.

[14] Pp. 147–227 (Columbus, 1885). See the Ohio section of Appendix 3 for a full description of the sources of Ohio incorporation data.

[15] The groupings in the Secretary's report were modified as follows:

a) Three companies were transferred from the Bank category: 1 of 1814 to Manufacturing, and 1 of 1816 and 1 of 1817 to Miscellaneous.

b) Four were transferred from the Bridge group to the Miscellaneous Other Public Utility group: 1 of 1832, 1 of 1837, 1 of 1849, and 1 of 1851.

c) Six of the Canal group were reclassified: 3 were transferred to Miscellaneous Transportation—1 of 1830, 1 of 1835, and 1 of 1848; 1 of 1836 to the Miscellaneous group; and 2 to Manufacturing—1 of 1837 and 1 of 1838.

d) The Cemetery group was put entirely under Real Estate.

e) Draining companies, except 1 of 1838, which was put in the general Miscellaneous group, were put in the Miscellaneous Other Public Utility group.

f) Harbor companies were transferred to Miscellaneous Transportation.

g) The entire Hotel group was accepted as listed.

h) Hydraulic companies were put in the Miscellaneous Other Public Utility group.

i) The entire Insurance group (except mutual companies, which were eliminated from the business incorporation series) was accepted as listed.

j) The Manufacturing and Mining groups, except 1 company of

TABLE 9

New York Business Incorporations
Under Special and General Laws, 1800–1845

	1800	'01	'02	'03	'04	'05	'06	'07	'08	'09	'10	'11	'12	'13	'14	'15	'16	'17	'18	'19	'20	'21	'22	'23	'24	'25	'26	'27	'28	'29	'30	'31	'32	'33	'34	'35	'36	'37	'38	'39	'40	'41	'42	'43	'44	'45
Total number	5	13	14	9	12	28	25	12	36	25	44	55	43	54	68	38	33	32	30	29	10	10	21	38	42	66	35	32	54	46	34	48	73	54	57	38	136	61	32	40	20	29	11	6	31	30
Mining																																														
Manufacturing																																														
By Special Act									1	8	15	1	3	2	2			5	5	1	1																								14	14
Under General Law									1	8	15	24	15	33	46	19	10			23																										
Public utilities	5	11	13	8	12	26	25	10	33	16	25	12	22	14	16	13	17	20	18	22	6	2	12	18	17	16	12	15	17	14		9	9	20	28	18	30	15	9	7	10	10	4	4	16	9
Transportation																																														
Railroad																											1	1	6																	
Steamboat																										5			5	3																
Canal					1	1	1		1		1			1							2					2	1	2	3	2																
Ferry																				1		1	4	4	2	2	2		7	4																
Misc.																							1	1	1	1	1		2												2				1	1
Communication																																														
Telegraph																																														
Misc.																			1							1				1	3	1		1	3						2				1	1
Others	5	11	13	8	12	26	24	10	32	16	24	22	22	12	15	13	17	20	18	22	6	2	12	18	17	16	12	15	17	14		9	9	13	14	14	30	15	9	7	10	10	4	4	16	9
Gas													1							1						3			1	1		2	3			1		2	2					2		
Water		1	4	1	4	8	3	1	6	1	2		3	1	1		1		2	3	2	1	5	9	9	3	3	5	5	2	2	5	2	2	3		9	5	1	3	4	3	2	1	3	3
Bridge		2	2	4	2		4	2	2		3	2	2	4			2	8	16		2	1	7	8	8	2	7	8	12	6	6	8	4	3	7	1	17	8	7	4	6	3	2	3	9	7
Turnpike	5	8	7	3	6	18	17	7	26	15	19	10	18	7	14	12	14	12		18	2	1				8									11	11	1					1				
Misc.																																														
Trade							1		1			1		1									2	2					1								1									
Service																																														
Hotel																																														
Amusement																																														
Misc.																																														
Finance																																														
Banking		2	1	1		2		2	1	1	3	7	3	4	4	2	3	6	6	5	1	4		4	14	24	1			13	12	12	15	19	12	1	26	2	4	9	2	2	2		14	
Bldg. & Loan		1										5	2	4			2	5	3	1	1	2		2	2	6				12	10	11	11	9	9		13				1	1	2			
Insurance		1	1	1		1		1	1		1	2	1		4	2	1		3	4		2	5	2	12	18	1			1	1	4	8	10		1	13	2	4	8	2					
Real Estate																														2	2			3							1					
Misc.																																														
Construction													1																		1		1						2							
Agriculture		1				1					2																						2		3											
Miscellaneous																																	1	1	1											

Compiled from state laws. See text.

17

Table 10
Ohio Business Incorporations
A By Special Acts, 1803–1851

	1803	'04	'05	'06	'07	'08	'09	'10	'11	'12	'13	'14	'15	'16	'17	'18	'19	'20	'21	'22	'23	'24	'25	'26	'27
Total number	2					2	3	1	1	2	1	3	1	18	18	3	2	2		1		2	3	8	7
Mining																		1							
Manufacturing									1			1				1								1	
Public utilities							2	1				2	1	5	12	1	1	1		1		2	3	5	6
Transportation												2	1	1								1		1	2
Railroad																									
Steamboat																									
Canal												1												1	2
Ferry																									
Misc.												1	1	1								1			
Communication																									
Telegraph																									
Misc.																									
Others							2	1						4	12	1	1	1		1		1	3	4	4
Gas																									
Water								1						1										1	
Bridge														2	1		1			1			2	1	3
Turnpike							2							1	11	1		1				1	1	2	1
Misc.																									
Trade																									
Service																									
Hotel																									
Amusement																									
Misc.																									
Finance	1					2	1			2	1			12	5	1	1							2	1
Banking						2	1			2	1			12	5	1									
Bldg. & Loan																									
Insurance																	1							2	1
Real Estate	1																								
Misc.																									
Construction																									
Agriculture																									
Miscellaneous	1													1	1										

	'28	'29	'30	'31	'32	'33	'34	'35	'36	'37	'38	'39	'40	'41	'42	'43	'44	'45	'46	'47	'48	'49	'50	'51
Total number	8	12	17	8	37	14	31	38	71	92	55	67	10	9	11	10	29	53	49	22	80	103	192	170
Mining										1	3								1				1	1
Manufacturing		2	6	1	5	1	3	11	9	26	11	16	2		2	1	2	4	5	1	1	1		7
Public utilities	8	7	9	4	29	11	13	22	55	55	38	47	8	9	8	3	22	42	38	19	73	94	176	137
Transportation	3		5	2	13	1	8	10	38	23	4	4	3	1	2	1	3	8	13	4	18	13	20	22
Railroad				1	11		5	7	32	10	2	4	2	1	2		3	8	11	4	15	12	19	21
Steamboat	1		2	1	2	1	2			4	1		1						1		2		1	
Canal	2		2				1	2	5	8	1					1								
Ferry																								
Misc.			1					1	1	1									1		1	1		1
Communication																						1	1	3
Telegraph																						1	1	3
Misc.																								
Others	5	7	4	2	16	10	5	12	17	32	34	43	5	8	6	2	19	34	25	15	55	80	155	112
Gas			1							1									2		1	2	1	1
Water		1	1			2		3	1	1	1							1			2		1	1
Bridge	2	2	1		6	2	1	4	5	6	9	5	1				2	2	4	1	12	4	3	5
Turnpike	3	3	1	2	9	6	4	5	11	19	20	34	4	7	6	2	17	30	12	14	37	73	148	103
Misc.		1			1					5	4	4		1				1	7		3	1	2	2
Trade																								
Service							1	1	1	1											1		1	8
Hotel							1	1	1	1											1		1	8
Amusement																								
Misc.																								
Finance		3	2	3	3	2	14	4	5	8	2	4			1	6	5	7	5	2	5	8	14	17
Banking		2		3	1	1	12		1		1					3	1	1		1	1	4	1	
Bldg. & Loan																								
Insurance		1	2		2	1	2	4	4	8	1	2						1	1		2	3	5	14
Real Estate												2			1	2	4	5	4	1	2	1	8	2
Misc.																1								1
Construction																								
Agriculture																								
Miscellaneous									1	1	1													

B Under General Laws, 1856–1899

	1856	'57	'58	'59	'60	'61	'62	'63	'64	'65	'66	'67	'68	'69	'70	'71	'72	'73	'74	'75	'76	'77	'78	'79	'80	'81	'82	'83	'84	'85	'86	'87	'88	'89	'90	'91	'92	'93	'94	'95	'96	'97	'98	'99
Total number	64	47	49	97	36	25	26	51	91	358	281	266	295	333	304	336	401	360	298	333	266	237	227	286	391	508	598	612	477	515	626	832	661	725	768	834	854	713	835	872	763	714	701	1005
Mining	6	7	3	1	5	9	2	4	36	245	106	25	28	47	32	25	56	35	35	30	17	6	13	24	34	29	42	30	29	38	72	163	49	44	51	55	51	37	62	70	94	66	37	116
Manufacturing	13	17	10	15	6	2	10	12	14	29	64	70	74	88	106	128	149	159	107	92	72	79	75	119	185	206	299	300	220	237	254	295	313	337	387	427	451		418	399	353	330	335	425
Public utilities	38	31	31	72	21	14	10	26	22	42	62	74	74	76	80	85	98	60	62	62	53	61	64	64	76	63	89	89	69	80	123	164	96	123	106	94	89	83	104	116	69	90	106	163
Transportation	7	3	4	4	6	6	6	8	8	21	27	27	46	45	61	74	84	49	48	52	35	46	42	45	48	102	71	47	35	31	64	77	48	67	67	58	61	67	48	71	40	46	42	78
Railroad	7	2	3	26	3	3	5	13	13	10	14	17	29	30	48	58	56	30	28	27	25	36	33	32	34	84	44	37	20	20	32	44	22	28	35	17	25	26	15	25	13	13	10	17
Steamboat										2	5	3	4	4	3	1	2	2	1		1	3		5	3		5	2		1	5	3	3	6	3	8	5	2	3	5	7	2	5	5
Canal																		1																										1
Ferry	1	1	1	19	6		1	6	5	9	7	7	13	11	10	15	21	16	9	25	8	7	7	7	12	17	22	8	12	10	27	30	23	33	27	33	31	36	30	41	20	31	27	55
Misc.											1		1	1	1	1	3	1	2	1	1		5	2	2	1	1	10	6	4	5	2	4	3	2	2	2	2	2	5	5	5	3	52
Communication																				3	4	5	4	2	3	3	5	9	6	3	4	5	2	2	1	3	2	2	1	1		2	2	3
Telegraph	1		1											1	1		1	2	1	3	4	5	5	5	18	13	1	9	6	3	4		2	2	1	3	3		1	28	15	26	38	49
Misc.																								7	9	39	12	32	27	45	54	82	44	45	37	31	24	14	30	16	14	16	24	33
Others	31	14	26	46	15	11	4	16	5	21	33	47	28	30	18	11	11	9	19	7	14	10	19	7	9	9	5	10	11	34	54	82	45	54	37	31	24	14	30	16	15	16	24	11
Gas	8	6	1	3	1	4		1		3	3	7	6	6	4	3	4	4	7	6	4	2	4	3	3	8	4	5	11	34	28	44	13	13	3	4	8	3	4	4	14	16	24	3
Water	4	1	1	1	3	3	1		1		2	2	3		2	1	1	1	1	1	1	2	1	1	3	3	2	4	2	2	4	2	4	3	3	2	2	2	2	4	5	5	2	3
Bridge	17	8	25	42	7	1	14	14	3	16	28	38	19	22	12	5	6	4	11	1	9	1	5	1	1	2	4	1	16	2	4	2		1	1	2		1	2				2	1
Turnpike																										23	21	17	22	9	15	25	35	41	46	65	77	8	24	12	7	10	14	18
Misc.	1				1										12	2		3		12		12		1	1	14	32	43	60	19	35	54	46	46	38	60	78	35	86	88	87	58	79	96
Trade										4		5	5	5	9	6	4	3	4	12	29	36	27	24	22	24	4	43	60	44	47	40	47	46	38	60	78	35	59	81	69	66	50	75
Service	3	2	3	8	1		2	6	13	3	3	6	8	10	3	3	20	10	29	23	21	23	18	16	16	14	8	26	36	34	26	24	30	31	26	35	44	20	34	46	37	43	24	30
Hotel					1					28	2	3	5	5	4	4	3	3	18	8	11	11	8	8	4	7	8	16	22	9	18	16	11	13	11	22	25	12	23	32	24	21	24	42
Amusement		3	3	8							15		91	85	64	89	66	90	9	95	57	41	35	47	60	63	94	115	65	65	79	102	109	111	115	112	89	55	75	90	69	70	59	89
Misc.				1	3			2	13		1	53	1		1	1		21	71	20	10		28	41	49	50	2	5	53	6	10	80	99	6	26	25	24	15	11	11	20	12	18	21
Finance								2				42	86	81	56	82	60	58	13	64	35	31			41		84	91	53	58	63	63	99	18	77	75	52	31	32	35	35	31	18	39
Banking	3	1	2	4	3		2	5	13	26	11	10	2	2	5	4	2	5	5	6	3	3	4	3	4	4	5	3	4	4	4	2	1	7	6	7	7	8	3	3	12	4	2	5
Bldg. & Loan	1	1						1	2	2			1	1	5	1	3	6	3	5	3	2	1	1	6	2		6	4	1	7	4	2	2	6	3	11	16	16	12	35	18	24	3
Insurance																										10	4	4	1		1	3	1		6	3	8	12	8	8	5	4	3	27
Real Estate																										2	7	7	2	1	7	7	7	3	6	9	4	6	6	8	5	11	8	9
Misc.				1							1	6	4	1	6	1	2	1	2	4	3	1	8	1	2			2	2	4	4	2	2	2	3									
Construction																							2	2																				
Agriculture	4	4	2	1				2	3	6		6	1	1	1		2	1	1	2	3	1	1	1	1	2	4	7	2	5	7	4	7	8	6	6	4	6	6	8	5	18	3	5
Miscellaneous	4		2	1				2	6	10	27	27	10	20	7	1	4	1	2	6	1	1	2	2	2	2	7	7	2	23	6	4	3	4	8	6	7	9	9	8	5	11	8	9

Compiled from sources cited in the Ohio section of Appendix 3.   For complete data, see Appendix 4.

19

adopted a constitutional provision requiring the incorporation of business enterprises under general laws. The first general comprehensive business incorporation law, however, was not passed until May 1, 1852.[16] Unfortunately no data have been published on Ohio incor-

TABLE 11
Incorporations Classified Industrially, Four States
Percentage Distribution by Decades, 1790-99 to 1890-99
Percentages of Total Incorporations Computed from Tables 7-10

INDUSTRIAL CATEGORIES	1790-1799	1800-1809	1810-1819	1820-1829	1830-1839	1840-1849	1850-1859	1860-1869	1870-1879	1880-1889	1890-1899
Maryland — Incorporations by Special Acts											
Mining & mfg.	.0	5.0	16.7	31.9	39.9	48.0	27.0[a]				
Banks	18.8	20.0	19.8	4.2	24.2	6.5	11.2[a]				
Public utilities	62.5	55.0	55.2	54.2	24.7	39.8	41.6[a]				
All others	18.8	20.0	8.3	9.7	11.2	5.7	20.2[a]				
New Jersey — Incorporations under Special and General Laws											
Mining & mfg.	9.1	4.7	19.0	41.9	41.6	41.5	25.5	38.7	36.5	58.1	58.9
Banks	.0	7.0	17.5	16.2	9.6	3.1	13.4	5.1	6.8	.8	.1
Public utilities	81.8	83.7	63.5	28.4	38.2	44.0	51.2	35.5	24.8	15.3	9.8
All others	9.1	4.7	.0	13.5	10.7	11.3	10.0	20.7	31.9	25.9	31.1
New York — Incorporations under Special and General Laws											
Mining & mfg.	9.5	5.0	43.2	26.8	28.3	42.5[b]					
Banks	14.3	2.8	5.4	7.1	10.5	2.4[b]					
Public utilities	66.7	88.8	46.2	53.7	49.9	52.0[b]					
All others	9.5	3.4	5.2	12.4	11.3	3.1[b]					
Ohio — Incorporations: by Special Acts, 1803-51; under General Laws, 1856-99											
Mining & mfg.		.0[c]	6.0	9.3	21.6	5.3	2.5[d] / 28.0[e]	49.7	44.6	53.4	56.4
Banks		42.9[c]	42.0	4.7	4.4	2.9	.3[d] / .4[e]	.3	2.4	1.1	2.1
Public utilities		28.6[c]	46.0	76.7	65.8	84.1	86.5[d] / 61.5[e]	23.9	22.1	17.9	12.6
All others		28.6[c]	6.0	9.3	8.1	7.7	10.8[d] / 10.1[e]	26.0	30.9	27.6	28.8

[a] For 1850-52.
[b] For 1840-45.
[c] For 1803-09.
[d] For 1850 and 1851. The break in the data makes two figures for the 1850's desirable.
[e] For 1856-59. See note d.

porations for 1852-55. But from 1855 through 1936, information on corporations chartered under general

1837, which was put in the Miscellaneous group, and 9 Gas companies, which were set up as a separate group under Public Utilities—Others, were accepted as listed.

k) The Navigation group, except 1 company of 1803, which was put in the Miscellaneous group, and 1 company of 1846, which was put in the Miscellaneous Transportation group, was put in the Steamboat group.

l) The Railroad, Road, Telegraph, and Water Company groups were accepted as listed.

m) Savings Associations, except 2, which were transferred to the Miscellaneous Finance group—1 of 1843 and 1 of 1851—were put with Banks.

[16] 50 Ohio Laws 274.

laws has been published (Table 10B).[17] Like the New Jersey figures in Table 8B, the data cover a longer period than that with which this chapter is concerned, but here also the purpose was to provide a longer series for use in Table 11.

The industrial classification of the 1800-75 incorporations of Maryland, New Jersey, New York, and Ohio was supplemented in various ways. The pre-1800 data published by Joseph S. Davis, some of the post-1875 material of this volume (as indicated above), and a portion of the information on early Pennsylvania incorporations prepared by William Miller and published in the *Quarterly Journal of Economics* were used.[18] The combined data reveal much about early incorporations. Many of them were tinged with public interest—utilities and banks. Such incorporations gradually formed a smaller and smaller percentage of the total as manufacturing and mining incorporations increased. Of course, the initial manufacturing corporations were not without public interest—witness *The Society for Establishing Useful Manufactures*[19]—but the public character soon gave way to private interest. Table 11, prepared to bring out the movements, utilizes decade (and partial decade) figures derived from Tables 7-10. Joseph S. Davis' published material, after mutual insurance companies had been excluded,[20] was used for 1790-99 in calculating the percentages for Maryland, New Jersey, and New York.

A general incorporation act passed in New York in 1811 stimulated manufacturing incorporations. Ohio incorporations, in sharp contrast to New York, were dominated by turnpike companies in the early part of the 19th century; manufacturing corporations constituted a small percentage of the total until the last four decades of the century, when the turnpike company was disappearing.

[17] The Ohio documents containing data on newly chartered corporations 1855-1936 are described in the Ohio section of Appendix 3. For 1855-71 the information on Ohio incorporations is similiar to that for the earlier period. Beginning in 1872, the office of the Secretary of State published a brief statement concerning the object of each newly formed corporation.

[18] A Note on the History of Business Corporations in Pennsylvania, 1800-1860, *Quarterly Journal of Economics*, LV, 1 (Nov. 1940), pp. 150-60. Of the Miller figures only those for total incorporations, turnpikes, and banks could be used because of differences in classification and the impossibility of rearranging the Miller material to parallel that set forth here. The Miller totals include mutual insurance companies, which, as mentioned above, were excluded from the business incorporation series of this study.

[19] Davis, I, 349-522.

[20] *Ibid.*, II, 22, 23. The three mutual insurance companies excluded from the percentage calculations were incorporated as follows: in Maryland, 1 in 1794 and 1 in 1798; in New York, 1 in 1798 (references to these companies will be found in Davis, II, Ch. 5).

The character of the early corporations may reflect a contemporary belief that the corporate form should not be resorted to unless the public interest was involved.[21] This link between the corporation and the numerous enterprises of a public nature that a large and rapidly developing country needed may in part explain the early growth of the corporation in this country, which appears phenomenal when compared with British and continental European experience. As more manufacturing enterprises were chartered and it became easier to get charters without demonstrating that the public interest was involved, the corporate form was adjusted to the new circumstances.

The long waves of incorporation mentioned above resulted largely from fluctuations in the number of charters granted turnpike and manufacturing enterprises. Turnpike undertakings bulked large in the total picture in every decade under consideration except the 'thirties (see Tables 7–10). Chart 2 was constructed from moving averages of data in Tables 7–10, supplemented by William Miller's Pennsylvania figures, to show the long waves in the turnpike incorporation series,[22] which extend roughly from 1792 to 1822, 1822 to 1842, 1842 to 1862, and from 1862 to 1884.[23] The dates of these waves, except the terminal date of the fourth wave, almost coincide with those of waves in total incorpora-

tions. The turnpike data are presented as five-item moving averages plotted at the central item.[24] (The period for the moving averages is longer than for some of the series in this chapter because the object was to concentrate attention on the long waves.) To avoid confusion concerning a point that will arise later in discussing the chartering of manufacturing enterprises, it should be noted that each unbroken curve on Chart 2 represents charters granted under *either* general laws *or* special acts. The Ohio material is, however, in two parts: the first is for charters under special laws; the second, dealing with the period following the constitutional provision of 1851, gives incorporations under general law.

For about a century turnpikes served as an outlet for private funds (Chart 2, supplemented by data in App. 4). Davis gives 1792 as the date of the first incorporation of a turnpike company.[25] After 1880 few turnpike companies were incorporated as private business enterprises, at least in Ohio, New Jersey, and Pennsylvania.

Incorporations of manufacturing enterprises were numerous and moved in long waves resembling those of turnpike concerns. The annual data, upon which the 5-item moving averages of Chart 3 were calculated, include incorporations under both general and special laws. During certain periods it was possible in many states to procure a charter for a manufacturing company under either type of law. The first long wave of incorporations for manufacturing purposes can scarcely be said to have begun before 1805 (at which time the first turnpike incorporation wave was well developed), but it ended about 1820, only slightly before the termination of the first turnpike wave. The trough of the second wave, 1842, coincided with that of turnpikes, while the third long wave probably ended in 1861 for manufacturing and in 1862 for turnpike incorporations. The end of the fourth wave in manufacturing incorporations was 1876, while 1884 appears to have been the end of the last wave in turnpike chartering.[26] Agreement on these two terminal dates could scarcely be expected, as almost no turnpikes were incorporated by the end of the period.

Long waves in the number of charters granted are to be observed sometimes in other industrial fields, but they are not as striking as the brief episodes. The railroad data, like the figures for turnpike and manufacturing companies, show long waves, but in the 1825–42 wave two, perhaps three, periods of intense chartering

---

[21] The phraseology of the preamble of many an early business charter suggests that a claim of public usefulness for a projected enterprise was important. See, for example, the charters in *Laws of Maryland, 1783*, Nov. Session, Ch. 23; *ibid., 1784*, Ch. 33; *ibid., 1804*, Ch. 41, 61, 63. The first two charters cited are for canals, the third for an insurance company, the fourth for a bank, and the fifth for a bridge company.

[22] Pennsylvania Turnpike Incorporations, 1800–1860:

	No.		No.		No.		No.		No.		No.
1800	0	1810	7	1820	3	1830	9	1840	5	1850	54
1801	1	1811	11	1821	2	1831	12	1841	7	1851	72
1802	0	1812	7	1822	3	1832	7	1842	7	1852	47
1803	4	1813	10	1823	4	1833	16	1843	8	1853	78
1804	8	1814	17	1824	1	1834	10	1844	7	1854	50
1805	3	1815	5	1825	6	1835	9	1845	8	1855	23
1806	4	1816	10	1826	11	1836	8	1846	6	1856	24
1807	5	1817	12	1827	5	1837	4	1847	9	1857	20
1808	2	1818	8	1828	10	1838	19	1848	26	1858	15
1809	5	1819	18	1829	8	1839	11	1849	46	1859	24
										1860	13

William Miller, pp. 158–9.

[23] The *annual* data indicate that 1821 would be a more appropriate date for the end of the first wave. The end of the second wave is not quite as clear in the annual figures. A low in the Pennsylvania annual figures occurred in 1840; in the New York annual figures in 1842; and in the Ohio annual figures in 1843. The year 1842 is thus fairly satisfactory. The end of the third wave is based upon only a few figures. The low point for the Ohio annual series, upon which the moving averages were constructed, occurred in 1862; the low point in the New Jersey annual series, however, was in 1861. From the little evidence there is, the fourth wave seems to have ended in the early 'eighties.

[24] Moving averages are omitted from this volume, for they are bulky and can be calculated easily from the basic data, which are given in full.

[25] Davis, II, 22–3.

[26] The original annual data for manufacturing incorporations (Tables 7–10) confirm the selection of 1820, 1861, and 1876 as troughs. On the basis of the original figures, 1843 would be slightly better than 1842.

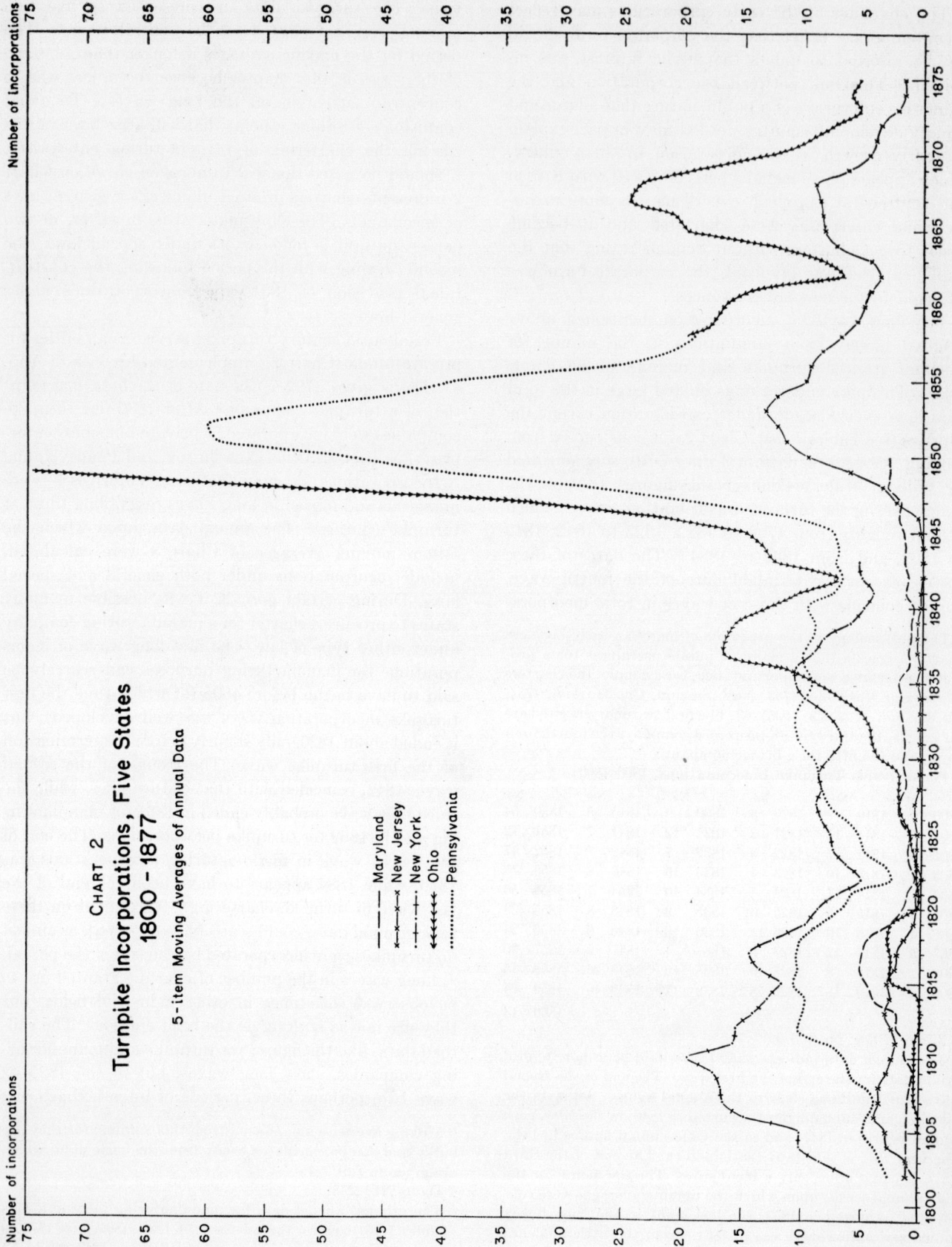

CHART 2

Turnpike Incorporations, Five States
1800 - 1877

5-item Moving Averages of Annual Data

Maryland
New Jersey
New York
Ohio
Pennsylvania

Number of incorporations

Source of annual data: Tables 7 to 10 and note 22.

Number of incorporations

CHART 3

Manufacturing Incorporations, Four States
1800-1877

5-item Moving Averages of Annual Data

Maryland — — —
New Jersey —x—x—x—
New York —·+·+·+·
Ohio <<<<<<

Number of incorporations

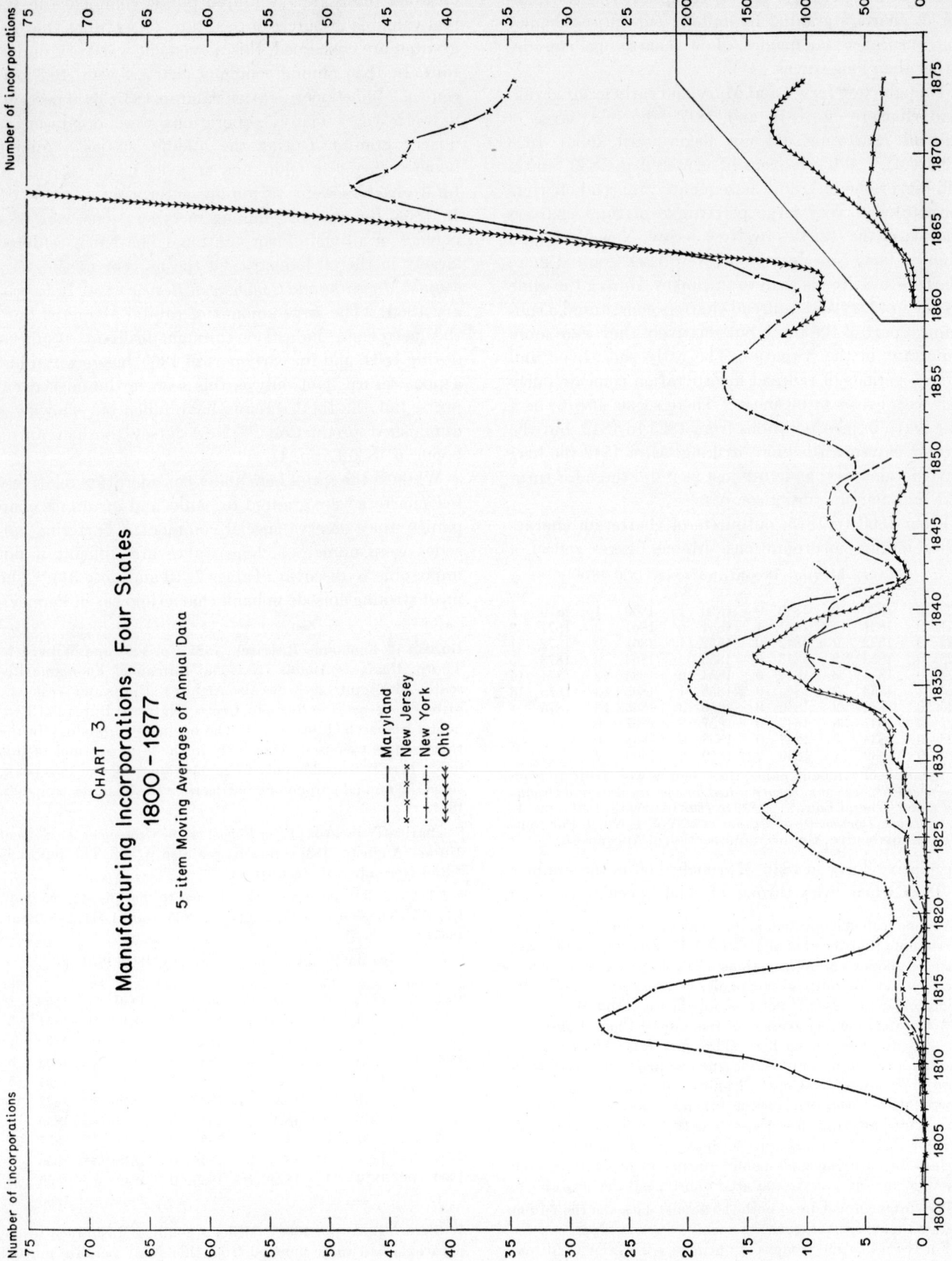

Source of annual data: Tables 7 to 10.

stand out more clearly. The series representing the number of charters granted for mining enterprises, banks, and insurance companies show chartering episodes rather than long waves.

Though New Jersey and Maryland early granted railroad charters—in 1815 and 1817—the first surge of railroad chartering did not begin until about 1828 (Chart 4).[27] A big movement centered in 1832, and a still bigger one in 1836. Consequently, railroad charters constituted a very large percentage of total charters granted in the 'thirties by New Jersey, New York, and Ohio; in fact, New Jersey and New York granted more charters to railroads than to turnpikes. During the same decade in Maryland, railroad charters constituted a substantial part of the total, but relatively they were more important in the 'twenties. The early short-lived and intense periods of railroad incorporation coincide fairly well with cycles in business.[28] There seems also to be a long wave in incorporations from 1825 to 1842, but the shorter movement is more striking. After 1842 the long wave dominates the picture just as it did those for turnpike and manufacturing companies.

From 1800 to 1875, outbursts of chartering characterize mining incorporations. Maine figures reflect a

MAINE MINING INCORPORATIONS, 1820–1876

	No.		No.		No.		No.		No.		No.
1820	0	1830	0	1840	0	1850	1	1860	1	1870	5
1821	0	1831	1	1841	1	1851	0	1861	0	1871	2
1822	0	1832	2	1842	0	1852	1	1862	0	1872	1
1823	0	1833	2	1843	0	1853	4	1863	0	1873	5
1824	0	1834	3	1844	0	1854	6	1864	2	1874	14
1825	1	1835	2	1845	0	1855	1	1865	3	1875	13
1826	0	1836	22	1846	0	1856	3	1866	12	1876	1
1827	0	1837	36	1847	0	1857	2	1867	6		
1828	0	1838	5	1848	0	1858	0	1868	5		
1829	0	1839	1	1849	2	1859	2	1869	2		

On the basis of company name, these figures were built up from *Business Corporations, Incorporated by Special Acts and Organized under General Law, . . . 1820 to 1892* (Augusta, 1891), pp. 3–71; or *Public Documents of Maine: 1892*, Vol. 1, No. 9. For comment on this source, see the Maine section of Appendix 3.

speculative flurry in 1836–37, touched off in the summer of 1835 when "the throng of wild speculators, who

crowded the State . . . injured public confidence in the real valuable resources of the State."[29] As far as charters granted are concerned, this movement was very important. In 1836 mining company charters were 16.8 percent of Maine incorporations and in 1837, 34.6 percent; in both years many corporations were organized to quarry granite. During the middle 'sixties a mining boom occurred in Ohio, and an even bigger portion of total charters went to mining enterprises (Table 10). In 1865, for example, mining incorporations were 68.4 percent of all Ohio incorporations. The boom centered largely in the oil industry. Of the movement the *Merchants' Magazine and Commercial Review* wrote in February 1866: "The large amount of capital attracted [into the petroleum industry] through brilliant promises during 1864, and the early part of 1865, has received but a poor return. Not only is this seen in diminished exports, but the total receipts have fallen off, showing a diminished production."[30] New Jersey too had an oil boom in 1865 (App. 4).

While in the states here under consideration relatively few charters were granted to banks and insurance companies, they deserve special comment. Chartering episodes were numerous; long waves are difficult if not impossible to discover (Tables 7–10 and note 31).[31] The most striking episode in bank chartering was in Pennsyl-

---

[27] Anyone calculating the moving average for New Jersey should note that the annual data for 1873 and subsequent years must be taken from both sections of Table 8. A general incorporation act for railroad companies was passed in 1873, but incorporation by special act was not then prohibited.

A five-item moving average of the data of Chart 4 obscures the episodes referred to here. This fact raises the question whether a two-item centered moving average would have been more appropriate for Charts 2 and 3. Moving averages of a shorter period were run on the turnpike and manufacturing data, and chartering episodes such as those in the railroad figures for 1825–42 did not appear. Since episodes were not important in turnpike and manufacturing incorporations, the five-item moving average was used to bring out the long waves.

[28] The statement is true of both the annual data and the 2-item centered moving averages.

For the peaks and troughs of business, see Wesley C. Mitchell, *Business Cycles: The Problem and Its Setting*, (National

Bureau of Economic Research, 1927), p. 426; and Willard L. Thorp, *Business Annals* (National Bureau of Economic Research, 1926), pp. 120–3. See also Arthur F. Burns and Wesley C. Mitchell, *Measuring Business Cycles* (National Bureau of Economic Research, 1946), Ch. 4. The business chronology in the third source was used extensively in the later portions of this book; here it is usable only in connection with the 1836 peak, since the annual chronology begins with the business trough in 1834.

[29] Charles T. Jackson, *First Report on the Geology of the State of Maine* (Augusta, 1837), p. viii; see also p. vii. The report is dated December 31, 1836 (p. 116).

[30] LIV, 122. For other minor references to the episode, see *ibid.*, LI, 415 (Nov. 1864); LII, 119 (Feb. 1865); and LIII, 205 (Sept. 1865).

[31] Pennsylvania Banking Incorporations, 1800–1860:

	No.		No.		No.		No.		No.		No.
1800	0	1810	0	1820	0	1830	0	1840	0	1850	3
1801	0	1811	0	1821	0	1831	1	1841	1	1851	3
1802	0	1812	0	1822	0	1832	6	1842	0	1852	1
1803	0	1813	0	1823	0	1833	4	1843	0	1853	6
1804	1	1814	41	1824	0	1834	8	1844	1	1854	5
1805	0	1815	0	1825	2	1835	5	1845	3	1855	14
1806	0	1816	0	1826	2	1836	8	1846	1	1856	1
1807	0	1817	0	1827	1	1837	2	1847	2	1857	28
1808	0	1818	0	1828	2	1838	0	1848	0	1858	2
1809	1	1819	1	1829	1	1839	0	1849	3	1859	1
										1860	6

William Miller, pp. 156–8. Miller's count of insurance incorporations had to be omitted from this study because mutual companies could not be excluded from his figures.

CHART 4

Railroad Incorporations, Four States, 1800–1876

2-item Centered Moving Averages of Annual Data

Number of incorporations

Maryland
New Jersey
New York
Ohio

Number of incorporations

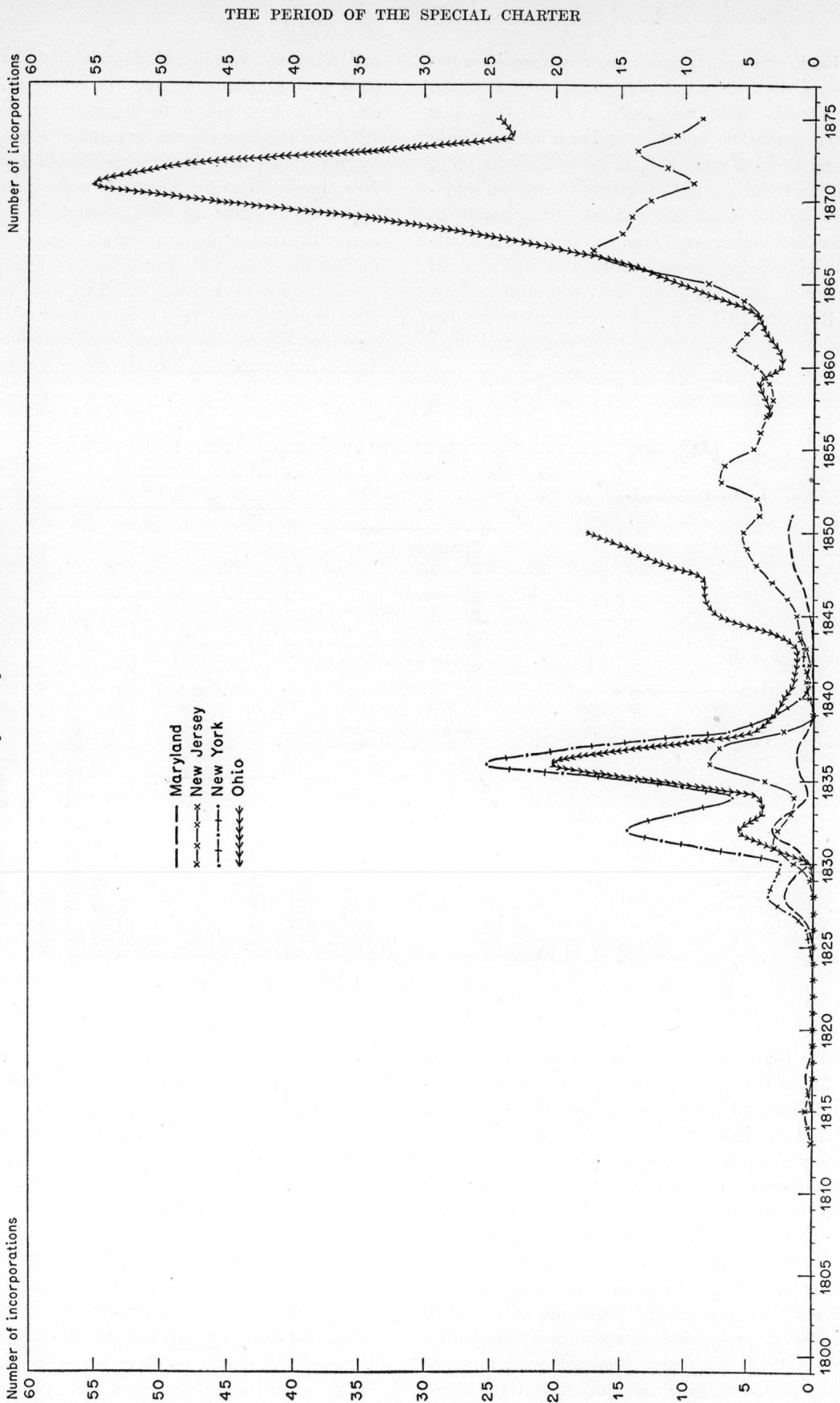

Source of annual data: Tables 7 to 10.

vania in 1814, when forty-one concerns were incorporated; during the four years preceding and following, not a single bank charter was issued. A few of the other outstanding chartering episodes in banking are those in Maryland in 1833 and 1836, in New York in 1836, and in Ohio in 1834. Toward the end of the period something in the nature of a long wave may be apparent in the data for New Jersey and Ohio. In insurance the outstanding brief periods of incorporating activity occurred in New York in 1824–25, 1833, and 1836, and in New Jersey in 1868 and 1871 (see Tables 7–10). A rather extended chartering movement in Ohio culminated in a peak in 1865.

and telegraph companies deserve little attention since they were granted infrequently before 1875. Maryland created a corporation to manufacture gas as early as 1817 and the first charter granted a telegraph company by the states here under consideration was issued by New Jersey in 1845. The real estate company charter appeared as early as 1803, though it was some time before the real estate corporation was regularly included among the chartered enterprises of each year.

Charts 5–8 were constructed to show in what industries, if any, a relatively large number of incorporations appeared outside the turnpike and manufacturing fields. Unless incorporations formed one-fifth of *total* incorpora-

CHART 5

Maryland Business Incorporations by Special Acts, 1800–1852
Excluding Turnpike and Manufacturing

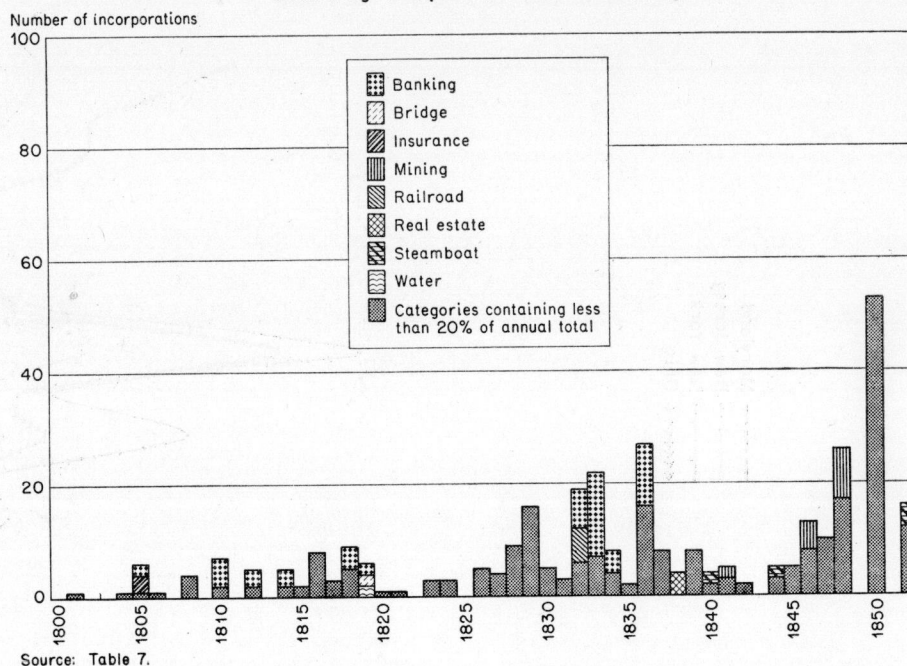

Source: Table 7.

Categories that contain only a few items—Ferries, Bridges, Trade Companies, Hotels, Amusement Companies, Building and Loan Associations (but see Ch. 3, note 3), and Agricultural Companies—are not commented upon (Tables 7–10). Some others, however, are worthy of notice. Canal incorporations were never very numerous, though in almost every year between 1800 and 1850 one canal charter was granted. After the middle of the century they were negligible. Before 1875 water company incorporations were relatively few except in New York around the beginning of the 19th century. The incorporation of steamboat companies was begun in 1813. Not many, however, were incorporated in the period under consideration, but the trend rose until the middle of the century. Charters for gas

tions of a state in a given year, they are not separately recorded (the other categories constitute what is called the 'residuum'—represented by gray areas). For example, in New York eighteen charters were issued to insurance enterprises in 1825; over and above those in the manufacturing and turnpike fields, forty charters were issued (Chart 7). The fact that the number of insurance company incorporations is registered on Chart 7 on the bar for 1825 indicates that the number (18) is at least 20 percent of *total* (66, including manufacturing and turnpike) incorporations in that year (Table 9). The absence of any other single category from the 1825 bar indicates that in no other (except perhaps the manufacturing or turnpike category) did the number of New York incorporations equal 20 percent of all charters granted that year.[32] Nothing is indicated in the chart about manufacturing and turnpike incorporations.

When Charts 5–8 are considered separately, the New York chart is the most interesting, particularly for 1821–43. Superimposed on the long wave in the chartering of turnpike and manufacturing undertakings are three important episodes: in insurance in 1824 and 1825, in banking about 1830, and in the railroad industry during the 'thirties. If any other one chart in the state

which few charters were issued (namely, all categories except turnpikes, manufacturing enterprises, and those industrial categories in which for the given year the charters granted equaled or exceeded one-fifth of total incorporations) are combined and plotted, the result is characterized roughly by the same long waves as those found in turnpike and manufacturing incorporations. Long waves in incorporations are thus noticeable not only in certain fields but in business generally.

CHART 6

New Jersey Business Incorporations by Special Acts, 1800–1845, and under Special and General Laws, 1846–1875
Excluding Turnpike and Manufacturing

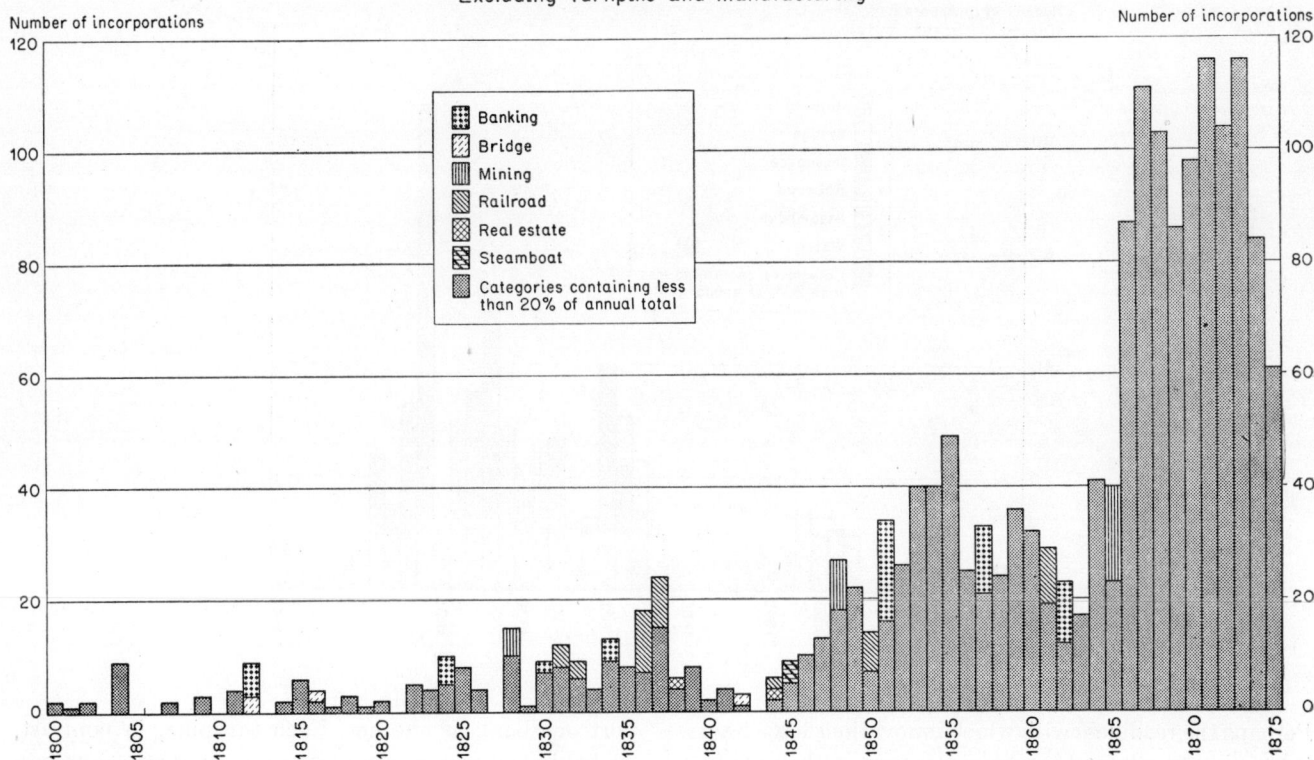

Source: Table 8.

series is to be singled out for comment, it should be that for Ohio (Chart 8). The boom in mining incorporations from 1864 to 1866, and the building and loan association charters of 1868–71 are outstanding features.

When Charts 5–8 are considered together, the importance of the railroad charter in the 'thirties is clear. Episodes in bank incorporations are many, but they occur at different times in the different states. Another feature is the long waves that appear in the residuum. That is, when for each year all industrial categories in

Long cycles and episodic movements in incorporation may perhaps be explained by differences in the rate a which some entrepreneurs copy the ideas of other entre preneurs. Imitation is as characteristic of entrepre neurial activity as innovation.[33] But it is easier for one group to imitate the ideas of another in a slightly modi fied version in some fields than in others. Whenever the rate of imitation is high and of short duration, an epi sode occurs; whenever it tends to be lower and sus tained, a long wave appears. In turnpike enterprises, the latter situation might be expected. Of course, the promotion of a turnpike from X to Y doubtless started

[32] Whenever total incorporations in a state were five or fewer in any one year, the percentages in the industrial categories were not calculated. No good purpose would have been served by making it possible for a single incorporation to be represented on Charts 5–8.

[33] See G. H. Evans, Jr., A Theory of Entrepreneurship, *Journal of Economic History* (Supplemental Issue, The Tasks of Economic History) Dec. 1942, pp. 142–6, particularly p. 144.

thinking about a road from X to Z. A community, however, does not need many turnpikes radiating from it. Certainly the idea of turnpike promotion spread from locality to locality, but the process was not as rapid as it would have been if one specific group of promoters had been interested.

For manufacturing also the hypothesis can be ventured that its very nature favors a low rate of imitation.

seem to be conducive to widespread imitations within a short period when the spirit of enterprise is expanding in a community. Competition among the members of each community for the distinction of being associated with a public enterprise together with the relatively small amount of capital needed to start business favored the creation of many banks when the fever was on. Moreover, bank promoters might be as willing to sup-

CHART 7
New York Business Incorporations under Special and General Laws, 1800-1845
Excluding Turnpike and Manufacturing

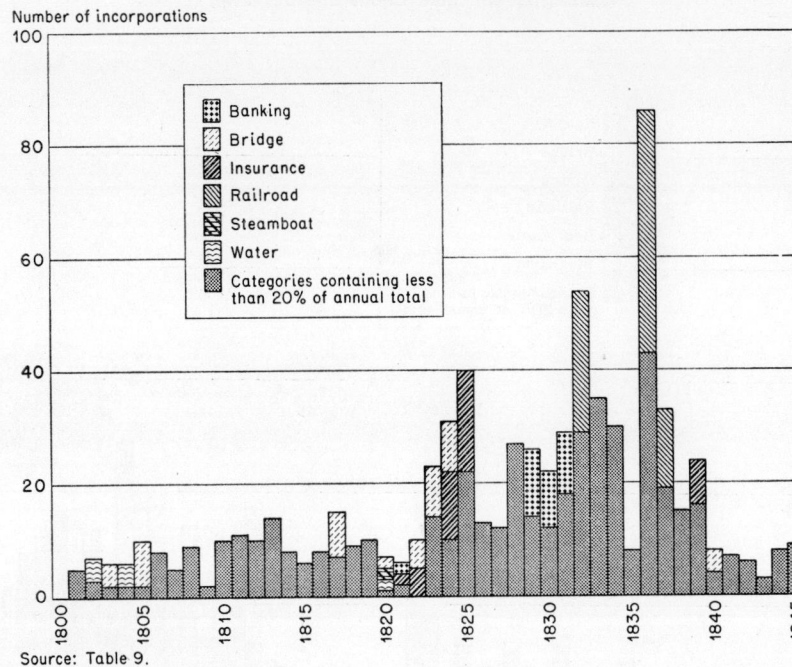

Source: Table 9.

Perhaps the readiness with which innovations have been taken up and adapted has been obscured in the present data by a lack of details for specific industries. As is well known, however, within each manufacturing industry businessmen strive to keep their processes secret and to differentiate their products—factors that work against quick imitation. It is highly probable too that many an early manufacturing corporation had formerly operated as a proprietorship or partnership. In the early period incorporation of manufacturing plants would thus be more closely associated with the general spread of the corporation idea than with the ups and downs of business cycles. Consequently, again, long waves rather than episodes are to be expected in manufacturing incorporations.

In both banking and insurance the nature of the business and the character of the promoting group would

port one bank as another. Each turnpike, in contrast, probably had many supporters who would not be among the promoters of another turnpike, and a large amount of capital was usually needed to complete a road. Banks and insurance companies are generalized projects; turnpikes and railroads are specialized. Moreover, changes in legislation and court decisions were more likely to affect the rate of imitation in the banking field than in turnpike construction and operation, since regulation was more minute and changes in the law more far-reaching. Finally, there were no obvious and precise limits to the number of banks a community could support, but there were for turnpikes.

In view of the similarities between railroads and turnpikes, the early episodes in railroad incorporations (the late 1820's and the 1830's) may seem difficult to explain.

Number of incorporations

313

Number of incorporations

CHART 8
Ohio Business Incorporations by Special Acts, 1803-1851,
and under General Laws, 1856-1875
Excluding Turnpike and Manufacturing

Banking
Bridge
Building and loan
Canal
Insurance
Mining
Railroad
Real estate
Categories containing less
than 20% of annual total

no data

1803 1805 1810 1815 1820 1825 1830 1835 1840 1845 1850 1855 1860 1865 1870 1875

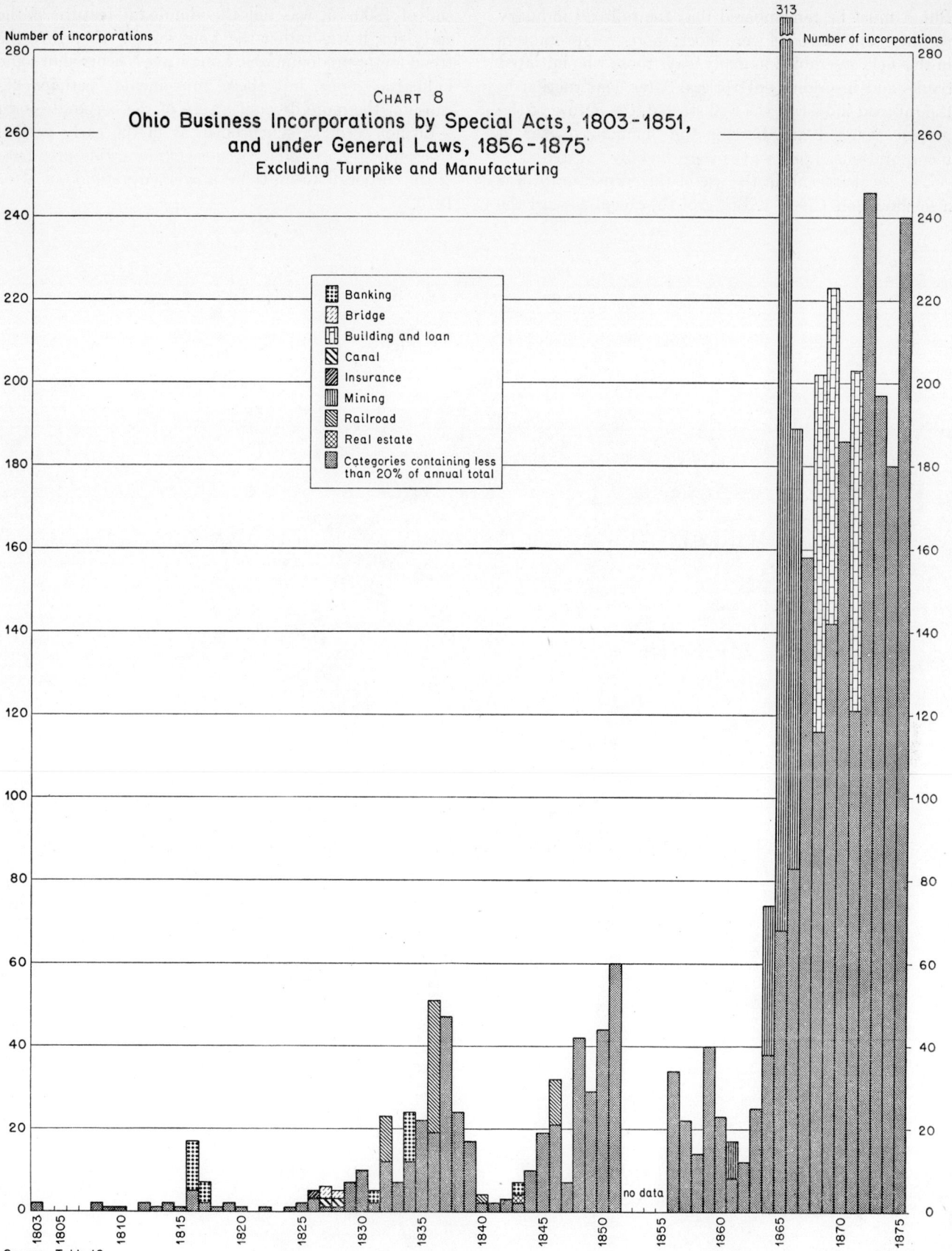

Source: Table 10.

But it must be remembered that the railroad industry was new and the roads were short; moreover, promoters in this field resembled in many ways those who initiated banks and insurance enterprises. After construction in the railroad industry was well started, the nature of the project changed and became the dominant factor in incorporations. Long waves were thereby favored.

The secular trend in the use of the corporate form is also shown on Chart 1. But growth, except toward the end of 1800–75, was not the dominant feature of the early era; it was rather the long waves. After 1875 the trend factor predominates. Long waves occurred in some industrial series, but these movements—perhaps because of the more diversified use of the corporate form —do not seem to synchronize as in the early period. Consequently, as well as because of more widespread use of the corporate form, trend movements stand out after 1875.

CHAPTER 4

Trends in Business Incorporations, 1875–1943

The year 1875 is a fitting date at which to drop from consideration corporations created by special acts and to concentrate attention on charters issued under general laws. As pointed out in the preceding chapter, by that time constitutional provisions requiring incorporation under general laws had become widespread. Only annual figures on special charters can be presented because legislatures are not continuously in session. To confine study to charters taken out under general laws has great advantages: monthly data can be compiled and the turning points of the cyclical movements of each incorporation series determined more precisely. The latter is important in studies of business cycles, which are related to incorporations in Chapter 9. For the present, however, annual figures on incorporations under general laws suffice because here trend movements are emphasized. The data compiled for this chapter are for the number of incorporations; capital stock figures are discussed later.

As was seen in Chapter 3, long cycles seem to dominate the early development of incorporations. Some readers, when examining the data for the Civil War years and the following decade, may have hesitated to concede this thesis. Had it not been desirable to treat the period of the special charter as a unit, the preceding chapter might have ended with 1860. Though a reasonable case can be made for a long wave lasting from 1861 to 1878, perhaps a better interpretation is that soon after the outbreak of hostilities the number of incorporations rose rapidly—in some states to a new level—and that the postwar readjustments produced substantially different effects in different states. In studying the curves of Chart 9 for this early period the Maine and New Jersey series should probably be omitted since the special charter in both was frequently used until 1875 and the series plotted on Chart 9 contain only data on the number of charters granted under general laws. If 1861–78 is not treated as a long cycle, it can be described as one of rapid growth during the Civil War followed by a little more than a decade of readjustment when the number of incorporations ceased to increase in some states and declined in others.

After 1878 trend movements seem clearly to dominate. Throughout the closing years of the 'seventies, the entire 'eighties, and the first few years of the 'nineties, the trend of each incorporation series is upward. Entrepreneurs, frequently using small corporations, were venturing into many new fields, at least new fields as far as the corporation was concerned (see Ch. 7 and 8).

It was the phenomenal expansion in the use of the corporate form, together with the impressive size of individual units, that led Edward Bellamy in 1888 to give the corporation a very vital role in his preview of the 20th century economy.[1] During the middle 'nineties the trend of each business incorporation series is practically horizontal—the growth of the preceding fourteen or fifteen years had been arrested. Big business was a feature of the years just prior to this period of quiescence and even more of the years around the turn of the century (Ch. 6).

From 1904 until 1917 the trends of the different series diverge somewhat. New York and Delaware incorporations, for example, grew rapidly; the number of Texas charters remained at about the same level throughout the period; in Maine the number fell off rapidly. To some extent this divergence in trends reflects the readiness of the different states to 'liberalize' their incorporation laws. The rate of growth in business incorporations seems to have been retarded somewhat after about 1904. Rapid expansion of the American market characterized our economy from the Civil War to the early years of the 20th century; and with this expansion one could expect a high rate of growth in incorporations. As the business-getting sections of each large corporation began to conquer the expanded market for its product, supplementary and complementary products were added to the corporation's line on a large scale; it may perhaps not be extravagant to give this change in the nature of business expansion a major role in the retardation of chartering.

Sharp curtailment of incorporations attended the priority regulations and the restrictions upon capital issues made during our participation in the first World War;[2] but a sharper rebound followed the cessation of hostilities, and was followed in turn by a decline during the depression that began in early 1920. All series traced the same pattern during 1917–21 except that the Maine and Arizona figures did not rebound in 1919 to heights exceeding those of 1917 and that the 1919 figures of Arizona, Maine, and New York exceeded their 1920 totals. From 1921 to 1929 the trends of several series seem to be continuations of the 1904–17 trends. Notice,

[1] *Looking Backward, 2000–1887* (Tickner & Co., 1888), pp. 71–5, 77–81.

[2] For a study of the control of capital issues during the war, see Woodbury Willoughby, *The Capital Issues Committee and War Finance Corporation* (Johns Hopkins University Studies in Historical and Political Science, Series LII, 2, 1934).

Number of incorporations

CHART 9

Business Incorporations, Sixteen States
Annually, 1860-1943

++++++ Arizona
———— Colorado
——◻—— Connecticut
——◇—— Delaware
——○—— Florida
····· Illinois
—··—·· Louisiana
———— Maine
—·—·— Maryland
——×—— Massachusetts
——+—— New Jersey
〈〈〈〈〈 New York
······ Ohio
——·—— Pennsylvania
—···—· Texas
—·—·— Virginia

Ratio scale

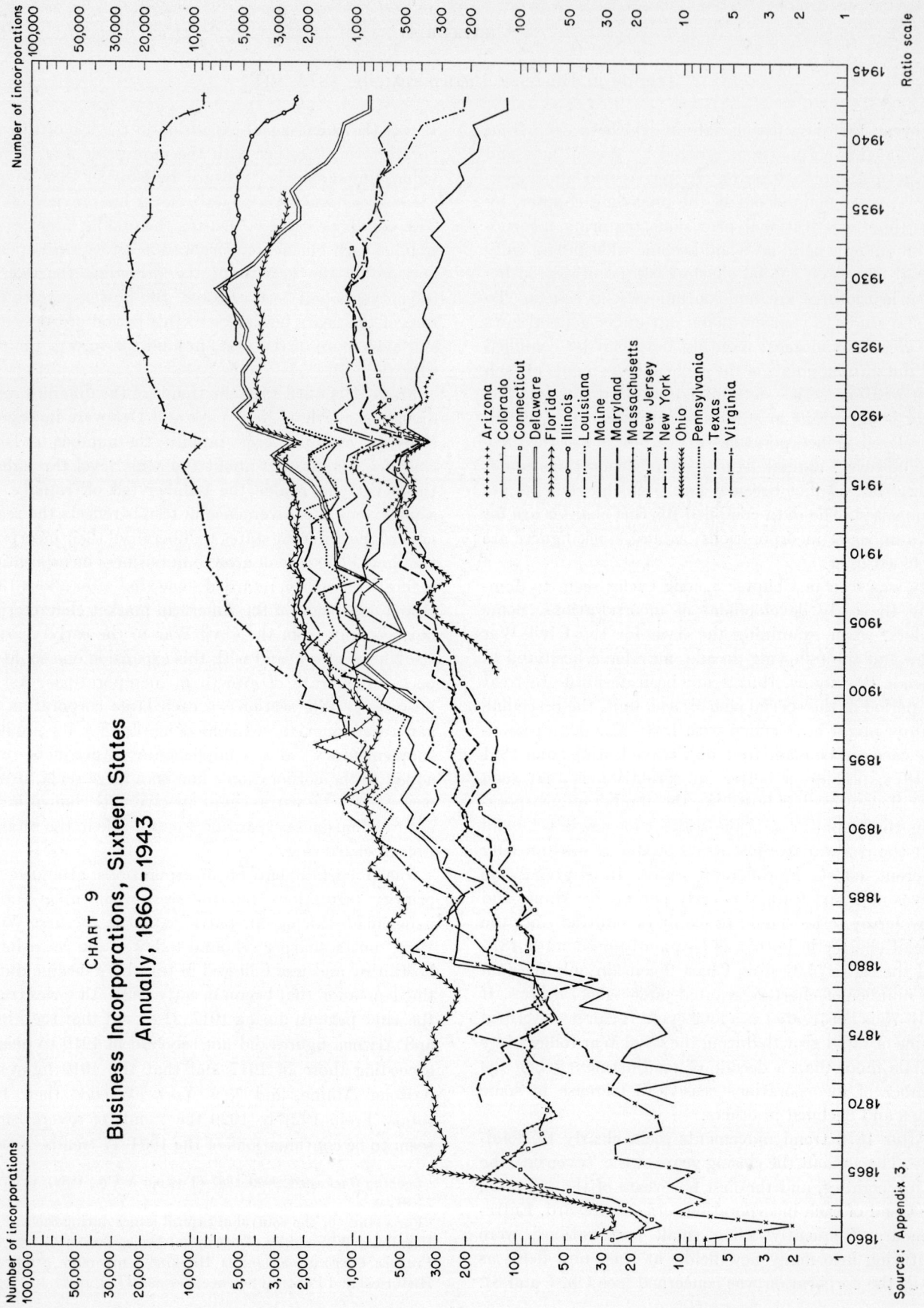

Source: Appendix 3.

for example, those for New York, Connecticut, and Maine. The Delaware series shows a somewhat slower growth than during the prewar era, though the 1926–29 rise is especially steep and therefore worthy of note. From 1929 to 1943 incorporations in each state declined almost continuously. The great depression in business, the various peacetime policies of the federal government that directly or indirectly affected the use of the corporate form, and the second World War with its various controls are possible explanations.

Chart 9 should be examined not only for some clues to the major periods in the growth of incorporations but also for information on the relative importance of each state as an incorporating agency and for the various movements in the different state series. Since 1900 New York has granted more charters than any other state treated. In Ohio, incorporations continued at a high level, and in Delaware many charters were issued in the 'twenties. In Connecticut and Maryland, incorporations rose almost steadily until the 1930's; in Maine they rose sharply until 1903, then declined steadily. The changes in the trends of the individual state series are difficult to explain. The whole problem of competition among states for the incorporating business of the country—a large subject beyond the scope of this study—is involved as well as shifts in industries.

Another difference in the state series is the amplitude of the waves of incorporation. In some states it is wide, in others, narrow. Contrast, for example, the Illinois and Pennsylvania series. Diversity of industry perhaps tends to reduce the amplitude, but another factor is also potent—the proportion of small corporations in the total. In Illinois from 1897 to 1917, about 92 percent of all companies chartered were small; each had an authorized capital stock of less than $100,000. In Pennsylvania, on the other hand, the percentage was 85. Because of differences in tax laws, there is risk in comparing the percentages of small corporations. Nevertheless, Illinois chartered a great many small corporations. In Chapter 6, where size is discussed, it is shown that in general the cyclical movement in the number of small companies chartered is much less than in the number of either medium or large corporations. Consequently, in states where small corporations constitute an exceptionally large portion of the total it may be expected that—other factors being equal—the number of incorporations will have a narrower amplitude than in states that chartered a great many large corporations.

While each curve of Chart 9 is a succession of waves, the peaks and troughs of the individual series do not coincide, partly because local conditions have had their effects. For example, the 1901 peak in the Texas series is due to oil discoveries. This and other important local episodes are treated in Chapter 8 in the section on random movements. Much of the cyclical variation from state to state, however, is more apparent than real. When monthly instead of annual figures are used—as they are subsequently—the cyclical movements in the different states are more similar.

Changes in the private corporation law of a state can affect drastically and abruptly the number of charters granted. A case in point is the sharp rise in Massachusetts incorporations in 1903 to a much higher level. That there are not similar pronounced breaks in other state incorporation series is rather astonishing. Except in the early years of corporate chartering and except in states that ordinarily do not charter many companies, the immediate effects of even radical changes in the law are generally fairly well obscured in total incorporations. Trends, it is true, may be altered greatly by a revision of the law, but the year-to-year and the month-to-month movements show the effects of legal innovations less than might be expected. In Pennsylvania, for example, corporations chartered to engage in wholesale trade were first created under general law in 1895, and retail trade companies could not be incorporated under general law until 1901 (Ch. 7, note 12). Surprisingly enough, these two extensions of the general incorporation law of Pennsylvania did not cause marked movements in total charters granted.

Annual Indexes

Such are the broad movements in the growth of incorporations and a few of the outstanding individual variations in the state series. To bring the broad movements out more clearly, two annual indexes of incorporations are set forth below. One was computed from medians of relatives, the other from simple aggregates.

In calculating the index from medians, the annual incorporations of each state, given in Appendix 3, were put into relatives with the first year of each section in Table 12 serving in turn as base. The simple median of the relatives for each year was then calculated. The indexes of the twenty-four sections were chained together on 1860 as the base; the base was then shifted to 1925 in order to facilitate comparison with the monthly indexes computed for use in Chapter 9 (Table 13).[3]

The other annual index is a byproduct of the monthly aggregate index of incorporations, which was constructed primarily to be used in studying the relation between business cycles and the number of corporate charters issued. It affords a series to check, or to dis-

[3] This annual index differs slightly from annual figures that could be computed from the monthly index of incorporations, calculated by the same method and described in Chapter 9, largely because for some states the annual index includes a longer run of figures than the monthly.

place, the annual index derived by the median of relatives method. As the monthly aggregate index is described in Chapter 9, there is no need to do more here than state that the annual aggregate index was computed from the seasonally unadjusted data compiled in the process of constructing the monthly index. Both aggregate indexes consist of two unspliced parts—the one ending in 1925, the other beginning in 1924—because the data on New York incorporations enter the computations in 1924 and seem to affect their cyclical behavior slightly (Table 13). Although the aggregate method gives more weight to the states issuing many charters, the two indexes are remarkably close except for the early period, 1867–80.

TABLE 12

States in the Annual Median Index of Incorporations with the Periods of Their Inclusion

SEC.	PERIOD OF INCLUSION	ARIZ.	COLO.	CONN.	DEL.	FLA.	ILL.	LA.	ME.	MD.	MASS.	N.J.	N.Y.	OHIO	PA.	TEXAS	VA.
1	1860–1870			X							X	X	X		X		
2	1870–1872								X	X	X	X			X		
3	1872–1881								X	X	X	X			X	X	
4	1881–1888			X					X	X	X	X			X	X	
5	1888–1891			X					X	X	X	X		X	X	X	
6	1891–1897		X	X					X	X	X	X		X	X	X	
7	1897–1899		X	X				X	X	X	X	X		X	X	X	
8	1899–1901		X	X	X				X	X	X	X		X	X	X	
9	1901–1904		X	X	X	X	X		X	X	X	X	X	X	X	X	
10	1904–1907		X	X	X	X	X		X	X	X	X	X	X	X	X	X
11	1907–1913			X	X	X	X		X	X	X	X	X	X	X	X	X
12	1913–1917	X		X	X	X	X		X	X	X	X	X	X	X	X	X
13	1917–1918	X		X	X	X			X	X	X	X	X	X	X	X	X
14	1918–1919	X		X	X	X			X	X	X	X		X	X	X	X
15	1919–1920	X		X	X	X			X	X	X	X		X	X	X	
16	1920–1921	X		X	X	X			X	X				X	X	X	
17	1921–1923	X		X	X				X	X				X	X	X	
18	1923–1925			X	X				X	X				X	X		X
19	1925–1932			X	X	X			X	X				X	X		X
20	1932–1936				X	X			X	X				X	X		X
21	1936–1937				X	X			X	X				X			X
22	1937–1939				X		X	X	X	X				X			X
23	1939–1941				X		X	X	X					X			X
24	1941–1943				X		X	X	X					X			

Several indexes of incorporations have been published for shorter periods than that covered here and should be compared with the data of Table 13.[4] Authorized capital stock figures for the companies chartered in eastern states with $1,000,000 or more of stock were published by the *New York Journal of Commerce and Commercial Bulletin* and are conveniently presented for 1901–19 in the *Review of Economic Statistics*.[5] This daily published

[4] In 1890 R. P. Falkner published some statistics on incorporations in several states. He did not compute an index; some of his figures are for calendar years while others are for fiscal years which vary from state to state. Falkner's data can, however, be compared with the series in Chart 9, but the fact that his figures are not always for calendar years must be borne in mind. See *Publications of the American Statistical Association*, II, N.S., No. 10 (June 1890), pp. 50–67.

[5] Preliminary Volume I (1919), pp. 148–9, 172–3, 198. The ambiguity concerning which states are covered by that capital stock series detracts from its usefulness. For a discussion of this point see *ibid.*, pp. 148–9.

a more comprehensive capital stock series covering companies chartered with $100,000 or more of capital stock. The more comprehensive series is readily accessible for 1907 through 1927 in the *Statistical Abstract of the United States, 1928*.[6] Comparison of those two series with the indexes of incorporations presented here brings out certain differences and similarities that are not surprising in the light of the data that either are in the next two chapters or can be developed from them. The cyclical movements of the capital stock series have wider

TABLE 13

Annual Aggregate and Median Indexes of Incorporations, 1860–1943
(1925:100.0)

	AGGREGATE	MEDIAN		AGGREGATE	MEDIAN		AGGREGATE		MEDIAN
1860	1.06	1.74	1890	25.9	29.6	1920	112.8		112.4
1861	.67	1.07	1891	27.1	28.0	1921	91.2		91.2
1862	.88	1.46	1892	29.5	29.7	1922	100.1		100.1
1863	1.66	2.13	1893	24.9	26.7	1923	99.3		100.0
1864	4.15	4.74	1894	24.4	26.0	1924	89.9	82.7*	92.3
1865	7.00	8.74	1895	26.5	29.3	1925	100.0	100.0	100.0
1866	6.26	8.38	1896	23.8	26.0	1926		100.3	97.5
1867	5.22	6.71	1897	26.3	27.1	1927		102.8	101.2
1868	5.52	6.09	1898	25.8	25.8	1928		110.0	107.9
1869	5.54	4.59	1899	36.9	33.9	1929		111.5	107.4
1870	5.30	5.05	1900	37.8	37.2	1930		99.6	96.1
1871	6.03	6.53	1901	50.2	44.7	1931		98.5	87.9
1872	6.37	6.11	1902	53.1	47.6	1932		95.1	85.9
1873	6.13	7.97	1903	56.0	52.3	1933		88.5	79.0
1874	5.75	8.07	1904	55.5	51.4	1934		73.7	68.0
1875	6.73	9.36	1905	63.6	59.3	1935		74.5	71.8
1876	5.31	9.51	1906	70.6	65.1	1936		75.4	70.9
1877	4.91	7.51	1907	68.6	61.7	1937		70.7	67.9
1878	4.76	7.68	1908	57.9	57.4	1938		62.6	58.4
1879	5.36	7.91	1909	71.5	68.3	1939		63.0	59.6
1880	9.81	11.0	1910	65.7	64.0	1940		61.8	57.0
1881	13.9	15.9	1911	67.2	63.5	1941		53.3	51.6
1882	13.9	15.7	1912	70.7	71.6	1942			32.5
1883	14.4	18.3	1913	70.9	76.3	1943			32.2
1884	12.6	15.3	1914	62.6	68.7				
1885	12.5	16.1	1915	67.7	76.1				
1886	15.0	17.3	1916	77.5	85.9				
1887	19.4	23.9	1917	77.1	80.3				
1888	18.8	20.8	1918	53.1	57.1				
1889	22.9	24.9	1919	100.5	105.4				

* For explanation of the overlap in 1924 and 1925, see the text.

amplitudes than those of indexes based upon the number of charters granted. This is the typical relation between capital stock and number series. The capital stock series based solely upon companies with $1,000,000 or more of stock has a wider amplitude than the series that includes companies with smaller authorized capital, again a typical relation. The trend of the capital stock series based on large corporations and covering 1901–19 is slightly downward. This is in accord with the trend of the data on large companies presented in the next two

[6] U. S. Department of Commerce, Washington, D. C., p. 309. It is doubtful that these capital stock figures are more useful than the less comprehensive series, again because of the ambiguity concerning which states are covered.

chapters but is in sharp contrast to the trend of the indexes of this chapter for the same period.[7] The timing of the cyclical movements of the capital stock series and the indexes are very similar, as is to be expected after reading Chapter 5.

A current index of incorporations is compiled by the Corporation Trust Company and published monthly in the *Survey of Current Business*. Extending back through 1925, it is an aggregate of the number of charters granted by four states—Delaware, Illinois, Maine, and New York.[8] When expressed on an annual basis, it moves in almost the same way as the aggregate index presented in this chapter. This similarity of movement might be expected, since the incorporations of the four states covered by the Corporation Trust Company figures are part of the data for the indexes given here. For the years since 1924 the indexes of this study cover at least five, and at times eight states.[9] Though more nonbusiness corporations are included in the figures of the Corporation Trust Company, this source of difference is not serious.[10] The Corporation Trust Company figures exceed the annual figures given in this volume for the business incorporations of Delaware, Illinois, Maine, and New York, though by less than 1 percent.

The total number of new business incorporations in the United States is now recorded monthly in *Dun's Statistical Review*. Total incorporations by each of 47 states are available for the last half of 1945; thereafter the tabulations include the figures for every state. Thus as long as this series continues, there will be no need for constructing indexes of total incorporations from sample data.[11]

[7] The substantial decline in the capital stock figures for large New Jersey companies, 1901–14, can be deduced from a comparison of the two capital stock series in Appendix 3 and from Table 17. New Jersey figures were included in the *Journal's* total, and during the early years of the 20th century would have constituted a large proportion of it.

[8] For the data, see the U. S. Department of Commerce, *Survey of Current Business*, Oct. 1947, p. S-3; March 1947, p. S-3; March 1946, p. S-3; March 1945, p. S-3; April 1944, p. S-18; and March 1943, p. S-16; and *1942 Supplement*, p. 73.

[9] Table 36 shows the coverage of both my annual and monthly aggregate indexes, Table 12 that of my annual median index, and Table 39 that of my monthly median index.

[10] Compare the definition of nonbusiness used in this study (Ch. 1) with the statement in the *1942 Supplement* to the *Survey of Current Business*, p. 205, note 4 for p. 73, concerning the compilation of the Corporation Trust Company: "Incorporations for fraternal and charitable purposes are excluded."

[11] New business incorporations were first published in the *Review* of Sept. 1946; the first issue to contain the data of all 48 states was that of February 1947.

The United States and the United Kingdom

To compare the growth in the use of the corporate form in this country and elsewhere is not a purpose of this study. Nevertheless, data for the United Kingdom are presented, since they may be interesting to some readers (Table 14). The course has in general been the same in

TABLE 14
Incorporations, United Kingdom, 1863–1937

	NUM-BER*	INDEX (1925: 100.0)		NUM-BER*	INDEX (1925: 100.0)		NUMBER*	INDEX (1925: 100.0)
1863	733	8.69	1890	3,005	35.6	1917	3,895	46.2
1864	944	11.19	1891	2,597	30.8	1918	3,385	40.1
1865	973	11.53	1892	2,505	29.7	1919	10,592	125.5
1866	726	8.61	1893	2,515	29.8			
1867	440	5.22	1894	2,885	34.2	1920	10,861	128.7
1868	425	5.04	1895	3,805	45.1	1921	6,692	79.3
1869	441	5.23	1896	4,658	55.2	1922	8,368	99.2
			1897	5,148	61.0	1923	8,400	99.6
1870	545	6.46	1898	5,065	60.0	1924	8,420	99.8
1871	741	8.78	1899	4,879	57.8	1925	8,437	100.0
1872	1,020	12.09				1926	8,178	96.9
1873	1,165	13.81	1900	4,859	57.6	1927	8,777	104.0
1874	1,157	13.71	1901	3,358	39.8	1928	9,442	111.9
1875	1,104	13.09	1902	3,850	45.6	1929	9,013	106.8
1876	924	10.95	1903	3,992	47.3			
1877	938	11.12	1904	3,765	44.6	1930	8,769	103.9
1878	815	9.66	1905	4,253	50.4	1931	8,696	103.1
1879	968	11.47	1906	4,766	56.5	1932	10,550	125.0
			1907	5,152	61.1	1933	11,844	140.4
1880	1,170	13.9	1908	4,932	58.5	1934	12,939	153.4
1881	1,495	17.7	1909	6,268	74.3	1935	13,519	160.2
1882	1,526	18.1				1936	14,180	168.1
1883	1,630	19.3	1910	7,091	84.0	1937	13,197	156.4
1884	1,443	17.1	1911	6,371	75.5			
1885	1,382	16.4	1912	7,268	86.1			
1886	1,785	21.2	1913	7,321	86.8			
1887	1,945	23.1	1914	6,097	72.3			
1888	2,465	29.2	1915	4,002	47.4			
1889	2,658	31.5	1916	3,317	39.3			

* Convenient sources for data on the number of incorporations chartered in the United Kingdom are: for 1863–1920, *Palgrave's Dictionary of Political Economy* (Higgs' Edition; London, 1926), I, 369 and 852; for 1921–30, *Statistical Abstract for the United Kingdom*, Seventy-fifth Number (London, 1932), p. 230; for 1931–37, *ibid.*, Eighty-second Number (London, 1939), p. 277.

There is some shifting in the geographical area covered, but it is not serious. The figures from *Palgrave's Dictionary* cover Great Britain and all Ireland. The figure for 1921 is for Great Britain alone, while the subsequent data are for Great Britain and Northern Ireland. Moreover, the figures from the two volumes of the *Statistical Abstract* cover only 'New Limited Companies with Nominal Capital', the series reproduced in *Palgrave's Dictionary*.

the two countries. The differences lie in certain episodes. The Civil War gave a great stimulus to the corporate form in this country. A smaller but similar movement occurred in Great Britain. From about 1869 to 1878, and again from 1892 to 1901, there was a pronounced surge in British incorporations. During the 1914–18 war, curtailment in incorporations was more drastic and protracted in Great Britain than in this country. Finally, the post-1929 years contrast sharply.

CHAPTER 5

The Number of Incorporations and Their Authorized Capital Stock

Had figures on total authorized capital stock been used in the preceding chapter instead of those on total incorporations, the series would have been shorter and for fewer states since information on capital stock is not as extensive as that on number. Moreover, series for total authorized capital stock fluctuate more violently and erratically. The major cyclical movements of the two series are much the same, though not identical, for each state. The total authorized capital stock figures are heavily weighted by big companies. A small company may be chartered with only a few hundreds of dollars of stock, while a big one may have an authorized capital stock of $50,000,000 or more; one large company can balance many small ones in authorized capital stock. To show the relation between the number of incorporations and authorized capital stock, eleven ratio charts were prepared. Only four are presented here and discussed in detail, since each of the others is more or less similar to one of the four. Arrows indicate the turning points of business cycles, but no use is made of them in this chapter. They were inserted so that the charts here may supplement those of Chapter 9, where the cyclical movements of incorporations are considered.

Each chart presents for a single state three 12-month moving averages plotted at the seventh month: total incorporations; their total authorized capital stock; and the stock figures less the authorized capital stock of the 'large' companies, defined as those having authorized capital stock of $1,000,000 or more.[1] Such a definition is of course arbitrary and its use in the analysis of a series covering a long period is open to the criticism that a million dollar capital has carried different connotations at different times. Examination of the detailed data, however, indicated that little violence would be done to the picture by its use. Moreover, the application of a flexible, more realistic gauge for 'large' would have been unduly burdensome. Further discussion of the problem of classifying corporations on the basis of size is reserved for the next chapter. But one more point must be made here. Nonpar shares make difficult, sometimes impossible, the compilation of a capital stock series. Whenever nonpar shares appeared,

they were taken into the data at the par value that the tax laws of the given state indicated to be the equivalent, provided the equivalent was a uniform figure. Many states tax nonpar shares in the same way as shares of $100 par value; for these states nonpar shares were treated as $100 par value shares. When nonpar value shares were taxed on the basis of a declared value that might differ from company to company, the construction of a capital stock series was not attempted after such a tax provision was enacted.

The incorporating activities of states produced four patterns of relation between the two authorized capital stock series, observable in Charts 10–13. The differences in the four patterns are caused by the character and frequency of the large incorporation. In pattern (1) the total authorized capital stock series is rather smooth and lies well above the capital stock series from which large companies have been eliminated, because the state chartered many very large companies. In pattern (2) the capital stock series lie close together and move in unison, because the state chartered neither many large companies nor any exceptionally large companies. In pattern (3) the two capital stock series also fluctuate in unison but they are further apart than in pattern (2), because the state chartered a fair number of large companies of almost uniform size. In pattern (4) the two capital stock series generally lie close together because the state habitually chartered few large companies; from time to time, however, the total stock series is featured by a 'hump' occasioned by the chartering of what, for the state, was an exceptionally large company.

Delaware is typical of states that incorporate many very large companies (Chart 10). Its total stock series is remarkably smooth, although it chartered some companies with a capital stock as high as $400,000,000. Of course, the reason that such a company does not cause a hump in the series at the time of its chartering is to be found in the high capitalization of all companies; that is, so many large companies were chartered that even a very large company does not have much effect on the moving average. Moreover, the moving average itself tends to produce a smooth curve by spreading an exceptional item over twelve months. In 1933, and again in 1936, the picture is different. Big humps in the total capital stock curve give this portion of the chart an appearance somewhat similar to that of the chart for Illinois, discussed below. The curve for those years could

---

[1] The 12-month moving average is used here and in certain other portions of the study to eliminate seasonal variation. Though not an entirely satisfactory method, it was the only practicable device when seasonal variation had to be eliminated from a large number of series. See Chapter 9 for a discussion of seasonal variation.

hardly be called characteristic of Delaware, which for decades has chartered annually many very large companies. The Maryland series for 1919–31 and the entire New Jersey series follow the Delaware pattern.

The Texas series (Chart 11) follows pattern (2). The curves representing total capital stock and the capital stock of all companies other than large corporations are very close, because almost no large companies were

abruptly as a single company affects the moving averages. The hump—and a similar one in the total capital stock series of Pennsylvania—was caused by the chartering of the New York Central Railroad Company with a capital stock of $300,000,000. This company took out charters simultaneously in these and other states.

Illinois is one of the states that chartered a few smaller corporations in the largest size group and from

CHART 10

Delaware Business Incorporations
Number and Authorized Capital Stock, 1916-1943

12-item Moving Averages

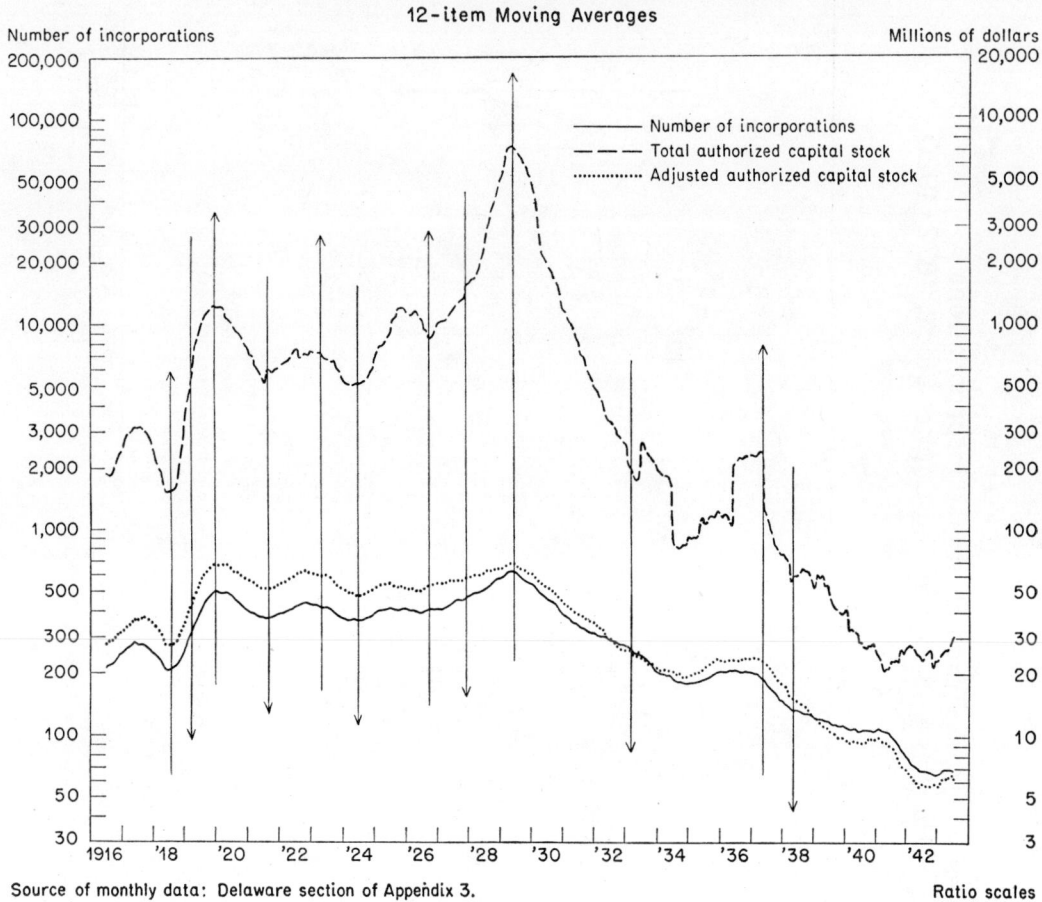

Source of monthly data: Delaware section of Appendix 3.

Ratio scales

chartered and those that were created were not capitalized at a figure greatly exceeding a million dollars. The Florida series and the Maryland series for the period prior to 1919 resemble in many respects that of Texas.

The figures for Colorado, Ohio, Pennsylvania, and Virginia illustrate the third pattern of relationship. Chart 12, which presents Ohio data, typifies the group. The total and the adjusted capital stock series are rather far apart and the total capital stock series is fairly smooth. An outstanding exception occurs in 1914–15, when total authorized capital stock rises and falls

time to time created one with a capital stock substantially in excess of $1,000,000, the lower limit for the capital stock of a large corporation. The dashed (total capital stock) and the dotted (adjusted capital stock) lines on Chart 13 are close together except when Illinois incorporated what for it was a relatively large company. For example, a $96,000,000 railroad company chartered in August 1909 is solely responsible for the hump in the total capital stock curve before and after that month. Similarly, a single company with a capital stock of $50,000,000 chartered in July 1913 causes another

CHART 11
Texas Business Incorporations
Number and Authorized Capital Stock, 1872-1920
12-item Moving Averages

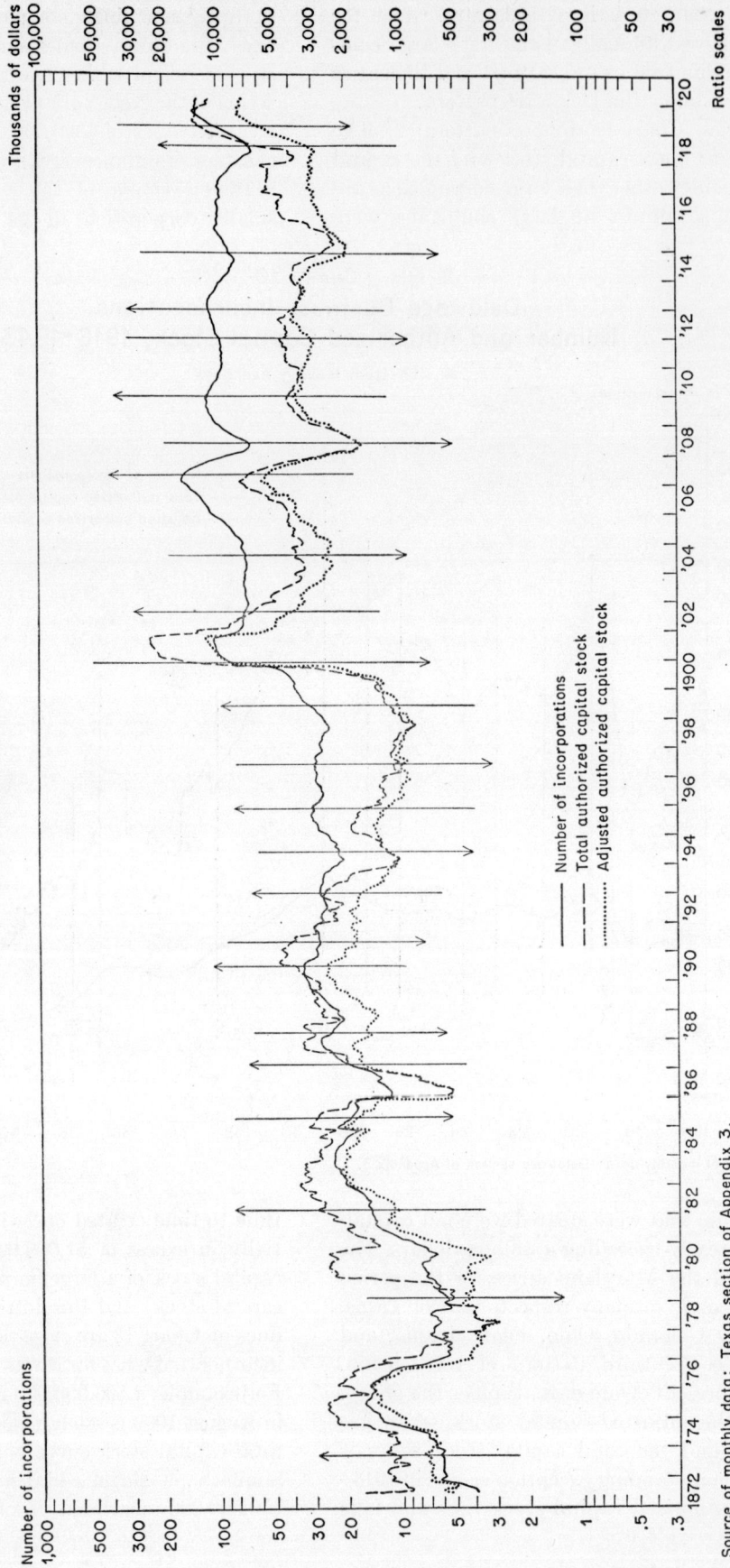

Number of incorporations
Total authorized capital stock
Adjusted authorized capital stock

Source of monthly data: Texas section of Appendix 3.

CHART 12

Ohio Business Incorporations
Number and Authorized Capital Stock, 1872–1918

12-item Moving Averages

Number of incorporations

Millions of dollars

Ratio scales

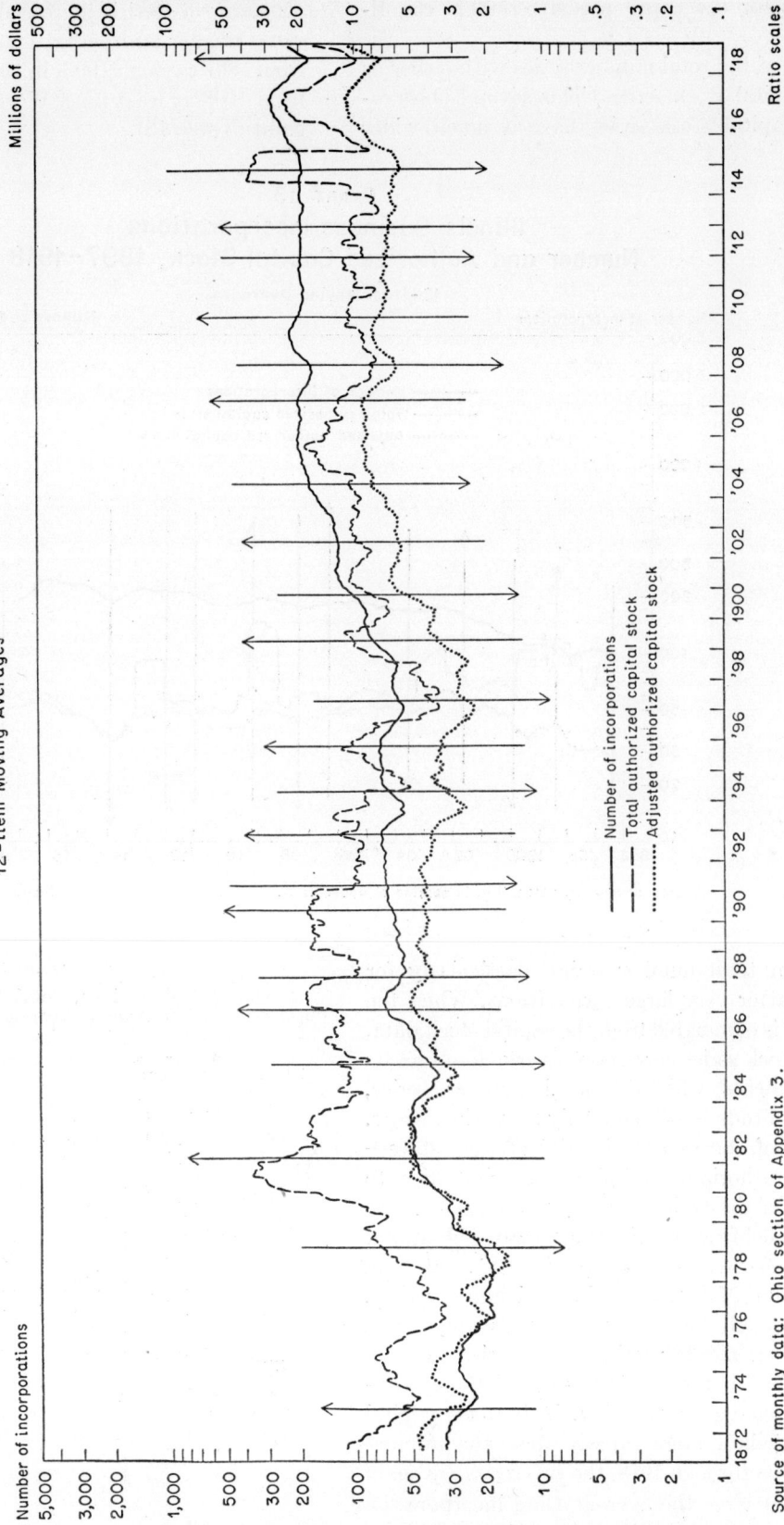

Source of monthly data: Ohio section of Appendix 3.

Number of incorporations
Total authorized capital stock
Adjusted authorized capital stock

hump. The Maryland series since 1932 and that of Massachusetts for the entire period resemble the Illinois series.

Comparison of the total number series with either or both of the capital stock series yields several observations. Total capital stock series have a much wider

sideration. From 1872 to 1880 the average size remained constant; in 1881 it increased; from 1881 to 1897 it became smaller and perhaps continued to shrink slightly from 1897 through 1906; in 1907 it shrank sharply; then, from 1908 at least until World War I, it remained constant (Table 15).

CHART 13

Illinois Business Incorporations
Number and Authorized Capital Stock, 1897-1918

12-item Moving Averages

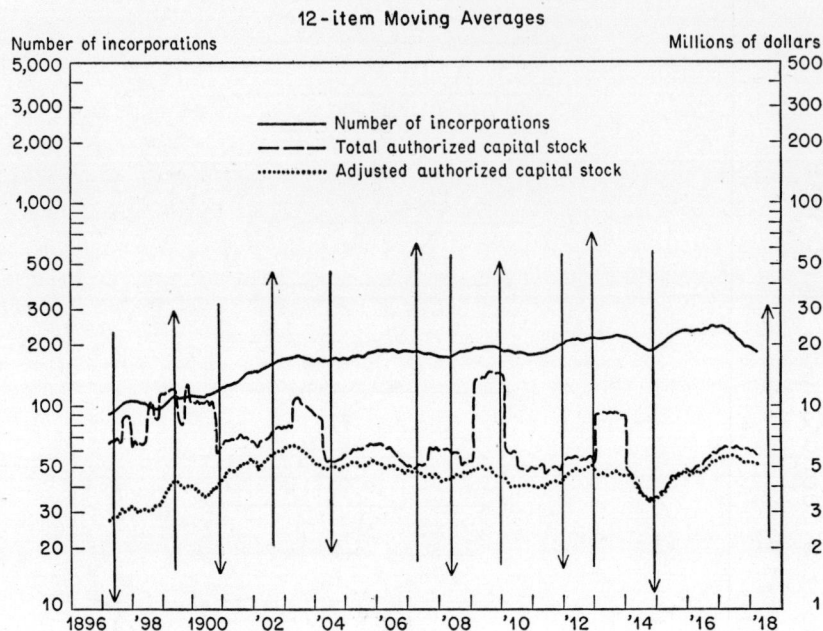

Source of monthly data: Illinois section of Appendix 3.　　　　　Ratio scales

amplitude than total number series, particularly for states that charter very large corporations. When the large company is eliminated from the capital stock data, the adjusted stock series corresponds very closely in its cyclical movements with the total number series, though its amplitude is still generally somewhat wider.

Comparison of the two total series of each state—number and authorized capital stock—gives rise to speculations. On the Ohio chart, for example, the two curves are parallel from 1872 through 1880. The capital stock curve then rises more sharply in 1881, but from that year until 1897 it falls while total number rises. From 1897 through 1906 the two trends are almost parallel; the total number series perhaps rises slightly more rapidly, but at the end of the period there is another clear-cut change in direction. In 1907 the capital stock series declines more rapidly than the number series. From 1908 through 1918, the two series are again parallel. By and large the average Ohio incorporation was becoming smaller throughout the period under con-

TABLE 15

Ohio Incorporations, Total Authorized Capital Stock
Annual Averages, 1872–1918

	AVERAGE CAP-ITAL STOCK		AVERAGE CAP-ITAL STOCK		AVERAGE CAP-ITAL STOCK
1872	$338,313	1887	$270,769	1902	$72,878
1873	208,990	1888	173,121	1903	68,480
1874	230,115	1889	279,339	1904	62,228
1875	289,147	1890	278,669	1905	80,982
1876	180,706	1891	146,770	1906	71,464
1877	198,590	1892	128,208	1907	56,773
1878	239,960	1893	222,463	1908	42,582
1879	354,394	1894	71,823	1909	41,486
1880	266,001	1895	125,391	1910	53,821
1881	743,780	1896	114,182	1911	50,666
1882	413,290	1897	71,447	1912	58,100
1883	345,546	1898	75,334	1913	38,816
1884	301,329	1899	129,929	1914	188,246
1885	209,182	1900	72,262	1915	39,581
1886	251,332	1901	86,011	1916	78,927
				1917	67,182
				1918	54,558

For basic data, see the Ohio section of Appendix 3.

A decrease in average size might be due to several circumstances. For example, there might be a relative increase in the number of small companies, other things remaining constant. An increase in average size for all corporations, on the other hand, might be due solely to an increase in either the relative number or average size of large incorporations. There is no need to recount all possible factors or combinations of factors governing average size. The object here is merely to emphasize that a constant average authorized capitalization does not necessarily imply a static situation in either the distribution or the average sizes of the subgroups. The next chapter provides some further insight into the movements of average capital stock, since there total incorporations are grouped on the basis of the size of the enterprise chartered.

CHAPTER 6

Large, Medium, and Small Business Corporations

To get a clearer idea of the various movements that combine to make up total incorporations, the figures for charters issued were divided into three groups on the basis of an index of the size of the corporation, that is, capital stock.[1] As might be imagined, capital stock is not entirely satisfactory as a criterion of size. But it is the only criterion common to the data from the various sources and is a fairly good rough indicator of relative size. A corner grocery store would not be expected to incorporate with a million dollars of capital stock, nor would a large railroad company be likely to have only a hundred thousand dollars of authorized capital stock. It is not contended that a given capital stock represents any particular absolute investment.[2] It is argued merely that a corporation with, say, $100,000 of capital stock is smaller in general than one with a million dollars. There is no attempt to say how much smaller or to make any precise statement about the absolute values of the capital assets involved.

Tests of correlation between the authorized capital stock and the size of a company seem to justify the use of authorized capital stock as a rough indicator of relative size. Three samples of Pennsylvania incorporations were drawn—for 1889, 1902, and 1916. The earliest and the latest of these years were determined by the progress that had been made in tabulating the charters of Pennsylvania enterprises. The in-between year, 1902, represents approximately the midpoint of the 1889–1916 span. The companies comprising each sample, 225, were looked up in the Bradstreet book of commercial ratings, published three years after the year for which the sample was drawn. Not all of the companies in each sample were found in the rating books, but, for each of those found, Bradstreet's "estimated pecuniary strength" was used as the index of size to correlate with the authorized capital stock.

Since the details of these tests are given in Appendix 5, the above brief description and a summary of the results will suffice here. In general, each of the three linear correlation coefficients between the two measures of size was fairly high when ungrouped data were used and a few items that had undue weight had been eliminated. The results obtained from ungrouped data were supplemented by a test on grouped data. After the details of many incorporations had been examined, it was decided arbitrarily to call a company small if its authorized capital stock was less than $100,000. A medium-sized corporation was defined as one with an authorized capital stock of $100,000–1,000,000, and a large company one with $1,000,000 or more. The corporations used for the ungrouped correlation test were then classified into these three size groups. About 82 percent were found to belong in the same size group on the basis of either criterion—authorized capital stock or Bradstreet's "estimated pecuniary strength".

As indicated in the preceding chapter, the definitions of large, medium, and small corporations are difficult to defend. They are arbitrary for any one point in time, and it is hard to justify the use of the same rigid criteria over a long period. The most defensible classification would perhaps be based upon: (1) the determination of values that at one point in time would divide the chartered enterprises into three groups containing the same number of items; (2) the extension, forward and backward, of these values, using some price index to determine the degree to which the class limits should be revised. Such a procedure was ruled out because of the large number of incorporations and the difficulty of procuring a satisfactory price index for the adjustment. For the initial determination of the class limits, resort was had to judgment based upon observation of a large number of companies; the decision to keep these intervals uniform over time was a practical necessity.

In many states small incorporations outnumber the medium and large by far; and they fluctuate in number less from year to year, partly because the limits of the size groups are rigid. Assume, for example, that the dividing line between large and small (for the sake of simplicity, the medium-sized group is excluded) is always $100,000. Companies that expect to do comparable volumes of business may organize in a period of prosperity with authorized capital stock of, say, $125,-000, but in a depression with only $75,000. In prosperity they would be classed as large, but in depression as small. Though the peaks in small incorporations may

---

[1] In Chapter 2, certain Maryland incorporations were classified into five size groups (see Ch. 2 and supplementary tables in Appendix 2).

[2] The U. S. Census Office has at various times expressed unwillingness to use capital stock as an index of size, but apparently it was thinking in terms of an indicator of the absolute amount of actual investment. See, for example, *Twelfth Census of the United States* (Washington, D. C., 1902), VII, Manufactures, Part I, p. cii, Sec. 13. Capital stock figures, however, have been used in other studies to indicate relative size. D. H. Macgregor, for example, in his *Enterprise, Purpose & Profit*, p. 133, used capitalization figures—for lack of anything better—to distinguish large and small enterprises.

thus be scaled down somewhat and the troughs filled up somewhat, it is believed that some valid statements can be made about the variations in the chartering of large, medium, and small companies.

Ratio Charts 14–19 show the twelve-month moving averages of total incorporations in each of six states and similar moving averages of the number of incorporations in each of the three size groups (see Ch. 5, note 1). In preparation for writing the rest of this chapter, these graphs were supplemented by similar ones for Florida, Massachusetts, Pennsylvania, Texas, and Virginia, which are not reproduced here since they do little more than confirm the observations derived from the six. The reader is warned to use with caution the moving averages based on the number of large incorporations. Some of these series were computed from very few incorporations. But it seemed better to compute and plot the small averages than to omit them. Their appearance on the charts makes possible a quick grasp of the relation between the numbers in the three size groups. Moreover, a few more observations of broad movements become feasible.

The amplitudes of the cyclical movements of the series representing the three size groups vary directly with the size of the incorporation, especially in periods of intense incorporating activity. At these times, it is strikingly clear that the rate at which large companies

CHART 14
Colorado Business Incorporations by Size Groups
1891-1908

12-item Moving Averages

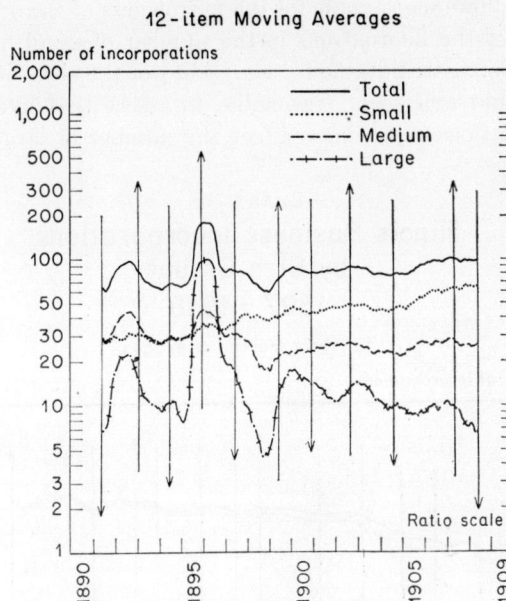

Source of monthly data: Colorado section of Appendix 3.

are chartered greatly exceeds that for medium-sized companies, which in turn is higher than that for small

CHART 15
Delaware Business Incorporations by Size Groups
1916 – 1943

12-item Moving Averages

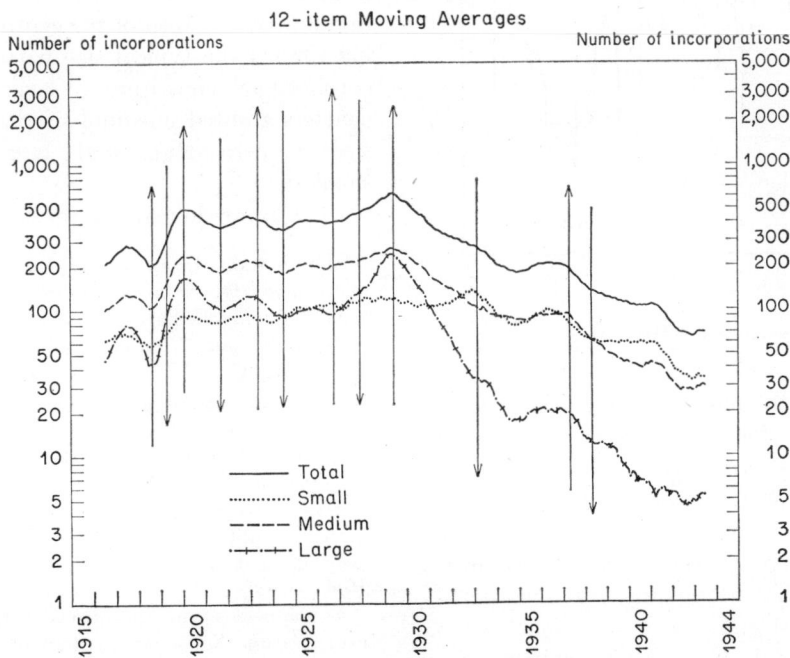

Source of monthly data: Delaware section of Appendix 3.   Ratio scale

companies. The relations are clearest in the Colorado chart for 1895–96 when a metal mining boom occurred. A similar pattern characterizes the Texas data for 1900–02 when an oil boom occurred.

If allowance is made for the narrowness of the amplitude of the fluctuations in the number of small incorporations attributable to the rigidity of the class limits, it would still seem reasonable to assert that cyclical fluctuations in business affect the number of large in-

CHART 16
Illinois Business Incorporations by Size Groups
1897 – 1918
12-item Moving Averages

Number of incorporations

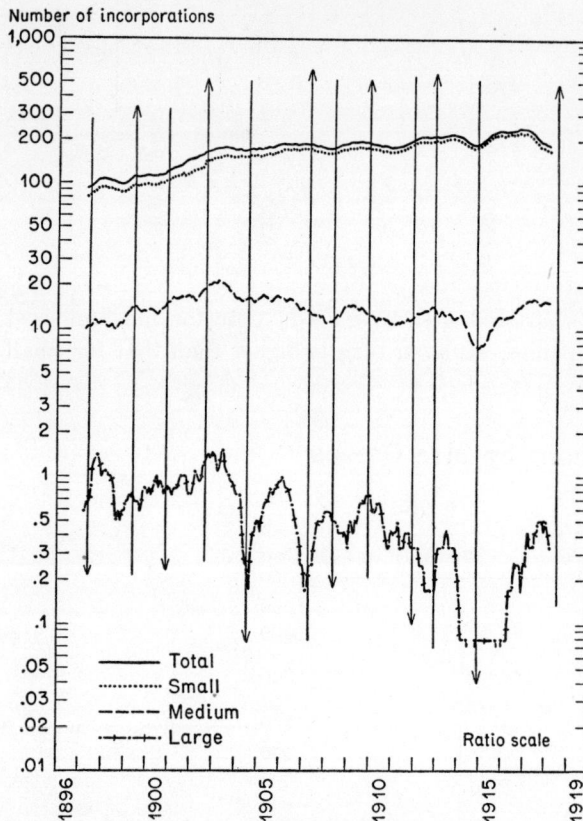

Source of monthly data: Illinois section of Appendix 3.

corporations most and the number of small incorporations least. The chart for Delaware is particularly interesting since for about half of the period covered the average number of charters granted large and small companies is roughly the same. The curves for the number of small and large incorporations are entwined from 1916 to 1930, and the series for large incorporations has a wider amplitude.

If one ignores series built upon a very few items, the peaks and troughs in the waves of incorporations occur

almost simultaneously in the three size groups. One of the interesting exceptions is the increase in the number of medium-sized Ohio corporations around 1877, which is associated with the chartering of numerous building and loan associations.

The data for the eleven states for which total incorporations can be classified by size revealed that in seven (Florida, Illinois, Massachusetts, Ohio, Pennsylvania, Texas, and Virginia) small incorporations constituted a very large proportion—in many cases well above 90 percent—of the total (see Charts 16 and 19 for Illinois and Ohio incorporations plotted by size groups).[3] Furthermore, each series representing the number of medium-sized incorporations in these seven states contains many more items than the series for large incorporations. Though the Pennsylvania figures do not conform closely to what might be called the typical size pattern, the state nevertheless belongs with the other six.

In Colorado, Delaware, Maryland, and New Jersey, small incorporations have not occupied as commanding a position as in the seven states, doubtless because of the liberality of the corporation laws. The size pattern of Colorado incorporations was greatly affected, at least before the beginning of the 20th century, by the number of large companies. Large Colorado incorporations, in turn, were dominated by mining companies, many of which were chartered with capital stock of a million dollars or more.[4] In the early 'nineties, except during the two periods when many charters were granted, the small and medium-sized incorporations were roughly the same percentage of the total. Then the number of medium-sized incorporations increased more rapidly. By the turn of the century Colorado was moving toward the typical size pattern in which small incorporations constitute a large percentage of total charters granted, medium-sized incorporations a much smaller percentage, and large incorporations the smallest.

In Delaware in many of the earlier years under study,

[3] Compare what Macgregor says concerning British joint-stock companies: "Over the period 1919 to 1925, of all companies registered, only 2.6 per cent. had a capitalization over £200,000, while more than 67 per cent. were capitalized below £10,000" (op. cit., p. 133).

[4] For example, at the peak of incorporations in May 1892, 39 of 43 incorporations with a capital stock of a million dollars or more were for mining, and at the peak in January 1896, of 343 large incorporations 340 were for mining. For the total figures on large incorporations, see the original data in the Colorado section of Appendix 3. The count of mining companies was based upon statements of corporate objectives in the sources cited there.

At the peak of incorporations in May 1892, 39 of 87 mining incorporations had a capital stock of a million or more, and at the peak of incorporations in January 1896, 340 of the 389 (ibid.).

CHART 17

Maryland Business Incorporations by Size Groups
1870 - 1939

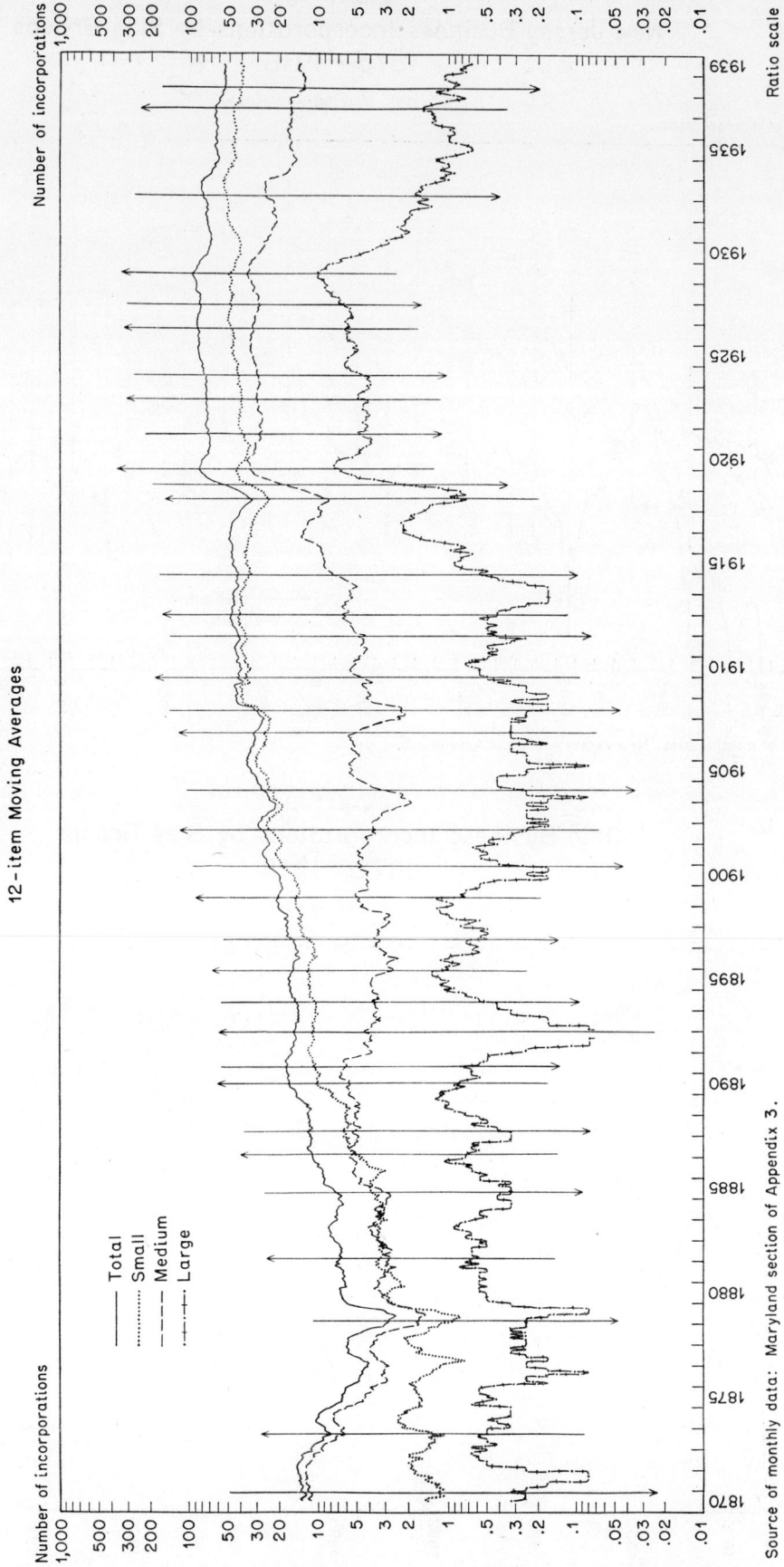

12-item Moving Averages

Number of incorporations

Number of incorporations

Ratio scale

Total
Small
Medium
Large

1870 1875 1880 1885 1890 1895 1900 1905 1910 1915 1920 1925 1930 1935 1939

1,000 500 300 200 100 50 30 20 10 5 3 2 1 .5 .3 .2 .1 .05 .03 .02 .01

Source of monthly data: Maryland section of Appendix 3.

CHART 18
New Jersey Business Incorporations by Size Groups
1875 – 1918

12-item Moving Averages

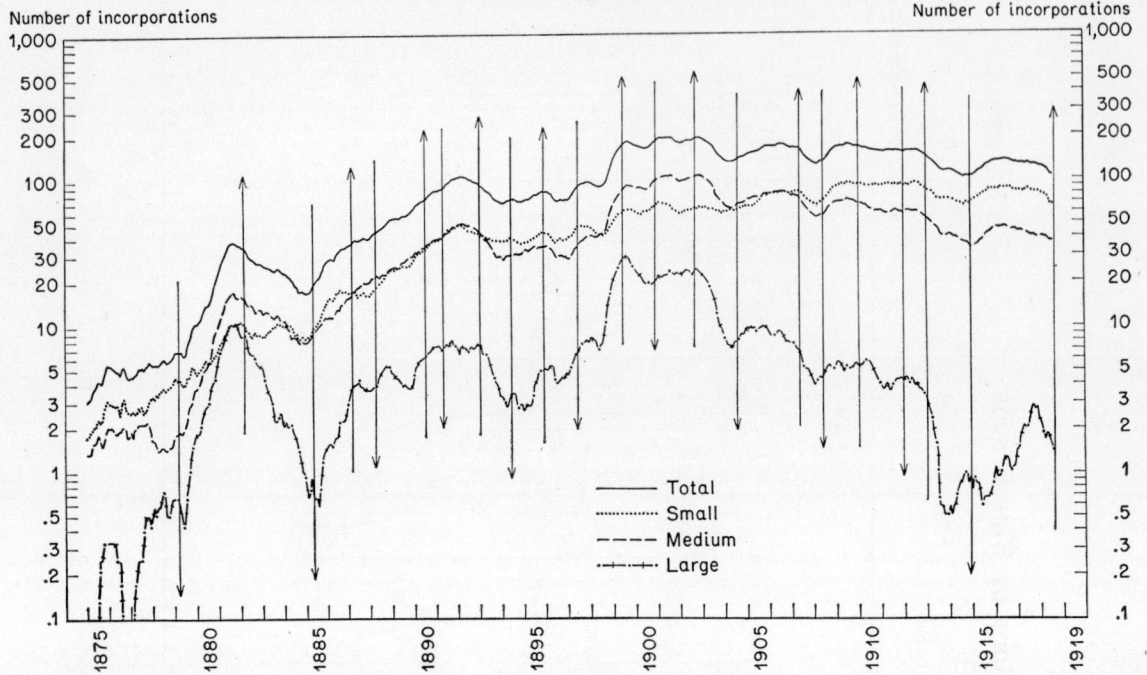

Source of monthly data: New Jersey section of Appendix 3.   Ratio scale

CHART 19
Ohio Business Incorporations by Size Groups
1872 – 1918

12-item Moving Averages

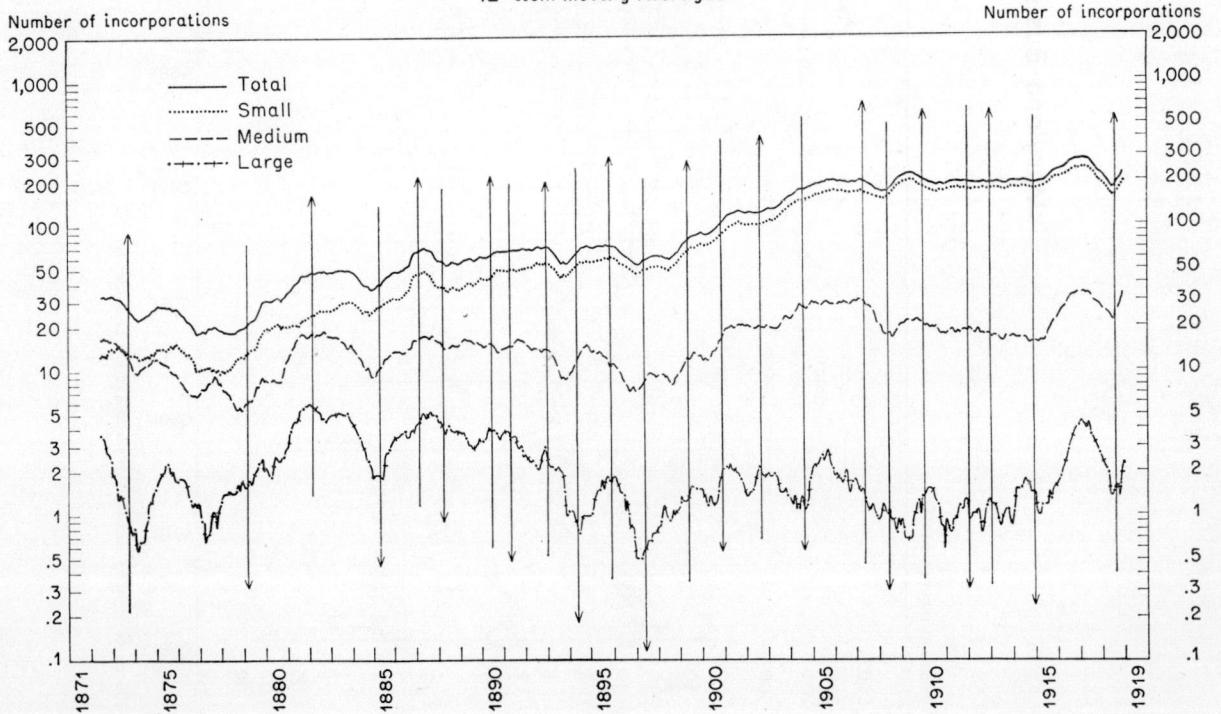

Source of monthly data: Ohio section of Appendix 3.   Ratio scale

small incorporations were less numerous than those of either of the other size groups. Not until after 1930 did the small incorporation assume relatively large importance, and even then it did not surpass the medium-sized; in this period large incorporations fell to a relatively insignificant proportion of the total. If the trend of recent years continues, the size pattern of incorporations by Delaware will approach the pattern of the seven states discussed above. In New Jersey from 1875 to 1907 small and medium-sized incorporations were approximately the same percentage of total incorporations; fewer large companies were incorporated. Between 1907 and 1918 the small incorporation became the dominant type, gradually moving from about one-half to roughly 65 percent of the total. In this state, likewise, the typical pattern of size relationships was apparently being approached by 1918. It is unfortunate that there are no post-1918 data to compare with those for Delaware and Maryland.

The Maryland chart can be divided into several more or less distinct sections. Through the 'seventies, incorporations of medium size dominated. They retained a high level through the 'eighties, though sharing the dominant position with small incorporations. From 1890 until about 1916, the size pattern was the typical one described above. But from 1916 through 1929 small companies declined in number while those of medium and large size increased appreciably. Thereafter the tendency was to revert to the typical size pattern.

To generalize about the trends of incorporations in the three size groups is not easy. Inasmuch as the small incorporations of many states are a very large percentage of total incorporations, it is clear that in general this trend in any given state is likely to be the same as that for the total series. Though from 1875 to 1929 incorporations as a whole and their largest component, small incorporations, were rising, the latter seem to have reached a peak later than the former—in 1932 rather than in 1929.

Concerning incorporations in the other size groups, generalizations are even more difficult to formulate. Perhaps it can be said that the trend in medium-sized incorporations is flat or inclined upward only slightly, but there are important exceptions. In Florida, Maryland, and New Jersey, each series representing medium-sized incorporations has a pronounced upward trend; and the corresponding series for Massachusetts shows a more than slightly upward trend during 1903–21.

Generalizations concerning the series representing large incorporations are complicated by the fact that some series rest upon few items. Moreover, at a maximum no more than eleven states could be studied and few of the series cover the full period 1875–1943. In an examination of large incorporations, one cannot take seriously the data for Florida, Illinois, and Texas. One

rather striking fact emerges from comparisons of the various series—the trend of large incorporations in New Jersey rises very sharply during the 'seventies and continues upward until about 1900. All or a part of this period is covered by the data for Colorado, Maryland, Massachusetts, Ohio, Pennsylvania, and Texas. In no one of these states is the trend for large companies upward. In Ohio and perhaps Pennsylvania one might say that the trend in large incorporations is downward. Though few would doubt that New Jersey was the chief home of the large corporation in this period, the extent to which it surpassed other states is surprising.

The figures on large New Jersey corporations in Chart 18 fail to disclose one feature with respect to size that should be noted here, although it interrupts the discussion somewhat. During the fifty-three years from 1846 through 1898 only twenty-five companies were chartered in New Jersey under general laws with a capital stock of more than $20,000,000 and only five of these before the 'nineties—in 1881 and 1882. In the single year 1899, fifty were chartered. In Table 16 the names of the New Jersey companies with a capitalization of $20,000,000 or more that were chartered under general laws between 1881 and 1902 are listed. These names stir memories of the large combines and enterprises that played a vital role in the development of the American economy. At the time some of these companies were organized, an intention to acquire almost complete control of the fields in which they were to operate was expressed. *The Commercial & Financial Chronicle*, for example, reported that the American Bicycle Co. would "control 95 percent of the bicycle-making industry in this country . . ."[5] The American Hide and Leather Company, it was stated, "controls about 85 percent of the total upper-leather output of the country."[6] In its article on the New Jersey charter for the American Ice Company, *The Commercial & Financial Chronicle* wrote: "The intention is said to be to bring under one control all the leading ice companies of the country."[7] A report of the pending consolidation that led to the chartering of the United States Worsted Company read: ". . . nineteen worsted yarn spinners, including most of the largest spinners in the country, have agreed to enter the trust."[8] There was no hesitation in these and many other instances to emphasize the monopolistic objectives or effects of the very large New Jersey corporations. Another New Jersey charter of the 1890's reflects the grandiose ideas of the period—that of the Electric Vehicle Company. This concern, which was somewhat smaller than those of Table 16, was chartered in September 1897 to manufacture, on its

---

[5] LXVIII, 974 (May 20, 1899).

[6] *Ibid.*, 925 (May 13, 1899).

[7] *Ibid.*, 522 (March 18, 1899).

[8] *Ibid.*, 1026 (May 27, 1899).

own and through certain subsidiaries, electrically driven automobiles; it adopted the policy of organizing trans-

portation companies in *every* state, each company being vested with the exclusive right to purchase for

TABLE 16

New Jersey Corporations with Authorized Capital Stock of $20,000,000 or more Chartered under General Laws, 1881–1902

	DATE OF FILING CERTIFICATE	AUTHORIZED CAPITAL STOCK ($ MILLION)		DATE OF FILING CERTIFICATE	AUTHORIZED CAPITAL STOCK ($ MILLION)
Gas Light Transportation Co.	May 1881	25.0	New England Electric Vehicle Transportation Co.	March 1899	25.0
New York, Susquehanna and Western Railroad Co.	June 1881	30.0	Panama Canal Company of America	December 1899	30.0
New York, West Shore and Buffalo Railway Co.	June 1881	40.0	Philadelphia Electric Co.	October 1899	25.0
Cosmopolitan Pipe-Protecting Co.	November 1882	40.0	Pressed Steel Car Co.	January 1899	25.0
Overland Railroad Construction Co.	April 1882	150.0	Railways and Light Company of America	September 1899	25.0
American Gas Investment Co.	June 1890	50.2	Republic Iron and Steel Co.	May 1899	55.0
American Tobacco Co.	January 1890	25.0	Royal Baking Powder Co.	March 1899	20.0
North American Co.	June 1890	50.0	Rubber Goods Manufacturing Co.	January 1899	50.0
American Sugar Refining Co.	January 1891	50.0	Scott-Janney Electric Co.	August 1899	30.0
National Lead Co.	December 1891	30.0	Sloss Sheffield Steel and Iron Co.	August 1899	20.0
Twin City Rapid Transit Co.	June 1891	20.0	Telephone, Telegraph and Cable Company of America	November 1899	30.0
United States Rubber Co.	March 1892	50.0	Union Bag and Paper Co.	February 1899	27.0
Union Typewriter Co.	March 1893	20.0	United Electric Company of New Jersey	May 1899	20.0
United States Cordage Co.	December 1893	34.0	United Fruit Co.	March 1899	20.0
American Securities Investment Co.	February 1896	20.0	United Fruit Co.	October 1899	20.0
American Malting Co.	September 1897	30.0	United Shoe Machinery Co.	February 1899	25.0
Glucose Sugar Refining Co.	August 1897	40.0	United States Cast Iron Pipe and Foundry Co.	March 1899	30.0
Marsden Company	February 1897	50.0	United States Flour Milling Co.	April 1899	25.0
American Linseed Co.	December 1898	33.5	United States Worsted Co.	April 1899	70.0
American Potteries Co.	December 1898	27.0	American Railways Co.	July 1900	25.0
American Tin Plate Co.	December 1898	50.0	American Sheet Steel Co.	March 1900	52.0
Federal Steel Co.	September 1898	200.0	American Snuff Co.	March 1900	25.0
International Silver Co.	November 1898	20.0	Carnegie Co.	March 1900	160.0
National Biscuit Co.	February 1898	55.0	Cosmopolitan Power Co.	April 1900	40.0
Standard Distilling & Distributing Co.	June 1898	24.0	Crucible Steel Company of America	July 1900	50.0
Amalgamated Copper Co.	April 1899	75.0	International Crude Rubber Co.	December 1900	30.0
American Alkali Co.	May 1899	30.0	Interoceanic Canal Co.	April 1900	100.0
American Beet Sugar Co.	March 1899	20.0	National Sugar Refining Company of New Jersey	June 1900	20.0
American Bicycle Co.	May 1899	80.0	National Telephone and Telegraph Co.	July 1900	50.0
American Car and Foundry Co.	February 1899	60.0	Siegel Copper Co.	April 1900	24.0
American Cereal Co.	February 1899	33.0	Allis-Chalmers Co.	May 1901	50.0
American Hide and Leather Co.	May 1899	70.0	American Can Co.	March 1901	88.0
American Ice Co.	March 1899	60.0	Consolidated Tobacco Co.	June 1901	30.0
American Plumbing Supply and Lead Co.	April 1899	35.0	Copper Range Consolidated Co.	December 1901	28.5
American Railways Co.	April 1899	25.0	Eastman Kodak Co.	October 1901	35.0
American Ship Building Co.	March 1899	30.0	George A. Fuller Co.	April 1901	20.0
American Smelting and Refining Co.	April 1899	65.0	Northern Securities Co.	November 1901	400.0
American Steel Hoop Co.	April 1899	33.0	Pacific Packing and Navigation Co.	July 1901	25.0
American Steel & Wire Company of New Jersey	January 1899	90.0	Pennsylvania Steel Co.	April 1901	50.0
American Woolen Co.	March 1899	65.0	Pocohontas Coal & Coke Co.	October 1901	40.0
American Writing Paper Co.	June 1899	25.0	United Electric Company of New Jersey	February 1901	20.0
Asphalt Company of America	June 1899	30.0	United States Cotton Duck Corporation	June 1901	50.0
Borden's Condensed Milk Co.	April 1899	20.0	American Steel Foundries	June 1902	40.0
Distilling Company of America	July 1899	125.0	Distillers Securities Corporation	September 1902	48.5
Electric Axle Light and Power Co.	July 1899	25.0	International Harvester Co.	August 1902	120.0
Electric Company of America	January 1899	25.0	International Nickel Co.	March 1902	24.0
Federal Printing Ink Co.	June 1899	20.0	North American Copper Co.	July 1902	20.0
General Carriage Co.	May 1899	20.0	Railway Steel-Spring Co.	February 1902	20.0
Havana Commercial Co.	March 1899	20.0	Railway Steel-Spring Co.	June 1902	27.0
Illinois Electric Vehicle Transportation Co.	May 1899	25.0	Rock Island Co.	July 1902	150.0
International Steam-Pump Co.	March 1899	27.5	United Copper Co.	April 1902	80.0
Jersey City, Hoboken and Paterson Street Railway Company	November 1899	20.0	United States Realty & Construction Co.	August 1902	66.0
Kentucky Distilleries & Warehouse Co.	February 1899	32.0	Western Telephone and Telegraph Co.	January 1902	32.0
National Enamel and Stamping Co.	January 1899	30.0			
National Steel Co.	February 1899	59.0			
National Tin Plate and Stamped Ware Co.	January 1899	20.0			

Constructed from the sources cited in the New Jersey section of Appendix 3.

operation and sale within its territory the product controlled by the Electric Vehicle Company.[9]

After 1902, incorporations of large companies in New Jersey began a long decline that reached a trough in 1913 (Chart 18). Charters for the biggest companies had been on the decline since 1899 (Table 17). The picture given by the New Jersey data is supplemented by more recent figures for Delaware. In the preparation of Table 18, nonpar shares were treated as shares of $100 par value, though this method of handling nonpar shares may overstate the totals. From the composite picture gained from the two series it appears that there have been three outstanding periods in the chartering of very large enterprises: 1899, 1920, and 1929.

TABLE 17

Number of New Jersey Corporations with Authorized Capital Stock of $20,000,000 or more Chartered under General Laws, 1880–1918

	NO.		NO.		NO.		NO.
1880	0	1890	3	1900	11	1910	0
1881	3	1891	3	1901	12	1911	3
1882	2	1892	1	1902	11	1912	4
1883	0	1893	2	1903	5	1913	2
1884	0	1894	0	1904	5	1914	0
1885	0	1895	0	1905	8	1915	0
1886	0	1896	1	1906	2	1916	0
1887	0	1897	3	1907	1	1917	0
1888	0	1898	7	1908	4	1918	1
1889	0	1899	50	1909	5		

Compiled from the sources cited in Appendix 3. As pointed out in the text, no companies of this size were chartered by New Jersey under general laws before 1881.

While large and very large New Jersey incorporations were decreasing from 1902 to 1913, large incorporations were increasing in Massachusetts, Pennsylvania, and Virginia. Large incorporations in these three states, however, were few except in Pennsylvania where the average increased from roughly 2 to 8 per month. In Florida, Illinois, and Texas after 1900 they were so few that they are hardly worth noting. But it may be pointed out that their trends in Florida and Texas are horizontal—provided in the case of Texas that allowance is made for the oil boom in 1901—and that the trend for Illinois large companies is downward. Unfortunately, data are not available for some of the more 'liberal' incorporating states for the first decade of the 20th century.

Few comments can be made on the trends in the chartering of large incorporations after 1910. The Maryland figures show a very interesting growth until 1929; and Massachusetts—and perhaps Pennsylvania

[9] Ibid., LXIX, 850 (Oct. 21, 1899). For the date of the charter and the amount of the originally authorized capital stock, see Corporations of New Jersey. List of Certificates Filed in the Department of State From 1895 to 1899, Inclusive. Compiled by the Secretary of State (Trenton, 1900), p. 167.

and Virginia—deserve attention because each has a rising trend during part of this period. Ohio, it should be noted particularly, has a flat trend from 1900 to 1918. After 1929 large incorporations in Delaware and Maryland declined markedly. In comparison with those in Delaware, however, total incorporations in Maryland have held up remarkably well, because the small incorporation has been much more important in the latter state.

TABLE 18

Number of Delaware Corporations with Authorized Capital Stock of $20,000,000 or more Chartered under General Laws, 1916–1943

	NO.		NO.		NO.		NO.
1916	11	1923	67	1930	253	1937	11
1917	27	1924	55	1931	121	1938	5
1918	10	1925	103	1932	41	1939	4
1919	96	1926	104	1933	12	1940	2
1920	110	1927	166	1934	8	1941	0
1921	51	1928	343	1935	12	1942	2
1922	77	1929	619	1936	12	1943	4

Compiled from the sources cited in Appendix 3.

In studying trends in large incorporations one should observe the absolute number of charters granted by the different states. In later years Delaware stands out strikingly as a home of the large corporation. Here again it is unfortunate that there are not data for more states.

Summary

The relative amplitude of the wave-like movements in the various series on the number of incorporations is closely correlated with the size of the incorporation. The widest relative amplitude is associated with the large, and the narrowest with the small incorporation. The trend of small incorporations is upward and steep until 1918; from 1918 to 1932 the rate of growth decreases; after 1932 the trend has a negative slope. The trends for the medium and large incorporations are for the most part either horizontal or inclined upward only slightly. The trend in the incorporation of big companies is less astonishing when one realizes that many large companies were first incorporated as small business units. The growth of some of these small companies has sometimes entailed the taking out of new charters for the enlarged units, but frequently original charters, though doubtless in amended form, have remained in use. Incorporations of small companies in most states far outnumber those of medium or large companies. Only in states with so-called liberal incorporation laws is the generalization questionable. Between 1880 and 1944 there were three peaks in high finance—1899, 1920, and 1929.

CHAPTER 7

An Industrial Classification of Incorporations

Through study of the kinds of business for which the corporations were chartered, that is, through study of what in corporation law are usually called the purposes or objects of incorporation, a fairly good picture of the United States at work and at play can be constructed. Be it the mania for skating rinks or Tom-Thumb golf courses or the feverish organization of 'trusts', an impress has been left upon business incorporations. Sometimes, a reading of the mere names of the newly chartered companies chronologically arranged suffices to indicate the nature of a wave of entrepreneurial activity. For example, a list of Ohio incorporations clearly reveals a fad for skating rinks in the winter of 1884-85 and one for miniature golf courses in the summer of 1930.[1] A simultaneous wave of Tom-Thumb golf courses occurred in New York, reaching such proportions that in August 1930 the Secretary of State of New York said:

"Hardly a day passed during the past month that did not witness anywhere from one to four or five companies incorporating to construct and maintain a Tom Thumb golf course. If one is to judge from the number of such courses already built, there must be tens of thousands of players each day."[2]

The company name—the chief basis for the industrial classifications of Chapter 3 except as noted otherwise—often furnishes a clue to the purpose for which a concern was chartered, but more precise information can be procured. The charter, of course, is a primary source of information, but it is not to be used without great care. The first difficulty encountered in an attempt to determine the main object of an incorporation from the purpose clauses of the charter is to select one purpose from the many that often seem of equal importance. This difficulty is not as great in the case of early charters as in that of more recent ones; the modern corporation is not modest in stating its objectives. Efforts to disguise the objects of the corporation are another source of difficulty. Concealed aims, however, have not been especially frequent since the enactment of general incorporation laws. Disguise characterizes chiefly the era of the special charter, when legislatures were averse to granting certain types freely. A third

difficulty must be faced by one who plans to classify industrially a large number of corporations. The average charter is so long that no investigator can read many from the first line to the last. Fortunately, some states have published brief abstracts of charter purpose statements. These abstracts, from which the basic information for the industrial classifications described in this and the next chapter was derived, represent the opinion of some local officer, and may or may not fairly interpret the main objects of the companies. The resulting errors are, however, probably not often serious, since contemporaneous judgments by local authorities, who are familiar with many of the incorporators or their agents, may be expected to have a rather high degree of reliability. Finally, these abbreviated statements of purpose may be misinterpreted.

Several supplementary types of information are aids to an industrial allocation, for example, the name of a company. An enterprise that could be classified from its charter description as either a mining company or a coal dealer, may well be placed in the mining category if the word mining appears in the corporate name. Occasionally the name can be allowed to play a more decisive role. For instance, the official summary of the charter purpose statement of the Pittsburgh Cigar Machine Company, incorporated by Pennsylvania on January 26, 1900, read: "Manufacturing iron and steel or both, or any article of commerce from wood, metal or both."[3] Despite the vagueness of this description, the company was put in the manufacturing subgroup that includes companies producing "specialized machinery other than transportation equipment and electric machinery"—class bta of Table 19.

The size and location of the corporation may also be items to note in deciding ambiguous cases. The amount of the authorized capital stock is seldom helpful in classifying corporations by objectives, but it frequently provides a clue to what is going on in the community. The sharp rise around 1899 in the number of very large New Jersey companies, which even a cursory survey of incorporations cannot fail to reveal, reflects combinations and monopolistic activities. The kind of articles produced or handled may also facilitate the determination of corporate purpose. For example, a company authorized "to manufacture, buy, and sell" a wide variety of articles usually stocked by drug stores can be treated—

[1] See the *Annual Report of the Secretary of State to the Governor of the State of Ohio, for the year 1885* (Columbus, 1885), p. 256, and the *Annual Report of the Secretary of State to the Governor and General Assembly of the State of Ohio for the Year Ending December 31, 1930* . . . (Cleveland, 1931). The golf course companies must be picked out of the group headed "Miscellaneous Companies", which appears on pages 36–71 of the latter *Report*.

[2] Press release on incorporations, dated August 1930.

[3] *List of charters of corporations enrolled in the office of the Secretary of the Commonwealth . . . June 1, 1899 . . . [to] June 1, 1901*, p. 69.

TABLE 19

Industrial Categories used in Classifying Incorporations

A Mining and Quarrying
  AA Metal mining
    aaa Iron
    aab Copper
    aac Lead and zinc
    aad Gold and silver
    aae Other metals (including manganese, aluminum, mercury, and radium)
    aaf Unallocable
  AB Coal mining
  AC Crude petroleum and natural gas production (including field service operations)
    aca Prospecting for petroleum
    acb Others
  AD Nonmetallic mining and quarrying
    ada Stone, sand, and gravel (including slate, marble, and limestone)
    adb Other mining and quarrying (including clay, asbestos, mica, rock salt, and those not allocable)
  AE Those not allocable to a two-letter group

A/B Mining and Manufacturing

B Manufacturing
  BA Food and kindred products
    baa Bakery products
    bab Confectionery and related products (including chocolate and cocoa products)
    bac Canning and preserving fruits, vegetables, and sea foods
    bad Meat products
    bae Grain-mill products
    baf Dairy products (including ice cream)
    bag Sugar (cane and beet)
    bah Others (including flavoring syrups)
    bai Unallocable
  BB Beverages
    bba Malt and malt liquors
    bbb Distilled, rectified, and blended liquors
    bbc Wines
    bbd Nonalcoholic beverages (including carbonated water, and birch and root beers)
    bbe Others (including those not allocable)
  BC Tobacco manufactures (including snuff)
  BD Textile-mill products
    bda Cotton
    bdb Woolen and worsted
    bdc Silk
    bdd Rayon and other synthetic textile-mill products
    bde Knit goods (including hosiery)
    bdf Hat bodies (except cloth and millinery)
    bdg Carpets
    bdh Dyeing and finishing textiles (except woolen and worsted)
    bdi Other textile-mill products
    bdj Unallocable
  BE Apparel and other finished products made from fabrics and similar materials
    bea Men's and boys' clothing (except fur and rubber clothing, and knitted goods)
    beb Women's, children's and infants' clothing (except fur and rubber clothing, and knitted goods)
    bec Fur goods
    bed Millinery
    bee Other apparel
    bef Unallocable
  BF Leather and leather products
    bfa Leather: tanned, curried, and finished
    bfb Footwear (except rubber)
    bfc Other leather products (including those not allocable)

  BG Rubber products
    bga Tires and inner tubes
    bgb Other rubber products and industries (including reclaimed rubber and those not allocable)
  BH Lumber and timber basic products
    bha Logging and sawmills
    bhb Planing mills
    bhc Others (including those not allocable)
    bhd Stream improvement for log movement
  BI Furniture and finished lumber products
    bia Furniture (wood and metal)
    bib Wooden containers (including barrels and boxes)
    bic Others (including matches regardless of material, cork products, and those not allocable)
  BJ Paper and allied products
  BK Printing, publishing, and allied industries
  BM Chemicals and allied products
    bma Paints, varnishes, and colors
    bmb Soap and glycerin
    bmc Drugs, toilet preparations, and insecticides
    bmd Rayon fibre and allied products
    bme Fertilizers
    bmf Animal and vegetable oils (excluding lubricants and cooking and salad oils; including cotton seed products and marine oil)
    bmg Plastic materials
    bmh Others (including industrial chemicals)
    bmi Unallocable
  BN Products of petroleum and coal
    bna Petroleum refining
    bnb Others (including those not allocable)
  BP Stone, clay, and glass products
    bpa Brick, tile, and other structural clay products
    bpb Pottery and related products (including porcelain)
    bpc Glass and glass products
    bpd Cement
    bpe Concrete, gypsum, and plaster products (including lime)
    bpf Others (including abrasives, asbestos products, graphite, and cut stone)
    bpg Unallocable
  BQ Iron and steel and their products
    bqa Blast furnaces, steel works, and rolling mills
    bqb Fabricated structural steel and ornamental metal work
    bqc Tin cans and other tinware
    bqd Tools and general hardware (except machine tools and cutlery)
    bqe Heating apparatus (except electric), enameled-iron sanitary ware, and boiler-shop products
    bqf Others (including cutlery, foundry and wire products [including cast iron pipe], and stamped metal)
        [for foundry and machine shop combined, see btb]
    bqg Unallocable
  BR Nonferrous metals and their products
    bra Clocks and watches
    brb Jewelry (excluding silverware and plated ware)
    brc Others (including those not allocable)
  BS Electrical machinery
    bsa Automotive electric equipment
    bsb Radio apparatus (including phonographs accessory to radios)
    bsc Electrical appliances (except refrigerators, washing machines, and sewing machines)
    bsd Others (including those not allocable)
  BT Machinery (except electrical)
    bta Special industry machinery (including textile machinery)
    btb General industrial machinery (including foundry and machine shops)

TABLE 19 (concl.)

btc   Metalworking machinery (including machine tools)
btd   Engines and turbines
bte   Construction and mining machinery
btf   Agricultural machinery and tractors
btg   Office and store machines, equipment, and supplies
bth   Others (including refrigerators, washing machines, and sewing machines)
bti   Unallocable

BU   Automobiles and automobile equipment
bua   Trailers
bub   Others (including those not allocable)

BV   Transportation equipment (except automobiles)
bva   Railroad equipment (including locomotives, and railroad and street cars)
bvb   Aircraft and parts
bvc   Ship and boat building
bvd   Motorcycles, bicycles, and parts
bve   Others (including wagons, carriages, sleighs, push carts, carts, and wheelbarrows)
bvf   Unallocable

BW   Miscellaneous manufacturing industries
bwa   Ice (natural and manufactured)
bwb   Others (including professional and scientific instruments, musical instruments, toys, pens, pencils, buttons, costume jewelry, brooms and brushes, and furs, dressed and dyed)
bwc   Phonographs and records (except phonographs accessory to radios)

BX   Those not allocable to a two-letter group

C   Public Utilities
CA   Transportation
caa   Railroads (including belt lines)
cab   Railway express
cac   Street railways (including interurban railways and subways)
cad   City and suburban bus lines (including omnibus lines)
cae   Interstate and interurban busses (including stages and terminals)
caf   Taxicabs (including horse-drawn cabs)
cag   Interstate and interurban motor freight carriers (including horse-drawn vehicles)
cah   Local trucking and warehousing
cai   Air transportation
caj   Pipe line transportation
cak   Water transportation other than ferries and canal construction and operation
cam   Canal construction and operation (including river improvement)
can   Ferries
cap   Others and allied services (including stockyards and ticket agents)
caq   Unallocable

CB   Communication
cba   Telephone
cbb   Telegraph
cbc   Radio broadcasting
cbd   Others (including those not allocable)

CC   Other public utilities
cca   Electric light and power
ccb   Gas production and distribution (except natural gas production)
ccc   Water (excluding irrigation companies)
ccd   Bridges
cce   Turnpikes
ccf   Others (including steam heat supply, sewerage, and tunnels)
ccg   Unallocable

D   Wholesale Trade (exclusively)
DA   Merchant wholesalers
DB   Commission merchants, manufacturers' agents, and merchandise brokers

DC   Others (including those not allocable to a two-letter group)

E   Retail Trade (including the combination of wholesale and retail trade)
EA   Department, general merchandise, and dry-goods stores
EB   Limited price variety stores
EC   Mail-order houses
ED   Food stores
EE   Drug stores
EF   Clothing stores
EG   House furnishings and furniture stores
EH   Restaurants and other eating and drinking places
EI   Automobile dealers (including sellers of parts and accessories)
EJ   Filling stations
EK   Hardware stores
EM   Lumber and building supplies yards
EN   Coal and fuel yards
EP   Others (including cigar stores, book stores, jewelry stores, florists, music stores, and ice dealers)
EQ   Those not allocable to a two-letter group

F   Service
FA   Domestic and personal
faa   Hotels, boarding houses, and camps
fab   Laundries (including cleaning and dyeing plants)
fac   Photographic studios (including commercial photography)
fad   Others (including barber shops, beauty shops, clothes cleaning and pressing shops, and undertaking establishments)
fae   Unallocable

FB   Business service
fba   Advertising
fbb   Others (including those not allocable)

FC   Auto repair services and garages

FD   Amusement
fda   Motion picture production and distribution
fdb   Motion picture theatres
fdc   Auditoriums, opera houses, and theatres
fdd   Others (including fairs, clubs, and those not allocable)

FE   Others (including political, charitable, and religious organizations, engineering and professional services, accountants, schools, colleges, hospitals, sanatoriums, and those not allocable to a two-letter group)

G   Finance, Insurance, Real Estate, and Lessors of Real Property
GA   Commercial banks, trust companies, and safe deposit companies (including nonmutual savings and loan associations)
GB   Building and loan associations (including mutual savings and loan associations)
GC   Other mortgage and title companies
GD   Investment trusts and companies
GE   Holding companies
GF   Stock, bond, and commodity brokers, and investment bankers
GG   Commercial credit and finance companies, and industrial and personal loan companies
GH   Other finance companies (including patent holding or buying and licensing)
GI   Insurance
GJ   Real estate (including townsite improvements)
GK   Those not allocable to a two-letter group (including equipment trusts)

H   Construction—contractors and subcontractors
HA   Construction of railways
HB   Other construction

I   Agriculture, Forestry, and Fishery (including cotton ginning, irrigation, compressing cotton, and baling hay)

J   Those not allocable to a major division

if other evidence is corroborative— as a trading rather than a manufacturing concern. The compilers of the state reports in which the data on incorporations are to be found have sometimes for publication purposes grouped companies along industrial lines; building and loan associations, for instance, are listed together. These classifications certainly cannot be accepted without question. They must be used merely as supplementary information. When there is doubt about the classification of a *large* corporation, resort may be had to the *Commercial & Financial Chronicle* and the Poor and Moody *Manuals*.

Even with the assistance of all available data, erroneous classifications may be made. For example, a concern may appear from the charter abstract and other printed material to be a planing mill with a builders' supply business tacked on, but upon examination firsthand, it may be found to be a lumber yard with an insignificant portion of its income derived from the mill operations. For this type of error, there is little check. Table 20, discussed below, gives evidence that there is no serious error in the classification work described in this chapter.

Short statements of the industrial purposes for which corporations have been created can be procured in readily accessible form for many years for at least three states: New Jersey, Ohio, and Pennsylvania.[4] In reports of the Secretary of State for each of these states, the newly chartered companies are listed, sometimes chronologically, sometimes alphabetically. Most of the data worked for this and the next chapter are derived from charters granted under general laws by New Jersey, 1875–1907, by Ohio, 1872–1930, and by Pennsylvania, 1888–1920 (App. 4). When desirable, this material is linked with that of Chapter 3, which for the most part is built upon less precise information. The state reports here utilized give the name of each company, its authorized capital stock, and a brief summary of its charter purpose statement. In addition, the companies are sometimes grouped in the reports by industries. In the Ohio reports, for example, manufacturing companies are listed together, subdivided into narrower groups.

On the basis of these abstracts, incorporations were classified according to the industrial categories of Table 19, which are similar to those in the *Standard Industrial Classification* of the Central Statistical Board.[5] In fact, the classification scheme of Table 19 for manufacturing

and mining is almost identical with that of the Board.[6] The other major categories of Table 19—those for Public Utilities, Wholesale Trade, Retail Trade, Services, Finance, Construction, and Agriculture—differ in internal arrangement from the Board's corresponding categories largely because they were set up before the Board had published its arrangement for the nonmanufacturing field. In comparing Table 19 with the Board's classification scheme it must be remembered that many companies were chartered in industrial fields that are no longer of great importance. To avoid losing detail on the early companies, some industrial classes had to be given more prominence than they would have had if present day corporations alone had been treated. On the other hand, the purpose statements abstracted from the charters of certain types of corporation were not explicit enough to warrant as much detail as that contained in the Board's classification scheme.

The 183 basic, that is, undivided, classes of Table 19 are not of equal scope.[7] Roughly 2 percent are one-letter classes. Agriculture, Construction, and an unallocable class (J) were the only one-letter categories used without subdivision in the grouping of Pennsylvania companies; for the New Jersey and Ohio data it was deemed advisable to have a Mining and Manufacturing class (A/B) for the companies that cut across those two major industrial groups and did not appear to belong really to either group. Of course, figures for other one-letter classes, such as Mining or Manufactur-

[4] Other states, including Colorado and Texas, have published information on the purposes for which corporations have been chartered. Some of these data have been used in part in the following pages to supplement the figures for New Jersey, Ohio, and Pennsylvania.

[5] (Washington, D. C., 1939–40), I, Parts 1–4, and II, Parts 1–3.

[6] In addition to the absence of a certain amount of detail from Table 19 and the prominence given certain currently obsolete industries, the important differences between Table 19 and the classification scheme of the Central Statistical Board are:
1) The manufacture of beverages appears in Table 19 as a two-letter category while in the C.S.B. classification it is a three-digit category in the *Food and Kindred Products* group.
2) The production of ice is likewise a part of food manufacture in the C.S.B. classification; but in Table 19 it appears as a type of *Miscellaneous Manufacturing*.
3) Cutlery manufacturing in Table 19 is in the *Others* class of the iron and steel group, while in the C.S.B. classification it is placed with tools and general hardware and as such constitutes a three-digit category in the iron and steel section. (In Table 19 *Tools and General Hardware* appears as a three-letter category.)
4) The manufacturing of phonographs and records appears in Table 19 as a subdivision of *Miscellaneous Manufacturing*; in the C.S.B. classification it is part of *Communication Equipment*, a subdivision of the *Electrical Machinery* group.
5) *Communication Equipment*, a subdivision of the *Electrical Machinery* manufacturing group of the C.S.B. classification, does not appear in Table 19 as such. The production of such material would appear in Table 19 under *Radio Apparatus* (a subdivision of *Electrical Machinery*) or *Phonographs and Records* (a subdivision of *Miscellaneous Manufacturing Industries*) or the *Others* class of the *Electrical Machinery* manufacturing group.

[7] As explained below, the two classes of Table 19 that are lettered A/B and HA were not used on the Pennsylvania data.

TABLE 20

A Sample of Pennsylvania Corporations Chartered in 1902 Classified on Basis of Bradstreet and Charter Descriptions

NAME OF COMPANY	BRADSTREET DESCRIPTION OF BUSINESS[a]	INDUSTRIAL CLASSIFICATION ON BASIS OF BRADSTREET DESCRIPTION	ABSTRACT OF CHARTER PURPOSES QUOTED FROM *List of Charters of Corporations*[b]	INDUSTRIAL CLASSIFICATION ON BASIS OF CHARTER ABSTRACT
Abington Dairy Co.	Dairy	baf[c]	Manufacture of butter, cheese, buttermilk and all other products made from milk	baf
Acme Department Store	Groceries, etc.	EA	Trading in merchandise at wholesale and retail	EA
Alcott-Ross Co.	Lumber & mill work	bhb	Manufacturing and selling lumber, mill-work, and builders' supplies	bhb
Allegheny Plumbing Co.	Plumbing	H	Carrying on the plumbing business	H
Allentown Bobbin Works	Bobbin works	bta	Manufacturing bobbins and other implements used in the manufacture of silk and cotton fabrics	bta
American Cement and Tile Manufacturing Co.	Cement and tile manufacturing	bpg	Manufacturing tile and all other articles of commerce from any material whatever, by patented and unpatented processes, either or both	bpg
American Foundry and Machine Company	Foundry and machine co.	btb	Making anything of iron, steel, brass, composition, wood, or a combination of any and all of them; for the purpose, generally, of carrying on the business of a machine-shop and iron and brass foundry	btb
American Manufacturing and Novelty Co.	Wooden specialties	bic	Manufacture of step ladders, lawn swings, iron or steel, or both, or of any other metal, or of any article of commerce from metal or wood, or both	bic
American Narrow Fabric Co.	Manufacturers	bdj	Manufacture of braided and woven narrow fabrics of cotton, linen and silk	bdj
American Planing Mill Co.	Planing mill	bhb	Manufacturing of and selling all kinds of lumber and builders' supplies	bhb
Arco Manufacturing Co.	Metal specialties	BX	Manufacture and sale of iron or steel, or both, or of any other metal, or articles of commerce from metal alone or in connection with other materials	BX
Armstrong County Trust Co.	Trust co.	GA	Insurance of owners of real estate, mortgagees, and others interested in real estate, from loss by reason of defective titles, liens and incumbrances	GC
Armure Tapestry Mill	Tapestry mill	bdj	Manufacturing textile fabrics	bdj
Autocrat Shirt Waist Manufacturing Co. of Wilkes-Barre	Shirt waist manufacture	beb	Manufacturing and selling of gentlemen's and ladies' shirt waists and wearing apparel and articles of a similar character	bef
Breon Table Co.	Manufacturers	bia	Manufacture and sale of tables, furniture and other articles made of wood	bia
Butler Silk Mill	Silk mill	bdc	Manufacturing, weaving and making silk, cotton, woolen and other textile goods, and of manufacturing and making silk, cotton, woolen thread and yarns	bdc
C. Schmidt & Sons Brewing Co.	Brewery	bba	Manufacture of beer and malt, and of brewed and malt liquors, and for the sale of the same so manufactured	bba
Cadwallader Tin Plate and Metal Co.	Manufacturers	bqa	Manufacture of iron or steel, or both, or of any other metal, or article of metal, wood, or both	bqa
Carnegie Mill and Lumber Co.	Mill and lumber co.	bhb	Acquiring and manufacturing lumber, doing mill-work, furnishing building supplies, acquiring and making all articles manufactured from wood, and selling and otherwise disposing of the same	bhb
Central Pennsylvania Trust Co.	Trust co.	GA	Insurance of owners of real estate, mortgagees, and others interested in real estate, from loss by reason of defective titles, liens and incumbrances	GC
Citizens' Ice Co.	Ice company	bwa	Manufacture of ice	bwa
Colonial Trust Co.	Trust co.	GA	Engaging in and carrying on the business of the insurance of owners of real estate, mortgagees, and others interested in real estate, from loss by reason of defective titles, liens and incumbrances	GC
Connellsville Distilling Co.	Distillery	bbb	Manufacturing and distilling spirituous liquors	bbb
Croton Limestone and Brick Co.	Limestone and brick company	bpa	Digging and quarrying clay and limestone, and manufacturing the various products therefrom	bpa
D. L. Clark Co.	Wholesale confectionery	DA	Manufacturing and dealing in crackers, candies and bakery and confection products and supplies generally	bai
Davis Textile Co.	Textile company	bdj	Manufacturing and selling textile fabrics	bdj

[a] The Bradstreet Company, *Bradstreet's Book of Commercial Ratings of Bankers, Merchants, Manufacturers in the United States and the Dominion of Canada* (Sept. 1905), Vol. 151.
[b] *List of Charters of Corporations enrolled in the office of Secretary of the Commonwealth during the two years beginning June 1, 1901, and ending June 1, 1903* . . . (1903), pp. 51–65.
[c] Unless a dairy was very small or there was specific reason to classify it as a mere distributor, it was treated as a manufacturing concern.

TABLE 20

NAME OF COMPANY	BRADSTREET DESCRIPTION OF BUSINESS[a]	INDUSTRIAL CLASSIFICATION ON BASIS OF BRADSTREET DESCRIPTION	ABSTRACT OF CHARTER PURPOSES QUOTED FROM *List of Charters of Corporations*[b]	INDUSTRIAL CLASSIFICATION ON BASIS OF CHARTER ABSTRACT
Donley Brick Co.	Brick company	bpa	Quarrying, mining and digging of limestone, sandstone, clay and shale, and the manufacturing from said limestone, sandstone, clay and shale of fire brick, pressed brick, stock brick, paving brick, common brick, decorative bricks and all manner of bricks, sewer pipe, tile pipe, building tile, crushed stone, paving stone, building stone, lime and sand, and the sale thereof, and the by-products thereof, to be used for any purpose, and for purchasing, leasing or holding, upon royalty or upon rental, clay or shale lands, from time to time, when and as the same shall become necessary or convenient in the transaction of the business of the said company	bpa
Excelsior Planing Mill Co. of Reading, Pennsylvania	Planing mill	bhb	Manufacture of doors, sash, blinds, shutters, window and door-frames, and other articles of commerce from wood	bhb
F. W. Crandall Co.	Manufacturers of toys and hardware specialties	bwb	Manufacture and sale of chairs, toys, novelties, building materials, lumber and other articles of metal or wood, or both	bic
Fayette R. Plumb & Sons, Inc.	Manufacturers of edge tools, etc.	bqf	Manufacture of railroad, miners' and blacksmiths' tools, and edge tools generally, and of all other similar articles of commerce of iron or steel, or both, or of any other metal	bqf
Finley Acker Co.	Grocers and manufacturers of confectionery	J	Manufacturing and selling all articles of food, confectionery, toilet articles, groceries and general merchandise	J
Fleischman Distilling Co.	Distillery	bbb	Engaging in and carrying on the business of dealing in spirituous and vinous liquors and rectifying and compounding the same and selling the same at wholesale	bbb
George C. Anderson and Sons, Inc.	Contractors	H	Erecting and constructing dwellings and other houses and buildings, and furnishing and supplying the necessary building materials	H
Germantown Telegraph Publishing Co.	Printers and publishers	BK	Publishing the Germantown Telegraph newspaper, and for the general purpose of the transaction of a printing and publishing business	BK
Greensburg Foundry and Machine Co.	Foundry and machine co.	btb	Manufacture of iron or steel, or both, or of any other metal, or of any article of commerce from wood or metal, or both	btb
H. H. Maus & Co., Inc.	Wholesale lumber and railroad ties	DA	Buying, selling, trading and dealing in lumber, railroad ties, wood, etc., at wholesale, under act approved 25th June, 1895	DA
Haney-White Co.	Builders' supplies	EM	Buying and selling merchandise	EQ
Herald Publishing Co. of Pittsburgh, Pa.	Publishing	BK	Transaction of a printing and publishing business	BK
Hyde Carbon Black Co.	Manufacturers of lampblack	bmb	Manufacturing, marketing and selling lampblack, carbon black, gas black, amorphous carbon, and other products, articles and materials of like nature and character	bmh
J. C. Lappe Tanning Co.	Tanning	bfa	Manufacture of all kinds of leather, and all articles of commerce composed wholly or partly of leather	bfa
J. W. Hodil Co.	Contractors	H	Purchase and sale of real estate, including power, from time to time, to subdivide lots or acreage, to sell, hold or lease the same, negotiate loans secured by mortgage thereon, or improve real estate by the erection of buildings or otherwise	GJ
James G. Corcoran Co.	Contractors	H	Carrying on the business of the construction of and contracting for buildings and railroads and general construction	H
John Crompton Co.	Manufacturers of paper boxes	BJ	Manufacturing paper, paper or pasteboard boxes, paper or pasteboard bags, paper goods and specialties, or any article of commerce manufactured from paper or pasteboard, either alone or in combination with wood, muslin, metal, glass or any other substance, and of selling such products so manufactured	BJ
Joseph Hendler Construction Co.	Construction	H	Conducting a general construction and contracting business	H

TABLE 20 (cont.)

NAME OF COMPANY	BRADSTREET DESCRIPTION OF BUSINESS[a]	INDUSTRIAL CLASSIFICATION ON BASIS OF BRADSTREET DESCRIPTION	ABSTRACT OF CHARTER PURPOSES QUOTED FROM *List of Charters of Corporations*[b]	INDUSTRIAL CLASSIFICATION ON BASIS OF CHARTER ABSTRACT
Joseph Woodwell Co.	Wholesale and retail hardware	EK	Buying, selling, trading and dealing in hardware, at wholesale and retail	EK
Kane Trust & Savings Co.	Trust and savings company	GK	Insuring owners of real estate, mortgagees, and others interested in real estate, from loss by reason of defective titles, liens and incumbrances	GC
Karl Schlatter Dye Works	Dye works	bdh	Manufacturing, dyeing and selling all kinds of fabrics, yarns and threads, made or to be made of cotton, wool, linen, silk or other materials	bdh
Kaufman Brothers	Department store	EA	Buying, selling and dealing in goods, wares and merchandise at retail	EQ
Keystone Sand and Supply Co.	Sand	EM	Buying and selling, trading and dealing in, sand, gravel, lime, cement, brick, and other and all kinds of building and builders' supplies	EM
Keystone Foundry Co.	Manufacturers of iron and steel	bqf	Manufacture of iron or steel, or both, or of any other metal, or article of commerce from metal, or wood, or both, and for the sale of the same	bqf
Keystone Silk Weaving Co.	Manufacturers of woven silk labels	bdc	Manufacturing and selling silk labels, shoe facing and other woven goods	bdc
Lackawaxen Creamery Co.	Creamery	baf	Manufacturing butter and cheese, and selling the same	baf
McCandless and Gordon Company	Men's furnishing	EF	Engaging in and carrying on the business of buying, selling, dealing in men's furnishing goods, at retail	EF
McKinney Manufacturing Company	Hinges	bqd	Manufacture of iron and steel, or both, or of any other metal, or of any articles of commerce from metal or wood, or both	BX
Nansen Supply Company	General store	EA	Buying, selling, vending, trading and dealing in any kind or kinds of goods, provisions, wares and merchandise, at retail or wholesale, or both retail and wholesale combined	EQ
Northern Trust and Savings Company	Trust and savings company	GK	Insurance of owners of real estate, mortgagees, and others interested in real estate, from loss by reason of defective titles, liens and incumbrances	GC
Ontwood Hotel Company	Hotel	faa	Maintaining and conducting an hotel	faa
P. C. Fulweiler and Bro. Company	Manufacturers of cigars	BC	Manufacture and sale of cigars, tobies, cheroots, and tobacco and any of its products, including cigarettes, snuff, smoking and chewing tobacco	BC
Patterson Coal and Supply Company	Coal and supply company	EM	Buying and selling coal, lumber, lime, cement, and a general line of builders' supplies	EM
Paxtang Electric Company	Electric company	cca	Supplying light, heat and power by means of electricity to the public of the city of Harrisburg, State of Pennsylvania, and to persons, partnerships and associations residing therein and adjacent thereto as may desire the same	cca
Penn Furniture Company	Manufacturers	bia	Manufacturing and selling all kinds of furniture, and to sell and manufacture any and all goods or materials used therein	bia
Peter Woll and Sons Feather Company	Manufacturers of bedding supplies	bia	Manufacture of bedding supplies	bia
Peter Woll and Sons Manufacturing Company	Upholsterers' and brush makers' supplies	bwb	Manufacture of upholsterers' mattress and brush supplies	bwb
Presque Isle Laundry Company	Laundry	fab	Cleansing, bleaching, starching and smoothing textile fabrics by the use of machinery and mechanical appliances and the application of skilled manual labor, and the carrying on of a laundry business	fab
Rambo and Regar, Inc.	Manufacturers of hosiery	bde	Manufacturing and selling knit goods and knitting machinery	bde
Reifler and Sons, Inc.	Lumber and manufacturers of acids	bmh	Manufacturing and selling lumber and wood alcohol, acetates, charcoal, and other products made from wood by destructive distillation	bmh
Ridgway Sandstone Company	Sandstone	ada	Mining, quarrying and selling stone and sand	ada
Robert W. Tunis Manufacturing Company	Printing presses	bta	Manufacture and sale of printing presses, type, printers supplies, and any article of commerce made from wood or metal, or both	bta
Rose Hill Hair Drawing Company	Wholesale horse hair	DA	Selling, drawing, and manufacturing horse hair, cow hair, bristles, and kindred articles and products	bwb
Rosenbaum Company	Department store	EA	Buying and selling, at wholesale and retail, drygoods, notions, millinery and general merchandise	EA

TABLE 20

NAME OF COMPANY	BRADSTREET DESCRIPTION OF BUSINESS[a]	INDUSTRIAL CLASSIFICATION ON BASIS OF BRADSTREET DESCRIPTION	ABSTRACT OF CHARTER PURPOSES QUOTED FROM *List of Charters of Corporations*[b]	INDUSTRIAL CLASSIFICATION ON BASIS OF CHARTER ABSTRACT
Saucony Shoe Manufacturing Company	Shoe manufacturing	bfb	Manufacturing boots and shoes from leather and other materials	bfb
Scranton Journal Publishing Company	Publishing	BK	Doing a general printing and publishing business in all its branches	BK
Shenandoah Trust Company	Trust company	GA	Insuring owners of real estate, mortgagees, and others interested in real estate, from loss by reason of defective titles, liens and incumbrances	GC
Smith Bros. Brick Company	Brick	bpa	Manufacture of brick, tile, terra-cotta and other products that can be manufactured from shale or clay	bpa
Sportsmen's Supply Company	Sporting goods	EP	Trading and dealing in goods and merchandise generally at wholesale and retail	EP
Spring Brewing Company	Brewery	bba	Manufacturing and selling lager beer, ale and porter	bba
Steelton Trust Company	Trust Company	GA	Insurance of owners of real estate, mortgagees, and others interested in real estate, from loss by reason of defective titles, liens and incumbrances	GC
Sterling Automatic Instantaneous Water Heater Company	Water heaters	bqe	Manufacturing the Sterling Automatic Instantaneous Water Heater, and any article of commerce of metal or wood, or both	bqe
Surburban Gas Company of Philadelphia	Gas company	ccb	Manufacture and supply of gas for light only to the public in the city of Chester, the township of Chester and Lower Chichester, and such boroughs as may be in existence or may be created within the territorial limits of the said townships, and to such persons, partnerships, corporations and associations residing therein and adjacent thereto as may desire the same	ccb
Susquehanna Dye Works	Dye works	bdh	Manufacturing and selling the ingredients and materials used in dyeing and cleansing thread, yarn or cloth, of silk, cotton, wool or other fabrics, and to dye thread, yarn, or cloth, or fabrics of silk, cotton, wool or other material, and to sell such dyed materials or products	bdh
Susquehanna Store Company	Store	EQ	Buying and selling any kind or kinds of goods, wares and merchandise, at wholesale and retail	EQ
Tacony Iron Company	Manufacturers of soil pipes	bqf	Manufacture of iron and steel, or both, or of any other metal, or of any article of commerce from metal or wood, or both	bqf
Tacony Soap Company	Manufacturers	bmb	Manufacturing soaps and soap makers' materials and supplies	bmb
Tarentum Savings and Trust Company	Savings and trust company	GK	Insurance in real estate, from loss by reason of defective titles, liens and incumbrances	GC
Union Razor Company	Manufacturers of cutlery	bqf	Manufacturing and selling cutlery	bqf
Union Trust Company of Donora	Trust company	GA	Engaging in and carrying on the business of the insurance of owners of real estate, mortgagees, and others interested in real estate, from loss by reason of defective titles, liens and incumbrances	GC
Wallis and Carley Company	Lumber and planing mill	bhb	Manufacture and sale of lumber, lath, shingles, doors, sash, blinds, frames, mantels, brackets, mouldings, and all kinds of furnishings and trimmings for houses and other buildings and the conduct of the general business of contracting and building	bhb
William T. Leggett Company	Wholesale cement	DA	Buying, selling, trading and dealing at wholesale in lime, cement, slate, plaster, and builders' and contractors' supplies of kindred character	DA
Wolf Company	Manufacturers of flour mill machinery	bta	Manufacture of mill machinery and supplies, and of iron or steel, or of any other metal, or of any article of commerce from metal or wood, or both, and the buying or selling of such articles	bta
Wrightsville Light and Power Co.	Light and power	ccg	Manufacturing light, heat or power by means of electricity in the borough of Wrightsville, or to such persons, partnerships and associations residing in or adjacent thereto as may desire the same	cca
Youghiogheny Stone Company	Stone	ada	Quarrying, mining, crushing and preparing for market stone, or other materials incidentally developed	ada

ing, can be built up by combining the proper basic classes; but that is a different matter. The 183 categories give the data in the most minute groupings feasible. Twenty percent of the classes are undivided two-letter ones. The manufacture of paper and of tobacco—both major subdivisions of the one-letter category, Manufacturing—are among the two-letter classes used. One two-letter category of Table 19—Construction of railways (HA)—was not part of the scheme when the Pennsylvania data were worked but was added when the New Jersey and Ohio companies were classified. In the latter two states there seemed to be enough such corporations to make it desirable to set up a separate class. Seventy-eight percent of the classes are three-letter ones, illustrated by the manufacture of paint, of soap, and of drugs. Each is a subdivision of the manufacture of chemicals (a two-letter class), which in turn is a major division of the broad one-letter class, Manufacturing.

The reliability of the published abstracts as an index of corporate purposes was tested by Pennsylvania data (App. 5). After all incorporations of that state in 1889, 1902, and 1916 had been classified industrially on the basis of the charter abstracts, a sample of 225 companies was drawn for each year. These companies were looked up in Bradstreet's rating books, and from their statements of objectives were again classified industrially. In both operations, company names were taken into account whenever they were a clue to the nature of the enterprise. The two classifications were made at periods sufficiently far apart to prevent the memory of the compiler from influencing the second. Identical classifications—using 181 categories of Table 19—were made for roughly 82 percent of the items classified for each year.[8] In view of the detail of the classification scheme, the 82 percent score seems very high. Moreover, many types of company whose purposes were obvious from the charter abstracts were not listed in Bradstreet's. Had all electric light concerns and building and loan associations, for example, been listed, it is hard to believe that they would have had industrial designations different from those determined from the abstracts. The test thus indicates a high degree of reliability for the Pennsylvania abstracts. To show how closely the results derived from the two sources agreed, the industrial descriptions of all companies in the 1902 sample for which

the purposes could be clearly determined from Bradstreet's (91) are presented in Table 20. A check of the eleven companies that were not classified 'identically' when both sources were used reveals that in only three did the allocations differ seriously.[9] Of course, this test assumes that the contemporary Bradstreet industrial designation was accurate.

The chartering episodes and pronounced waves of incorporation in many industries that were revealed by the industrial classification suggested another group of tests. These movements, together with tests of the accuracy of the incorporation figures, are treated in Chapter 8. An example of these tests is given in Table 21. The discrepancies between the number of charters granted title guarantee and trust companies by Pennsylvania in the early years of the 20th century as reported by the Pennsylvania Banking Commissioner and as compiled from the charter abstracts published by the

TABLE 21
Title Guarantee and Trust Incorporations
Pennsylvania, December 1899–November 1904

DECEMBER TO NOVEMBER		ACCORDING TO BANKING COMMISSIONER REPORTS[a]	AS COMPILED FROM CHARTER ABSTRACTS[b]
1899	1900	16	17
1900	1901	47	47
1901	1902	69	68
1902	1903	75	76
1903	1904	16	14

[a] *Sixth Annual Report of the Commissioner of Banking . . . for . . . 1900* (1901), Part 1, pp. II–III; *Seventh Annual Report . . . for . . . 1901* (1902), Part 1, pp. II–III; *Eighth Annual Report . . . for . . . 1902* (1903), Part 1, pp. II–IV; *Ninth Annual Report . . . for . . . 1903* (1904), Part 1, pp. II–V; *Tenth Annual Report . . . for . . . 1904* (1905), Part 1, pp. II–III.
[b] *List of Charters of Corporations enrolled in the office of the Secretary of the Commonwealth during the two years beginning June 1, 1899, and ending June 1, 1901 . . .* (1901); *List of Charters . . . beginning June 1, 1901, and ending June 1, 1903 . . .* (1903); *List of Charters . . . beginning June 1, 1903 and ending May 31, 1905 . . .* (Harrisburg, 1905).

Secretary of the Commonwealth are unimportant and easily explained. For instance, a comparison of the two sources for December 1, 1901–November 30, 1902 reveals the following differences:
1) The Banking Commissioner omitted a trust company listed by the Secretary of the Commonwealth (Penn Savings and Trust Company, incorporated February 11, 1902).
2) The Banking Commissioner listed a company that does not appear in the Secretary's report (Mortgage Banking Company, incorporated March 3, 1902).
3) The Banking Commissioner classified a safe deposit company (Armored Safe Deposit Co. of Pittsburgh, incorporated February 6, 1902) as a trust company, but the Secretary's description suggests that the concern is

---

[8] The term 'identical classification' was stretched in the case of the 1902 test. The nine companies that in one source were listed as trust and savings companies and in the other as title guarantee and trust companies were considered to belong to the same industrial category. For further information on the test, see Appendix 5.

The 181 categories were those of Table 19 minus the two classes A/B and HA.

[9] See items 25, 41, and 69 in Table 20.

more properly classified with commerical banks (GA of Table 19).

Another test—less valid as a check upon the quality of the incorporation data but nevertheless interesting—consists of comparing the percentage distribution of incorporations among the major categories of Table 19 with the distribution of corporations reporting to the Office of Internal Revenue. As the industrial distribution of newly chartered companies is compared with that of all existing corporations, there are obvious drawbacks. The results, however, were such that it seemed desirable to give them here.

If the wholesale and retail trade categories of Table 19 are merged, the major groups are mining, manufacturing, public utilities, trade, service, finance, construction, agriculture, and a miscellaneous group. These were the categories by which the Office of Internal Revenue classified corporations reporting for income tax purposes (Table 22). The absolute figures were converted into percentages of the total in order to portray better the industrial distributions of the corporations in existence at each date. The comparable percentage figures for incorporations, Table 23, were computed from the basic data in Appendix 4. The most striking feature of Chart 20 is the closeness with which the industrial distribution based upon the Internal Revenue data ties in with that for the incorporation figures. One is tempted to predict that if data similar to those of the Office of Internal Revenue could be compiled for the pre-1916 period, they would yield industrial distributions similar to those of the incorporation figures. Such a prediction is dangerous because it entails such assumptions as a uniform rate of death among corporations of the various industrial groups; but in the almost complete absence of more definite data on the total population of corporations existing at that time, the distribution indicated by the incorporation data may be accepted as a rough approximation. Of course, the corporations existing at any one time bear a relation to the number previously created. The factor, however, that makes the movements in the industrial pattern of incorporations a questionable index of variation in the total picture of existing corporations is that mentioned above, namely, the possible differences in the rates at which companies in different industries abandon or lose their charters.

From reading and working over the charter abstracts and purpose descriptions utilized in classifying incorporations along industrial lines my assistants and I gained impressions about the quality of the source material that must be mentioned to caution the reader against hasty generalizations. The results obtained from the Pennsylvania and Ohio data seem to us quite reliable. The Pennsylvania descriptions were fairly complete; the brevity of the Ohio descriptions was offset

TABLE 22
Corporations Reporting for Income Taxation
Percentage Distribution by Major Industrial Categories
New Jersey, Ohio, and Pennsylvania, 1916–1918 and 1921–1930

	1916	1917	1918	1921	1922	1923	1924	1925	1926	1927	1928	1929	1930
Mining													
N.J.	1.7	1.8	.6	1.0	1.0	.9	.8	.8	.8	.7	.6	.6	.6
Ohio	3.7	4.3	4.3	5.2	4.7	4.7	4.1	4.0	3.9	3.5	3.4	3.1	3.0
Pa.	6.1	7.0	8.1	10.4	9.9	9.5	9.1	9.0	8.2	8.0	7.6	7.1	6.6
Manufacturing													
N.J.	30.0	28.8	28.2	30.2	29.1	27.5	26.5	24.9	22.8	21.1	20.2	19.4	18.9
Ohio	31.8	32.5	30.2	28.5	27.5	27.1	26.6	26.2	26.1	25.2	25.0	24.3	23.9
Pa.	31.4	29.9	29.4	31.4	29.9	30.2	29.2	29.3	29.4	28.6	28.2	27.8	26.9
Public Utilities													
N.J.	5.0	6.3	5.8	4.6	4.8	4.4	4.8	4.9	4.6	3.6	3.4	3.4	3.5
Ohio	6.1	7.8	5.2	4.5	4.4	4.3	4.5	4.6	4.7	3.9	3.9	3.7	3.7
Pa.	10.1	10.4	8.8	7.2	7.4	7.2	7.1	7.2	7.5	6.6	6.2	6.2	5.9
Trade													
N.J.	a	20.5	15.4	19.1	19.8	20.3	20.1	20.0	19.3	20.4	20.7	20.9	21.1
Ohio	a	28.6	21.3	24.6	24.9	25.1	25.1	26.2	26.1	27.2	27.8	27.9	27.5
Pa.	a	17.3	14.9	18.8	19.4	19.6	20.3	20.9	20.5	21.6	22.3	22.5	23.0
Service													
N.J.	a	5.7	4.6	6.1	6.6	6.7	6.4	6.6	6.7	6.5	6.5	6.8	7.2
Ohio	a	5.8	4.8	5.4	5.8	6.0	6.2	6.5	6.8	7.0	7.2	7.6	8.1
Pa.	a	4.0	4.3	4.3	5.0	5.2	5.2	5.5	6.0	6.3	6.4	6.7	7.0
Finance													
N.J.	a	22.0	24.7	25.0	26.3	27.4	28.5	32.0	36.2	37.7	38.9	38.9	38.9
Ohio	a	13.7	18.5	20.6	21.6	22.0	23.0	24.2	24.7	24.8	24.7	25.1	25.3
Pa.	a	12.6	16.7	17.4	17.5	17.6	17.9	18.8	19.9	20.2	20.3	20.3	20.4
Construction													
N.J.	a	5.3	4.3	5.4	5.3	5.7	5.7	6.1	6.0	6.1	6.3	6.5	6.1
Ohio	a	4.5	3.4	4.0	4.0	3.9	4.0	4.2	4.3	4.3	4.5	4.7	4.7
Pa.	a	3.1	2.5	2.9	2.9	3.2	3.4	3.7	3.6	3.7	3.9	4.2	4.3
Agriculture													
N.J.	1.3	1.7	1.4	1.3	1.2	1.2	1.0	1.0	1.0	1.0	.9	1.0	1.1
Ohio	.9	1.1	1.1	1.0	1.0	1.0	1.1	1.0	1.1	1.2	1.2	1.2	1.2
Pa.	.8	.8	.8	.9	.8	.8	.8	.9	.9	.9	.9	.9	.9
Others													
N.J.	62.0	8.1[b]	14.9	7.3	5.9	6.0	6.2	3.6	2.5	2.8	2.4	2.4	2.8
Ohio	57.5	1.7[b]	11.2	6.2	6.1	5.8	5.5	3.1	2.2	2.9	2.2	2.3	2.6
Pa.	51.6	14.9[b]	14.6	6.8	7.2	6.7	7.1	4.6	4.0	4.1	4.2	4.3	5.1

[a] Not ascertainable.

[b] Computed from the total and the amounts in the other categories. Data for 1919 and 1920 are not available.

Percentages were calculated from data in the following sources: U.S., (Office of) Internal Revenue, *Statistics of Income . . . for 1916 . . .* (Washington, D.C., 1918), Table 9, pp. 35-6, and Table 10a, pp. 281-323; *for 1917*, Tables 12-20, pp. 53-70; *for 1918*, Table 10, pp. 92-3, and Table 13, pp. 135-41; *for 1919*, Table 8, pp. 54-5; *for 1920*, Table 8, pp. 60-1; *for 1921*, Table 8, pp. 56-7, and Table 10, pp. 86-91; *for 1922*, Table 8, following p. 95, and Table 10, pp. 123-8; *for 1923*, Table 8, facing p. 77, and Table 10, pp. 87-117; *for 1924*, Table 8, following p. 121, and Table 12, pp. 161-7; *for 1925*, Table 8, facing p. 104, and Table 12, pp. 119-39; *for 1926*, Table 12, following p. 313, and Table 16, pp. 335-55; *for 1927*, Table 12, following p. 309, and Table 17, pp. 332-64; *for 1928*, Table 12, pp. 314-6, and Table 17, pp. 341-74; *for 1929*, Table 12, pp. 263-5, and Table 17, pp. 294-326; *for 1930*, Table 12, pp. 209-11, and Table 17, pp. 240-59.

somewhat by the fact that the Office of the Secretary of State grouped incorporations along industrial lines for

TABLE 23
Incorporations under General Laws
Percentage Distribution by Major Industrial Categories
New Jersey, Ohio, and Pennsylvania, 1872–1930

Mining

	1872	1873	1874	1875	1876	1877	1878	1879	1880	1881	1882	1883	1884	1885	1886	1887	1888	1889	1890	1891	1892	1893	1894	1895	1896	1897	1898	1899	1900	1901
N. J.				.0	7.1	3.1	5.5	6.3	15.5	23.8	15.7	5.8	3.9	4.7	3.4	6.4	4.1	3.2	3.1	3.8	3.6	3.7	4.8	3.2	5.1	8.2	5.3	8.1	8.6	8.5
Ohio	14.0	9.7	11.7	9.0	6.4	2.5	5.7	8.4	8.7	5.7	7.0	4.9	6.1	7.4	11.5	19.6	7.4	6.1	6.6	6.6	6.0	5.2	7.4	8.0	12.3	9.2	5.3	11.5	10.7	7.8
Pa.																	10.9	10.3	11.4	8.9	9.1	8.1	8.7	6.8	7.7	6.7	4.8	7.4	12.2	8.9

Manufacturing

	1872	1873	1874	1875	1876	1877	1878	1879	1880	1881	1882	1883	1884	1885	1886	1887	1888	1889	1890	1891	1892	1893	1894	1895	1896	1897	1898	1899	1900	1901
N. J.				52.9	41.1	54.7	41.1	53.2	38.7	38.3	49.0	49.5	54.3	54.3	51.0	48.9	55.6	53.3	59.4	56.6	56.8	53.8	56.6	53.4	53.1	49.3	52.4	50.0	53.2	52.3
Ohio	37.2	44.2	35.9	27.6	27.1	33.3	33.0	41.6	47.3	40.6	50.0	49.0	46.1	46.0	40.6	35.5	47.4	46.5	50.4	51.2	52.8	53.2	50.1	45.8	46.3	46.2	47.8	42.3	45.5	42.7
Pa.																	39.2	33.9	38.2	50.3	42.6	47.2	45.2	48.9	50.6	49.1	52.3	54.7	46.7	44.8

Public Utilities

	1872	1873	1874	1875	1876	1877	1878	1879	1880	1881	1882	1883	1884	1885	1886	1887	1888	1889	1890	1891	1892	1893	1894	1895	1896	1897	1898	1899	1900	1901
N. J.				21.6	35.7	15.6	26.0	24.1	26.8	13.6	12.3	16.3	21.1	17.3	19.2	11.7	12.7	14.3	9.8	7.9	8.7	9.6	10.0	10.7	11.3	9.7	10.4	10.2	9.2	9.4
Ohio	24.4	16.7	16.1	18.6	19.9	25.7	27.8	22.4	19.4	30.3	14.9	14.5	14.5	15.5	19.6	19.7	14.5	17.0	13.8	11.3	10.4	11.6	12.5	13.3	9.0	12.6	15.1	16.2	16.2	17.0
Pa.																	18.7	23.3	22.5	17.0	22.8	22.7	21.3	26.5	22.8	22.8	24.4	20.7	23.2	22.0

Wholesale and Retail Trade

	1872	1873	1874	1875	1876	1877	1878	1879	1880	1881	1882	1883	1884	1885	1886	1887	1888	1889	1890	1891	1892	1893	1894	1895	1896	1897	1898	1899	1900	1901
N. J.				.0	1.8	7.8	.0	.0	1.2	.2	2.0	2.7	1.7	3.5	4.4	3.2	4.4	3.9	5.8	7.6	8.4	10.1	8.1	9.9	8.0	8.1	8.3	11.2	8.8	8.1
Ohio	1.0	.8	1.3	3.6	10.9	5.1	1.8	1.4	2.3	2.8	3.5	2.8	4.6	3.7	5.6	6.5	5.3	6.3	6.0	7.8	9.0	12.2	10.3	10.1	11.4	8.1	11.3	9.6	7.4	9.3
Pa.																	.2	.1	.0	.0	.0	.0	.0	.2	2.8	2.4	3.1	2.0	2.7	5.3

Service

	1872	1873	1874	1875	1876	1877	1878	1879	1880	1881	1882	1883	1884	1885	1886	1887	1888	1889	1890	1891	1892	1893	1894	1895	1896	1897	1898	1899	1900	1901
N. J.				11.8	7.1	4.7	11.0	7.6	4.8	2.7	4.0	4.1	4.7	5.1	6.0	7.0	4.9	4.5	5.2	6.4	6.0	6.7	7.4	7.3	7.2	7.9	6.9	5.9	5.8	4.5
Ohio	5.0	2.8	9.7	9.6	12.8	15.2	11.9	8.4	5.6	4.7	5.4	7.0	12.6	8.5	7.5	4.8	7.1	6.3	5.0	7.2	9.1	4.9	7.1	9.3	9.0	9.2	7.1	7.5	6.8	6.1
Pa.																	.8	.8	1.4	1.2	1.2	1.3	1.9	1.2	1.1	2.4	1.2	1.2	1.5	2.5

Finance

	1872	1873	1874	1875	1876	1877	1878	1879	1880	1881	1882	1883	1884	1885	1886	1887	1888	1889	1890	1891	1892	1893	1894	1895	1896	1897	1898	1899	1900	1901
N. J.				13.7	3.6	12.5	12.3	5.1	4.8	6.7	4.8	9.8	7.8	5.9	6.0	11.2	10.9	12.1	9.3	11.5	10.1	9.3	6.9	9.0	8.9	8.1	10.1	7.4	8.0	10.2
Ohio	16.5	25.0	23.8	28.5	21.4	17.3	15.4	16.4	15.3	12.4	15.7	18.8	13.6	12.6	12.6	12.3	16.5	15.3	15.0	13.4	10.4	7.7	9.0	10.3	9.0	9.8	8.4	8.9	11.3	13.8
Pa.																	29.6	30.8	25.3	21.7	23.4	20.0	22.0	16.1	14.3	14.6	12.4	12.8	12.6	15.1

Construction

	1872	1873	1874	1875	1876	1877	1878	1879	1880	1881	1882	1883	1884	1885	1886	1887	1888	1889	1890	1891	1892	1893	1894	1895	1896	1897	1898	1899	1900	1901
N. J.				.0	.0	.0	1.4	1.3	6.0	10.7	7.7	6.4	2.2	3.1	6.5	7.6	3.9	5.0	4.0	4.1	3.4	4.1	2.7	4.1	3.5	5.3	3.9	3.5	3.3	4.5
Ohio	.5	.3	.0	1.2	1.1	.4	.0	.3	.5	2.0	.7	.7	.2	.8	.5	.5	1.1	.8	.8	.7	.9	2.2	1.9	1.4	1.6	2.5	3.4	2.7	1.9	2.6
Pa.																	.4	.1	.7	.5	.1	.7	.2	.0	.6	1.1	1.2	.3	.6	.9

Agriculture

	1872	1873	1874	1875	1876	1877	1878	1879	1880	1881	1882	1883	1884	1885	1886	1887	1888	1889	1890	1891	1892	1893	1894	1895	1896	1897	1898	1899	1900	1901
N. J.				.0	3.6	.0	1.4	2.5	.0	.7	.9	3.4	2.6	2.0	1.8	1.3	.7	.9	1.2	.6	1.1	1.1	1.5	.5	1.0	.9	.4	1.1	1.3	1.0
Ohio	.5	.3	.7	.0	.4	.0	3.5	.7	.3	.4	1.7	1.1	1.9	1.0	1.1	.4	.3	1.1	1.4	1.1	.5	1.7	.7	.9	.7	.7	.4	.5	.1	.3
Pa.																	.0	.1	.4	.2	.1	.0	.0	.2	.0	.2	.2	.3	.0	.3

Unallocable*

	1872	1873	1874	1875	1876	1877	1878	1879	1880	1881	1882	1883	1884	1885	1886	1887	1888	1889	1890	1891	1892	1893	1894	1895	1896	1897	1898	1899	1900	1901
N. J.				.0	.0	1.6	1.4	.0	2.4	3.3	3.7	2.0	1.7	3.9	1.8	2.8	2.8	2.8	2.1	1.5	1.9	1.5	2.0	1.9	1.9	2.6	2.3	2.6	1.8	1.6
Ohio	1.0	.3	.7	1.8	.0	.4	.9	.3	.5	1.2	1.2	1.1	.4	4.5	1.0	.8	.5	.6	1.0	.7	.8	1.3	1.1	.9	.7	1.5	1.1	.9	.1	.4
Pa.																	.2	.4	.0	.2	.7	.0	.9	.2	.0	.7	.4	.6	.5	.3

* In the cases of New Jersey and Ohio, the unallocable class is a composite of the categories J and A/B of Table 19. In the case of Pennsylvania it consists of only category J, since the A/B class was not used in grouping Pennsylvania incorporations.
Percentages were calculated from data in Appendix 4.

TABLE 23

Incorporations under General Laws
Percentage Distribution by Major Industrial Categories
New Jersey, Ohio, and Pennsylvania, 1872–1930

Mining

State	1902	1903	1904	1905	1906	1907	1908	1909	1910	1911	1912	1913	1914	1915	1916	1917	1918	1919	1920	1921	1922	1923	1924	1925	1926	1927	1928	1929	1930
N. J.	8.4	6.3	6.2	4.6	4.1	3.9																							
Ohio	10.2	11.2	10.0	8.3	6.0	6.6	11.2	13.2	7.4	5.8	5.0	5.0	11.2	5.4	5.6	11.4	10.6	5.2	8.1	6.6	4.7	4.6	3.7	3.4	2.5	3.0	2.9	3.1	2.4
Pa.	8.8	10.4	8.7	7.0	7.5	6.0	6.1	6.1	5.6	4.3	6.3	5.5	7.3	7.5	7.3	23.1	18.6	6.9	10.6										

Manufacturing

State	1902	1903	1904	1905	1906	1907	1908	1909	1910	1911	1912	1913	1914	1915	1916	1917	1918	1919	1920	1921	1922	1923	1924	1925	1926	1927	1928	1929	1930
N. J.	50.6	50.1	45.9	39.7	35.7	35.8																							
Ohio	45.0	44.1	48.8	48.1	46.2	44.1	43.7	39.6	41.1	43.0	39.4	37.2	34.2	33.4	33.0	29.6	33.9	35.3	33.2	31.8	32.8	28.3	26.0	25.1	24.4	25.8	25.2	23.8	21.1
Pa.	41.7	40.1	41.5	42.0	39.9	38.6	39.5	37.5	32.6	30.4	30.6	25.1	36.1	34.4	31.5	25.1	32.5	31.0	26.7										

Public Utilities

State	1902	1903	1904	1905	1906	1907	1908	1909	1910	1911	1912	1913	1914	1915	1916	1917	1918	1919	1920	1921	1922	1923	1924	1925	1926	1927	1928	1929	1930
N. J.	7.1	6.6	6.8	7.3	4.7	4.5																							
Ohio	13.5	13.1	8.6	9.3	9.0	6.3	5.4	5.2	5.1	4.3	4.6	4.6	4.0	4.7	4.2	4.1	4.3	3.9	3.4	3.4	3.4	4.6	4.2	4.3	4.9	3.9	5.2	5.1	4.6
Pa.	17.3	15.5	14.9	17.4	12.0	11.0	12.0	14.8	19.9	26.4	26.8	36.7	7.2	11.5	12.7	8.4	5.5	5.4	5.2										

Wholesale and Retail Trade

State	1902	1903	1904	1905	1906	1907	1908	1909	1910	1911	1912	1913	1914	1915	1916	1917	1918	1919	1920	1921	1922	1923	1924	1925	1926	1927	1928	1929	1930
N. J.	8.6	10.3	11.9	13.2	17.2	14.0																							
Ohio	8.2	8.1	10.0	10.8	12.8	14.6	14.4	14.7	16.4	16.0	18.2	20.4	18.5	21.3	21.5	22.3	24.5	19.7	20.6	22.4	20.9	21.8	22.2	24.2	26.6	24.3	25.3	26.5	30.2
Pa.	8.9	10.1	12.0	11.1	12.6	14.0	16.4	13.7	13.1	13.8	13.8	11.0	17.3	17.2	17.1	19.0	19.3	22.1	22.0										

Service

State	1902	1903	1904	1905	1906	1907	1908	1909	1910	1911	1912	1913	1914	1915	1916	1917	1918	1919	1920	1921	1922	1923	1924	1925	1926	1927	1928	1929	1930
N. J.	6.1	7.0	6.6	7.3	8.4	8.4																							
Ohio	6.0	7.1	8.3	7.2	8.5	9.2	8.7	10.3	8.8	10.5	11.0	11.7	11.2	12.7	10.8	9.5	8.5	9.7	8.8	9.8	9.7	8.9	10.8	10.3	11.2	12.4	11.2	11.0	13.1
Pa.	3.6	3.0	3.9	4.9	5.6	6.8	6.3	7.8	7.3	6.0	4.7	5.6	8.0	7.8	6.0	5.2	6.1	6.2	5.8										

Finance

State	1902	1903	1904	1905	1906	1907	1908	1909	1910	1911	1912	1913	1914	1915	1916	1917	1918	1919	1920	1921	1922	1923	1924	1925	1926	1927	1928	1929	1930
N. J.	11.4	11.8	13.5	15.1	16.5	21.2																							
Ohio	12.3	12.5	8.4	11.0	12.4	13.5	11.6	11.5	14.8	14.5	16.1	14.7	14.3	15.6	19.0	16.4	13.2	20.9	20.1	19.3	23.3	25.3	25.8	26.1	22.8	22.0	21.9	22.4	21.8
Pa.	16.2	17.7	14.0	13.2	16.3	18.2	14.0	15.1	17.6	15.0	12.8	11.7	18.1	17.0	19.7	14.4	12.5	23.8	25.6										

Construction

State	1902	1903	1904	1905	1906	1907	1908	1909	1910	1911	1912	1913	1914	1915	1916	1917	1918	1919	1920	1921	1922	1923	1924	1925	1926	1927	1928	1929	1930
N. J.	4.7	4.5	4.3	6.6	6.3	7.6																							
Ohio	2.3	2.4	3.0	3.2	3.8	3.6	3.3	3.1	3.7	3.5	3.4	3.5	4.2	4.1	4.1	5.0	3.1	3.4	3.4	4.1	3.9	4.3	4.8	4.6	6.1	6.6	6.0	6.1	4.6
Pa.	2.7	2.5	3.3	3.1	4.0	3.5	3.5	3.7	2.8	2.8	3.7	2.9	3.5	3.0	3.5	2.9	2.7	3.2	2.6										

Agriculture

State	1902	1903	1904	1905	1906	1907	1908	1909	1910	1911	1912	1913	1914	1915	1916	1917	1918	1919	1920	1921	1922	1923	1924	1925	1926	1927	1928	1929	1930
N. J.	1.2	1.5	1.0	1.4	1.5	.9																							
Ohio	.8	.3	1.1	.9	.6	.5	.8	.9	1.3	1.0	.6	.8	.7	1.1	.6	.7	.7	.7	1.1	.7	.4	.9	1.0	.7	.9	1.1	1.3	1.1	1.3
Pa.	.5	.3	.7	.5	.9	.6	.7	.5	.5	1.1	1.0	.6	1.4	1.0	.7	.6	.7	.4	.5										

Unallocable*

State	1902	1903	1904	1905	1906	1907	1908	1909	1910	1911	1912	1913	1914	1915	1916	1917	1918	1919	1920	1921	1922	1923	1924	1925	1926	1927	1928	1929	1930
N. J.	1.7	1.9	3.8	4.7	5.6	3.9																							
Ohio	1.7	1.3	1.8	1.4	.6	1.5	.8	1.4	1.4	1.4	1.7	1.9	1.9	1.6	1.1	1.0	1.1	1.2	1.4	1.8	.9	1.4	1.4	1.2	.6	1.1	1.0	.9	1.0
Pa.	.4	.4	.8	.7	1.2	1.4	1.4	.8	.7	.2	.4	.7	1.1	.7	1.6	1.4	2.3	1.1	1.1										

* In the cases of New Jersey and Ohio, the unallocable class is a composite of the categories J and A/B of Table 19. In the case of Pennsylvania it consists of only category J, since the A/B class was not used in grouping Pennsylvania incorporations.
Percentages were calculated from data in Appendix 4.

CHART 20

Incorporations under General Laws and Corporations Reporting for Income Taxation

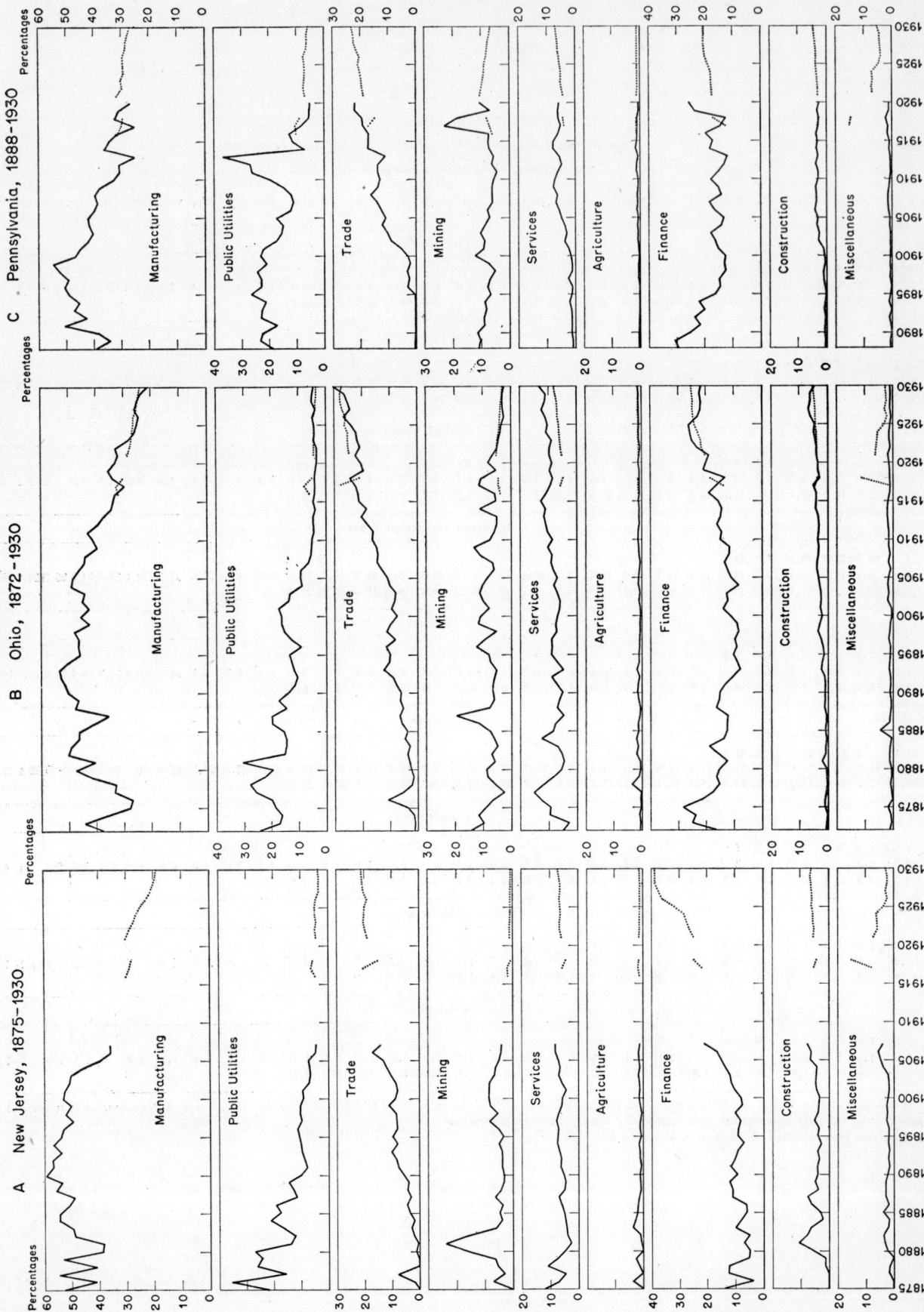

Percentage Distribution by Major Industrial Categories

——— Incorporations

············· Corporations reporting for income taxation

A   New Jersey, 1875-1930

B   Ohio, 1872-1930

C   Pennsylvania, 1888-1930

Manufacturing

Public Utilities

Trade

Mining

Services

Agriculture

Finance

Construction

Miscellaneous

Sources: Tables 22 and 23.

TABLE 24
Number and Percentage of Basic Categories of Table 19 Used in Classifying Industrially the Incorporations of Each Year, 1800–1930
New Jersey, Ohio, and Pennsylvania

Year	NEW JERSEY Total basic classes used	Basic classes used 1st time	% total used is of total basic classes[a]	OHIO Total basic classes used	Basic classes used 1st time	% total used is of total basic classes[a]	PENNSYLVANIA Total basic classes used	Basic classes used 1st time	% total used is of total basic classes[a]
1800	2	2	1.1						
1801	3	2	1.6						
1802	3	1	1.6						
1803	0	0	.0	2	2	1.1			
1804	7	4	3.8	0	0	.0			
1805	0	0	.0	0	0	.0			
1806	1	0	.5	0	0	.0			
1807	3	0	1.6	0	0	.0			
1808	1	0	.5	1	1	.5			
1809	4	0	2.2	2	1	1.1			
1810	0	0	.0	1	1	.5			
1811	5	1	2.7	1	1	.5			
1812	2	0	1.1	1	0	.5			
1813	2	1	1.1	1	0	.5			
1814	5	2	2.7	3	2	1.6			
1815	7	2	3.8	1	0	.5			
1816	5	0	2.7	6	1	3.3			
1817	2	0	1.1	4	0	2.2			
1818	2	0	1.1	3	1	1.6			
1819	2	0	1.1	2	1	1.1			
1820	2	1	1.1	2	1	1.1			
1821	1	0	.5	0	0	.0			
1822	3	1	1.6	1	0	.5			
1823	5	1	2.7	0	0	.0			
1824	9	2	4.9	2	0	1.1			
1825	10	3	5.5	2	0	1.1			
1826	5	0	2.7	6	1	3.3			
1827	0	0	.0	4	0	2.2			
1828	10	3	5.5	4	1	2.2			
1829	4	1	2.2	8	2	4.4			
1830	9	1	4.9	12	3	6.6			
1831	9	0	4.9	5	1	2.7			
1832	7	0	3.8	10	1	5.5			
1833	12	4	6.6	7	0	3.8			
1834	8	0	4.4	11	3	6.0			
1835	8	1	4.4	11	0	6.0			
1836	11	2	6.0	15	2	8.2			
1837	19	8	10.4	23	6	12.6			
1838	7	0	3.8	15	2	8.2			
1839	11	1	6.0	12	1	6.6			
1840	5	2	2.7	6	0	3.3			
1841	6	1	3.3	3	0	1.6			
1842	4	0	2.2	4	0	2.2			
1843	1	0	.5	6	1	3.3			
1844	5	0	2.7	7	0	3.8			
1845	11	2	6.0	11	0	6.0			
1846	10	1	5.5	14	2	7.7			
1847	15	2	8.2	6	0	3.3			
1848	19	2	10.4	13	0	7.1			
1849	13	0	7.1	11	1	6.0			
1850	15	5	8.2	14	1	7.7			
1851	12	1	6.6	15	1	8.2			
1852	20	4	10.9						
1853	26	2	14.2						
1854	29	1	15.8						
1855	31	5	16.9						
1856	25	3	13.7	18	4	9.8			
1857	19	1	10.4	20	6	10.9			
1858	25	2	13.7	16	5	8.7			
1859	21	2	11.5	16	3	8.7			
1860	22	1	12.0	17	2	9.3			
1861	21	0	11.5	9	0	4.9			
1862	13	1	7.1	16	2	8.7			
1863	20	3	10.9	19	1	10.4			
1864	29	4	15.8	19	1	10.4			
1865	38	4	20.8	31	3	16.9			
1866	51	6	27.9	54	11	29.5			
1867	55	5	30.1	48	8	26.2			
1868	55	2	30.1	54	7	29.5			
1869	52	0	28.4	56	6	30.6			
1870	57	4	31.1	57	4	31.1			
1871	46	0	25.1	62	3	33.9			
1872	47	1	25.7	69	7	37.7			
1873	47	0	25.7	67	3	36.6			
1874	51	2	27.9	67	1	36.6			
1875	43	2	23.5	62	3	33.9			
1876	31	3	16.9	63	3	34.4			
1877	40	5	21.9	59	0	32.2			
1878	35	1	19.1	64	3	35.0			
1879	47	1	25.7	72	3	39.3			
1880	57	4	31.1	89	3	48.6			
1881	89	3	48.6	95	5	51.9			
1882	93	3	50.8	101	5	55.2			
1883	89	6	48.6	112	3	61.2			
1884	76	1	41.5	103	3	56.3			
1885	88	3	48.1	89	0	48.6			
1886	103	2	56.3	103	1	56.3			
1887	109	2	59.6	105	0	57.4	57[b]	57[b]	
1888	119	5	65.0	104	2	56.8	84	35	46.4
1889	117	0	63.9	114	2	62.3	92	16	50.8
1890	137	6	74.9	113	0	61.7	87	8	48.1
1891	133	1	72.7	124	2	67.8	92	4	50.8
1892	138	2	75.4	117	3	63.9	98	3	54.1
1893	126	1	68.9	113	0	61.7	92	1	50.8
1894	124	0	67.8	125	1	68.3	83	1	45.9
1895	128	0	69.9	119	1	65.0	90	2	49.7
1896	131	2	71.6	114	0	62.3	95	5	52.5
1897	136	0	74.3	117	0	63.9	94	2	51.9
1898	136	0	74.3	118	1	64.5	88	1	48.6
1899	154	2	84.2	131	0	71.6	94	1	51.9
1900	150	2	82.0	127	1	69.4	97	2	53.6
1901	148	0	80.9	140	1	76.5	122	14	67.4
1902	144	0	78.7	128	0	69.9	127	7	70.2
1903	149	0	81.4	132	1	72.1	131	3	72.4
1904	148	0	80.9	140	2	76.5	124	0	68.5
1905	151	0	82.5	142	0	77.6	133	2	73.5
1906	152	0	83.1	144	1	78.7	136	0	75.1
1907	148	1	80.9	144	2	78.7	135	1	74.6
1908				140	0	76.5	134	1	74.0
1909				146	1	79.8	137	3	75.7
1910				141	1	77.0	145	3	80.1
1911				142	1	77.6	139	1	76.8
1912				150	0	82.0	141	1	77.9
1913				141	2	77.0	143	2	79.0
1914				138	0	75.4	139	0	76.8
1915				144	2	78.7	142	1	78.5
1916				147	0	80.3	139	0	76.8
1917				146	1	79.8	136	0	75.1
1918				143	0	78.1	126	1	69.6
1919				149	2	81.4	144	1	79.6
1920				153	0	83.6	141	0	77.9
1921				145	0	79.2			
1922				150	0	82.0			
1923				145	0	79.2			
1924				139	0	76.0			
1925				151	0	82.5			
1926				141	0	77.0			
1927				143	0	78.1			
1928				142	0	77.6			
1929				147	0	80.3			
1930				145	0	79.2			

Compiled from data in Appendix 4.
[a] The 183 basic categories were used in classifying New Jersey and Ohio incorporations, while two fewer (the 183 classes minus A/B and HA) were used in classifying Pennsylvania incorporations.
[b] These data are for less than a full calendar year.

presentation in the published documents. Work on the New Jersey material was hampered by brief descriptions unaided by any purpose grouping by the incorporating office; consequently, the results for this state are not as trustworthy as those for Pennsylvania and Ohio, but they show broad movements, and in many cases even the small categories are highly reliable. We attempted to classify New Jersey incorporations beyond 1907 along industrial lines, but decided that the quality of the descriptions deteriorated and too much reliance had to be placed upon the name of the corporation. Accordingly, we terminated the New Jersey industrial material with 1907. The Ohio industrial classification goes through 1930, though beginning with the Secretary of State's report for 1925 the charter descriptions can be relied upon less implicitly.[10] All published Pennsylvania charter abstracts were used; their quality did not seem to vary appreciably.

Before the results yielded by classifying incorporations along industrial lines are discussed in detail, the reader should note the percentage of total industrial categories of Table 19 that were utilized in grouping the corporations of each state in each year (Table 24). For example, in 1890 approximately 75 percent of the 183 categories were used in classifying New Jersey corporations by industrial objectives, about 48 percent of the 181 categories for Pennsylvania corporations, and roughly 62 percent of the 183 categories for Ohio corporations. From 1803 to 1851 in Ohio, corporations were created only by special acts. Since the state constitutional provision of 1851 practically stopped the granting of special charters, the later Ohio data are for concerns incorporated under general laws alone. The New Jersey data for the pre-1846 period are for charters granted by special statutes; since from 1846 to 1875 many charters were procured under both general and special laws, the data of Table 24 for that period apply to both types of charter; and since not many special charters were granted after 1875, the figures thereafter are for incorporations under general law only. In Pennsylvania, incorporation was accomplished primarily under general law in the period covered by the Pennsylvania section of Table 24; the data of that state, therefore, apply solely to corporations chartered under general laws.

Table 24 supplements Charts 1 and 9. When studying

the three, it must be remembered that an upward movement of percentages in Table 24 may be due to one or both of two factors: incorporations in new fields of enterprise; continued use in the old fields. Of course, the continued use of the corporate form in old fields is partly a function of the number of incorporations, since the more charters granted the greater the likelihood—other things being equal—that an incorporation will be found in any industrial category in which the corporate form had been customary.

The second column in each state section of Table 24 gives the number of basic categories of Table 19 that were used for the first time when classifying industrially the business incorporations of each year. For example, when the New Jersey incorporations of 1804 were classified by industry, seven of the basic categories of Table 19 were used, four of which had not been used in classifying the incorporations of the preceding years. Generally speaking, the corporate form seems to have entered new fields around 1837, throughout the 1850's, during and after the Civil War, and in the late 1870's and early 1880's; in New Jersey, in addition, there was extension in the use of the corporation around 1890. Some of the large rise in the New Jersey percentages in the late 'eighties and almost all of it in the late 'nineties seem to be due to more incorporations in established lines.

The Pennsylvania data of Table 24 seem to indicate a pronounced expansion into new fields in the early years of the 20th century, but some of the expansion is deceptive. In the first place, the initial full year for the Pennsylvania series is 1888, and some types of enterprise that had to be recorded as originally chartered in the early 1900's would doubtless have appeared among the incorporations of an earlier year if the series had begun as early as, say, 1850; in the second place, the general corporation law was broadened in 1901 to include concerns in any lawful business.[11] Corporations engaged in retail trade and certain other types of business procured special charters before 1901,[12] and they would not have been considered in compiling the Penn-

---

[10] Reports of the Secretary of State of Ohio contain statements of the industrial objectives for newly chartered companies from 1872 through 1936. The data for 1931–36 were worked for this and the next chapters, and will be made available by the author to anyone who wants to see them. Except for some major categories and certain minor subdivisions, the figures for these last six years, however, are not considered worthy of publication.

[11] *Pennsylvania Laws, 1901* (July 9, 1901), p. 624.

[12] When classifying the charter abstracts published by the Secretary of State, four companies chartered before July 9, 1901—the date on which it became possible to procure under general law a charter for a retail trading company (the incorporation of a wholesaling company under Pennsylvania general law having been permitted on June 25, 1895)—had to be treated as concerns engaged in retail trade. Thus either the charter abstracts in these cases were poorly written or the concerns were to engage primarily in retail trade, though for chartering purposes they were treated by the Secretary's office as engaged in some other type of business.

sylvania series since special acts were ignored. The differences between the Ohio and New Jersey series, on the one hand, and the Pennsylvania series, on the other, are to some extent explained by the fact that in building the former some account was taken of incorporations by special acts whereas in the latter they did not figure at all. In studying Table 24 it should also be borne in mind that broad incorporation laws similar to that passed by Pennsylvania in 1901 took effect in New Jersey in April 1875, and in Ohio in January 1880.[13]

[13] *New Jersey Revised Statutes, 1875*, p. 6; *Ohio Revised Statutes, 1880*, Vol. 1, Sec. 3235.

Chapter 8

Fields of Corporate Enterprise

The Major Industrial Categories

In Chart 20 similarities between the incorporation data of this study and the figures on corporations reporting for income tax purposes are observable. The diagrams, supplemented when necessary by the percentages in Tables 22 and 23 and the basic purpose data (App. 4), reveal other points. The three state series for each of the major (one-letter) industrial categories resemble one another closely. Incorporations in agriculture, construction, and the miscellaneous group were few and these categories can be disposed of promptly. The construction group is the only one that cannot be dismissed without comment. The New Jersey series reflects a fair amount of activity in this industry during the 'eighties, which is largely attributable to the chartering of railroad construction companies.

Both the Ohio and the Pennsylvania series for finance have falling trends until the late 'nineties—to be explained on slightly different grounds. In the case of Pennsylvania the downward movement was caused chiefly by a drop in the number of building and loan associations chartered. In Ohio, building and loan incorporations declined from 1875 to 1878. After 1879 this decline—by no means uninterrupted—was relative rather than absolute until in the middle 'nineties incorporations of building and loan associations became negligible both absolutely and relatively. The reason the New Jersey financial series does not have a similar trend is perhaps because it does not contain figures for building and loan associations. (The data were not given in the New Jersey sources that had to be used for the compilation of the incorporations by that state.) The upward trend in all three state series, beginning about 1900, is not unexpected.

The fluctuations prior to 1890 in the incorporation of companies that supply services (other than public utility services) were due largely to the incorporation of amusement companies in New Jersey and Ohio. Hotel incorporations in New Jersey were also substantial. For 1890–1930 the slowly rising trends of the series in this category are worthy of note.

The fairly horizontal trends of the three mining series on Chart 20 are less interesting than the bulges in the curves. The three largest bulges are: the one for New Jersey that reached its peak in 1881, reflecting gold and silver mining activity; the one for Ohio that reached its peak in 1887, reflecting natural gas discoveries and attempts to exploit them; and the one for Pennsylvania

that reached its peak in 1917, reflecting expansion in the coal mining industry during the war. The minor movement in the Ohio series that matches this Pennsylvania episode was also caused by activity in the coal industry. The other minor wave-like movements in the Ohio series reflect activity in either the petroleum and natural gas producing industry or coal mining.

As might be expected, the three state series for wholesale and retail trade are dominated by an upward trend. The low percentages for the first portion of the Pennsylvania series may seem somewhat surprising. As mentioned in the preceding chapter, the incorporation of wholesale trading enterprises under general law was first authorized in June 1895; companies organized to carry on retail trade could not be incorporated under general law until July 1901. Nevertheless, four companies incorporated before 1895 had, in accordance with the descriptions in the charter abstracts, to be classified as trading concerns. The Pennsylvania trade series rises in 1895 and jumps substantially in 1901; thereafter it keeps pace with the other two series.

Public utility incorporations continued the downtrend shown in Table 11, chiefly because the corporate form entered other fields, such as trade and the services. In Pennsylvania the upsurge that reached a peak in 1913 is explained largely by certain state legal provisions, discussed in the latter part of this chapter.

Complementing the declines in the financial and public utilities series, incorporations in manufacturing rose until approximately the early 'nineties. The falling per-

TABLE 25

Business Incorporations
Percentage Distribution by One-Letter Industrial Categories
New Jersey, Ohio, and Pennsylvania

	NEW JERSEY			OHIO					PENNSYLVANIA		
	1880–1889	1890–1899	1900–1907	1880–1889	1890–1899	1900–1909	1910–1919	1920–1929	1890–1899	1900–1909	1910–1919
Total	100	101	99	102	101	100	99	99	100	101	98
Mining & quarrying	8	5	6	9	8	9	7	4	8	8	9
Manufacturing	50	54	46	45	48	45	36	28	48	41	30
Public utilities	15	10	7	18	13	9	4	4	22	16	16
Trade (wholesale & retail)	3	9	11	5	10	12	20	23	1	11	16
Service	5	7	7	7	8	8	10	10	1	5	6
Finance	9	9	13	15	10	12	16	23	19	15	16
Construction	6	4	5	1	2	3	4	5	1	6	3
Agriculture	1	1	1	1	1	1	1	1	0*	1	1
Unallocable	3	2	3	1	1	1	1	1	0*	1	1

* Less than .5 per cent.
Percentages were computed from data in Appendix 4.

centages that set in during the 'nineties are associated with the rising trends in trade, service, and finance.

A few final comments concerning incorporations grouped according to the one-letter categories are in order. Manufacturing incorporations have constituted a large percentage of all charters granted each year since 1875. In contrast, incorporations for agricultural, construction, and miscellaneous purposes have constituted small percentages of the annual totals. The charters granted wholesale and retail trading enterprises have greatly increased; charters issued for public utilities have declined as a percentage of the total (Table 25).

The Secondary Industrial Categories

As Agriculture, a one-letter category, has no subdivisions, incorporations in it are not discussed here; nor are the secondary (two-letter) categories of Trade and Construction. The latter industry can be dismissed with a few remarks in appropriate places, since only two subdivisions were utilized. Trade incorporations presented more difficulties. The reason they are not discussed is that the tally of incorporations in this field is deemed somewhat less reliable than the two-letter tallies of the other industrial groups.

Incorporations in the two-letter mining categories of New Jersey, Ohio, and Pennsylvania (App. 4 and Table 26) reveal contrasts that might have been predicted by one reasonably well acquainted with both industrial life in these three states and the activities of promoters procuring corporate charters from them. Many New Jersey incorporations had to be placed in the unallocable mining group because the descriptions of their corporate objectives were either too vague or too comprehensive to warrant assignment to other two-letter categories. Many New Jersey mining companies of that period were doubtless organized to function outside the state on properties inadequately explored, and

their promoters wanted broad corporate powers so that they could take advantage of any and all opportunities. In Pennsylvania, coal mining is the chief field for incorporation. In Ohio it shares the dominant position with petroleum and natural gas production. In New Jersey metal mining is the largest mining subgroup; on occasion, for example in 1881, it completely eclipsed the other groups. There was a parallel metal mining movement in Ohio in the early 'eighties.

To discuss all of the two-letter manufacturing subgroups would flood the text with details. Accordingly, the only two-letter manufacturing categories treated are those that in any one of the years under study contained a number of incorporations equal to at least $7\frac{1}{2}$ per cent of total charters granted manufacturing enterprises. Industries that from an incorporation point of view were important throughout the period as well as both those that had an important position and lost it and those that grew from insignificance to prominence are included. The rule, however, excluded a few interesting cases. For the most part they are new industries that developed rapidly, but in which incorporations did not total the minimum percentage ($7\frac{1}{2}$) of manufacturing charters granted by the state.

No one industry dominates the manufacturing incorporations of any one of the three states (Table 27). In the New Jersey section of Table 27 there are seven subgroups, in the Pennsylvania section, eight, and in the Ohio section, ten. The differences in the number of subcategories are not surprising. The Ohio data, covering the longest period and extending to the most recent date, contain the largest number of subgroups that qualified for inclusion in Table 27. The Pennsylvania data are for more recent years than the New Jersey and cover a slightly longer period; the Pennsylvania section has one more two-letter category.

Six two-letter manufacturing categories are common to the three states: Food and kindred products; Printing, publishing, and allied industries; Chemicals and allied products; Stone, clay, and glass products; Iron and steel and their products; Machinery (except electrical). One subgroup, Textile-mill products, is to be found in both the New Jersey and the Pennsylvania figures. The Ohio section contains percentages for four manufacturing subgroups that do not appear for either of the other states: Furniture and finished lumber products; Electrical machinery; Automobiles and automobile equipment; and Transportation equipment (except automobiles). The Pennsylvania section contains only one manufacturing subgroup, Beverages, that does not appear for either of the other states. Since it may be of interest to some readers to record the first dates when incorporations in the categories of Table 27 became

TABLE 26

Mining and Quarrying Incorporations
Percentage Distribution by Two-Letter Industrial Categories
New Jersey, Ohio, and Pennsylvania

	NEW JERSEY			OHIO					PENNSYLVANIA		
	1880–1889	1890–1899	1900–1907	1880–1889	1890–1899	1900–1909	1910–1919	1920–1929	1890–1899	1900–1909	1910–1919
Total	100	100	101	100	100	101	100	100	99	100	101
Metal mining	37	28	23	9	2	2	1	1	1	1	1
Coal mining	4	9	9	25	22	26	34	34	56	61	73
Crude petroleum & natural gas production	1	3	8	47	56	56	49	54	16	16	13
Nonmetallic mining & quarrying	12	19	15	5	9	4	6	4	21	17	10
Unallocable	46	41	46	14	11	13	10	7	5	5	4

Percentages were computed from data in Appendix 4.

sufficiently numerous to warrant inclusion, Table 28 was compiled.

Incorporations in the two-letter subgroups of the public utility category are more like those previously given for mining than those just discussed for manufacturing (Table 29). While no single subgroup dominates New Jersey public utility incorporations, charters granted

Ohio section of Table 29 was made revealed long cycles in each series representing a subgroup. Although these cycles do not coincide, there is also a long wave in total public utility incorporations, largely because incorporations in transportation bulk large in total public utility incorporations. Consequently, the total moves much as the transportation subgroup does. Since long cycles are

TABLE 27

Percentages of Total Manufacturing Incorporations that Fitted into Certain Two-Letter Industrial Categories
New Jersey, Ohio, and Pennsylvania

	NEW JERSEY			OHIO					PENNSYLVANIA		
	1880–1889	1890–1899	1900–1907	1880–1889	1890–1899	1900–1909	1910–1919	1920–1929	1890–1899	1900–1909	1910–1919
Food & kindred products	4	5	5	7	11	9	9	9	7	7	10
Beverages	a	a	a	a	a	a	a	a	4	4	3
Textile-mill products	6	5	5	a	a	a	a	a	6	9	12
Furniture & finished lumber products	a	a	a	6	5	5	3	4	a	a	a
Printing, publishing, & allied industries	6	8	6	11	10	8	7	8	8	8	7
Chemicals & allied products	9	8	8	7	7	7	8	9	7	7	7
Stone, clay, & glass products	8	5	8	5	9	9	6	5	10	11	6
Iron & steel & their products	12	7	9	17	11	11	10	9	19	11	9
Electrical machinery	a	a	a	1	3	3	4	6	a	a	a
Machinery (except electrical)	12	9	10	13	10	11	13	10	7	8	9
Automobiles & automobile equipment	a	a	a	0	0b	2	6	5	a	a	a
Transportation equipment (except automobiles)	a	a	a	6	6	3	2	1	a	a	a

Percentages were computed from data in Appendix 4.
a This category did not contain in any one *year* as much as 7½ percent of the total incorporations for manufacturing purposes in the given state.
b Less than .5 percent.

TABLE 28

Years in which Annual Incorporations in Certain Manufacturing Industries First Equaled or Exceeded 7½ Percent of the Total Annual Manufacturing Incorporations
New Jersey, Ohio, and Pennsylvania

MANUFACTURING INDUSTRY	SYMBOL FROM TABLE 19	NEW JERSEY	OHIO	PENN-SYL-VANIA
Food & kindred products	BA	1881	1883	1893
Beverages	BB			1897
Textile-mill products	BD	1887		1888
Furniture & finished lumber products	BI		1892	
Printing, publishing, & allied industries	BK	1883	1881	1889
Chemicals & allied products	BM	1881	1881	1892
Stone, clay, & glass products	BP	1881	1882	1888
Iron & steel & their products	BQ	1881	1881	1888
Electrical machinery	BS		1922	
Machinery (except electrical)	BT	1881	1881	1888
Automobiles & automobile equipment	BU		1917	
Transportation equipment (except automobiles)	BV		1881	

Based on data in Appendix 4.

transportation companies were a relatively large percentage of the total throughout the period. Another feature of the New Jersey section of the table is the importance of the miscellaneous group, which includes gas, electric light, power, water, bridge, and turnpike companies. Annual incorporations in the communications field, though few, have a very interesting long cycle (Chart 21A). Study of the annual data from which the

TABLE 29

Public Utility Incorporations
Percentage Distribution by Two-Letter Industrial Categories
New Jersey, Ohio, and Pennsylvania

	NEW JERSEY			OHIO					PENNSYLVANIA		
	1880–1889	1890–1899	1900–1907	1880–1889	1890–1899	1900–1909	1910–1919	1920–1929	1890–1899	1900–1909	1910–1919
Total	99	100	100	101	100	100	100	100	100	100	100
Transportation	43	47	50	56	57	52	66	77	11	10	15
Communication	13	9	9	7	20	29	7	6	9	13	4
Others*	43	44	41	38	23	19	27	17	80	77	81

Percentages were computed from data in Appendix 4.
* The unallocable group, ccg, is part of this group. For New Jersey it constitutes 8% of all public utility incorporations of the 80's, 11% of the 90's, and 14% in 1900–07. For Ohio, similar figures for the successive decades beginning with the 80's are 2, 1, 2, 1, and 1 percent. For Pennsylvania, similar figures for the successive decades beginning with the 90's are 3, 5, and 3 percent.

treated below, further comment on these series is postponed. In the Pennsylvania section of the table, the miscellaneous category clearly dominates the total public utility group; it also shows a long wave when annual figures are studied.

Among the two-letter service categories, incorporations in the amusement field were a large, though generally declining, percentage of total charters granted (Table 30). Next largest was the group of incorporations that had as their objective the supply of domestic and personal services—hotels, laundries, etc. Charters granted corporations in this group were especially numerous in Pennsylvania from 1888 to 1903. Incorporations of automobile repair shops and garages were remarkably similar for all three states.

Incorporations in the two-letter financial categories are summarized in part in Table 31. Though all two-letter financial categories are not represented, the most important are. Real estate companies and building and loan associations together have dominated financial incorporations in Ohio and Pennsylvania. In both states the figures, when expressed as percentages of the

TABLE 30
Incorporations of Companies Supplying Services
Percentage Distribution by Two-Letter Industrial Categories
New Jersey, Ohio, and Pennsylvania

	NEW JERSEY			OHIO					PENNSYLVANIA		
	1880–1889	1890–1899	1900–1907	1880–1889	1890–1899	1900–1909	1910–1919	1920–1929	1890–1899	1900–1909	1910–1919
Total	100	100	100	100	100	99	100	100	100	100	100
Domestic & personal	21	16	23	10	16	20	20	20	69	28	24
Business	19	29	20	13	12	10	12	13	1	10	10
Auto repair, etc.	0	*	2	0	0	3	12	16	0	3	17
Amusement	48	35	29	63	55	45	41	35	24	40	36
Other	12	20	26	14	17	21	15	16	6	19	13

Percentages were computed from data in Appendix 4.
* Less than .5 percent.

TABLE 31
Percentages of Total Incorporations of Financial Enterprises
that Fitted into Certain Two-Letter Industrial Categories
New Jersey, Ohio, and Pennsylvania

	NEW JERSEY			OHIO					PENNSYLVANIA		
	1880–1889	1890–1899	1900–1907	1880–1889	1890–1899	1900–1909	1910–1919	1920–1929	1890–1899	1900–1909	1910–1919
Commercial banks, etc.	9	1	0	8	21	22	6	2	1	*	6
Building & loan associations	3	1	*	82	46	7	4	4	57	27	40
Real estate	75	74	70	5	27	56	73	69	36	55	42

Percentages were computed from data in Appendix 4.
* Less than .5 percent.

total, move inversely. The percentages for building and loan associations in New Jersey are very small because the sources from which New Jersey incorporations were compiled did not contain complete information on charters granted those institutions. Since the long waves in annual incorporations of building and loan associations are discussed below, they are merely mentioned at this point.

The Rise of the Corporation in Certain Industries

To discuss and present graphically all incorporation series for the three-letter categories of Table 19 would make the trees obscure the woods. Accordingly, a few categories were picked to show when the corporation attained an established position in various industrial fields. First, each Ohio three-letter category in which annual incorporations equaled or exceeded 15—a number chosen more or less arbitrarily—was singled out. This step eliminated industrial categories in which throughout the period 1872–1930 incorporations were very few. Each selected series and the similar industrial series for New Jersey and Pennsylvania were then plotted on roughly drawn charts. (Ohio incorporations were used as the base because they cover the longest period.) From 73 preliminary charts those in which the series of the three states showed somewhat the same development—32 in all—were chosen for further study. The charts thereby excluded were chiefly those for highly localized industries. For example, the chart showing rubber tire manufacturing was eliminated because of this lack of parallelism, a parallelism that could scarcely be expected since Ohio is the home of rubber manufacture. Charts presenting the miscellaneous categories were also excluded.

The full industrial data are presented in Appendix 4 in order that anyone can similarly chart the progress of incorporations in other industries. The 32 charts revealed such information as the following. The corporation attained prominence during the 1880's in the manufacture of heating apparatus and in the electric light and power industry; into the latter field it was introduced very rapidly. By the early 'nineties it was common in the manufacture of dairy products, bricks and tiles, and general industrial machinery, and toward the end of the decade in hotels, drug manufacturing, and stone, sand, and gravel quarrying. During the closing years of the 19th century many automobile manufacturers and local truckers and haulers were incorporated.

Laundries, auditoriums, and paint manufacturing establishments had on occasion been organized as corporations at least as early as the 'seventies, but not until the first decade of the 20th century were there many corporations in these types of enterprise. The manufacture of confectionery might be said to have progressed by 1910 to the point where the corporation was a suitable form of business organization, but the date might better be put between 1910 and 1920. In that decade the corporate form was taken up by advertisers and by manufacturers of bakery products, nonalcoholic beverages, and metal-working machinery.

An increase in incorporations reflects both growth in the size of business units and the development of industries themselves. Series for industries in which incorporations rose during the 1920's illustrate the two features. For example, the rise of footwear manufacturing incorporations is doubtless due to the growth of

CHART 21

Long Cycles in Incorporations
New Jersey, Ohio, and Pennsylvania, 1872–1930

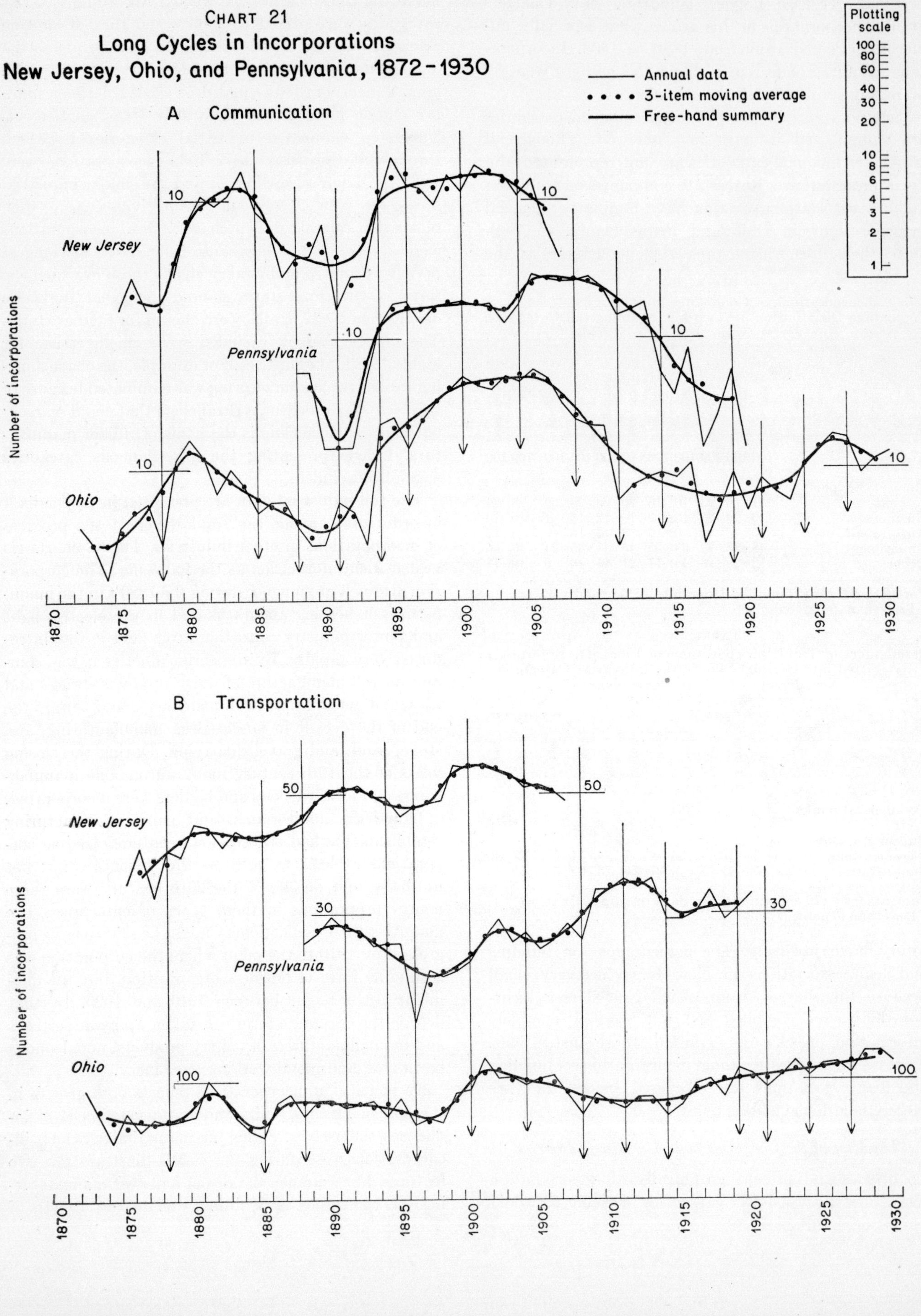

A　Communication

——— Annual data
• • • • 3-item moving average
——— Free-hand summary

Plotting scale
100
80
60
40
30
20
10
8
6
4
3
2
1

Number of incorporations

New Jersey

10

10

Pennsylvania

10

10

Ohio

10

10

1870 1875 1880 1885 1890 1895 1900 1905 1910 1915 1920 1925 1930

B　Transportation

Number of incorporations

New Jersey

50

50

Pennsylvania

30

30

Ohio

100

100

1870 1875 1880 1885 1890 1895 1900 1905 1910 1915 1920 1925 1930

CHART 21 (CONCL.)
Long Cycles in Incorporations
New Jersey, Ohio, and Pennsylvania, 1872-1930

C Other Public Utilities

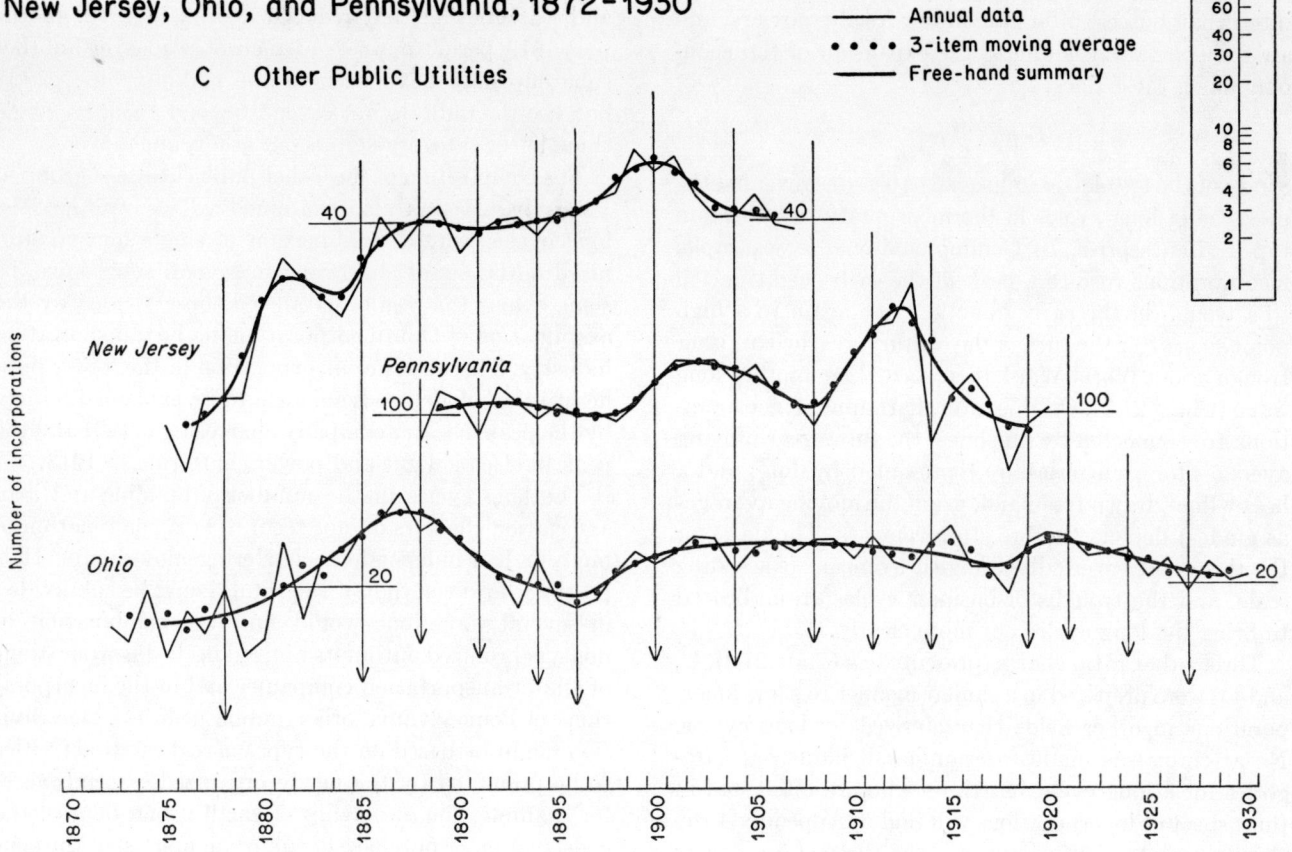

D Building and Loan Associations

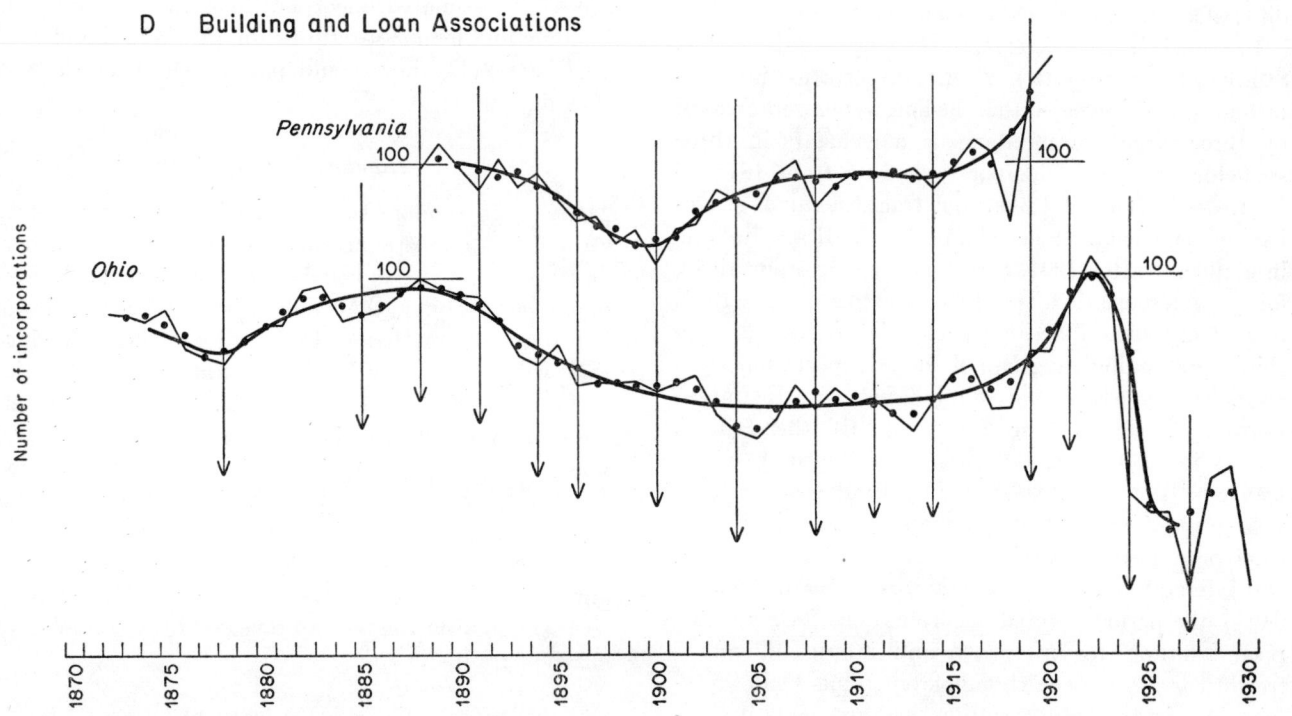

Source of annual data: Appendix 4.

large scale enterprise; while the rise of incorporations in the manufacture of radios and of aircraft and parts, as well as in city and suburban bus lines, interstate and interurban busses, interstate motor freight carriers, and air transportation is due to the expansion of the economy along these lines.

Long Cycles

Study of the two-letter industrial categories revealed the presence of long cycles in the incorporations of certain types of enterprise. In Communications, for example, incorporations rose to a peak in the early 'eighties, fell to a trough in the early 'nineties, rose again to a high point soon after the turn of the century, reached another trough about World War I, then started on another long wave (Chart 21A). On this ratio chart annual incorporations are connected by fine lines; the three-year moving averages for each series are represented by dots; and a heavy line (drawn free-hand, using the moving averages as guides) depicts the broad movements. The data for the three states were disentangled by means of a sliding scale, and the troughs of business cycles are indicated to bring the long cycles out more clearly.

Three other ratio charts (presented as Chart 21 B, C, and D) were prepared in a similar manner to show incorporations in other fields characterized by long cycles. No attempt was made to examine all industrial categories for a long cycle, but those who are interested in this aspect of incorporations will find in Appendix 4 the necessary data. Long waves for the three states rarely coincide at either peaks or troughs, doubtless because of differences in the regional economies.

In some instances at least, the long wave is deceptive. Study of the composition of all transportation incorporations in Ohio revealed that the long waves were created by three large nonsimultaneous movements in three subfields. Railroad incorporations rose from 1875 to 1881, declined until 1898, then traced a minor wave-like movement that reached a peak in 1901 and became insignificant after 1907. Street railway incorporations, fairly numerous as early as 1886, rose to a peak in 1901, then declined and became negligible after 1912. The third outstanding subgroup of the transportation category, local trucking and warehousing, rose to importance about 1902, reached a peak in 1919, then fell off, though in 1930 it still bulked large in the total for the transportation field. About 1919 several other categories, most of which center around the automobile, became prominent—taxicabs, city and suburban bus lines, and interstate and interurban busses. Toward the very end of the period covered, incorporations for air transportation and for interstate and interurban motor freight carriers were fairly numerous. Thus Ohio incorporations in the transportation field are made up primarily of three major chartering movements: one in rail-

roads that reached a major peak in 1881; one in street railways that reached a peak in 1901 (railroads had a minor peak at the same time); and one in local trucking and warehousing that reached a peak in 1919. In the post-1919 period a wave of incorporations in another subgroup may have been in the making; but, partly because the data do not extend beyond 1930, no single three-letter category stands out as a prime mover.

The composition of the 'other public utilities' group in Pennsylvania was also examined to see whether the long cycles were a combination of single nonsynchronized outbursts of chartering in several subgroups. To some extent the results paralleled those yielded by the examination of Ohio incorporations in the transportation industry. The waves of incorporation in the 'other public utilities' of Pennsylvania are to be explained largely by the peak in water company chartering in 1901 and the peak in electric light and power chartering in 1913.

The long cycles in the number of building and loan association charters do not seem to be a combination of more or less independent chartering movements. It is possible, however, that, if the totals could be subdivided in several ways, one would find the combination of nonsynchronized outbursts noticed in the incorporations of Ohio transportation companies and in the incorporations of Pennsylvania 'other public utilities'. One division might be based on the types of real estate activities to be promoted by the newly organized associations— for example, the ownership of small urban houses, the construction or purchase of suburban houses, or the conversion of dwellings in the building of local shopping areas. If estimated incorporations for Pennsylvania building and loan associations for 1875-87 were plotted on Chart 21D, they would parallel the Ohio data in striking fashion.[1]

Random Movements

Many large random movements in the various state series for total incorporations were explained, and others discovered, as the industrial data were worked. Frequently very brief, they reflect intense activity in an industry. Several have already been referred to since they were sufficiently large to dominate a state series and cause a significant 'bulge' in it. The Texas chartering episode of 1901, which was just a phase of the oil boom that had repercussions over a wide area, for example, was cited in Chapter 4. Table 32 gives Texas monthly incorporations in all fields and in oil. Items in the *Commercial & Financial Chronicle* of May 4 and June 1, 1901 that attest the feverishness of oil activity in Texas confirm the picture revealed by the number of charters granted.[2]

---

[1] See the Pennsylvania section of Appendix 3.

[2] LXXII, 842, col. 2, and 1054, col. 1.

TABLE 32
Oil Incorporations as a Percentage of Total Business Incorporations, Texas, 1901

INCORPORATIONS	JAN.	FEB.	MAR.	APR.	MAY	JUNE	JULY	AUG.	SEPT.	OCT.	NOV.	DEC.	TOTAL
Total business	81	75	87	196	289	105	107	77	47	55	47	68	1,234
Oil	7	15	17	147	193	25	32	21	6	15	6	16	500
Oil as % of total	8.6	20.0	19.5	75.0	66.8	23.8	29.9	27.3	12.8	27.3	12.8	23.5	40.5

Based on reports of the Secretary of State of Texas (described in the Texas section of Appendix 3), which state briefly the purposes of each newly chartered company.

Incorporations in both Ohio and Pennsylvania reflect outstanding episodes in the natural gas field during the 'eighties (Table 33). In Pennsylvania borings for gas wells were numerous in 1883 and the early months of 1884. Gas drilling did not reach its peak, however, until May 1884, when an immense gas well was struck inside the limits of Pittsburgh.[3] Incorporations for gas companies reached their peak the same year; unfortunately, these annual data cannot be divided into monthly figures. High-pressure gas was discovered in northwestern Ohio in November 1884, but the first big well in that area was not opened until January 1886. In central Ohio, large high-pressure gas discoveries were made in 1887.[4] Gas company incorporations in Ohio reached their peak in April 1887.[5]

TABLE 33
Gas Incorporations, Ohio and Pennsylvania, 1880–1893

	1880	1881	1882	1883	1884	1885	1886	1887	1888	1889	1890	1891	1892	1893
Ohio	2	4	5	12	18	55	76	176	30	31	41	25	21	14
Pa.	6	15	24	70	116	68	18	29	24	51	42	18	18	8

The numbers of producing and distributing companies were combined. The figures (from Appendix 4) are the sum of the data of two purpose categories, acb and ccb.

The chartering of companies to mine gold and silver was a feature of Colorado incorporations in 1892 and 1896 (Table 34). Between 1891 and 1897 Colorado charters granted business corporations outside the mining field ranged from 461 to 571; total incorporations ranged from 738 to 1,841. It was thus the great variation in the number of companies created to engage in mining that produced the wide fluctuations in the number of charters granted by Colorado between 1891 and

[3] Albert Williams, Jr., U.S. Geological Survey, *Mineral Resources of the United States, Calendar Years 1883 and 1884* (Washington, D. C., 1885), pp. 240–2.

[4] Edward Orton, *First Annual Report of the Geological Survey of Ohio (Third organization)*, (Columbus, Ohio, 1890), pp. 105 and 229.

[5] Combined monthly incorporations of producing and distributing gas companies in Ohio in 1887 were as follows: Jan., 7; Feb., 18; March, 24; April, 53; May, 25; June, 14; July, 7; Aug., 4; Sept., 4; Oct., 10; Nov., 8; Dec., 2. These data were compiled from the sources cited for the annual figures in Appendix 4.

1897. As would be expected, most of the mining enterprises were organized as gold and silver mining companies.

TABLE 34
Mining and Total Business Incorporations
Colorado, 1891–1897

	1891	1892	1893	1894	1895	1896	1897
Total business incorporations	738	1,164	822	829	1,164	1,841	990
Mining	223	593	312	368	690	1,324	508
Nonmining	515	571	510	461	474	517	482

Based on reports of the Secretary of State of Colorado (described in the Colorado section of Appendix 3), which briefly state the purposes of each newly chartered company. In some cases the company name was also used in determining the industrial objective.

The tabulation of water supply companies from the lists of incorporations published by the Secretary of State of Pennsylvania recorded a surge of water charters with a high peak in 1901; this is confirmed by the 1907 report by the Water Supply Commission. The peak of

PENNSYLVANIA WATER INCORPORATIONS, 1888–1907, ACCORDING TO TWO SOURCES

	1888	1889	1890	1891	1892	1893	1894	1895	1896	1897	1898	1899	1900	1901	1902	1903	1904	1905[c]	1905[d]	1906	1907
Water Supply Commission[a]	33	62	41	27	71	64	38	58	40	38	30	50	101	153	118	116	104	71	7	30	32
Secretary of State[b]	33	61	42	28	74	63	41	52	35	37	31	50	101	151	87	90	97	83	2	22	27

[a] *Report of the Water Supply Commission of Pennsylvania, 1907* (Harrisburg, 1908), pp. 14, 15, and 16.
[b] Compiled from reports described in Pennsylvania section of Appendix 3.
[c] January to June.
[d] June through December.
  The discrepancies in the two sets of figures are not large in view of the fact that companies supplying water solely for manufacturing and power purposes were excluded from the water company count based upon the reports of the Secretary of State. In that count, water power companies were placed in the unallocable group of Other Public Utilities—Table 19, category ccg.

1901 seems to have developed because certain rights of eminent domain that attached to Pennsylvania water companies made it highly advantageous for speculators to acquire water company charters. The widespread seizure and holding of water supplies, which is reflected in incorporations, led to an alteration in the powers of water companies and to the establishment of the Water Supply Commission, whose control in 1905 caused a drastic reduction in water company charters. In the first five months of that year, 71 water companies were chartered according to the Commission, while only seven were incorporated in the rest of the year when the Commission was functioning.[6]

The 615 charters Pennsylvania granted to electric light companies in 1913 have already been referred to, but some further description of the episode is not inappropriate since so many incorporations were involved.[7] The incorporation of such a large number of electric light companies is reflected in contemporary journals and was probably due partly to a provision of an old Pennsylvania law that required the organization of a separate company for each township or municipality in which a lighting franchise was obtained.[8] In conse-

quence of this law and an effort to consolidate the servicing of several localities, a group of related companies —often a holding company and its operating units— would be chartered at the same time. Perhaps, too, chartering activity in the electric light field at that time was stimulated by efforts to establish a Pennsylvania Public Service Commission with extensive powers of control. The law creating such a commission was enacted on July 26, 1913.[9]

These and similar random movements have from time to time caused bulges in incorporations, but on the whole they have warped neither the trend nor the cyclical movements unduly. They indicate, however, that most state incorporation series should be considered in the light of state business annals. Such a task would be far beyond the scope of this study, especially in view of the paucity of such annals.

---

[6] For further information on the Pennsylvania water situation of 1901, see *Message of the Governor of Pennsylvania to the General Assembly, January 3, 1905* (1905), p. 15; *Message of the Governor of Pennsylvania to the General Assembly, Extraordinary Session, January 15, 1906* (Harrisburg, 1906), p. 1; *Penna. Laws, 1901*, No. 177, pp. 270–1, and *ibid., 1905*, No. 109 and 236.

[7] For data of this and adjacent years, see category cca in Pennsylvania section of Appendix 4.

[8] *Pennsylvania Laws, 1874*, No. 32 (April 29, 1874), Sec. 34, clauses 1 and 3. See also news item, entitled 'Pennsylvania

Properties Consolidated', in *The Electrical World*, Vol. 61, No. 17 (April 26, 1913), pp. 903 and 904.

Pennsylvania Laws, 1913, No. 854.

[9]

CHAPTER 9

Incorporations and Business Cycles

Fluctuations in the number of incorporations have frequently been regarded as an index of business conditions. For example, the Secretary of the Commonwealth of Massachusetts, reporting to the Legislature in 1864 on the great increase in the number of corporate charters issued in 1863, wrote: "It is gratifying to observe this large increase in the number of corporations established under general law, *indicating, as it does, prosperity in manufacturing and mining interests*, and an appreciation by capitalists of the facilities afforded by standing laws for the establishment of corporate bodies without the delay involved in obtaining special charters, and the expense for the Commonwealth of legislative time and public money."[1] To be sure, more space is devoted to the effect of general incorporation laws, but the reference to prosperity comes first. There were many later statements. In 1902, for example, the chief of the Maryland Bureau of Industrial Statistics stated that the increase in 1901 over 1900 in both the number and the capitalization of new corporations reflected the "energy and enterprise in the State". Moreover, the large amount of capital stock for the numerous companies chartered in the counties evoked the comment: "This certainly is an indication of thrift and energy in the counties that ought to be gratifying to all our citizens."[2]

More recent comments of state officials can be cited. In the press releases dealing with incorporations put out by the Office of the Secretary of State of New York, increases in the number of incorporations are almost always said to indicate 'better business'. From the many statements that could be quoted the following have been selected:

These figures are given as showing the vast strides that are being made this year in the number of companies incorporating in New York state, and which must be regarded as reflecting an optimism toward the future and the belief that business conditions are not only fundamentally strong at the present time, but present a most excellent future.

Press Release, June 1925

There is evidence of a coming real estate boom, judging from the large number of companies that are incorporating these days, mainly from New York city and from Nassau and Westchester counties.

Press Release, May 1926

The 343 stock companies that incorporated last month outside of the metropolis were distributed over 35 counties, a good feature, and showing business and industrial activity as being general over the state, rather than confined to any particular locality or to the larger cities.

Press Release, Feb. 1927

More stock companies were incorporated in New York State during the month of January than during any one month since last May. This indicates a confidence in the business future and is in sharp contrast to the slump that followed the stock market crash of last October and November, when the number of companies incorporating dropped to a low figure.

Press Release, Feb. 1930

Commenting on the increase [in the number of incorporations], Secretary Walsh said, "The rise for the year was very gratifying to me. I believe that the yearly totals of the stock company incorporations might well be regarded as a fair sort of business barometer. An upswing in the number of charterings, I think, indicated better business conditions throughout the state."

Press Release, Jan. 1940

"The substantial numerical rise in stock company formations in the past six months," Secretary Curran said, "may well indicate that the 1942 total will be equaled and in all probability exceeded when the final count for the 1943 twelve month period is completed ... If the chartering of stock companies is a fair barometer of business conditions—and I believe it is—it would appear there has been a marked improvement in the state within the past six months."

Press Release, Dec. 1943

Most of such comments upon the relation between incorporations and business cycles refer either to the upturn or the continued rise in the number of incorporations as a favorable business sign or to incorportaions as a general barometer of business. It should be noted, for future reference, that they suggest that a rise in incorporations precedes a business revival. Among the few comments in which a decline in incorporations is associated with a recession in business is a press release by the Secretary of State of New York, dated September 1927:

There is probably no better criterion of general business conditions in New York state than the corporation bureau located in the Department of State, and which is the largest in the world today. A let up in business is almost immediately reflected in the number of companies incorporating through the bureau, while confidence in the future is easy to recognize in the influx of companies incorporating and with heavy capitalization.

According to Alfred Marshall, on the contrary, "most promotions of new companies, and reorganizations of old companies, are made in the years just before an inflation of credit and prices reaches its bursting point."[3]

---

[1] *Abstract of the Attested Returns of Corporations organized during 1863, under General Statutes of Massachusetts* (*Massachusetts Public Documents, 1863*, no. 13) (Boston, 1864), p. 3 (italics mine).

[2] *Tenth Annual Report of the Bureau of Industrial Statistics of Maryland* (Baltimore, 1902), p. 195.

[3] *Industry and Trade* (Macmillan, London, 1919), p. 334.

Marshall's statement is not supported by factual data, though perhaps an examination of the British material of that and prior periods would substantiate it. Each of the other quotations seems to be tied primarily to a particular situation. All serve to indicate the prevalence of the opinion that business incorporations have had a definite relation to cyclical movements in general business. Efforts to define the relation have not been lacking. The indexes of incorporation referred to in Chapter 4 —the *New York Journal of Commerce* indexes and the Corporation Trust Company index—are perhaps evidence of efforts to establish the bases for a careful examination. The Harvard University Committee on Economic Research tried to use the *Journal's* indexes in its studies of business cycles but concluded that the data were collected in such a manner that the compilations were of questionable value.[4]

D. H. Macgregor showed that in general in Great Britain from 1865 to 1910 turning points in new joint-stock registrations preceded turning points in employment, which in turn preceded those in prices. It is unfortunate that his data were not monthly, but on the basis of annual figures he concludes "that enterprisers have got themselves out of depression[s], rather than that they have been led out of them by actual price policies."[5] Marshall's statement concerning peaks in incorporation seems to be substantiated and is, in fact, referred to by Macgregor.

The remaining sections of this chapter are devoted to some results of explorations concerning the relation between incorporations and business cycles. These explorations are a beginning in the treatment of a subject that deserves full investigation. It is hoped that the new evidence presented in this monograph will stimulate further research.

Initial Investigations

Before cyclical movements in business incorporations were studied, seasonal movements were calculated. A casual examination substantiated the observation of others that seasonal movements were pronounced. The Secretary of State of New York on several occasions called attention to a seasonal decline in incorporations during the midsummer months.[6] And a quarterly index of seasonal variation constructed by the Harvard University Committee on Economic Research from one of the incorporation indexes of the *New York Journal of Commerce* also indicated a midsummer slump in the granting of new charters.[7]

[4] *Review of Economic Statistics*, Preliminary Volume 1 (1919), pp. 148–9.

[5] *Op. cit.*, pp. 62–94, particularly pp. 81–6.

[6] See, for example, his press releases on incorporations for August 1925 and August 1927.

[7] *Review of Economic Statistics*, Preliminary Volume 1 (1919), pp. 172–3.

To confirm or refute first impressions derived from an examination of the series compiled for this study, six indexes of seasonal variation were calculated for Maine, Ohio, and Texas for the 1880's and for a later decade. For Maine and Ohio, the later seasonal index covered the 1920's, but for Texas 1910–19 had to be used since data for the 'twenties were not available. Each index was based upon ratios of the monthly data to the corresponding twelve-month moving averages.[8] The ten ratios for each month were averaged separately by taking an arithmetic mean of the six central items. The representative monthly figures thus procured were adjusted by dividing each by the average of the twelve (Table 35).

TABLE 35

Indexes of Seasonal Variation in Business Incorporations Maine, Ohio, and Texas

	MAINE		OHIO		TEXAS	
	1880–89	1920–29	1880–89	1920–29	1880–89	1910–19
Jan.	83.2	119.9	120.5	114.3	101.8	109.5
Feb.	83.6	111.1	117.4	106.7	104.9	116.2
Mar.	111.4	112.4	132.4	124.6	124.5	121.1
Apr.	131.8	110.0	107.6	111.5	125.2	107.2
May	116.5	114.6	100.1	104.4	114.2	124.2
June	107.4	94.3	91.4	96.7	119.4	107.8
July	93.0	81.2	88.4	90.3	97.9	104.8
Aug.	92.7	92.6	77.3	89.9	84.6	92.0
Sept.	89.2	80.9	81.5	88.0	93.1	86.6
Oct.	92.6	89.3	86.1	91.2	81.9	81.4
Nov.	99.6	93.3	88.4	82.5	67.1	72.4
Dec.	99.0	100.4	109.2	100.0	85.4	76.8

Calculated as described in the text from the basic data given in Appendix 3.

While the seasonal movement in the charters granted by Maine has changed somewhat, in both Ohio and Texas it has remained very much the same. If any change is common to all three states, it is the decrease in the amplitude of the variation. Moreover, the seasonal patterns of the three states are more or less similar. Finally, it is clear that the seasonal variation in chartering is so large that account must be taken of it.

To facilitate study of the relation between incorporations and business cycles, twelve-item moving averages, entered at the seventh item, were calculated for the monthly series of incorporations of sixteen states. This procedure eliminated seasonal variation crudely and made it possible to compare the peaks and troughs in each state incorporation series with the turning points of business.[9] A more refined procedure for eliminating seasonal variation was not used because there were so many series to be treated.

The movements of the Maine series, one of the four important series plotted on Chart 22, clearly suggest

[8] The 12-month moving averages were entered at the seventh month.

[9] For the turning points of business, see Burns and Mitchell, p. 78.

CHART 22

Business Incorporations, Four States, 1881–1907

12-item Moving Averages

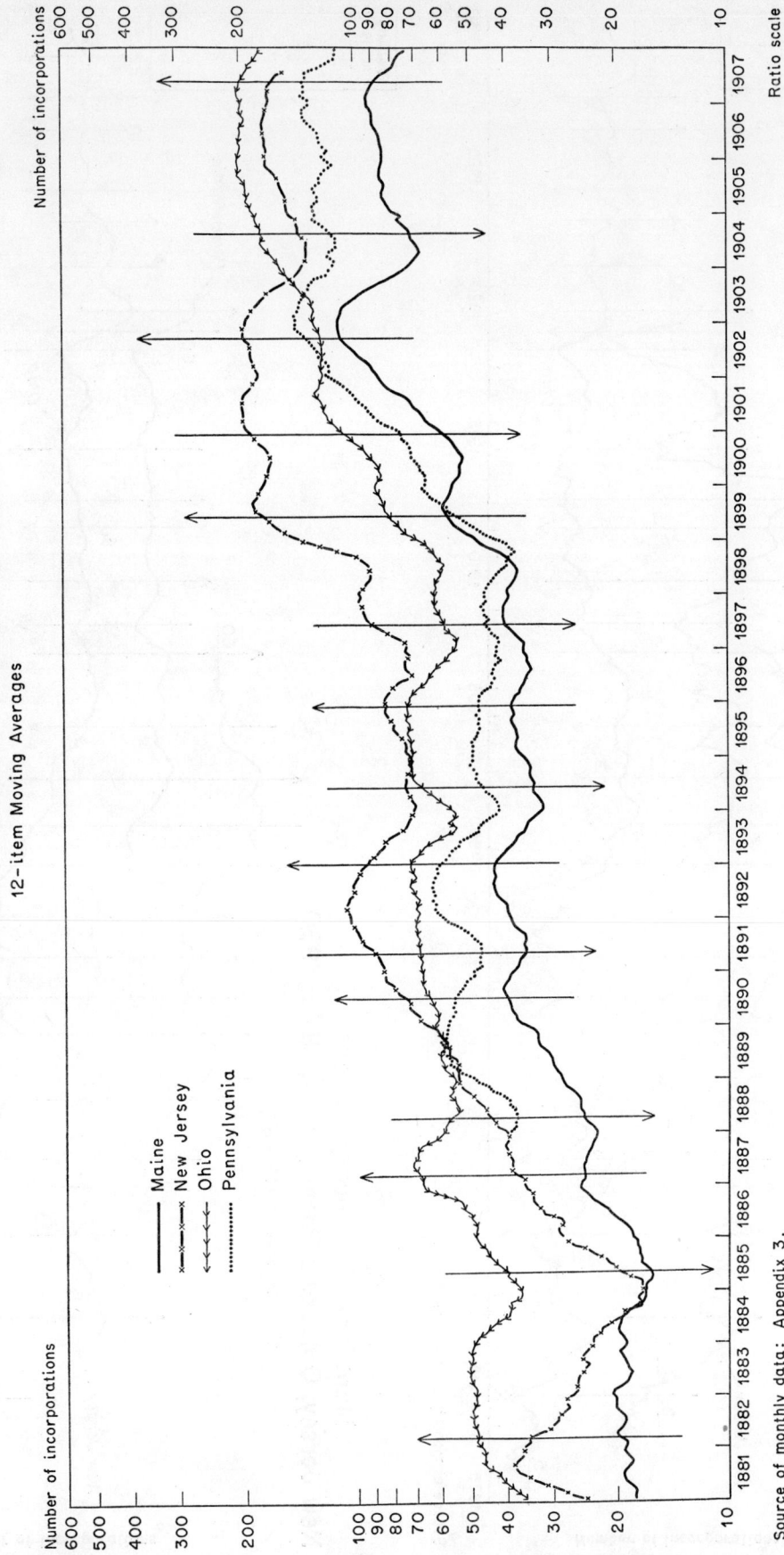

Number of incorporations

Maine
New Jersey
Ohio
Pennsylvania

Ratio scale

Source of monthly data: Appendix 3.

CHART 23
Public Utility Incorporations
New Jersey, Ohio, and Pennsylvania, 1875–1930
12–item Moving Averages

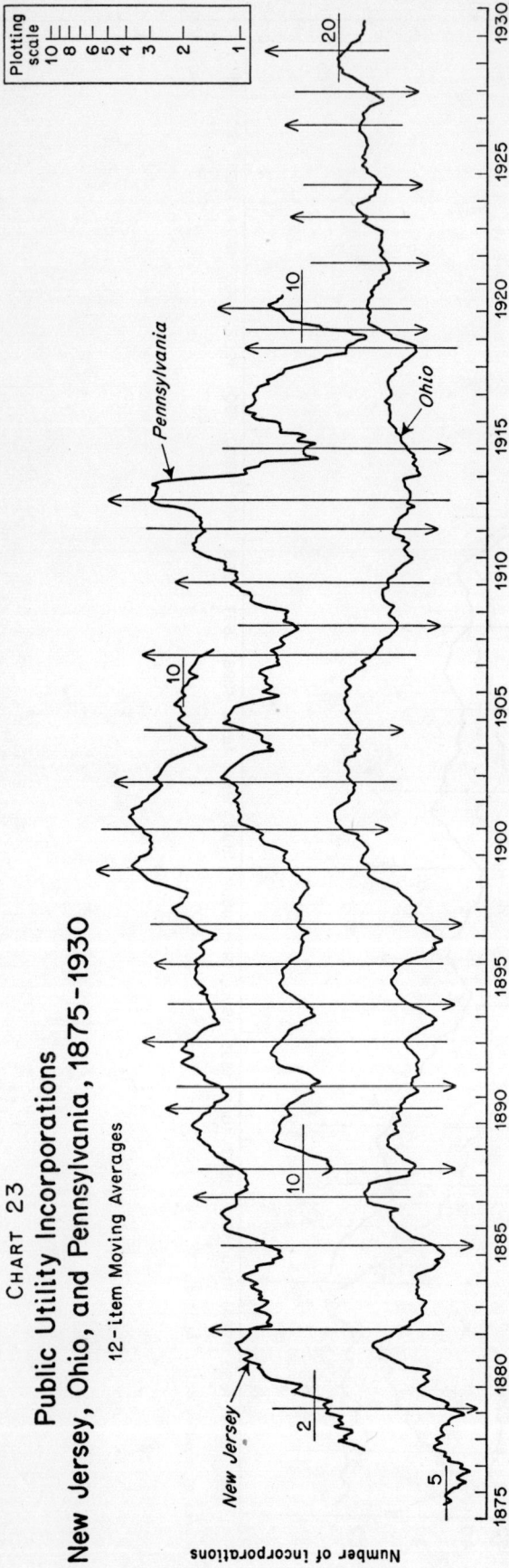

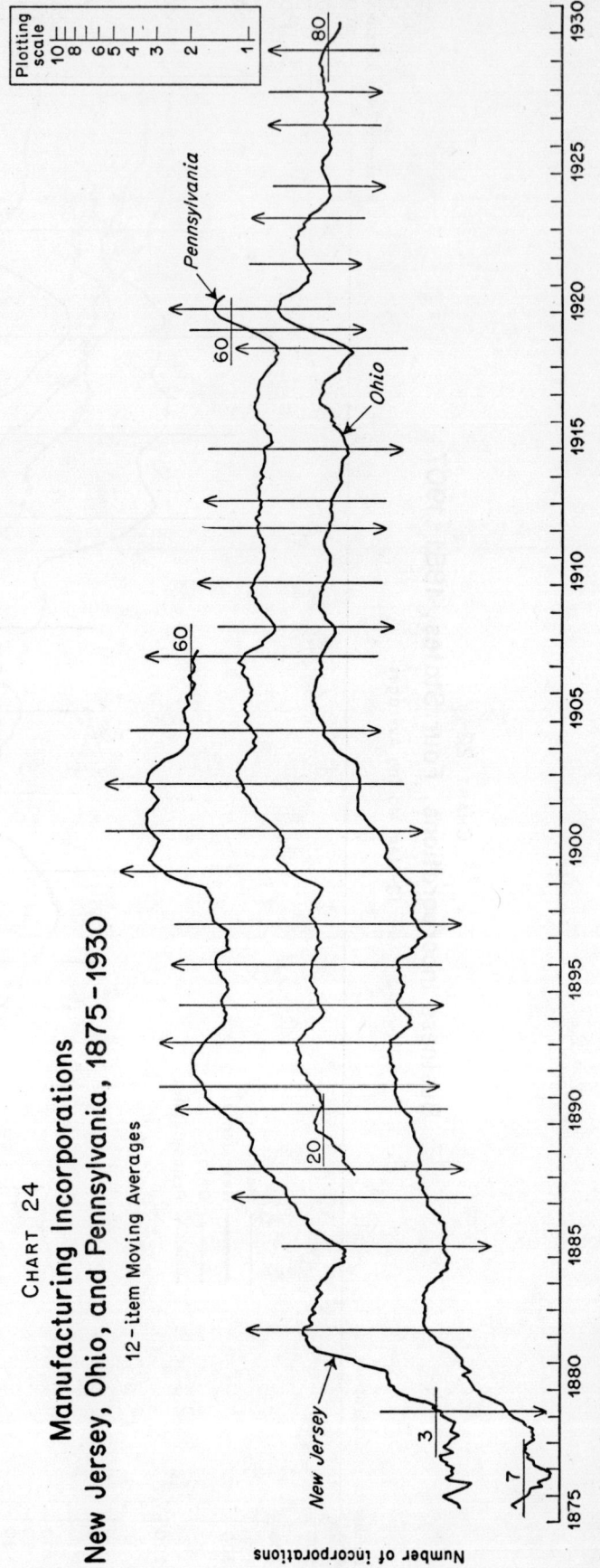

Number of Incorporations

Source of monthly data: Appendix 4.

CHART 24
Manufacturing Incorporations
New Jersey, Ohio, and Pennsylvania, 1875–1930
12–item Moving Averages

Number of incorporations

Source of monthly data: Appendix 4.

that a trough in incorporations usually precedes a trough in business. The same is true of the three other series. At peaks the relation is less uniform. Study of the moving averages of all sixteen states—which cannot advantageously be reproduced on a single chart—gave rise to a firm conviction that incorporations usually turned upward some months before business began to revive.

When the peaks and troughs of the twelve-month moving averages for incorporations in the major industrial categories were compared with the turning points in business, several relations were observed. First, the various New Jersey series seemed to show a very pronounced tendency to turn up before business reached a trough. All except one of the Ohio incorporation series—that for mining—also showed this tendency, but less regularly. Several Pennsylvania series seemed to lag behind business troughs about as often as they led them. That troughs in the various incorporation series of New Jersey usually preceded business troughs was not unexpected in view of the 'liberal' character of its laws. The weaker tendency in the other two states suggests the hypothesis that, as long as state laws for the organization of corporations differ substantially and as long as states are the chief agencies for granting charters, the incorporation series of 'liberal' states are likely to be better indicators of general business activity. But there seems to be no plausible reason why Ohio incorporations reached *crests* before business more regularly than the parallel series of the other two states.

When attention was directed to industries, it was found that changes in the number of charters granted manufacturing and public utility companies were closely correlated with turning points in business. In both these industrial fields there has been a strong tendency for an *upturn* in incorporations to precede a *trough* in business. To facilitate observation of the relation, incorporations of public utilities in three states are brought together in Chart 23, and incorporations of manufacturing enterprises in Chart 24. The tendency of incorporations in public utilities to reach a trough before business seems reasonable in view of the importance of capital in this field and of the low interest rates that are likely to prevail as a recession spends itself. The same argument applies to manufacturing concerns, but with less force. With the exception of manufacturing incorporations in New Jersey, the series plotted on Charts 23 and 24 seem to attain *peaks* before business. They are not as regular in this respect, however, as they are in turning upward before business reaches a trough.

Monthly Aggregate and Median Indexes of Incorporations

To bring the study of the relation between incorporations and business cycles within more manageable proportions and be in a position to describe any ob-

served relation more precisely, incorporation data for a number of states—the figures for no one of which are available for the entire eighty-three years covered—were combined and attention was focused upon the composite picture. Two monthly indexes of incorporations covering the period 1860–1943 were constructed.[10] That based on simple aggregates was designed specifically for studying the relation between the number of incorporations and business cycles. The other, computed as a simple median of relatives, was developed as a general purpose index and is less elaborate in construction. It provides, however, a good check on the results obtained from the aggregate index.

a) *Monthly aggregate index*

In computing the monthly aggregate index care was taken to see that the data of no state were allowed to enter or leave the index near a peak or trough, and thereby affect the timing of the turning points. Con-

TABLE 36

States in the Monthly Aggregate Index of Incorporations with the Periods of Their Inclusion

SEC.	PERIOD OF INCLUSION	CONN.	DEL.	FLA.	ILL.	LA.	ME.	MD.	MASS.	N. J.	N. Y.	OHIO	PA.	TEXAS	VA.
1	1860–1869	x							x	x		x			
2	1870–1871						x	x	x	x		x			
3	1872–1880						x	x	x	x		x		x	
4	1881–1887	x					x	x	x	x		x		x	
5	1888–1896	x					x	x	x	x		x	x	x	
6	1897–1903	x			x		x	x	x	x		x	x	x	
7	1904–1917	x		x	x		x	x	x	x		x	x	x	x
8	1918–6/1919	x	x	x			x	x	x			x	x	x	x
9	7/1919–1925	x	x				x	x				x			x
10	1924	x	x				x					x	x		x
11	1925–1932	x	x		x		x	x				x	x		x
12	1933–1936		x		x		x	x				x	x		x
13	1937–1939		x		x		x	x				x			x
14	1940–1941		x		x	x	x					x			x

Arizona data, available for 1912–24, and Colorado data, available for 1891–1908, were not used.

The following additional data were not used: for Florida, 1901–03 and 1920–21; for New Jersey, 1918; for Massachusetts, 1920–21; for Pennsylvania, 1920–21; and for Louisiana, 1937–39.

sequently, some portions of the incorporation series set forth in Appendix 3 could not be used, and the data for Colorado (available for 1891–1908) and Arizona (avail-

[10] Had an index been constructed from total capital stock figures, the data of Chapter 5 indicate that the results would have been much the same with respect to timing, but such an index would have fluctuated more violently than an index based on total incorporations. Moreover, total capital stock is more erratic than the number of incorporations because of the effect a few very large companies may produce. The adjusted capital stock series (that is, the total figures less the capital of the companies with authorized stock of $1,000,000 or more) would have produced results very similar to a total number index, but any capital stock series would have been inferior to the total number series because the coverage of states could not have been as large—there are not as many data on stock as on number.

TABLE 37

Seasonal Indexes used in Computing the Monthly Aggregate Index of Incorporations

MONTH	PERIODS USED IN CALCULATIONS									
	1863–69	1871–79	1873–79	1880–95	1897–04	1905–16	1920–25	1924–28	1929–32	1934–38
January	125	103	104	111	119	114	114	116	111	118
February	123	108	103	109	108	109	104	102	101	97
March	150	120	129	125	125	124	118	117	112	112
April	131	115	124	113	111	111	111	107	109	105
May	117	121	118	108	111	107	107	105	106	103
June	98	102	104	99	100	100	99	101	103	100
July	71	91	91	92	89	93	90	90	94	95
August	80	94	90	82	82	86	89	87	94	92
September	62	80	76	80	80	86	86	83	90	86
October	77	85	80	88	89	88	91	94	96	96
November	71	83	80	88	86	86	87	91	88	94
December	94	99	100	103	100	97	104	108	96	103
Periods to which indexes were applied	1860–70	1871	1872–79	1880–96	1897–04	1905–18	1919–24	1924–28	1929–32	1933–41

Computed as described in the text from the basic data in Appendix 3 as totaled in Appendix 6.

TABLE 38

Monthly Aggregate Index of Incorporations, 1860–1941

(1925:100.0)

	JAN.	FEB.	MAR.	APR.	MAY	JUNE	JULY	AUG.	SEPT.	OCT.	NOV.	DEC.
1860	1.41	1.41	.85	.28	.99	.85	.56	1.41	1.55	1.13	.99	1.69
1861	.99	.42	1.27	.71	.71	.71	.00	.56	.42	.56	.85	.14
1862	1.13	.56	.85	.71	.85	.71	1.55	.56	1.13	.71	1.98	.56
1863	1.13	1.13	1.55	1.41	1.27	1.84	1.55	1.13	.71	2.97	2.40	3.25
1864	3.25	1.84	4.66	4.80	4.38	3.95	5.51	4.52	4.94	3.67	3.39	5.65
1865	7.48	10.45	7.48	5.65	5.65	6.78	6.21	6.35	9.32	5.51	6.92	6.07
1866	6.78	7.34	4.10	6.50	6.64	6.35	4.52	5.93	7.91	6.21	7.91	6.07
1867	5.51	4.66	4.38	4.24	5.08	5.08	6.78	6.50	4.94	6.07	5.93	5.37
1868	6.35	6.35	4.80	4.94	5.79	4.80	4.52	7.06	5.51	5.93	5.79	4.80
1869	4.24	4.38	5.93	6.50	6.21	5.51	5.79	5.65	6.21	5.37	5.37	5.79
1870	4.77	4.65	5.11	4.43	4.65	4.65	6.13	4.99	6.92	3.86	9.42	6.47
1871	6.92	5.45	5.79	5.33	6.81	5.33	5.79	5.79	4.99	8.17	6.01	6.24
1872	5.09	8.70	5.62	6.36	6.26	6.47	7.43	6.47	6.58	5.52	7.64	4.77
1873	6.47	7.11	7.21	5.94	5.94	6.36	6.05	7.64	5.83	4.46	4.24	5.30
1874	4.77	5.09	5.83	5.09	5.52	5.62	5.20	7.00	7.21	7.53	5.52	5.52
1875	6.26	6.68	7.21	6.90	5.94	6.90	6.58	6.38	9.12	6.79	6.15	6.36
1876	5.41	5.52	6.36	7.74	5.52	5.73	4.88	3.92	5.30	3.08	4.46	4.03
1877	4.24	4.56	4.46	3.71	5.62	4.67	5.62	4.67	4.77	6.58	5.52	5.30
1878	5.73	4.77	4.24	4.67	4.46	4.03	4.67	4.56	3.08	5.73	6.15	5.30
1879	5.73	4.99	3.61	4.35	5.20	5.20	5.52	4.88	4.77	5.20	7.53	8.49
1880	9.7	11.7	9.7	12.0	8.8	8.0	8.8	8.7	10.5	9.4	10.6	9.8
1881	9.5	10.9	14.8	11.9	14.2	13.2	14.7	14.9	15.2	17.6	16.7	15.7
1882	13.0	12.7	13.3	13.0	13.8	16.2	13.1	15.8	13.6	15.0	15.2	13.6
1883	12.6	14.2	13.2	13.8	15.0	16.7	14.0	16.2	14.3	15.8	13.9	14.7
1884	14.2	15.1	13.9	14.6	12.8	13.1	13.1	11.2	11.3	10.6	8.2	11.4
1885	12.3	11.3	10.8	9.7	10.3	20.8	12.5	12.5	13.2	13.4	11.4	13.7
1886	14.0	15.2	13.2	14.1	13.2	14.7	16.1	12.2	14.2	15.6	20.0	18.2
1887	18.1	16.8	19.4	23.7	21.7	20.2	16.3	19.5	19.3	21.1	19.9	16.3
1888	20.1	17.9	18.3	17.4	19.7	18.1	17.2	19.7	20.7	18.1	18.5	21.3
1889	21.9	20.7	22.0	21.4	23.0	20.1	27.8	24.9	27.0	20.3	26.8	22.2
1890	22.7	24.5	24.1	25.3	26.0	27.0	30.5	24.9	27.5	27.6	26.6	26.6
1891	26.4	26.7	24.1	24.5	24.4	29.6	27.9	25.1	29.0	28.9	27.4	33.5
1892	28.8	30.3	30.6	29.2	28.1	29.5	27.6	35.0	26.7	27.1	28.3	32.5
1893	31.9	27.8	26.1	29.3	30.7	24.5	23.6	20.9	18.9	17.8	20.3	21.9
1894	23.7	21.3	26.2	22.2	25.4	23.2	23.2	26.3	25.1	27.4	26.1	24.3
1895	25.3	21.7	24.7	26.6	23.7	24.8	28.9	29.1	28.3	30.4	29.6	27.9
1896	25.9	26.6	26.4	25.6	24.7	24.2	26.1	20.8	17.6	20.6	19.1	25.2
1897	24.6	24.2	25.9	24.8	23.2	24.2	24.9	27.6	31.7	28.2	30.0	29.7
1898	29.7	27.9	28.6	25.3	21.7	25.7	22.0	23.5	23.8	25.2	28.6	25.7
1899	31.6	31.8	36.4	36.0	36.3	40.0	41.5	40.6	38.1	37.9	39.5	36.6
1900	36.4	35.3	35.3	36.7	38.6	36.6	37.1	35.6	39.4	38.9	41.6	43.5
1901	40.8	43.9	47.1	57.1	60.7	52.9	52.9	54.5	45.7	48.1	49.4	50.3
1902	49.1	50.3	48.5	50.7	54.7	50.7	58.5	54.5	55.3	60.3	54.1	55.2
1903	59.0	59.9	55.2	57.6	53.6	55.1	55.5	50.3	57.5	55.5	51.6	59.0

	JAN.	FEB.	MAR.	APR.	MAY	JUNE	JULY	AUG.	SEPT.	OCT.	NOV.	DEC.
1904	51.1	53.9	51.0	49.2	54.0	54.7	58.0	62.4	58.1	57.3	57.8	64.0
1905	65.0	58.9	61.1	58.5	67.2	62.2	60.6	65.1	65.0	66.6	69.8	65.2
1906	72.2	67.6	71.1	65.2	73.1	72.1	61.1	72.7	67.3	74.4	74.8	75.1
1907	78.2	73.2	72.7	73.9	72.8	73.7	76.6	67.3	62.5	64.6	51.2	48.7
1908	51.2	53.3	52.8	57.2	53.8	57.9	60.1	59.7	62.6	62.3	61.2	67.6
1909	66.3	74.0	73.6	70.4	68.2	70.6	74.9	67.7	75.4	66.6	75.9	74.7
1910	65.7	71.0	62.5	69.0	66.7	66.8	58.1	66.4	62.6	61.7	70.9	65.6
1911	68.2	66.3	69.4	65.0	63.8	68.5	63.4	69.8	68.2	67.1	69.5	66.9
1912	68.8	69.8	67.9	67.8	67.8	67.0	77.3	73.2	71.9	76.1	71.9	71.8
1913	74.4	74.0	70.2	75.5	73.2	65.7	68.8	67.8	71.0	72.5	61.2	72.6
1914	63.6	64.2	69.2	66.6	65.1	64.6	68.6	56.4	57.7	58.1	56.0	54.7
1915	60.7	58.5	62.6	66.1	65.7	64.7	69.4	72.8	67.9	70.4	76.1	83.0
1916	69.5	75.1	76.2	74.8	77.8	78.2	73.7	73.2	83.2	81.9	84.5	85.1
1917	87.5	79.2	83.7	76.8	77.7	76.0	78.8	75.1	69.3	80.4	76.5	58.5
1918	55.9	56.1	54.7	57.7	60.5	51.5	58.7	53.6	44.9	41.6	41.6	53.8
1919	68.2	75.7	76.5	89.6	92.6	102.4	120.2	115.5	116.8	119.6	121.2	129.2
1920	128.0	124.2	122.8	121.1	112.7	115.4	110.2	106.6	107.4	107.0	101.8	88.4
1921	86.5	89.3	94.6	93.6	90.3	90.5	88.5	96.9	93.9	87.5	95.3	88.2
1922	89.6	93.9	94.8	94.4	110.0	105.0	100.6	99.5	104.7	106.0	101.2	105.7
1923	104.5	102.8	103.5	108.9	98.7	98.5	100.4	100.3	83.0	88.6	100.1	97.2
1924	93.4	93.5	89.3	88.5	85.0	84.5	86.2	81.5	94.0	95.9	84.7	100.5
1925	98.0	98.5	93.6	94.4	98.1	101.1	108.6	106.8	102.7	103.0	98.6	100.6
1924*	86.4	87.8	83.2	85.6	81.3	73.5	77.8	75.3	82.8	79.1	80.8	94.7
1925*	89.4	91.5	93.3	94.6	97.0	99.1	103.9	109.9	109.4	110.8	102.8	104.6
1926	104.4	99.0	98.7	98.2	98.1	105.8	104.3	96.5	100.4	100.7	99.8	96.8
1927	99.7	98.8	106.0	104.2	99.7	103.5	99.6	103.3	105.4	100.3	107.4	104.6
1928	104.7	112.2	106.5	105.6	116.6	114.0	108.2	109.6	102.0	115.3	116.8	107.9
1929	119.0	116.6	116.4	116.4	118.2	105.6	110.8	112.3	106.7	108.2	105.3	99.0
1930	99.2	102.0	99.0	99.6	104.5	97.9	100.5	90.6	101.6	100.8	97.9	100.8
1931	94.4	96.1	101.0	99.7	96.9	100.8	101.4	95.8	92.2	98.4	102.4	103.4
1932	98.8	96.7	95.2	93.9	90.1	100.3	91.2	103.1	98.3	90.0	91.6	91.1
1933	93.7	96.9	78.7	85.7	107.9	98.0	85.7	88.3	83.0	79.3	82.8	80.2
1934	79.7	72.8	76.2	76.2	75.8	72.3	71.6	73.1	69.8	74.4	72.7	66.2
1935	72.6	75.3	69.9	74.3	75.1	72.1	75.4	75.0	77.9	79.6	73.0	74.6
1936	76.3	77.3	74.5	73.1	73.6	77.2	76.7	70.4	77.5	74.6	73.0	80.1
1937	74.7	76.9	77.4	77.3	69.7	72.4	68.7	67.0	66.0	63.6	65.8	64.9
1938	61.6	61.4	62.8	60.8	62.9	62.8	63.2	66.3	63.2	60.3	63.6	62.6
1939	62.4	62.8	66.4	60.7	71.4	58.5	60.8	62.8	57.6	62.9	65.6	61.8
1940	67.1	67.2	59.7	72.3	68.7	54.5	60.8	59.3	60.3	57.4	53.4	57.7
1941	59.0	59.8	56.2	57.6	56.7	50.9	57.1	48.8	52.1	49.2	44.0	45.6

* See text.

able for 1912–24) had to be discarded. Fourteen overlapping sections including different groups of states were set up (Table 36). Next, the monthly aggregates within each section were adjusted by seasonal indexes calculated by the ratios-to-moving-average method (Table 37). The seasonally adjusted data of the first nine sections were then spliced and converted to an index based upon the monthly average of the original data for 1925. The last five sections of the adjusted data were similarly spliced to form the second part of the index.[11] The index was built in two overlapping parts—

[11] The splicing ratios were computed from annual totals of the original data except in one instance, when a six-month total of the original data was used.

Sections spliced	Period used to obtain splicing ratio	Splicing ratio
2/1	1870	1.2444444
3/2	1872	1.0697329
4/3	1881	1.0540369
5/4	1888	1.2122830
6/5	1897	1.3061761
7/6	1904	1.0674811
8/7	July–Dec. 1917	.9591558
9/8	1919	.6409781

(Continued on page 84)

TABLE 39

States in the Monthly Median Index of Incorporations with the Periods of Their Inclusion

SEC.	PERIOD OF INCLUSION	ARIZ.	COLO.	CONN.	DEL.	FLA.	ILL.	LA.	ME.	MD.	MASS.	N. J.	N. Y.	OHIO	PA.	TEXAS	VA.
1	1/60–7/70			x								x	x	x			
2	7/70–7/72									x	x	x	x	x			
3	7/72–7/81									x	x	x	x	x		x	
4	7/81–7/88			x						x	x	x	x	x		x	x
5	7/88–7/91			x						x	x	x	x	x	x	x	x
6	7/91–7/97		x	x						x	x	x	x	x	x	x	x
7	7/97–7/01		x	x			x			x	x	x	x	x	x	x	x
8	7/01–7/04		x	x				x	x	x	x	x	x	x	x	x	x
9	7/04–7/07		x	x		x		x	x	x	x	x	x	x	x	x	x
10	7/07–7/13			x		x		x	x	x	x	x	x	x	x	x	x
11	7/13–7/16	x		x		x		x	x	x	x	x	x	x	x	x	x
12	7/16–7/17	x		x	x	x	x		x	x	x	x	x			x	x
13	7/17–7/18	x		x	x	x			x	x	x	x	x			x	x
14	7/18–7/19	x		x	x	x			x	x	x					x	x
15	7/19–7/20	x		x	x	x			x	x	x	x				x	x
16	7/20–7/21	x		x	x	x			x	x					x		x
17	7/21–7/23	x		x	x				x	x					x		x
18	7/23–7/24			x	x				x	x					x		x
19	7/24–7/25			x	x				x	x			x		x		x
20	7/25–7/32			x	x		x		x	x					x	x	x
21	7/32–7/36			x		x		x	x						x		x
22	7/36–7/37			x		x		x	x						x		x
23	7/37–7/39			x		x	x	x	x						x		x
24	7/39–7/41			x		x	x	x	x						x		x
25	7/41–7/43			x		x	x	x	x						x		

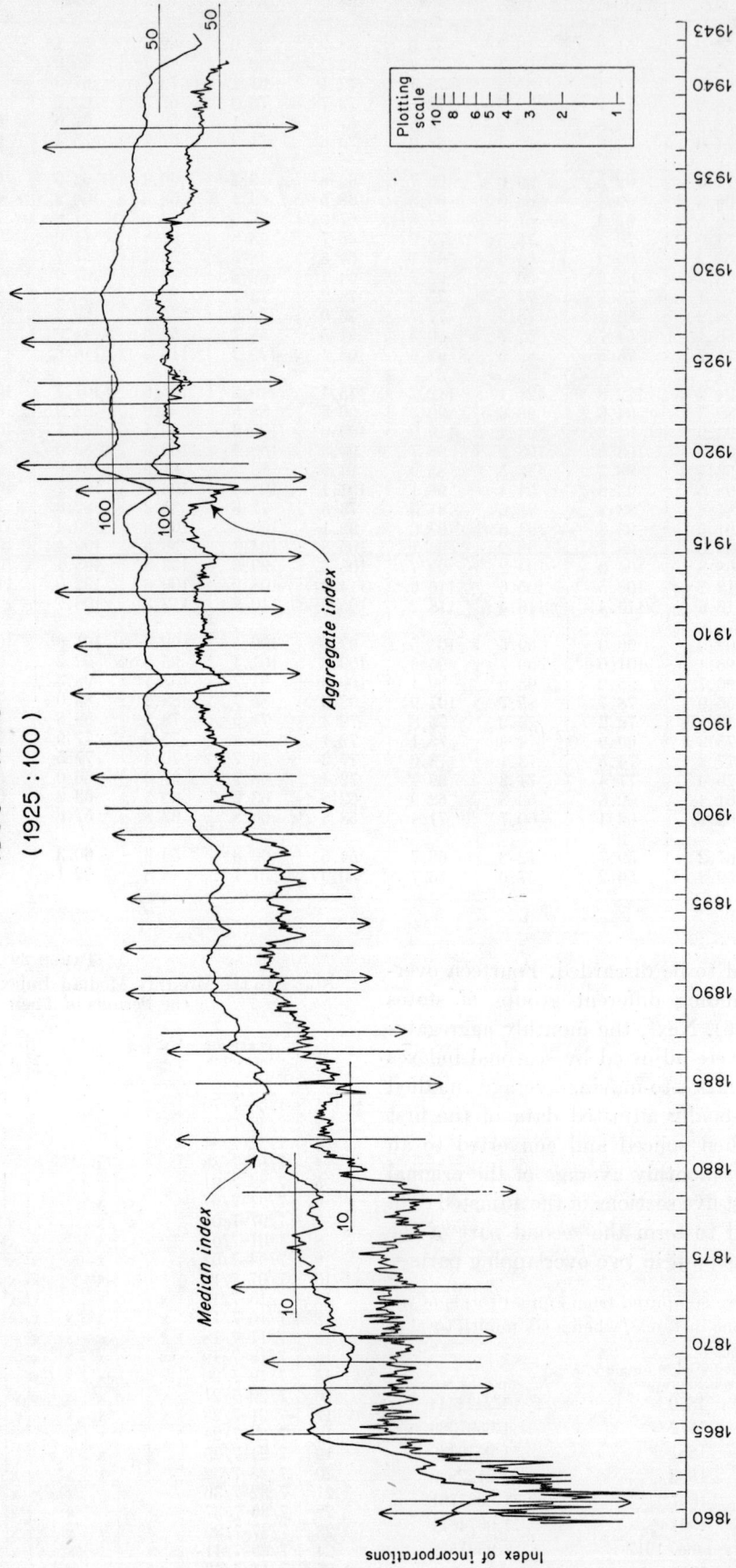

CHART 25

Monthly Aggregate and Median Indexes of Business Incorporations
1860 - 1943
(1925 : 100)

Index of incorporations

Sources: Tables 38 and 40.

TABLE 40
Monthly Median Index of Incorporations, 1860–1943
(1925:100.0)

	JAN.	FEB.	MAR.	APR.	MAY	JUNE	JULY	AUG.	SEPT.	OCT.	NOV.	DEC.
1860	1.56	1.46	1.59	1.53	1.42	1.37	1.34	1.26	1.14	1.20	1.28	1.24
1861	1.21	1.14	1.09	1.06	1.00	.99	.81	.78	.81	.68	.67	.77
1862	.82	.93	.96	.97	.94	1.28	1.46	1.36	1.41	1.63	1.70	1.84
1863	1.98	1.95	2.05	1.77	1.87	1.54	1.62	1.71	1.81	1.93	2.10	2.20
1864	2.32	2.67	2.86	3.06	3.26	3.35	3.66	4.29	5.38	6.29	6.76	7.15
1865	7.49	7.43	7.61	8.03	8.26	8.60	8.67	8.65	8.32	7.83	7.95	8.11
1866	8.20	8.22	8.31	8.17	8.14	8.21	8.20	8.04	7.56	7.44	6.93	6.65
1867	6.33	6.62	6.84	6.79	6.78	6.55	6.68	6.39	6.67	6.68	6.86	7.01
1868	7.00	6.83	6.90	6.97	6.93	6.89	6.64	5.95	5.38	5.34	5.09	5.05
1869	5.29	5.10	5.02	5.10	4.96	4.97	4.81	4.78	5.04	5.06	5.22	5.07
1870	4.67	4.80	4.62	4.67	4.57	4.75	5.11	5.30	5.21	5.18	5.21	5.35
1871	5.35	5.66	6.47	6.47	7.23	7.02	6.60	5.89	6.20	6.44	6.68	6.07
1872	6.24	6.37	6.44	6.37	6.21	6.21	6.21	6.50	6.53	6.40	6.72	6.92
1873	6.83	6.39	6.87	7.46	7.83	7.96	8.10	7.86	7.71	8.27	7.88	8.02
1874	8.01	8.17	8.05	7.60	7.80	7.88	8.20	8.75	9.12	8.17	8.24	7.78
1875	8.51	8.73	8.86	9.62	9.48	9.75	9.51	9.24	9.61	10.01	9.39	11.37
1876	11.33	10.56	8.78	8.74	9.83	9.60	9.68	9.49	10.64	10.08	8.70	8.28
1877	7.67	7.27	7.17	6.99	7.39	7.25	7.62	7.59	7.35	8.01	8.61	8.63
1878	8.25	8.40	8.29	7.95	7.42	7.76	7.79	8.14	8.11	7.53	6.90	7.41
1879	7.64	7.41	7.37	7.49	7.63	8.10	8.04	8.29	8.85	8.89	9.75	9.70
1880	9.9	10.2	10.5	11.3	11.5	11.1	11.2	10.6	10.6	11.3	11.0	11.8
1881	12.2	12.4	13.4	13.5	14.3	15.2	16.1	16.4	16.5	16.6	16.7	16.7
1882	16.9	16.7	16.7	16.3	16.4	16.5	15.9	16.5	16.3	17.0	16.9	17.3
1883	17.3	17.5	17.9	18.4	18.8	18.8	18.6	19.0	17.7	18.1	18.6	18.4
1884	17.6	17.6	16.9	17.0	16.6	15.9	15.5	15.1	15.2	14.7	14.1	14.0
1885	14.1	14.3	14.6	15.3	15.1	15.8	16.4	16.9	17.3	17.1	16.5	17.1
1886	15.0	15.7	15.4	16.2	16.3	17.4	17.6	18.1	19.1	19.8	20.5	21.0
1887	21.7	22.4	24.2	24.1	25.8	25.5	24.3	23.6	23.6	22.6	21.5	22.1
1888	22.1	22.1	22.1	21.7	20.8	20.6	21.1	21.1	21.4	21.5	21.5	21.7
1889	21.4	22.6	23.1	24.1	24.7	25.3	25.3	25.3	25.4	25.7	26.5	27.2
1890	27.9	28.6	28.4	28.6	29.9	29.9	30.1	29.8	29.3	28.4	27.5	27.3
1891	27.9	29.1	28.6	28.4	28.1	28.2	28.4	28.7	29.1	30.2	30.5	30.3
1892	31.0	30.2	31.6	31.5	31.1	31.4	30.2	31.6	30.2	29.3	29.3	29.8
1893	29.6	29.4	28.2	27.8	27.3	27.3	27.1	26.8	26.8	25.2	24.8	23.4
1894	23.2	24.1	24.8	25.6	26.6	27.1	26.4	26.9	27.8	27.0	27.7	27.5
1895	28.3	29.1	29.5	29.6	29.1	29.4	29.7	29.6	30.4	30.2	29.8	30.0
1896	29.8	29.6	28.8	27.9	26.9	26.4	26.3	26.1	25.7	24.9	25.8	25.6
1897	25.5	25.1	25.4	26.4	26.8	27.5	27.5	27.9	28.3	28.6	28.4	28.4
1898	28.5	28.0	27.5	26.8	26.5	26.2	26.2	27.1	27.4	27.9	28.6	29.3
1899	30.2	31.2	31.7	32.6	33.5	33.2	34.4	34.4	35.2	36.3	36.0	36.6
1900	37.0	36.8	36.2	36.3	36.8	37.1	37.6	36.8	38.1	38.8	40.2	40.4
1901	40.9	41.5	43.5	44.8	45.5	46.6	47.9	48.5	48.7	48.9	48.5	48.1
1902	48.4	48.5	48.1	48.1	48.7	49.3	48.7	50.3	52.5	52.1	52.0	51.8
1903	52.5	51.4	56.8	55.8	54.8	54.2	56.0	56.8	56.6	56.6	56.2	56.2
1904	55.8	55.4	56.8	56.6	54.7	55.0	55.0	56.3	56.6	57.4	58.3	60.3
1905	61.2	61.7	61.0	61.1	61.9	63.4	63.5	64.7	65.9	66.7	67.0	66.2
1906	66.7	68.0	68.3	67.9	68.8	69.4	69.7	69.8	69.8	69.3	69.2	69.7
1907	69.9	69.6	68.7	69.2	68.2	65.8	64.5	62.0	61.1	58.5	58.5	56.6
1908	54.6	53.8	53.5	54.7	55.4	55.6	57.6	59.7	62.0	63.4	61.1	63.6
1909	65.4	67.7	67.8	67.7	67.5	68.3	68.7	68.6	68.6	67.8	67.9	68.2
1910	68.5	66.7	66.5	66.3	66.0	65.2	64.0	64.4	64.3	64.3	64.2	64.7
1911	65.4	64.9	65.1	65.5	66.0	65.6	66.2	65.7	65.9	65.9	66.0	65.9
1912	66.4	67.0	65.8	66.6	67.4	68.4	66.6	70.2	71.5	74.1	74.8	75.2
1913	75.8	74.9	74.5	74.6	75.4	75.9	76.2	74.5	73.9	72.4	72.8	73.4
1914	73.9	73.4	72.4	71.0	69.5	69.4	67.9	66.7	65.9	65.5	65.4	66.0
1915	64.8	64.5	65.7	67.7	69.1	71.3	75.1	77.7	78.6	80.9	81.2	81.1
1916	82.2	81.6	81.5	83.2	84.9	85.2	84.9	87.1	88.3	89.2	88.4	88.3
1917	87.5	88.8	87.7	87.4	85.4	84.9	82.3	79.8	76.8	74.0	71.7	70.0
1918	67.7	65.6	64.4	61.0	59.5	57.1	57.2	58.2	59.1	62.6	64.7	68.8
1919	73.3	76.8	82.3	87.2	93.1	98.5	106.4	112.0	117.4	121.0	123.1	124.6
1920	125.0	124.9	123.6	121.9	120.4	119.2	115.0	111.3	107.6	104.4	101.6	100.0
1921	98.1	95.0	94.9	94.3	93.4	92.5	92.2	93.1	94.1	94.1	93.2	95.7
1922	95.1	98.0	97.9	97.3	98.7	99.0	101.1	102.1	98.5	100.0	101.5	103.4
1923	102.2	102.3	102.6	101.8	100.0	100.3	100.6	101.1	101.3	100.2	100.1	98.1
1924	96.0	94.8	93.5	93.7	93.4	92.6	92.1	92.4	92.4	92.4	93.9	95.1
1925	94.8	96.6	98.1	100.1	100.1	100.6	101.8	102.2	101.5	101.4	101.3	101.5
1926	101.1	100.8	100.1	100.1	99.8	100.0	99.3	99.2	99.3	100.2	101.0	101.1

TABLE 40 (concl.)

	JAN.	FEB.	MAR.	APR.	MAY	JUNE	JULY	AUG.	SEPT.	OCT.	NOV.	DEC.
1927	102.0	101.0	101.5	102.0	103.4	103.3	103.0	103.0	103.3	103.7	104.6	106.7
1928	107.0	106.7	108.0	107.2	109.0	109.2	109.8	110.4	110.0	109.6	109.5	109.6
1929	109.1	109.2	111.4	112.3	112.9	112.6	109.4	107.5	106.3	105.3	104.9	102.8
1930	102.3	101.4	99.0	98.1	98.1	97.4	97.8	97.8	96.7	97.2	97.8	96.6
1931	95.0	93.5	92.6	91.1	90.3	89.8	89.5	89.4	89.9	89.7	89.4	89.3
1932	90.7	90.5	90.7	90.7	90.5	89.5	87.4	87.6	87.3	85.2	84.9	85.8
1933	85.3	84.9	83.8	83.3	82.3	81.2	80.4	78.5	77.6	79.3	77.4	76.2
1934	74.6	73.4	71.9	70.7	71.1	70.5	69.2	69.8	71.2	71.0	71.4	71.7
1935	71.3	73.3	73.4	73.0	73.4	74.7	73.1	70.3	71.1	72.3	71.8	71.6
1936	72.9	73.2	73.0	71.9	71.2	70.5	72.1	72.2	72.1	72.3	72.3	72.2
1937	71.9	71.4	71.4	70.9	70.4	70.0	69.1	67.6	66.3	67.1	65.4	63.1
1938	62.2	62.6	62.1	60.4	60.2	59.5	59.4	59.0	59.9	59.1	60.2	61.6
1939	62.7	62.5	61.0	61.4	60.3	60.3	60.7	60.0	61.0	60.9	62.2	61.4
1940	61.1	61.0	60.8	61.0	60.0	58.6	58.1	57.4	55.9	55.6	55.0	56.0
1941	56.3	56.6	56.0	55.1	54.6	53.9	52.5	50.3	49.2	47.3	46.2	44.3
1942	42.5	40.5	39.1	37.8	37.0	34.8	33.1	32.1	31.0	30.8	29.9	29.3
1943	29.6	30.0	30.4	31.1	31.5	32.1	32.7					

the one ending with December 1925, the other beginning with January 1924 (Table 38 and Chart 25)—because the inclusion of New York data not only swelled the aggregates to a very much higher level but seemed to make some difference in the cyclical behavior of the figures.[12]

Inasmuch as the monthly aggregate index was designed to be a means of exploring the relation between

Sections spliced	Period used to obtain splicing ratio	Splicing ratio
Sections 9 and 10 were not spliced		
11/10	1925	1.1507252
11/12	1932	1.0272145
12/13	1936	1.1003406
13/14	1939	1.0074579

In general, of two overlapping sections the one containing the larger number of incorporations was used in the index as far as it was available. When the 1916–19 and 1918–25 sections were spliced on the basis of the 1919 ratio, the first section, being the more comprehensive, should have been used through 1919 and the second from January 1920 on. Had the general rule been adhered to, however, January 1920 would have become the peak of the cycle in the spliced index, whereas December 1919 is the peak of the actual numbers (seasonally adjusted) in the 1918–25 section. Since this is the only section from which the peak can be dated precisely (December 1919 is the highest point reached by the 1916–19 section, but since the section ends at that date the peak cannot actually be dated from that section), it is desirable to make the spliced index consistent with it. Comparison of the annual splicing ratio for 1919 with ratios for the individual months in 1919 indicated that the annual ratio represents the relation between the two sections adequately, and that a ratio based on December 1919 alone (which, of course, would effect the required adjustment and make December 1919 the peak) would not be representative. Hence the less comprehensive (1918–25) section was used back to July 1919 for the purposes of the spliced index.

[12] The monthly average of the original data for 1925, on which the first part of the index is based, is 1,033; the comparable figure for the second part is 3,557.

incorporations and business cycles, the reader should note that the cyclical turning points in it are the same as those dated from the more comprehensive of the overlapping sections in actual incorporations—with one exception. February 1900 is a trough in total incorporations, while in the index February and March are identical lows; under the rules used in cyclical work by the National Bureau of Economic Research, March was chosen as the trough for the index.

b) *Monthly median index*

Like the aggregate index, the median index consists of overlapping sections representing the number of incorporations in varying groups of states (Table 39). The overlap here, however, was only one month. To reduce the labor of calculation no state was taken into or dropped from the index except at the beginning or end of a calendar year. This meant that the series were spliced at July, because the index was constructed from twelve-month moving averages of monthly figures, entered at the seventh month. These moving averages were developed in connection with the exploratory investigations. Since the index begins with January 1860 and is built upon these moving averages, the basic incorporation data for the last half of 1859 were used in calculating the moving averages from which the index for the early months of 1860 was made. The moving averages for each state were put into relatives based in turn on the first month of each section. The simple median of the relatives of each month was determined, and the sections were chained together on January 1860 as base. The base was then shifted to the arithmetic mean of the figures for 1925 (Table 40 and Chart 25).

Cyclical Analysis

The first step in the study of the relation between cyclical movements in business incorporations and turning points in business was to select the peaks and troughs in total incorporations.[13] Since choice is a matter of judgment, the results may easily be questioned. It is believed, however, that in general the dates selected as peaks and troughs are satisfactory (Table 41). The leads and lags of the peaks and troughs in

'reference dates'.[14] Twenty-two cycles in total incorporations were marked out for 1861–1939. On the average, as shown in Table 41, a peak in them leads a peak in business by 2.5 months (average deviation, 4.6 months), and their trough leads a trough in business by 3.6 months (average deviation, 6.0 months). Moreover, in relatively few instances does a turn in incorporations lag behind a turn in business, and exceptions occur at peaks more frequently than at troughs.[15]

TABLE 41
Timing of Cycles in Total Incorporations

| | DATES OF SPECIFIC CYCLES | | | LEAD (−) OR LAG (+) AT REFERENCE | | | |
| | | | | Peak | | Trough | |
	Trough	Peak	Trough	No. of months	Reference date	No. of months	Reference date
			7/1861			+1	6/1861
1	7/1861	2/1865	5/1870	−2	4/1865	−7*	12/1870
			4/1870			−8	12/1870
2	4/1870	2/1872	11/1873				
3	11/1873	9/1875	10/1876				
4	10/1876	10/1877	9/1878			−6*	3/1879
			9/1878			−6	3/1879
5	9/1878	6/1883	11/1884	+15	3/1882	−6	5/1885
6	11/1884	4/1887	12/1887	+1	3/1887	−4*	4/1888
			12/1887			−4	4/1888
7	12/1887	7/1890	3/1891	0	7/1890	−2	5/1891
8	3/1891	8/1892	10/1893	−5	1/1893	−8	6/1894
9	10/1893	10/1895	9/1896	−2	12/1895	−9*	6/1897
			9/1896			−9	6/1897
10	9/1896	9/1897	5/1898				
11	5/1898	7/1899	2/1900	+1	6/1899	−10	12/1900
12	2/1900	5/1901	9/1901				
13	9/1901	2/1903	4/1904	+5	9/1902	−4*	8/1904
			4/1904			−4	8/1904
14	4/1904	1/1907	12/1907	−4	5/1907	−6	6/1908
15	12/1907	11/1909	7/1910	−2	1/1910	−18	1/1912
16	7/1910	7/1912	12/1914	−6	1/1913	0	12/1914
17	12/1914	1/1917	11/1918	−19	8/1918	−5	4/1919
			9/1918			−7*	4/1919
18	9/1918	12/1919	1/1921	−1	1/1920	−8	9/1921
19	1/1921	4/1923	8/1924	−1	5/1923	+1*	7/1924
			6/1924			−1	7/1924
20	6/1924	10/1925	12/1926	−12	10/1926	−12	12/1927
21	12/1926	1/1929	12/1934	−5	6/1929	+21*	3/1933
			12/1934			+21	3/1933
22	12/1934	12/1936	9/1939	−5	5/1937	+16	5/1938
	9/1939	4/1940					
Average, 22 cycles, 1861–1939				−2.5		−3.6	
Average deviation				4.6		6.0	

* Excluded from the averages.
No peaks or troughs of incorporations were selected for comparison with the following reference dates: 10/1860(peak), 12/1867(trough), 6/1869(peak), and 10/1873(peak).

incorporations were determined with respect to the National Bureau's turning points in business, called

TABLE 42
Timing of Cycles in the Monthly Median Index of Incorporations

| | DATES OF SPECIFIC CYCLES | | | LEAD (−) OR LAG (+) AT REFERENCE | | | |
| | | | | Peak | | Trough | |
	Trough	Peak	Trough	No. of months	Reference date	No. of months	Reference date
			11/1861			+5	6/1861
1	11/1861	3/1863	6/1863				
2	6/1863	7/1865	1/1867	+3	4/1865	−11	12/1867
3	1/1867	12/1867	5/1870	−18	6/1869	−7	12/1870
4	5/1870	5/1871	8/1871				
5	8/1871	12/1875	4/1877	+26	10/1873		
6	4/1877	12/1877	11/1878			−4	3/1879
7	11/1878	1/1882	7/1882	−2	3/1882		
8	7/1882	8/1883	12/1884			−5	5/1885
9	12/1884	5/1887	6/1888	+2	3/1887	+2	4/1888
10	6/1888	7/1890	12/1890	0	7/1890	−5	5/1891
11	12/1890	3/1892	1/1894	−10	1/1893	−5	6/1894
12	1/1894	9/1895	2/1897	−3	12/1895	−4	6/1897
13	2/1897	10/1897	7/1898				
14	7/1898	8/1903	5/1904	+11	9/1902	−3	8/1904
15	5/1904	1/1907	3/1908	−4	5/1907	−3	6/1908
16	3/1908	7/1909	7/1910	−6	1/1910	−18	1/1912
17	7/1910	7/1913	2/1915	+6	1/1913	+2	12/1914
18	2/1915	10/1916	6/1918	−22	8/1918	−10	4/1919
19	6/1918	1/1920	7/1921	0	1/1920	−2	9/1921
20	7/1921	12/1922	7/1924	−5	5/1923	0	7/1924
21	7/1924	8/1925	8/1926	−14	10/1926	−16	12/1927
22	8/1926	5/1929	12/1931	−1	6/1929		
23	12/1931	4/1932	7/1934			+16	3/1933
24	7/1934	6/1935	8/1938	−23	5/1937	+3	5/1938
	8/1938	1/1939					
Average, 24 cycles, 1861–1938				−3.3		−3.4	
Average deviation				8.4		5.3	

No peaks or troughs of incorporations were selected for comparison with the following reference dates: 10/1860(peak), 6/1899(peak), and 12/1900(trough).

The monthly median index was similarly analyzed although it was believed to be inferior to the number of actual incorporations for the purpose of relating turning points in incorporations and in business (Table 42). After the middle 'seventies, the two measurements of cyclical movements resemble each other closely.

The pattern of the cycles of a series (cycles that

[13] Total incorporations (App. 6) were used here instead of the aggregate index derived from them. As they were spliced only when a cycle had to be completed, dates overlap in Table 41, and in the analysis there are 9 sections (separated by spaces in Table 41) instead of the original 14.

[14] Burns and Mitchell, p. 78.

[15] In studying the relation between incorporations and business cycles, some investigators may deem it desirable to eliminate from consideration the August 1918 peak in business and the April 1919 trough because wartime controls vitiated the normal relation.

CHAPTER 9

TABLE 43
Specific-Cycle Patterns in Total Incorporations

	DATES OF SPECIFIC CYCLES			AVERAGES OF SPECIFIC-CYCLE RELATIVES AT NINE STAGES OF THE CYCLES								
				I	II	III	IV	V	VI	VII	VIII	IX
				Three months centered on initial trough	Expansion			Three months centered on peak	Contraction			Three months centered on terminal trough
	Trough	Peak	Trough		First third	Middle third	Last third		First third	Middle third	Last third	
1	7/1861	2/1865	5/1870	9.7	17.3	33.1	99.9	193.3	147.9	123.4	125.3	106.3
2	4/1870	2/1872	11/1873	77.2	94.5	97.7	98.2	105.4	105.1	105.1	98.2	76.0
3	11/1873	9/1875	10/1876	77.6	88.4	105.1	110.6	123.5	102.7	104.5	82.5	71.1
4	10/1876	10/1877	9/1878	90.8	91.7	97.5	104.6	119.3	117.0	96.2	93.8	94.5
5	9/1878	6/1883	11/1884	39.0	57.8	102.5	123.8	133.0	129.6	124.1	103.4	87.6
6	11/1884	4/1887	12/1887	64.9	80.1	87.9	108.3	139.7	135.7	118.9	132.8	120.2
7	12/1887	7/1890	3/1891	82.1	81.9	96.9	107.6	120.1	114.6	117.8	116.2	109.8
8	3/1891	8/1892	10/1893	90.6	94.9	107.0	104.8	107.6	103.5	105.3	79.3	68.6
9	10/1893	10/1895	9/1896	96.0	92.1	101.4	103.9	117.7	111.2	103.1	94.7	78.6
10	9/1896	9/1897	5/1898	76.5	86.8	96.9	97.0	113.3	113.1	113.1	104.7	94.1
11	5/1898	7/1899	2/1900	74.1	72.7	87.6	113.9	124.7	120.6	118.5	111.7	109.2
12	2/1900	5/1901	9/1901	81.3	84.0	88.6	105.9	129.6	120.5	120.7	124.1	112.6
13	9/1901	2/1903	4/1904	92.1	92.1	98.6	105.8	108.1	103.1	100.8	100.7	96.0
14	4/1904	1/1907	12/1907	78.1	90.0	99.2	107.1	114.8	111.4	110.4	90.3	76.6
15	12/1907	11/1909	7/1910	77.6	85.0	101.5	108.6	111.5	108.1	103.9	102.8	98.2
16	7/1910	7/1912	12/1914	94.5	98.3	98.6	101.0	107.4	108.5	100.8	92.5	84.6
17	12/1914	1/1917	11/1918	82.5	94.0	107.0	115.1	121.3	112.9	93.1	76.0	66.0
18	9/1918	12/1919	1/1921	45.4	56.4	90.7	120.0	127.6	125.4	112.5	102.3	85.0
19	1/1921	4/1923	8/1924	92.2	96.0	101.0	108.1	108.6	100.8	99.0	90.8	91.4
20	6/1924	10/1925	12/1926	80.5	82.2	96.3	107.9	111.8	106.7	105.0	103.2	102.6
21	12/1926	1/1929	12/1934	101.3	104.5	108.5	114.2	117.4	107.5	99.3	83.6	72.3
22	12/1934	12/1936	9/1939	102.8	106.4	109.2	107.5	109.9	101.8	90.5	90.4	87.7
	9/1939	4/1940		93.2*	98.1*	98.4*	96.9*	102.1*				
Average, 22 cycles, 1861–1939				77.6	84.0	96.0	107.9	121.2	114.0	107.5	100.0	90.6
Average deviation				14.2	12.6	8.4	4.7	11.2	9.0	8.3	11.6	12.6

* Computed on the base of the inverted cycle December 1936–April 1940. Excluded from the averages.

in National Bureau terminology are called 'specific cycles') can be determined neatly by a technique developed by Arthur F. Burns and Wesley C. Mitchell.[16] First, an average monthly value, called the cycle base

CHART 26
Average Cyclical Patterns of Monthly Aggregate Incorporations

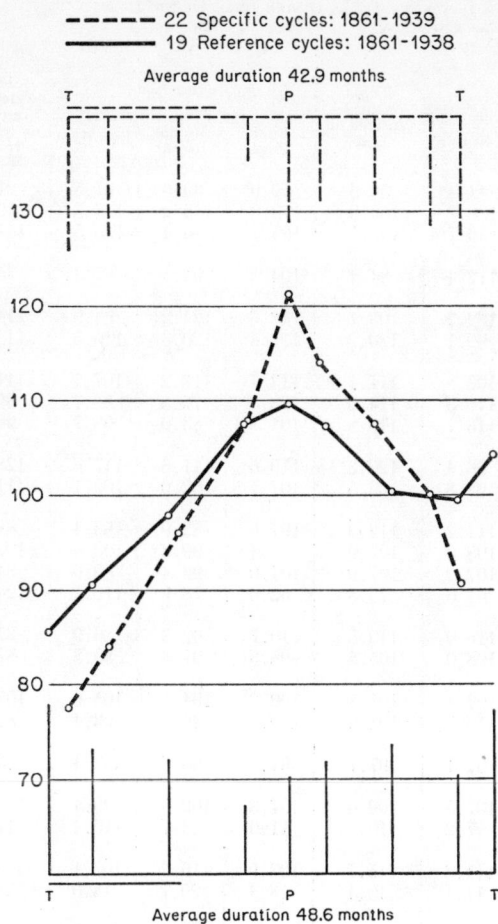

- - - - 22 Specific cycles: 1861-1939
——— 19 Reference cycles: 1861-1938

Average duration 42.9 months

Average duration 48.6 months

Data from Tables 43 and 44.
For method of construction, see Burns and Mitchell, *op. cit.*, pp. 170 ff.

number, for each cycle measured from trough to trough is computed. Each cycle is then divided into nine segments, and the average value for each segment is calculated and expressed as a relative of the average value for the whole cycle.[17] Finally, to procure a composite

[16] *Op. cit.*, pp. 144 ff.

[17] Three of the nine segments—those centering on the initial trough, the peak, and the terminal trough—are indicated with sufficient clarity in Table 43. For those unfamiliar with the Burns-Mitchell technique, it should be added that the expansion phase of a cycle begins with the month after the initial trough and ends with the month before the cyclical peak. This phase is subdivided into three parts as nearly equal as may be without using fractions of a month. The contraction phase of

specific-cycle pattern, an average standing of the relatives for each of the nine segments is calculated. This technique was applied to aggregate incorporations (Table 43 and Chart 26). The typical cycle of incorporations is simple: it rises steadily to a peak, then recedes rather steadily for a shorter period.

The reference-cycle pattern, likewise traced on Chart 26, is derived similarly. The essential difference is that the dates for the troughs and the peaks as well as periods of intervening expansions and contractions are determined by the reference dates instead of by the turning points of the specific cycles. Table 44 gives for each phase of each cycle the relative standing of aggregate incorporations. It gives also average standings for the nineteen reference cycles as a whole, as well as average standings for the reference cycles in three component periods: 1861–88, 1888–1912, 1912–38. The calculations for these three component periods suggest that the peak of incorporations has shifted somewhat. In the average pattern for 1861–88 it occurred during the first third of the contraction phase of the reference cycle. In 1888–1912 it coincided with the reference-cycle peak. By 1912–38 it had shifted back to the middle third of the reference-cycle expansion. The evidence that the trough has shifted is less strong. In the earliest of the three periods the trough in incorporations occurs in the last third of the reference-cycle contraction. In the last two periods it occurs in the middle third of the reference-cycle contraction.

Chart 26 suggests that the reference-cycle analysis yields results somewhat at variance with Table 41. The former shows no lead at the peak, whereas the latter shows a lead of two and a half months. The explanation is found in the coarse time unit employed in the reference-cycle pattern. Since the average duration of a third of an expansion phase is 8.3 months, a lead of merely two and a half months can easily be obliterated in the reference-cycle pattern. This is what happens at the peak of the pattern. At the trough no such difficulty arises.

The Burns-Mitchell measures of conformity indicate also that, when the tendency of incorporations to lead turns in business is allowed for, total incorporations move preponderantly in the same direction as business cycles.[18] The indexes of conformity, which have a theoretical range from −100 to +100, are: to reference expansions, +68; to reference contractions, +60; to full business cycles, +84.

The evidence, in summary and in detail, indicates a

the cycle—the interval beginning with the month after the peak and ending with the month before the terminal trough—is similarly divided into thirds. Thus, each specific cycle is divided into nine segments.

[18] *Op. cit.*, pp. 176 ff.

high degree of correlation between movements in incorporations and business generally. Since incorporations belong to the preparatory stage of enterprise, troughs in incorporations on the average lead troughs in business. Peaks in incorporations also lead peaks in business, but by a smaller average interval and less regularly, perhaps because, even in the face of slackening business conditions, many promoting groups whose organizational work is at an advanced stage will complete the legal procedures and incorporate their enterprises. Their only additional costs would probably be state incorporation fees. Once they had charters, the organizers would be ready to float securities and begin operations if the downturn in business proved temporary. One might almost have been led to predict that peaks in incorporations would follow peaks in business. Promoters, however, seem to sense the approach of a recession, or at least grow wary, and curtail incorporating activities while prosperity still has a high degree of momentum. Their bearishness doubtless contributes toward bringing on a recession. On the other hand, their preparations for a revival precede an upturn and most certainly contribute to the spirit of optimism that characterizes expansions.

TABLE 44
Reference-Cycle Patterns in Total Incorporations

	DATES OF REFERENCE CYCLES			CYCLE BASE NUMBER	AVERAGES OF REFERENCE-CYCLE RELATIVES AT NINE STAGES OF THE CYCLES								
					I	II	III	IV	V	VI	VII	VIII	IX
						Expansion				Contraction			
	Trough	Peak	Trough		Three months centered on initial trough	First third	Middle third	Last third	Three months centered on peak	First third	Middle third	Last third	Three months centered on terminal trough
		10/1860	6/1861	15.9[a]				41.4[b]	54.6[b]	59.9[b]	39.9[b]	31.5[b]	21.0[b]
1	6/1861	4/1865	12/1867	27.9	12.0	17.9	39.9	128.7	159.0	170.0	156.2	136.3	149.5
2	12/1867	6/1869	12/1870	39.1	106.5	99.7	104.3	96.7	105.7	103.1	86.4	106.5	141.5
3	12/1870	10/1873	3/1879	54.1	132.5	105.2	112.1	112.4	84.4	104.5	94.5	87.3	75.2
4	3/1879	3/1882	5/1885	118	36.4	57.5	81.5	122.2	109.1	118.5	124.2	94.9	114.2
5	5/1885	3/1887	4/1888	165	81.8	83.8	86.4	99.1	120.2	123.4	120.3	110.5	113.2
6	4/1888	7/1890	5/1891	282	78.9	83.0	99.7	103.8	117.1	113.7	113.2	107.1	111.7
7	5/1891	1/1893	6/1894	323	97.7	104.4	112.0	110.3	114.6	103.3	76.8	88.7	89.3
8	6/1894	12/1895	6/1897	302	95.4	101.2	97.3	113.7	110.8	101.8	83.0	98.7	96.5
9	6/1897	6/1899	12/1900	514	73.8	87.9	74.6	96.4	120.3	119.6	111.6	117.0	128.5
10	12/1900	9/1902	8/1904	837	78.9	95.4	93.1	98.8	106.5	107.7	102.9	100.1	111.2
11	8/1904	5/1907	6/1908	1093	91.4	93.7	104.7	111.2	112.9	107.6	82.9	83.4	88.0
12	6/1908	1/1910	1/1912	1128	85.2	92.7	105.0	108.0	104.9	97.4	99.3	100.0	102.0
13	1/1912	1/1913	12/1914	1143	100.7	100.4	106.6	107.2	107.9	104.0	99.4	89.6	84.0
14	12/1914	8/1918	4/1919	1161	82.6	99.5	115.1	94.0	75.8	62.6	78.9	110.1	124.9
15	4/1919	1/1920	9/1921	1098	80.0	98.8	109.2	116.0	119.5	110.7	92.3	86.9	87.3
16	9/1921	5/1923	7/1924	998	96.0	94.7	106.4	108.0	105.5	98.8	97.8	89.8	87.0
17	7/1924	10/1926	12/1927	3506	76.6	88.1	106.2	102.1	101.8	100.2	104.1	105.6	107.1
18	12/1927	6/1929	3/1933	3644	103.0	107.3	107.8	113.0	108.9	100.1	96.1	93.4	85.1
19	3/1933	5/1937	5/1938	2355	116.6	109.9	98.8	101.1	97.7	91.6	86.5	82.4	83.1
Average, 19 cycles, 1861–1938					85.6	90.6	97.9	107.5	109.6	107.3	100.3	99.4	104.2
Average deviation					17.9	13.2	12.1	7.2	10.3	11.9	13.7	10.4	17.3
Average, 5 cycles, 1861–1888					73.8	72.8	84.8	111.8	115.7	123.9	116.3	107.1	118.7
Average deviation					39.7	28.1	19.3	11.1	19.1	18.4	20.7	13.0	21.4
Average, 7 cycles, 1888–1912					85.9	94.0	98.1	106.0	112.4	107.3	95.7	99.3	103.9
Average deviation					7.7	5.4	8.3	5.5	4.3	5.5	12.7	7.7	11.4
Average, 7 cycles, 1912–1938					93.6	99.8	107.2	105.9	102.4	95.4	93.6	94.0	94.1
Average deviation					11.9	5.2	3.0	5.9	9.2	10.5	6.6	7.9	12.5

[a] Inverted cycle 1860–1865.
[b] Computed on the base of the inverted cycle 1860–1865. Excluded from the averages.

APPENDIX 1

Private Nonbusiness Incorporations

Arizona, 1912–1924
Connecticut, 1837–70, 1880–97, 1905–32
Delaware, 1916–1943
Ohio, 1803–51, 1872–1936

This Appendix includes some data on nonbusiness incorporations that may be used in exploring the relation between business cycles and the chartering of nonbusiness enterprises. The following table contains by no means all series that could be compiled from public documents.

	1803	1804	1805	1806	1807	1808	1809	1810	1811	1812	1813	1814	1815	1816	1817	1818	1819	1820	1821	1822	1823	1824	1825	1826	1827	1828	1829	1830	1831	1832	1833	1834	1835	1836	1837	1838	1839	1840	1841	1842	1843
Arizona[a]																																									
Connecticut[b]																																			1	2	0	0	0	2	4
Delaware[c]																																									
Ohio[d]	1	1	2	0	5	5	1	6	5	4	5	7	7	4	0	2	5	1	1	4	1	9	7	12	19	30	40	34	49	57	60	87	94	106	102	99	127	83	90	108	131

	1844	1845	1846	1847	1848	1849	1850	1851	1852	1853	1854	1855	1856	1857	1858	1859	1860	1861	1862	1863	1864	1865	1866	1867	1868	1869	1870	1871	1872	1873	1874	1875	1876	1877	1878	1879	1880	1881	1882
Arizona[a]																																							
Connecticut[b]	1	2	2	2	4	9	10	11	9	17	12	8		10	5	6	8	11	6	6	7	11	4	14	14	13	17	16									1*	6	20
Delaware[c]																																							
Ohio[d]	129	130	17	10	19	31	68	96																					11	23	30	29	60	77	64	67	169	244	320

	1883	1884	1885	1886	1887	1888	1889	1890	1891	1892	1893	1894	1895	1896	1897	1898	1899	1900	1901	1902	1903	1904	1905	1906	1907	1908	1909	1910	1911	1912
Arizona[a]																														27*
Connecticut[b]	20	18	18	19	26	25	53	56	45	59	65	70	86	53	68*								59*	137	159	131	187	180	198	188
Delaware[c]																														
Ohio[d]	259	282	296	323	427	398	446	485	453	485	437	514	454	425	433	356	400	450	399	439	485	501	533	558	542	490	551	653	617	590

	1913	1914	1915	1916	1917	1918	1919	1920	1921	1922	1923	1924	1925	1926	1927	1928	1929	1930	1931	1932	1933	1934	1935	1936	1937	1938	1939	1940	1941	1942	1943
Arizona[a]	17	14	14	8	5	12	18	23	38	19	23	7*																			
Connecticut[b]	168	189	185	173	175	117	218	226	203	192	187	208	222	196	186	175	210	238	216	198											
Delaware[c]				28	27	18	46	33	40	45	40	58	54	44	56	67	60	65	71	71	122	197	124	85	95	64	63	81	81	83	82
Ohio[d]	514	704	643	557	474	374	539	621	673	634	541	622	625	575	583	645	546	581	513	423	553	635	593	605							

* Not a full year.

[a] The sources of the raw data are those set forth in full in the Arizona section of Appendix 3. The nonbusiness concerns were selected entirely on the basis of name. Note 3 in Chapter 1 gives the types of corporation treated as nonbusiness enterprises.

[b] The volumes cited in the two Connecticut sections of Appendix 3 contain the raw data for the nonbusiness figures given here. In those volumes the lists of nonbusiness incorporations appear beside or immediately following the lists of business incorporations. The comments in the Connecticut sections of Appendix 3 will make clear the nature of the nonbusiness series given here.

[c] Nonbusiness incorporations were tallied from the sources indicated in the Delaware section of Appendix 3 for 1916–43. The special comments there will make clear their nature.

[d] The sources of the raw data are those given in the Ohio sections of Appendix 3. The special comments there will make clear the nature of this series.

Appendix 2

Maryland Business Incorporations

Classified According to

Authorized Capital Stock

COMPANIES CHARTERED WITH CAPITAL STOCK IN 1926, 1927, AND 1928 THAT WERE ON THE FEBRUARY 28, 1932 MARYLAND FORFEITURE LIST

AUTHORIZED CAPITAL STOCK	1926		1927		1928	
	No.	% of Total	No.	% of Total	No.	% of Total
Under $25,000	17	32.7	23	28.4	125	32.9
$25,000– 50,000	3	5.8	7	8.6	43	11.3
$50,000– 100,000	10	19.2	18	22.2	46	12.1
$100,000–1,000,000	18	34.6	29	35.8	148	38.9
$1,000,000 & over	4	7.7	4	4.9	18	4.7
All size groups	52	100.0	81	99.9	380	99.9

COMPANIES CHARTERED WITH CAPITAL STOCK IN 1927, 1928, AND 1929 THAT WERE ON THE FEBRUARY 10, 1933 MARYLAND FORFEITURE LIST

AUTHORIZED CAPITAL STOCK	1927		1928		1929	
	No.	% of Total	No.	% of Total	No.	% of Total
Under $25,000	24	34.8	35	29.9	138	33.3
$25,000– 50,000	12	17.4	18	15.4	42	10.1
$50,000– 100,000	7	10.1	19	16.2	52	12.6
$100,000–1,000,000	21	30.4	36	30.8	155	37.4
$1,000,000 & over	5	7.2	9	7.7	27	6.5
All size groups	69	99.9	117	100.0	414	99.9

COMPANIES CHARTERED WITH CAPITAL STOCK IN 1928, 1929, AND 1930 THAT WERE ON THE FEBRUARY 16, 1934 MARYLAND FORFEITURE LIST

AUTHORIZED CAPITAL STOCK	1928		1929		1930	
	No.	% of Total	No.	% of Total	No.	% of Total
Under $25,000	18	30.0	29	25.7	162	41.1
$25,000– 50,000	7	11.7	12	10.6	43	10.9
$50,000– 100,000	11	18.3	18	15.9	40	10.2
$100,000–1,000,000	16	26.7	44	38.9	135	34.3
$1,000,000 & over	8	13.3	10	8.8	14	3.6
All size groups	60	100.0	113	99.9	394	100.1

COMPANIES CHARTERED WITH CAPITAL STOCK IN 1929, 1930, AND 1931 THAT WERE ON THE FEBRUARY 1935 MARYLAND FORFEITURE LIST

AUTHORIZED CAPITAL STOCK	1929		1930		1931	
	No.	% of Total	No.	% of Total	No.	% of Total
Under $25,000	10	16.9	31	33.0	159	39.5
$25,000– 50,000	9	15.3	5	5.3	56	13.9
$50,000– 100,000	6	10.2	15	16.0	51	12.7
$100,000–1,000,000	32	54.2	41	43.6	130	32.3
$1,000,000 & over	2	3.4	2	2.1	7	1.7
All size groups	59	100.0	94	100.0	403	100.1

COMPANIES CHARTERED WITH CAPITAL STOCK IN 1930, 1931, AND 1932 THAT WERE ON THE FEBRUARY 1936 MARYLAND FORFEITURE LIST

AUTHORIZED CAPITAL STOCK	1930		1931		1932	
	No.	% of Total	No.	% of Total	No.	% of Total
Under $25,000	26	46.4	31	40.3	179	47.0
$25,000– 50,000	6	10.7	7	9.1	42	11.0
$50,000– 100,000	5	8.9	15	19.5	53	13.9
$100,000–1,000,000	17	30.4	20	26.0	99	26.0
$1,000,000 & over	2	3.6	4	5.2	8	2.1
All size groups	56	100.0	77	100.1	381	100.0

COMPANIES CHARTERED WITH CAPITAL STOCK IN 1931, 1932, AND 1933 THAT WERE ON THE FEBRUARY 1937 MARYLAND FORFEITURE LIST

AUTHORIZED CAPITAL STOCK	1931		1932		1933	
	No.	% of Total	No.	% of Total	No.	% of Total
Under $25,000	15	48.4	28	39.4	193	49.7
$25,000– 50,000	2	6.5	7	9.9	35	9.0
$50,000– 100,000	3	9.7	9	12.7	24	6.2
$100,000–1,000,000	11	35.5	26	36.6	134	34.5
$1,000,000 & over	0	.0	1	1.4	2	.5
All size groups	31	100.1	71	100.0	388	99.9

COMPANIES CHARTERED WITH CAPITAL STOCK IN 1932, 1933, AND 1934 THAT WERE ON THE FEBRUARY 1938 MARYLAND FORFEITURE LIST

AUTHORIZED CAPITAL STOCK	1932		1933		1934	
	No.	% of Total	No.	% of Total	No.	% of Total
Under $25,000	24	60.0	45	60.8	139	48.9
$25,000– 50,000	4	10.0	4	5.4	29	10.2
$50,000– 100,000	2	5.0	8	10.8	47	16.5
$100,000–1,000,000	10	25.0	15	20.3	67	23.6
$1,000,000 & over	0	.0	2	2.7	2	.7
All size groups	40	100.0	74	100.0	284	99.9

COMPANIES CHARTERED WITH CAPITAL STOCK IN 1933, 1934, AND 1935 THAT WERE ON THE FEBRUARY 1939 MARYLAND FORFEITURE LIST

AUTHORIZED CAPITAL STOCK	1933		1934		1935	
	No.	% of Total	No.	% of Total	No	% of Total
Under $25,000	27	45.8	51	59.3	156	52.9
$25,000– 50,000	7	11.9	7	8.1	27	9.2
$50,000– 100,000	10	16.9	10	11.6	31	10.5
$100,000–1,000,000	15	25.4	17	19.8	79	26.8
$1,000,000 & over	0	.0	1	1.2	2	.7
All size groups	59	100.0	86	100.0	295	100.1

COMPANIES CHARTERED WITH CAPITAL STOCK IN 1935, 1936, AND 1937 THAT WERE ON THE OCTOBER 1939 MARYLAND FORFEITURE LIST

AUTHORIZED CAPITAL STOCK	1935		1936		1937	
	No.	% of Total	No.	% of Total	No.	% of Total
Under $25,000	58	56.3	190	54.9	157	60.9
$25,000– 50,000	10	9.7	31	9.0	28	10.9
$50,000– 100,000	16	15.5	31	9.0	21	8.1
$100,000–1,000,000	19	18.4	93	26.9	52	20.2
$1,000,000 & over	0	.0	1	.3	0	.0
All size groups	103	99.9	346	100.1	258	100.1

COMPANIES CHARTERED WITH CAPITAL STOCK IN 1936, 1937, AND 1938 THAT WERE ON THE OCTOBER 1940 MARYLAND FORFEITURE LIST

AUTHORIZED CAPITAL STOCK	1936		1937		1938	
	No.	% of Total	No.	% of Total	No.	% of Total
Under $25,000	15	45.5	20	43.5	109	54.2
$25,000– 50,000	6	18.2	7	15.2	27	13.4
$50,000– 100,000	6	18.2	9	19.6	24	11.9
$100,000–1,000,000	6	18.2	9	19.6	40	19.9
$1,000,000 & over	0	.0	1	2.2	1	.5
All size groups	33	100.1	46	100.1	201	99.9

ALL MARYLAND BUSINESS INCORPORATIONS, 1928–1938

AUTHORIZED CAPITAL STOCK	1928		1929		1930		1931		1932		1933		1934		1935		1936		1937		1938	
	No.	% of Total	No.	% of Total	No.	% of Total	No.	% of Total	No.	% of Total	No.	% of Total	No.	% of Total	No.	% of Total	No.	% of Total	No.	% of Total	No.	% of Total
Under $25,000	323	30.5	337	29.5	317	35.1	331	38.0	393	44.2	498	49.2	404	49.5	397	51.5	382	50.5	387	51.7	315	49.0
$25,000– 50,000	113	10.7	110	9.6	80	8.8	103	11.8	93	10.4	80	7.9	78	9.6	71	9.2	78	10.3	66	8.8	76	11.8
$50,000– 100,000	146	13.8	138	12.1	108	11.9	129	14.8	118	13.3	95	9.4	116	14.2	92	11.9	82	10.8	77	10.3	84	13.1
$100,000–1,000,000	377	35.6	432	37.9	350	38.7	280	32.2	264	29.7	320	31.6	205	25.1	203	26.3	201	26.6	202	27.0	158	24.6
$1,000,000 & over	99	9.4	124	10.9	49	5.4	27	3.1	22	2.5	19	1.9	13	1.6	8	1.0	14	1.8	16	2.1	10	1.6
All size groups	1,058	100.0	1,141	100.0	904	99.9	870	99.9	890	100.1	1,012	100.0	816	100.1	771	99.9	757	100.0	748	99.9	643	100.1

Appendix 3

Business Incorporations

and

Their Authorized Capital Stock

Arizona, under General Laws, 1912–1924
Colorado, under General Laws, 1890–1908
Connecticut, under General Laws, 1837–1870, 1880–1932
Delaware, under General Laws, 1899–1943
Florida, under General Laws, 1901–1922
Illinois, under General Laws, 1896–1918, 1925–1943
Louisiana, under General Laws, 1937–1943
Maine, by Special Acts, 1820–1891
      under General Laws, 1870–1943
Maryland, by Special Acts, 1800–1852
      under General Laws, 1870–1939
Massachusetts, under General Laws, 1851–1921
New Jersey, by Special Acts, 1800–1875
      under General Laws, 1846–1918
New York, under Special and General Laws, 1800–1845
      under General Laws, 1901–1943
Ohio, by Special Acts, 1803–1851
      under General Laws, 1855–1936
Pennsylvania, by Special Acts, 1800–1860
      under General Laws, 1875–1921
Texas, under General Laws, 1872–1920
Virginia, under General Laws, 1903–1941

Note: If in the notes the place and date of publication are omitted, it is because they were not given in the source cited.

ARIZONA BUSINESS INCORPORATIONS UNDER GENERAL LAWS, 1912–1924

YEAR	JAN.	FEB.	MAR.	APR.	MAY	JUNE	JULY	AUG.	SEPT.	OCT.	NOV.	DEC.	TOTAL
1912		46*	146	118	90	73	80	77	76	62	66	72	
1913	66	61	69	66	54	55	65	43	54	43	50	42	668
1914	51	47	68	51	38	53	47	41	33	43	30	28	530
1915	36	33	46	52	33	50	45	43	73	85	86	74	656
1916	79	83	117	97	102	70	73	70	78	98	99	118	1,084
1917	130	93	122	108	107	77	57	49	67	64	110	45	1,029
1918	55	54	68	59	49	45	66	33	23	27	33	37	549
1919	47	49	66	70	86	45	59	53	52	79	55	56	717
1920	66	56	60	70	46	44	41	47	43	34	24	36	567
1921	49	32	30	29	28	35	18	19	29	39	25	26	359
1922	46	24	25	35	33	32	49	23	18	38	25	26	374
1923	41	25	27	38	30	20	26	22	36	34	18	21	338
1924	32	28	29	27	30	12							

* Not a full month. Arizona became a state on February 14, 1912.

1) Sources of Raw Data

First Annual Report of the Arizona Corporation Commission, State of Arizona . . . February 14, 1912 to December 1, 1913 (Phoenix), pp. 967–1020; *Second Annual Report . . . December 1, 1913 to June 30, 1914*, pp. 353–68; *Third Annual Report . . . July 1, 1914 to June 30, 1915*, pp. 568–86; *Fourth Annual Report . . . July 1, 1915 to June 30, 1916*, pp. 708–42; *Fifth Annual Report . . . June 30, 1916–June 30, 1917*, pp. 339–80; *Sixth Annual Report . . . June 30, 1917–June 30, 1918*, pp. 563–90; *Seventh Annual Report . . . July 1, 1918, to June 30, 1919* (Phoenix), pp. 443–66; *Eighth Annual Report . . . July 1, 1919, to June 30, 1920* (Phoenix), pp. 483–509; *Ninth Annual Report . . . . July 1, 1920, to June 30, 1921* (Phoenix), pp. 543–61; *Triennial Report . . . Including Tenth, Eleventh, and Twelfth Annual Reports . . . July 1, 1921, to June 30, 1924*, pp. 811–25, 830–42, and 847–62.

2) Special Comments

a) In the above mentioned sources the name of each company is listed together with the date of its incorporation. Since no capital stock figures are given and since business and nonbusiness concerns appear together, the nonbusiness were eliminated on the basis of name. No information on corporate purposes is given. (For the number of nonbusiness corporations chartered by Arizona, see Appendix 1.)

b) The series extends from the date on which Arizona became a state to June 30, 1924, when the Corporation Commission discontinued the publication of the raw data.

c) Entries such as the following—from the *Sixth Annual Report*, p. 564—were treated as incorporations and were not viewed as mere changes of name for an existing corporation: All Metal Aeroplane Company (name changed to International Air Ship Company) . . . Nov. 27, 1917. That is, the above entries were regarded as applying to companies that had been chartered on the date indicated but had changed their names before the Commission's report was published. There were not many such entries in any one report.

COLORADO BUSINESS INCORPORATIONS UNDER GENERAL LAWS, 1890–1908

YEAR	JAN.	FEB.	MAR.	APR.	MAY	JUNE	JULY	AUG.	SEPT.	OCT.	NOV.	DEC.	TOTAL
A Total Incorporations													
1890												86	
1891	70	71	67	70	65	72	59	52	61	51	49	51	738
1892	85	94	146	121	139	102	87	94	76	71	63	86	1,164
1893	95	88	92	90	78	75	53	39	49	45	54	64	822
1894	74	80	81	79	79	62	43	63	65	64	64	75	829
1895	81	58	69	73	62	61	61	71	77	98	152	301	1,164
1896	451	333	244	149	117	104	59	45	92	75	64	108	1,841
1897	87	89	103	106	73	81	79	75	83	64	63	87	990
1898	94	90	98	73	74	68	36	39	53	50	54	52	781
1899	75	73	73	84	65	64	70	78	93	80	69	88	912
1900	98	96	117	80	90	80	87	68	76	71	68	77	1,008
1901	89	88	103	67	100	78	94	69	72	87	68	68	983
1902	104	89	101	88	99	54	97	81	82	86	76	90	1,047
1903	122	101	92	86	86	79	74	80	81	70	72	64	1,007
1904	89	78	80	98	87	76	76	69	73	62	66	77	931
1905	97	89	96	80	97	73	63	68	90	76	83	78	990
1906	143	99	121	107	89	82	78	94	87	94	93	84	1,171
1907	139	106	98	99	134	94	91	98	94	92	67	81	1,193
1908	86	99	141	119	107	107	84	88	90	95	86		
B Small Incorporations													
1890												36	
1891	28	38	31	31	22	34	29	30	28	20	21	19	331
1892	36	32	46	42	31	20	24	24	25	30	19	42	371
1893	41	34	37	39	28	31	21	21	22	17	21	29	341
1894	34	40	35	33	26	24	17	28	25	28	30	40	360

YEAR	JAN.	FEB.	MAR.	APR.	MAY	JUNE	JULY	AUG.	SEPT.	OCT.	NOV.	DEC.	TOTAL
1895	31	29	30	42	20	24	27	28	24	33	20	48	356
1896	45	46	48	38	40	36	20	20	44	26	22	35	420
1897	37	25	49	46	36	40	39	31	37	32	30	40	442
1898	58	52	56	49	45	29	21	31	40	35	41	36	493
1899	43	48	41	51	36	33	34	43	39	42	32	45	487
1900	60	46	76	44	48	46	47	36	33	27	41	40	544
1901	46	48	60	39	64	34	56	28	39	44	41	37	536
1902	55	58	59	51	61	34	50	37	39	47	44	47	582
1903	66	55	54	51	49	46	45	44	42	31	43	32	558
1904	52	50	53	52	50	48	50	41	32	25	38	48	539
1905	63	56	63	53	59	39	38	36	48	39	51	50	595
1906	88	64	80	70	53	55	50	53	55	59	45	54	726
1907	95	58	68	62	81	61	55	63	64	57	44	49	757
1908	61	67	110	85	60	69	58	52	65	60	51		

C Medium Incorporations

YEAR	JAN.	FEB.	MAR.	APR.	MAY	JUNE	JULY	AUG.	SEPT.	OCT.	NOV.	DEC.	TOTAL
1890												42	
1891	35	28	32	32	33	30	23	18	24	22	25	20	322
1892	39	42	62	43	65	53	42	46	35	34	35	28	524
1893	45	43	36	31	36	27	22	16	22	24	28	24	354
1894	34	33	25	31	37	27	20	26	32	27	26	27	345
1895	37	24	30	28	29	32	32	30	31	33	43	48	397
1896	63	66	64	54	43	37	22	13	35	29	23	35	484
1897	32	37	31	39	26	30	27	28	36	27	24	36	373
1898	24	25	34	20	21	30	11	7	10	13	12	12	219
1899	26	21	25	25	24	17	25	24	25	15	19	21	267
1900	26	30	27	23	19	26	25	15	28	28	17	25	289
1901	20	25	31	19	22	31	23	31	23	31	15	24	295
1902	37	23	29	29	27	12	32	28	29	23	20	30	319
1903	39	26	24	23	23	23	19	24	22	24	24	21	292
1904	28	16	24	31	27	19	21	18	28	30	16	19	277
1905	19	23	25	21	26	27	20	27	35	27	24	17	291
1906	38	28	30	25	31	19	22	26	24	25	35	25	328
1907	34	30	21	24	42	23	31	28	23	24	16	26	322
1908	19	25	27	26	39	28	16	32	24	28	27		

D Large Incorporations

YEAR	JAN.	FEB.	MAR.	APR.	MAY	JUNE	JULY	AUG.	SEPT.	OCT.	NOV.	DEC.	TOTAL
1890												8	
1891	7	5	4	7	10	8	7	4	9	9	3	12	85
1892	10	20	38	36	43	29	21	24	16	7	9	16	269
1893	9	11	19	20	14	17	10	2	5	4	5	11	127
1894	6	7	21	15	16	11	6	9	8	9	8	8	124
1895	13	5	9	3	13	5	2	13	22	32	89	205	411
1896	343	221	132	57	34	31	17	12	13	20	19	38	937
1897	18	27	23	21	11	11	13	16	10	5	9	11	175
1898	12	13	8	4	8	9	4	1	3	2	1	4	69
1899	6	4	7	8	5	14	11	11	29	23	18	22	158
1900	12	20	14	13	23	8	15	17	15	16	10	12	175
1901	23	15	12	9	14	13	15	10	10	12	12	7	152
1902	12	8	13	8	11	8	15	16	14	16	12	13	146
1903	17	20	14	12	14	10	10	12	17	15	5	11	157
1904	9	12	3	15	10	9	5	10	13	7	12	10	115
1905	15	10	8	6	12	7	5	5	7	10	8	11	104
1906	17	7	11	12	5	8	6	15	8	10	13	5	117
1907	10	18	9	13	11	10	10	5	7	7	11	7	114
1908	6	7	4	8	8	10	10	4	1	7	8		

E Total Authorized Capital Stock
(thousands of dollars)

YEAR	JAN.	FEB.	MAR.	APR.	MAY	JUNE	JULY	AUG.	SEPT.	OCT.	NOV.	DEC.	TOTAL
1890												23,929	
1891	29,934	29,614	13,517	21,051	46,541	19,958	14,984	9,785	19,977	22,292	13,652	29,066	270,371
1892	30,004	46,457	90,135	61,646	82,578	58,451	44,713	39,475	27,434	31,313	18,504	30,068	560,778
1893	29,873	25,162	38,034	42,839	26,598	33,020	29,056	8,376	14,192	10,067	15,906	26,242	299,365
1894	22,742	18,730	38,130	25,898	27,060	20,908	12,376	15,218	20,701	22,760	15,088	16,927	256,538
1895	27,730	15,020	17,442	13,985	24,045	15,010	9,306	19,635	43,038	53,306	128,501	284,708	651,726
1896	483,881	332,471	196,605	93,443	61,098	54,289	22,827	18,231	24,613	34,812	27,239	67,865	1,417,374
1897	32,798	48,872	39,261	36,900	21,912	24,513	24,594	29,816	22,972	23,764	17,749	22,693	345,844
1898	24,894	22,063	23,993	10,336	13,038	19,485	6,701	3,572	6,586	9,049	4,717	55,449	199,883
1899	12,874	10,777	27,382	18,456	11,612	28,752	20,774	23,361	46,166	42,352	30,744	41,142	314,392

Colorado Business Incorporations under General Laws, 1890–1908 (concl.)

E Total Authorized Capital Stock (concl.)
(thousands of dollars)

YEAR	JAN.	FEB.	MAR.	APR.	MAY	JUNE	JULY	AUG.	SEPT.	OCT.	NOV.	DEC.	TOTAL
1900	23,648	35,832	25,939	23,647	33,937	17,754	31,774	29,122	35,698	31,509	19,459	20,011	328,330
1901	44,924	28,622	31,995	19,546	37,315	25,261	26,864	22,905	19,596	27,709	22,583	22,887	330,207
1902	27,208	27,600	31,061	20,635	27,338	17,160	55,847	33,037	30,461	30,404	27,903	31,938	360,592
1903	37,741	43,950	27,040	26,438	35,895	27,592	15,744	28,476	27,846	24,942	15,556	18,901	330,121
1904	22,315	23,895	13,349	32,116	27,436	15,210	15,748	18,736	28,870	17,586	21,921	19,058	256,240
1905	25,480	19,399	19,571	13,631	20,371	17,646	13,924	17,149	20,796	18,247	25,740	17,686	229,640
1906	34,678	17,960	31,801	23,162	19,542	26,691	11,876	29,129	22,111	25,049	50,744	13,511	306,254
1907	26,618	30,149	25,433	23,598	34,650	28,479	14,433	17,396	15,899	25,472	13,316	14,932	270,375
1908	13,134	20,343	14,568	24,850	25,241	26,965	110,123	13,258	8,736	19,945	16,808		

F Total Authorized Capital Stock Excluding Large Companies
(thousands of dollars)

YEAR	JAN.	FEB.	MAR.	APR.	MAY	JUNE	JULY	AUG.	SEPT.	OCT.	NOV.	DEC.	TOTAL
1890												9,905	
1891	7,434	7,614	8,017	10,051	10,541	7,958	5,984	5,535	6,977	5,792	7,652	5,566	89,121
1892	12,504	11,207	23,035	16,796	23,503	20,701	15,063	13,525	7,684	11,563	8,754	8,068	172,403
1893	11,623	14,162	9,784	9,889	11,098	8,020	6,056	5,376	5,692	6,067	9,406	7,041	104,214
1894	12,042	9,530	8,280	7,898	9,060	6,408	5,376	6,018	10,951	7,260	6,088	6,727	95,638
1895	11,480	6,520	7,192	8,985	8,345	9,010	7,106	6,285	7,288	7,806	13,251	16,258	109,526
1896	16,431	22,121	17,955	14,743	13,848	10,289	4,827	2,481	9,113	8,662	5,489	8,415	134,374
1897	9,048	9,172	9,861	10,850	7,162	9,513	10,094	6,716	8,472	7,764	6,249	9,093	103,994
1898	7,144	7,063	9,993	6,336	5,038	8,485	2,201	2,572	3,586	4,049	3,717	3,749	63,933
1899	6,124	6,277	8,382	6,206	5,862	4,052	7,024	8,111	6,966	5,852	5,294	7,142	77,292
1900	6,648	7,332	8,589	8,397	5,687	7,504	9,174	5,172	8,448	7,709	5,459	6,511	86,630
1901	6,424	6,872	8,745	6,046	7,065	9,011	8,364	9,155	7,846	9,709	5,083	8,287	92,607
1902	10,458	8,100	10,061	8,635	8,838	4,460	11,047	9,337	10,461	8,304	7,903	10,938	108,542
1903	12,191	7,600	8,040	6,438	8,045	8,292	4,494	6,476	7,246	7,192	8,556	6,401	90,971
1904	9,815	5,895	7,349	10,616	8,286	5,460	7,248	5,736	8,620	9,336	6,921	5,308	90,590
1905	6,230	5,899	7,571	6,131	6,371	7,146	7,724	6,649	10,296	6,997	8,490	5,686	85,190
1906	11,328	8,960	9,051	7,562	9,792	5,691	5,626	8,629	6,611	6,549	10,244	7,011	97,054
1907	11,118	8,599	6,983	6,848	12,650	7,479	7,433	9,396	8,149	7,472	5,116	7,432	98,675
1908	4,884	8,243	9,068	8,350	12,741	8,965	6,123	8,758	7,236	9,945	8,208		

1) Sources of Raw Data

Biennial Report of the Secretary of State of Colorado for the fiscal years ending November 30, 1891, and November 30, 1892 (Colorado Springs, 1893), pp. 10–67; and similar reports for fiscal years ending in *1893* and *1894* (1894) pp. 10–102, *1895* and *1896* (1896) pp. 18–174, *1897* and *1898* (1898) pp. 16–114, *1899* and *1900* (1901) pp. 18–133, *1901* and *1902* (1902) pp. 18–141, *1903* and *1904* (1904) pp. 8–125, *1905* and *1906* (1906) pp. 8–130, *1907* and *1908* (1908) pp. 8–139. All reports except that of 1893 were published in Denver; the years of publication are given in parentheses.

December 1894 incorporations do not appear in the above mentioned volume for the year ending November 30, 1895. The missing data were supplied by the Office of the Secretary of State of Colorado.

2) Special Comments

a) The biennial reports of the Secretary of State of Colorado for the years preceding and following this series do not contain the incorporation data needed to extend the series to either earlier or later years.

b) Incorporation data in the Secretary's reports referred to in note 1 include the date of each incorporation, the name of each company, its purpose, and capital stock.

c) Incorporations are listed in the Reports chronologically within an alphabetical division.

d) Two lists are given in each report: "Domestic Corporations" and "Foreign Corporations". Some foreign corporations are listed among the domestic with the designation "foreign" either immediately following the name of the corporation or in the column headed "Objects". A check of a few of these names showed that they were listed under foreign corporations also. Accordingly, they were excluded from the tally of domestic corporations.

e) Renewals, designated as such, were listed with incorporations but not tallied.

f) Nonbusiness companies (i.e., those for which no capital stock was given) are listed in each Report among corporations organized with a view to profits; they were not counted as business incorporations.

Connecticut Business Incorporations under General Laws, 1837–1870

YEAR	JAN.	FEB.	MAR.	APR.	MAY	JUNE	JULY	AUG.	SEPT.	OCT.	NOV.	DEC.	TOTAL
1837						0*	1	3	3	3	0	2	
1838	2	5	2	4	3	1	2	2	0	1	1	0	23
1839	1	0	1	1	3	2	0	0	0	0	0	1	9
1840	1	1	0	1	0	0	0	0	0	0	1	0	4
1841	0	2	0	2	1	0	1	2	1	0	1	0	10
1842	0	1	1	1	0	0	0	1	0	0	0	0	4
1843	1	0	0	2	0	0	0	3	0	0	0	2	8
1844	2	0	0	0	1	1	2	0	1	1	0	1	9

YEAR	JAN.	FEB.	MAR.	APR.	MAY	JUNE	JULY	AUG.	SEPT.	OCT.	NOV.	DEC.	TOTAL
1845	1	5	1	1	2	0	1	0	3	2	0	4	20
1846	4	3	3	1	2	0	0	0	1	1	2	1	18
1847	2	1	2	3	5	2	4	1	1	2	2	1	26
1848	2	1	0	2	1	2	1	0	1	1	3	0	14
1849	4	1	2	6	2	2	0	5	3	0	2	2	29
1850	4	4	3	4	5	0	3	4	4	2	2	3	38
1851	4	4	3	8	8	3	2	3	0	3	3	3	44
1852	11	8	6	10	8	6	7	6	2	6	6	9	85
1853	10	13	13	10	15	8	9	8	17	14	5	11	133
1854	15	8	8	13	14	8	5	7	15	4	3	6	106
1855	5	7	6	2	11	4	3	0	2	2	3	3	48
1856	1	3	1	4	5	3	1	2	1	3	1	1	26
1857	3	1	2	2	6	2	2	3	2	3	1	1	28
1858	0	1	3	3	1	2	3	1	1	0	1	3	18
1859	3	1	2	2	1	1	0	1	3	3	3	2	22
1860	7	2	3	0	2	2	2	0	1	2	1	4	26
1861	3	0	4	0	0	2	0	0	2	1	2	0	14
1862	3	1	0	2	3	4	2	1	0	0	2	0	18
1863	4	1	1	2	3	2	3	1	3	2	1	4	27
1864	6	6	7	5	9	7	12	7	6	5	3	3	76
1865	7	7	12	8	6	6	4	1	13	12	6	11	93
1866	13	16	12	13	13	11	6	9	9	9	8	4	123
1867	6	5	6	4	5	5	7	8	2	9	6	3	66
1868	8	7	4	11	3	4	7	6	3	7	9	3	72
1869	4	7	10	4	7	7	4	7	6	2	7	3	68
1870	3	7	7	8	7	2	7	6	4	4	6	1	62

* First general act was approved June 10, 1837.

1) Source of Raw Data

Special Laws of the State of Connecticut Compiled and Published under Authority of the General Assembly (Hartford, 1872), VI (1866–70), 957–1002.

2) Special Comments

a) The corporations chartered are listed by name in the Appendix of the above mentioned volume in a table entitled: "Corporations formed under General Laws." The eight subdivisions are: (1) "Joint Stock Companies", with the note, "The First Act Relating to Joint Stock Companies was approved June 10th, 1837". (2) "Library Companies", with the note, "The *Act Concerning Library Companies* was passed at the October Session, 1818". (3) "Academies", with the note, "Organized under *An Act concerning Academies and Schools*, approved June 1, 1838". (4) "Cemetery Associations", with the note, "Organized under *An Act concerning Burying Grounds and Places of Sepulture*, approved June 2, 1841". (5) "Telegraph Companies", with the note, "Organized under *An Act concerning Telegraph Companies*, approved June 24, 1848". (6) "Benevolent Societies", with the note, "Organized under *An Act in addition to An Act concerning Communities and Corporations*, approved June 17th, 1852". (7) "Parsonage Associations", with the note, "Organized under *An Act in addition to An Act concerning Communities and Corporations*, approved

June 28th, 1852". (8) "Miscellaneous", which includes bands, medical societies, etc.

In the tally of business corporations, the items in only two of the above groups were used: Joint Stock Companies and Telegraph Companies. The former includes manufacturing, mining, and quarrying corporations and also steamboat and transportation companies. An examination of the names of the companies revealed that the list contains also a very few service, financial, and public utility companies. Several types of corporation common in other state incorporation lists for this period do not appear in the Connecticut data. For example, there are no Connecticut turnpike or bridge companies, probably because Connecticut townships were supplying these facilities (see *The General Laws and Liberties of Connecticut Colonie*, p. 28; and *Connecticut Public Statutes, 1795*, p. 229, *1824*, p. 220, and *1861*, p. 68).

b) The companies tabulated were arranged by date of incorporation with the month, day, and year of certificate filing given under the column headings "Corporate name", "Location", "Certificate Filed". An occasional notation such as "[Chartered May Session, 1864.]" was ignored in making the tally on the ground that it gave merely the date on which a joint-stock company already chartered under a general law procured a special act of incorporation.

c) As indicated above, the series presented here, applying as it does only to incorporations under general laws, cannot be extended backward to earlier years.

CONNECTICUT BUSINESS INCORPORATIONS UNDER GENERAL LAWS, 1880–1932

YEAR	JAN.	FEB.	MAR.	APR.	MAY	JUNE	JULY	AUG.	SEPT.	OCT.	NOV.	DEC.	TOTAL
1880									5	7	2	4	
1881	11	6	13	10	8	6	5	3	2	5	9	7	85
1882	5	5	13	12	6	8	8	3	3	7	4	9	83
1883	9	14	10	8	8	8	5	9	6	9	4	8	98
1884	11	7	12	11	7	7	4	3	3	1	3	8	77
1885	10	11	6	10	3	5	12	5	8	8	7	5	90
1886	11	11	5	7	6	7	14	4	6	7	14	11	103
1887	14	10	10	19	9	12	8	9	4	16	12	5	128
1888	10	10	5	13	12	12	8	9	10	5	6	10	110
1889	6	12	13	7	12	7	16	6	8	6	9	8	110

CONNECTICUT BUSINESS INCORPORATIONS UNDER GENERAL LAWS, 1880–1932 (concl.)

YEAR	JAN.	FEB.	MAR.	APR.	MAY	JUNE	JULY	AUG.	SEPT.	OCT.	NOV.	DEC.	TOTAL
1890	8	8	12	17	9	6	7	10	5	9	12	15	118
1891	12	21	11	18	15	11	17	11	5	18	7	17	163
1892	19	24	20	16	16	10	10	18	6	13	11	10	173
1893	27	16	15	12	16	9	14	7	6	2	7	6	137
1894	15	14	20	9	13	13	7	10	12	8	9	11	141
1895	10	15	9	5	9	9	12	9	18	13	17	13	139
1896	10	14	17	22	9	11	8	8	6	6	8	12	131
1897	20	10	18	11	6	8	6	9	9	14	16	10	137
1898	19	19	19	16	14	16	8	12	6	13	8	15	165
1899	11	18	20	25	21	14	19	7	5	13	11	15	179
1900	28	16	18	20	21	12	17	10	9	10	16	21	198
1901	20	24	23	24	20	14	14	21	16	16	19	25	236
1902	18	19	25	27	23	23	17	9	16	22	19	21	239
1903	27	37	33	24	26	27	16	17	6	17	16	30	276
1904	31	32	26	33	26	27	16	20	24	19	27	32	313
1905	37	34	26	29	26	19	26	19	25	21	27	33	322
1906	37	40	47	31	42	28	44	26	32	32	36	42	437
1907	31	41	36	35	40	27	24	19	30	27	16	17	343
1908	23	31	36	46	21	25	21	21	21	27	23	34	329
1909	34	21	43	34	34	35	38	38	27	26	26	34	390
1910	36	48	31	36	25	31	23	20	28	29	33	29	369
1911	43	45	40	39	33	28	40	28	27	30	32	36	421
1912	47	39	49	33	38	17	31	38	23	35	27	60	437
1913	47	55	50	60	43	34	41	33	28	32	35	41	499
1914	30	37	53	38	37	44	46	31	20	29	26	37	428
1915	31	38	46	43	41	32	38	39	34	32	43	56	473
1916	36	44	56	60	52	47	36	39	49	49	42	42	552
1917	63	42	59	52	50	46	44	35	44	34	31	27	527
1918	49	30	30	36	40	32	29	31	17	29	14	38	375
1919	41	50	59	44	70	61	49	54	62	57	60	90	697
1920	79	79	88	81	75	78	67	63	43	56	51	51	811
1921	47	44	72	63	67	67	36	45	48	37	56	41	623
1922	60	58	71	66	62	57	63	64	54	49	39	70	713
1923	68	55	64	87	67	60	47	72	49	60	46	68	743
1924	71	58	89	69	73	73	63	48	64	51	50	85	794
1925	78	63	71	75	72	67	55	64	68	80	73	82	848
1926	83	91	85	61	67	68	59	73	69	48	70	77	851
1927	78	74	94	91	73	85	76	72	61	80	58	91	933
1928	73	86	127	99	98	85	65	91	71	82	79	91	1,047
1929	134	97	110	116	111	96	74	100	91	86	79	88	1,182
1930	97	87	103	102	102	103	67	74	71	72	79	86	1,043
1931	104	92	92	86	89	80	83	75	70	69	55	111	1,006
1932	109	92	92	90	95	83	99	92	93	68	64	98	1,075

1) Sources of Raw Data

Special Laws of Connecticut, vol. 9 (1881–84), pp. 1047–57; vol. 10 (1885–89), pp. 1377–90; vol. 11 (1893), pp. 1180–95; vol. 12, part 1 (1895), pp. 649–55; vol. 12, part 2 (1897), pp. 1221–8; vol. 13, part 1 (1899), pp. 571–8; vol. 13, part 2 (1901), pp. 1249–59; vol. 14, part 1 (1903), pp. 499–517; vol. 14, part 2 (1905), pp. 1123–41; vol. 15, part 2 (1909), pp. 1155–99; vol. 16 (1911–13), pp. 1301–62; vol. 17 (1915–17), pp. 1257–331; vol. 18 (1919 and 1921), pp. 1093–184; vol. 19 (1923 and 1925), pp. 1159–238; vol. 20 (1927 and 1929), pp. 1263–393; vol. 21 (1931 and 1933), pp. 1283–402.

For compiling the data for September 1880 to May 1889, the following volumes of the *Special Laws of Connecticut* also may be used: *1883*, pp. 877–83; *1884*, pp. 1047–50; *1885*, pp. 196–8; *1886*, pp. 398–400; *1887*, pp. 773–6; *1889*, pp. 1377–82. Figures gathered from these volumes will yield almost exactly the same results as those from the sources cited above, if the compiler is very careful to spot and eliminate reinstated companies and companies that were merely changing their names.

2) Special Comments

a) In the Connecticut series set forth here and in the preceding section of this Appendix, there is a hiatus from 1870 to 1880. A list of companies *in existence* in 1880, published in *Special Laws of Connecticut*, vol. 8 (1876–80), pp. 449 ff., to comply with a legislative directive addressed to the Secretary of State (*ibid.*, p. 397), would bridge this gap imperfectly. It was not used, for it is almost certainly not comparable with the lists of incorporations used, because of the probability that many corporations created between 1870 and 1880 forfeited their charters before 1880.

b) Publication of the type of data used for this study was discontinued after the appearance of the volume (cited in note 1) that contained the information on incorporations through December 1932.

c) The titles of the tables from which the incorporation series was compiled change as follows: Volume 9 (1881–84), "Joint Stock Corporations"; Volume 10 (1885–89) through Volume 13, Part 1 (1899), "Joint Stock Companies"; subsequent volumes, "Corporations under the General Law". During the early years only joint-stock companies were created under general laws; corporate charters were procured by special acts. The corporations, as such, for the early years were not counted, since—being created by special statutes—they could not have reflected business fluctuations sensitively.

The tables in Volumes 9–15 must be inspected carefully in order to spot reinstated companies and companies merely changing their names. In Volume 9 this means that a company name must not be counted if it is followed by parentheses containing a statement to the effect that the company was formerly the such and such company. The certificate filing date in such an instance appears to be merely the date on which the company changed its name. In Volumes 10–15, companies merely changing their names are more difficult to identify; the word *named* in the column headed *Location* was a clue. There is no difficulty in determining which companies were reinstated.

d) In the lists of joint-stock companies there is an occasional note after a company name to the effect that the concern was incorporated on such and such date, the date always being subsequent to the date of joint-stock company organization. These references to incorporations were ignored in the tabulation since, as mentioned above, the incorporation was by special statute.

e) When, as happened occasionally, an incorporation was designated as a reorganization, it was counted as an incorporation.

f) Small supplementary lists of mergers and consolidations appear as early as Volume 14, Part 1 (1903), p. 519. They were not tabulated, since the companies did not appear to be organized under general laws.

g) No data on capital stock were available in the above-mentioned lists.

h) The evidence that the joint-stock enterprises tabulated were business enterprises is two-fold. In the first place, the very term *joint-stock* suggests business enterprises, since non-business units usually organize without capital stock. In the second place, the volumes referred to above include also lists either of associations or of corporations organized without capital or capital stock. These lists of cemetery, benevolent, and ecclesiastical associations were used in compiling the Connecticut nonbusiness incorporation series in Appendix 1.

DELAWARE BUSINESS INCORPORATIONS UNDER GENERAL LAWS, 1899–1915

1899	1900	1901	1902	1903	1904	1905	1906	1907	1908	1909	1910	1911	1912	1913	1914	1915
421	552	734	872	746	493	550	587	671	872	1,318	1,325	1,342	1,427	1,613	1,661	1,916

1) Source
Russell Carpenter Larcom, *The Delaware Corporation* (Baltimore, 1937), p. 156.

2) Special Comments
The annual figures from the source cited above are slightly larger than they should be for a business incorporation series. They doubtless include companies without capital stock. This inflation of the figures is, however, negligible in view of the large number of total incorporations and of the very small differences between the 1916–36 totals presented by Larcom and those excluding nonstock companies presented in the Delaware section for 1916–43 (see also the Delaware nonbusiness series in Appendix 1).

DELAWARE BUSINESS INCORPORATIONS UNDER GENERAL LAWS, 1916–1943

YEAR	JAN.	FEB.	MAR.	APR.	MAY	JUNE	JULY	AUG.	SEPT.	OCT.	NOV.	DEC.	TOTAL
					A Total Incorporations								
1916	186	206	228	191	223	226	188	189	182	219	204	279	2,521
1917	274	218	316	311	336	282	270	271	240	293	307	196	3,314
1918	259	238	278	245	230	205	192	183	151	137	146	196	2,460
1919	302	260	352	357	380	385	479	410	403	434	440	529	4,731
1920	630	521	598	561	520	482	420	391	406	436	364	387	5,716
1921	442	410	427	410	418	375	330	368	291	334	354	368	4,527
1922	382	384	447	451	496	465	384	382	381	406	403	467	5,048
1923	453	454	519	529	441	400	378	356	290	347	407	456	5,030
1924	403	338	404	395	336	345	306	303	336	393	317	446	4,322
1925	416	403	477	393	436	461	432	374	351	406	365	483	4,997
1926	387	354	447	446	452	442	387	363	345	327	340	444	4,734
1927	454	430	500	461	439	473	346	400	393	449	450	572	5,367
1928	506	495	472	514	590	518	488	449	396	550	552	653	6,183
1929	673	621	690	726	682	513	624	653	610	614	515	553	7,474
1930	492	457	503	533	637	471	458	392	412	412	347	432	5,546
1931	393	379	421	384	320	323	357	306	276	331	306	370	4,166
1932	298	294	359	320	271	333	252	277	278	265	230	316	3,493
1933	289	300	256	253	295	295	228	183	180	200	226	267	2,972
1934	232	175	189	207	194	176	175	183	160	198	192	192	2,273
1935	166	172	180	177	180	195	187	184	180	205	205	243	2,274
1936	224	210	194	229	204	200	208	171	232	191	215	237	2,515
1937	213	169	234	206	199	171	179	159	156	163	126	159	2,134
1938	152	125	148	131	135	153	117	124	98	134	131	147	1,595
1939	125	108	132	131	101	108	122	112	94	114	129	111	1,387
1940	100	118	110	115	119	90	81	108	106	103	100	123	1,273
1941	111	108	116	113	111	109	101	94	78	96	88	85	1,210
1942	78	69	68	73	72	67	66	48	61	77	64	86	829
1943	70	60	58	68	55	77	70	90	62	73	69	80	832
					B Small Incorporations								
1916	57	52	74	66	59	72	68	55	54	67	50	78	752
1917	73	53	76	93	88	70	62	60	57	74	69	54	829
1918	63	53	64	69	66	61	54	53	66	47	44	57	697
1919	70	57	91	76	66	81	94	98	63	85	78	84	943

DELAWARE BUSINESS INCORPORATIONS UNDER GENERAL LAWS, 1916–1943 (cont.)

YEAR	JAN.	FEB.	MAR.	APR.	MAY	JUNE	JULY	AUG.	SEPT.	OCT.	NOV.	DEC.	TOTAL
B Small Incorporations (concl.)													
1920	118	109	118	93	90	83	77	88	102	80	77	76	1,111
1921	104	90	92	72	87	79	77	89	76	74	89	76	1,005
1922	95	84	97	92	94	91	83	112	104	78	88	96	1,114
1923	91	91	107	107	86	92	63	68	72	84	84	94	1,039
1924	93	84	89	106	71	84	78	84	99	105	93	105	1,091
1925	104	104	106	105	111	125	108	99	98	92	81	100	1,233
1926	100	104	106	111	171	122	101	128	91	86	87	98	1,305
1927	127	104	128	102	89	115	90	89	102	114	114	202	1,376
1928	115	107	107	114	124	121	115	126	93	123	104	118	1,367
1929	136	138	139	143	120	84	99	133	110	116	107	124	1,449
1930	124	97	97	112	137	115	107	102	90	107	65	113	1,266
1931	134	116	109	125	91	97	116	98	99	106	96	135	1,322
1932	121	104	141	113	93	142	122	133	125	127	178	123	1,522
1933	131	178	118	120	144	125	102	80	76	80	90	151	1,395
1934	119	82	92	90	82	70	64	69	63	90	93	72	986
1935	81	72	90	86	75	86	83	69	83	90	89	109	1,013
1936	111	102	80	101	93	100	102	82	123	100	85	98	1,177
1937	101	72	96	88	80	73	71	59	55	87	53	73	908
1938	70	62	64	61	52	72	57	55	48	67	58	69	735
1939	58	46	62	72	54	54	68	62	43	61	63	64	707
1940	49	65	60	66	66	47	48	58	54	56	60	74	703
1941	70	61	52	49	61	66	53	58	37	52	46	41	646
1942	39	40	33	39	40	32	30	25	33	50	36	31	428
1943	35	36	20	32	28	40	33	50	32	31	35	34	406
C Medium Incorporations													
1916	89	103	114	91	124	104	86	93	78	97	103	139	1,221
1917	129	100	142	134	154	132	136	126	111	140	133	106	1,543
1918	124	118	141	119	114	122	102	99	64	72	72	89	1,236
1919	164	133	182	183	193	186	242	183	191	202	193	271	2,323
1920	300	231	275	294	259	230	196	188	190	229	178	200	2,770
1921	199	213	202	212	230	198	160	186	133	164	173	183	2,253
1922	190	191	238	238	267	251	201	166	184	207	189	214	2,536
1923	232	234	268	264	235	188	202	176	143	182	222	226	2,572
1924	218	164	203	199	188	169	156	129	159	197	145	227	2,154
1925	211	203	261	195	229	221	219	179	168	216	192	245	2,539
1926	176	154	225	228	191	225	192	162	172	158	187	228	2,298
1927	218	237	252	239	223	223	179	195	171	213	205	209	2,564
1928	241	242	241	276	260	241	217	192	181	252	243	279	2,865
1929	282	239	291	287	288	222	268	281	262	275	235	234	3,164
1930	196	206	248	232	258	209	216	180	192	177	178	205	2,497
1931	151	172	201	160	155	139	146	139	121	164	144	164	1,856
1932	114	141	148	155	122	142	101	105	125	99	37	155	1,444
1933	121	91	106	94	112	128	93	73	82	99	108	81	1,188
1934	85	73	85	99	98	90	85	94	84	94	90	93	1,070
1935	66	84	73	70	93	88	86	96	81	91	93	107	1,028
1936	89	89	94	111	91	78	84	69	98	79	101	109	1,092
1937	95	84	110	97	92	83	92	87	88	61	53	69	1,011
1938	73	52	74	57	73	67	50	54	44	54	58	60	716
1939	58	48	59	49	39	45	38	46	41	42	54	44	563
1940	42	49	41	43	49	35	27	40	43	39	38	41	487
1941	35	42	56	61	44	40	43	32	38	32	37	34	494
1942	32	23	32	30	30	30	30	19	25	23	24	47	345
1943	28	21	32	33	21	32	33	35	22	37	29	39	362
D Large Incorporations													
1916	40	51	40	34	40	50	34	41	50	55	51	62	548
1917	72	65	98	84	94	80	72	85	72	79	105	36	942
1918	72	67	73	57	50	22	36	31	21	18	30	50	527
1919	68	70	79	98	121	118	143	129	149	147	169	174	1,465
1920	212	181	205	174	171	169	147	115	114	127	109	111	1,835
1921	139	107	133	126	101	98	93	93	82	96	92	109	1,269
1922	97	109	112	121	135	123	100	104	93	121	126	157	1,398
1923	130	129	144	158	120	120	113	112	75	81	101	136	1,419
1924	92	90	112	90	77	92	72	90	78	91	79	114	1,077

YEAR	JAN.	FEB.	MAR.	APR.	MAY	JUNE	JULY	AUG.	SEPT.	OCT.	NOV.	DEC.	TOTAL
1925	101	96	110	93	96	115	105	96	85	98	92	138	1,225
1926	111	96	116	107	90	95	94	73	82	83	66	118	1,131
1927	109	89	120	120	127	135	77	116	120	122	131	161	1,427
1928	150	146	124	124	206	156	156	131	122	175	205	256	1,951
1929	255	244	260	296	274	207	257	239	238	223	173	195	2,861
1930	172	154	158	189	242	147	135	110	130	128	104	114	1,783
1931	108	91	111	99	74	87	95	69	56	61	66	71	988
1932	63	49	70	52	56	49	29	39	28	39	15	38	527
1933	37	31	32	39	39	42	33	30	22	21	28	35	389
1934	28	20	12	18	14	16	26	20	13	14	9	27	217
1935	19	16	17	21	12	21	18	19	16	24	23	27	233
1936	24	19	20	17	20	22	22	20	11	12	29	30	246
1937	17	13	28	21	27	15	16	13	13	15	20	17	215
1938	9	11	10	13	10	14	10	15	6	13	15	18	144
1939	9	14	11	10	8	9	16	4	10	11	12	3	117
1940	9	4	9	6	4	8	6	10	9	8	2	8	83
1941	6	5	8	3	6	3	5	4	3	12	5	10	70
1942	7	6	3	4	2	5	6	4	3	4	4	8	56
1943	7	3	6	3	6	5	4	5	8	5	5	7	64

E Total Authorized Capital Stock
(millions of dollars*)

YEAR	JAN.	FEB.	MAR.	APR.	MAY	JUNE	JULY	AUG.	SEPT.	OCT.	NOV.	DEC.	TOTAL
1916	263.7	276.0	114.7	114.5	233.3	259.3	98.5	113.7	164.9	283.4	155.8	194.6	2,272.5
1917	231.5	229.1	307.1	341.9	412.5	351.1	436.0	373.9	266.6	312.7	359.2	142.6	3,764.2
1918	302.9	191.4	197.8	218.2	173.4	138.3	106.4	96.3	115.4	54.4	87.8	147.9	1,830.3
1919	335.6	207.7	232.3	651.6	657.2	1,183.2	1,045.1	698.1	1,297.2	2,320.9	1,132.6	1,316.3	11,077.9
1920	1,479.2	1,073.1	936.9	1,190.4	1,188.0	968.9	1,052.4	691.1	1,307.4	733.0	661.9	1,029.2	12,311.2
1921	983.6	508.3	705.6	688.7	441.0	511.4	348.8	651.9	374.9	378.9	382.3	616.6	6,591.9
1922	584.1	1,569.8	464.4	722.8	692.4	649.0	582.5	689.5	571.6	572.3	818.2	1,212.0	9,128.5
1923	588.7	654.7	629.1	999.6	555.5	1,081.4	533.5	592.8	558.5	512.3	470.9	947.7	8,124.6
1924	573.1	469.5	661.0	397.6	333.1	447.1	366.6	404.1	563.3	459.9	543.5	971.7	6,190.5
1925	605.7	596.2	712.9	736.3	736.6	1,334.6	1,116.2	1,122.7	622.0	663.7	1,237.0	1,309.7	10,793.5
1926	2,589.2	754.2	2,305.5	722.4	773.2	713.9	528.5	1,143.2	1,039.1	962.8	377.6	1,002.3	12,911.9
1927	1,126.4	703.4	1,069.9	967.2	1,248.2	1,869.0	934.5	1,189.1	1,008.1	1,523.0	1,056.1	1,527.2	14,222.2
1928	1,767.1	1,194.9	1,350.6	1,389.4	3,793.7	2,329.5	2,065.6	993.3	1,625.3	4,011.1	3,163.4	5,402.2	29,086.1
1929	7,378.6	5,311.8	6,382.7	5,268.4	10,443.1	6,916.2	7,457.1	9,751.2	15,444.9	5,008.0	3,771.1	2,590.1	85,723.4
1930	2,639.3	2,555.5	1,913.9	2,826.2	2,998.3	2,689.6	1,264.0	1,485.5	1,472.9	1,253.7	1,788.8	874.4	23,762.0
1931	1,533.8	768.3	1,285.3	812.4	863.2	779.0	981.1	636.0	513.4	811.9	503.5	302.7	9,790.4
1932	358.0	599.4	374.6	231.1	361.1	285.1	835.0	244.4	296.9	198.4	61.8	244.8	4,090.5
1933	332.8	306.7	112.8	146.5	182.7	239.0	185.9	115.8	94.4	71.2	144.6	1,292.0	3,224.4
1934	123.2	89.6	49.8	62.1	59.5	43.9	116.0	57.6	94.7	69.2	40.7	249.8	1,056.1
1935	64.7	74.9	70.2	86.5	49.3	153.6	73.4	87.3	78.5	251.9	164.4	121.5	1,276.4
1936	90.1	189.9	61.2	57.3	160.5	66.9	105.4	72.3	45.2	114.1	1,443.8	188.5	2,595.2
1937	219.9	125.5	160.5	88.0	149.2	62.4	83.1	80.6	207.9	67.8	55.2	79.5	1,379.6
1938	41.8	58.3	41.9	47.0	103.1	64.7	32.3	60.1	27.5	115.2	52.8	81.9	726.5
1939	105.5	36.2	34.7	37.0	24.1	27.3	140.0	22.4	52.6	30.7	58.1	17.3	585.8
1940	41.4	17.3	25.0	18.9	21.5	52.1	33.1	33.7	39.9	26.9	14.0	20.5	344.4
1941	20.1	16.3	35.9	16.9	29.0	19.8	20.9	14.9	16.6	27.9	13.6	43.6	275.3
1942	22.1	21.7	21.9	65.0	11.7	41.6	27.5	12.1	7.8	9.6	10.8	27.0	278.8
1943	34.7	36.8	30.5	10.6	29.2	45.6	43.0	19.2	18.1	12.5	30.8	56.4	367.4

* The totals of this table were rounded from totals in dollars.

F Total Authorized Capital Stock Excluding Large Companies
(thousands of dollars)

YEAR	JAN.	FEB.	MAR.	APR.	MAY	JUNE	JULY	AUG.	SEPT.	OCT.	NOV.	DEC.	TOTAL
1916	24,230	26,849	32,749	25,658	31,085	30,771	24,940	24,984	24,976	23,674	28,583	35,523	334,022
1917	34,639	24,262	42,020	38,177	41,530	36,728	39,864	37,294	29,976	41,423	40,426	31,179	437,518
1918	34,911	37,597	40,597	30,440	29,692	29,656	24,418	23,772	16,721	18,928	16,342	24,115	327,189
1919	41,381	34,060	53,782	52,464	55,494	56,418	63,805	55,246	53,963	56,758	59,263	77,074	659,708
1920	86,981	66,287	77,722	83,489	70,166	68,451	54,774	55,690	53,537	61,517	52,037	58,928	789,579
1921	50,225	63,728	56,784	62,919	65,402	52,182	49,251	49,184	32,888	44,947	47,248	47,938	622,696
1922	52,018	54,702	63,786	69,454	72,696	73,923	55,453	47,892	53,666	59,952	52,830	63,250	719,622
1923	65,866	63,514	80,990	69,618	68,262	56,261	50,339	52,592	39,805	53,927	57,612	67,332	726,118
1924	53,151	43,095	49,848	51,986	48,858	50,924	43,366	32,253	41,299	54,121	38,684	66,558	574,143
1925	52,404	52,138	67,858	49,812	56,774	64,563	56,428	44,023	46,320	56,339	50,012	60,135	656,806
1926	45,763	38,625	63,105	59,511	46,600	60,887	48,816	44,608	47,485	42,245	45,787	58,332	601,764
1927	57,767	66,233	69,351	60,888	57,325	62,324	45,517	50,431	46,802	58,802	54,579	53,261	683,280
1928	60,890	64,781	62,882	76,810	68,782	60,363	61,473	56,093	44,554	63,188	56,772	74,502	751,090
1929	74,195	60,384	75,895	76,614	75,745	56,158	68,002	76,333	71,243	65,143	58,831	58,005	816,548

DELAWARE BUSINESS INCORPORATIONS UNDER GENERAL LAWS, 1916–1943 (concl.)

YEAR	JAN.	FEB.	MAR.	APR.	MAY	JUNE	JULY	AUG.	SEPT.	OCT.	NOV.	DEC.	TOTAL

F Total Authorized Capital Stock Excluding Large Companies (concl.)
(thousands of dollars)

YEAR	JAN.	FEB.	MAR.	APR.	MAY	JUNE	JULY	AUG.	SEPT.	OCT.	NOV.	DEC.	TOTAL
1930	48,984	52,712	62,328	61,918	58,433	53,281	55,023	42,596	49,791	46,721	47,863	49,087	628,737
1931	38,880	40,346	48,402	43,717	37,443	35,664	39,157	35,508	30,091	43,317	33,378	39,889	465,792
1932	33,438	36,015	36,592	37,148	29,486	34,244	21,629	25,180	30,642	22,995	8,528	41,553	357,450
1933	29,556	20,984	24,652	23,526	30,335	31,524	22,368	18,254	18,514	21,150	25,191	20,047	286,101
1934	21,795	15,507	22,753	24,365	22,405	19,741	19,384	19,295	20,661	20,435	19,454	20,686	246,481
1935	15,178	17,881	16,906	19,582	21,385	24,298	22,419	22,913	21,766	22,204	24,233	30,033	258,798
1936	21,623	23,031	25,020	25,547	22,982	19,403	22,567	17,876	29,015	21,266	23,217	25,478	277,025
1937	25,894	24,898	29,854	24,533	23,405	20,618	21,339	20,842	24,764	14,912	15,374	17,302	263,735
1938	18,831	14,314	19,174	14,209	18,425	15,255	12,629	13,700	11,465	12,747	12,721	14,773	178,243
1939	13,873	11,305	14,672	10,750	8,207	10,640	10,288	9,915	8,088	9,035	10,899	11,690	129,362
1940	8,014	10,293	8,767	10,146	11,578	7,828	6,032	10,056	9,931	8,610	9,726	10,413	111,394
1941	8,026	9,916	13,509	12,758	8,924	7,847	8,728	6,041	8,556	8,353	7,561	7,538	107,757
1942	6,307	5,042	6,919	5,514	5,722	7,229	5,717	3,144	4,598	5,572	4,538	9,964	70,266
1943	5,245	4,828	7,038	6,578	5,180	5,568	8,299	7,432	4,514	6,405	7,543	6,361	74,991

1) Sources of Raw Data

Monthly pamphlets issued by the Secretary of State of Delaware from January 1916 through December 1943 under the title: *Delaware Corporations . . . List of Corporations Organized in the Month of . . . , under The General Corporation Law of the State of Delaware.* Similar pamphlets were published before 1916, but the state offices at Dover do not have a complete set and only scattered monthly issues for the earlier years could be found elsewhere.

2) Special Comments

a) In each pamphlet the corporations chartered during the given month are listed by name. Moreover, the capital stock figures of each company are almost always stated. During the four months March–June 1927, however, capital stock figures were omitted; these had to be gathered from the official records at Dover. From five other monthly lists containing information on companies with and without stock, the capital stock figure for a single company was omitted. These missing data were also procured from the records at Dover. The only other irregularity in the statement of stock figures is in the July 1933 pamphlet; its treatment is explained in (b) below.

b) In the tally of business incorporations made from the pamphlets of the Secretary of State, companies whose capital stock is given as "none" were eliminated as nonbusiness. The sixteen companies for which there is no information on capital stock in the July 1933 pamphlet were likewise treated as nonbusiness; in the list of incorporations for that month no company had a capital stock listing of "none" and the names of the sixteen companies suggested that they were not chartered to engage in business. Since the monthly series given above is confined to business corporations and Larcom's figures (see preceding section of this Appendix) are for total incorporations, a slight error would be involved in using the Larcom figures to extend the annual totals of the monthly series backward. But comparison of the Larcom figures with those given above for the period of their overlap shows the smallness of the differences. The reader can compare also the Delaware nonbusiness incorporation series of Appendix 1 with the business series.

c) Renewals of charters were not tallied as incorporations.

d) In 1915 Delaware authorized the use of nonpar shares (*Revised Code of 1915*, Ch. 65, Sec. 13). Accordingly, throughout the period covered by the series given above, nonpar shares were issued. In constructing the capital stock figures and in classifying the incorporations on the basis of size, nonpar shares were treated as $100 par value shares. Under Delaware law such equality has not always existed but it was present to a sufficient degree to warrant this method of equating the two types of share. See, for example, Josiah Marvel, *Delaware Corporations and Receiverships* (4th ed., Wilmington, 1929), pp. 59, 207–8, 308.

FLORIDA BUSINESS INCORPORATIONS UNDER GENERAL LAWS, 1901–1922

YEAR	JAN.	FEB.	MAR.	APR.	MAY	JUNE	JULY	AUG.	SEPT.	OCT.	NOV.	DEC.	TOTAL

A Total Incorporations

YEAR	JAN.	FEB.	MAR.	APR.	MAY	JUNE	JULY	AUG.	SEPT.	OCT.	NOV.	DEC.	TOTAL
1901	12	10	14	14	17	11	9	14	5	10	10	6	132
1902	12	4	16	11	13	6	9	6	17	8	19	20	141
1903	12	11	12	17	17	8	11	21	14	13	13	18	167
1904	15	11	23	17	11	24	11	22	16	16	24	21	211
1905	27	17	35	18	38	17	25	23	22	29	22	32	305
1906	25	26	30	29	25	32	16	30	25	28	26	32	324
1907	36	25	42	31	30	33	31	34	31	22	26	9	350
1908	18	28	20	16	23	18	17	19	26	27	18	23	253
1909	28	27	31	26	29	21	23	27	24	25	30	33	324
1910	45	33	37	38	28	39	38	32	26	39	32	39	426
1911	44	44	51	41	39	37	39	23	32	38	37	45	470
1912	35	45	59	35	57	38	54	55	35	40	37	33	523
1913	56	39	69	59	43	39	50	49	44	52	39	39	578
1914	43	43	39	51	35	40	37	37	25	30	30	26	436
1915	53	43	46	27	44	31	34	28	36	29	39	29	439
1916	34	32	51	48	41	49	35	37	34	42	43	32	478
1917	48	54	62	36	40	40	38	22	35	35	38	40	488
1918	42	30	44	37	47	20	29	23	26	12	19	28	357
1919	20	35	38	52	52	61	47	44	41	71	53	54	568
1920	70	64	61	80	61	70	74	49	44	44	54	54	725
1921	52	48	53	59	71	41	58	80	42	62	64	71	701
1922	72	77	93	74	98	81	83	90					

YEAR	JAN.	FEB.	MAR.	APR.	MAY	JUNE	JULY	AUG.	SEPT.	OCT.	NOV.	DEC.	TOTAL
B Small Incorporations													
1901	12	8	11	12	14	8	8	9	4	8	9	5	108
1902	10	4	12	8	12	6	9	6	13	6	14	18	118
1903	11	8	10	13	17	7	8	16	12	12	11	16	141
1904	12	9	19	13	10	24	9	17	11	15	19	17	175
1905	23	11	29	13	33	10	22	21	19	24	22	24	251
1906	19	22	24	21	23	25	13	25	19	22	22	24	259
1907	28	21	34	26	26	30	28	28	28	21	24	8	302
1908	13	23	18	13	23	15	16	16	22	24	16	19	218
1909	23	23	26	21	23	19	15	25	20	23	26	32	276
1910	38	22	32	28	22	34	31	25	21	36	28	34	351
1911	37	37	41	36	34	35	32	20	27	34	29	39	401
1912	31	36	50	31	54	30	43	46	26	31	27	26	431
1913	42	29	58	49	37	31	43	45	38	44	32	36	484
1914	37	36	35	42	30	37	35	33	21	28	27	23	384
1915	47	40	41	24	38	25	29	24	33	24	36	24	385
1916	30	26	44	40	36	45	31	31	27	36	36	29	411
1917	42	47	53	31	34	33	34	20	29	31	37	33	424
1918	35	26	37	32	40	16	25	22	20	8	14	24	299
1919	17	28	33	40	44	51	39	35	31	53	42	39	452
1920	53	48	48	58	45	51	60	36	24	32	37	33	525
1921	33	30	40	40	55	31	42	69	29	45	49	59	522
1922	57	57	62	61	81	69	68	75					
C Medium Incorporations													
1901	0	2	2	2	3	3	1	5	0	2	1	1	22
1902	2	0	4	1	1	0	0	0	4	1	5	2	20
1903	1	3	2	3	0	1	2	5	2	1	2	2	24
1904	3	2	4	4	1	0	2	4	5	1	3	4	33
1905	4	5	6	4	5	5	3	2	3	4	0	8	49
1906	5	4	6	8	2	7	3	4	6	5	3	8	61
1907	6	2	8	5	4	3	3	5	3	1	2	1	43
1908	5	4	2	3	0	2	0	3	4	3	1	3	30
1909	5	4	5	5	5	2	8	1	4	2	4	1	46
1910	5	11	4	8	6	5	7	6	5	3	4	5	69
1911	4	6	9	4	4	2	5	2	5	4	8	6	59
1912	4	9	7	4	3	7	9	7	6	7	9	6	78
1913	13	9	10	10	6	8	7	4	6	7	6	2	88
1914	6	6	4	9	5	3	2	4	4	2	3	3	51
1915	6	3	5	2	6	4	5	4	3	5	3	5	51
1916	4	4	6	8	5	4	3	5	7	6	6	3	61
1917	5	6	9	4	5	5	4	2	5	4	1	7	57
1918	7	3	7	5	5	4	3	1	5	4	5	3	52
1919	2	7	5	11	7	10	8	8	9	17	10	14	108
1920	15	13	10	20	15	18	13	13	18	12	16	21	184
1921	19	17	11	18	15	10	15	11	12	17	13	12	170
1922	14	20	27	11	16	11	14	15					
D Large Incorporations													
1901	0	0	1	0	0	0	0	0	1	0	0	0	2
1902	0	0	0	2	0	0	0	0	0	1	0	0	3
1903	0	0	0	1	0	0	1	0	0	0	0	0	2
1904	0	0	0	0	0	0	0	1	0	0	2	0	3
1905	0	1	0	1	0	2	0	0	0	1	0	0	5
1906	1	0	0	0	0	0	0	1	0	1	1	0	4
1907	2	2	0	0	0	0	0	1	0	0	0	0	5
1908	0	1	0	0	0	1	1	0	0	0	1	1	5
1909	0	0	0	0	1	0	0	1	0	0	0	0	2
1910	2	0	1	2	0	0	0	1	0	0	0	0	6
1911	3	1	1	1	1	0	2	1	0	0	0	0	10
1912	0	0	2	0	0	1	2	2	3	2	1	1	14
1913	1	1	1	0	0	0	0	0	0	1	1	1	6
1914	0	1	0	0	0	0	0	0	0	0	0	0	1
1915	0	0	0	1	0	2	0	0	0	0	0	0	3
1916	0	2	1	0	0	0	1	1	0	0	1	0	6
1917	1	1	0	1	1	2	0	0	1	0	0	0	7
1918	0	1	0	0	2	0	1	0	1	0	0	1	6
1919	1	0	0	1	1	0	0	1	1	1	1	1	8
1920	2	3	3	2	1	1	1	0	2	0	1	0	16
1921	0	1	2	1	1	0	1	0	1	0	2	0	9
1922	1	0	4	2	1	1	1	0					

FLORIDA BUSINESS INCORPORATIONS UNDER GENERAL LAWS, 1901–1922 (concl.)

E Total Authorized Capital Stock
(thousands of dollars)

YEAR	JAN.	FEB.	MAR.	APR.	MAY	JUNE	JULY	AUG.	SEPT.	OCT.	NOV.	DEC.	TOTAL
1901	191	1,029	1,350	557	722	434	220	706	2,070	736	363	355	8,733
1902	430	24	897	2,408	581	79	68	75	1,400	3,588	1,893	1,192	12,635
1903	770	554	433	1,988	439	436	1,760	870	976	386	572	1,014	10,198
1904	720	568	1,528	681	264	579	508	2,342	1,676	392	2,786	954	12,998
1905	1,622	2,411	1,514	2,222	1,560	6,040	1,128	827	1,404	2,778	504	1,709	23,719
1906	2,308	914	1,698	1,647	852	1,982	744	2,051	1,769	2,131	11,222	2,308	29,626
1907	7,496	3,213	2,555	1,513	2,070	1,732	900	2,499	894	686	998	236	24,792
1908	950	2,298	723	630	598	1,552	1,340	1,054	1,488	938	1,415	1,727	14,713
1909	1,459	1,160	1,469	1,055	4,062	541	1,685	1,627	1,745	867	1,044	1,044	17,758
1910	4,790	3,736	6,840	6,127	2,155	2,004	1,985	2,686	1,525	1,466	1,411	1,524	36,249
1911	7,362	8,156	3,797	3,410	3,545	1,234	3,387	1,976	1,602	1,942	2,705	2,047	41,163
1912	1,806	2,571	6,303	1,253	1,446	2,860	3,948	4,556	6,580	5,656	3,164	4,422	44,565
1913	4,051	13,114	3,924	2,949	1,710	2,192	1,805	1,899	1,976	3,180	4,461	2,935	44,196
1914	1,534	3,236	1,583	2,766	1,407	1,773	858	1,730	1,457	1,121	1,045	1,473	19,983
1915	2,506	1,424	1,834	2,686	2,320	4,955	1,544	998	860	1,617	1,322	1,346	23,412
1916	1,205	3,368	4,005	3,056	1,424	1,268	2,321	3,038	1,725	1,715	3,420	1,429	27,974
1917	2,480	3,022	2,948	3,112	5,531	3,313	2,384	792	5,958	1,428	924	1,894	33,786
1918	2,729	2,088	2,618	1,768	5,578	1,478	2,287	732	2,400	805	1,206	3,566	27,255
1919	2,844	2,044	1,663	3,855	2,858	3,541	2,583	3,502	5,285	5,436	8,617	5,692	47,920
1920	6,612	7,098	7,414	9,444	5,354	7,411	6,236	2,701	6,418	3,160	6,760	5,518	74,126
1921	6,752	8,290	8,955	6,880	4,544	2,994	6,281	4,750	3,540	5,637	8,154	3,134	69,911
1922	6,934	6,946	13,290	6,003	6,016	4,352	6,338	5,834					

F Total Authorized Capital Stock Excluding Large Companies
(thousands of dollars)

YEAR	JAN.	FEB.	MAR.	APR.	MAY	JUNE	JULY	AUG.	SEPT.	OCT.	NOV.	DEC.	TOTAL
1901	191	1,029	350	557	722	434	220	706	70	736	363	355	5,733
1902	430	24	897	408	581	79	68	75	1,400	588	1,893	1,192	7,635
1903	770	554	433	988	439	436	760	870	976	386	572	1,014	8,198
1904	720	568	1,528	681	264	579	508	1,342	1,676	392	786	954	9,998
1905	1,622	1,411	1,514	1,222	1,560	2,040	1,128	827	1,404	1,778	504	1,709	16,719
1906	1,308	914	1,698	1,647	852	1,982	744	1,051	1,769	1,131	1,222	2,308	16,626
1907	1,496	1,213	2,555	1,513	2,070	1,732	900	1,499	894	686	998	236	15,792
1908	950	1,298	723	630	598	552	340	1,054	1,488	938	415	727	9,713
1909	1,459	1,160	1,469	1,055	1,562	541	1,685	627	1,745	867	1,044	1,044	14,258
1910	2,290	3,736	1,840	2,127	2,155	2,004	1,985	1,686	1,525	1,466	1,411	1,524	23,749
1911	1,862	3,156	2,797	1,410	2,545	1,234	1,387	976	1,602	1,942	2,705	2,047	23,663
1912	1,806	2,571	3,053	1,253	1,446	1,860	1,948	2,556	2,255	2,656	2,164	2,422	25,990
1913	3,051	3,114	2,924	2,949	1,710	2,192	1,805	1,899	1,976	2,180	1,961	935	26,696
1914	1,534	2,236	1,583	2,766	1,407	1,773	858	1,730	1,457	1,121	1,045	1,473	18,983
1915	2,506	1,424	1,834	1,486	2,320	1,455	1,544	998	860	1,617	1,322	1,346	18,712
1916	1,205	1,368	1,505	3,056	1,424	1,268	1,321	2,038	1,725	1,715	2,420	1,429	20,474
1917	1,480	2,022	2,948	1,862	2,531	1,313	2,384	792	1,958	1,428	924	1,894	21,536
1918	2,729	838	2,618	1,768	2,578	1,478	1,287	732	1,150	805	1,206	1,066	18,255
1919	844	2,044	1,663	2,855	1,858	3,541	2,583	2,502	2,785	4,436	2,617	4,692	32,420
1920	4,112	3,098	4,414	5,944	4,354	6,411	4,236	2,701	4,418	3,160	4,760	5,518	53,126
1921	6,752	4,790	2,455	5,380	3,544	2,994	5,281	4,750	2,540	5,637	4,654	3,134	51,911
1922	5,934	6,946	7,290	3,003	5,016	3,352	5,288	5,834					

1) Sources of Raw Data

Report of the Secretary of State of the State of Florida for the period beginning January 1, 1901, and ending December 31, 1902 (1902), pp. 116–70; and similar reports for *1903* and *1904* (1904) pp. 187–255, for *1905* and *1906* (1906) pp. 241–376, for *1907* and *1908* (1909) pp. 130–304, for *1909* and *1910* (1911) pp. 372–587, for *1911* and *1912* (1913) pp. 529–806; *Biennial Report of the Secretary of State of the State of Florida for the period beginning January 1, 1913, and ending December 31, 1914* (1914), Part 2, pp. 5–295; and similar reports for *1915* and *1916* (1916), Part 2, pp. 5–260; for *1917* and *1918* (1918), Part 2, pp. 5–239; for *1919* and *1920* (1920), Part 2, pp. 5–359; for *1921* and *1922* (1922), Part 2, pp. 5–469. All reports were published in Tallahassee; the years of publication are given in parentheses.

2) Special Comments

a) On the basis of the published data the series has to end with 1922, since in the Secretary's later reports the dates of incorporation are not attached to the names of the companies chartered. The series could perhaps be extended into the years prior to 1901, but the few companies created annually in that early period would not add much to the total picture of incorporations presented by this study.

b) In the sources given in note 1, the names of the incorporated companies are listed alphabetically with their authorized capital stock and two dates, labeled "filed" and "letters patent issued". In tallying incorporations, the "filed" date was used except in the few instances when, owing to its omission, resort was had to the other date.

c) Nonbusiness incorporations, considered to be those without capital stock, were not included in the series set forth above.

d) Although the last Secretary's report used purports to cover the incorporations of 1922, it was decided to end the monthly series with August 1922. Each volume cited in note 1 contains many incorporations of the last quarter of the preceding year, particularly of December. The compiled figures for incorporations during the last four months of 1922 were therefore believed to be incomplete and accordingly were not counted.

ILLINOIS BUSINESS INCORPORATIONS UNDER GENERAL LAWS, 1896–1918

YEAR	JAN.	FEB.	MAR.	APR.	MAY	JUNE	JULY	AUG.	SEPT.	OCT.	NOV.	DEC.	TOTAL
						A Total Incorporations							
1896										66	78	95	
1897	111	93	112	106	85	85	89	85	88	86	98	127	1,165
1898	144	124	146	108	99	84	76	71	75	82	95	104	1,208
1899	126	127	126	111	99	106	107	109	107	113	103	85	1,319
1900	131	126	131	121	122	101	100	96	107	111	102	125	1,373
1901	117	146	149	160	138	133	106	137	103	137	113	128	1,567
1902	173	188	189	193	160	130	140	117	143	160	132	157	1,882
1903	229	199	223	217	165	166	148	130	147	175	145	183	2,127
1904	201	179	205	202	147	161	150	155	120	156	152	189	2,017
1905	231	198	207	172	181	162	134	156	176	147	179	184	2,127
1906	210	201	264	197	184	185	179	154	165	154	166	202	2,261
1907	225	189	199	225	194	206	169	157	151	170	158	146	2,189
1908	197	189	217	204	167	179	153	152	157	167	168	200	2,150
1909	211	213	251	201	192	194	192	155	154	161	195	212	2,331
1910	209	213	223	205	201	156	158	155	163	151	166	173	2,173
1911	223	209	215	179	172	176	157	165	167	159	186	201	2,209
1912	244	245	248	214	207	195	223	193	184	202	166	221	2,542
1913	229	224	257	239	221	216	192	179	186	231	181	232	2,587
1914	254	234	287	215	200	192	178	164	145	133	156	161	2,319
1915	227	211	231	226	214	237	214	216	181	210	251	249	2,667
1916	250	268	247	246	230	233	185	212	214	231	259	240	2,815
1917	294	251	326	256	226	200	215	196	151	216	174	181	2,686
1918	187	183	223	196	227	180	163	177	114				
						B Small Incorporations							
1896										63	66	81	
1897	102	84	95	95	75	75	82	71	77	76	88	111	1,031
1898	123	106	135	100	85	77	68	68	63	74	80	97	1,076
1899	109	109	107	101	87	86	93	98	91	95	91	74	1,141
1900	122	112	117	104	109	81	84	83	93	97	92	116	1,210
1901	103	126	132	141	114	108	92	109	94	124	103	114	1,360
1902	154	172	169	171	137	114	122	102	128	137	115	135	1,656
1903	199	179	192	189	143	141	131	117	125	156	130	163	1,865
1904	181	166	187	179	134	148	136	140	106	141	140	164	1,822
1905	208	184	192	159	165	139	118	139	153	135	167	167	1,926
1906	194	184	243	174	167	167	163	138	153	144	147	186	2,060
1907	213	177	187	209	187	185	150	148	141	158	147	133	2,035
1908	184	177	203	193	156	166	141	142	144	156	152	183	1,997
1909	192	206	231	178	174	181	178	146	137	150	184	200	2,157
1910	192	197	211	190	184	144	148	148	153	145	147	164	2,023
1911	204	194	208	165	161	166	145	160	156	149	173	185	2,066
1912	228	227	234	206	196	180	206	179	176	193	148	203	2,376
1913	212	209	241	222	209	208	184	172	174	212	172	215	2,430
1914	234	219	275	206	189	182	167	154	143	126	151	153	2,199
1915	218	203	224	219	207	226	199	206	177	198	235	231	2,543
1916	242	251	233	232	218	223	175	200	208	217	240	223	2,662
1917	279	231	302	238	215	181	204	177	140	202	157	158	2,484
1918	173	168	208	179	209	159	150	163	104				
						C Medium Incorporations							
1896										3	12	13	
1897	8	9	17	11	8	7	7	14	11	9	10	14	125
1898	16	16	10	7	14	7	7	3	12	8	15	6	121
1899	15	18	17	10	11	20	12	11	15	18	12	11	170
1900	7	14	13	16	10	20	15	12	14	13	9	8	151
1901	14	19	17	19	20	25	13	28	8	12	9	12	196
1902	18	15	20	22	22	16	17	13	12	23	17	20	215
1903	26	18	30	27	22	24	16	12	22	17	12	18	244
1904	20	12	18	23	13	13	14	14	14	15	12	24	192
1905	23	14	13	12	16	22	16	17	22	11	11	16	193
1906	15	16	20	21	17	16	16	15	12	10	18	16	192
1907	12	12	12	15	7	21	19	9	10	11	10	13	151
1908	12	11	13	10	11	13	11	10	13	10	16	17	147
1909	18	7	19	22	18	13	14	7	17	11	10	12	168

Illinois Business Incorporations under General Laws, 1896–1918 (concl.)

YEAR	JAN.	FEB.	MAR.	APR.	MAY	JUNE	JULY	AUG.	SEPT.	OCT.	NOV.	DEC.	TOTAL
C Medium Incorporations (concl.)													
1910	15	15	11	14	16	12	10	7	10	6	17	9	142
1911	18	15	7	14	10	9	12	5	11	9	13	16	139
1912	15	17	14	8	11	14	17	14	8	9	18	18	163
1913	17	14	16	17	12	7	7	6	12	19	9	16	152
1914	20	15	12	9	11	10	11	10	2	7	5	8	120
1915	9	8	7	6	7	11	15	10	4	12	16	18	123
1916	8	17	14	14	11	10	10	12	6	13	19	17	151
1917	14	20	24	18	11	18	11	18	10	14	17	23	198
1918	12	15	14	17	18	21	12	14	10				
D Large Incorporations													
1896										0	0	1	
1897	1	0	0	0	2	3	0	0	0	1	0	2	9
1898	5	2	1	1	0	0	1	0	0	0	0	1	11
1899	2	0	2	0	1	0	2	0	1	0	0	0	8
1900	2	0	1	1	3	0	1	1	0	1	1	1	12
1901	0	1	0	0	4	0	1	0	1	1	1	2	11
1902	1	1	0	0	1	0	1	2	3	0	0	2	11
1903	4	2	1	1	0	1	1	1	0	2	3	2	18
1904	0	1	0	0	0	0	0	1	0	0	0	1	3
1905	0	0	2	1	0	1	0	0	1	1	1	1	8
1906	1	1	1	2	0	2	0	1	0	0	1	0	9
1907	0	0	0 •	1	0	0	0	0	0	1	1	0	3
1908	1	1	1	1	0	0	1	0	0	1	0	0	6
1909	1	0	1	1	0	0	0	2	0	0	1	0	6
1910	2	1	1	1	1	0	0	0	0	0	2	0	8
1911	1	0	0	0	1	1	0	0	0	1	0	0	4
1912	1	1	0	0	0	1	0	0	0	0	0	0	3
1913	0	1	0	0	0	1	1	1	0	0	0	1	5
1914	0	0	0	0	0	0	0	0	0	0	0	0	0
1915	0	0	0	1	0	0	0	0	0	0	0	0	1
1916	0	0	0	0	1	0	0	0	0	1	0	0	2
1917	1	0	0	0	0	1	0	1	1	0	0	0	4
1918	2	0	1	0	0	0	1	0	0				
E Total Authorized Capital Stock (thousands of dollars)													
1896										1,467	3,122	3,974	
1897	13,406	2,438	5,008	1,753	4,545	34,271	2,754	3,260	2,432	3,635	3,055	6,626	83,183
1898	8,932	6,776	27,574	3,821	3,136	3,138	7,628	1,395	2,748	2,390	4,272	27,391	99,201
1899	36,001	4,967	7,730	2,621	35,148	4,993	7,374	3,814	6,313	5,409	4,519	2,813	121,702
1900	12,265	3,286	24,377	44,294	7,493	4,156	4,937	8,220	2,976	5,156	4,492	6,285	127,937
1901	3,513	11,296	4,237	6,755	11,836	6,175	8,867	8,450	4,388	5,910	4,107	8,390	83,924
1902	6,132	6,490	6,141	6,715	9,290	4,652	8,101	5,064	9,274	5,969	5,653	8,535	82,016
1903	12,621	8,253	9,183	8,305	6,760	7,857	7,446	6,457	6,440	39,151	9,871	7,976	130,320
1904	5,772	5,958	6,306	5,773	4,351	4,905	3,978	5,122	4,308	4,862	3,624	8,254	63,216
1905	6,396	4,947	7,664	6,527	5,634	7,822	4,555	4,750	7,662	4,729	4,792	7,391	72,869
1906	7,229	7,240	7,596	8,584	5,368	7,021	4,923	5,974	3,909	3,532	5,802	5,421	72,599
1907	5,400	4,910	4,345	6,926	3,331	6,674	5,282	3,355	3,796	6,004	6,518	3,573	60,114
1908	7,126	6,194	15,972	4,735	5,284	3,975	6,010	3,482	4,390	4,911	3,864	5,686	71,629
1909	7,214	3,504	7,970	7,279	5,057	4,913	4,544	100,258	6,478	4,236	8,341	3,995	163,789
1910	18,343	6,198	4,671	5,102	5,482	4,056	3,684	3,264	3,096	2,427	11,420	3,542	71,285
1911	6,517	5,401	3,986	4,351	6,174	6,110	3,466	2,785	3,702	4,483	4,087	6,311	57,373
1912	7,517	5,878	5,144	3,486	3,564	11,044	6,629	4,517	3,689	4,259	5,870	5,370	66,967
1913	5,017	6,283	4,869	5,349	5,256	4,384	53,252	4,943	4,199	5,139	4,335	6,986	110,012
1914	5,701	5,883	5,675	3,499	3,691	3,802	3,589	3,172	1,860	2,458	2,461	3,074	44,865
1915	4,724	4,321	3,723	5,329	3,227	4,458	5,299	3,839	2,236	4,633	5,948	5,799	53,536
1916	4,109	5,558	5,004	4,999	5,847	4,583	3,439	4,392	3,673	6,759	6,085	6,450	60,898
1917	7,490	6,432	7,923	7,091	4,318	7,415	4,504	6,164	4,933	4,835	5,921	6,374	73,400
1918	9,070	5,483	6,144	7,272	5,273	5,425	5,088	5,003	2,907				
F Total Authorized Capital Stock Excluding Large Companies (thousands of dollars)													
1896										1,467	3,122	2,974	
1897	3,082	2,438	5,008	1,753	2,045	2,271	2,754	3,260	2,432	2,635	3,055	3,626	34,359
1898	3,932	4,776	3,574	2,221	3,136	3,138	2,128	1,395	2,748	2,390	4,272	2,391	36,101
1899	4,501	4,967	5,230	2,621	3,148	4,993	4,874	3,814	4,313	5,409	4,519	2,813	51,202

YEAR	JAN.	FEB.	MAR.	APR.	MAY	JUNE	JULY	AUG.	SEPT.	OCT.	NOV.	DEC.	TOTAL
1900	2,915	3,286	4,377	4,294	3,493	4,156	3,437	3,720	2,976	4,156	3,492	3,285	43,587
1901	3,513	5,296	4,237	6,755	5,336	6,175	3,867	8,450	3,388	3,910	3,107	5,390	59,424
1902	5,132	5,490	6,141	6,715	7,090	4,652	4,601	3,064	5,774	5,969	5,653	5,535	65,816
1903	8,121	5,753	8,183	7,055	6,760	6,857	6,446	3,357	6,440	6,151	4,071	5,876	75,070
1904	5,772	4,333	6,306	5,773	4,354	4,905	3,978	4,122	4,308	4,862	3,624	7,254	59,591
1905	6,396	4,947	4,914	4,527	5,634	5,822	4,555	4,750	6,562	3,729	3,792	5,376	61,004
1906	5,729	5,740	6,096	6,084	5,368	4,821	4,923	4,274	3,909	3,532	4,802	5,421	60,699
1907	5,400	4,910	4,345	5,926	3,331	6,674	5,282	3,355	3,796	4,004	4,018	3,573	54,614
1908	4,626	5,194	5,972	3,735	5,284	3,975	4,010	3,482	4,390	3,911	3,864	5,686	54,129
1909	6,214	3,504	6,970	5,279	5,057	4,913	4,544	3,008	6,478	4,236	4,341	3,995	58,539
1910	5,343	5,198	3,671	4,102	4,482	4,056	3,684	3,264	3,096	2,427	5,395	3,542	48,260
1911	5,517	5,401	3,986	4,351	4,174	3,610	3,466	2,785	3,702	2,883	4,087	6,311	50,273
1912	6,017	4,878	5,144	3,486	3,564	5,044	6,629	4,517	3,689	4,259	5,870	5,370	58,467
1913	5,017	5,283	4,869	5,349	5,256	3,384	3,252	2,942	4,199	5,139	4,335	5,986	55,011
1914	5,701	5,883	5,675	3,499	3,691	3,802	3,589	3,172	1,860	2,458	2,461	3,074	44,865
1915	4,724	4,321	3,723	4,179	3,227	4,458	5,299	3,839	2,236	4,633	5,948	5,799	52,386
1916	4,109	5,558	5,004	4,999	4,347	4,583	3,439	4,392	3,673	4,059	6,085	6,450	56,698
1917	5,490	6,432	7,923	7,091	4,318	6,015	4,504	5,164	3,433	4,835	5,921	6,374	67,500
1918	4,570	5,483	5,144	7,272	5,273	5,425	4,088	5,003	2,907				

1) Sources of Raw Data

Biennial Report of the Secretary of State of the State of Illinois for the Fiscal Years, Beginning October 1, 1896, and Ending September 30, 1898, pp. 57–90, 103. Also similar biennial reports for fiscal years ending in: *1900*, pp. 45–82 and 97–8; *1902* (1902), pp. 66–115 and 143–4; *1904* (1905), pp. 68–131; *1906* (1906), pp. 61–133; *1908* (1908), pp. 76–142; *1910* (1910), pp. 86–150; *1912* (1913), pp. 87–154; *1914* (1915), pp. 94–163; *1916* (1916), pp. 26–94; *1918* (1919), pp. 61–128. All reports except those for which no years of publication are given (in parentheses) were published in Springfield.

2) Special Comments

a) The primary lists used for tallying business incorporations are headed in the following or a similar fashion: "List of Domestic Corporations for Pecuniary Profit". They include companies with capital stock. The corporations chartered without capital stock are listed separately and usually appear in tables headed somewhat as follows: "List of Domestic Corporations not for Profit".

In the reports of the Secretary of State published in the early portion of the period under study, railway incorporations are listed separately, though the segregation seems incomplete. In the later reports newly chartered railways are in the major lists of business incorporations. To make the business incorporation series uniform, the railways listed separately were included in the tally of chartered business enterprises.

Building and loan associations likewise are given in separate tables in the earlier reports, and they would have been tallied as business incorporations had they appeared at all in later reports. The power to issue charters to such associations was transferred in 1899 to another state official who did not publish the information essential for tallying. Had the associations chartered by the Secretary of State in the early period been counted, the series built upon the documents cited in note 1 above would not have been uniform.

A few insurance companies are listed in separate tables but, since capital stock figures are not given, they were not tallied as business enterprises.

b) In the lists of business enterprises chartered, two dates relating to the incorporation of each company are frequently given: one is for "Statement filed and license issued" or "Articles filed"; the other is for "Final certificate issued". The former date was used in tallying because the latter is not always to be found in the lists and because incorporators' intentions were the primary object of study.

c) The series could not be extended beyond September 1918 because the reports of the Secretary of State covering the subsequent period did not contain comparable material. Moreover, the reports covering the period before October 1896 were without the information necessary to extend the above series backward.

ILLINOIS BUSINESS INCORPORATIONS UNDER GENERAL LAWS, 1925–1943

YEAR	JAN.	FEB.	MAR.	APR.	MAY	JUNE	JULY	AUG.	SEPT.	OCT.	NOV.	DEC.	TOTAL
1925	570	508	512	523	454	419	431	399	426	479	360	510	5,591
1926	581	450	519	466	448	426	478	392	429	485	416	438	5,528
1927	506	441	560	535	479	492	412	403	437	428	438	484	5,615
1928	544	551	582	508	585	585	438	509	462	422	532	446	6,164
1929	480	633	605	629	604	618	477	489	471	460	536	408	6,410
1930	430	585	526	559	554	548	460	457	444	469	456	420	5,908
1931	468	587	560	588	612	571	456	458	468	455	568	471	6,262
1932	609	580	579	534	411	455	354	456	446	521	301	320	5,566
1933	611	539	479	510	674	434	334	472	403	423	427	490	5,796
1934	563	453	566	517	456	393	377	345	369	432	404	381	5,256
1935	458	420	463	526	499	409	498	427	441	520	411	452	5,524
1936	511	445	600	454	435	471	458	401	376	395	430	471	5,447
1937	455	474	532	494	463	452	432	417	398	405	417	455	5,394
1938	445	402	472	434	419	403	400	386	376	370	367	425	4,899
1939	433	339	464	390	578	366	395	347	316	368	377	363	4,736
1940	415	407	427	523	429	349	362	335	322	341	241	332	4,483
1941	318	330	382	363	393	295	303	257	261	319	254	274	3,749
1942	228	224	277	254	254	163	183	161	200	192	146	160	2,442
1943	244	158	167	183	244	203	214	191	174	179	179	203	2,339

ILLINOIS BUSINESS INCORPORATIONS UNDER GENERAL LAWS, 1925–1943 (concl.)

1) Source

The U. S. Department of Commerce supplied the figures given above, which it had procured from the Corporation Trust Company.

2) Special Comments

These data, together with incorporation figures for Delaware, Maine, and New York, have been published since 1925 as an incorporation series in the *Survey of Current Business.* According to a footnote in that publication (1942 Supplement, p. 205), incorporations for fraternal and charitable purposes were excluded from the data before the figures were combined. This Illinois series, however, probably contains some corporations that would have been excluded as nonbusiness if the series had been compiled for this study (for a discussion of this point, see Ch. 4).

LOUISIANA BUSINESS INCORPORATIONS UNDER GENERAL LAWS, 1937–1943

YEAR	JAN.	FEB.	MAR.	APR.	MAY	JUNE	JULY	AUG.	SEPT.	OCT.	NOV.	DEC.	TOTAL
1937	56	46	59	75	69	59	69	67	63	67	62	53	745
1938	62	71	60	71	38	45	40	34	37	53	35	26	572
1939	55	32	48	40	62	32	46	38	31	38	36	33	491
1940	41	32	36	43	50	37	41	24	27	38	42	32	443
1941	42	34	37	34	42	35	40	21	29	24	34	23	395
1942	23	23	28	26	27	22	21	14	9	11	4	12	220
1943	14	16	26	21	26	19	20	16	8	23	21	7	217

1) Source

Bureau of Business Research, College of Commerce, Louisiana State University, *Louisiana Business Review:*

VOLUME 1		VOLUME 2		VOLUME 3		VOLUME 4		VOLUME 5		VOLUME 6		VOLUME 7		VOLUME 8	
No.	Page	No.	Page	No.	Page	No.	Page	No.	Page	No.	Page	No.	Page	No.	Page
2	6	1	8	1	9	1	8	1	8	1	11	2	12	1	14
3	9	2	8	2	7	2	8	2	6	2	12	3	12		
4	6	3	7	3	8	3	7	3	7	3	13	4	12		
5	9	4	8	4	8	4	8	4	8	4	12	5	15–6		
6	9	5	7	5	7	5	8	5	7	5	11	6	13–4		
7	7	6	7	6	7	6	8	6	7	6	11	7	14		
8 & 9	6	7	7	7	8	7	8	7	8	7	12	8	14		
10	7	8 & 9	6	8 & 9	7	8 & 9	7	8 & 9	8	8	12	9	14		
11	8	10	6	10	8	10	8	10	10	9	12	10	14		
12	8	11	7	11	8	11	8	11	10	10	13	11	14, 15		
		12	11	12	8	12	8	12	10	11	12	12	14		
										12	12				

Louisiana incorporations for July 1940 and July 1941 were not recorded in the *Review.* The data for these months were therefore obtained directly from the Office of the Secretary of State at Baton Rouge.

2) Special Comments

a) The incorporation series was not compiled for this study, but—except for the above mentioned two figures procured from the Secretary of State of Louisiana—is made up of figures transcribed from the *Louisiana Business Review.* Corporations were not listed by name; the *Review* gave merely the total number of companies chartered each month and an industrial distribution. No data on capital stock have appeared in the *Review.* The series seems to represent business incorporations as defined in this study, except that some mutual companies were included; it was not practicable to eliminate them.

b) Data on Louisiana incorporations are available for some years around 1900 in the reports of the Secretary of State of Louisiana, but their number was not determined since it seemed impossible to link them with the above series.

MAINE BUSINESS INCORPORATIONS BY SPECIAL ACTS, 1820–1891

YEAR	NO.	YEAR	NO.	YEAR	NO.	YEAR	NO.	YEAR	NO.	YEAR	NO.	YEAR	NO.	YEAR	NO.	YEAR	NO.	YEAR	NO.	YEAR	NO.	YEAR	NO.	YEAR	NO.	YEAR	NO.	YEAR	NO.
1820	3	1825	17	1830	13	1835	24	1840	3	1845	30	1850	27	1855	33	1860	31	1865	38	1870	68	1875	66	1880	21	1885	32	1890	0
1821	13	1826	18	1831	20	1836	131	1841	18	1846	44	1851	8	1856	38	1861	16	1866	61	1871	54	1876	11	1881	34	1886	0	1891	98
1822	10	1827	19	1932	21	1837	104	1842	11	1847	32	1852	52	1857	39	1862	19	1867	55	1872	58	1877	4	1882	0	1887	81		
1823	13	1828	12	1833	25	1838	34	1843	10	1848	27	1853	61	1858	14	1863	16	1868	50	1873	68	1878	9	1883	36	1888	0		
1824	10	1829	17	1834	47	1839	14	1844	17	1849	34	1854	63	1859	29	1864	33	1869	65	1874	93	1879	11	1884	0	1889	96		

1) Source of Raw Data

State of Maine, *Business Corporations, Incorporated by Special Acts and Organized under General Law, . . . 1820 to 1892* (Augusta, 1891), pp. 3–71; or *Public Documents of Maine: 1892,* Vol. 1, No. 9.

2) Special Comments

a) The incorporation data in the above source (the names of the corporations chartered, together with the dates of incorporation) were checked against similar data in *Statistics of Industries and Finances of Maine for the year 1884, Third*

Report, by the Secretary of State, (Augusta, 1884), App. pp. 3–48. The 1891 volume corrects several errors in the list of 1884 but seems to have omitted the East Lamoine Water Company which, according to the 1884 volume, was incorporated in 1883. The above table does not include this water company; it was built solely upon the 1891 volume.

b) Since the constitution of Maine was amended in 1876 to require incorporation under general laws when feasible (New York State Constitutional Convention Committee, *Constitutions of the States and the United States*, Albany, 1938, Art. IV, Sec. 14, p. 707), the data for 1876–91 were examined to determine the type of company chartered by special acts. The names of such companies indicate that most were water companies, banks and trust companies, telephone and telegraph companies, railroads, dam and river improvement companies, light and power companies, street railways, insurance companies, ferries, and bridges.

c) The companies tabulated were designated in the document as "Business Corporations". Thus, even though capital stock figures were not given, corporations that on the basis of name appeared to be nonbusiness were not removed from the list. In the 1884 volume there is a note that seems also to apply to the 1891 list at least through 1883: "Cemetery, Park, State Bank, Agriculture & Horticultural, Social, Charitable, Literary and Municipal Corporations, are not included in the foregoing." The post-1883 material in the 1891 volume contains some banking corporations and a very few cemetery, agricultural and horticultural, social, and charitable corporations; all were tallied since they were designated in the document as business corporations.

d) Two general incorporation acts were passed before the constitutional provision requiring incorporation under general law, when feasible, was adopted in 1876. These acts were: *Acts and Resolves . . . of the State of Maine, 1862*, Ch. 152 and *1870*, Ch. 93. Neither seems to have affected appreciably the number of special charters granted. No evidence has been found of chartering under the 1862 act and only 91 charters were issued from 1870 through 1875 under the General Act of 1870.

e) Since Maine did not become a state until March 1820, the series presented here cannot be extended to cover earlier years.

MAINE BUSINESS INCORPORATIONS UNDER GENERAL LAWS, 1870–1943

YEAR	JAN.	FEB.	MAR.	APR.	MAY	JUNE	JULY	AUG.	SEPT.	OCT.	NOV.	DEC.	TOTAL
1870	0	0	0	0	2	1	2	1	3	0	2	0	11
1871	1	3	2	1	2	1	0	3	0	1	2	3	19
1872	0	2	0	1	0	0	0	1	0	2	0	0	6
1873	1	2	0	1	3	6	1	3	1	0	2	3	23
1874	2	3	2	4	3	1	0	1	0	1	2	1	20
1875	0	0	1	1	2	1	1	3	0	2	1	0	12
1876	0	1	1	0	6	1	0	0	0	4	1	0	14
1877	0	3	7	4	9	2	4	3	2	2	2	3	41
1878	3	2	3	3	4	3	2	0	2	1	3	2	28
1879	8	1	4	4	7	5	3	3	3	1	4	12	55
1880	15	28	32	27	24	12	20	18	13	15	16	21	241
1881	12	23	20	18	17	21	21	18	11	29	19	22	231
1882	12	14	16	22	23	26	12	24	28	17	20	14	228
1883	13	18	24	26	19	32	15	17	10	19	13	16	222
1884	19	18	27	33	18	21	20	17	22	13	14	12	234
1885	14	12	15	24	19	20	18	19	10	20	11	26	208
1886	15	12	17	23	23	20	28	15	22	21	27	29	252
1887	22	26	27	33	31	29	16	15	18	26	26	23	292
1888	26	16	28	26	30	23	21	25	30	24	31	28	308
1889	22	19	35	42	43	21	27	30	43	22	38	28	370
1890	38	33	34	46	42	43	60	29	46	37	36	32	476
1891	47	42	37	31	38	34	44	27	40	27	26	43	436
1892	44	37	44	59	39	45	43	40	32	42	44	50	519
1893	50	39	41	55	47	39	40	23	23	29	28	42	456
1894	40	18	48	39	34	29	29	34	22	45	36	31	405
1895	47	32	36	49	31	42	42	43	27	37	35	36	457
1896	53	43	29	40	49	30	46	24	22	34	23	39	432
1897	41	33	48	35	55	44	31	35	44	31	51	42	490
1898	43	36	46	36	37	46	36	28	30	28	44	42	452
1899	58	42	73	58	80	56	59	64	48	50	50	59	697
1900	71	42	52	55	68	57	50	42	39	57	45	53	631
1901	71	59	59	71	86	82	80	75	61	58	76	84	862
1902	68	109	118	108	107	94	107	90	75	119	114	106	1,215
1903	129	131	128	123	112	98	99	72	77	64	81	64	1,178
1904	78	78	72	67	65	71	64	62	49	62	89	96	853
1905	80	80	98	100	94	94	70	72	72	79	75	79	993
1906	101	101	92	101	75	98	67	78	77	84	81	87	1,042
1907	132	98	100	99	107	96	79	65	68	68	45	70	1,027
1908	69	85	81	98	77	63	65	51	72	54	52	83	850
1909	96	88	87	94	74	78	72	60	56	66	68	81	920
1910	67	70	58	67	61	57	59	64	53	47	47	72	722
1911	70	52	66	72	48	59	56	59	61	55	48	64	710
1912	66	72	73	56	50	52	61	54	66	56	45	55	706
1913	66	57	54	48	47	49	41	38	54	46	26	46	572
1914	42	37	63	59	61	51	39	28	42	30	45	31	528
1915	38	32	59	33	38	34	43	44	34	30	51	49	485
1916	51	60	52	62	47	65	54	49	43	55	50	66	654
1917	57	62	66	42	53	48	40	30	40	40	43	27	548
1918	41	34	36	31	30	34	36	33	18	15	13	24	345
1919	45	27	32	42	50	31	38	43	36	53	39	49	485

MAINE BUSINESS INCORPORATIONS UNDER GENERAL LAWS, 1870–1943 (concl.)

YEAR	JAN.	FEB.	MAR.	APR.	MAY	JUNE	JULY	AUG.	SEPT.	OCT.	NOV.	DEC.	TOTAL
1920	70	60	44	52	35	32	36	27	23	24	38	41	482
1921	31	40	35	36	32	24	30	39	25	31	28	40	391
1922	35	45	34	47	41	42	34	22	23	39	33	34	429
1923	39	30	37	39	70	33	27	28	29	26	37	32	427
1924	42	34	45	35	40	31	28	24	27	25	35	28	394
1925	40	35	47	35	35	23	20	34	31	22	30	34	386
1926	48	33	35	30	31	29	15	24	25	28	27	24	349
1927	36	37	33	42	41	31	25	32	26	34	20	33	390
1928	33	29	31	29	32	42	24	34	30	30	25	28	367
1929	40	31	48	23	41	32	24	40	22	30	27	31	389
1930	30	27	42	36	33	24	17	19	24	26	30	31	339
1931	21	33	21	33	29	36	26	16	22	28	16	26	307
1932	38	16	25	24	35	21	21	25	17	18	21	26	287
1933	39	17	24	34	29	40	29	35	26	31	20	28	352
1934	19	20	33	22	29	31	13	19	24	30	18	31	289
1935	31	38	20	41	30	29	18	22	25	22	25	27	328
1936	15	26	19	25	24	19	21	22	22	22	21	25	261
1937	19	13	20	20	24	28	12	20	18	9	24	13	220
1938	25	9	30	23	20	22	19	24	9	19	14	24	238
1939	24	13	21	8	19	11	15	17	11	15	12	17	183
1940	18	19	25	19	10	12	12	17	11	10	9	15	177
1941	18	11	18	12	25	18	16	14	15	17	14	15	193
1942	8	9	17	9	12	23	8	9	6	6	6	7	120
1943	6	5	16	6	8	7	9	14	12	10	8	19	120

1) Sources of Raw Data

State of Maine, *Business Corporations, Incorporated by Special Acts and Organized under General Law, . . . 1820 to 1892* (Augusta, 1891), pp. 72–201; or *Public Documents of Maine: 1892*, Vol. 1, No. 9. Subsequent documents contain reports, published annually in pamphlet form, listing by name the companies chartered. The title of each report is the same as that given above except for a change in the dates to which the report relates. The dates of the successive reports covering the twelve months January 1 to January 1 and the pages from which the incorporation data were compiled are: *1892–93*, pp. 3–15; *1893–94*, pp. 3–13; *1894–95*, pp. 3–14; *1895–96*, pp. 3–13; *1896–97*, pp. 3–16; *1897–98*, pp. 3–17; *1898–99*, pp. 3–16; *1899–1900*, pp. 3–23; *1900–01*, pp. 3–20; *1901–02*, pp. 3–27; *1902–03*, pp. 3–38; *1903–04*, pp. 3–30; *1904–05*, pp. 3–21; *1905–06*, pp. 3–24; *1906–07*, pp. 3–26; *1907–08*, pp. 3–32; *1908–09*, pp. 3–27; *1909–10*, pp. 3–27; *1910–11*, pp. 3–23; *1911–12*, pp. 1–20; *1912–13*, pp. 1–19; *1913–14*, pp. 1–16; *1914–15*, pp. 1–15; *1915–16*, pp. 1–13; *1916–17*, pp. 1–18; *1917–18*, pp. 1–15; *1918–19*, pp. 3–12; *1919–20*, pp. 1–11; *1920–21*, pp. 3–13; *1921–22*, pp. 1–9; *1922–23*, pp. 2–11; *1923–24*, pp. 2–11; *1924–25*, pp. 2–10; *1925–26*, pp. 2–10; *1926–27*, pp. 2–9; *1927–28*, pp. 2–11; *1928–29*, pp. 2–10; *1929–30*, pp. 2–10; *1930–31*, pp. 2–9; *1931–32*, pp. 2–10; *1932–33*, pp. 2–9; *1933–34*, pp. 2–10; *1934–35*, pp. 2–9; *1935–36*, pp. 2–10; *1936–37*, pp. 2–8; *1937–38*, pp. 2–7; *1938–39*, pp. 2–8; *1939–40*, pp. 2–6; *1940–41*, pp. 2–6.

The monthly data for January 1, 1941 through December 31, 1943 were supplied to the writer by the State of Maine, Department of State, Corporation Division.

2) Special Comments

a) Since the published lists of incorporations are for *business* concerns, no effort was made to eliminate companies that on the basis of name might be assumed to have incorporated as nonprofit organizations. Capital stock figures, used elsewhere to segregate business from nonbusiness incorporations, could not be utilized since merely the names and dates of incorporated enterprises are given in the sources.

b) In each pamphlet used there are two lists of incorporations: one for charters procured under general laws; the other for charters granted by special acts. Only companies organized under general laws were tallied. The exclusion of companies created by special acts must be borne in mind when these figures are compared with other published data.

c) Despite the enactment on March 19, 1862 of the first Maine general incorporation law that applied to manufacturing, mechanical, mining, and quarrying businesses (*Acts and Resolves . . . of the State of Maine, 1862*, Ch. 152, Sec. 2, p. 119), there are no data on general incorporations in the above sources for the period prior to 1870. Nor is there evidence in other public documents that charters were issued under general laws during these eight years.

d) Several relatively minor decisions were made in the process of tallying: (1) Whenever two dates appeared after the name of a corporation, the first was taken as the date of incorporation; the second was assumed to be that of an amendment to or renewal of the charter. (2) Whenever a date was obviously a misprint, it was corrected to accord with the surrounding evidence. (3) Supplementary data on stock increases and changes of name were ignored. Thus, when a company's name was followed by the notation, "name changed *from . . .*", the company was not tallied as an incorporation. When the company's name and date of incorporation were followed by information about a name subsequently used by the company, this additional material was ignored. (4) The few company names given without any date of incorporation or with only the year were ignored.

e) On the rare occasion when an entry was duplicated, the second item was, of course, not counted.

MARYLAND BUSINESS INCORPORATIONS BY SPECIAL ACTS, 1800–1852

See Table 7 of text.

1) Source

Joseph G. Blandi, *Maryland Business Corporations, 1783–1852* (The Johns Hopkins University Studies in Historical and Political Science, LII, 2, Baltimore, 1934), pp. 14, 93–111.

2) Special Comments

a) The list of charters in the Appendix of the Blandi volume was compiled from the statutes of the State of Maryland. For the present study mutual insurance companies were eliminated because, whenever possible, they were excluded from the business incorporation series.

b) Each Maryland business company chartered before the spring of 1852 was incorporated by special statute. A constitutional provision requiring business charters to be procured under general law was ratified in June 1851 (New York State Constitutional Convention Committee, *Constitutions of the States and the United States*, Albany, 1938, Art. III, Sec. 48, p. 735), but general incorporating statutes passed in compliance with the constitutional provision were not enacted until the spring of 1852 (*Maryland Laws, 1852*, Ch. 322, 338, and 369).

c) Data for the pre-1800 period on special charters for Maryland business corporations are available in the Blandi volume and in J. S. Davis, *Essays in the Earlier History of American Corporations*, II (Harvard Economic Studies, Vol. XVI, No. iv; 1917). The series presented here can therefore be extended backward.

MARYLAND BUSINESS INCORPORATIONS UNDER GENERAL LAWS, 1870–1939

YEAR	JAN.	FEB.	MAR.	APR.	MAY	JUNE	JULY	AUG.	SEPT.	OCT.	NOV.	DEC.	TOTAL
A Total Incorporations													
1870	11	14	25	16	16	8	12	11	11	11	16	10	161
1871	17	6	17	15	26	12	9	8	11	20	14	17	172
1872	8	12	14	24	24	12	12	11	11	13	12	10	163
1873	5	11	21	10	7	16	12	7	7	6	2	5	109
1874	9	5	10	13	15	17	11	13	11	13	5	3	125
1875	6	5	9	9	9	6	8	7	8	4	5	4	80
1876	4	7	5	8	8	7	3	4	1	2	6	3	58
1877	4	3	7	6	8	3	4	2	4	6	8	9	64
1878	7	8	5	7	10	2	3	3	2	8	5	3	63
1879	3	4	1	3	1	1	2	1	2	6	3	5	32
1880	7	5	8	13	11	5	8	3	3	8	4	5	80
1881	8	4	12	2	14	4	9	5	4	4	6	6	78
1882	6	8	13	10	7	10	4	4	1	8	4	4	79
1883	8	6	16	9	11	14	6	4	8	7	2	8	99
1884	7	9	14	6	7	7	6	9	3	8	4	7	87
1885	4	9	7	9	8	11	3	6	8	12	7	8	92
1886	10	15	15	5	9	8	9	5	10	9	9	10	114
1887	19	11	20	11	13	8	10	6	10	15	14	10	147
1888	12	11	17	13	9	14	8	12	12	10	6	18	142
1889	11	15	13	14	13	12	13	8	10	6	19	10	144
1890	21	21	19	21	21	10	14	10	15	21	20	13	206
1891	20	21	27	20	15	17	17	10	14	23	12	20	216
1892	24	17	19	18	10	12	18	14	11	13	14	23	193
1893	14	16	19	19	15	16	11	11	13	13	16	9	172
1894	21	9	25	14	20	13	13	13	9	17	17	17	188
1895	16	21	23	18	24	15	11	15	16	12	15	22	208
1896	17	13	23	19	14	13	15	14	15	10	12	7	172
1897	17	27	19	12	19	17	15	13	20	15	9	22	205
1898	28	18	26	15	18	14	22	12	11	15	27	6	212
1899	27	29	38	20	27	19	18	12	18	21	11	12	252
1900	23	22	33	15	29	25	16	15	23	16	13	17	247
1901	31	29	43	32	33	30	22	23	16	27	22	25	333
1902	28	27	30	27	21	24	30	26	17	38	20	30	318
1903	36	36	45	31	27	21	16	16	23	13	17	20	301
1904	20	18	43	31	23	34	28	28	22	21	15	26	309
1905	40	34	41	32	42	34	35	23	32	28	37	29	407
1906	41	43	65	30	37	42	22	28	20	29	28	27	412
1907	40	29	49	36	30	39	20	35	27	23	17	9	354
1908	34	23	43	30	35	20	32	48	35	30	41	9	380
1909	50	100	76	47	29	24	49	20	46	34	39	25	539
1910	56	58	30	58	54	41	35	34	31	27	29	42	495
1911	55	52	65	50	40	45	48	38	34	38	34	32	531
1912	47	40	55	34	58	47	54	40	46	43	47	55	566
1913	40	56	55	52	49	36	45	43	53	43	34	35	541
1914	52	52	68	34	66	35	40	37	36	25	27	49	521
1915	59	45	55	50	51	34	60	41	39	44	41	43	562
1916	47	51	74	49	42	46	48	40	41	46	43	53	580
1917	62	65	60	44	50	39	41	43	33	38	45	43	563
1918	44	44	48	40	42	30	37	24	21	21	25	27	403
1919	61	54	63	64	57	73	72	74	82	92	66	106	864
1920	92	90	108	81	81	74	73	68	64	82	65	68	946
1921	71	57	87	92	65	65	57	79	71	72	66	70	852
1922	78	88	83	68	92	77	72	63	65	69	60	66	881
1923	84	84	97	83	74	72	80	68	59	67	77	58	903
1924	94	78	88	90	71	91	65	58	68	84	59	88	934
1925	104	85	96	87	95	72	83	73	89	84	64	100	1,032
1926	110	81	105	103	69	76	77	93	71	89	85	90	1,049
1927	87	109	109	104	82	75	89	79	81	70	91	69	1,045
1928	86	87	106	97	89	96	91	65	70	86	73	112	1,058
1929	123	98	101	90	95	95	90	105	81	109	86	68	1,141
1930	89	71	101	89	64	83	85	67	61	68	60	66	904
1931	64	73	79	78	79	68	74	81	59	58	76	81	870
1932	75	77	89	78	82	89	70	80	75	65	56	54	890
1933	100	69	83	85	98	94	109	88	71	79	62	74	1,012
1934	93	68	79	93	64	79	56	68	41	63	56	56	816
1935	54	82	67	63	57	63	80	65	48	66	68	58	771
1936	72	47	62	79	67	64	67	60	51	65	48	75	757
1937	72	57	59	84	81	60	56	55	65	53	53	53	748
1938	49	43	74	66	52	54	60	55	42	50	46	52	643
1939	45	52	66	68	61	65	48	55	42	48	51	66	667

MARYLAND BUSINESS INCORPORATIONS UNDER GENERAL LAWS, 1870–1939 (cont.)

YEAR	JAN.	FEB.	MAR.	APR.	MAY	JUNE	JULY	AUG.	SEPT.	OCT.	NOV.	DEC.	TOTAL
					B	Small	Incorporations						
1870	1	3	5	1	1	2	1	0	1	1	0	1	17
1871	2	2	1	2	1	2	0	1	2	0	2	2	17
1872	3	0	2	6	2	1	2	1	1	2	1	0	21
1873	1	5	2	2	0	1	0	2	1	0	1	1	16
1874	2	1	5	2	4	3	5	0	3	2	1	0	28
1875	2	2	1	3	1	2	2	1	3	1	1	1	20
1876	2	2	2	3	2	1	3	3	0	0	1	0	19
1877	0	1	2	2	1	0	1	1	0	2	3	3	16
1878	3	3	0	2	4	1	2	1	1	3	0	0	20
1879	1	2	0	2	1	1	0	0	1	2	0	3	13
1880	2	3	7	6	5	2	3	1	0	2	3	1	35
1881	1	2	6	0	7	2	3	3	2	2	3	3	34
1882	3	6	7	2	5	4	1	2	1	1	3	4	39
1883	5	2	5	6	4	8	1	1	2	1	2	5	42
1884	3	2	10	1	4	3	4	3	0	5	0	2	37
1885	3	6	5	5	5	6	3	1	5	6	1	2	48
1886	4	3	7	5	2	5	2	0	3	3	5	4	43
1887	11	4	7	6	8	2	7	3	6	5	7	6	72
1888	9	3	10	7	5	10	2	5	8	5	2	5	71
1889	6	9	9	9	5	7	6	4	4	3	8	4	74
1890	14	12	12	15	8	4	9	6	11	16	12	8	127
1891	11	14	11	11	5	10	12	9	11	19	8	13	134
1892	13	13	13	15	7	12	14	10	9	10	7	15	138
1893	10	10	15	17	10	11	8	11	12	8	11	7	130
1894	13	7	15	10	17	10	9	11	8	11	12	11	134
1895	14	16	14	12	14	12	9	10	13	7	11	15	147
1896	15	9	17	17	12	11	10	9	13	4	8	6	131
1897	11	20	17	9	14	13	9	8	16	12	6	17	152
1898	24	15	22	13	12	11	17	9	10	11	18	3	165
1899	24	22	25	13	18	13	17	7	12	16	6	9	182
1900	17	16	28	14	20	19	14	13	17	13	9	13	193
1901	24	26	34	25	27	21	18	20	13	24	15	20	267
1902	23	19	27	20	18	19	26	21	16	33	19	29	270
1903	29	31	40	25	24	14	14	15	21	11	15	20	259
1904	17	17	39	29	21	30	25	26	18	18	13	22	275
1905	31	28	29	30	36	26	29	18	26	25	31	27	336
1906	34	35	56	23	33	36	18	27	15	23	21	22	343
1907	30	25	39	30	25	30	17	30	26	22	13	5	292
1908	30	23	39	28	32	19	28	47	34	27	38	6	351
1909	43	94	62	41	26	21	48	20	42	31	35	21	484
1910	46	50	25	50	46	34	28	29	26	22	26	39	421
1911	46	46	59	46	36	37	46	33	31	35	30	23	468
1912	40	37	48	32	47	46	44	32	40	40	41	45	492
1913	34	50	43	45	46	28	42	38	46	35	27	31	465
1914	44	51	58	30	60	28	36	31	33	22	18	41	452
1915	47	37	41	38	35	27	51	29	31	36	33	37	442
1916	37	40	61	34	31	35	33	30	34	30	28	36	429
1917	36	41	38	31	40	27	33	34	26	26	29	27	388
1918	31	37	30	30	31	25	20	19	15	18	20	18	294
1919	41	33	44	37	37	47	40	45	41	56	36	49	506
1920	36	41	55	46	38	34	36	36	31	30	26	35	444
1921	41	28	52	47	30	32	25	45	42	44	36	41	463
1922	32	55	50	43	51	38	35	38	39	44	36	31	492
1923	44	43	49	46	36	36	39	46	35	37	35	30	476
1924	52	45	44	53	42	57	42	26	37	49	22	45	514
1925	55	47	48	47	55	39	45	45	56	42	36	53	568
1926	53	36	61	61	33	45	36	52	39	53	47	54	570
1927	48	55	66	58	46	50	55	49	44	36	58	39	604
1928	55	41	55	57	57	53	48	41	36	41	35	63	582
1929	64	53	60	45	47	46	48	51	41	61	39	30	585
1930	51	37	53	46	45	40	46	40	35	37	35	40	505
1931	39	48	38	55	45	41	49	54	42	44	57	51	563
1932	48	53	63	54	57	57	49	53	51	39	40	40	604
1933	69	49	60	55	69	58	52	59	44	56	44	58	673
1934	69	43	58	67	47	69	34	54	32	44	42	39	598
1935	39	58	52	43	43	45	56	54	38	46	44	42	560
1936	56	28	46	56	46	49	44	45	35	45	39	53	542
1937	52	42	46	60	56	44	41	36	45	39	36	33	530
1938	34	30	58	53	42	39	44	47	33	34	31	30	475
1939	33	38	49	56	42	56	28	40	29	35	38	50	494

YEAR	JAN.	FEB.	MAR.	APR.	MAY	JUNE	JULY	AUG.	SEPT.	OCT.	NOV.	DEC.	TOTAL
					C Medium Incorporations								
1870	9	11	20	15	15	5	11	11	9	10	16	8	140
1871	15	4	16	13	24	10	9	7	9	20	12	15	154
1872	5	12	12	18	21	9	10	9	8	11	11	9	135
1873	4	6	18	8	7	14	10	5	6	5	1	3	87
1874	6	4	5	11	11	13	6	13	7	10	3	3	92
1875	4	3	8	6	8	3	5	3	5	3	4	2	54
1876	2	4	3	5	6	6	0	1	0	2	5	3	37
1877	4	2	4	4	6	3	3	1	4	4	4	6	45
1878	3	5	5	4	6	1	1	2	1	4	5	2	39
1879	2	1	1	1	0	0	2	1	1	4	3	2	18
1880	5	1	1	5	5	3	4	1	3	6	1	4	39
1881	6	1	6	1	5	2	5	2	1	2	3	3	37
1882	3	1	2	8	2	4	3	2	0	6	1	0	32
1883	3	3	9	3	6	5	4	1	6	6	0	2	48
1884	2	6	3	5	3	4	2	5	2	3	4	5	44
1885	1	2	1	4	3	4	0	4	3	6	6	6	40
1886	6	10	8	0	4	2	7	5	6	5	4	6	63
1887	7	6	9	4	5	6	3	3	4	10	6	4	67
1888	3	6	6	6	4	4	6	7	3	5	3	11	64
1889	4	6	3	4	8	3	7	2	5	1	10	5	58
1890	6	8	4	6	13	5	4	4	4	5	5	5	69
1891	8	7	15	9	9	6	4	1	2	3	4	7	75
1892	11	4	5	3	3	0	4	4	2	3	7	8	54
1893	4	6	4	2	5	5	2	0	1	4	5	2	40
1894	8	2	9	3	3	3	2	2	1	5	3	6	47
1895	2	4	7	5	7	2	2	3	2	5	3	5	47
1896	2	1	4	1	2	2	4	5	2	4	1	1	29
1897	6	6	2	3	4	4	6	4	3	1	3	4	46
1898	4	3	4	1	6	0	4	3	1	3	5	1	35
1899	3	5	13	6	8	6	1	4	5	2	5	3	61
1900	5	5	5	1	9	6	2	2	6	3	4	3	51
1901	6	3	9	7	5	7	4	3	2	2	7	5	60
1902	4	7	3	6	3	5	3	5	1	5	1	1	44
1903	7	4	5	6	3	6	2	1	1	2	2	0	39
1904	3	1	4	1	2	4	3	2	4	1	2	4	31
1905	9	5	11	1	6	8	6	5	6	3	6	2	68
1906	7	8	9	5	3	6	4	1	5	6	6	5	65
1907	10	4	10	6	3	9	2	5	1	1	3	4	58
1908	4	0	4	2	2	0	4	1	1	3	3	3	27
1909	7	6	13	5	3	3	1	0	3	3	4	4	52
1910	10	7	3	8	6	7	6	5	4	5	3	2	66
1911	8	5	6	3	4	8	2	4	3	3	3	8	57
1912	7	3	7	2	9	1	9	8	5	3	5	10	69
1913	5	6	12	6	3	8	2	5	7	8	7	4	73
1914	8	1	10	3	6	7	3	6	3	3	8	8	66
1915	11	7	14	10	15	7	9	9	7	7	7	6	109
1916	10	10	13	14	11	10	12	9	7	14	12	14	136
1917	22	22	20	11	6	11	6	7	7	10	12	14	148
1918	12	7	14	10	9	5	16	4	6	3	5	9	100
1919	18	19	18	26	18	23	30	23	34	31	25	45	310
1920	40	47	43	27	36	36	26	26	29	48	34	31	423
1921	28	28	31	35	31	30	25	30	27	23	27	23	338
1922	39	30	26	23	37	36	32	19	21	22	23	28	336
1923	37	35	42	31	33	34	36	19	21	26	31	23	368
1924	37	31	41	33	26	30	22	29	27	28	29	34	367
1925	40	31	38	36	30	29	37	26	32	35	22	42	398
1926	49	40	37	31	31	26	39	32	28	29	33	30	405
1927	36	42	36	40	31	19	28	24	34	33	25	25	373
1928	25	35	45	26	26	30	37	20	29	32	31	41	377
1929	46	31	34	36	39	33	35	41	31	37	40	29	432
1930	33	30	40	37	18	41	32	20	25	28	22	24	350
1931	22	24	36	23	33	23	22	26	15	13	18	25	280
1932	23	21	25	24	24	28	20	26	23	24	15	11	264
1933	31	19	20	28	27	36	53	28	24	22	18	14	320
1934	23	25	21	26	17	8	19	13	8	17	12	16	205
1935	15	24	14	19	13	18	23	11	10	19	22	15	203
1936	15	18	13	22	20	15	23	15	16	18	8	18	201
1937	18	13	11	22	25	15	15	19	17	12	17	18	202
1938	15	12	16	13	9	13	13	7	9	15	15	21	158
1939	11	12	16	12	18	9	19	14	12	13	13	16	165

MARYLAND BUSINESS INCORPORATIONS UNDER GENERAL LAWS, 1870–1939 (cont.)

YEAR	JAN.	FEB.	MAR.	APR.	MAY	JUNE	JULY	AUG.	SEPT.	OCT.	NOV.	DEC.	TOTAL
						D Large Incorporations							
1870	1	0	0	0	0	1	0	0	1	0	0	1	4
1871	0	0	0	0	1	0	0	0	0	0	0	0	1
1872	0	0	0	0	1	2	0	1	2	0	0	1	7
1873	0	0	1	0	0	1	2	0	0	1	0	1	6
1874	1	0	0	0	0	1	0	0	1	1	1	0	5
1875	0	0	0	0	0	1	1	3	0	0	0	1	6
1876	0	1	0	0	0	0	0	0	1	0	0	0	2
1877	0	0	1	0	1	0	0	0	0	0	1	0	3
1878	1	0	0	1	0	0	0	0	0	1	0	1	4
1879	0	1	0	0	0	0	0	0	0	0	0	0	1
1880	0	1	0	2	1	0	1	1	0	0	0	0	6
1881	1	1	0	1	2	0	1	0	1	0	0	0	7
1882	0	1	4	0	0	2	0	0	0	1	0	0	8
1883	0	1	2	0	1	1	1	2	0	0	0	1	9
1884	2	1	1	0	0	0	0	1	1	0	0	0	6
1885	0	1	1	0	0	1	0	1	0	0	0	0	4
1886	0	2	0	0	3	1	0	0	1	1	0	0	8
1887	1	1	4	1	0	0	0	0	0	0	1	0	8
1888	0	2	1	0	0	0	0	0	1	0	1	2	7
1889	1	0	1	1	0	2	0	2	1	2	1	1	12
1890	1	1	3	0	0	1	1	0	0	0	3	0	10
1891	1	0	1	0	1	1	1	0	1	1	0	0	7
1892	0	0	1	0	0	0	0	0	0	0	0	0	1
1893	0	0	0	0	0	0	1	0	0	1	0	0	2
1894	0	0	1	1	0	0	2	0	0	1	2	0	7
1895	0	1	2	1	3	1	0	2	1	0	1	2	14
1896	0	3	2	1	0	0	1	0	0	2	3	0	12
1897	0	1	0	0	1	0	0	1	1	2	0	1	7
1898	0	0	0	1	0	3	1	0	0	1	4	2	12
1899	0	2	0	1	1	0	0	1	1	3	0	0	9
1900	1	1	0	0	0	0	0	0	0	0	0	1	3
1901	1	0	0	0	1	2	0	0	1	1	0	0	6
1902	1	1	0	1	0	0	1	0	0	0	0	0	4
1903	0	1	0	0	0	1	0	0	1	0	0	0	3
1904	0	0	0	1	0	0	0	0	0	2	0	0	3
1905	0	1	1	1	0	0	0	0	0	0	0	0	3
1906	0	0	0	2	1	0	0	0	0	0	1	0	4
1907	0	0	0	0	2	0	1	0	0	0	1	0	4
1908	0	0	0	0	1	1	0	0	0	0	0	0	2
1909	0	0	1	1	0	0	0	0	1	0	0	0	3
1910	0	1	2	0	2	0	1	0	1	0	0	1	8
1911	1	1	0	1	0	0	0	1	0	0	1	1	6
1912	0	0	0	0	2	0	1	0	1	0	1	0	5
1913	1	0	0	0	0	0	1	0	0	0	0	0	3
1914	0	0	0	1	0	0	1	0	0	0	1	0	3
1915	1	1	0	2	1	0	0	3	1	1	1	0	11
1916	0	1	0	1	0	1	3	1	0	2	3	3	15
1917	4	2	2	2	4	1	2	2	0	2	4	2	27
1918	1	0	4	0	2	0	1	1	0	0	0	0	9
1919	2	2	1	1	2	3	2	6	7	5	5	12	48
1920	16	2	10	8	7	4	11	6	4	4	5	2	79
1921	2	1	4	10	4	3	7	4	2	5	3	6	51
1922	7	3	7	2	4	3	5	6	5	3	1	7	53
1923	3	6	6	6	5	2	5	3	3	4	11	5	59
1924	5	2	3	4	3	4	1	3	4	7	8	9	53
1925	9	7	10	4	10	4	1	2	1	7	6	5	66
1926	8	5	7	11	5	5	2	9	4	7	5	6	74
1927	3	12	7	6	5	6	6	6	3	1	8	5	68
1928	6	11	6	14	6	13	6	4	5	13	7	8	99
1929	13	14	7	9	9	16	7	13	9	11	7	9	124
1930	5	4	8	6	1	2	7	7	1	3	3	2	49
1931	3	1	5	0	1	4	3	1	2	1	1	5	27
1932	4	3	1	0	1	4	1	1	1	2	1	3	22
1933	0	1	3	2	2	0	4	1	3	1	0	2	19
1934	1	0	0	0	0	2	3	1	1	2	2	1	13
1935	0	0	1	1	1	0	1	0	0	1	2	1	8
1936	1	1	3	1	1	0	0	0	0	2	1	4	14
1937	2	2	2	2	0	1	0	0	3	2	0	2	16
1938	0	1	0	0	1	2	3	1	0	1	0	1	10
1939	1	2	1	0	1	0	1	1	1	0	0	0	8

YEAR	JAN.	FEB.	MAR.	APR.	MAY	JUNE	JULY	AUG.	SEPT.	OCT.	NOV.	DEC.	TOTAL

E   Total Authorized Capital Stock
(thousands of dollars*)

YEAR	JAN.	FEB.	MAR.	APR.	MAY	JUNE	JULY	AUG.	SEPT.	OCT.	NOV.	DEC.	TOTAL
1870	2,759	2,726	3,377	3,349	2,660	1,807	1,905	1,639	2,744	2,629	2,995	2,175	30,765
1871	2,206	968	3,094	2,395	6,588	1,290	1,505	2,390	1,680	3,705	2,962	2,306	31,089
1872	885	2,639	2,154	4,292	5,848	3,640	2,224	2,805	3,685	2,860	2,205	3,600	36,838
1873	665	2,026	4,878	1,870	1,750	5,285	5,454	1,008	933	1,925	250	2,680	28,724
1874	2,825	1,400	1,235	2,764	2,830	4,119	1,633	2,132	3,210	5,052	3,155	1,300	31,656
1875	745	565	1,965	2,756	1,223	1,488	3,635	3,487	681	590	552	1,963	19,650
1876	635	1,552	860	1,386	1,454	1,095	70	246	1,000	800	1,110	630	10,838
1877	737	250	2,345	581	4,470	388	454	350	500	816	2,034	1,220	14,145
1878	2,085	955	700	4,030	1,752	101	262	305	104	3,635	1,734	1,750	17,414
1879	205	2,805	100	681	25	50	500	600	250	610	310	627	6,763
1880	1,117	1,396	580	6,800	3,857	452	2,061	1,118	562	1,320	250	500	20,014
1881	3,380	8,666	1,836	5,100	5,604	950	2,320	530	5,331	450	855	537	35,559
1882	854	1,538	6,380	1,850	1,155	7,656	709	1,041	50	2,273	240	81	23,827
1883	1,122	1,326	5,405	884	4,477	4,814	2,360	2,223	1,898	1,362	25	1,526	27,422
1884	11,450	3,307	2,016	1,120	365	740	745	2,761	1,200	679	1,150	1,220	26,753
1885	160	1,382	1,196	1,234	1,188	2,084	7	1,725	824	2,143	1,310	1,279	14,532
1886	1,121	4,980	2,486	110	3,708	1,412	1,651	1,060	3,171	2,398	1,608	2,245	25,951
1887	7,478	2,626	7,226	2,894	885	1,396	926	564	1,156	3,468	3,335	1,765	33,717
1888	740	5,350	3,892	1,637	1,218	1,379	1,130	1,785	1,708	2,898	6,170	21,263	49,171
1889	2,872	1,782	3,329	2,170	2,667	3,495	1,668	2,875	3,088	3,775	3,560	4,325	35,605
1890	3,780	4,634	7,800	1,844	3,196	1,843	2,965	864	2,006	1,966	8,364	1,145	40,407
1891	3,381	2,524	6,190	2,521	3,678	2,092	2,458	375	1,913	2,034	1,084	2,213	30,464
1892	2,529	1,418	3,138	1,305	572	314	1,029	942	745	482	1,090	2,042	15,607
1893	564	904	996	1,170	1,733	1,038	26,252	267	381	1,720	1,147	559	36,731
1894	1,875	598	7,578	1,946	1,026	998	12,539	530	545	2,773	5,182	2,282	37,873
1895	1,105	2,439	4,851	4,226	6,885	2,934	840	12,108	2,454	1,626	13,060	4,774	57,300
1896	670	4,540	11,747	2,599	566	574	1,918	1,240	471	4,463	21,902	221	50,912
1897	785	11,834	1,018	1,095	2,252	1,094	1,348	1,703	1,938	4,533	857	2,931	31,389
1898	1,361	1,797	857	2,033	1,787	4,443	2,341	1,136	144	2,076	12,095	6,538	36,609
1899	1,195	3,601	3,656	2,971	4,235	2,162	348	1,718	6,256	21,810	894	414	49,259
1900	11,976	11,656	1,427	400	1,700	1,025	482	1,190	913	900	1,026	2,952	35,645
1901	2,278	862	3,154	2,153	6,028	3,262	1,475	1,022	5,540	4,008	1,295	1,932	33,009
1902	7,293	4,162	964	3,145	993	962	1,870	1,436	341	1,939	369	669	24,142
1903	2,315	2,491	1,185	2,486	1,126	2,444	689	344	3,486	576	703	296	18,141
1904	1,006	818	1,918	1,976	704	947	864	628	778	3,986	403	1,909	15,935
1905	2,752	8,274	5,755	1,750	2,219	2,942	1,716	1,055	1,467	951	1,348	833	31,061
1906	2,868	1,974	4,182	3,781	2,960	1,980	872	559	1,076	1,572	3,765	2,320	27,907
1907	3,174	1,930	2,891	1,534	3,384	3,509	1,760	2,283	450	719	3,469	856	25,958
1908	1,455	174	1,330	1,215	2,161	1,140	688	747	937	856	1,510	450	12,662
1909	1,996	2,272	4,780	3,714	642	884	938	289	2,534	1,029	1,440	1,023	21,541
1910	2,585	23,637	3,088	2,668	4,350	1,862	3,332	909	2,659	1,668	1,057	2,322	50,136
1911	3,094	3,550	2,400	2,817	1,343	2,257	937	2,869	1,743	1,036	2,890	4,321	29,256
1912	2,226	1,364	1,833	1,375	5,314	783	3,719	2,855	3,156	695	3,676	3,373	30,368
1913	2,262	2,937	3,890	5,395	1,824	1,865	2,276	1,369	1,601	2,042	2,246	1,092	28,800
1914	3,609	832	3,490	2,265	2,671	3,480	2,700	2,499	867	726	3,169	1,901	28,209
1915	16,526	6,226	3,522	5,071	5,453	2,464	2,248	9,066	5,630	4,014	3,630	1,601	65,451
1916	3,243	8,405	3,343	10,577	3,199	3,799	34,544	3,122	2,647	7,833	17,558	57,110	155,380
1917	40,620	9,458	9,645	5,960	10,337	3,868	4,730	6,010	2,136	6,953	32,328	6,592	138,636
1918	5,247	2,029	34,438	2,266	5,863	1,408	4,852	2,248	1,365	1,346	1,394	4,180	66,637
1919	6,648	10,352	8,356	10,195	9,806	41,068	11,962	27,852	30,630	30,050	16,331	63,678	266,929
1920	82,754	13,314	40,556	16,819	38,750	88,028	183,656	31,578	139,508	18,468	38,703	10,040	702,173
1921	12,703	8,852	15,166	25,387	12,404	11,608	75,760	13,178	7,704	28,162	11,658	23,977	246,560
1922	61,459	12,346	165,829	9,331	65,349	13,350	16,892	142,472	23,456	10,631	8,636	50,749	580,500
1923	21,357	23,220	70,896	43,957	162,492	12,375	17,330	8,975	29,990	83,280	76,679	160,545	711,095
1924	41,860	10,313	23,484	12,344	11,112	29,144	13,425	11,971	25,058	300,179	786,132	267,500	1,532,522
1925	170,248	218,055	191,663	402,987	634,028	15,423	19,070	9,767	11,197	1,250,639	130,688	490,431	3,544,195
1926	3,049,277	44,757	341,596	293,034	112,779	81,500	70,911	80,574	108,685	411,565	28,219	78,014	4,700,909
1927	56,117	238,870	36,454	37,648	123,987	245,428	162,272	45,902	23,725	26,220	34,379	39,086	1,070,086
1928	209,916	159,445	70,170	509,344	375,022	304,092	167,780	31,032	123,444	1,033,019	314,877	102,516	3,400,656
1929	1,346,914	943,256	60,281	126,058	122,731	392,465	269,259	699,022	2,478,917	430,605	76,217	724,407	7,670,131
1930	21,344	32,187	633,653	51,431	5,625	9,544	53,256	367,872	104,026	14,110	56,333	6,109	1,355,490
1931	18,305	34,281	222,263	4,475	8,595	18,037	8,038	10,540	47,670	8,473	5,641	21,761	408,078
1932	30,861	36,329	6,030	4,265	12,760	39,799	8,202	50,049	6,407	10,307	7,468	16,214	228,691
1933	5,420	23,648	109,167	12,204	32,449	6,334	15,910	7,358	7,898	29,401	3,279	6,473	259,542
1934	6,595	3,955	4,604	5,291	3,670	3,688	8,737	3,826	3,970	6,905	6,245	5,556	63,043
1935	2,270	3,835	12,492	5,099	3,804	3,285	5,107	2,195	2,276	4,431	13,378	7,820	65,992
1936	4,912	8,305	6,823	5,716	14,278	3,078	4,042	3,233	2,910	17,633	3,774	28,548	103,251
1937	38,605	4,762	3,952	7,150	4,754	15,010	3,424	3,563	19,027	5,789	2,781	182,742	291,558
1938	2,332	3,349	3,409	2,306	9,024	27,715	6,252	2,849	1,840	12,813	3,367	5,242	80,497
1939	3,261	22,098	3,874	2,025	4,617	2,005	4,242	3,408	5,404	2,855	1,983	3,941	59,710

* The totals of this table were rounded from totals in dollars.

YEAR	JAN.	FEB.	MAR.	APR.	MAY	JUNE	JULY	AUG.	SEPT.	OCT.	NOV.	DEC.	TOTAL

F   Total Authorized Capital Stock Excluding Large Companies
(thousands of dollars)

YEAR	JAN.	FEB.	MAR.	APR.	MAY	JUNE	JULY	AUG.	SEPT.	OCT.	NOV.	DEC.	TOTAL
1870	1,759	2,726	3,377	3,349	2,660	807	1,905	1,639	1,744	2,629	2,995	1,175	26,765
1871	2,206	968	3,094	2,395	4,988	1,290	1,505	2,390	1,680	3,705	2,962	2,306	29,489
1872	885	2,639	2,154	4,292	4,648	1,640	2,224	1,765	1,685	2,860	2,205	2,600	29,597
1873	665	2,026	3,878	1,870	1,750	3,285	2,954	1,008	933	925	250	680	20,224
1874	1,825	1,400	1,225	2,764	2,830	3,119	1,633	2,132	2,210	2,052	555	1,300	23,055
1875	745	565	1,965	2,756	1,223	488	1,635	487	681	590	552	463	12,150
1876	635	552	860	1,386	1,454	1,095	70	246	0	800	1,110	630	8,835
1877	737	250	1,345	581	2,470	388	454	350	500	816	1,034	1,220	10,145
1878	1,085	955	700	1,030	1,752	101	262	305	104	635	1,734	750	9,413
1879	205	305	100	681	25	50	500	600	250	610	310	627	4,263
1880	1,117	396	580	800	2,357	452	561	118	562	1,320	250	500	9,013
1881	1,380	416	1,836	100	1,104	950	820	530	331	450	855	537	9,309
1882	854	288	630	1,850	1,155	656	709	1,041	50	1,273	240	81	8,827
1883	1,122	326	2,565	884	1,477	1,814	860	223	1,898	1,362	25	526	13,082
1884	450	2,267	1,016	1,120	365	740	745	1,761	200	679	1,150	1,220	11,713
1885	160	342	196	1,234	1,188	1,084	7	725	824	2,143	1,310	1,279	10,492
1886	1,121	2,940	2,486	110	708	412	1,651	1,060	2,131	898	1,608	2,245	17,370
1887	2,478	1,626	1,886	894	885	1,396	926	564	1,156	3,468	1,335	1,765	18,379
1888	740	2,270	1,892	1,637	1,218	1,379	1,130	1,785	708	2,898	1,170	3,263	20,090
1889	1,872	1,782	1,249	1,170	2,667	1,495	1,668	375	1,138	275	2,560	825	17,076
1890	2,780	2,554	800	1,844	3,196	843	1,165	864	2,006	1,966	1,364	1,145	20,527
1891	2,341	2,524	4,110	2,521	1,678	1,092	1,458	375	913	1,034	1,084	2,213	21,343
1892	2,529	1,418	2,138	1,305	572	314	1,029	942	745	482	1,090	2,042	14,606
1893	564	904	996	1,170	1,733	1,038	1,252	267	381	720	1,147	559	10,731
1894	1,875	598	2,578	946	1,026	998	539	530	545	1,473	1,182	2,282	14,572
1895	1,105	1,139	1,471	1,626	1,685	434	840	1,108	1,454	1,626	1,060	974	14,522
1896	670	240	747	519	566	574	918	1,240	471	963	602	221	7,731
1897	785	1,834	1,018	1,095	952	1,094	1,348	703	938	433	857	1,431	12,488
1898	1,361	1,797	857	733	1,787	143	1,341	1,136	144	776	1,095	538	11,708
1899	1,195	1,351	3,656	1,671	1,235	2,162	348	718	1,256	810	894	414	15,710
1900	1,976	1,656	1,427	400	1,700	1,025	482	1,190	913	900	1,026	952	13,647
1901	1,278	862	3,154	2,153	1,028	1,262	1,475	1,022	540	758	1,295	1,932	16,759
1902	2,293	1,562	964	1,845	993	962	870	1,436	341	1,939	369	669	14,243
1903	2,315	1,491	1,185	2,486	1,126	1,444	689	344	376	576	703	296	13,031
1904	1,006	818	1,918	776	704	947	864	628	778	486	403	1,909	11,237
1905	2,752	2,274	4,555	750	2,219	2,942	1,716	1,055	1,467	951	1,348	833	22,862
1906	2,868	1,974	4,182	1,531	1,460	1,980	872	559	1,076	1,572	1,685	2,320	22,079
1907	3,174	1,930	2,891	1,534	1,534	3,509	760	2,283	450	719	869	856	20,359
1908	1,455	174	1,330	1,215	1,161	140	688	747	937	856	1,510	450	10,663
1909	1,996	2,272	3,480	2,214	642	884	938	289	1,034	1,029	1,440	1,023	17,241
1910	2,585	2,837	848	2,668	2,350	1,862	2,240	909	1,463	1,668	1,057	1,022	21,509
1911	1,794	2,250	2,400	1,817	1,343	2,257	937	1,269	1,743	1,036	890	2,321	20,057
1912	2,226	1,364	1,833	1,375	3,114	783	2,679	2,855	1,656	695	1,476	3,373	23,429
1913	1,262	2,937	3,890	2,395	1,824	1,865	1,276	1,369	1,601	2,042	2,246	1,092	23,799
1914	3,609	832	3,490	765	2,671	3,480	1,700	2,499	867	726	2,169	1,901	24,709
1915	2,926	1,726	3,522	2,821	4,353	2,464	2,248	2,466	3,830	3,014	2,130	1,601	33,101
1916	3,243	3,405	3,343	3,577	3,199	2,299	3,544	2,121	2,647	4,833	2,758	3,610	38,579
1917	8,220	6,958	6,645	2,960	1,987	2,868	2,230	2,710	2,136	2,953	3,328	4,192	47,187
1918	4,247	2,029	3,798	2,266	2,463	1,408	3,852	1,248	1,365	1,346	1,394	4,180	29,596
1919	4,148	4,352	5,956	7,945	5,556	5,168	5,862	6,502	9,518	8,500	6,731	11,688	81,926
1920	10,304	11,314	12,356	6,529	10,650	10,628	8,231	7,278	7,488	11,168	7,503	6,040	109,489
1921	6,203	7,852	8,466	9,587	7,554	7,908	6,470	7,228	5,404	6,912	7,358	6,337	87,279
1922	7,219	7,086	6,989	6,131	9,174	8,350	7,942	5,332	6,206	6,341	6,136	7,209	84,115
1923	10,357	8,618	10,596	7,157	8,152	7,875	7,330	5,475	6,840	6,830	7,679	5,245	92,154
1924	8,210	6,313	9,584	8,020	5,862	9,144	6,425	6,071	6,558	5,269	7,092	7,500	86,048
1925	10,728	8,127	8,063	9,487	6,708	9,423	9,070	5,767	9,197	8,989	5,613	10,931	102,103
1926	12,277	8,154	7,596	8,494	7,279	7,350	8,411	6,969	5,285	6,065	6,919	7,514	92,313
1927	7,117	7,820	8,464	9,148	6,081	5,428	7,767	5,902	6,225	6,220	6,129	4,836	81,137
1928	7,066	9,145	8,170	6,144	6,022	5,892	8,780	4,032	4,569	7,519	6,877	9,516	83,732
1929	9,714	6,006	7,051	8,758	8,231	7,365	7,884	8,122	7,417	8,105	8,862	4,542	92,057
1930	6,300	6,087	7,903	6,731	4,625	6,944	5,456	4,022	4,026	6,610	4,033	4,024	66,761
1931	3,954	4,281	6,763	4,475	6,595	3,737	4,598	5,540	2,670	3,473	3,641	4,699	54,426
1932	3,761	4,079	5,030	4,265	5,260	5,779	3,202	4,549	4,730	4,307	2,468	2,614	50,044
1933	5,420	3,648	3,167	4,954	4,949	6,334	9,310	6,358	3,898	4,400	3,279	2,873	58,590
1934	4,595	3,955	4,604	5,291	3,670	1,688	3,487	2,826	1,345	3,905	2,245	3,056	40,667
1935	2,270	3,835	2,492	3,099	2,804	3,285	4,107	2,195	2,276	3,431	3,680	3,070	36,544
1936	3,912	4,305	2,783	3,716	4,278	3,078	4,042	3,233	2,910	3,123	2,274	3,548	41,202
1937	3,605	2,762	1,952	3,750	4,754	2,635	3,424	3,563	3,451	2,289	2,781	3,771	38,737
1938	2,332	2,349	3,409	2,306	1,924	2,425	2,952	1,809	1,840	2,813	3,367	3,567	31,093
1939	2,261	2,098	2,874	2,025	3,617	2,005	2,882	2,408	2,404	2,855	1,983	3,941	31,353

1) Sources of Raw Data

Seventh Annual Report of the [Md.] Bureau of Industrial Statistics for 1898 (1899), pp. 143–203; *Eighth Annual Report . . . 1899* (1900), pp. 49–161; *Ninth Annual Report of the Bureau of Industrial Statistics of Maryland, 1900* (1901), pp. 139–56; *Tenth Annual Report . . . 1901* (1902), pp. 196–206; *Eleventh Annual Report of the Bureau of Statistics and Information of Maryland, 1903* (1903), pp. 301–13; also succeeding annual reports, published in years given in parentheses or brackets: (1904), pp. 279–92; [1905], pp. 161–79; (1906), pp. 282–303; (1907), pp. 170–91; (1908), pp. 173–92; (1908), pp. 377–97; (1910), pp. 215–40; (1911), pp. 320–48; (1912), pp. 331–62. All reports were published in Baltimore. The Charter Records in the office of the Maryland State Tax Commission were used for 1912–39.

2) Special Comments

a) Maryland Charter Records from 1908 to date are available for examination in the office of the Maryland State Tax Commission in Baltimore. They were not, however, utilized for the years prior to 1912 because the reports listed above provided a source that could be worked much more rapidly without seriously reducing the accuracy of the compiled incorporation series. The Maryland State Tax Commission has approved charters only since June 1, 1916. From April 16, 1914 through May 31, 1916, Maryland charters were issued by the Secretary of State of Maryland. Until then, courts scattered throughout the state acted as charter approving bodies.

b) The quality and completeness of the incorporation data published by the Bureau of Industrial Statistics and its successor were checked for 1870, 1880, and 1890. The check for even these years could not be complete because for the period before 1908 the incorporation records of Maryland are scattered throughout the courts of the state; it was therefore feasible merely to compare the published data for Baltimore city with the original charter records of the Superior Court in Baltimore. About ten minor errors were found in the published data of each year; they had no effect upon the compilation of the incorporation series. In addition, there were a fairly small number of serious errors, but they do not distort the total picture appreciably. For example, in 1890 the total of charters granted in Baltimore city is the same in both sources; the monthly figures, however, differ here and there by one or two incorporations. The Superior Court records for 1880 show four more incorporations than those of the Bureau; these four additions affect three monthly figures. The serious differences between the published and the original incorporation data for Baltimore for 1870 are of about the same order as those for 1880. Since the total charters granted through the Superior Court in Baltimore in 1870, 1880, and 1890 numbered 157, 70, and 139, respectively, the errors found in the figures published by the Bureau were not considered large enough to discredit the published material as a basis for a description of the general course of incorporations. The errors in the information on charters granted by the courts outside Baltimore, however, are likely to be somewhat more numerous. But even if they are, the series for the state as a whole would not be seriously affected since the number of charters granted through the Superior Court at Baltimore greatly exceeded the total granted through the other courts.

c) In the above mentioned publications of the Bureau, the listings of incorporations in any given year were often scattered over two—and once even over three—successive volumes. Accordingly, the incorporation figures for 1911 are probably smaller than they should be because the *Twenty-first Annual Report of the Bureau of Statistics and Information of Maryland, 1912* did not contain data on incorporations similar to those previously published.

d) When compiling the incorporation data from the publications of the Bureau the few companies for which the month of incorporation or the capital stock was not given had to be omitted—the former because it was desirable to have monthly and annual figures agree, the latter because it was necessary to preserve a balance between the series for the number of incorporations and those for capital stock.

Amendments to charters are presented in the tables from which the incorporation data were gathered but, of course, were not tallied for the series on incorporations.

e) The above figures on business incorporations differ from those on total incorporations published by the Maryland State Tax Commission. In assembling data on incorporations for this study, companies chartered without capital stock were treated as nonbusiness.

f) Whenever nonpar shares appeared in authorized capital stock, they were treated as shares of a par value of $100, since from 1916 (when Maryland authorized the issue of nonpar shares) to 1941 these two types of share were equated in that fashion for the computation of annual franchise taxes. This relation may be traced from *Maryland Laws, 1916*, Ch. 596, Sec. 9, through the various tax laws to *The Annotated Code of the Public General Laws of Maryland* (1939 ed.), Art. 81, Sec. 144, and finally to *Maryland Laws, 1941*, Ch. 912, Sec. 8, which established a new method for determining the value of nonpar shares for the levy of the annual franchise tax. The 1941 change does not affect the Maryland series set forth above since it ends with 1939.

g) Renewed charters and amended certificates were not tallied as incorporations.

h) When working the Maryland forfeiture lists for Chapter 2, a negligible number of companies that had changed from nonstock to stock corporations had to be disposed of. They were added to the business incorporation series as of the month in which they became stock companies. This method of treating transfers aligned the data on forfeitures and incorporations without causing more than slight changes in the compiled series on incorporations. No attempt was made to add to the business incorporation series *all* companies that changed from nonstock to stock units.

MASSACHUSETTS BUSINESS INCORPORATIONS UNDER GENERAL LAWS, 1851–1921

YEAR	JAN.	FEB.	MAR.	APR.	MAY	JUNE	JULY	AUG.	SEPT.	OCT.	NOV.	DEC.	TOTAL
A Total Incorporations													
1851						1	0	2	0	3	0	2	
1852	4	1	2	3	2	0	2	3	0	1	0	2	20
1853	1	4	3	3	3	2	0	1	0	2	1	1	21
1854	2	0	2	4	2	0	0	1	0	0	2	0	13
1855	2	0	0	3	4	3	4	2	1	3	9	0	31
1856	3	2	1	2	6	3	1	2	2	0	2	2	26
1857	2	2	1	5	3	5	1	2	3	1	1	0	26
1858	1	0	0	1	1	1	0	1	1	1	1	3	11
1859	2	1	3	1	3	5	2	1	2	0	0	0	20
1860	2	1	2	2	2	1	0	4	2	1	1	3	21
1861	1	1	3	1	3	2	0	2	0	1	1	1	16
1862	5	1	2	2	0	0	3	1	1	2	2	1	20
1863	1	2	7	5	0	6	4	2	0	10	8	11	56
1864	15	6	35	27	24	16	8	16	8	2	9	8	174
1865	18	17	16	10	10	13	11	10	7	6	9	9	136
1866	16	15	7	10	12	10	2	7	5	7	7	5	103
1867	6	11	8	5	11	7	7	6	4	5	6	11	87
1868	17	11	10	5	8	6	5	8	4	7	2	6	89
1869	6	0	6	4	5	9	3	6	4	7	3	3	56

MASSACHUSETTS BUSINESS INCORPORATIONS UNDER GENERAL LAWS, 1851–1921 (cont.)

YEAR	JAN.	FEB.	MAR.	APR.	MAY	JUNE	JULY	AUG.	SEPT.	OCT.	NOV.	DEC.	TOTAL
A Total Incorporations (concl.)													
1870	6	5	8	5	2	4	4	3	6	4	7	11	65
1871	12	6	7	6	8	8	12	2	7	6	5	5	84
1872	3	10	10	9	9	6	9	3	6	6	6	4	81
1873	9	9	6	5	6	10	9	5	7	5	5	12	88
1874	10	5	6	6	6	3	7	8	6	10	7	6	80
1875	14	4	6	8	8	8	9	8	8	3	7	3	86
1876	7	7	10	5	6	7	2	2	7	4	1	5	63
1877	2	11	7	6	7	5	7	8	4	11	4	8	80
1878	8	3	7	8	4	2	11	5	2	4	6	9	69
1879	5	4	9	9	12	1	12	2	2	4	8	9	77
1880	15	10	10	16	9	13	13	10	15	9	13	12	145
1881	11	12	11	7	17	12	11	12	9	12	13	22	149
1882	14	10	14	8	17	14	9	12	4	12	10	8	132
1883	11	12	16	11	14	9	13	7	9	5	12	13	132
1884	21	12	18	17	13	8	7	5	7	5	7	23	143
1885	15	8	11	7	11	10	6	6	7	12	5	13	111
1886	14	17	8	13	16	12	12	11	7	12	13	11	146
1887	10	15	18	11	21	20	12	12	7	9	8	10	153
1888	20	23	18	16	29	11	13	9	13	13	14	16	195
1889	22	21	15	12	19	21	24	15	28	22	17	17	233
1890	20	18	15	24	20	20	13	10	9	16	14	20	199
1891	19	21	22	18	26	22	13	8	11	12	11	20	203
1892	18	27	30	20	20	14	22	21	18	9	25	21	245
1893	24	23	16	28	24	19	21	8	10	12	12	30	227
1894	35	18	21	22	17	19	16	16	14	11	19	20	228
1895	16	21	23	16	24	16	20	15	18	31	20	31	251
1896	23	25	20	27	17	19	20	16	14	14	16	24	235
1897	21	21	29	30	18	26	13	19	17	23	21	21	259
1898	22	18	27	37	16	17	13	8	19	17	16	22	232
1899	20	22	27	23	30	25	24	9	14	20	18	24	256
1900	26	24	21	20	28	28	21	10	12	8	13	28	239
1901	37	20	16	28	27	24	18	11	17	19	13	24	254
1902	27	29	27	21	26	25	22	13	19	12	17	20	258
1903	33	29	32	19	23	25	13	59	61	86	75	80	535
1904	95	83	100	78	103	90	78	90	80	89	76	105	1,067
1905	130	95	118	99	144	99	103	105	85	106	89	99	1,272
1906	131	112	132	104	136	102	108	87	82	104	100	116	1,314
1907	146	122	144	109	121	96	102	69	73	83	55	93	1,213
1908	116	116	104	115	108	115	111	95	81	81	98	136	1,276
1909	114	101	160	119	144	116	96	78	90	94	119	112	1,343
1910	126	115	130	119	121	104	78	80	85	88	110	127	1,283
1911	153	105	148	125	122	99	89	107	93	108	110	124	1,383
1912	133	119	132	133	123	108	134	111	96	120	119	147	1,475
1913	140	149	141	142	139	118	99	109	95	119	106	144	1,501
1914	163	143	167	167	128	124	149	107	106	111	94	136	1,595
1915	158	141	176	154	143	143	137	129	110	136	137	155	1,719
1916	165	152	198	177	180	179	146	136	129	141	159	184	1,946
1917	252	187	216	183	152	171	150	118	114	150	139	133	1,965
1918	125	111	152	181	134	115	150	102	78	84	89	143	1,464
1919	200	184	184	230	237	194	230	252	201	238	217	311	2,678
1920	331	235	309	298	260	255	221	184	189	199	152	187	2,820
1921	207	194	250	233	197	197	182	186	170	158	178		
B Small Incorporations													
1851						1	0	2	0	1	0	2	
1852	3	1	2	2	2	0	2	2	0	1	0	2	17
1853	1	3	1	3	1	2	0	1	0	2	1	1	16
1854	0	0	2	3	1	0	0	1	0	0	2	0	9
1855	2	0	0	2	3	3	1	2	0	3	9	0	25
1856	3	2	1	1	5	2	1	1	1	0	2	2	21
1857	2	2	1	5	3	3	1	2	2	1	1	0	23
1858	1	0	0	1	1	1	0	1	1	1	1	2	10
1859	0	1	0	1	2	5	2	0	1	0	0	0	12
1860	2	1	1	1	2	0	0	2	2	0	1	3	15
1861	1	0	3	1	1	2	0	1	0	1	1	1	12
1862	4	0	2	2	0	0	3	1	0	1	2	1	16
1863	1	0	2	2	0	2	0	2	0	1	6	2	18

YEAR	JAN.	FEB.	MAR.	APR.	MAY	JUNE	JULY	AUG.	SEPT.	OCT.	NOV.	DEC.	TOTAL
1864	5	2	5	2	4	2	2	4	1	1	4	2	34
1865	6	5	6	1	1	3	5	1	2	2	3	4	39
1866	6	9	2	6	2	5	2	2	1	3	5	1	44
1867	2	6	4	1	7	3	4	2	2	4	6	8	49
1868	10	6	6	3	2	3	2	5	2	4	2	1	46
1869	4	0	5	3	2	4	2	2	1	3	2	2	30
1870	2	3	4	3	1	4	4	3	4	3	4	6	41
1871	7	5	5	4	5	4	8	1	3	2	2	3	49
1872	2	3	9	5	6	2	6	2	5	3	3	2	48
1873	7	4	6	2	5	7	5	4	3	4	3	9	59
1874	8	2	5	4	3	1	4	6	5	9	7	5	59
1875	11	3	6	6	6	6	5	5	5	3	7	3	66
1876	6	6	9	3	5	4	2	1	5	3	1	3	48
1877	2	10	5	3	6	5	5	7	1	4	4	5	57
1878	6	1	6	7	4	2	8	3	0	3	5	7	52
1879	4	4	5	6	11	1	8	2	2	4	6	6	59
1880	9	7	9	10	7	10	7	8	6	5	9	9	96
1881	6	8	6	5	11	8	7	8	6	9	8	15	97
1882	12	7	11	7	14	13	8	8	2	11	7	3	103
1883	4	9	13	10	10	7	11	6	7	4	11	11	103
1884	16	9	14	15	10	7	5	3	6	3	6	14	108
1885	9	6	10	6	10	7	6	5	7	9	5	11	91
1886	10	14	7	11	15	9	12	11	7	9	11	10	126
1887	10	14	16	9	18	17	10	10	7	6	7	9	133
1888	18	19	14	13	22	10	10	9	11	10	14	13	163
1889	19	16	12	9	17	17	21	12	27	20	15	17	202
1890	20	16	14	20	19	14	10	10	9	12	12	19	175
1891	17	19	20	15	22	19	12	6	10	12	10	17	179
1892	15	21	23	16	18	11	16	18	14	9	24	17	202
1893	17	20	15	25	18	17	18	8	9	10	12	22	191
1894	27	18	18	20	14	19	15	12	13	10	19	18	203
1895	13	21	20	15	20	13	19	12	17	25	19	25	219
1896	20	25	19	26	17	16	17	15	14	11	12	21	213
1897	18	19	27	26	14	25	11	16	16	23	19	20	234
1898	19	16	27	35	14	16	13	8	17	14	12	20	211
1899	19	16	26	22	28	24	21	9	11	18	13	20	227
1900	24	22	19	18	27	25	19	10	10	7	13	28	222
1901	32	18	13	25	24	23	17	10	17	18	10	21	228
1902	24	26	25	19	25	22	22	12	19	11	17	19	241
1903	31	26	31	17	21	24	9	50	53	67	59	63	451
1904	80	70	84	59	79	75	65	74	66	68	63	83	866
1905	104	77	106	81	116	80	94	93	73	91	75	84	1,074
1906	115	99	113	91	120	81	91	69	66	90	82	90	1,107
1907	120	103	123	92	104	88	91	58	60	75	50	78	1,042
1908	108	106	86	101	100	102	95	81	70	76	86	114	1,125
1909	101	82	154	103	134	96	89	70	85	80	101	102	1,197
1910	112	102	114	104	109	93	70	74	76	79	96	113	1,142
1911	134	91	127	114	105	88	77	91	81	95	102	112	1,217
1912	115	98	111	117	103	91	115	95	80	104	96	121	1,246
1913	126	123	121	132	119	92	83	102	83	96	93	121	1,291
1914	140	122	138	137	105	109	129	95	91	104	84	121	1,375
1915	133	126	149	136	127	123	113	116	97	123	113	128	1,484
1916	138	130	162	144	160	154	123	121	109	128	133	139	1,641
1917	213	165	173	157	132	146	125	98	95	130	109	106	1,649
1918	108	93	138	159	111	104	132	92	69	74	78	117	1,275
1919	162	154	155	188	195	153	188	214	160	180	178	225	2,152
1920	254	183	245	230	200	174	157	129	126	136	113	128	2,075
1921	145	139	185	175	151	142	121	140	133	126	133		

C   Medium Incorporations

YEAR	JAN.	FEB.	MAR.	APR.	MAY	JUNE	JULY	AUG.	SEPT.	OCT.	NOV.	DEC.	TOTAL
1851						0	0	0	0	2	0	0	
1852	1	0	0	1	0	0	0	1	0	0	0	0	3
1853	0	1	2	0	2	0	0	0	0	0	0	0	5
1854	2	0	0	1	1	0	0	0	0	0	0	0	4
1855	0	0	0	1	1	0	3	0	1	0	0	0	6
1856	0	0	0	1	1	1	0	1	1	0	0	0	5
1857	0	0	0	0	0	2	0	0	1	0	0	0	3
1858	0	0	0	0	0	0	0	0	0	0	0	1	1
1859	2	0	3	0	1	0	0	1	1	0	0	0	8

MASSACHUSETTS BUSINESS INCORPORATIONS UNDER GENERAL LAWS, 1851–1921 (cont.)

YEAR	JAN.	FEB.	MAR.	APR.	MAY	JUNE	JULY	AUG.	SEPT.	OCT.	NOV.	DEC.	TOTAL
					C Medium Incoporations (concl.)								
1860	0	0	1	1	0	1	0	1	0	1	0	0	5
1861	0	1	0	0	2	0	0	1	0	0	0	0	4
1862	1	1	0	0	0	0	0	0	1	1	0	0	4
1863	0	2	5	3	0	4	4	0	0	9	2	9	38
1864	10	4	30	25	20	14	6	12	7	1	5	6	140
1865	12	12	10	9	9	10	6	9	5	4	6	5	97
1866	10	6	5	4	10	5	0	5	4	4	2	4	59
1867	4	5	4	4	4	4	3	4	2	1	0	3	38
1868	7	5	4	2	6	3	3	3	2	3	0	5	43
1869	2	0	1	1	3	5	1	4	3	4	1	1	26
1870	4	2	4	2	1	0	0	0	2	1	3	5	24
1871	5	1	2	2	3	4	4	1	4	4	3	2	35
1872	1	7	1	4	3	3	3	1	1	3	3	2	32
1873	2	5	0	3	1	3	4	1	4	0	2	3	28
1874	2	3	1	2	3	2	3	2	1	1	0	1	21
1875	3	1	0	2	2	2	4	3	3	0	0	0	20
1876	1	1	1	2	1	3	0	1	2	1	0	2	15
1877	0	1	2	3	1	0	1	0	1	3	0	2	14
1878	2	1	1	1	0	0	3	2	2	0	1	2	15
1879	1	0	4	2	1	0	4	0	0	0	2	3	17
1880	6	3	1	5	2	3	6	2	9	4	4	3	48
1881	5	4	4	2	6	3	4	4	3	3	5	7	50
1882	2	3	2	1	3	1	1	4	2	1	3	5	28
1883	7	2	3	1	4	2	2	1	2	1	1	2	28
1884	5	3	4	2	3	1	2	2	1	2	1	9	35
1885	6	2	1	1	1	3	0	1	0	3	0	2	20
1886	4	3	1	2	1	3	0	0	0	3	2	1	20
1887	0	1	2	2	3	3	2	2	0	3	1	1	20
1888	2	3	4	3	7	1	3	0	2	3	0	3	31
1889	3	5	3	3	2	4	3	3	1	2	2	0	31
1890	0	2	1	4	1	6	3	0	0	4	2	1	24
1891	2	2	2	3	4	3	1	2	1	0	1	3	24
1892	3	6	7	4	2	3	6	3	3	0	1	4	42
1893	7	3	1	3	6	2	3	0	1	2	0	8	36
1894	8	0	2	2	3	0	1	4	1	1	0	2	24
1895	3	0	3	1	3	3	1	3	1	6	1	6	31
1896	3	0	1	1	0	2	3	1	0	3	4	3	21
1897	3	2	2	4	4	1	2	3	1	0	2	1	25
1898	3	2	0	1	2	1	0	0	2	3	4	2	20
1899	1	6	1	1	2	1	3	0	3	2	5	3	28
1900	2	2	2	2	0	3	2	0	2	1	0	0	16
1901	5	2	3	3	2	1	1	1	0	1	3	3	25
1902	2	3	2	2	1	2	0	1	0	1	0	1	15
1903	2	3	1	1	2	1	2	9	8	18	14	17	78
1904	15	12	14	18	22	15	12	16	13	21	12	21	191
1905	26	18	12	17	27	18	9	12	12	15	12	14	192
1906	13	13	18	11	15	19	17	17	16	14	17	24	194
1907	24	19	21	16	16	8	9	11	12	8	5	15	164
1908	8	10	18	14	7	13	16	14	11	5	12	21	149
1909	12	18	6	14	9	19	7	7	5	14	16	9	136
1910	13	13	16	14	10	9	7	6	9	9	11	13	130
1911	13	11	19	11	16	9	11	15	11	13	6	11	146
1912	17	20	14	14	17	14	15	15	15	14	21	22	198
1913	12	21	17	9	17	23	16	7	11	22	11	21	187
1914	20	20	24	28	20	13	19	11	13	6	10	14	198
1915	23	14	26	18	13	20	22	10	11	13	22	22	214
1916	25	19	31	28	16	22	22	14	20	12	23	42	274
1917	35	18	40	21	16	22	24	18	16	17	29	20	276
1918	15	14	12	18	22	10	17	9	9	10	11	25	172
1919	37	27	28	38	35	33	33	32	37	49	34	75	458
1920	62	46	55	61	55	67	55	51	56	61	36	56	661
1921	59	50	62	51	44	49	58	46	37	29	43		

D Large Incorporations

From June 1851 through Dec. 1902, large business incorporations were as follows: 1860, Aug. *1*; 1872, June *1*; 1873, Oct. *1*; 1877, July *1*, Aug. *1*, Sept. *2*, Oct. *4*, Dec. *1*; 1878, Feb. *1*, Oct. *1*; 1879, Apr. *1*; 1880, Apr. *1*; 1881, Mar. *1*, June *1*; 1882, Mar. *1*; 1883, Feb. *1*; 1888, Feb. *1*; 1892, Sept. *1*; 1894, Mar. *1*; 1895, May *1*; 1896, June *1*; 1898, Apr. *1*; 1899, Dec. *1*; 1900, May *1*; 1901, May *1*; 1902, Jan. *1*, June *1*.

YEAR	JAN.	FEB.	MAR.	APR.	MAY	JUNE	JULY	AUG.	SEPT.	OCT.	NOV.	DEC.	TOTAL
1903	0	0	0	1	0	0	2	0	0	1	2	0	6
1904	0	1	2	1	2	0	1	0	1	0	1	1	10
1905	0	0	0	1	1	1	0	0	0	0	2	1	6
1906	3	0	1	2	1	2	0	1	0	0	1	2	13
1907	2	0	0	1	1	0	2	0	1	0	0	0	7
1908	0	0	0	0	1	0	0	0	0	0	0	1	2
1909	1	1	0	2	1	1	0	1	0	0	2	1	10
1910	1	0	0	1	2	2	1	0	0	0	3	1	11
1911	6	3	2	0	1	2	1	1	1	0	2	1	20
1912	1	1	7	2	3	3	4	1	1	2	2	4	31
1913	2	5	3	1	3	3	0	0	1	1	2	2	23
1914	3	1	5	2	3	2	1	1	2	1	0	1	22
1915	2	1	1	0	3	0	2	3	2	0	2	5	21
1916	2	3	5	5	4	3	1	1	0	1	3	3	31
1917	4	4	3	5	4	3	1	2	3	3	1	7	40
1918	2	4	2	4	1	1	1	1	0	0	0	1	17
1919	1	3	1	4	7	8	9	6	4	9	5	11	68
1920	15	6	9	7	5	14	9	4	7	2	3	3	84
1921	3	5	3	7	2	6	3	0	0	3	2		

E Total Authorized Capital Stock
(thousands of dollars)

YEAR	JAN.	FEB.	MAR.	APR.	MAY	JUNE	JULY	AUG.	SEPT.	OCT.	NOV.	DEC.	TOTAL
1851						30	0	56	0	255	0	69	
1852	319	5	35	205	30	0	85	202	0	5	0	100	986
1853	50	315	955	92	420	75	0	12	0	48	45	20	2,032
1854	350	0	65	174	125	0	0	24	0	0	45	0	783
1855	50	0	0	262	285	59	437	37	300	50	246	0	1,726
1856	102	50	40	158	264	195	21	510	305	0	95	72	1,812
1857	80	71	50	94	85	1,057	22	82	148	6	5	0	1,700
1858	110	0	0	50	40	72	0	10	15	10	45	212	564
1859	300	24	820	25	145	165	60	120	116	0	0	0	1,775
1860	22	60	405	275	95	350	0	1,835	35	360	8	80	3,525
1861	6	100	125	25	270	25	0	120	0	10	15	50	746
1862	340	150	108	75	0	0	90	25	200	132	86	5	1,211
1863	24	200	1,355	445	0	1,280	1,425	100	0	2,935	964	2,150	10,878
1864	2,580	1,460	8,625	8,250	6,320	3,480	1,980	5,615	2,340	130	1,605	1,493	43,878
1865	4,660	2,355	2,976	2,337	3,200	2,805	1,960	1,720	970	988	890	1,455	26,316
1866	2,830	1,720	870	854	2,305	1,498	130	1,074	711	665	570	1,224	14,451
1867	1,028	1,564	865	520	1,030	1,244	625	1,196	374	292	224	760	9,722
1868	2,201	1,194	655	261	1,594	1,000	946	652	394	448	17	1,508	10,870
1869	648	0	345	203	910	1,087	180	624	810	1,278	200	170	6,455
1870	950	420	1,152	687	160	121	131	105	422	246	666	1,025	6,085
1871	1,096	222	375	430	968	1,565	1,776	160	1,048	431	1,129	538	9,738
1872	145	2,182	356	1,520	1,036	1,575	948	417	286	849	965	309	10,588
1873	592	1,059	153	734	276	872	1,007	1,017	711	1,097	480	679	8,677
1874	977	370	260	1,175	700	660	608	470	230	407	240	213	6,310
1875	1,052	425	172	349	607	343	1,063	635	592	41	117	107	5,503
1876	204	168	728	492	348	552	11	183	826	183	1	405	4,101
1877	55	346	546	531	320	106	1,250	1,270	2,510	4,762	133	1,499	13,328
1878	398	1,205	272	287	29	11	1,205	358	400	1,035	298	593	6,091
1879	217	80	1,311	1,310	392	5	1,225	28	41	111	678	640	6,038
1880	1,603	957	414	9,570	788	643	982	565	1,946	742	870	653	19,733
1881	1,636	571	1,942	506	1,795	1,922	802	790	921	601	1,073	2,240	14,799
1882	509	1,055	2,361	456	938	385	316	1,434	330	291	469	807	9,351
1883	1,871	1,529	1,190	402	1,245	315	1,091	272	636	171	429	562	9,713
1884	1,137	789	1,112	676	632	400	742	290	456	355	294	2,793	9,676
1885	1,207	314	254	321	810	732	70	171	119	894	97	474	5,463
1886	668	821	246	365	392	506	235	230	73	789	761	427	5,513
1887	271	518	486	424	727	1,128	536	873	107	729	339	268	6,406
1888	590	2,794	1,484	826	1,497	496	788	178	548	531	250	612	10,594
1889	754	1,673	757	962	979	997	711	1,319	537	935	638	408	10,670
1890	426	460	409	1,271	803	1,334	449	253	126	1,237	511	656	7,935
1891	894	940	802	1,438	1,106	1,021	410	324	494	221	273	997	8,920
1892	1,012	1,300	2,290	1,281	856	1,130	970	1,158	2,096	127	586	896	13,702
1893	1,996	1,059	375	927	1,087	848	994	82	411	364	270	1,762	10,175
1894	1,504	302	1,607	779	790	284	603	940	425	299	401	1,104	9,038
1895	523	530	1,110	329	2,060	1,351	601	1,079	358	1,688	472	2,019	12,120
1896	783	555	535	712	658	1,445	788	522	179	476	782	1,189	8,624
1897	848	784	1,071	937	590	614	456	998	507	381	1,454	419	9,059
1898	987	622	339	1,898	698	364	249	166	514	763	659	798	8,057
1899	551	1,295	880	462	820	694	1,150	123	900	591	1,153	5,161	13,780

Massachusetts Business Incorporations under General Laws, 1851–1921 (concl.)

YEAR	JAN.	FEB.	MAR.	APR.	MAY	JUNE	JULY	AUG.	SEPT.	OCT.	NOV.	DEC.	TOTAL

E Total Authorized Capital Stock (concl.)
(thousands of dollars)

YEAR	JAN.	FEB.	MAR.	APR.	MAY	JUNE	JULY	AUG.	SEPT.	OCT.	NOV.	DEC.	TOTAL
1900	968	1,106	567	488	2,086	1,172	1,106	93	594	700	177	618	9,675
1901	2,164	1,180	1,451	964	2,128	542	559	426	422	618	1,672	1,030	13,156
1902	2,519	1,117	998	1,447	551	1,726	539	434	295	287	314	679	10,906
1903	1,062	827	930	4,933	522	708	90,530	3,042	2,846	6,871	10,146	4,297	126,714
1904	4,159	4,311	6,049	5,128	8,246	4,552	5,514	5,118	8,612	4,608	4,842	6,290	67,429
1905	6,080	6,370	5,027	6,210	7,550	4,787	3,507	4,863	4,000	4,898	5,752	5,858	64,902
1906	9,538	3,781	7,396	17,126	8,454	7,456	5,199	5,070	4,515	4,394	7,243	7,446	87,618
1907	8,314	7,462	6,724	5,680	6,464	2,772	5,810	2,962	5,045	2,978	1,920	5,083	61,214
1908	4,818	3,562	5,167	4,427	5,076	3,716	4,935	4,399	3 486	2,333	3,924	7,648	53,491
1909	5,956	7,083	4,388	7,041	6,905	9,708	3,056	5,034	3,222	4,409	9,135	5,161	71,098
1910	7,032	4,716	7,500	6,546	9,049	8,208	4,312	3,504	3,270	3,708	7,962	5,597	71,404
1911	22,734	11,371	13,856	4,213	6,382	6,758	5,626	6,552	13,247	5,230	8,141	10,747	114,857
1912	9.824	8,374	16,350	11,150	23.091	14,990	48,826	8,408	14,721	20,221	26,635	22,318	224,908
1913	31,840	36,893	13,227	6,020	10,279	10,656	4,877	3,570	5,086	18,346	8,970	11,644	161,408
1914	12,015	8,313	21,275	13,404	11,857	13,075	10,149	5,329	7,165	4,471	4,496	7,874	119,423
1915	17,136	7,354	16,027	6,653	13,154	6,407	8,619	8,993	7,379	6,164	7,852	13,768	119,506
1916	15,405	68,596	68,785	24,295	13,193	13,744	9,050	6,334	5,109	9,099	16,449	17,421	267,480
1917	20,037	19,273	17,671	15,277	12,478	14,160	10,128	8,057	8,273	9,296	11,302	30,704	176,656
1918	15,980	13,281	9,192	20,585	14,156	5,621	7,103	6,118	4,326	4,203	4,794	8,822	114,181
1919	12,612	14,110	12,610	21,298	23,841	36,327	40,001	22,583	17,855	32,118	21,971	50,306	305,632
1920	62,373	32,203	31,780	50,320	32,446	105,746	33,127	19,713	44,858	18,272	20,436	21,720	472,994
1921	25,353	35,153	24,231	28,539	14,933	30,302	35,166	12,270	9,598	12,984	12,673		

F Total Authorized Capital Stock Excluding Large Companies
(thousands of dollars)

From June 1851 through Dec. 1902, capital stock figures excluding large companies are the same as those for total capital stock (see E above), except that the total stock figures of the following dates are larger by the indicated amounts in thousands of dollars: 1860, Aug. *1,650;* 1872, June *1,000;* 1873, Oct. *1,000;* 1877, July *1,000,* Aug. *1,000,* Sept. *2,000,* Oct. *4,000,* Dec. *1,000;* 1878, Feb. *1,000,* Oct. *1,000;* 1879, Apr. *1,000;* 1880, Apr. *7,350;* 1881, Mar. *1,000,* June *1,000;* 1882, Mar. *1,000;* 1883, Feb. *1,000;* 1888, Feb. *1,000;* 1892, Sept. *1,000;* 1894, Mar. *1,000;* 1895, May *1,000;* 1896, June *1,000;* 1898, Apr. *1,000;* 1899, Dec. *4,030;* 1900, May *1,600;* 1901, May *1,000;* 1902, Jan. *1,500,* June *1,100.*

YEAR	JAN.	FEB.	MAR.	APR.	MAY	JUNE	JULY	AUG.	SEPT.	OCT.	NOV.	DEC.	TOTAL
1903	1,062	827	930	433	522	708	530	3,042	2,846	5,371	3,246	4,297	23,814
1904	4,159	3,311	4,049	4,128	6,246	4,552	4,514	5,118	3,812	4,608	3,842	5,290	53,629
1905	6,080	6,370	5,027	5,210	6,550	3,787	3,507	4,863	4,000	4,898	3,752	4,858	58,902
1906	5,138	3,781	6,196	4,126	5,454	5,456	5,199	4,070	4,515	4,394	6,043	5,446	59,818
1907	6,314	7,462	6,724	4,180	4,964	2,772	3,810	2,962	3,545	2,978	1,920	5,083	52,714
1908	4,818	3,562	5,167	4,427	3,926	3,716	4,935	4,399	3,486	2,333	3,924	6,448	51,141
1909	4,956	5,583	4,388	5,041	5,205	7,208	3,056	3,034	3,222	4,409	4,635	3,661	54,398
1910	4,432	4,716	7,500	5,546	5,949	5,708	3,062	3,504	3,270	3,708	3,639	4,547	55,581
1911	4,484	3,871	5,856	4,213	5,382	3,008	4,626	5,052	3,247	5,230	4,141	5,147	54,257
1912	6,824	5,874	6,040	6,650	6,591	6,840	5,826	4,408	4,721	5,721	7,535	7,818	74,848
1913	5,840	8,393	7,659	5,020	6,279	6,156	4,877	3,570	4,086	5,846	3,970	6,394	68,090
1914	7,915	7,313	11,025	10,104	7,157	6,325	7,149	4,329	4,915	4,915	4,496	5,374	79,573
1915	7,236	5,354	9,027	6,653	5,704	6,407	6,619	4,793	4,409	6,164	5,852	6,988	75,206
1916	8,405	5,596	9,285	9,595	6,543	8,744	7,550	5,284	5,109	5,599	9,199	11,671	92,580
1917	14,337	7,023	13,921	9,277	7,028	9,160	9,128	6,057	5,273	5,796	10,302	6,854	104,156
1918	4,980	5,081	6,692	6,835	8,156	4,621	6,103	3,618	4,326	4,203	4,794	7,822	67,231
1919	11,112	8,110	11,360	13,798	11,241	10,827	13,976	13,083	12,155	16,268	11,421	23,756	157,107
1920	20,973	15,103	19,780	22,570	18,146	21,246	13,677	12,703	14,273	15,672	11,086	17,720	202,949
1921	16,973	13,653	17,731	14,439	11,433	15,802	13,191	12,270	9,598	9,384	10,473		

1) Sources of Raw Data

Documents of the Commonwealth of Massachusetts: for 1851–62, *Abstract of Returns of Joint Stock Companies in Massachusetts, required by Chapter 61 of General Statutes* (Boston, 1863), pp. 4–20; for 1863, *Abstract of the Attested Returns of Corporations Organized during 1863, under General Statutes of Massachusetts* (Boston, 1864), pp. 4–7. The other documents used for this study were published annually under similar titles. For 1864–71 the title of each document is the same, or about the same, as for 1863, while the remaining volumes, for 1872–1921, are entitled *Abstract of the Certificates of Corporations....* The periods covered by successive reports and the pages from which the incorporation data were compiled are: *1864,* pp. 5–17; *1865,* pp. 4–13; *1866,* pp. 4–11; *1867,* pp. 4–9; *1868,* pp. 4–9; *1869,* pp. 4–7; *1870,* pp. 4–5, 10–12; *1871,* pp. 5–11; *1872,* pp. 6–13; *1873,* pp. 6–13; *1874,* pp. 6–13; *1875,* pp. 4–14; *1876,* pp. 4–12; *1877,* pp. 5–9; *1878,* pp. 5–9; *1879,* pp. 5–9; *1880,* pp. 5–9; *1881,* pp. 5–9; *1882,* pp. 5–9; *1883,* pp. 5–9; *1884,* pp. 5–10; *1885,* pp. 5–8; *1886,* pp. 5–10; *1887,* pp. 5–10; *1888,* pp. 5–11; *1889,* pp. 5–12; *1890,* pp. 5–11; *1891,* pp. 5–11; *1892,* pp. 5–12; *1893,* pp. 5–12; *1894,* pp. 5–12; *1895,* pp. 5–13; *1896,* pp. 5–12; *1897,* pp. 5–13; *1898,* pp. 5–12; *1899,* pp. 5–13; *1900,* pp. 5–12; *1901,* pp. 5–13; *1902,* pp. 5–13; *1903,* pp. 5–25; *1904,* pp. 5–46; *1905,* pp. 5–53; *January 1, 1906–November 30, 1906,* pp. 5–50; *December 1, 1906–November 30, 1907,* pp. 5–51; *December 1, 1907–November 30, 1908,* pp. 5–50; *December 1, 1908–November 30, 1909,* pp. 5–55; *December 1, 1909–November 30, 1910,* pp. 5–52; *December 1, 1910–November 30, 1911,* pp. 5–58; *December 1, 1911–November 30, 1912,* pp. 5–59;

December 1, 1912–November 30, 1913, pp. 5–61; *December 1, 1913–November 30, 1914*, pp. 5–53; *December 1, 1914–November 30, 1915*, pp. 5–56; *December 1, 1915–November 30, 1916*, pp. 5–63; *December 1, 1916–November 30, 1917*, pp. 5–66; *December 1, 1917–November 30, 1918*, pp. 5–48; *December 1, 1918–November 30, 1919*, pp. 5–79; *December 1, 1919–November 30, 1920*, pp. 5–97; *December 1, 1920–November 30, 1921*, pp. 6–80.

2) Special Comments

a) The data were taken from the main table of certificates, or articles, of organization in each of the above volumes. Frequently other very small tables appear (often containing only 2 or 3 items) such as those giving the details of organization for railroad, insurance, electric, water, drainage, gas, and trust companies. These corporations were not included in the tally of companies chartered under general laws, but they should have been counted to make the Massachusetts total incorporation series strictly comparable with the other state series. Various calculations, however, were made from the above figures for Massachusetts incorporations, and it was considered unnecessary to recompute, using more inclusive figures. The alterations would have been both time consuming and negligible in effect. The data tabulated for this study are clearly indicated above; anyone who cares to add the information in the small supplementary tables referred to may easily do so.

A rather large table containing a few companies with capital stock, but a majority with no capital stock, appears frequently in the volumes cited above. As these corporations were non business, they were not tallied.

b) Computed totals differ slightly from official totals partly because the few companies whose capital stock was given as "not fixed" or as "none" were not tallied. To have counted them would have destroyed the balance between the series on number and those on capital stock. An exception was made when working the early volumes: on the rare occasions when capital stock does not appear but a figure called "amount of capital" does, the latter was used. When other differences between computed and official figures were found, the computed totals were checked carefully; if a difference persisted, the official totals were deemed to be in error as far as the published data are concerned.

c) Reorganizations, which were few, were not tallied.

d) The date used in tallying was the date of 'charter' or of 'incorporation', not of 'organization'. (For 1870 and earlier years the date was designated as 'certificate of organization when filed', which seemed very similar in meaning.)

e) Nonpar stock, first appearing in the above cited 1919–20 volume, was treated as having a value of $100 per share because in the volume for 1920–21 (see p. 1309) the law was said to require that the rates used for settling filing and recording fees for the articles of organization of trading companies should be 1/20 of 1% of the total authorized capital stock with par value and 5¢ per share for all authorized shares without par value.

NEW JERSEY BUSINESS INCORPORATIONS BY SPECIAL ACTS, 1800–1870

See Table 8 of text.

1) Source of Raw Data

John Hood, *Index of Titles of Corporations chartered under general and special laws by the Legislature of New Jersey... 1693–1870...* (Trenton, 1871) (a report to the Governor of New Jersey), pp. 31–196.

2) Special Comments

a) In the above mentioned source, the names and dates of incorporation of both business and nonbusiness enterprises are given. Companies created under general and special laws are listed separately. The information on the former was not used anywhere in this study; instead, the source cited in the 1846–1918 New Jersey section of this Appendix was used.

b) The data on nonbusiness corporations chartered by special acts are incomplete since Hood notes that he excluded "Agricultural, Benevolent, Cemetery, City, Educational, Fire, Meadow, Medical, Military, Religious and Town Associations". In separating business from nonbusiness corporations his industrial groupings were utilized. Only two groups contained nonbusiness corporations: Insurance Companies and Hall Companies. In the former, mutual insurance companies were treated as nonbusiness enterprises; in the latter, library associations and lodges were similarly treated. The name of the company within each group served to indicate whether the concern was a business or nonbusiness enterprise, since capital stock figures were not given. Hood's industrial groups are:

Banks [including Loan Companies, Savings Institutions, and Trust Companies]
Bridge Companies
Canal Companies
Docks and Wharves
Express Companies
Gas Companies
Hall Companies
Hotel Companies
Ice Companies
Improvement Companies [including Land Companies, and Building Associations]
Insurance Companies
Manufacturing Companies [including Mining Companies]
Market Companies
Miscellaneous Companies [including Oil Companies, Transportation Companies, and Warehouse Companies]
Navigation Companies
Railroad Companies
Steamboat and Steamship Companies [including Ferry Companies]
Telegraph Companies
Turnpike Road Companies [including Plank Road Companies]
Water Companies and Water Works

c) Hood's figures must be used with great care because his list contains companies chartered by other states that were authorized by special act to do business in New Jersey. These were not tabulated as New Jersey corporations. The following were excluded on these grounds but unfortunately there may have been others that should have been excluded: First Union Co-operative Land and Building Association (of New York), 1869; National Land and Mining Company, of New York, 1866 (see next paragraph)*; New York Co-operative Building Lot Association, of New York, 1869; Fire Insurance Company of Northampton County, Pennsylvania, 1861; North American Transit Insurance Company of Philadelphia, 1865; Allentown Iron Company, of Pennsylvania, 1863; Lehigh Crane Iron Company of Pennsylvania, 1862 (see next paragraph)*; Susquehanna and Wyoming Valley Railroad and Coal Company of Pennsylvania, 1866; South Side Railroad Company of Pennsylvania, 1869; Thomas Iron Company of Pennsylvania, 1862 (see next paragraph)*; Lehigh Water Company, of Easton, Pennsylvania, 1861. The above were authorized to do business during the 'sixties. Several other companies that appeared to be foreign corporations were found to be New Jersey corporations when looked up in the laws.

The list contains 75 duplications, which were eliminated. A bridge and ferry company, for example, is listed among Bridge as well as among Ferry Companies. Three of the 75 were not tallied because they were foreign corporations (the 3 items with asterisks in the preceding paragraph); 2 others appeared three times in Hood's list, but of course were tallied only once.

Sixteen items which represent the grant to an individual of certain rights, for example, the right to construct a bridge or to operate a ferry, were not counted as charters of incorporation. In the process of eliminating them, several other items were looked up in the New Jersey laws to determine whether they were incorporations. This attempt to eliminate Hood entries that were not incorporations involved looking up in the statutes all items in which the following words or phrases did not appear in the name of the enterprise: company, works, mill, factory, manufactory, president and directors of, or the proprietors of. This procedure was not applied to Banks or Hall Associations; all items in these two groups were treated as incorporations.

In a few cases the same company name appears with different incorporation dates. While these were probably all merely reincorporations upon the expiration of an original charter, they were tallied as new incorporations.

NEW JERSEY BUSINESS INCORPORATIONS BY SPECIAL ACTS, 1800–1870 (concl.)

d) The series of New Jersey corporations created under special acts can be extended into the period before 1800 by the use of J. S. Davis, *Essays in the Earlier History of American Corporations*, II (Harvard Economic Studies, 1917, Vol. XVI, No. iv).

e) While a general incorporation law for manufacturing companies was enacted on February 25, 1846 (*New Jersey Laws, 1846*, p. 64), charters for manufacturing purposes continued to be procured by special acts until the constitutional provision of 1875 (New York State Constitutional Convention Committee, *Constitutions of the States and the United States*, Albany, 1938, Art. iv, Sec. 11, p. 1056). Other acts providing for the incorporation of business enterprises under general laws were likewise enacted between 1846 and 1875, but as in the case of the 1846 law, it was not compulsory to procure a charter under general law (for other general incorporation laws, see *N. J. Laws: 1849*, p. 300; *1873*, Ch. CCCXIII).

NEW JERSEY BUSINESS INCORPORATIONS BY SPECIAL ACTS, 1871–1875

See Table 8 of text.

1) Source of Raw Data
Laws of New Jersey, 1871, 1872, 1873, 1874, and 1875.

2) Special Comments
See the portions of the text that relate to Table 8.

NEW JERSEY BUSINESS INCORPORATIONS UNDER GENERAL LAWS, 1846–1918

YEAR	JAN.	FEB.	MAR.	APR.	MAY	JUNE	JULY	AUG.	SEPT.	OCT.	NOV.	DEC.	TOTAL
A Total Incorporations													
1846			0	0	0	1	0	1	1	0	1	0	
1847	0	0	1	1	0	0	1	2	0	0	0	0	5
1848	2	0	0	0	0	0	1	0	0	1	0	1	5
1849	0	1	0	0	0	0	0	0	0	0	0	0	1
1850	1	0	1	2	1	0	0	1	0	1	0	0	7
1851	0	1	0	2	5	2	1	2	2	1	0	2	18
1852	4	2	0	0	0	1	1	2	1	0	1	1	13
1853	2	3	4	1	0	0	0	2	1	5	1	0	19
1854	0	3	2	2	2	1	1	1	4	3	2	0	21
1855	1	2	0	2	0	1	4	1	1	2	2	0	16
1856	0	2	1	0	2	0	0	3	0	0	0	0	8
1857	0	1	3	1	2	2	0	0	1	1	0	0	11
1858	3	4	1	3	2	1	1	2	1	2	0	0	20
1859	1	1	0	0	0	0	0	0	1	1	0	1	5
1860	1	2	1	0	2	0	0	0	1	0	0	0	7
1861	1	0	1	0	0	0	0	0	0	0	0	0	2
1862	0	0	2	0	0	0	0	0	3	0	4	2	11
1863	1	2	0	0	1	1	0	1	0	1	0	0	7
1864	2	1	1	2	0	1	1	0	1	3	0	0	12
1865	0	1	0	0	0	3	0	1	1	0	0	2	8
1866	1	1	2	4	1	1	1	2	3	3	4	2	25
1867	5	1	0	1	1	1	1	6	3	4	2	0	25
1868	0	1	0	2	0	0	2	1	2	2	2	1	13
1869	1	1	2	0	0	1	0	3	2	1	0	3	14
1870	4	1	1	2	1	1	2	1	1	0	3	2	19
1871	2	0	3	2	1	1	5	4	1	4	1	3	27
1872	1	2	2	2	3	2	3	4	0	0	1	3	23
1873	3	1	2	5	4	2	0	7	4	3	3	1	35
1874	1	1	7	1	5	4	4	3	1	3	3	5	38
1875	4	4	0	1	1	8	5	4	6	4	5	9	51
1876	3	2	7	6	8	6	5	2	5	1	7	4	56
1877	10	4	0	1	8	8	4	5	5	7	6	6	64
1878	7	7	2	5	5	7	4	6	3	10	9	8	73
1879	3	7	3	8	8	14	4	4	4	4	9	11	79
1880	16	15	15	17	13	12	10	8	19	14	19	10	168
1881	24	33	47	32	36	39	41	26	41	54	34	42	449
1882	30	36	36	22	32	38	27	28	17	24	30	31	351
1883	29	24	26	26	32	24	20	29	15	22	21	27	295
1884	22	37	25	18	23	22	20	16	13	11	8	17	232
1885	21	14	26	22	16	21	22	16	28	26	13	29	254
1886	26	32	39	48	30	33	29	18	17	31	51	32	386
1887	41	41	39	51	47	37	27	41	31	30	46	41	472
1888	48	45	46	38	49	45	55	46	44	44	49	58	567
1889	68	55	69	57	62	46	55	54	35	51	78	55	685

YEAR	JAN.	FEB.	MAR.	APR.	MAY	JUNE	JULY	AUG.	SEPT.	OCT.	NOV.	DEC.	TOTAL
1890	71	67	83	67	76	97	88	55	65	75	72	81	897
1891	101	101	94	108	82	107	81	74	79	96	94	138	1,155
1892	111	121	141	103	111	110	88	92	76	78	68	113	1,212
1893	119	109	115	101	93	73	69	54	49	51	62	75	970
1894	77	79	100	86	88	61	57	75	56	71	71	69	890
1895	79	65	82	91	100	71	78	80	69	61	92	95	964
1896	71	88	109	100	71	83	68	52	39	62	42	74	859
1897	100	92	111	72	94	79	81	91	97	106	87	108	1,118
1898	119	100	119	97	70	96	51	68	75	101	96	112	1,104
1899	160	146	242	224	206	207	162	155	150	157	174	203	2,186
1900	176	167	195	202	182	153	151	130	128	157	153	201	1,995
1901	207	203	285	248	238	229	168	133	127	160	172	183	2,353
1902	235	153	214	207	204	178	208	162	160	177	173	184	2,255
1903	245	228	216	220	165	179	158	128	120	121	119	136	2,035
1904	126	146	148	153	145	136	128	125	121	121	116	170	1,635
1905	170	151	173	152	208	158	137	127	131	145	143	177	1,872
1906	200	187	223	210	182	190	118	149	112	171	157	187	2,086
1907	203	184	186	198	162	166	162	136	102	136	107	98	1,840
1908	127	111	160	149	128	141	140	129	135	156	112	155	1,643
1909	189	191	220	204	182	169	150	151	153	136	152	194	2,091
1910	175	174	193	192	172	175	133	136	120	145	132	162	1,909
1911	174	162	185	176	171	171	119	120	149	143	137	149	1,856
1912	193	168	184	166	157	138	169	126	125	175	129	170	1,900
1913	187	144	124	137	132	100	106	103	101	108	98	105	1,445
1914	139	116	120	147	124	111	102	80	79	90	83	89	1,280
1915	110	110	149	128	122	114	126	111	98	124	103	133	1,428
1916	159	130	185	143	151	125	111	115	127	127	117	132	1,622
1917	146	106	153	149	132	117	119	116	96	155	131	95	1,515
1918	118	134	140	136	106	105	110	98	82	68	73	102	1,272

B Small Incorporations

From March 1846 through December 1865, small business incorporations were as follows: 1846, June *1*, Sept. *1*; 1848, Jan. *1*; 1850, Jan. *1*, Mar. *1*, Apr. *1*, Aug. *1*; 1851, May *1*, Sept. *1*; 1852, Jan. *2*, July *1*, Aug. *1*, Sept. *1*; 1853, Feb. *1*, Mar. *3*; 1854, Mar. *1*, Apr. *2*, June *1*, Sept. *2*, Oct. *3*, Nov. *1*; 1855, Apr. *2*, July *2*, Oct. *1*; 1856, Mar. *1*, Aug. *1*; 1857, Feb. *1*; 1858, Jan. *2*, Apr. *1*, May *1*, Aug. *1*, Sept. *1*, Oct. *1*; 1859, Feb. *1*, Sept. *1*, Oct. *1*; 1860, Feb. *2*, May *1*, Sept. *1*; 1862, Mar. *1*, Sept. *1*, Nov. *2*; 1863, Jan. *1*, Feb. *1*, May *1*, June *1*, Aug. *1*; 1864, Jan. *1*, Feb. *1*, Mar. *1*, Apr. *1*, July *1*, Oct. *1*; 1865, Feb. *1*, June *1*, Aug. *1*, Dec. *2*.

Year	Jan.	Feb.	Mar.	Apr.	May	June	July	Aug.	Sept.	Oct.	Nov.	Dec.	Total
1866	1	0	2	2	0	0	1	2	1	1	2	0	12
1867	1	0	0	0	0	1	0	3	1	2	0	0	8
1868	0	0	0	1	0	0	2	0	2	1	0	1	7
1869	0	1	2	0	0	1	0	2	1	1	0	2	10
1870	1	0	1	1	0	1	1	1	0	0	2	1	9
1871	1	0	0	2	0	1	2	2	0	0	1	2	13
1872	0	1	1	0	1	1	0	2	0	0	1	2	9
1873	0	1	0	1	2	1	0	4	0	1	1	0	11
1874	1	0	4	0	2	1	1	2	1	2	2	5	21
1875	1	0	0	0	1	6	2	3	3	2	3	7	28
1876	0	0	5	2	5	4	2	2	3	1	4	2	30
1877	7	2	0	0	4	4	3	1	3	4	3	4	35
1878	3	3	1	5	5	5	2	4	2	7	4	5	46
1879	1	5	1	7	7	9	1	2	3	3	4	6	49
1880	7	5	10	7	4	5	5	3	5	6	10	1	68
1881	7	7	15	9	8	13	11	5	15	8	11	17	126
1882	6	5	16	9	13	14	7	4	4	7	8	10	103
1883	9	12	10	8	16	10	7	8	8	8	11	15	122
1884	9	19	8	8	13	8	9	10	7	6	3	7	107
1885	11	5	15	11	8	8	13	6	16	17	4	16	130
1886	11	18	21	26	16	21	17	8	8	16	30	14	206
1887	22	13	20	26	16	16	13	12	13	14	12	19	196
1888	25	21	16	18	16	24	21	15	24	17	24	22	243
1889	34	30	35	25	25	22	20	24	20	21	34	20	310
1890	33	29	37	33	40	43	38	27	27	35	27	37	406
1891	40	58	37	54	41	45	37	31	41	45	44	67	540
1892	54	42	66	47	63	54	33	34	33	36	29	46	537
1893	52	46	52	53	53	35	38	30	25	19	36	38	477
1894	40	43	58	49	50	34	37	35	27	40	33	34	480
1895	31	35	46	49	40	43	40	38	37	45	45	37	486
1896	41	43	69	56	37	33	34	30	20	29	23	44	459

New Jersey Business Incorporations under General Laws, 1846–1918 (cont.)

YEAR	JAN.	FEB.	MAR.	APR.	MAY	JUNE	JULY	AUG.	SEPT.	OCT.	NOV.	DEC.	TOTAL
					B	Small Incorporations (concl.)							
1897	54	51	58	43	50	48	39	44	44	56	52	46	585
1898	51	48	56	49	35	46	22	31	24	50	42	42	496
1899	68	54	73	77	70	70	63	48	54	49	55	75	756
1900	57	69	69	79	60	49	50	45	45	73	55	71	722
1901	78	84	98	86	78	80	52	38	39	61	55	59	808
1902	68	52	79	73	73	57	64	57	51	59	55	58	746
1903	75	80	65	95	56	71	58	45	48	42	62	62	759
1904	68	61	67	68	77	72	57	48	64	53	41	74	750
1905	73	70	73	70	103	62	68	50	56	72	66	84	847
1906	100	96	105	100	82	90	59	62	54	73	73	87	981
1907	113	93	98	92	82	84	80	79	55	71	55	52	954
1908	72	65	82	73	70	77	76	64	72	85	66	82	884
1909	97	103	128	117	98	91	77	90	85	76	79	102	1,143
1910	99	90	104	117	102	99	75	71	71	79	81	96	1,084
1911	105	101	112	86	113	93	78	74	93	85	79	80	1,099
1912	110	92	116	96	92	82	100	72	79	111	83	104	1,137
1913	98	76	73	84	78	65	71	64	70	74	64	62	879
1914	91	76	66	102	72	63	65	56	50	65	50	61	817
1915	70	70	103	83	90	81	85	70	66	81	68	83	950
1916	96	76	132	89	94	76	77	81	88	74	73	86	1,042
1917	99	70	95	87	87	75	78	77	69	105	96	58	996
1918	74	82	92	85	68	59	71	66	53	46	43	64	803
					C	Medium Incorporations							
1846			0	0	0	0	0	1	0	0	1	0	
1847	0	0	1	1	0	0	1	2	0	0	0	0	5
1848	1	0	0	0	0	0	1	0	0	1	0	1	4
1849	0	1	0	0	0	0	0	0	0	0	0	0	1
1850	0	0	0	1	1	0	0	0	0	1	0	0	3
1851	0	1	0	2	4	2	1	2	1	1	0	2	16
1852	2	2	0	0	0	1	0	1	0	0	1	1	8
1853	2	2	1	1	0	0	0	2	1	5	1	0	15
1854	0	3	1	0	2	0	1	1	1	0	1	0	10
1855	1	2	0	0	0	1	2	1	1	1	2	0	11
1856	0	2	0	0	2	0	0	2	0	0	0	0	6
1857	0	0	3	1	2	2	0	0	1	1	0	0	10
1858	1	2	1	2	1	1	1	1	0	1	0	0	11
1859	1	0	0	0	0	0	0	0	0	0	0	1	2
1860	1	0	1	0	1	0	0	0	0	0	0	0	3
1861	1	0	1	0	0	0	0	0	0	0	0	0	2
1862	0	0	1	0	0	0	0	0	2	0	2	2	7
1863	0	1	0	0	0	0	0	0	0	1	0	0	2
1864	1	0	0	1	0	1	0	0	1	2	0	0	6
1865	0	0	0	0	0	2	0	0	1	0	0	0	3
1866	0	1	0	2	1	1	0	0	2	1	2	2	12
1867	4	1	0	1	1	0	1	3	2	1	2	0	16
1868	0	1	0	1	0	0	0	1	0	1	2	0	6
1869	1	0	0	0	0	0	0	1	1	0	0	1	4
1870	3	1	0	1	1	0	1	0	1	0	1	1	10
1871	1	0	3	0	1	0	3	1	1	2	0	1	13
1872	1	1	1	2	2	1	2	2	0	0	1	1	13
1873	2	0	2	1	1	1	0	2	4	1	2	1	17
1874	0	1	2	1	1	2	3	1	0	1	1	0	13
1875	3	4	0	1	0	2	3	1	3	1	2	2	22
1876	1	2	1	4	3	2	3	0	2	0	3	2	23
1877	3	2	0	1	3	4	1	3	2	2	3	2	26
1878	3	2	1	0	0	1	1	2	0	2	4	2	18
1879	2	2	2	0	0	4	2	2	1	1	5	3	24
1880	6	8	3	4	6	4	4	5	8	5	6	6	65
1881	11	16	26	15	14	11	21	15	17	24	11	18	199
1882	16	22	11	9	15	18	12	15	7	14	16	15	170
1883	10	9	14	16	13	8	13	19	7	12	7	11	139
1884	10	15	13	6	10	11	9	6	6	2	5	10	103
1885	8	9	10	10	8	12	9	9	10	9	9	13	116
1886	14	11	14	18	13	10	11	9	8	13	20	18	159
1887	12	25	15	21	26	13	10	22	16	12	34	17	223
1888	23	21	28	15	29	13	29	23	18	22	19	28	268
1889	30	20	29	29	32	23	31	25	13	27	39	30	328

YEAR	JAN.	FEB.	MAR.	APR.	MAY	JUNE	JULY	AUG.	SEPT.	OCT.	NOV.	DEC.	TOTAL
1890	33	35	42	31	30	45	37	21	31	36	39	37	417
1891	53	37	53	43	36	52	30	36	37	44	43	58	522
1892	53	71	63	53	43	49	50	42	40	38	33	58	593
1893	58	54	53	43	31	32	25	23	19	29	26	35	428
1894	35	31	36	34	37	21	16	40	27	26	34	31	368
1895	46	30	34	37	38	32	34	30	23	42	39	45	430
1896	26	39	34	40	32	45	30	20	14	29	18	24	351
1897	41	34	44	27	36	29	34	39	41	41	31	48	445
1898	58	45	53	43	31	39	25	31	47	47	42	57	518
1899	67	63	125	108	104	104	74	82	71	79	93	106	1,076
1900	94	75	99	103	101	90	82	69	72	66	78	111	1,040
1901	98	104	160	136	129	122	93	83	75	76	97	88	1,261
1902	141	93	109	102	102	95	121	89	86	98	102	101	1,239
1903	144	117	123	103	92	91	85	74	64	70	55	66	1,084
1904	49	81	76	71	62	54	62	73	49	64	63	87	791
1905	87	73	88	70	92	80	62	70	70	67	72	80	911
1906	88	81	104	100	90	91	57	78	54	89	74	88	994
1907	85	83	83	95	72	73	73	80	54	58	51	45	823
1908	50	41	73	70	53	60	60	60	58	65	44	67	701
1909	83	81	87	84	79	68	68	58	67	58	65	87	885
1910	69	76	84	68	65	69	52	62	44	62	44	63	758
1911	65	58	71	88	55	73	38	42	48	57	53	61	709
1912	78	71	66	67	62	54	62	51	43	58	44	61	717
1913	82	67	49	51	54	34	34	39	31	34	34	43	552
1914	48	39	53	43	52	46	37	23	29	23	32	28	453
1915	39	38	45	45	31	33	39	41	32	43	35	49	470
1916	62	52	52	53	54	47	34	34	38	51	43	45	565
1917	47	36	56	61	38	40	37	36	25	49	33	34	492
1918	40	49	48	49	37	45	39	31	25	22	30	37	452

D Large Incorporations

From Mar. 1846 through Dec. 1877, large business incorporations were as follows: 1854, Sept. *1*; 1858, Feb. *2*; 1866, Oct. *1*; 1867, Oct. *1*; 1871, Aug. *1*; 1872, July *1*; 1873, Jan. *1*, Apr. *3*, May *1*, Aug. *1*, Oct. *1*; 1874, Mar. *1*, May *2*, June *1*; 1875, Oct. *1*; 1876, Jan. *2*, Mar. *1*; 1877, May *1*, Aug. *1*, Oct. *1*.

YEAR	JAN.	FEB.	MAR.	APR.	MAY	JUNE	JULY	AUG.	SEPT.	OCT.	NOV.	DEC.	TOTAL
1878	1	2	0	0	0	1	1	0	1	1	1	1	9
1879	0	0	0	1	1	1	1	0	0	0	0	2	6
1880	3	2	2	6	3	3	1	0	6	3	3	3	35
1881	6	10	6	8	14	15	9	6	9	22	12	7	124
1882	8	9	9	4	4	6	8	9	6	3	6	6	78
1883	10	3	2	2	3	6	0	2	0	2	3	1	34
1884	3	3	4	4	0	3	2	0	0	3	0	0	22
1885	2	0	1	1	0	1	0	1	2	0	0	0	8
1886	1	3	4	4	1	2	1	1	1	2	1	0	21
1887	7	3	4	4	5	8	4	7	2	4	0	5	53
1888	0	3	2	5	4	8	5	8	2	5	6	8	56
1889	4	5	5	3	5	1	4	5	2	3	5	5	47
1890	5	3	4	3	6	9	13	7	7	4	6	7	74
1891	8	6	4	11	5	10	14	7	1	7	7	13	93
1892	4	8	12	3	5	7	5	16	3	4	6	9	82
1893	9	9	10	5	9	6	6	1	5	3	0	2	65
1894	2	5	6	3	1	6	4	0	2	5	4	4	42
1895	2	0	2	5	1	3	6	1	1	5	11	11	48
1896	4	6	6	4	2	5	4	2	5	4	1	6	49
1897	5	7	9	2	8	2	8	8	12	9	4	14	88
1898	10	7	10	5	4	11	4	6	4	4	12	13	90
1899	25	29	44	39	32	33	25	25	25	29	26	22	354
1900	25	23	27	20	21	14	19	16	11	18	20	19	233
1901	31	15	27	26	31	27	23	12	13	23	20	36	284
1902	26	8	26	32	29	26	23	16	23	20	16	25	270
1903	26	31	28	22	17	17	15	9	8	9	2	8	192
1904	9	4	5	14	6	10	9	4	8	4	12	9	94
1905	10	8	12	12	13	16	7	7	5	6	5	13	114
1906	12	10	14	10	10	9	2	9	4	9	10	12	111
1907	5	8	5	11	8	9	2	3	3	7	1	1	63
1908	5	5	5	6	5	4	4	5	5	6	2	6	58
1909	9	7	5	3	5	10	5	3	1	2	8	5	63
1910	7	8	5	7	5	7	•6	3	5	4	7	3	67
1911	4	3	2	2	3	5	3	4	8	1	5	8	48

NEW JERSEY BUSINESS INCORPORATIONS UNDER GENERAL LAWS, 1846–1918 (cont.)

YEAR	JAN.	FEB.	MAR.	APR.	MAY	JUNE	JULY	AUG.	SEPT.	OCT.	NOV.	DEC.	TOTAL
D Large Incorporations (concl.)													
1912	5	5	2	3	3	2	7	3	3	6	2	5	46
1913	7	1	2	2	0	1	1	0	0	0	0	0	14
1914	0	1	1	2	0	2	0	1	0	2	1	0	10
1915	1	2	1	0	1	0	2	0	0	0	0	1	8
1916	1	2	1	1	3	2	0	0	1	2	1	1	15
1917	0	0	2	1	7	2	4	3	2	1	2	3	27
1918	4	3	0	2	1	1	0	1	4	0	0	1	17
E Total Authorized Capital Stock (thousands of dollars)													
1846			0	0	0	65	0	100	10	0	100	0	
1847	0	0	300	100	0	0	120	250	0	0	0	0	770
1848	250	0	0	0	0	0	100	0	0	100	0	250	700
1849	0	300	0	0	0	0	0	0	0	0	0	0	300
1850	50	0	10	310	100	0	0	10	0	200	0	0	680
1851	0	500	0	700	1,750	600	500	1,000	506	500	0	500	6,556
1852	752	1,000	0	0	0	250	13	325	25	0	200	100	2,665
1853	1,000	1,080	372	150	0	0	0	400	250	2,250	150	0	5,652
1854	0	650	300	39	800	3	120	100	2,300	32	125	0	4,469
1855	100	200	0	70	0	150	468	250	150	360	620	0	2,368
1856	0	400	30	0	625	0	0	760	0	0	0	0	1,815
1857	0	50	700	300	500	700	0	0	500	500	0	0	3,250
1858	535	2,600	150	700	210	100	500	350	10	515	0	0	5,670
1859	500	75	0	0	0	0	0	0	10	50	0	100	735
1860	100	96	500	0	160	0	0	0	60	0	0	0	916
1861	200	0	100	0	0	0	0	0	0	0	0	0	300
1862	0	0	150	0	0	0	0	0	1,050	0	1,058	1,000	3,258
1863	50	165	0	0	20	30	0	25	0	300	0	0	590
1864	550	50	30	350	0	500	96	0	600	715	0	0	2,891
1865	0	16	0	0	0	475	0	50	100	0	0	112	753
1866	30	200	100	635	300	100	25	31	850	1,250	505	750	4,776
1867	1,400	100	0	225	100	72	120	1,005	650	10,264	660	0	14,596
1868	0	200	0	200	0	0	40	100	140	710	220	50	1,660
1869	300	50	60	0	0	20	0	375	205	10	0	270	1,290
1870	1,160	500	50	550	300	25	170	25	150	0	162	513	3,605
1871	244	0	475	55	500	10	515	3,653	100	400	50	600	6,602
1872	100	120	125	1,300	750	180	3,700	600	0	0	40	180	7,095
1873	5,600	14	650	13,329	3,262	350	0	1,721	700	1,465	560	250	27,901
1874	50	100	1,610	200	11,146	1,465	1,220	145	10	291	585	132	16,954
1875	340	750	0	150	10	406	830	300	564	3,800	318	436	7,904
1876	3,500	600	1,272	707	584	652	658	35	672	40	452	850	10,022
1877	1,230	307	0	750	1,630	564	264	1,902	402	1,370	404	700	9,523
1878	1,897	11,450	160	140	122	1,540	10,159	730	5,014	1,916	2,070	2,101	37,299
1879	520	278	260	1,194	1,800	3,048	3,066	700	156	275	1,160	4,861	17,318
1880	4,623	12,141	6,532	25,907	8,391	6,386	11,239	2,070	30,359	17,682	14,519	6,275	146,124
1881	24,546	19,589	26,524	19,821	70,674	107,159	29,256	14,872	16,681	41,835	24,312	21,734	417,003
1882	19,585	42,775	27,576	156,756	11,145	18,946	16,630	41,373	9,910	18,975	54,314	15,796	433,781
1883	38,666	8,393	19,158	7,425	11,104	13,514	3,790	9,241	1,363	8,176	7,418	4,477	132,725
1884	6,767	6,470	9,906	5,477	1,988	11,009	4,704	1,419	1,920	4,045	638	2,270	56,613
1885	3,875	3,081	3,556	3,050	2,322	4,218	1,808	3,350	4,720	1,889	1,965	3,058	36,892
1886	4,853	18,743	11,674	11,418	4,614	7,312	3,599	4,510	3,009	4,413	6,446	4,113	84,704
1887	12,733	8,398	20,579	14,644	14,615	22,548	7,644	15,240	4,944	6,731	6,439	11,378	145,893
1888	5,919	8,476	12,354	15,169	16,096	25,362	18,184	13,889	10,144	10,256	15,049	19,562	170,460
1889	23,834	15,153	15,958	13,094	13,316	8,107	10,793	13,993	6,212	12,200	23,131	17,033	172,824
1890	38,672	13,157	14,414	18,851	24,682	129,012	51,855	30,336	15,132	13,428	23,880	27,206	400,625
1891	72,094	19,295	14,424	49,906	13,886	49,068	28,860	35,657	10,238	25,054	28,835	60,188	407,505
1892	20,388	29,743	85,721	19,314	21,642	20,886	22,239	55,968	18,037	37,882	23,312	34,954	390,086
1893	31,334	43,109	69,783	18,292	28,779	33,326	18,128	5,989	18,493	10,639	7,076	43,991	328,939
1894	11,802	17,324	17,098	11,315	12,024	18,798	21,134	9,094	9,308	17,404	20,375	13,583	179,259
1895	11,284	5,912	12,033	15,282	10,494	11,546	17,912	7,551	11,197	16,162	33,842	26,498	179,713
1896	14,234	40,796	20,855	22,554	17,381	15,911	13,476	6,461	9,995	10,397	4,471	18,468	194,999
1897	20,670	68,351	34,988	9,902	18,259	9,162	16,900	64,089	77,267	27,379	22,811	50,565	420,343
1898	48,674	85,204	36,611	29,351	10,475	44,964	13,702	18,232	233,426	15,583	62,193	211,674	810,089
1899	320,438	333,497	534,436	482,340	427,290	212,286	255,100	145,069	94,693	165,960	151,334	139,465	3,261,908

YEAR	JAN.	FEB.	MAR.	APR.	MAY	JUNE	JULY	AUG.	SEPT.	OCT.	NOV.	DEC.	TOTAL
1900	93,697	72,396	296,326	249,726	82,432	71,315	183,509	49,540	37,914	61,813	42,243	88,892	1,329,803
1901	96,196	88,721	177,035	149,931	145,546	167,665	91,427	40,095	49,075	140,787	468,310	165,058	1,779,846
1902	123,385	53,716	145,657	168,090	116,070	144,200	255,963	231,364	110,231	53,787	43,829	71,363	1,517,655
1903	129,980	137,041	189,142	65,918	181,562	45,392	76,420	41,238	52,004	37,625	15,758	27,871	999,951
1904	23,075	27,760	26,179	54,832	50,336	37,517	45,919	17,243	20,538	196,040	80,612	61,508	641,559
1905	49,545	40,438	150,574	142,869	116,875	76,082	38,110	35,563	30,032	23,344	22,669	42,969	769,070
1906	73,558	49,735	75,030	49,688	38,448	36,549	13,325	49,120	38,313	42,276	54,146	75,927	596,115
1907	35,874	30,230	24,802	44,605	25,504	48,603	18,872	15,753	10,986	19,880	18,715	10,547	304,371
1908	29,084	74,770	21,388	24,001	39,018	32,652	22,027	15,697	22,304	54,442	61,718	83,132	480,233
1909	53,642	41,901	40,355	20,056	22,256	127,328	21,734	15,038	93,780	61,787	82,030	64,676	644,583
1910	39,262	45,998	23,361	22,399	22,475	43,519	17,871	24,690	14,624	16,908	21,799	17,150	310,056
1911	20,680	60,132	18,080	17,487	19,754	36,276	12,505	13,299	33,642	12,230	79,356	40,931	364,372
1912	35,577	19,387	43,726	19,692	19,832	21,117	66,570	13,329	35,514	23,037	13,688	116,745	428,214
1913	108,860	11,632	10,528	14,186	8,761	36,598	7,599	6,238	5,802	5,514	5,665	7,371	228,754
1914	9,096	8,094	10,106	10,874	8,424	11,634	7,293	5,126	4,558	6,839	8,005	5,511	95,560
1915	9,025	9,603	9,436	7,432	8,136	7,005	12,867	8,278	6,757	10,718	5,577	10,344	105,178
1916	12,335	13,052	11,566	9,946	17,314	23,273	7,323	7,016	8,509	19,784	9,802	9,706	149,626
1917	8,711	7,687	19,327	12,255	38,263	9,705	13,076	10,271	16,624	11,776	8,839	14,149	170,683
1918	12,690	11,969	9,010	10,808	8,279	8,504	7,345	8,300	150,546	3,874	4,898	10,630	246,853

F   Total Authorized Capital Stock Excluding Large Companies
(thousands of dollars)

From Mar. 1846 through Dec. 1877, the capital stock figures excluding large companies are the same as those for total capital stock (see E above), except that the total stock figures of the following dates are larger by the indicated amounts in thousands of dollars: 1854, Sept. *2,000;* 1858, Feb. *2,000;* 1866, Oct. *1,000;* 1867, Oct. *10,000;* 1871, Aug. *3,500;* 1872, July *2,500;* 1873, Jan. *5,000,* Apr. *13,000,* May *3,000,* Aug. *1,000,* Oct. *1,200;* 1874, Mar. *1,000,* May *11,000,* June *1,000;* 1875, Oct. *3,500;* 1876, Jan. *3,000,* Mar. *1,000;* 1877, May *1,000,* Aug. *1,000,* Oct. *1,000.*

YEAR	JAN.	FEB.	MAR.	APR.	MAY	JUNE	JULY	AUG.	SEPT.	OCT.	NOV.	DEC.	TOTAL
1878	397	450	160	140	122	540	159	730	14	916	1,070	851	5,549
1879	520	278	260	194	300	1,048	475	700	156	275	1,160	861	6,227
1880	1,623	1,141	1,032	1,107	1,391	1,386	1,239	2,070	2,359	1,642	1,519	1,775	18,284
1881	4,546	5,589	7,024	4,321	5,674	3,659	6,256	3,872	6,431	9,335	4,312	6,384	67,403
1882	5,585	7,275	3,576	3,256	5,145	5,946	3,880	4,373	1,910	2,975	4,314	4,296	52,531
1883	2,266	2,893	3,158	3,425	4,104	2,014	3,790	4,741	1,363	3,676	2,918	3,277	37,625
1884	2,767	3,470	2,906	1,477	1,988	3,509	1,704	1,419	1,920	545	638	2,270	24,613
1885	1,875	3,081	2,556	2,050	2,322	3,218	1,808	2,350	2,720	1,889	1,965	3,058	28,892
1886	3,853	2,743	4,174	4,418	3,414	3,312	2,599	2,510	1,809	2,413	5,446	4,113	40,804
1887	3,233	4,398	3,579	5,444	5,615	3,548	2,144	5,490	2,944	1,781	6,439	4,378	48,993
1888	5,919	4,476	7,354	4,169	8,096	3,862	7,384	4,889	5,644	5,256	4,549	8,562	70,160
1889	6,834	5,153	6,758	5,594	7,216	7,107	6,793	6,493	4,212	8,200	10,131	8,533	83,024
1890	8,672	9,907	10,164	7,851	7,182	12,812	9,905	6,836	5,632	9,428	9,880	8,706	106,975
1891	13,094	10,045	10,424	10,306	7,286	11,318	7,510	8,307	9,238	12,304	10,335	13,188	123,355
1892	12,888	16,373	15,521	12,814	10,142	11,786	12,489	10,968	10,037	8,882	8,312	15,954	146,166
1893	14,084	12,109	11,283	10,292	10,279	7,926	6,128	4,989	4,593	7,139	7,076	7,491	103,389
1894	8,802	8,124	8,098	7,315	9,724	4,798	4,434	9,094	6,308	6,404	6,875	7,383	87,359
1895	8,784	5,912	9,533	10,282	8,994	7,546	9,162	6,551	4,697	11,162	7,642	8,998	99,263
1896	6,234	8,846	8,605	9,054	7,201	8,411	7,476	3,961	2,995	4,897	3,471	6,168	77,319
1897	9,970	7,351	10,488	6,402	7,259	5,912	6,900	9,489	10,985	8,179	6,286	11,565	100,786
1898	12,174	9,204	10,861	10,351	6,275	9,164	5,702	7,132	10,426	10,583	7,393	12,174	111,439
1899	15,838	24,397	27,086	23,190	23,840	22,536	17,400	20,069	17,993	17,410	20,146	26,065	255,970
1900	21,697	15,296	20,026	26,476	23,682	24,365	19,159	16,540	14,214	12,963	16,193	25,292	235,903
1901	24,746	25,221	37,785	32,731	29,316	29,890	19,077	17,895	15,875	17,287	20,135	21,058	291,016
1902	30,135	21,216	29,007	19,715	24,870	19,150	30,113	18,414	19,981	20,037	22,179	23,113	277,930
1903	33,480	28,591	24,442	24,163	23,312	18,977	19,016	15,488	11,754	14,325	12,508	13,771	239,827
1904	9,625	17,510	15,179	15,132	13,836	10,117	12,919	13,243	10,788	13,040	12,812	18,558	162,759
1905	17,545	13,378	17,499	15,061	17,875	15,182	14,295	13,813	16,032	11,844	15,169	17,819	185,512
1906	17,408	18,035	23,330	21,038	15,448	19,049	10,675	17,520	13,313	17,526	16,646	18,526	208,514
1907	18,774	17,480	15,602	19,905	14,504	15,603	15,872	10,753	7,986	11,330	8,715	9,547	166,071
1908	9,684	8,770	14,388	12,801	11,518	11,652	11,981	10,697	13,304	14,442	10,718	15,632	145,587
1909	14,242	16,201	16,355	17,056	16,756	15,028	11,784	10,038	13,780	10,787	15,329	20,176	177,532
1910	13,162	16,373	14,861	12,899	14,275	14,919	9,871	12,690	9,124	11,903	9,644	11,650	151,371
1911	14,180	11,532	15,980	15,487	13,754	13,576	8,405	7,999	11,142	10,730	11,013	11,431	145,229
1912	15,077	12,887	12,726	13,472	12,332	12,117	13,482	9,129	9,514	11,537	10,413	11,245	143,931
1913	15,110	10,632	8,528	8,186	8,761	6,598	6,599	6,238	5,802	5,514	5,665	7,371	95,004
1914	9,096	7,094	9,106	7,839	8,424	8,384	7,293	4,126	4,558	4,639	6,255	5,511	82,325
1915	8,025	6,857	8,436	7,432	6,136	7,005	8,367	8,278	6,757	10,718	5,577	8,344	91,932
1916	11,335	9,052	10,066	8,946	8,814	8,285	7,323	7,016	7,309	8,784	7,802	8,706	103,438
1917	8,711	7,687	12,077	11,005	8,913	7,705	7,076	6,771	5,624	10,776	6,839	6,649	99,833
1918	7,690	8,469	9,010	8,808	7,029	7,254	7,345	7,100	5,046	3,874	4,898	9,130	85,653

New Jersey Business Incorporations under General Laws, 1846–1918 (concl.)

1) Sources of Raw Data

Corporations of New Jersey. List of Certificates filed in the Department of State from 1846 to 1894, inclusive, Compiled by the Secretary of State (Trenton, 1895), pp. 2–482. Subsequent reports compiled by the Secretary of State were published under the same title with different dates. The periods covered and the pages from which the incorporation data were compiled are: *1895–99,* pp. 6–568; *1900,* pp. 6–240; *1901,* pp. 6–257; *1902,* pp. 6–224; *1903,* pp. 6–315; *1904,* pp. 6–266; *1905,* pp. 6–276; *1906,* pp. 6–302; *1907,* pp. 6–297; *1908,* pp. 7–265; *1909,* pp. 6–296; *1912,* pp. 6–287; *1913,* pp. 6–286; *1914,* pp. 6–257; *1915–16,* pp. 6–546; *1917,* pp. 6–291; *1918,* pp. 6–256.

For 1910 and 1911, *Corporations of New Jersey. List of Certificates to December 31, 1911* (Trenton, 1914), Part I, List of Corporations in Existence December 31st, 1911, pp. 6–777, had to be used.

2) Special Comments

a) The first two volumes of the reports utilized present data, arranged alphabetically for the entire period. Consequently, the task of tallying was more difficult than in the case of the other reports, which—except for that used for 1910 and 1911—are annual compilations.

b) The series begins with incorporations under the Corporation Law of 1846 (*New Jersey Laws, 1846,* p. 22) and is carried through World War I. The Corporation Law of 1846 was not a general incorporation law in the sense that it prescribed a procedure by which a company could be chartered without further action of the legislature. It merely established uniform provisions to be used by the legislature—unless it should see fit not to use them—in its subsequent charter grants. Charters granted under that act are frequently referred to as having been issued under general law, though a general incorporation statute, as that term is usually employed, was not enacted by New Jersey until 1849 (*New Jersey Laws, 1849,* p. 300). The charters of 1846–49 presented here as granted under general laws are not duplicated in the section of the Appendix that lists charters granted by special acts. This is in harmony with the interpretation put upon the Law of 1846 by the Office of the Secretary of State (see, for example, the first volume cited in note 1, and the Hood volume cited in the preceding section of this Appendix). For discussions of the development of New Jersey Corporation Law, see: E. Q. Keasbey, New Jersey and the Great Corporations, *Harvard Law Review* (Nov. 1899), XIII, 198 ff., especially pp. 203–6; and H. W. Stoke, Economic Influences upon the Corporation Laws of New Jersey, *Journal of Political Economy* (Oct. 1930), XXXVIII, 551 ff., especially pp. 559–61.

c) Each entry in the above listed volumes includes the name of the company, its date of incorporation, a brief purpose statement, the authorized capital stock, and quite frequently the general law under which the company was organized.

d) The report from which the 1910 and 1911 data were compiled lists corporations *in existence* on December 31, 1911. The tally for these two years is perhaps smaller than it would be if it included all incorporations: some business units probably gave up or lost their charters within a year or two after incorporating, and would presumably not be listed in a report on corporations *in existence.* The error, however, is apparently not large since the movements of the New Jersey series of this period resemble those of other state series.

e) To compile from the above mentioned reports all data on consolidations one must watch carefully the statements that occasionally follow an entry described in (c) above.

f) Annual figures, which vary slightly from those tabulated above, were published in Stoke, *op. cit.,* p. 574. Covering 1901–28, they could have been used to supplement for 1919–28 the figures presented here. They were not used because they were annual and did not tie in exactly with the above tabulation.

New York Business Incorporations under Special and General Laws, 1800–1845

See Table 9 of text and the related discussion.

New York Business Incorporations under General Laws, 1901–1923

1901	1902	1903	1904	1905	1906	1907	1908	1909	1910	1911	1912
2,670	3,577	3,887	4,420	5,609	6,347	6,599	7,185	8,328	7,998	8,357	8,668

1913	1914	1915	1916	1917	1918	1919	1920	1921	1922	1923
9,090	9,327	10,521	11,830	10,536	8,504	15,274	15,103	16,097	18,160	19,530

1) Source

State of New York, *Annual Report of the Department of State. . .* (Albany, 1943), pp. 13–4, or Legislative Document (1943), No. 34.

2) Special Comments

The data in the above source correct errors in New York Legislative Manuals.

New York Business Incorporations under General Laws, 1924–1943

YEAR	JAN.	FEB.	MAR.	APR.	MAY	JUNE	JULY	AUG.	SEPT.	OCT.	NOV.	DEC.	TOTAL
1924	1,999	1,764	1,920	1,817	1,699	1,432	1,363	1,276	1,289	1,396	1,512	2,082	19,549
1925	1,966	1,755	2,230	1,995	2,087	2,106	1,887	2,019	1,892	2,257	2,080	2,429	24,703
1926	2,640	2,139	2,392	2,181	2,193	2,333	1,908	1,685	1,665	2,022	1,954	2,276	25,388
1927	2,452	2,077	2,585	2,310	2,261	2,160	1,828	1,833	1,743	1,932	2,089	2,400	25,670
1928	2,598	2,351	2,589	2,304	2,489	2,312	1,958	1,808	1,610	2,242	2,153	2,403	26,817
1929	2,757	2,282	2,518	2,417	2,397	2,086	2,015	1,949	1,771	1,982	1,683	1,898	25,755

YEAR	JAN.	FEB.	MAR.	APR.	MAY	JUNE	JULY	AUG.	SEPT.	OCT.	NOV.	DEC.	TOTAL
1930	2,280	2,005	2,229	2,107	2,089	1,968	1,866	1,651	1,853	1,990	1,773	2,056	23,867
1931	2,219	1,936	2,390	2,266	2,133	2,222	2,028	1,914	1,679	2,024	1,881	2,136	24,828
1932	2,357	2,036	2,235	2,191	2,134	2,296	1,900	2,141	1,915	1,785	1,896	2,015	24,901
1933	2,365	1,981	1,909	1,868	2,360	2,155	1,795	1,686	1,477	1,636	1,698	1,729	22,659
1934	2,027	1,439	1,706	1,626	1,627	1,557	1,472	1,450	1,223	1,465	1,466	1,479	18,537
1935	1,936	1,520	1,683	1,562	1,606	1,535	1,435	1,413	1,341	1,515	1,400	1,678	18,624
1936	1,902	1,536	1,681	1,580	1,604	1,589	1,487	1,312	1,385	1,540	1,440	1,749	18,805
1937	1,922	1,568	1,811	1,689	1,428	1,509	1,313	1,238	1,093	1,231	1,272	1,381	17,455
1938	1,548	1,244	1,434	1,316	1,357	1,296	1,235	1,280	1,127	1,195	1,279	1,338	15,649
1939	1,624	1,358	1,602	1,340	1,484	1,223	1,189	1,234	1,041	1,287	1,327	1,404	16,113
1940	1,818	1,414	1,431	1,586	1,523	1,162	1,250	1,159	1,091	1,171	1,119	1,316	16,040
1941	1,630	1,259	1,348	1,310	1,195	1,070	1,187	972	968	976	867	1,033	13,815
1942	1,035	867	940	850	745	629	627	613	545	610	562	673	8,696
1943	708	580	714	727	710	721	729	728	728	711	780	824	8,660

1) Sources

Press releases on incorporations issued monthly by the Secretary of State of New York State from June 1925 through December 1943.

2) Special Comments

a) The figures published in the above mentioned releases cover the charters granted by New York to stock corporations. Thus, according to the definition used in this study, the series is for business enterprises.

b) Annual figures built from the monthly data of the press releases are identical with the yearly figures published in the *Annual Report of the Department of State . . .* (Albany, 1943), p. 14, or Legislative Document (1943), No. 34.

OHIO BUSINESS INCORPORATIONS BY SPECIAL ACTS, 1803–1851

See Table 10, Section A, of text.

1) Source of Raw Data

Secretary of State, *Annual Report of the Secretary of State, to the Governor of the State of Ohio, For the Year 1885* (Columbus, 1885), pp. 147–227.

2) Special Comments

a) The incorporation data in the above mentioned source (the names of the corporations chartered together with the dates of incorporation) pertain to both business and nonbusiness concerns. They are grouped industrially and the companies of each group are arranged alphabetically.

b) In separating business from nonbusiness incorporations, the groupings of the report were utilized. The name also served to indicate whether the company was a business or a nonbusiness enterprise, since capital stock figures were not given. The name proved to be a necessary supplementary indicator only in the insurance and miscellaneous groups. The following lists indicate the groups considered to be in business and nonbusiness fields:

TYPES OF BUSINESS ENTERPRISE	TYPES OF NONBUSINESS ENTERPRISE
Banks	Agricultural and Horticultural Societies
Bridge Companies	Art Unions
Canal Companies	Athenaeums
Cemeteries, Cemetery Associations, Companies and Societies	Beneficial, Benevolent, and Charitable Societies and Institutions
Draining	Churches
Harbor, Pier, Wharf, etc., Companies	Church Societies
Hotel Companies	Church Educational and Other Institutions and Societies—Miscellaneous
Hydraulic Associations and Companies	Commercial Exchange Companies
Insurance Companies (except mutuals)	Educational Institutions

TYPES OF BUSINESS ENTERPRISE	TYPES OF NONBUSINESS ENTERPRISE
Manufacturing and Mining Companies	Fire and Hook and Ladder Companies and Associations
Navigation and Transportation Companies	Insurance Companies (mutuals)
Railroads	Library Companies and Societies
Road Companies	Literary Societies
Savings Societies and Institutions	Medical Colleges and Institutions
Telegraph Companies	Medical Societies
Water Companies	Musical Societies and Institutions
	School Associations and Districts
	Social Clubs and Societies

The Miscellaneous category was divided between the two fields. Municipal and other governmental corporations were not included in either.

c) Ohio became a state on March 1, 1803. In April the first charters were issued to both business and nonbusiness enterprises.

d) In the report cited in note 1, a company name occasionally appears twice with different dates of incorporation. These may have represented reincorporation upon the expiration of a charter, but, since there was no specific evidence for or against such an hypothesis, the second appearance of the name was counted as an incorporation.

e) A constitutional provision requiring incorporation under general law was adopted and became effective in 1851 (New York State Constitutional Convention Committee, *Constitutions of the States and the United States*, Albany, 1938, Art. XIII, Sec. 1, p. 1216). The first general comprehensive incorporation law, however, was not passed until May 1, 1852 (see 50 *Ohio Laws* 274). Several business incorporation acts of limited scope had been passed prior to the act of 1852; see, for example, 44 *Ohio Laws* 37 (Feb. 9, 1846), 46 *Ohio Laws* 25 (Jan. 5, 1848), 46 *Ohio Laws* 79 (Feb. 24, 1848), and 49 *Ohio Laws* 88 (Jan. 17, 1851).

OHIO BUSINESS INCORPORATIONS UNDER GENERAL LAWS, 1855–1936

YEAR	JAN.	FEB.	MAR.	APR.	MAY	JUNE	JULY	AUG.	SEPT.	OCT.	NOV.	DEC.	TOTAL
A Total Incorporations													
1855											1*	6	
1856	6	9	4	7	6	6	5	6	6	2	1	6	64
1857	3	7	4	8	3	6	5	3	2	2	1	3	47
1858	3	10	4	5	2	6	4	0	4	1	3	6	49
1859	11	10	14	11	12	11	7	7	3	4	5	2	97
1860	2	7	3	1	2	3	1	4	3	3	3	4	36
1861	4	3	5	6	3	1	0	1	0	1	1	0	25
1862	2	3	4	2	4	1	3	1	1	2	2	1	26
1863	4	5	9	6	7	4	1	2	0	3	3	7	51
1864	6	3	6	11	3	3	7	3	7	10	5	27	91
1865	41	66	51	34	31	25	16	24	20	12	20	18	358
1866	30	32	22	33	29	22	14	16	18	15	21	29	281
1867	32	23	33	29	25	22	19	17	13	15	16	22	266
1868	31	36	37	28	37	23	9	25	15	16	16	22	295
1869	26	30	45	52	40	21	22	16	15	19	17	30	333
1870	32	30	34	28	27	26	18	19	17	11	21	31	304
1871	31	37	32	30	35	26	20	31	16	30	22	26	336
1872	33	52	37	37	31	36	35	33	28	17	36	26	401
1873	39	36	49	36	36	25	26	37	21	17	15	23	360
1874	23	27	32	27	22	19	20	27	29	22	20	30	298
1875	24	35	43	33	23	34	23	24	26	24	19	25	333
1876	28	28	34	40	24	19	15	15	19	8	13	23	266
1877	15	19	27	21	28	20	21	17	14	18	20	17	237
1878	24	21	19	19	23	21	12	20	12	18	17	21	227
1879	23	28	21	24	23	22	22	25	20	20	21	37	286
1880	36	53	43	43	25	28	17	22	22	28	32	42	391
1881	32	33	64	52	45	37	34	37	42	36	48	48	508
1882	65	50	59	56	46	47	49	36	37	46	55	52	598
1883	56	62	49	48	49	48	46	50	40	56	50	58	612
1884	51	54	52	50	43	39	37	27	23	38	27	36	477
1885	48	48	55	23	39	43	46	41	38	32	49	53	515
1886	64	60	60	45	50	51	44	38	42	45	49	78	626
1887	71	71	101	118	89	62	45	50	60	66	48	51	832
1888	73	63	85	55	67	43	45	40	48	37	41	64	661
1889	89	76	69	55	54	50	69	54	53	48	45	63	725
1890	69	67	85	71	72	57	50	61	51	61	55	69	768
1891	94	74	95	67	72	65	54	53	65	63	55	77	834
1892	85	87	94	74	71	61	40	68	59	53	79	83	854
1893	102	80	74	89	85	56	35	33	38	36	33	52	713
1894	68	60	104	64	81	76	63	53	63	64	56	83	835
1895	86	62	106	86	70	68	57	63	65	71	68	70	872
1896	83	86	100	72	77	61	53	42	36	41	54	58	763
1897	66	62	76	67	52	52	48	45	55	67	53	71	714
1898	75	78	84	66	52	55	40	52	42	51	55	51	701
1899	100	89	105	83	77	88	87	77	66	82	74	77	1,005
1900	105	97	119	103	91	82	61	67	81	89	100	107	1,102
1901	128	117	173	135	145	117	99	120	93	114	100	127	1,468
1902	168	135	144	130	120	107	116	112	95	102	100	130	1,459
1903	175	153	148	150	144	121	124	89	121	105	122	205	1,657
1904	207	197	207	171	199	137	163	134	166	167	163	175	2,086
1905	236	189	242	207	206	190	177	187	147	187	179	191	2,338
1906	277	230	237	210	221	175	161	174	165	179	173	195	2,397
1907	221	217	277	231	211	177	206	183	131	171	135	146	2,306
1908	195	194	202	189	171	170	174	151	145	169	175	211	2,146
1909	229	301	294	253	236	216	211	168	187	188	191	207	2,681
1910	217	235	231	230	195	188	147	161	138	176	166	191	2,275
1911	207	241	258	198	178	201	185	188	154	192	165	201	2,368
1912	229	185	262	220	174	173	180	176	159	182	182	206	2,328
1913	218	231	219	192	198	175	194	172	180	177	128	185	2,269
1914	217	215	277	223	217	185	195	152	178	188	148	179	2,374
1915	200	209	216	239	201	203	208	172	197	187	184	244	2,460
1916	249	260	339	261	281	226	217	216	243	223	258	325	3,098
1917	354	295	382	301	263	252	245	237	207	213	237	180	3,166
1918	226	217	220	233	208	168	166	155	119	114	140	185	2,151
1919	297	335	331	377	363	382	362	362	347	352	366	477	4,352

YEAR	JAN.	FEB.	MAR.	APR.	MAY	JUNE	JULY	AUG.	SEPT.	OCT.	NOV.	DEC.	TOTAL
1920	474	439	520	486	423	384	329	319	325	326	291	327	4,643
1921	329	324	417	375	330	303	293	282	298	275	288	341	3,855
1922	380	349	424	361	414	338	275	293	331	336	300	432	4,233
1923	469	378	427	404	341	328	293	304	246	259	250	351	4,050
1924	367	381	364	330	316	249	264	242	265	278	231	353	3,640
1925	378	380	358	396	362	316	331	342	289	288	288	323	4,051
1926	356	351	405	348	316	338	336	277	281	304	266	315	3,893
1927	406	342	410	341	269	303	311	297	286	291	251	301	3,808
1928	373	366	401	361	367	369	312	332	301	349	287	333	4,151
1929	378	344	454	404	417	349	301	228	282	329	291	271	4,148
1930	381	348	349	335	364	306	323	290	320	319	253	284	3,872
1931	384	276	363	356	302	298	290	287	311	323	236	273	3,699
1932	327	312	312	329	285	327	289	302	253	276	240	211	3,463
1933	338	270	241	308	320	283	263	271	250	201	214	226	3,185
1934	262	236	308	232	273	220	216	210	202	218	188	178	2,743
1935	235	227	227	257	240	201	213	219	231	244	208	175	2,677
1936	335	268	273	238	230	253	228	210	188	214	181	240	2,858

* Not a full month.

B   Small Incorporations, 1871–1919

YEAR	JAN.	FEB.	MAR.	APR.	MAY	JUNE	JULY	AUG.	SEPT.	OCT.	NOV.	DEC.	TOTAL
1871												9	
1872	16	21	9	11	9	7	18	16	11	6	20	16	160
1873	13	17	21	21	11	7	9	25	18	8	9	12	171
1874	10	16	16	17	11	7	9	15	17	11	11	15	155
1875	11	14	25	13	12	20	12	15	14	13	8	13	170
1876	18	20	19	22	17	10	9	9	11	5	6	15	161
1877	11	13	10	6	19	10	11	11	9	8	9	8	125
1878	12	8	10	11	9	17	7	14	10	9	13	14	134
1879	18	17	10	15	10	15	14	17	14	14	11	19	174
1880	22	40	21	29	22	16	15	15	17	16	20	26	259
1881	20	20	33	21	23	20	15	19	18	16	18	23	246
1882	35	31	30	31	26	23	24	20	20	22	29	27	318
1883	29	32	30	30	29	22	28	28	25	35	33	36	357
1884	28	33	36	34	21	22	25	18	16	28	15	27	303
1885	36	35	36	15	29	31	33	25	26	18	35	32	351
1886	38	45	37	28	33	34	29	23	28	31	36	56	418
1887	43	52	73	86	62	41	29	28	34	49	37	35	569
1888	45	38	52	36	44	33	28	30	38	22	26	43	435
1889	61	47	41	34	36	32	45	40	40	38	35	42	491
1890	47	43	52	49	56	43	33	46	34	42	39	56	540
1891	74	59	71	49	49	47	33	36	46	46	40	53	603
1892	62	69	73	58	55	47	27	55	47	41	61	62	657
1893	79	65	54	64	64	46	28	27	33	32	26	42	560
1894	57	55	87	46	63	60	49	46	48	54	43	65	673
1895	64	46	88	60	57	60	48	50	56	59	52	52	692
1896	71	69	84	62	68	45	48	36	32	37	47	49	648
1897	56	54	66	53	42	45	42	38	49	56	42	53	596
1898	61	67	76	52	46	44	33	43	34	46	43	40	585
1899	91	80	88	65	66	74	71	63	51	65	66	62	842
1900	86	82	108	90	78	73	52	50	71	70	79	86	925
1901	108	94	138	118	113	92	83	101	75	93	87	104	1,206
1902	144	106	118	105	99	84	97	96	79	86	84	100	1,198
1903	145	129	124	130	113	100	108	77	105	91	109	169	1,400
1904	166	160	168	152	178	121	138	107	140	135	132	145	1,742
1905	200	163	204	167	172	155	161	154	128	158	151	157	1,970
1906	228	196	211	181	189	147	144	141	136	156	131	165	2,025
1907	187	188	239	191	174	155	175	153	110	152	118	118	1,960
1908	167	171	184	172	158	157	149	138	135	153	154	182	1,920
1909	214	276	269	219	218	192	185	154	166	168	176	178	2,415
1910	199	202	204	207	175	167	134	142	124	157	150	167	2,028
1911	185	220	246	179	159	179	168	168	129	172	159	180	2,144
1912	197	172	239	198	155	158	152	162	144	166	166	179	2,088
1913	206	215	197	167	179	162	177	150	168	163	115	168	2,067
1914	206	190	247	206	198	165	174	137	166	174	130	162	2,155
1915	189	194	197	220	181	184	190	159	177	172	168	213	2,244
1916	218	234	300	230	257	193	185	191	205	200	218	265	2,696
1917	302	256	341	264	228	217	214	209	181	184	198	148	2,742
1918	201	184	188	204	188	152	140	134	107	96	115	162	1,871
1919	241	294	277	310	296								

Ohio Business Incorporations under General Laws, 1855–1936 (cont.)

C Medium Incorporations, 1871–1919

YEAR	JAN.	FEB.	MAR.	APR.	MAY	JUNE	JULY	AUG.	SEPT.	OCT.	NOV.	DEC.	TOTAL
1871												14	
1872	13	24	22	24	18	22	14	15	11	11	16	8	198
1873	23	17	26	13	23	18	15	11	3	8	6	11	174
1874	12	10	15	9	10	11	11	12	11	10	9	13	133
1875	11	16	17	17	9	12	9	8	9	10	8	9	135
1876	8	7	13	17	7	7	3	5	5	3	6	7	88
1877	4	6	14	15	8	10	9	5	5	9	10	6	101
1878	10	13	9	5	12	2	3	5	2	7	4	4	76
1879	3	10	9	8	8	6	7	6	5	5	9	12	88
1880	11	9	20	11	3	10	2	7	5	8	5	11	102
1881	10	9	27	28	18	14	14	11	19	14	24	18	206
1882	18	15	23	20	16	18	22	11	12	22	20	20	217
1883	22	24	16	12	13	19	14	17	11	16	12	18	194
1884	18	15	11	14	19	11	11	7	5	9	9	8	137
1885	10	11	15	8	8	10	11	14	10	13	12	18	140
1886	17	11	19	13	13	13	12	13	11	11	11	17	161
1887	24	15	19	28	24	12	12	18	17	12	11	14	206
1888	19	19	28	15	20	7	12	9	5	13	11	17	175
1889	23	23	24	16	17	14	20	12	12	9	10	17	197
1890	19	18	27	16	12	12	13	12	15	12	15	11	182
1891	16	10	20	16	16	14	16	14	17	16	12	21	188
1892	20	18	19	12	15	9	9	12	11	10	16	20	171
1893	21	14	14	19	16	10	7	6	4	3	5	8	127
1894	10	5	16	16	16	15	14	7	15	10	12	17	153
1895	19	15	17	24	11	7	8	11	8	10	15	14	159
1896	12	14	13	9	8	13	4	6	4	4	6	9	102
1897	8	7	10	13	10	7	5	7	6	10	10	17	110
1898	12	10	7	13	6	10	6	7	6	5	12	11	105
1899	7	6	17	16	11	12	13	13	13	17	7	12	144
1900	17	13	11	11	13	7	8	16	10	17	20	20	163
1901	18	20	30	14	28	23	14	19	16	21	13	21	237
1902	24	26	23	23	19	23	17	15	14	15	13	27	239
1903	26	23	23	18	29	20	15	11	13	14	12	36	240
1904	37	36	37	19	19	16	25	24	26	31	31	27	328
1905	34	26	35	34	30	32	15	30	18	26	26	34	340
1906	44	32	25	27	31	27	15	32	28	21	39	27	348
1907	34	29	34	38	35	22	31	30	19	18	17	26	333
1908	28	22	15	16	12	13	24	11	9	16	20	29	215
1909	15	25	23	31	18	23	26	14	20	20	14	26	255
1910	17	31	24	23	16	20	12	18	13	19	16	23	232
1911	22	20	12	19	18	17	17	20	24	18	6	19	212
1912	30	13	23	20	18	14	28	13	14	14	15	27	229
1913	12	15	19	22	17	13	17	21	12	14	13	16	191
1914	10	23	27	16	18	17	16	14	12	14	16	15	198
1915	11	13	19	18	19	19	15	12	18	15	14	29	202
1916	28	26	36	29	23	32	28	22	33	21	35	53	366
1917	47	34	35	32	33	31	29	26	24	22	38	31	382
1918	22	31	28	27	20	14	26	20	12	18	24	20	262
1919	52	39	53	61	60								

D Large Incorporations, 1871–1919

YEAR	JAN.	FEB.	MAR.	APR.	MAY	JUNE	JULY	AUG.	SEPT.	OCT.	NOV.	DEC.	TOTAL
1871												3	
1872	4	7	6	2	4	7	3	2	6	0	0	2	43
1873	3	2	2	2	2	0	2	1	0	1	0	0	15
1874	1	1	1	1	1	1	0	0	1	1	0	2	10
1875	2	5	1	3	2	2	2	1	3	1	3	3	28
1876	2	1	2	1	0	2	3	1	3	0	1	1	17
1877	0	0	3	0	1	0	1	1	0	1	1	3	11
1878	2	0	0	3	2	2	2	1	0	2	0	3	17
1879	2	1	2	1	5	1	1	2	1	1	1	6	24
1880	3	4	2	3	0	2	0	0	0	4	7	5	30
1881	2	4	4	3	4	3	5	7	5	6	6	7	56
1882	12	4	6	5	4	6	3	5	5	2	6	5	63
1883	5	6	3	6	7	7	4	5	4	5	5	4	61
1884	5	6	5	2	3	6	1	2	2	1	3	1	37
1885	2	2	4	0	2	2	2	2	2	1	2	3	24
1886	9	4	4	4	4	4	3	2	3	3	2	5	47
1887	4	4	9	4	3	9	4	4	9	5	0	2	57
1888	9	6	5	4	3	3	5	1	5	2	4	4	51
1889	5	6	4	5	1	4	4	2	1	1	0	4	37

YEAR	JAN.	FEB.	MAR.	APR.	MAY	JUNE	JULY	AUG.	SEPT.	OCT.	NOV.	DEC.	TOTAL
1890	3	6	6	6	4	2	4	3	2	7	1	2	46
1891	4	5	4	2	7	4	5	3	2	1	3	3	43
1892	3	0	2	4	1	5	4	1	1	2	2	1	26
1893	2	1	6	6	5	0	0	0	1	1	2	2	26
1894	1	0	1	2	2	1	0	0	0	0	1	1	9
1895	3	1	1	2	2	1	1	2	1	2	1	4	21
1896	0	3	3	1	1	3	1	0	0	0	1	0	13
1897	2	1	0	1	0	0	1	0	0	1	1	1	8
1898	2	1	1	1	0	1	1	2	2	0	0	0	11
1899	2	3	0	2	0	2	3	1	2	0	1	3	19
1900	2	2	0	2	0	2	1	1	0	2	1	1	14
1901	2	3	5	3	4	2	2	0	2	0	0	2	25
1902	0	3	3	2	2	0	2	1	2	1	3	3	22
1903	4	1	1	2	2	1	1	1	3	0	1	0	17
1904	4	1	2	0	2	0	0	3	0	1	0	3	16
1905	2	0	3	6	4	3	1	3	1	3	2	0	28
1906	5	2	1	2	1	1	2	1	1	2	3	3	24
1907	0	0	4	2	2	0	0	0	2	1	0	2	13
1908	0	1	3	1	1	0	1	2	1	0	1	0	11
1909	0	0	2	3	0	1	0	0	1	0	1	3	11
1910	1	2	3	0	4	1	1	1	1	0	0	1	15
1911	0	1	0	0	1	5	0	0	1	2	0	2	12
1912	2	0	0	2	1	1	0	1	1	2	1	0	11
1913	0	1	3	3	2	0	0	1	0	0	0	1	11
1914	1	2	3	1	1	3	5	1	0	0	2	2	21
1915	0	2	0	1	1	0	3	1	2	0	2	2	14
1916	3	0	3	2	1	1	4	3	5	2	5	7	36
1917	5	5	6	5	2	4	2	2	2	7	1	1	42
1918	3	2	4	2	0	2	0	1	0	0	1	3	18
1919	4	2	1	6	7								

E   Total Authorized Capital Stock, 1871–1919
(thousands of dollars)

YEAR	JAN.	FEB.	MAR.	APR.	MAY	JUNE	JULY	AUG.	SEPT.	OCT.	NOV.	DEC.	TOTAL
1871												8,015	
1872	10,424	18,965	17,965	10,968	16,992	19,854	6,748	7,271	13,195	3,013	4,386	5,884	135,665
1873	11,290	7,852	7,968	10,314	12,315	4,015	7,716	4,520	1,242	3,605	2,084	2,315	75,236
1874	3,770	4,856	4,378	17,604	4,753	4,125	3,662	2,809	5,234	6,291	2,671	8,421	68,574
1875	7,621	13,402	7,243	7,615	5,145	5,184	13,552	3,802	6,514	6,663	10,745	8,801	96,287
1876	3,423	3,744	8,008	6,060	1,896	3,513	5,311	3,254	4,546	1,652	2,738	3,923	48,068
1877	1,324	1,479	7,263	3,880	4,004	3,446	5,658	2,739	1,974	4,355	3,612	7,333	47,067
1878	7,058	2,633	3,252	4,212	6,322	8,252	4,050	2,301	622	4,269	1,522	9,978	54,471
1879	12,116	14,002	5,894	3,127	14,401	11,389	3,866	6,478	3,369	6,296	4,071	16,349	101,358
1880	7,264	13,598	10,198	13,378	1,447	4,946	710	1,342	2,038	21,410	14,014	13,662	104,007
1881	15,028	20,237	33,423	44,804	10,030	11,365	98,567	35,526	32,995	35,180	20,894	19,791	377,840
1882	75,312	11,554	28,247	14,086	18,588	22,393	9,284	15,281	9,720	8,286	17,336	17,058	247,145
1883	17,753	34,488	12,702	20,348	39,940	12,207	8,263	9,910	7,698	19,401	15,104	13,662	211,476
1884	13,748	10,788	8,960	6,186	8,307	11,690	7,222	7,620	3,607	3,300	58,262	4,042	143,732
1885	5,185	6,573	11,188	2,144	12,394	10,496	7,067	5,378	26,374	4,364	5,832	10,732	107,727
1886	31,392	13,086	12,821	19,003	10,550	27,478	8,445	5,002	5,722	6,794	5,498	11,542	157,333
1887	18,892	9,814	18,423	11,823	14,584	32,058	10,620	20,789	54,034	12,418	3,619	18,207	225,281
1888	17,177	10,774	13,015	8,038	9,804	6,586	10,342	4,277	10,596	6,142	7,508	10,174	114,433
1889	20,782	12,601	11,094	23,763	6,826	36,960	9,519	56,361	4,480	4,094	2,737	13,304	202,521
1890	8,030	23,621	17,218	20,195	11,180	5,554	17,466	82,184	6,048	12,528	4,160	5,833	214,017
1891	11,185	8,668	20,732	6,224	12,108	17,080	10,222	6,456	6,461	4,202	6,330	12,737	122,405
1892	8,985	4,498	23,251	9,968	5,623	7,572	23,824	4,851	3,450	4,567	6,620	6,283	109,492
1893	7,690	6,288	27,586	25,381	21,600	2,439	1,498	2,343	3,545	2,344	44,511	13,395	158,620
1894	4,310	1,771	6,532	9,601	10,458	5,236	3,156	2,353	3,874	2,872	2,578	7,232	59,973
1895	9,476	5,182	5,088	11,298	18,584	2,903	17,871	8,307	4,250	11,737	5,380	9,265	109,341
1896	3,786	21,794	28,203	3,788	5,274	5,886	7,703	1,754	1,030	1,962	3,309	2,631	87,120
1897	13,204	4,067	3,299	4,364	2,420	2,031	2,746	1,593	1,667	4,512	5,395	5,715	51,013
1898	5,012	4,578	3,645	12,280	2,130	4,092	2,946	4,260	5,860	2,323	2,900	2,786	52,812
1899	6,665	30,904	4,716	29,653	3,699	6,621	13,246	10,876	5,311	4,627	4,903	9,358	130,579
1900	11,630	7,573	4,330	10,055	4,754	6,881	4,584	6,044	2,792	5,788	7,596	7,606	79,633
1901	10,104	10,822	14,926	13,029	14,023	9,441	17,028	4,846	12,917	5,758	3,843	9,525	126,262
1902	7,260	10,965	9,559	7,924	13,602	5,580	9,641	6,240	6,166	7,236	11,940	10,215	106,328
1903	19,419	10,818	7,605	13,987	13,102	10,482	5,905	4,336	8,215	4,086	5,444	10,070	113,469
1904	17,734	16,987	12,254	6,512	11,898	5,837	6,982	12,496	7,736	10,125	8,152	13,094	129,807
1905	14,637	8,014	13,966	24,660	40,420	15,554	7,364	21,478	6,418	14,258	14,550	8,016	189,335
1906	32,657	20,913	15,314	10,219	10,345	9,446	11,667	9,693	8,217	10,917	18,793	13,119	171,300
1907	10,237	9,712	24,194	12,232	14,736	6,763	9,332	7,085	8,434	7,162	5,315	15,718	130,920
1908	7,828	7,010	11,762	7,252	5,613	4,978	9,246	8,441	5,594	5,359	9,823	8,472	91,378
1909	6,567	10,712	12,433	14,257	7,676	9,400	8,582	5,906	8,481	6,339	7,125	13,747	111,225

OHIO BUSINESS INCORPORATIONS UNDER GENERAL LAWS, 1855–1936 (concl.)

E   Total Authorized Capital Stock, 1871–1919 (concl.)

YEAR	JAN.	FEB.	MAR.	APR.	MAY	JUNE	JULY	AUG.	SEPT.	OCT.	NOV.	DEC.	TOTAL
1910	8,229	30,070	13,928	8,107	10,697	6,587	8,158	10,274	5,179	6,564	5,834	8,818	122,445
1911	8,576	9,221	6,808	6,954	8,666	35,152	5,779	7,278	7,950	8,372	4,006	11,217	119,979
1912	25,069	5,218	9,314	8,615	7,322	7,343	8,672	6,198	6,462	11,288	31,035	8,720	135,256
1913	7,233	7,285	11,506	11,632	9,964	5,362	5,826	8,161	4,965	5,314	3,721	7,104	88,073
1914	8,456	9,090	17,184	8,228	8,655	15,400	30,970	6,837	4,309	4,540	27,048	306,180	446,897
1915	5,008	8,961	6,204	8,080	7,892	7,851	9,896	6,121	9,471	6,223	9,185	12,476	97,368
1916	14,894	10,589	17,887	12,150	15,182	11,068	12,172	14,601	22,860	10,902	25,329	76,886	244,520
1917	21,082	22,935	21,410	21,306	12,818	24,311	14,944	13,045	11,338	20,939	14,098	14,470	212,696
1918	13,339	13,839	12,676	12,933	6,626	7,180	6,932	11,714	4,110	5,092	8,460	14,453	117,354
1919	20,151	20,676	15,876	34,718	47,197								

F   Total Authorized Capital Stock Excluding Large Companies, 1871–1919
(thousands of dollars)

YEAR	JAN.	FEB.	MAR.	APR.	MAY	JUNE	JULY	AUG.	SEPT.	OCT.	NOV.	DEC.	TOTAL
1871												4,015	
1872	3,424	5,965	5,690	5,968	4,992	6,354	3,748	4,271	3,195	3,013	4,386	2,384	53,390
1873	6,290	5,852	5,968	3,814	8,315	4,015	3,716	3,520	1,242	1,605	2,084	2,315	48,736
1874	2,770	2,856	3,378	2,604	2,753	3,125	3,662	2,809	3,234	4,291	2,671	4,621	38,774
1875	4,121	6,877	5,243	4,615	2,645	2,684	2,552	2,802	3,014	3,663	2,195	2,301	42,712
1876	1,423	2,744	4,508	5,060	1,896	1,513	2,036	1,979	1,046	1,652	1,448	1,923	27,228
1877	1,324	1,479	3,138	3,880	3,004	3,446	3,258	1,739	1,974	2,855	2,612	1,333	30,042
1878	3,058	2,633	3,252	1,212	3,322	752	550	1,301	622	1,369	1,522	978	20,571
1879	1,116	4,002	2,144	1,927	2,401	1,389	1,666	1,978	1,869	1,296	3,071	4,349	27,208
1880	3,264	3,098	6,698	3,878	1,447	2,946	710	1,342	2,038	1,810	1,464	2,262	30,957
1881	3,028	3,737	8,423	6,804	5,030	3,365	4,067	3,976	4,495	3,430	6,894	5,791	59,040
1882	5,312	4,554	6,747	6,086	3,688	4,893	6,284	2,281	3,720	5,786	6,336	5,558	61,245
1883	7,053	6,688	5,102	3,348	3,940	5,007	4,263	4,910	3,698	6,401	3,854	5,162	59,426
1884	3,748	3,788	2,960	4,186	5,307	3,190	3,582	1,620	1,607	2,300	2,662	3,042	37,992
1885	3,185	3,373	5,188	2,144	2,674	4,146	4,067	3,378	4,224	3,364	3,832	4,232	43,807
1886	5,592	3,086	4,789	3,803	3,960	3,073	3,195	3,002	2,722	2,794	3,498	5,042	44,556
1887	7,852	4,814	4,923	7,323	7,584	4,483	3,620	3,839	5,034	3,318	3,619	3,882	60,291
1888	6,177	4,574	7,015	4,038	5,804	1,686	2,842	2,777	1,696	3,942	3,508	4,674	48,733
1889	6,782	6,601	7,094	4,763	4,426	3,460	5,119	3,361	3,480	3,094	2,737	4,304	55,221
1890	4,030	4,621	7,738	5,195	3,180	3,554	3,466	4,744	4,048	3,528	3,160	3,833	51,097
1891	5,185	3,668	5,732	4,224	5,108	4,520	4,222	2,956	4,461	3,202	3,330	5,737	52,345
1892	5,985	4,498	5,951	3,768	4,623	2,572	2,324	3,351	2,450	2,567	3,970	5,283	47,342
1893	5,690	4,288	4,586	6,381	3,800	2,439	1,498	2,343	1,545	1,344	1,511	2,395	37,820
1894	3,310	1,771	5,532	3,351	4,458	4,236	3,156	2,353	3,874	2,872	578	5,232	40,723
1895	5,476	4,182	4,088	6,298	3,084	1,903	1,871	3,077	2,250	3,337	4,380	3,765	43,711
1896	3,786	4,294	5,203	2,788	4,274	2,786	1,703	1,754	1,030	1,962	2,309	2,631	34,520
1897	2,204	3,067	3,299	3,364	2,420	2,031	1,746	1,593	1,667	3,512	3,395	4,715	33,013
1898	3,012	3,578	2,645	3,280	2,130	2,092	1,946	2,260	1,860	2,323	2,900	2,786	30,812
1899	2,665	2,904	4,716	4,153	3,699	4,621	4,246	3,876	2,811	4,627	2,903	3,558	44,779
1900	5,630	3,573	4,330	3,055	4,754	2,881	3,234	4,394	2,792	3,788	6,596	6,606	51,633
1901	6,104	6,572	8,926	5,529	9,773	7,441	4,028	4,846	5,917	5,758	3,843	6,025	74,762
1902	7,260	6,965	6,559	5,924	6,102	5,580	6,141	4,040	4,166	4,736	3,440	7,215	68,128
1903	8,669	7,818	6,605	6,987	6,602	6,132	4,655	3,136	4,165	4,086	4,444	10,070	73,369
1904	9,484	10,987	10,004	6,512	6,898	5,837	6,982	5,996	7,736	7,625	8,152	8,094	94,307
1905	12,137	8,014	10,066	10,160	9,170	10,554	6,364	7,978	5,418	7,758	8,550	8,016	104,185
1906	12,907	10,913	10,314	8,219	9,345	7,746	5,667	7,693	7,217	8,167	10,793	8,119	107,100
1907	10,237	9,712	10,594	10,232	11,236	6,763	9,332	7,085	6,184	6,162	5,315	6,718	99,570
1908	7,828	6,010	6,562	6,252	4,613	4,978	7,746	4,941	4,594	5,359	6,823	8,472	74,178
1909	6,567	10,712	9,933	9,257	7,676	8,400	8,582	5,906	6,981	6,339	5,275	10,247	95,875
1910	7,229	9,070	8,928	8,107	6,697	5,587	5,158	6,274	4,179	6,564	5,834	7,618	81,245
1911	8,576	8,221	6,808	6,954	6,666	7,652	5,779	7,278	6,950	6,372	4,006	7,217	82,479
1912	9,069	5,218	9,314	6,615	6,322	5,843	8,672	4,948	5,462	5,288	6,035	8,720	81,506
1913	7,233	6,285	6,656	6,882	6,914	5,362	5,826	7,161	4,965	5,314	3,721	6,104	72,423
1914	5,956	6,490	9,884	7,028	7,655	6,400	6,470	4,337	4,309	4,540	6,048	5,180	74,297
1915	5,008	5,961	6,204	6,580	6,892	7,851	5,896	4,821	5,971	6,223	5,685	9,476	76,568
1916	11,894	10,589	13,787	8,400	9,182	10,068	7,422	7,851	10,360	6,902	12,329	14,216	123,000
1917	14,582	11,185	13,060	11,056	10,618	9,311	9,994	9,045	7,838	6,739	11,598	11,470	126,496
1918	8,339	9,089	8,476	10,683	6,626	5,180	6,932	6,714	4,110	5,092	7,210	8,453	86,904
1919	16,001	15,176	14,876	21,218	18,397								

1) Sources of Raw Data

Reports of the Secretary of State of Ohio issued each year—but not always covering operations for exactly twelve months—and to be found in the Executive and the Assembly Documents of the State. The title is almost always: *Annual Report of the Secretary of State . . . for the year* ——. The exceptions are: the annual reports for the years ending November 15, 1911, November 15, 1912, and November 15, 1914 where the word *Statistical* is inserted between the words *Annual* and *Report;* and the report for November 16, 1914–June 30, 1915, which is styled *Statistical Report of the Secretary of State . . . .* The successive reports used and the pages from which the incorporation data were compiled are:[1]

PERIOD COVERED	PAGES	PERIOD COVERED	PAGES	PERIOD COVERED	PAGES	PERIOD COVERED	PAGES
1856	210–4	1876	190–211	1896ᵃ	486–513	1916ᵇ	11–69
1857	18–9	1877	118–41	1897ᵃ	533–55	1917ᵇ	10–69
1858	9–11	1878	120–40	1898ᵃ	401–25	1918ᵇ	8–59
1859	322–8	1879	114–38	1899ᵃ	450–81	1919ᵇ	8–66
1860	6–7	1880	130–61	1900ᵃ	442–81	1920ᵇ	8–90
1861	8–10	1881	222–41	1901ᵃ	545–91	1921ᵇ	8–75
1862	7–8	1882	104–38	1902ᵃ	512–59	1922ᵇ	8–78
1863	394–5	1883	154–86	1903ᵃ	783–833	1923ᵇ	8–80
1864	6–9	1884	172–205	1904ᵃ	839–91	1924ᵇ	8–75
1865	447–61	1885	231–62	1905ᵃ	482–544	1925ᵇ	8–76
1866	17–27	1886	118–46	1906ᵃ	469–514	1926ᵇ	8–89
1867	23–34	1887	364–400	1907ᵃ	187–236	1927ᵇ	8–74
1868	193–206	1888	359–90	1908ᵃ	609–52	1928ᵇ	12–83
1869	9–21	1889	299–333	1909ᵃ	281–336	1929ᶜ	16–90 & 172–204
1870	103–13	1890ᵃ	411–50	1910ᵃ	489–541	1930	12–81
1871	32–44, 2d. ed.	1891ᵃ	464–96	1911ᵃ	11–80	1931	12–83
1872	38–63	1892ᵃ	376–417	1912ᵃ	11–76	1932	13–70
1873	54–77	1893ᵃ	491–527	1913ᵃ	11–75	1933	9–63
1874	42–64	1894ᵃ	462–87	1914ᵃ	11–58	1934	9–64
1875	194–216	1895ᵃ	486–512	11/16/14– 6/30/15	11–56	1935	9–62
						1936	9–66

ᵃ Fiscal year ending Nov. 15.
ᵇ Fiscal year ending June 30.
ᶜ Fiscal year ending June 30, 1929, but includes Report of the Corporation Dept. for 7/1/29–12/31/29.
[1] Usually, particularly for the later years, the page references are for the separate reports; when a report was bound with other executive or legislative documents, the page references are those of the document series. Error in using these page references cannot arise if one takes care to look for the table on incorporations.

2) Special Comments

a) The data used in compiling this series are not presented in the reports in a uniform manner. From November 16, 1855 to November 15, 1871 the names of the chartered companies, sometimes classified by industry, are listed with their dates of incorporation but without capital stock figures. One clue to whether a company was a business or nonbusiness enterprise was its industrial group. The only other clue to a nonbusiness enterprise was its name. The number of nonprofit seeking companies eliminated on the basis of name was not large and included such incorporations as churches (see Ch. 1).

The lists of incorporations for November 15, 1871–December 31, 1936 give information on the capital stock of each company as well as its date of incorporation and a brief statement of its objectives. Since capital stock figures were given, neither the industrial groupings of companies nor their names were employed in eliminating the nonbusiness enterprises.

An Ohio series for nonbusiness incorporations, compiled for 1803–51 and 1872–1936 appears in Appendix 1.

b) Consolidations and reorganizations were tallied as new companies, though a few obviously business units were omitted because their capital stock was not given although they appeared in lists purporting to give the capital stock of all business units. The exclusion of those few was necessary to preserve the balance between the series on the number of incorporations and those on capital stock.

Reorganizations are important for ten or eleven months after May 1923, a peak in business activity; the succeeding trough occurred in July 1924.

c) Occasionally a company appeared to be entered twice. Since it was not feasible to check the entries and there were no indications that the second entries were amendments to charters, the few seeming duplications were treated as incorporations.

d) Capital stock figures could be compiled for November 16, 1871 through May 31, 1919 and used to classify corporations according to size. For subsequent months neither procedure was feasible, because nonpar value shares were issued and there was no simple scheme that could be used to equate even roughly the par and the nonpar value shares of Ohio corporations. For the statute authorizing stock without par value, see 108 *Laws of Ohio* (1919), Part 1, p. 507.

e) While in 1851 an amendment to the Ohio state constitution made it necessary for business corporations to be formed under general laws rather than by special acts (Table 5 of text), the series in this section could not be extended back to that year. The data to link this series with the Ohio figures of the preceding section were apparently not published. This series has to end with 1936, because publication of incorporation data such as those used for this study was discontinued.

PENNSYLVANIA BUSINESS INCORPORATIONS BY SPECIAL ACTS, 1800–1860

See Table 6 of text and also Ch. 3, notes 22 and 31.

1) Source

William Miller, A Note on the History of Business Corporations in Pennsylvania, 1800–1860, *Quarterly Journal of Economics*, LV, No. 1 (Nov. 1940), pp. 150–60.

2) Special Comments

See portions of the text that relate to Table 6.

PENNSYLVANIA BUSINESS INCORPORATIONS UNDER GENERAL LAWS, 1875–1887

Calculated total annual figures, together with the calculated number in each of three industrial categories; see note 2a below.

	1875	1876	1877	1878	1879	1880	1881	1882	1883	1884	1885	1886	1887
Total incorporations	188	163	135	116	155	215	252	288	344	399	441	482	467
Building & loan assns.	79	64	58	57	55	57	63	68	74	78	90	102	108
Oil producing corps.	2	2	5	4	3	6	4	2	2	2	18	34	33
Gas distributing corps.	7	7	7	4	4	6	15	24	70	116	68	18	11

1) Sources of Raw Data

Pennsylvania Laws: 1875, pp. 81–101; *1876*, pp. 223–50; *1877*, pp. 103–22; *1878*, pp. 234–55; *1879*, pp. 213–28; *1881*, pp. 189–245; *1883*, pp. 251–334; *1885*, pp. 342–469; *1887*, pp. 449–585; *1889*, pp. a1–a143.

2) Special Comments

a) In the 1889 volume of *Pennsylvania Laws*, business corporations chartered by Pennsylvania from July 1, 1887 to May 31, 1889 are listed by name, and the incorporation date and other facts are given for each company. Preceding volumes give merely the names of the corporations chartered during specified periods. Since the periods vary in length from volume to volume, a series of estimated annual figures was built up from the table in (c) below. The period covered in each volume was converted to the nearest number of half weeks and, on the assumption of regular chartering throughout each calendar year, annual figures (of 52 weeks each) were calculated.

b) The incorporations in a few industrial categories were

PENNSYLVANIA BUSINESS INCORPORATIONS UNDER GENERAL LAWS, 1875–1887 (concl.)

selected by name from the lists referred to in (a). The original counts made on the data appear in (c). Annual figures for these industrial categories were estimated in the same manner as for the total number, described in (a). All estimated figures are given in the table above.
c) The original counts:

Period	7/14/1874–5/1/1875	5/1/1875–6/7/1876	6/7/1876–5/1/1877	5/1/1877–7/1/1878	7/1/1878–7/14/1879	7/14/1879–7/1/1881	7/1/1881–7/1 1883	7/1/1883–7/1/1885	7/1/1885–6/30/1887	7/1/1887–12/31/1887
No. of wks. in specified period	41½	57½	46½	60½	54	102	104	104	104	26
Total incorporations	153	206	130	152	105	421	577	798	965	226
Bldg. & loan assns.	64	86	47	71	56	111	137	157	203	57
Oil producing corps.	0	3	1	7	1	11	5	4	67	16
Gas distributing corps.	10	5	8	7	2	12	48	233	37	2
Reference: *Penna. Laws*	*1875*, pp. 81–101	*1876*, pp. 223–50	*1877*, pp. 103–22	*1878*, pp. 234–55	*1879*, pp. 213–28	*1881*, pp. 189–245	*1883*, pp. 251–334	*1885*, pp. 342–469	*1887*, pp. 449–585	*1889*, pp. al–al43

PENNSYLVANIA BUSINESS INCORPORATIONS UNDER GENERAL LAWS, 1887–1921

YEAR	JAN.	FEB.	MAR.	APR.	MAY	JUNE	JULY	AUG.	SEPT.	OCT.	NOV.	DEC.	TOTAL
A Total Incorporations													
1887							46	37	32	41	30	40	
1888	54	31	44	49	31	37	34	37	27	43	35	55	477
1889	55	47	80	61	66	57	76	55	55	38	57	70	717
1890	47	66	58	55	63	55	69	39	45	48	54	68	667
1891	36	46	53	43	34	60	41	46	43	44	56	70	572
1892	58	60	74	73	70	79	63	64	34	59	43	83	760
1893	62	53	66	62	74	57	49	43	25	31	42	40	604
1894	37	52	49	40	52	48	54	48	38	53	51	56	578
1895	46	48	61	51	45	46	55	46	42	38	43	52	573
1896	50	49	70	36	49	46	51	33	21	31	33	61	530
1897	46	41	52	55	45	45	42	38	42	39	48	47	540
1898	61	43	62	39	50	45	32	33	23	29	34	33	484
1899	61	33	48	53	61	82	67	55	47	52	63	65	687
1900	69	65	80	70	85	70	65	60	64	60	86	80	854
1901	72	73	91	103	84	98	127	106	95	88	106	128	1,171
1902	98	105	126	140	155	146	100	115	125	156	107	157	1,530
1903	130	136	194	192	153	144	115	74	117	140	73	140	1,608
1904	99	125	151	87	133	110	106	122	98	94	78	142	1,345
1905	143	153	185	170	108	131	108	86	95	117	102	71	1,469
1906	146	129	157	127	150	157	70	132	117	129	113	101	1,528
1907	205	165	161	125	106	150	147	98	119	134	85	116	1,611
1908	84	85	97	112	104	96	92	68	83	89	87	117	1,114
1909	109	126	148	142	123	152	125	93	139	108	111	141	1,517
1910	118	142	144	166	136	123	94	124	121	81	171	103	1,523
1911	154	136	190	171	148	160	124	145	109	85	114	122	1,658
1912	114	157	160	183	172	173	140	98	147	105	137	73	1,659
1913	209	189	302	264	235	124	118	91	140	107	114	202	2,095
1914	113	105	172	122	119	137	129	69	93	100	81	82	1,322
1915	136	101	136	114	103	92	59	126	100	82	106	211	1,366
1916	137	166	136	138	172	150	121	86	168	143	129	148	1,694
1917	167	186	186	177	230	181	156	127	136	155	143	114	1,958
1918	120	137	109	108	140	105	101	78	117	98	54	110	1,277
1919	108	134	170	208	179	175	227	181	224	183	267	241	2,297
1920	306	277	294	271	261	265	207	185	222	181	225	224	2,918
1921	184	171	215	182	169								
B Small Incorporations													
1887							19	21	19	27	17	26	
1888	33	17	25	32	17	21	19	24	20	27	23	30	288
1889	36	24	48	37	39	44	44	32	35	20	38	41	438
1890	35	39	38	38	42	35	45	23	32	32	36	45	440
1891	24	28	37	31	23	37	28	30	25	32	40	46	381
1892	42	36	46	48	49	64	43	40	27	34	31	59	519
1893	41	41	45	44	57	39	38	33	20	24	35	31	448
1894	23	38	35	24	39	35	38	34	28	36	34	40	404
1895	31	40	42	39	34	35	41	37	28	31	30	40	428

YEAR	JAN.	FEB.	MAR.	APR.	MAY	JUNE	JULY	AUG.	SEPT.	OCT.	NOV.	DEC.	TOTAL
1896	36	40	51	28	32	40	37	27	18	26	26	44	405
1897	36	33	41	41	37	28	33	31	33	31	33	38	415
1898	48	35	49	36	41	42	27	29	19	25	30	28	409
1899	51	23	35	43	43	64	56	45	39	39	42	51	531
1900	49	53	64	59	70	52	58	50	56	54	71	65	701
1901	57	52	76	82	73	86	109	94	82	75	88	99	973
1902	81	86	108	113	134	127	91	102	102	129	93	133	1,299
1903	105	109	155	154	120	121	85	56	94	121	60	107	1,287
1904	84	106	131	69	118	90	97	105	86	83	68	119	1,156
1905	126	132	163	146	99	115	97	74	80	102	86	58	1,278
1906	111	104	129	99	128	130	60	112	98	113	93	84	1,261
1907	170	131	140	101	88	119	126	87	99	114	66	98	1,339
1908	71	75	83	98	94	86	79	60	73	76	78	100	973
1909	99	106	132	123	105	130	104	80	123	86	99	121	1,308
1910	97	121	115	141	115	94	79	111	104	64	154	84	1,279
1911	133	110	164	155	121	142	107	126	96	72	104	105	1,435
1912	98	137	132	166	154	152	119	87	136	86	115	63	1,445
1913	166	167	276	246	208	105	102	82	135	92	101	167	1,847
1914	100	96	139	107	108	115	121	58	84	93	73	75	1,169
1915	115	93	118	101	87	70	50	114	88	66	88	185	1,175
1916	112	143	114	119	143	129	107	72	145	118	99	119	1,420
1917	138	147	146	137	200	149	133	106	117	134	120	99	1,626
1918	100	114	91	93	114	86	82	65	103	88	44	91	1,071
1919	79	97	122	135	130	131	172	131	170	138	197	163	1,665
1920	211	197	182	199	179	176	141	140	152	132	146	160	2,015
1921	124	114	155	141	123								

C Medium Incorporations

YEAR	JAN.	FEB.	MAR.	APR.	MAY	JUNE	JULY	AUG.	SEPT.	OCT.	NOV.	DEC.	TOTAL
1887							22	9	5	11	9	9	
1888	16	12	13	12	9	14	13	11	6	8	7	16	137
1889	11	15	23	16	14	5	22	17	12	12	13	19	179
1890	8	19	18	12	14	15	17	10	9	12	13	18	165
1891	9	18	15	12	10	19	12	13	11	6	11	18	154
1892	9	16	16	20	14	12	15	13	6	17	7	20	165
1893	16	9	11	11	14	14	8	6	3	4	2	5	103
1894	11	10	9	9	7	4	10	6	8	5	9	7	95
1895	9	7	15	11	4	7	8	6	6	4	8	11	96
1896	6	9	10	7	13	5	10	3	3	4	3	14	87
1897	6	6	9	8	6	12	5	3	3	7	11	8	84
1898	8	7	7	2	5	1	3	3	3	4	1	3	47
1899	8	8	12	8	15	13	9	8	6	10	14	10	121
1900	17	11	13	10	12	15	6	8	7	6	12	13	130
1901	11	20	12	11	10	11	14	10	10	13	16	23	161
1902	12	16	15	22	18	16	8	12	22	21	11	22	195
1903	18	24	37	32	24	19	28	16	21	12	8	26	265
1904	6	16	13	13	5	12	9	13	9	10	9	16	131
1905	13	15	17	15	8	12	7	12	12	7	13	9	140
1906	26	17	20	21	13	20	8	13	16	6	10	10	180
1907	24	24	16	11	10	19	13	9	15	12	12	7	172
1908	6	5	9	9	7	5	10	7	10	8	7	14	97
1909	9	14	8	8	11	16	18	12	10	18	5	12	141
1910	9	16	25	11	11	15	9	10	8	10	11	12	147
1911	12	17	17	8	14	14	8	9	7	11	6	8	131
1912	10	11	16	9	7	12	15	9	7	12	10	4	122
1913	22	14	15	10	13	10	13	7	4	6	4	21	139
1914	9	8	15	9	6	15	7	6	6	1	4	4	90
1915	10	4	9	5	9	14	5	10	4	6	6	11	93
1916	14	10	5	11	12	11	9	7	12	14	10	13	128
1917	19	17	24	21	18	24	21	14	16	17	15	8	214
1918	15	17	13	9	20	16	14	9	9	8	10	17	157
1919	16	22	18	36	20	25	28	23	32	24	35	35	314
1920	47	38	45	28	35	31	33	27	35	29	37	36	421
1921	39	30	31	25	27								

D Large Incorporations

YEAR	JAN.	FEB.	MAR.	APR.	MAY	JUNE	JULY	AUG.	SEPT.	OCT.	NOV.	DEC.	TOTAL
1887							5	7	8	3	4	5	
1888	5	2	6	5	5	2	2	2	1	8	5	9	52
1889	8	8	9	8	13	8	10	6	8	6	6	10	100

PENNSYLVANIA BUSINESS INCORPORATIONS UNDER GENERAL LAWS, 1887–1921 (concl.)

D Large Incorporations (concl.)

YEAR	JAN.	FEB.	MAR.	APR.	MAY	JUNE	JULY	AUG.	SEPT.	OCT.	NOV.	DEC.	TOTAL
1890	4	8	2	5	7	5	7	6	4	4	5	5	62
1891	3	0	1	0	1	4	1	3	7	6	5	6	37
1892	7	8	12	5	7	3	5	11	1	8	5	4	76
1893	5	3	10	7	3	4	3	4	2	3	5	4	53
1894	3	4	5	7	6	9	6	8	2	12	8	9	79
1895	6	1	4	1	7	4	6	3	8	3	5	1	49
1896	8	0	9	1	4	1	4	3	0	1	4	3	38
1897	4	2	2	6	2	5	4	4	6	1	4	1	41
1898	5	1	6	1	4	2	2	1	1	0	3	2	28
1899	2	2	1	2	3	5	2	2	2	3	7	4	35
1900	3	1	3	1	3	3	1	2	1	0	3	2	23
1901	4	1	3	10	1	1	4	2	3	0	2	6	37
1902	5	3	3	5	3	3	1	1	1	6	3	2	36
1903	7	3	2	6	9	4	2	2	2	7	5	7	56
1904	9	3	7	5	10	8	0	4	3	1	1	7	58
1905	4	6	5	9	1	4	4	0	3	8	3	4	51
1906	9	8	8	7	9	7	2	7	3	10	10	7	87
1907	11	10	5	13	8	12	8	2	5	8	7	11	100
1908	7	5	5	5	3	5	3	1	0	5	2	3	44
1909	1	6	8	11	7	6	3	1	6	4	7	8	68
1910	12	5	4	14	10	14	6	3	9	7	6	7	97
1911	9	9	9	8	13	4	9	10	6	2	4	9	92
1912	6	9	12	8	11	9	6	2	4	7	12	6	92
1913	21	8	11	8	14	9	3	2	1	9	9	14	109
1914	4	1	18	6	5	7	1	5	3	6	4	3	63
1915	11	4	9	8	7	8	4	2	8	10	12	15	98
1916	11	13	17	8	17	10	5	7	11	11	20	16	146
1917	10	22	16	19	12	8	2	7	3	4	8	7	118
1918	5	6	5	6	6	3	5	4	5	2	0	2	49
1919	13	15	30	37	29	19	27	27	22	21	35	43	318
1920	48	42	67	44	47	58	33	18	35	20	42	28	482
1921	21	27	29	16	19								

E Total Authorized Capital Stock
(thousands of dollars)

YEAR	JAN.	FEB.	MAR.	APR.	MAY	JUNE	JULY	AUG.	SEPT.	OCT.	NOV.	DEC.	TOTAL
1887							14,212	9,562	10,632	6,241	6,910	8,928	
1888	9,785	5,176	10,268	9,680	7,354	7,796	7,241	5,036	3,102	9,910	6,888	13,405	95,641
1889	12,346	13,666	15,354	12,991	18,331	9,654	16,747	10,988	12,386	10,812	9,509	16,127	158,911
1890	6,135	20,231	6,415	8,489	11,928	12,147	13,907	8,895	7,276	8,644	8,977	10,015	123,059
1891	6,033	3,296	5,763	2,922	3,783	9,040	4,036	6,883	10,198	8,114	8,992	12,121	81,181
1892	10,839	12,894	17,602	11,136	11,065	7,070	9,581	14,220	2,820	15,010	8,272	10,264	130,773
1893	10,404	5,844	15,336	12,024	7,272	7,681	6,188	6,092	3,127	4,976	6,440	6,279	91,663
1894	6,538	7,068	9,094	9,130	8,540	11,721	9,137	10,131	4,314	41,050	11,164	13,124	141,011
1895	27,252	3,410	8,043	13,866	8,750	6,205	7,806	5,600	9,742	4,122	7,644	3,601	106,041
1896	9,552	2,746	12,656	3,244	7,225	3,362	7,617	4,768	772	2,103	5,314	6,103	65,462
1897	5,354	4,781	4,866	8,377	4,974	9,056	5,889	5,254	7,066	4,068	6,645	3,612	69,942
1898	7,433	2,801	10,516	2,214	5,306	3,137	3,535	1,992	2,030	1,162	3,913	2,934	46,973
1899	4,749	4,374	4,616	4,858	6,905	9,603	4,004	4,872	3,491	7,701	10,388	7,870	73,431
1900	7,059	4,724	35,814	4,073	9,546	6,323	3,191	3,967	7,323	2,370	5,678	6,446	96,514
1901	6,752	6,011	10,382	12,528	4,606	3,811	7,772	5,058	15,484	3,346	6,142	22,133	104,025
1902	10,528	36,587	7,941	10,537	14,618	7,588	12,854	5,325	6,160	11,774	6,187	8,592	138,691
1903	11,826	9,603	12,602	15,749	15,002	22,126	9,846	5,391	7,985	15,638	7,378	13,922	147,068
1904	11,862	7,852	12,774	8,718	14,127	14,627	3,568	8,400	6,716	4,004	3,845	12,036	108,529
1905	8,232	11,236	15,448	13,762	4,671	9,339	7,192	3,559	9,396	11,120	8,054	7,652	109,661
1906	18,232	12,688	23,848	12,929	15,126	13,320	4,819	11,158	8,836	12,796	13,524	10,324	157,600
1907	18,849	16,037	11,198	17,466	11,112	18,597	13,268	6,540	11,656	11,864	10,046	14,630	161,263
1908	13,478	7,580	9,104	8,315	8,156	6,912	6,439	3,016	3,354	8,065	4,298	8,062	86,779
1909	4,449	11,688	14,444	15,484	12,162	11,820	8,944	8,013	11,734	8,054	14,286	13,441	134,519
1910	24,299	10,389	10,830	19,736	19,778	25,228	9,985	7,034	19,426	9,948	10,142	10,172	176,967
1911	17,490	14,763	15,352	13,054	20,040	9,580	18,310	19,146	9,063	8,193	6,784	22,988	174,763
1912	19,708	16,253	17,797	13,050	23,536	14,816	11,350	4,945	7,420	10,512	22,119	7,755	169,261
1913	40,023	17,481	25,251	15,000	20,270	14,564	6,574	4,695	3,300	13,959	11,176	30,707	203,060
1914	7,654	4,686	24,048	10,114	8,641	12,258	4,310	6,782	4,812	9,912	15,850	305,103	414,170
1915	15,708	6,408	13,374	16,370	16,211	12,646	15,210	6,262	11,562	15,406	17,852	22,076	169,085
1916	93,962	16,875	35,470	13,611	23,451	20,268	8,079	15,061	48,739	33,164	25,657	123,417	457,754
1917	16,508	104,419	30,003	36,375	25,522	84,961	7,898	47,444	9,628	10,545	16,544	24,490	414,337

YEAR	JAN.	FEB.	MAR.	APR.	MAY	JUNE	JULY	AUG.	SEPT.	OCT.	NOV.	DEC.	TOTAL
1918	11,966	19,918	14,587	9,940	14,471	8,127	9,146	9,347	9,231	5,326	2,436	8,582	123,077
1919	21,762	29,976	38,692	61,615	40,625	46,727	59,791	44,729	41,272	51,431	70,703	102,128	609,451
1920	94,138	76,801	140,968	71,423	105,963	108,088	62,024	37,734	83,637	53,098	114,892	74,442	1,023,208
1921	55,492	53,466	72,296	47,997	44,043								

F Total Authorized Capital Stock Excluding Large Companies
(thousands of dollars)

YEAR	JAN.	FEB.	MAR.	APR.	MAY	JUNE	JULY	AUG.	SEPT.	OCT.	NOV.	DEC.	TOTAL
1887							7,712	2,562	2,632	3,241	2,910	3,928	
1888	4,785	3,176	4,268	4,580	2,354	5,796	5,241	3,036	2,102	1,910	1,888	3,905	43,041
1889	4,346	5,666	6,354	4,991	4,331	1,654	6,747	4,488	3,386	4,812	3,509	5,927	56,211
1890	2,135	6,231	4,415	3,489	4,928	3,147	5,107	2,695	3,276	4,644	3,977	4,015	48,059
1891	3,033	3,296	4,263	2,922	2,583	5,040	3,036	3,883	3,198	2,114	3,992	6,121	43,481
1892	3,839	4,894	5,602	6,136	4,065	4,070	4,581	3,220	1,820	4,610	2,272	6,264	51,373
1893	5,404	2,844	4,736	5,024	4,272	3,681	3,188	2,092	1,127	1,976	1,440	2,279	38,063
1894	3,538	3,068	2,594	2,130	2,340	2,721	3,137	2,131	2,314	2,050	3,164	2,324	31,511
1895	3,252	2,410	4,043	3,866	1,750	2,205	1,806	2,600	1,742	1,122	2,644	2,601	30,041
1896	1,552	2,746	3,656	2,244	3,225	2,362	3,117	1,768	772	1,103	1,314	3,103	26,962
1897	1,354	2,781	2,866	2,377	2,974	3,056	1,889	1,004	1,066	3,068	2,645	2,612	27,692
1898	2,433	1,801	3,016	1,214	1,306	1,137	1,535	992	1,030	1,162	913	934	17,473
1899	2,749	2,374	3,116	2,858	3,905	4,103	2,004	2,872	1,491	2,701	3,388	3,870	35,431
1900	4,059	3,724	3,564	3,073	3,546	3,323	2,191	1,967	2,323	2,370	2,678	4,446	37,264
1901	2,752	5,011	3,382	2,528	3,606	2,811	3,772	3,058	3,484	3,346	3,892	7,133	44,775
1902	3,328	4,587	4,941	5,537	6,618	4,588	2,854	4,325	5,160	5,774	3,187	6,592	57,491
1903	4,226	5,603	10,602	9,749	6,002	6,126	7,846	3,391	5,985	4,638	2,378	6,922	73,468
1904	2,862	4,852	5,274	3,718	3,627	4,733	3,568	4,400	3,216	3,004	2,645	5,036	46,935
1905	4,232	5,036	6,448	4,762	3,671	4,839	3,192	3,559	4,396	3,120	4,054	3,652	50,961
1906	8,232	4,688	6,648	5,679	4,426	6,320	2,819	4,158	5,836	2,796	3,524	3,324	58,450
1907	7,849	6,037	6,198	4,466	3,112	6,597	5,268	4,540	5,656	3,864	3,046	3,630	60,263
1908	2,478	2,080	4,104	3,315	4,156	1,912	3,439	2,016	3,354	3,065	2,298	5,062	37,279
1909	3,449	5,188	3,944	2,984	5,162	4,707	5,944	3,013	3,534	4,054	2,286	5,441	49,706
1910	4,049	5,389	6,705	4,736	3,778	5,469	2,985	4,034	3,918	2,948	4,142	2,672	50,825
1911	4,490	4,763	5,852	3,554	4,840	5,580	4,028	3,514	2,563	4,693	2,284	2,988	49,149
1912	3,398	3,565	4,797	5,050	3,661	4,246	5,350	2,945	3,420	3,512	3,884	1,755	45,583
1913	7,553	4,661	6,686	5,060	5,270	4,714	3,574	2,695	2,300	2,459	2,176	7,921	55,069
1914	3,654	3,686	5,298	3,114	3,641	5,258	3,310	1,782	1,812	1,912	1,850	2,103	37,420
1915	4,708	2,408	3,374	2,370	2,961	3,646	1,909	3,262	2,562	2,406	3,307	4,466	37,379
1916	3,962	3,875	2,470	3,611	4,451	3,268	3,079	3,061	3,839	5,164	3,057	3,717	43,554
1917	5,508	4,919	8,003	6,375	6,522	2,961	5,898	4,444	5,128	6,545	4,944	3,515	64,762
1918	5,966	5,318	3,657	2,940	6,171	4,127	4,146	2,997	4,231	3,326	2,436	5,582	50,897
1919	5,262	6,976	5,692	7,115	5,625	7,027	8,791	7,329	9,422	7,931	10,548	9,628	91,346
1920	12,638	12,801	12,044	10,583	10,863	9,988	8,024	7,734	12,017	7,098	10,892	10,042	124,724
1921	9,392	8,466	10,296	7,395	8,043								

1) Sources of Raw Data

a) For July 1887 through May 1899. *Laws of Pennsylvania: 1889*, pp. a1–a143; *1891*, pp. a1–a172; *1893*, pp. a1–a185; *1895*, pp. a1–a145; *1897*, pp. 571–730; *1899*, pp. 435–571.

b) For June 1, 1899 through May 31, 1909. *List of Charters of Corporations enrolled in the office of the Secretary of the Commonwealth during the two years beginning June 1, 1899, and ending June 1, 1901, . . . (1901)*, pp. 3–233. Also successive biennial reports for periods ending May 31: *1903*, pp. 1–206; *1905*, pp. 1–196; *1907*, pp. 1–205; *1909*, pp. 3–188. All sources cited here and in (c), except those of 1901 and 1903, were published in Harrisburg; the years of publication are the same as the terminal dates of the reports except that the report covering the years ending May 1921 was published in 1922.

c) For June 1, 1909 through May 31, 1921. *Alphabetical List of Charters . . . Beginning June 1, 1909, and Ending May 31, 1911* (1911), pp. 3–237. Also successive biennial reports for periods ending May 31: *1913*, pp. 3–308; *1915*, pp. 3–193; *1917*, pp. 3–231; *1919*, pp. 3–244; *1921*, pp. 3–421.

2) Special Comments

a) The above sources give the name of each company chartered, together with its date of incorporation, its authorized capital stock, and a fairly complete statement of corporate objectives.

b) In many lists of incorporations, the companies are grouped by industry. These groupings were sometimes helpful in classifying the corporations.

c) Rechartered, renewals, and extensions of charters were not tallied as incorporations.

d) The occasional company that had a date of incorporation outside the period covered by the list in which it appeared was not tallied unless the arrangement of the list was such that the assumed misprint could with good reason be corrected.

YEAR	JAN.	FEB.	MAR.	APR.	MAY	JUNE	JULY	AUG.	SEPT.	OCT.	NOV.	DEC.	TOTAL
A Total Incorporations													
1872	5	6	6	1	3	7	5	3	2	4	3	2	47
1873	6	10	10	13	10	3	4	6	2	3	5	6	78
1874	2	8	14	9	10	11	3	7	5	8	5	7	89
1875	13	17	29	29	23	11	10	8	17	14	9	19	199
1876	11	9	21	32	9	16	17	10	6	4	6	3	144
1877	11	4	6	5	2	8	8	5	5	6	2	7	69
1878	7	5	16	13	4	4	8	5	1	2	6	7	78
1879	14	4	6	3	7	8	4	6	3	4	12	6	77
1880	12	9	6	12	8	4	8	6	7	4	4	5	85
1881	6	7	17	12	15	11	13	20	12	14	17	14	158
1882	11	14	14	16	17	16	11	22	18	17	10	21	187
1883	13	18	23	27	28	29	23	16	26	20	19	20	262
1884	26	26	25	29	26	25	26	14	19	16	8	13	253
1885	23	20	14	13	14	95	7	9	6	7	7	6	221
1886	14	18	20	17	8	14	11	8	9	11	12	15	157
1887	23	8	26	22	23	31	31	26	24	23	20	27	284
1888	26	36	33	27	29	31	6	16	15	16	14	15	264
1889	20	26	37	44	30	26	28	24	28	22	21	25	331
1890	30	42	56	44	35	34	37	32	29	25	19	33	416
1891	24	25	23	28	35	37	42	19	22	23	29	30	337
1892	26	25	39	35	29	20	22	29	22	21	16	20	304
1893	28	29	46	33	46	23	22	28	18	14	16	18	321
1894	24	30	27	28	26	18	18	11	28	21	17	15	263
1895	38	21	33	46	27	22	43	28	26	28	21	29	362
1896	39	31	30	32	35	25	28	17	17	20	14	37	325
1897	38	31	44	45	31	25	23	22	26	14	23	20	342
1898	45	38	34	28	23	31	30	19	18	17	12	20	315
1899	29	35	37	32	33	33	38	36	25	23	30	36	387
1900	52	40	46	36	48	48	38	29	33	37	35	52	494
1901	81	75	87	196	289	105	107	77	47	55	47	68	1,234
1902	104	90	81	32	139	71	80	59	46	58	50	63	873
1903	102	68	66	30	121	86	89	64	51	57	50	70	854
1904	108	71	49	36	110	90	76	67	44	64	52	85	852
1905	92	77	93	41	92	78	88	96	89	72	83	97	998
1906	140	102	132	91	178	123	106	117	125	110	105	126	1,455
1907	172	174	188	175	197	198	209	117	116	79	40	41	1,706
1908	65	69	76	53	73	82	65	79	91	57	55	80	845
1909	138	110	142	103	115	106	141	101	125	87	92	107	1,367
1910	132	131	136	104	137	115	85	89	80	75	73	75	1,232
1911	109	109	136	84	115	99	86	76	95	70	78	58	1,115
1912	134	112	118	107	118	120	96	106	101	95	81	87	1,275
1913	138	129	109	124	127	141	111	111	85	83	63	81	1,302
1914	81	114	98	95	120	82	93	66	59	70	62	51	991
1915	75	86	97	128	151	99	93	88	80	87	68	91	1,143
1916	97	119	130	126	105	102	107	67	91	76	65	89	1,174
1917	118	112	113	95	121	101	112	96	78	77	62	53	1,138
1918	63	78	97	70	97	57	80	61	47	24	38	53	765
1919	101	107	122	120	118	144	134	127	133	104	107	114	1,431
1920	187	140	148	135	117	119	141	110					
B Small Incorporations													
1872	4	2	3	1	1	4	4	1	1	0	0	2	23
1873	4	7	7	10	3	1	2	3	2	2	0	1	42
1874	0	7	8	5	4	8	3	7	2	7	2	4	57
1875	9	11	16	23	17	8	7	4	11	9	4	10	129
1876	5	7	12	21	5	13	11	8	5	2	5	1	95
1877	6	4	5	3	2	5	7	4	4	3	2	6	51
1878	5	5	14	13	1	3	5	4	1	2	4	5	62
1879	10	3	5	3	4	6	3	5	3	3	9	2	56
1880	9	8	3	9	3	4	4	3	7	4	4	4	62
1881	3	4	15	6	7	7	10	12	7	11	15	9	106
1882	8	8	4	10	10	9	8	15	12	14	6	10	114
1883	9	9	14	20	12	18	12	13	21	8	11	12	159
1884	17	20	14	22	16	13	16	11	17	10	5	11	172
1885	10	11	9	8	11	52	6	7	5	4	7	5	135
1886	9	14	17	14	8	11	9	7	9	7	8	10	123
1887	18	6	19	12	18	20	18	24	24	20	18	24	221
1888	16	24	23	21	22	20	4	13	10	11	9	11	184
1889	16	19	26	36	21	20	19	19	22	14	15	14	241

YEAR	JAN.	FEB.	MAR.	APR.	MAY	JUNE	JULY	AUG.	SEPT.	OCT.	NOV.	DEC.	TOTAL
1890	23	29	37	31	24	21	27	21	25	19	12	24	293
1891	14	15	19	22	24	27	27	16	19	20	24	15	242
1892	20	15	32	26	21	9	16	21	17	17	9	17	220
1893	24	22	36	25	39	18	17	25	14	13	14	16	263
1894	21	25	17	19	24	14	14	10	22	16	14	12	208
1895	29	16	28	33	24	19	36	27	23	23	19	25	302
1896	37	29	23	29	31	22	24	13	17	19	12	32	288
1897	34	28	38	43	28	23	20	22	23	13	22	19	313
1898	40	31	25	28	22	28	28	18	16	15	12	18	281
1899	27	30	32	27	29	32	36	32	23	21	28	34	351
1900	49	37	40	28	38	43	33	26	32	33	30	39	428
1901	71	63	68	54	122	72	70	59	38	39	31	43	730
1902	75	66	58	25	112	54	66	51	37	46	41	53	684
1903	80	57	55	22	108	73	75	52	50	51	46	68	737
1904	95	61	39	30	91	81	68	60	39	54	44	70	732
1905	90	69	85	36	83	68	77	82	77	66	71	90	894
1906	126	91	119	86	170	111	97	103	113	99	89	108	1,312
1907	163	145	168	158	175	184	179	114	111	75	38	37	1,547
1908	63	65	72	52	68	74	63	76	89	52	49	77	800
1909	134	107	133	99	105	98	122	88	112	83	86	96	1,263
1910	124	120	123	97	126	101	70	82	71	67	67	64	1,112
1911	98	99	118	77	109	87	75	70	89	69	72	57	1,020
1912	124	103	103	98	104	105	83	97	91	85	74	77	1,144
1913	124	118	97	116	117	134	104	107	77	80	56	75	1,205
1914	69	99	92	79	108	73	88	57	56	67	58	45	891
1915	73	83	91	125	146	89	84	82	78	81	65	83	1,080
1916	95	111	119	117	96	91	97	63	83	68	58	79	1,077
1917	115	98	103	85	110	93	101	84	71	70	56	47	1,033
1918	54	71	83	61	80	48	71	52	38	18	30	44	650
1919	85	85	97	91	86	113	108	110	98	84	88	83	1,128
1920	152	113	126	112	92	93	110	99					

C Medium Incorporations

YEAR	JAN.	FEB.	MAR.	APR.	MAY	JUNE	JULY	AUG.	SEPT.	OCT.	NOV.	DEC.	TOTAL
1872	0	4	3	0	2	3	1	2	1	3	2	0	21
1873	2	1	3	3	7	2	2	2	0	1	5	3	31
1874	2	0	6	3	6	3	0	0	3	1	2	3	29
1875	3	5	13	5	6	3	3	4	5	5	5	9	66
1876	5	2	9	11	3	3	6	1	1	2	1	2	46
1877	3	0	1	2	0	2	1	1	1	3	0	1	15
1878	2	0	2	0	3	1	3	1	0	0	2	2	16
1879	4	1	1	0	2	2	1	1	0	1	3	3	19
1880	3	1	2	2	2	0	4	2	0	0	0	1	17
1881	2	3	1	6	6	4	3	8	4	3	2	5	47
1882	3	5	8	4	5	6	1	4	6	3	4	10	59
1883	3	9	9	5	14	10	10	3	5	12	7	8	95
1884	8	6	10	6	9	10	10	3	2	6	3	2	75
1885	11	7	5	5	3	37	1	2	1	3	0	1	76
1886	5	4	3	3	0	3	2	1	0	4	4	5	34
1887	5	2	7	10	4	10	11	2	0	3	2	3	59
1888	9	10	9	6	6	10	2	3	5	4	4	4	72
1889	4	7	8	8	8	6	9	5	5	7	6	11	84
1890	7	13	18	13	10	13	8	10	3	5	6	9	115
1891	8	8	2	6	11	9	13	3	3	1	5	14	83
1892	6	8	6	9	8	11	6	8	5	4	6	3	80
1893	4	7	8	6	6	5	5	3	4	1	2	2	53
1894	3	5	10	9	2	4	4	1	6	5	3	3	55
1895	9	5	5	12	3	2	5	1	3	5	2	4	56
1896	2	2	7	3	4	3	3	3	0	1	2	5	35
1897	4	2	6	2	3	2	3	0	3	1	1	1	28
1898	4	7	9	0	1	3	2	1	2	2	0	2	33
1899	2	5	5	4	4	1	2	4	2	2	1	2	34
1900	3	3	6	8	10	5	5	3	1	3	5	13	65
1901	8	10	18	125	153	31	30	16	8	10	15	20	444
1902	24	23	21	6	25	15	13	8	9	12	8	8	172
1903	21	9	10	8	11	12	12	12	1	6	4	2	108
1904	13	9	9	6	17	8	8	6	5	9	8	14	112
1905	2	6	7	4	8	9	11	14	11	6	12	7	97
1906	13	10	13	5	8	12	9	12	11	11	15	16	135
1907	9	28	20	15	21	14	29	3	5	4	2	4	154

Texas Business Incorporations under General Laws, 1872–1920 (cont.)

YEAR	JAN.	FEB.	MAR.	APR.	MAY	JUNE	JULY	AUG.	SEPT.	OCT.	NOV.	DEC.	TOTAL
C Medium Incorporations (concl.)													
1908	2	4	4	1	5	8	2	3	2	5	6	3	45
1909	4	3	9	4	9	7	19	13	13	4	5	11	101
1910	8	11	12	7	11	13	15	7	9	8	6	11	118
1911	11	10	18	7	6	10	9	5	4	1	6	1	88
1912	10	9	13	9	13	13	12	9	10	10	7	10	125
1913	14	11	12	8	10	7	7	4	7	3	7	6	96
1914	12	15	6	15	12	8	3	8	2	3	3	5	92
1915	2	3	6	3	5	10	8	6	2	6	3	7	61
1916	2	8	9	8	9	9	9	2	8	7	7	10	88
1917	3	14	10	10	10	6	10	11	7	7	6	6	100
1918	9	6	14	9	16	8	9	9	9	5	8	8	110
1919	15	21	23	24	29	26	25	16	31	18	17	27	272
1920	34	26	19	22	23	25	30	11					
D Large Incorporations													
1872	1	0	0	0	0	0	0	0	0	1	1	0	3
1873	0	2	0	0	0	0	0	1	0	0	0	2	5
1874	0	1	0	1	0	0	0	0	0	0	1	0	3
1875	1	1	0	1	0	0	0	0	1	0	0	0	4
1876	1	0	0	0	1	0	0	1	0	0	0	0	3
1877	2	0	0	0	0	1	0	0	0	0	0	0	3
1878	0	0	0	0	0	0	0	0	0	0	0	0	0
1879	0	0	0	0	1	0	0	0	0	0	0	1	2
1880	0	0	1	1	3	0	0	1	0	0	0	0	6
1881	1	0	1	0	2	0	0	0	1	0	0	0	5
1882	0	1	2	2	2	1	2	3	0	0	0	1	14
1883	1	0	0	2	2	1	1	0	0	0	1	0	8
1884	1	0	1	1	1	2	0	0	0	0	0	0	6
1885	2	2	0	0	0	6	0	0	0	0	0	0	10
1886	0	0	0	0	0	0	0	0	0	0	0	0	0
1887	0	0	0	0	1	1	2	0	0	0	0	0	4
1888	1	2	1	0	1	1	0	0	0	1	1	0	8
1889	0	0	3	0	1	0	0	0	1	1	0	0	6
1890	0	0	1	0	1	0	2	1	1	1	1	0	8
1891	2	2	2	0	0	1	2	0	0	2	0	1	12
1892	0	2	1	0	0	0	0	0	0	0	1	0	4
1893	0	0	2	2	1	0	0	0	0	0	0	0	5
1894	0	0	0	0	0	0	0	0	0	0	0	0	0
1895	0	0	0	1	0	1	2	0	0	0	0	0	4
1896	0	0	0	0	0	0	1	1	0	0	0	0	2
1897	0	1	0	0	0	0	0	0	0	0	0	0	1
1898	1	0	0	0	0	0	0	0	0	0	0	0	1
1899	0	0	0	1	0	0	0	0	0	0	1	0	2
1900	0	0	0	0	0	0	0	0	0	1	0	0	1
1901	2	2	1	17	14	2	7	2	1	6	1	5	60
1902	5	1	2	1	2	2	1	0	0	0	1	2	17
1903	1	2	1	0	2	1	2	0	0	0	0	0	9
1904	0	1	1	0	2	1	0	1	0	1	0	1	8
1905	0	2	1	1	1	1	0	0	1	0	0	0	7
1906	1	1	0	0	0	0	0	2	1	0	1	2	8
1907	0	1	0	2	1	0	1	0	0	0	0	0	5
1908	0	0	0	0	0	0	0	0	0	0	0	0	0
1909	0	0	0	0	1	1	0	0	0	0	1	0	3
1910	0	0	1	0	0	1	0	0	0	0	0	0	2
1911	0	0	0	0	0	2	2	1	2	0	0	0	7
1912	0	0	2	0	1	2	1	0	0	0	0	0	6
1913	0	0	0	0	0	0	0	0	1	0	0	0	1
1914	0	0	0	1	0	1	2	1	1	0	1	1	8
1915	0	0	0	0	0	0	1	0	0	0	0	1	2
1916	0	0	2	1	0	2	1	2	0	1	0	0	9
1917	0	0	0	0	1	2	1	1	0	0	0	0	5
1918	0	1	0	0	1	1	0	0	0	1	0	1	5
1919	1	1	2	5	3	5	1	1	4	2	2	4	31
1920	1	1	3	1	2	1	1	0					

YEAR	JAN.	FEB.	MAR.	APR.	MAY	JUNE	JULY	AUG.	SEPT.	OCT.	NOV.	DEC.	TOTAL

E Total Authorized Capital Stock (thousands of dollars)

YEAR	JAN.	FEB.	MAR.	APR.	MAY	JUNE	JULY	AUG.	SEPT.	OCT.	NOV.	DEC.	TOTAL
1872	10,070	1,379	780	25	695	1,212	235	300	220	1,400	3,600	60	19,976
1873	720	2,330	796	1,017	2,175	650	658	1,399	25	514	900	2,660	13,844
1874	600	1,136	1,464	2,995	1,374	739	95	121	656	505	2,520	823	13,028
1875	3,080	3,513	2,541	11,685	1,611	570	807	863	2,373	985	1,350	2,095	31,473
1876	2,503	655	2,327	2,902	4,575	1,082	1,421	5,633	621	545	240	275	22,779
1877	2,933	90	300	600	50	2,970	612	420	578	430	110	142	9,235
1878	694	62	555	231	510	159	396	621	25	11	1,138	516	4,918
1879	594	195	452	66	2,118	828	146	175	180	246	697	2,370	8,067
1880	805	217	5,305	5,712	11,960	52	462	2,260	135	130	64	188	27,290
1881	2,955	1,325	1,446	806	6,377	757	1,260	1,735	4,536	980	1,364	1,052	24,593
1882	563	1,858	5,675	3,054	4,459	2,448	3,362	5,481	1,730	1,106	1,162	3,480	34,378
1883	4,067	2,638	2,326	9,048	5,234	4,233	2,894	715	1,082	3,391	2,480	1,692	39,800
1884	5,402	1,726	3,402	2,605	3,381	5,488	2,376	1,158	576	1,786	815	736	29,451
1885	5,334	6,400	968	972	1,038	16,954	290	680	215	401	76	579	33,907
1886	730	1,028	1,004	764	126	470	558	280	216	578	1,190	1,219	8,163
1887	2,125	555	2,125	2,735	2,728	4,486	4,403	1,640	434	1,025	623	1,082	23,961
1888	12,707	6,116	3,480	2,626	3,258	2,972	595	738	1,577	2,819	3,749	931	41,568
1889	1,106	2,210	9,892	2,607	3,479	1,508	2,735	1,511	2,569	3,788	1,819	2,318	35,542
1890	1,446	3,698	5,650	3,286	3,209	2,556	5,112	4,835	3,090	6,568	2,480	2,461	44,391
1891	12,635	4,292	2,719	1,488	2,306	5,103	7,070	731	1,653	2,996	1,402	4,200	46,595
1892	1,232	3,952	3,070	2,032	2,183	1,909	1,514	2,125	1,756	1,540	4,456	950	26,719
1893	1,144	2,010	6,294	5,078	3,200	1,096	980	1,428	566	294	546	958	23,594
1894	728	1,686	1,710	2,018	761	1,110	1,309	292	1,087	904	1,742	798	14,145
1895	2,013	1,716	1,224	3,253	1,491	2,217	4,990	649	1,285	1,099	686	896	21,519
1896	1,658	1,046	1,930	1,337	1,245	621	2,876	1,500	312	508	503	1,668	15,204
1897	1,301	1,935	1,585	911	814	1,196	635	450	1,322	545	508	666	11,868
1898	2,491	2,105	2,050	445	608	824	1,169	414	483	611	318	579	12,097
1899	1,208	1,610	1,466	2,008	1,097	886	1,172	1,671	506	504	1,572	770	14,470
1900	1,340	1,579	1,810	1,882	2,071	1,577	1,220	912	749	3,784	1,305	4,762	22,991
1901	4,970	6,080	6,364	63,202	84,586	13,110	55,341	8,530	3,326	12,356	5,604	12,699	276,168
1902	12,900	8,500	8,642	5,240	10,365	16,379	4,343	2,626	2,371	3,319	7,073	5,174	86,932
1903	7,026	5,963	4,628	2,286	7,518	5,176	7,509	2,843	1,601	2,024	1,276	1,294	49,144
1904	3,462	3,670	2,937	1,696	11,840	3,970	2,565	3,373	1,298	3,382	2,315	4,264	44,772
1905	1,982	4,627	3,306	3,874	4,897	4,183	3,569	4,781	5,282	2,272	2,837	2,806	44,416
1906	5,936	4,362	4,830	2,504	4,312	4,854	3,911	5,738	6,449	3,188	7,102	9,349	62,535
1907	5,122	9,743	8,124	11,233	7,954	6,581	8,677	2,212	2,696	2,132	1,316	1,235	67,025
1908	1,235	1,707	1,747	979	1,794	2,875	1,398	1,650	1,701	1,460	1,960	2,017	20,523
1909	3,048	2,959	3,408	2,307	4,080	5,924	5,549	3,458	4,745	1,772	4,068	3,525	44,843
1910	2,897	4,137	6,004	2,817	4,522	5,987	3,692	2,561	2,568	2,422	2,301	2,904	42,812
1911	3,114	3,600	5,409	3,369	3,543	5,867	10,024	3,899	3,861	1,430	3,424	1,218	48,758
1912	3,759	2,973	8,746	2,685	5,720	6,226	5,131	4,513	3,245	2,772	2,752	3,173	51,695
1913	6,034	4,217	3,364	3,187	3,472	3,471	4,073	2,877	4,170	1,723	2,131	2,665	41,384
1914	4,757	4,851	3,245	6,334	4,629	4,249	4,459	3,516	3,017	1,233	2,303	2,353	44,946
1915	1,526	1,818	1,953	2,665	3,156	3,003	3,376	1,877	1,199	2,858	1,527	3,521	28,479
1916	1,778	3,427	6,137	4,752	2,959	6,891	13,391	3,497	3,179	3,599	2,175	2,779	54,564
1917	2,313	4,432	3,435	3,167	4,504	20,879	8,847	5,165	2,366	2,684	2,902	1,716	62,410
1918	2,916	3,493	4,085	2,529	11,410	3,603	3,104	3,632	2,333	6,368	2,132	12,814	58,419
1919	16,972	10,583	11,355	15,186	16,205	27,218	7,779	10,546	16,918	7,254	10,174	13,479	163,669
1920	11,585	9,185	18,333	7,955	11,400	10,993	10,102	4,019					

F Total Authorized Capital Stock Excluding Large Companies (thousands of dollars)

YEAR	JAN.	FEB.	MAR.	APR.	MAY	JUNE	JULY	AUG.	SEPT.	OCT.	NOV.	DEC.	TOTAL
1872	70	1,379	780	25	695	1,212	235	300	220	400	1,100	60	6,476
1873	720	330	796	1,017	2,175	650	658	399	25	514	900	660	8,844
1874	600	136	1,464	995	1,374	739	95	121	656	505	520	823	8,028
1875	1,080	1,513	2,541	1,685	1,611	570	807	863	1,373	985	1,350	2,095	16,473
1876	1,503	655	2,327	2,902	1,575	1,082	1,421	293	621	545	240	275	13,439
1877	933	90	300	600	50	470	612	420	578	430	110	142	4,735
1878	694	62	555	231	510	159	396	621	25	11	1,138	516	4,918
1879	594	195	452	66	868	828	146	175	180	246	697	370	4,817
1880	805	217	305	712	960	52	462	260	135	130	64	188	4,290
1881	455	1,325	446	806	1,877	757	1,260	1,735	786	980	1,364	1,052	12,843
1882	563	858	2,175	1,054	819	1,448	362	981	1,730	1,106	1,162	2,480	14,738
1883	1,067	2,638	2,326	1,548	3,234	3,233	1,894	715	1,082	3,391	1,480	1,692	24,300
1884	2,402	1,726	2,402	1,605	2,381	2,988	2,376	1,158	576	1,786	815	736	20,951
1885	2,834	1,900	968	972	1,038	9,954	290	680	215	401	76	579	19,907

TEXAS BUSINESS INCORPORATIONS UNDER GENERAL LAWS, 1872–1920 (concl.)

YEAR	JAN.	FEB.	MAR.	APR.	MAY	JUNE	JULY	AUG.	SEPT.	OCT.	NOV.	DEC.	TOTAL
			F Total Authorized Capital Stock Excluding Large Companies (concl.) (thousands of dollars)										
1886	730	1,028	1,004	764	126	470	558	280	216	578	1,190	1,219	8,163
1887	2,125	555	2,125	2,735	1,728	3,486	2,403	1,640	434	1,025	623	1,082	19,961
1888	2,707	2,116	2,480	2,626	1,258	1,972	595	738	1,577	819	749	931	18,568
1889	1,106	2,210	1,892	2,607	2,479	1,508	2,735	1,511	1,569	1,788	1,819	2,318	23,542
1890	1,446	3,698	3,650	3,286	2,209	2,556	2,862	3,835	1,090	1,568	1,480	2,461	30,141
1891	1,635	2,292	719	1,488	2,306	3,103	2,570	731	1,653	496	1,402	3,200	21,595
1892	1,232	1,952	2,070	2,032	2,183	1,909	1,514	2,125	1,756	1,540	1,456	950	20,719
1893	1,144	2,010	2,294	1,578	2,200	1,096	980	1,428	566	294	546	958	15,094
1894	728	1,686	1,710	2,018	761	1,110	1,309	292	1,087	904	1,742	798	14,145
1895	2,013	1,716	1,224	2,253	1,491	1,217	1,490	649	1,285	1,099	686	896	16,019
1896	1,658	1,046	1,930	1,337	1,245	621	876	500	312	508	503	1,668	12,204
1897	1,301	935	1,585	911	814	1,196	635	450	1,322	545	508	666	10,868
1898	1,491	2,105	2,050	445	608	824	1,169	414	483	611	318	579	11,097
1899	1,208	1,610	1,466	1,008	1,097	886	1,172	1,671	506	504	572	770	12,470
1900	1,340	1,579	1,810	1,882	2,071	1,577	1,220	912	749	1,384	1,305	4,762	20,591
1901	2,970	3,080	5,364	33,702	45,836	8,610	8,841	5,530	2,326	3,281	4,604	6,699	130,843
1902	7,400	7,500	6,642	2,240	7,865	3,379	3,343	2,626	2,371	3,319	2,573	3,174	52,432
1903	6,026	3,713	3,628	2,286	3,518	4,176	4,009	2,843	1,601	2,024	1,276	1,294	36,394
1904	3,462	2,670	1,937	1,696	4,340	2,970	2,565	2,373	1,298	2,382	2,315	3,264	31,272
1905	1,982	2,077	2,306	1,874	2,897	3,183	3,569	4,781	4,032	2,272	2,837	2,806	34,616
1906	4,936	3,362	4,830	2,504	4,312	4,854	3,911	3,738	3,449	3,188	3,602	5,849	48,535
1907	5,122	7,343	8,124	5,733	6,954	6,581	7,677	2,212	2,696	2,132	1,316	1,235	57,125
1908	1,235	1,707	1,747	979	1,794	2,875	1,398	1,650	1,701	1,460	1,960	2,017	20,523
1909	3,048	2,959	3,408	2,307	3,080	3,424	5,549	3,458	4,745	1,772	2,568	3,525	39,843
1910	2,897	4,137	5,004	2,817	4,522	4,487	3,692	2,561	2,568	2,422	2,301	2,904	40,312
1911	3,114	3,600	5,409	3,369	3,543	3,367	3,964	1,899	1,861	1,430	3,424	1,218	36,198
1912	3,759	2,973	4,746	2,685	4,420	3,976	4,131	4,513	3,245	2,772	2,752	3,173	43,145
1913	6,034	4,217	3,364	3,187	3,472	3,471	4,073	2,877	2,870	1,723	2,131	2,665	40,084
1914	4,757	4,851	3,245	5,184	4,629	2,999	2,259	2,266	1,017	1,233	1,303	1,353	35,096
1915	1,526	1,818	1,953	2,665	3,156	3,003	2,006	1,877	1,199	2,858	1,527	2,521	26,109
1916	1,778	3,427	3,137	3,752	2,959	3,391	2,891	1,497	3,179	2,599	2,175	2,779	33,564
1917	2,313	4,432	3,435	3,167	3,504	2,879	4,147	3,165	2,366	2,684	2,902	1,716	36,710
1918	2,916	2,493	4,085	2,529	5,410	2,603	3,104	3,632	2,333	1,368	2,132	2,779	35,384
1919	4,972	5,583	7,855	6,827	9,705	8,718	6,779	6,546	8,918	5,254	6,174	7,279	84,610
1920	10,585	8,185	6,333	6,955	7,400	7,993	8,102	4,019					

1) Sources of Raw Data

Biennial Report of the Secretary of State of the State of Texas, 1894 (1895), pp. 2–146. Also similar biennial reports for periods ending in: *1896* (1897), pp. 8–35; *1898* (1899), pp. 14–37; *1900* (1900), pp. 32–61; *1902* (1902), pp. 6–12, 14–73; *1904* (1905), pp. 11–55; *1906* (1907), pp. 3–65; *1908* (1908), pp. 3–79; *1910* (1910), pp. 28–104; *1912* (1912), pp. 28–103; *1914* (1914), pp. 28–106; *1916* (1916), pp. 36–106; *1918*, pp. 35–113; *1920*, pp. 49–152. All reports were published in Austin; the year of publication, when given in source, appears in parentheses.

2) Special Comments

a) All business incorporations in the above mentioned volumes were tallied if they appeared in tables headed in the following fashion: "Domestic Charters Filed from . . . to . . . ". In each volume there is also a table of railroad incorporations. The latter were not used, because at the time of compilation it was not known that in 1876 the legislature of Texas had provided by general law for the incorporation of railroads. Their omission reduces annual incorporations by about ten on the average.

b) In the Secretary's letter of transmittal in the 1894 Report (p. 111), there is some indication that the table from which the business incorporation series was compiled contained corporations chartered under both special and general laws. But when the laws of Texas were examined for special charters and many incorporations checked against the Secretary's list, none was found. Not all companies receiving special charters were checked, but enough were examined to lead to the conclusion that few of the corporations created by special acts were listed in the first compilation published by the Secretary of State. There are other grounds for believing that there were not many

companies with special charters in any of the above mentioned Secretary's publications. In the early '70's general incorporation laws of wide scope were enacted by Texas (*General Laws . . . of Texas: 1871*, 2d Sess., Ch. LXXX; and *1874*, Jan. Sess., Ch. XCVII). Furthermore, as set forth in Table 5, a Texas constitutional provision requiring incorporation under general law was adopted in 1876. Despite this constitutional provision and the breadth of the early general incorporation laws, apparently no general law concerning the chartering of commercial banks was enacted before 1905. Many commercial banking corporations appear in the Secretary's report for 1905; few such companies are listed for preceding years.

c) Companies chartered without capital stock, companies with capital stock entered at an "estimated value" (frequently indicated by "E.V."), and companies with capital stock designated "exempt" were not included in the tally of business incorporations. Their names also indicated that they were nonbusiness units. In the reports of the Secretary of State of Texas, capital stock is not a very good index of whether a corporation was organized for profit. Some churches, high schools, etc. are listed with capital stock (usually less than $500); on the other hand, the names of several companies without capital stock indicate incorporation for business purposes. For determining the purpose of organization, the presence or absence of capital stock, however, seemed a better criterion than the name of a company. It was therefore used to separate business from nonbusiness units.

d) Each table of the Secretary's reports used in compiling the incorporation series is chronologically arranged within each letter of the alphabet, and this order helped to uncover obvious errors in dates. For example, a company for which the date of incorporation was given as November 1904 was treated as an incorporation of November 1903, if in the table it was preceded and succeeded by companies listed as chartered in November 1903. Such a correction was always made if the Secretary's report was not supposed to contain incorporations of November 1904. Assumptions were made also concerning misprints in capital stock figures. For example, $1 ,000 was treated as $10,000.

e) Companies listed twice in a table were tallied only once, the second listing being assumed to be an amendment. Whenever the word "revised" followed a company name the entry was likewise assumed to have been made in consequence of a charter amendment. Entries that appeared to relate to mere changes of name were omitted.

VIRGINIA BUSINESS INCORPORATIONS UNDER GENERAL LAWS, 1903–1941

A Total Incorporations

YEAR	JAN.	FEB.	MAR.	APR.	MAY	JUNE	JULY	AUG.	SEPT.	OCT.	NOV.	DEC.	TOTAL
1903						62	44	39	74	69	38	43	
1904	41	39	46	42	45	39	47	34	40	47	42	34	496
1905	59	51	56	70	68	63	43	47	65	53	73	70	718
1906	74	67	102	86	84	79	64	75	53	80	95	108	967
1907	87	97	132	113	110	50	47	60	54	42	56	48	896
1908	52	45	64	54	59	64	68	50	58	64	55	54	687
1909	72	77	81	90	67	74	73	87	88	60	73	71	913
1910	78	80	89	72	70	93	58	65	60	54	64	56	839
1911	73	59	90	76	80	76	47	60	64	74	63	57	819
1912	76	95	74	82	64	65	65	60	57	72	68	63	841
1913	95	82	82	91	82	72	78	51	60	73	60	72	898
1914	85	79	98	90	62	84	63	44	50	52	57	49	813
1915	75	55	94	91	72	68	72	58	71	79	76	92	903
1916	107	92	118	84	98	91	90	60	63	78	56	76	1,013
1917	115	90	119	97	79	81	70	65	67	75	62	60	980
1918	57	66	79	51	75	63	60	51	28	56	38	36	660
1919	78	82	104	109	90	127	117	118	107	136	118	136	1,322
1920	162	144	138	126	112	130	99	112	93	82	105	76	1,379
1921	98	84	115	96	85	92	77	78	101	74	64	87	1,051
1922	119	85	96	89	110	94	107	90	76	97	74	66	1,103
1923	117	103	118	106	97	114	108	94	64	74	83	79	1,157
1924	122	115	98	95	103	75	75	74	75	70	69	80	1,051
1925	138	92	92	96	84	95	88	95	84	88	66	59	1,077
1926	102	91	121	104	86	91	79	81	80	63	72	53	1,023
1927	93	75	120	82	81	99	101	81	84	70	80	66	1,032
1928	106	105	125	106	104	89	88	104	73	94	81	79	1,154
1929	112	83	111	108	110	81	99	92	89	84	80	65	1,114
1930	118	84	91	101	96	85	84	81	68	87	67	66	1,028
1931	74	75	96	75	89	95	76	65	65	71	66	63	910
1932	86	68	101	76	85	71	64	76	70	77	58	69	901
1933	88	79	61	59	71	91	62	79	65	66	47	47	815
1934	62	54	75	72	64	49	48	55	59	69	44	45	696
1935	85	69	73	76	67	63	50	58	53	73	58	28	753
1936	57	64	62	51	60	79	54	67	53	52	40	59	698
1937	92	65	74	62	64	59	61	52	57	61	54	43	744
1938	69	52	55	39	57	49	58	50	59	53	43	42	626
1939	66	47	57	67	72	69	48	52	54	68	46	43	689
1940	83	47	60	85	79	51	59	61	62	59	56	39	741
1941	54	70	63	58	58	64	47	43	48	43	35	39	622

B Small Incorporations, 1903–1918

YEAR	JAN.	FEB.	MAR.	APR.	MAY	JUNE	JULY	AUG.	SEPT.	OCT.	NOV.	DEC.	TOTAL
1903						51	41	33	63	61	30	33	
1904	35	29	39	36	34	30	40	25	33	40	34	28	403
1905	52	37	48	60	60	50	34	39	52	41	63	54	590
1906	61	54	89	64	66	60	47	60	46	66	77	87	777
1907	75	77	112	100	94	46	38	47	45	36	37	41	748
1908	44	34	57	57	50	52	52	54	45	55	46	44	577
1909	61	69	72	76	59	60	65	76	75	56	65	52	786
1910	68	71	72	59	50	75	52	59	54	43	54	46	703
1911	64	51	78	62	63	62	39	52	48	66	57	47	689
1912	66	76	63	65	52	56	49	49	48	57	49	48	678
1913	72	71	66	82	70	48	68	39	56	60	49	55	736
1914	73	60	86	70	53	65	47	39	46	46	47	39	671
1915	64	43	72	73	58	58	52	52	58	65	62	72	729
1916	83	72	83	69	74	69	66	51	47	56	39	53	762
1917	87	73	89	77	54	63	60	47	54	58	42	38	742
1918	37	48	57	40	58	48	47	39	24	50	30	31	509

VIRGINIA BUSINESS INCORPORATIONS UNDER GENERAL LAWS, 1903–1941 (concl.)

YEAR	JAN.	FEB.	MAR.	APR.	MAY	JUNE	JULY	AUG.	SEPT.	OCT.	NOV.	DEC.	TOTAL
C Medium Incorporations, 1903–1918													
1903						11	3	5	10	8	8	9	
1904	6	9	7	6	9	7	6	9	7	7	7	6	86
1905	6	14	8	9	8	13	8	8	13	11	10	16	124
1906	12	12	13	21	16	16	17	15	6	14	17	20	179
1907	11	20	20	13	12	4	8	12	8	5	17	6	136
1908	8	11	7	4	7	11	13	5	14	8	9	10	107
1909	10	8	9	13	6	12	8	9	12	4	8	17	116
1910	9	9	17	11	18	14	6	6	6	9	9	10	124
1911	8	7	10	12	14	12	8	8	15	8	4	8	114
1912	10	16	10	17	9	7	12	11	5	10	15	13	135
1913	20	8	14	6	9	18	9	10	4	8	11	14	131
1914	8	16	10	16	7	13	14	5	3	4	9	9	114
1915	9	9	17	12	12	12	12	6	11	14	7	17	138
1916	17	14	26	12	21	17	16	8	10	15	14	17	187
1917	24	13	23	15	22	16	7	13	9	15	14	16	187
1918	16	18	18	11	14	14	10	11	3	6	7	5	133
D Large Incorporations, 1903–1918													
1903						0	0	1	1	0	0	1	
1904	0	1	0	0	2	2	1	0	0	0	1	0	7
1905	1	0	0	1	0	0	1	0	0	1	0	0	4
1906	1	1	0	1	2	3	0	0	1	0	1	1	11
1907	1	0	0	0	4	0	1	1	1	1	2	1	12
1908	0	0	0	0	0	1	1	0	0	1	0	0	3
1909	1	0	0	1	2	2	0	2	1	0	0	2	11
1910	1	0	0	2	2	4	0	0	0	2	1	0	12
1911	1	1	2	2	3	2	0	0	1	0	2	2	16
1912	0	3	1	0	3	2	4	0	4	5	4	2	28
1913	3	3	2	3	3	6	1	2	0	5	0	3	31
1914	4	3	2	4	2	6	2	0	1	2	1	1	28
1915	2	3	5	6	2	4	2	0	2	0	7	3	36
1916	7	6	9	3	3	5	8	1	6	7	3	6	64
1917	4	4	7	5	3	2	3	5	4	2	6	6	51
1918	4	0	4	0	3	1	3	1	1	0	1	0	18
E Total Authorized Capital Stock, 1903–1918 (thousands of dollars)													
1903						3,553	2,998	3,142	5,253	3,206	2,798	7,894	
1904	1,616	3,166	2,722	2,329	15,531	15,316	3,726	3,048	2,176	1,820	11,901	1,566	64,917
1905	3,047	4,627	2,303	4,491	3,227	3,873	10,662	2,104	4,139	3,667	3,442	3,604	49,186
1906	10,593	10,236	5,497	11,122	21,104	60,110	3,989	4,906	3,706	4,409	32,086	7,456	175,214
1907	15,161	6,389	7,428	3,932	23,275	2,584	10,646	7,502	7,950	2,710	19,658	7,755	114,990
1908	2,936	3,055	2,272	1,782	2,214	4,972	5,966	1,772	3,796	22,103	3,078	2,531	56,477
1909	7,342	2,855	4,018	6,562	6,640	23,542	3,513	14,944	9,106	2,212	2,480	14,274	97,488
1910	6,497	4,438	5,594	11,124	22,446	14,086	2,756	1,926	2,515	6,756	4,531	5,074	87,743
1911	8,078	3,920	15,957	11,330	32,025	30,523	3,339	2,846	9,734	2,946	10,614	9,428	140,740
1912	2,885	19,313	5,050	5,277	51,721	24,040	9,545	3,851	88,872	78,304	67,918	16,465	373,241
1913	12,222	15,872	29,472	14,142	16,595	69,890	10,558	11,656	2,248	13,847	4,050	11,833	212,385
1914	9,029	13,900	13,946	68,289	17,100	23,768	22,849	1,962	2,900	4,172	5,708	12,792	196,415
1915	5,809	30,930	11,504	14,585	6,999	10,448	10,914	2,640	6,094	4,449	160,090	11,469	275,931
1916	35,000	35,444	185,786	54,938	61,346	37,161	39,336	4,549	20,217	35,366	26,368	43,918	579,429
1917	69,159	26,798	85,256	129,167	33,998	10,070	7,852	17,680	7,158	6,668	27,210	25,458	446,474
1918	41,820	5,229	13,222	2,830	33,809	5,228	20,678	10,952	2,489	2,319	9,248	1,901	149,725
F Total Authorized Capital Stock Excluding Large Companies, 1903–1918 (thousands of dollars)													
1903						3,553	2,998	2,142	3,753	3,206	2,798	2,894	
1904	1,616	2,166	2,722	2,329	2,531	2,316	2,226	3,048	2,176	1,820	1,901	1,566	26,417
1905	2,047	4,627	2,303	3,091	3,227	3,873	3,162	2,104	4,139	2,667	3,442	3,604	38,286
1906	3,093	5,236	5,497	5,122	4,604	5,110	3,989	4,906	2,706	4,409	7,086	5,956	57,714
1907	5,161	6,389	7,428	3,932	5,475	2,584	2,846	5,002	2,950	1,710	4,658	2,755	50,890
1908	2,936	3,055	2,272	1,782	2,214	3,372	3,966	1,772	3,796	2,103	3,078	2,531	32,877
1909	4,342	2,855	4,018	4,522	3,140	3,542	3,513	3,944	4,106	2,212	2,480	5,274	43,948

YEAR	JAN.	FEB.	MAR.	APR.	MAY	JUNE	JULY	AUG.	SEPT.	OCT.	NOV.	DEC.	TOTAL
1910	3,997	4,438	5,594	3,084	5,446	5,086	2,756	1,926	2,515	2,756	3,531	5,074	46,203
1911	3,078	2,920	3,457	4,330	4,025	4,523	3,339	2,846	3,984	2,946	2,114	2,628	40,190
1912	2,885	5,313	3,550	5,277	2,421	3,040	3,045	3,851	2,372	3,804	4,418	3,965	43,941
1913	6,812	2,872	4,472	3,142	4,345	5,290	3,808	2,656	2,248	2,847	4,050	4,833	47,375
1914	3,329	3,650	3,946	5,989	3,700	6,118	2,849	1,962	1,900	1,672	2,708	2,792	40,615
1915	2,809	4,368	4,904	4,555	4,249	3,448	3,914	2,640	3,944	4,449	4,590	5,869	49,739
1916	5,250	5,194	6,786	4,188	6,846	5,911	5,636	2,549	4,967	5,466	4,368	5,918	63,079
1917	7,659	4,948	7,506	6,167	6,998	4,570	2,852	3,680	2,658	4,418	4,710	4,658	60,824
1918	4,570	5,229	5,722	2,830	5,309	4,228	3,428	3,452	1,289	2,319	2,248	1,901	42,525

1) Sources of Raw Data

First Annual Report of the State Corporation Commission of Virginia For the Year Ending December 31, 1903 (Richmond, 1904), Part I, pp. 55–68. Also succeeding annual reports, all published in Richmond in years given in parentheses (for the 1905–08 volumes, the references are to pages in Part I; for the 1909–42 volumes, they are to pages in the General Report): (1905), pp. 133–48; (1906), pp. 351–68; (1907), pp. 338–61; (1908), pp. 419–39; (1909), pp. 89–106; (1910), pp. 82–103; (1911), pp. 80–100; (1912), pp. 104–22; (1913), pp. 76–94; (1914), pp. 237–58; (1915), pp. 216–35; (1916), pp. 240–60; (1917), pp. 226–48; (1918), pp. 646–68; (1919), pp. 324–39; (1920), pp. 146–78, 198; (1921), pp. 310–44, 375, 376; (1922), pp. 238–65, 288–89; (1923), pp. 112–41, 166; (1924), pp. 150–81, 207; (1925), pp. 226–55, 277; (1926), pp. 113–42, 167; (1927), pp. 223–40, 250; (1928), pp. 116–18, 120, 140, 150; (1929), pp. 225–26, 228–48, 257, 258; (1930), pp. 421–42, 453; (1931), pp. 316, 318–36, 345; (1932), pp. 445–62, 470; (1933), pp. 260–76, 282, 283; (1934), pp. 288–302, 309; (1935), pp. 329–40, 348; (1936), pp. 262–76, 283; (1937), pp. 345–57, 364; (1938), pp. 437, 439–51, 459; (1939), pp. 438–50, 456; (1940), pp. 557–70, 576, 577; (1941), pp. 526–40, 546; (1942), pp. 545–57, 563.

2) Special Comments

a) Prior to the issue of the *Twenty-fifth Annual Report* (1928), the Virginia Corporation Commission published two lists of incorporations: in one the companies are arranged chronologically, in the other industrially. The former list was used in tallying the incorporation series set forth above, since the latter often lacked the miscellaneous group and was thus incomplete. The few companies that appear in the industrial and not in the chronological list were added to the tally from the chronological list. Beginning with the *Twenty-fifth Annual Report* the industrial classification alone was published and seems to be complete.

b) Since capital stock figures were given, incorporations without capital stock were treated as nonbusiness units. The name of the company was not used as a criterion for nonbusiness enterprises.

c) Virginia authorized the issuance of nonpar shares in 1919. By employing the method utilized by the state taxing authorities, namely, treating a nonpar share as a share of par value of $100, par value and nonpar value shares could have been equated for the purposes of this study. Virginia capital stock figures for the post-1918 period, however, were not used because by the time the Virginia series were being compiled sufficient evidence for the purposes of this study had been developed concerning the relationships brought out by capital stock data.

d) Mergers were included in the tally of incorporations, but amendments were not.

APPENDIX 4

Industrial Classification of Business Incorporations

New Jersey Business Incorporations*
    By Special Acts, 1800-1875
    Under General Laws, 1846-1907

Ohio Business Incorporations*
    By Special Acts, 1803-1851
    Under General Laws, 1856-1930

Pennsylvania Business Incorporations under General Laws, 1888-1920*

Manufacturing and Public Utility Incorporations (monthly)
    A   New Jersey, 1875-1907
    B   Ohio, 1875-1930
    C   Pennsylvania, 1887-1920

* In these tables the industrial categories are the same as those of Table 19 and are similarly lettered. In each segment of each table there appear only those industrial categories of Table 19 that were used when the incorporations of a given span of years were classified industrially. While merely annual data are presented here, the author can make available the monthly figures for incorporations under general laws.

New Jersey Business Incorporations by Special Acts, 1800–1875*

INDUSTRIAL CATEGORIES	'00	'01	'02	'03	'04	'05	'06	'07	'08	'09	'10	'11	'12	'13	'14	'15	'16	'17	'18	'19	'20	'21	'22	'23	'24	'25	'26	'27	'28	'29	'30	INDUSTRIAL CATEGORIES
Total	2	3	3	0	12	0	9	4	5	5	0	11	9	4	9	13	9	2	3	3	2	1	5	5	13	13	5	0	25	5	10	Total
A												1									1				1	1			5		1	A
AA												1													1	1	1		5			AA
aab												1											1		1	1	1					aab
AB																													3			AB
AD																					1											AD
ada																					1											ada
AE		1																											2		1	AE
B		1								1		1		1	1	4	4	1				1		1	3	3	1		9	4	1	B
BD													1	1	1	1								1	1				1	1		BD
bda																														1			bda
bdb														1																			bdb
bdh																									1							bdh
bdj															1	1														1		bdj
BP																									1	1						BP
bpb																										1						bpb
bpc																									1							bpc
BQ																														1		BQ
bqg																														1		bqg
BX		1								1		1				3	3	1			1		2	1	2	6	1		8	2	1	BX
C	2	2	3		8		9	3	5	4		9	3	3	5	7	7	2	1	3	1		2	2	2	6	1		6	1	5	C
CA	1	2	1		2										1	3	1	1	1		1		2	2	2	2	1		4	1	4	CA
caa																1															1	caa
cak																2										1			3	1	1	cak
cam	1		1		2												1				1		2	1	1	1	1		1		1	cam
can															1			1	1					1	1						1	can
CC	1	2	2		6		9	3	5	4		9	3	3	4	4	6	1		3					4				2		1	CC
ccb																									1							ccb
ccc	1	1			2			1		1		2					2													1		ccc
ccd					1					2		1	3		1																	ccd
cce		1	1		3		9	2	5	1		6		3	3	3	4	1		2					2				1			cce
ccg		1														1				1									1			ccg
E																															1	E
EQ																														1	1	EQ
G					4			1				6				2	1		2				2	1	6	2	1		5		2	G
GA					2			1				6				2	1		2				2		5	2			3		2	GA
GJ					1																											GJ
GK					1																											GK
GI																							1	1	1		1		2			GI
I																										1		1				I
J																							1	1	1							J

INDUSTRIAL CATEGORIES	'31	'32	'33	'34	'35	'36	'37	'38	'39	'40	'41	'42	'43	'44	'45	'46	'47	'48	'49	'50	'51	'52	'53	'54	'55	'56	'57	'58	'59	'60	'61	INDUSTRIAL CATEGORIES
Total	14	11	13	14	13	35	45	9	14	6	6	6	1	7	18	21	20	28	31	20	36	44	46	51	66	41	43	27	49	43	37	Total
A	1	1	1	2	1	1	1		1		1					1	2	9	1				1	3	2	1	1			2		A
AA												1						1					1	1						1		AA
aac																		1														aac
aaf												1											1	1						1		aaf
AB		1	1																						2					1		AB
AD																									2					1		AD
ada																														1		ada
AE	1			2	1	1	1		1							1	2	8	1				2	2	1	1						AE
A/B							1									3		1					1								1	A/B
B	2	2	8	1	5	17	20	3	5	4	2	3	1	1	9	11	7		1	4	5	6	9	10	12	10	7	8	12		7	B
BA			1				1			4																						BA
baa										1																						baa
baf			1																													baf
bag							1																									bag
BD						5	4		2							3					1				1	1			1			BD
bda																1																bda
bdb																1																bdb
bdc						5	3		2												1											bdc
bdh							1																		1	1			1			bdh
bdi																1																bdi
BF																													1			BF
bfa																													1			bfa
BG							1									1													1			BG
bgb							1									1													1			bgb
BJ			1																													BJ
BM			1				1															1	1	1	1			1				BM
bma																						1	1	1	1							bma
bme																												1				bme
bmf			1																													bmf
bmi							1																									bmi
BP			2			2				1													1	1	1	1	2	2	1	1	1	BP
bpa																									1		2					bpa
bpb			1																				1	1				1	1			bpb
bpc			1			2																		1				1		1		bpc
bpg									1																1			1			1	bpg
BQ						1	1				1	1			1		1					1	2	2	3	2	1		4	3	2	BQ
bqa							1																		1				1	1	1	bqa
bqf						1																1	1	1	2	1			1	2	1	bqf
bqg												1				1		1				1	1	1	1	1			2			bqg
BR																1	1					1		2							2	BR
bra																1																bra
brc																	1					1		2							2	brc
BT						1	1								1										1	2	1	1	1	1	1	BT
bta																1																bta
btb						1	1																		1	2		1		1	btb
btc																													1			btc
btf																												1				btf
BV																				1			1		1	1	1					BV

* Classification is based upon data in: the Hood volume referred to in both Ch. 3 and the New Jersey 1800–70 section of App. 3; statutes cited in the New Jersey 1871–75 section of App. 3.

INDUSTRIAL CATEGORIES	'31	'32	'33	'34	'35	'36	'37	'38	'39	'40	'41	'42	'43	'44	'45	'46	'47	'48	'49	'50	'51	'52	'53	'54	'55	'56	'57	'58	'59	'60	'61	INDUSTRIAL CATEGORIES
bva																			1		1	1			1		1	1		1		b va
BW			1						1																1							BW
bwa																														1		bwa
bwb			1						1																					1	1	bwb
BX	2	2	2	1	5	9	11	2	2	2	1	2	1	1	4	9	5	14	24	17	3	2	1	2	3	5	4	2		6	1	BX
C	9	5	4		6	4	15	1	6	2	3	2		4	9	5	7	10	8	10	29	33	34	31	30	24	24	13	32	22	21	C
CA	5	4	2	5	1	13	12	1	6	2	1			3	5	4	5	10	4	10	11	11	11	11	14	14	8	3	15	11	15	CA
caa	4	3	1	2	1	11	9							2		3	2	6	4	7	4	2	10	7	4	4	5	1	6	1	10	caa
cac																														7	3	cac
cad																														8		cad
cah																									1	2	1					cah
cak	1	1		2		1	1	1	1	1				1	4	1	2	1			1	6		3	3	2	1			2	1	cak
cam			1	1			1		1								1								1	2						cam
can									1		1							2		3	2	4	3	1	1	3	1	1	2		1	can
cap							1								1							2			1			1				cap
caq																					1	1			2	2					1	caq
CB															1			1				2		2	2				1	1	1	CB
cbb																		1			1	1	2		2				1	1	1	cbb
CC	4	1	2	1	3	2	1		4	1	1	2		1	3	1	2	4	16	6	16	22	21	20	17	10	16	10	16	11	5	CC
ccb															1			1	3	2	1	7	2	4	1		2	2	4	5	3	ccb
ccc	1		1		1				1						2	1		1	2		2	2	1	3		2			2			ccc
ccd	2	1	1	1	2	2			1		1	2			1		1	1	1	1			1				2	2	2	2		ccd
cce			1				1		1					1	1		1		9	6	14	19	10	13	11	9	7	8	8	3	2	cce
ccf									1																1					1		ccf
ccg	1													1					1												1	ccg
E																															1	E
EQ															1																1	EQ
F						1											1		2	1	1	2	3	3		2		3		1	3	F
FA																					1	1	1	2	1		1	3		1	1	FA
faa																					1	1	1	2	1		1			1	1	faa
FD						1											1		2			1	1	1		1					2	FD
fdd						1													2			1	1	1		1					2	fdd
G	2	3		5	1	1	8	3	2			1		2		1	3	4	4	1	2	4	2	4	21	2	8	4	9	6	4	G
GA	1	2		4		1	5		2								1	2	2					1	14	5	1	1	4	3	2	GA
GI	1	1		1	1		2	1				1											2	2		3	3	1	4	1	1	GI
GJ							1	2						2	1		1					2	3	7	1				1	2	1	GJ
I								1																								I
J					1	1	2	1																								J

INDUSTRIAL CATEGORIES	'62	'63	'64	'65	'66	'67	'68	'69	'70	'71	'72	'73	'74	'75	INDUSTRIAL CATEGORIES	INDUSTRIAL CATEGORIES	'62	'63	'64	'65	'66	'67	'68	'69	'70	'71	'72	'73	'74	'75	INDUSTRIAL CATEGORIES
Total	22	30	60	69	123	140	148	128	135	122	119	133	83	44	Total	bnb					1										bnb
A		3	1	17	9	15	6	3		4	9	5	3		A	BP	1	2	2	2	4	4	4	9	6	2	1	5	1		BP
AA			1	1	3	6	3			2	2				AA	bpa					4	3	3	3	2	1					bpa
aaa				1	1										aaa	bpb			1	2	1	1						3			bpb
aab		1													aab	bpc	1	2	1		2	1		2	1	1		1			bpc
aad				3	5	3			2	2					aad	bpe					1			1							bpe
AB					1	2					2				AB	bpf													1		bpf
AC			1	11	1										AC	bpg					1		2	1			1	1			bpg
acb			1	11	1										acb	BQ		2	9	4	6	6	12	6	4	4	3	7	3		BQ
AD		2		2	6	3	2		4	4	3	3			AD	bqa		1			1	1	1						1		bqa
ada		1			3				3	4	2	2			ada	bqb													1		bqb
adb		1		2	2	3	2		1	1	1	2			adb	bqd							1		1				1		bqd
AE				4	2		1			3					AE	bqe							1		1			1			bqe
A/B										1	1	3			A/B	bqf			1	3	3	4	4	2	4	3	7	1			bqf
B	6	11	19	22	32	36	43	44	36	20	29	37	22	5	B	bqg			1	6	6	3	1	5							bqg
BA				2	4	2					1	1			BA	BR	1		1	1	1	1	1			1					BR
bac				2	1	1	1				1	1			bac	bra				1	1					1					bra
bae					1								1		bae	brc	1		1			1	1	1		1					brc
bag					1	1									bag	BT			3	1		2	4	4	4	1	1		2		BT
bai					1								1		bai	bta								1					1		bta
BB					1										BB	btb			2	1			3	1					1		btb
bba					1										bba	btd								1	1						btd
BD			1	3	5	2	2	5	1	1	6	1	1		BD	btf							1	1		1					btf
dba								1			1				dba	bth								1	1						bth
bdb			1	1	1	1	2								bdb	bti			1			1									bti
bdc				1							1				bdc	BV		2	2	1	2	1	1	2	1	1	2	1			BV
bde			1					1			1				bde	bva		1	2	1	2	1	1	1	1	1	2	1			bva
bdg											1	1			bdg	bvc		1							1						bvc
bdh											1	1			bdh	bve								1							bve
bdi				1	1			3			2		1		bdi	BW						1	5	3	2	2	2	3			BW
bdj			2	3											bdj	bwa						1	4	1				3			bwa
BF						1	1	1					1		BF	bwb							1								bwb
bfb						1	1	1					1		bfb	BX	3	5	3		8	10	10	7	10	6	6	11	4		BX
BG			1	1			1	1	1	1	2				BG	C	13	14	29	22	52	45	48	43	47	29	29	29	16	15	C
bgb			1	1			1	1	1	1	2	1			bgb	CA	5	5	17	11	32	31	32	29	25	20	21	6		6	CA
BH					1		1		2	3	1	1			BH	caa	4	3	7	5	16	20	13	14	16	7					caa
bha								1	1						bha	cac			2	2	4	4	5	7		6	4	1		1	cac
bhb				1			1			2					bhb	cad									1	1					cad
bhc						1	1			2	1	1			bhc	cae					1		1								cae
BI						1	2	1							BI	cah			1	2	1	4	1	1	1	2	2			1	cah
bic						1	2	1							bic	cak	1		1	2	2	3	1	2		1			2		cak
BJ			1								1	1			BJ	cam					1		2	1	1				2		cam
BK		1		2						1	1	2	4	4	BK	can		2	1	1	3	2	4	3	2				1	1	can
BM							1	4	2	1	4	3	2	1	BM	cap							2	2							cap
bma							1	1							bma	caq								1	3	1	1			3	caq
bmb											1				bmb	CB							1	1			2		2	3	CB
bmc								1							bmc	cbb		1	1						2				2	3	cbb
bme					1	1						2			bme	CC	8	9	12	11	20	14	15	13	22	8	9	8	8	6	CC
bmh					1		1	1				1	1	1	bmh	ccb	3	3	5	2	2	1	4	2	5	2	2	3	2	1	ccb
bmi							1		1	1		1	1		bmi	ccc	1		2	2	1		2	2	3	2	5		1		ccc
BN	1			1	1										BN	ccd			1				2	2	1			1			ccd
bna	1			1	1										bna	cce	4	5	4	7	17	9	6	5	9	3		3	3	2	cce

New Jersey Business Incorporations by Special Acts, 1800–1875 (concl.)

INDUSTRIAL CATEGORIES	'62	'63	'64	'65	'66	'67	'68	'69	'70	'71	'72	'73	'74	'75	INDUSTRIAL CATEGORIES	INDUSTRIAL CATEGORIES	'62	'63	'64	'65	'66	'67	'68	'69	'70	'71	'72	'73	'74	'75	INDUSTRIAL CATEGORIES
ccf									3					1	ccf	fdd				3	1	1	3		2	1	6	3			fdd
E ccg	1			1		4	1 2	2 1	1 2	1	1	1 2		2	E ccg	FE					1		1	1	3	5	3	6	2		FE
ED			1				2	1	2						ED	G GA	3 3	2 1	2	2 4 1	20	27 7	33 1	23	33 13	56 24	33 9	42 13	25 7	12 5	G GA
EM					1	1	1				2		1	2	EM	GB								9	1	2	4	3	2	1	GB
EQ					1	1	1	5	3	8 8	8 4	9 2	2	7	EQ	GC								1							GC
F FA		8 8	2 2	8 5	7 5	5 6	8 6	8 5		1 1	4 4	4	2		F FA	GI		1		2 1	5 15	3 14	13 2	5 8	7 1	8 9	12 13	6 13	7 18	9 7	GI
faa		8	2	5											faa	GJ															GJ
FB					1	1						1		1	FB	GK											2	2	1		GK
fbb					1	1	1		1			1	1	4	fbb	H HB			1	1	1	1 1	3 1	7	2	2	2	2	1		H HB
FD			3	1	1		3	1	3	2	1	1		1	FD	I				1	1	5 2	7	5	6	4	8	6	3	1 2	I
fdc														1	fdc	J															J

New Jersey Business Incorporations under General Laws, 1846–1907*

INDUSTRIAL CATEGORIES	'46	'47	'48	'49	'50	'51	'52	'53	'54	'55	'56	'57	'58	'59	'60	'61	'62	'63	'64	'65	'66	'67	'68	'69	'70	'71	'72	'73	'74	'75	'76	INDUSTRIAL CATEGORIES
Total	4	5	5	1	7	18	13	19	21	16	8	11	20	5	7	2	11	7	12	8	25	25	13	14	19	27	23	35	38	51	56	Total
A															1						3	4						1	1		4	A
AA															1							2							1		2	AA
aaa																						1						1				aaa
aac																						1										aac
aad																															2	aad
aaf															1																	aaf
AD																					2	2										AD
ada																			1			1										ada
adb																			1			1										adb
AE																			1										1		2	AE
A/B		1																								1 9						A/B
B	4	4	5	1	6	2	7	9	10	12	3	4	8	2	3	1		4	8	8	12	9	9	7	11	10	12	12	27		23	B
BA					1																		1						2	4	1	BA
bac																														3		bac
bad																															1	bad
bae					1																		1									bae
baf																													2	1		baf
BB																					2	1				1					1	BB
bba																						1										bba
bbb																								1								bbb
bbc																															1	bbc
bbd																			1													bbd
bbe																			1													bbe
BD		1	1					1		2								1			1	1	2		1		1		1	1	2	BD
bda		1																				1			1							bda
bdb								1										1								1						bdb
bde								1																								bde
bdf																														1		bdf
bdg																																bdg
bdh																						1					1				2	bdh
bdi		1																						1					1			bdi
bdj										1														1								bdj
BF								1		2		1			1				1	1		1		1		1		2	2	1		BF
bfa								1														1				1						bfa
bfb																			1										2	1		bfb
bfc										2		1			1					1				1					2	1		bfc
BG	1				1		2	3		1											1		1						1		2	BG
bgb	1				1		2	3		1						1						1							1		2	bgb
BH					1					1														3				1	1	1	1	BH
bha					1					1														2								bha
bhb																							1	1				1	1	1	bhb
bhc																							1					1	1	1	1	bhc
BI							1			1											1					1						BI
bia										1																						bia
bic							1														1					1						bic
BJ													1																1	1	1	BJ
BK																			1										1	2	1	BK
BM		1					2	1			1	1	2						1			1	1	1	1	1				1	1	BM
bma		1					1																	1								bma
bmb								1																						1		bmb
bmc																														1		bmc
bme											1		1											1		1						bme
bmh								1				1										1				1					1	bmh
bmi													1																			bmi
BN																			1							1						BN
bna																			1													bna
bnb																										1						bnb
BP			1		1	1		3	2	2	2	1	1	2			1	2	2	2	2	1		1	2	2			3	1	BP
bpa								1	2		1											1				1				1		bpa
bpb						1		1			1						1		1	1	1				1							bpb
bpc					1		1								1																1	bpc
bpd									1			1	1						2		1		1			1				2		bpd
bpe															2																	bpe
bpf													1	1								1		1								bpf
bpg	3		1	1	1		2	1	4	2								1	2	1	2	2	2	3		2		2	2	6	6	bpg
BQ			1					1											2				1		2		1		1	2		BQ
bqa							1		1	1																						bqa
bqd	3			1	1		1	1	3	1								1		1	2	1		2				2	1	3	6	bqd
BR		2	1					1				1									1				1	1		1	1	3	3	BR
bra												1																1			1	bra
brc		2	1					1		1														2	1		1	1	3		2	brc
BT																	1	1	2						1	1	1			3	2	BT
bta																	1	1	2						2	1	1		1			bta

*Classification is based upon data cited in the New Jersey 1846–1918 section of App. 3.

INDUSTRIAL CATEGORIES	'46	'47	'48	'49	'50	'51	'52	'53	'54	'55	'56	'57	'58	'59	'60	'61	'62	'63	'64	'65	'66	'67	'68	'69	'70	'71	'72	'73	'74	'75	'76	INDUSTRIAL CATEGORIES
btb								1																1						1	1	btb
btf																						1						2		1	1	btf
bth																												2		1	1	bth
BV														1														2			1	BV
bva																										1		1			1	bva
bve														1												1		1			1	bve
BW										1			3				1	1		1	1					1	1	1		2		BW
bwa											1		1								1	1				1	1	1		2		bwa
bwb													2				1	1		1						1	2	1		2		bwb
BX			1			1	1	2												1			1						12	11	20	BX
C							2	5	6	1	1		5		2	1	3	2	3		3	3		2		3	3	11	12	11	17	C
CA							1	2	1				2		1	1	2				3	3				2	2	11	10	8	10	CA
caa																												10	9			caa
cab																											1				1	cab
cac																1						1									2	cac
cad																															1	cad
cae													1																			cae
cak						1																							1		2	cak
can																	1															can
cap																1										1						cap
caq							2	1					1			1	1				3	2				1			1	1	2	caq
CB							3	5	1				1		1		1		1							1			1	1	2	CB
cbb							3	5	1				1		1		1									1			1	2	1	cbb
CC						1					1		2					2	2				2			1			1		1	CC
ccb											1		2					2	2				2									ccb
ccc																							1							1	1	ccc
ccd																														1		ccd
ccf						1																				1			1		1	ccf
E																																E
EA																	1				1					1			2		1	EA
ED																											1					ED
EM																										1				1		EM
EN																													1			EN
EP																								1								EP
F						1																				1		1	4	6	4	F
FA																													1	3	2	FA
faa																														3		faa
fab																													1			fab
FB					1																									1		FB
fbb					1																								1			fbb
FD																												1	1	3	1	FD
fdc																														2		fdc
fdd																													1	1	1	fdd
FE																													1	1	1	FE
G						16	4	4	5	3	4	7	6	2	1		8		1		3	8	4	2	7	9	10	10	5	7	2	G
GA						16	4	4	3	2	3	7	6	2	1		8		1			1				2	1		1			GA
GB																						1	2									GB
GI									1	1	1			1	1																	GI
GJ									1												3	6	2	2	6	7	9	10	4	7	2	GJ
H																										1			1			H
HA																													1			HA
HB																										1	1					HB
I													1									2	1				2		1		2	I
J							1						1													1	1					J

INDUSTRIAL CATEGORIES	'77	'78	'79	'80	'81	'82	'83	'84	'85	'86	'87	'88	'89	'90	'91	'92	'93	'94	'95	'96	'97	'98	'99	'00	'01	'02	'03	'04	'05	'06	'07	INDUSTRIAL CATEGORIES
Total	64	73	79	168	449	351	295	232	254	386	472	567	685	897	1155	1212	970	890	964	859	1118	1104	2186	1995	2353	2255	2035	1635	1872	2086	1840	Total
A	2	4	5	26	107	55	17	9	12	13	30	23	22	28	44	44	36	43	31	44	92	59	176	172	200	190	129	102	87	85	71	A
AA	2	1	4	10	45	25	2	2	3	2	16	6	5	8	5	11	4	9	11	13	25	10	74	60	46	45	21	12	20	19	11	AA
aaa			1	3	8	5		2			5	2	4	3	1		3			1			3	6	1	1	8	5		1	1	aaa
aab					2	4	2	2	1					1					2			1	25	17	18	7	4	2	8	5	5	aab
aac					1					1				2	1	2						1	30	15	5	12		3	4	4		aac
aad	2	1	3	7	33	16			2		10	4	2	1	1	8	1	9	7	12	24	7	10	20	18	17	10	4	3	4	2	aad
aae											1	1		1								1	1	2	1	2	1	2	2	5	2	aae
aaf				1									1	1	1					1		1	5	3	4	1		2	2		1	aaf
AB			1			2	1				1	1	4	5	2	7		3	6	3	3	6		4	11	12	20	16	15	12	10	7	5	AB
AC							1		1				1	2			2	2	2	3			4	10	20	25	10	4	6	3	2	AC
acb							1						1	2			2	2	3				4	10	20	25	10	4	6	3	2	acb
AD		1	1	1	3	2	3	2	4	5	9	4	5	8	12	15	11	7	6	10	9	12	26	16	31	18	18	16	17	17	18	AD
ada			1	1	1	1	3	2	3	4	8	3	5	7	11	14	10	7	5	9	8	7	20	10	17	12	12	9	14	14	15	ada
adb		1		2	1	1	3	1	1	1	1	1	1	1	1	1	1		1	1	1	5	6	6	14	6	6	7	3	3	3	adb
AE		2	15	59	26	10	1	5	5	5	4	9	6	8	20	13	13	18	9	15	52	33	61	74	83	86	65	58	34	39	35	AE
A/B				4	13	10	1	5	5	3	4	7	5	5	4	5	3	2		1	4	7	5	1	2	3	8	4			1	A/B
B	35	30	42	65	172	172	146	126	138	197	231	315	365	533	654	689	522	504	515	456	551	578	1093	1062	1231	1141	1019	751	743	745	658	B
BA	1		1	1	22	6	8	4	9	8	9	10	8	30	33	34	25	19	19	19	25	24	55	53	47	59	55	37	39		32	BA
baa							1	2					2	1	2		3	2	4	2	5	9	7	4	10	7	6	4	2	4	baa
bab						1			1	1	1		1	1		3	3		2	4	3	5	9	4	3	5	3	4	7	bab
bac			1		3	1	2	1	1	1	1	2	2	3	5	5	6	2	5	2	2	4	8	3	5	7	7	2	5	3	bac
bad					1			2			3	1	1	5	6		3	2		1	3	1	5	1	5	1	7	3	6	8	1	bad
bae				1								3	5	6	8		2	3		5	5	8	10	5	15	6	8	1	bae
baf		1		14	1	2	1	3				2		2	5	5		1		2	6		11	9	3	6	10	4	6	7	8	baf
bag				4		2	1	1			1			1	2	6		3		1	6		10	5	12	10	6	3	2	4	3	bag
bah	1				1	1	1		1		2	3	1	6	3	5	3	3	3	3	1	4	7	2	6	8	10	3	4	2	3	bah
bai					1	1	1			1	1	2	2	3	3	5	2		3	3	4	4	7	8	6	8	2	3	6	5	3	bai
BB	1		1	2	4	1	2	6	3	3	3	5	4	14	17	9	9	11	11	6	14	9	28	18	34	20	16	12	11	15	19	BB
bba	1		1	1	1	1	2	6	3	3	3		4	10	12	2	3	5		3	9		12	7	6	7	5	7	4	7	4	bba
bbb			1	1				3	1			1		2	2	2							2	2	7	3	4	2	1	7	4	bbb
bbc								1	2		1										1	1		5	5	2	6	4	1			bbc
bbd			1	1				1	1			1	1	1	3	6	4	5	1	1	4	2	8	7	14	5	6	2	1	3	8	bbd
bbe			1	1	1							1		1	1	1		1	2				2	6	2	4		4	1	1		bbe
BC						1		1		1			1	2	7	5	5	4	1	3	1	2	16	11	14	13	8	10	6	3	6	BC
BD	3		4	4	11	11	6	6	7	14	22	18	17	29	38	42	15	25	25	32	26	26	54	34	53	43	47	46	61	42	48	BD

New Jersey Business Incorporations under General Laws, 1846–1907 (concl.)

Industrial Categories	'77	'78	'79	'80	'81	'82	'83	'84	'85	'86	'87	'88	'89	'90	'91	'92	'93	'94	'95	'96	'97	'98	'99	'00	'01	'02	'03	'04	'05	'06	'07	Industrial Categories
bda					1			1		2									1		1		2	4	2	3		2	1	2	4	bda
bdb					3			3	1				2		2	1	1	1	1	1	2	1	7	3	7	4	4		7	3		bdb
bdc			1	1	4	3	1		3	3	8	7	7	10	13	12	3	6	6	15	9	9	15	4	17	18	17	14	19	22	17	bdc
bde					1		1			1		2		2	2	6	1	1	3	3	3	2	1	1	2	5	3	4	8	4	1	bde
bdf										1		1		2	2	4	1	1					5	1		3	3	1	1	1	3	bdf
bdg						1				1	1	1		3	2	2	3	1	2	1	3	1	2	1	2	1	1	3	3	1	9	bdg
bdh	2		1	2		2	1		1	1	2	1	1	4	3	5	2	3	8	3	1	2	11	7	6	3	9	3	8	2	9	bdh
bdi				2	2	2	1		3	1	5	2	1	4	3	5	5	1	7	1	2	7	3	9	3	3	4	3	3	7	7	bdi
bdj	1		2	1	3	1	3	1		5	5	5	3	5	11	7		4	4	3	4	6	7	7	6	6	6	13	11		6	bdj
BE		1		2	3		1	1	2	2	2	2	6	14	12	11	2	5	4	6	8	5	12	12	7	15	13	12	15	18	17	BE
bea			1	2				1		1			1	3	3	3		3	1	1	2	1	1	2		4	1	3	1	2	1	bea
beb									1			1		2	1	1	1	1	1	1	2	1	1	5	1	1	3	3	2	1	1	beb
bec														1		1					1		1	1		1	1	1	1	1	1	bec
bed														1	3		1			2	1		1	1		1	1	1		1		bed
bee		1			1					1	1			2	2	4			1	2	2		2	2	3	4	6	4	7	9	8	bee
bef				1				1	1		1	1	1	5	5	4	1	1	1	1	2	1	6	1	3	6	9	2	3	3	4	bef
BF			1	2	3	1	2	1	4	7	4	3	9	15	12	18	16	10	12	10	16	11	16	16	27	29	25	17	27	20	22	BF
bfa			1	1	1	1	1				2	3	1	4	6	5	6	2	6	4	4	5	8	6	11	15	12	12	16	11	10	bfa
bfb				2	1			3	4	2			6	8	2	7	8	6	5	1	8	2	5	5	5	8	5	2	4	5	5	bfb
bfc			1					1	1	1			2	3	4	6	2	2	1	5	4	4	3	5	11	6	8	3	7	4	7	bfc
BG			1		3	2	4			5	1	2	5	5	6	7	12	4	4	9	8	13	21	13	14	19	14	9	7	11	14	BG
bga														2	1	1	3	1	4	1	5	7	4	4	2	2	1		3		5	bga
bgb			1		3	2	4			5	1	2	5	3	5	6	9	3	4	3	10	15	16	15	11	11	8	20	19	22		bgb
BH			1	2	2	5	1	3	2	4	6		7	11	9	5	11	9	7	4	3	10	15	16	15	11	11	8	20	19	22	BH
bha				1	2	3		1					1	2	3	2	4	3	5	1	1	2	2	5	8	3	3	5	7	12	16	bha
bhb									1	2			3	4	4	1	4	2	2		1	3	4	2	5	1	1	1	4	5	5	bhb
bhc			1		2	1	2	1	2	6	3	3	2	6	2	2	2	4	3	1	5	9	9	6	7	7	1	1	9	2	1	bhc
BI	3	2	1	2		6	3	2	5	7	8	12	10	12	8	17	20	11	13	9	9	9	28	24	27	25	15	18	21	26	12	BI
bia	1	1				4		1	3	3		4	5	4	4	4	7	5	2	2	2	10	10	8	11	4	5	9	9	8	3	bia
bib	1				1	2		1	1	1		1	3	3		7	4	2	1	2	3		6	4	4	8	3	6	1	6	2	bib
bic	1	1	1	2		2	1	3	3	5	7	2	5	4	6	9	4	8	5	5	12	12	12	13	7	7	11	12	7			bic
BJ	1		1	2	1	3	4	4	1	4	4	8	7	12	17	20	10	10	7	7	7	8	24	12	12	13	9	14	14	13	6	BJ
BK	3		1	5	8	10	11	8	10	16	11	20	23	39	59	66	43	46	25	35	38	46	66	64	70	53	54	54	40	55	52	BK
BM	2	4	3	2	14	13	15	12	17	24	18	20	32	53	64	59	43	39	39	30	50	70	79	81	83	72	60	85	73	63		BM
bma	1	1	1		4	2		3	3	3	2		3	4	7	8	9			2	3	6	4	7	4	9	12	14	7	6		bma
bmb		1	1		2			2						4	4	4		5	3	1	1	1	1	4	5	2	3	4	3	4	4	bmb
bmc		1			2			2	3	4	6	5	2	8	16	14	23	15	8	12	7	2	15	18	19	28	20	14	18	31	31	22	bmc
bme					2		2	2		1	3	2	3	4	1	2	2	1	1	3	2	1	3	4	2	3	3		2	2	2	bme
bmf								1		1	2	3	4	3	1	1		1				3	4	1	2	1		2	1			bmf
bmg													1			1							1									bmg
bmh	1	1	1	1	6	6	3	4	5	2	4	4	8	10	17	5	11	11	8	12	10	17	23	30	26	25	17	10	19	18	9	bmh
bmi				1	2	1	8	1	1	7	2	4	4	6	12	19	16	9	12	13	11	10	15	19	15	26	24	15	13	12	20	bmi
BN			1		2	4	1	5	4	4	1	10		8	5	3	5	5	5	1	5	6	7	8	8	6	6	2	6	8	8	BN
bna			1		1	3		2		1	1		4		1		3	3	2		3	3	1	3	3		1	2	1	2	1	bna
bnb				1	1	1	1	3		3		10	4	5	2	5	6	4	3	1	2	3	4	6	4	5	6	1	4	1	7	bnb
BP	4	1	4	3	13	12	17	7	13	18	15	26	30	39	34	45	20	23	20	22	31	29	62	66	90	79	56	57	78	71	55	BP
bpa	2		1	1	3	5	2			1	3	4	7	9	10	7	11	6	3	4	5	8	17	13	19	14	13	14	15	26	17	bpa
bpb	1		2	1	3	1	1			3	2	1	6	6	3	6	2	3	3	4	6	3	9	6	2	2	9	2	9	4	1	bpb
bpc					1	1		4		6	4	4	4	7	10	7	4	3	6	5	7	6	9	11	22	15	12	11	12	9	11	bpc
bpd													1	4	1	4	1	1	5	1		2	11	9	14	8	9	8	7	11	12	bpd
bpe						1	1	1					1		5	4	1	1	1	2			5	2	4	5	5	4	10	3		bpe
bpf	1	1	1		3	4	6	4	4	5	3	9	5	8	5	12	6	7	4	5	10	7	10	21	17	23	9	8	11	4	7	bpf
bpg				1	3	1	2	1	1	3	2	2	4	4	4	4	1	2	2	1	4	5	8	8	5	8	6	10	14	14	7	bpg
BQ	3	7	10	11	22	19	15	22	14	22	28	42	35	45	38	49	30	24	47	25	37	39	115	83	111	99	85	51	74	60	74	BQ
bqa		1		2	3	1	2	1	3	3	5			5	6	6	8	1		6	6	5	36	16	28	14	9	7	12	4	7	bqa
bqb													1		1	1			1	1	1		1	5	2	2	4	5	5	2		bqb
bqc												1								2		1	2	10	7	3	2	1	1	1	1	bqc
bqd		1	1	1	6	2	5	8	1	6	4	9	7	8	7	6	4	5	11	6	11	6	13	15	16	18	19	8	7	3	5	bqd
bqe				4	3	5	4	1	5		9		10	6	14	11	12	11	10	13	4	1	21	17	22	17	18	16	20	14	17	bqe
bqf	2	6	9	5	11	9	5	11	7	12	8	12	15	14	13	20	14	9	12	8	18	19	36	28	30	36	30	13	27	31	39	bqf
bqg	1									1	2	4	1	1	1				2		1	2	4		4	5	5	3	4	2	3	bqg
BR		2	2	2	3	6	6	3	3	3	1	12	15	14	18	18	21	12	21	13	15	19	18	34	33	44	32	33	27	35	40	28	BR
bra		1				1	1			1	1		3		6	1	5	2	2	4	1	1	4	4	6		6	2	1	8	2	3	bra
brb						1	1		1		1	1		3	4	2	2	4	1	5	2	1	1	1		1	1	8	2	2		brb
brc		1	2	2	3	5	5	3	2	2		10	12	12	9	13	14	8	15	10	14	17	17	29	28	38	26	29	25	25	35	25	brc
BS	1		1	1	6	11	5	2	5	5	13	17	20	24	29	26	23	20	23	13	15	16	28	29	28	39	30	22	26	17	18	BS
bsc						1					2	1		2	2	3	3	1	3	2			1		1	1	1	1	8	1	1	bsc
bsd	1		1	1	6	10	5	2	5	5	11	16	20	22	27	23	20	19	23	10	14	14	28	29	28	39	29	18	18	16	17	bsd
BT	7	6	5	7	28	21	19	16	13	14	26	39	41	57	75	09	56	45	40	40	54	81	89	108	115	93	78	81	76	63		BT
bta		1	2	3	3	5	6	6	4	6	4	12	11	11	25	17	18	15	10	11	11	16	19	22	26	22	25	15	17	13	10	bta
btb	2			1	5	5	4	2	4	2	4	9	10	18	14	16	9	10	12	18	12	20	25	23	34	37	22	22	15	27	23	btb
btc					1	1					1		2		1	1			1	1		1	1	4	1	2	3	1	1	1	7	btc
btd			1		1	4	2		2	2	3		3		2	7	4	4	5	2		5	4	9	17	14	18	9	11	12	7	btd
bte	1				1			2	2		1	1	1		1				1		1		3	4	1	4	3	3	2	2	2	bte
btf		2			3	2		2	1					3	2	2		6			1	1	3	4	7	2	3	1	5	3	1	btf
btg							1			4	6	4	8	13	10	4	8	6	6	7	7	4	11	11	11	14	12	14	12	4	5	btg
bth	2	1	1	2	5	1	1			1	2		3	4	4	3	3		1	4	2	3	3	3	4	4	4	5	4	4	5	bth
bti	2	2	1	1	9	3	5	2	3	2	5	7	8	7	9	13	7	5	8	6	3	4	16	12	8	16	2	8	16	10	12	bti
BU																					3	3	24	34	18	16	11	5	13	9	8	BU
bub																					1	1	24	34	18	16	11	5	13	9	8	bub
BV	2	1	3	1	8	10	8	6	5	10	11	9	14	16	29	29	22	8	29	16	27	16	37	26	24	35	38	14	20	16	14	BV
bva	2	1			4	6	5	4	2	6	6	6	7	13	13	11	11	5	8	7	7		19	13	11	21	21	10	7	8	2	bva
bvb																1				1	1										3	bvb
bvc			1		2	2	1			1	2		1	2		1			3	1			7	7	7	9	5	4	8	3	6	bvc
bvd									1	1				6	4	3	2		17	6	17	4	5	5	3	1	1		1		1	bvd
bve			2	1		1	2			1	1	1	3	1	5	8	3		1	1	1		5	4	11				2	3	2	bve
bvf					2	1		2	2	1	2	1	2	1	1	2	1				1		5	1	3					2	2	bvf

INDUSTRIAL CATE-GORIES	'77	'78	'79	'80	'81	'82	'83	'84	'85	'86	'87	'88	'89	'90	'91	'92	'93	'94	'95	'96	'97	'98	'99	'00	'01	'02	'03	'04	'05	'06	'07	INDUSTRIAL CATE-GORIES
BW		2	2	3	5	5	3	6	8	8	16	15	21	38	58	41	29	39	23	23	26	41	56	82	76	67	57	73	44	63	45	BW
bwa					1	1			1		1	2	1	15	7	4	1	8	5	3	4	12	15	25	16	11	10	9	3	17	7	bwa
bwb		2	2	3	4	4	3	6		7	8	14	11	19	22	49	37	27	31	18	19	21	27	38	56	57	56	47	63	39	44	bwb
bwc						1					1	2	1	1	1	2	1		1	2	3	3	1	3	1						37	bwc
BX	4	4	19	13	14	26	15	14	14	19	21	35	56	55	88	111	110	126	148	116	165	143	245	262	324	268	269	108	26	53	32	BX
C	10	19	45	61	43	48	49	44	74	55	72	98	88	91	105	93	89	103	97	108	115	224	183	221	161	135	111	136	99	82		C
CA	6	16	14	28	26	17	24	20	19	24	25	28	44	57	55	62	48	48	32	39	42	45	93	88	96	85	76	58	62	56	44	CA
caa	3	11	10	18	14	7	10	8	7	10	7	10			9	10	4	8	7	8	6	3	7	8	13	17	17	16	15	12	5	caa
cab												1			2	2																cab
cac	1			2				1	2	4	6	2	6	14	7	23	20	15	10	4	11	7	10	11	12	19	15	7	6	6	3	cac
cad						1			1																	1			1			cad
cae				1																											1	cae
caf																							17	2	1		1			1	1	caf
cag																								2								cag
cah		1	2	1		1	1	1	3	1		3	2	7	12	9	11	6	2	4	4	5	15	18	24	13	12	20	14	10	20	cah
caj					1											1								1				1				caj
cak		3	1	6	3	5	8	4	2	5	2	3	5	7	9	5	3	6	2	3	8	8	14	28	12	12	9	3	8	9	4	cak
cam		1							1		1				1				1				4	1	1		1	1		2		cam
can		1				3	3	2	1	1	2	1		1		1		3		2		3	2			1				2		can
cap	1				3	3	2	4	3	2	5	2	3	1	11	5	5	6	2	5	7	10	13	12	10	9	7	4	9	9	4	cap
caq	1		1	1		4	3	2	1	1	3	5	3	5	5	5	5	6		25	14	13	9	17	12	21	17	17	11	16	6	caq
CB	1		2	6	11	9	11	19	8	6	2	3	3	6	1	2	2	9	25	14	13	9	17	12	21	17	17	11	16	6	3	CB
cba				1	5	2	3	3	3	4	3	1	1		2	2	5	7	4	6	6	5	3	5	7	7	5	8	4	3		cba
cbb	1		1	5	4	3	3	7	4	3	1	2		3		1			2		1	1		4								cbb
cbd			1		2	4	5	9		2			1	2			1		2	18	9	6	12	9	12	10	6	8				cbd
CC	3	3	3	11	24	17	13	10	17	44	28	41	51	25	35	41	43	32	46	44	53	61	114	83	104	59	42	42	58	37	35	CC
cca				1	4	6	6	7	10	15	6	17	22	8	14	13	15	16	3	11	30	20	20	9	8	10	16	3	6			cca
ccb	1			2	1	1			3	3	4	6	1	3	6	2	4	5	3	12	8	28	8	20	10	7	7	7	8	7		ccb
ccc	1	2		7	14	4	2	1	2	17	7	5	9	6	8	11	9	13	17	17	22	19	14	15	26	13	7	9	18	9	10	ccc
ccd		1									2											2	1	1	1		3	1		1	1	ccd
cce				1	1	1		1		2			1	1		1			1				1						1			cce
ccf	1			1	1	1			1	3	1	3	1	1	7	2	1	2	4	5	7	6	4	3	3	1		6	1	2		ccf
ccg			3	1	3	4	2	2	1	7	8	10	12	8	10	11	10	6	10	4	10	17	33	34	34	24	14	14	11	14	9	ccg
D					4	4																								43	36	D
DA						4	3	2	1	1	5	4	9	10	17	20	14	14	21	6	15	29	28	97	10	15	20	17	25	47	62	DA
DB					1	1		1	1		1	3	3	6	4	1	3	6	3	2	5	5	6	4	8	4	12	5				DB
DC						1	1	1		1		1	1	5	4	3	3	2	2	2	3	11	4	10	11	4	4	2	2			DC
E	5			2	1	3	2	1	6	15	8	18	14	31	61	75	80	53	72	45	58	59	136	157	159	165	178	160	193	282	215	E
EA						1	1			2	1	4	2	5	6	7	14	3	13	5	6	6	26	20	19	18	26	16	21	16	21	EA
EB																1								1	1							EB
ED	1			1		1			3	3	2	2	2	2	8	9	7	7	6	6	7	10	26	25	28	27	29	38	25	45	35	ED
EE										1	1	1	1	8	1	2	3	7	4	4	2	9	10	9	13							EE
EF											1				4	3	2	3	5	1	4	2	8	7	11	5	10	3	3	10	11	EF
EG															1	1	1	2		2	2	3	2	3	6	4	5	5	5	5	5	EG
EH														1				1	2		1	1	2	11	8	6	3	5	6	6	24	EH
EI																							5	4	3		3	15	30			EI
EK										1		1	1	2	4	3		4	1	2	1	3	2	3	2	5	5	5	5			EK
EM										2	2	4	2	2	12	13	17	7	14	7	7	15	20	14	16	20	22	23	46	21		EM
EN	1						1	1		2	2	2	1	3	1	5	4	6	3	5	4	4	5	9	25	15	10	9				EN
EP					1		1			3	2	2	3	5	12	16	17	7	14	14	9	11	29	38	48	45	37	27	54	73	54	EP
EQ	3			1				2	2	2	1	2	12	14	15	10	16	11	4	13	7	12	15	13	13	10	19	17	28	17		EQ
F	3	8	6	8	12	14	12	11	13	23	33	28	31	47	74	73	65	66	70	62	88	76	129	116	106	138	142	108	137	176	154	F
FA	2	2	1	1	2	4	1	1	2	6	6	10	6	9	21	17	13	8	9	5	10	8	21	23	22	36	28	36	25	40	34	FA
faa	1	2	1	1	1	2	4	1	6	6	8	18	14	12	7	5	3	1	3	4	6	7	12	14	14	18	21	28	18	23	19	faa
fab						1	1	4	2	2	2	1	1	3	1	3	4	6	7	11	3	7	5	11	10							fab
fac					1						1				1		1					1	1	1				1	3	2		fac
fad	1					2					1			1	2	1				1			2	1		1	7	4	1	3	3	fad
fae																							2									fae
FB		1	1		2	2	4	5		6	5	5	7	15	15	15	15	17	25	10	34	28	41	25	27	27	34	18	29	31	21	FB
fba							1						1		3	2	5	3	2	3	11	10	6	10	6	13	4	9	8	8	6	fba
fbb		1	1		2	2	3	5		6	5	5	6	15	12	13	13	12	22	3	31	17	31	19	17	21	21	14	20	23	15	fbb
FC																						1				1	2	5	5	7		FC
FD	1	5	3	6	7	4	4	5	11	11	17	10	13	15	29	27	20	24	26	32	31	20	35	23	22	43	26	23	52	59	67	FD
fdb																															1	fdb
fdc			1		2	1	1		2	2	3	3	2	3	1	2	2	3		4	2		1	5	1	1	2	2	7	7	8	fdc
fdd	1	5	2	6	5	3	3	5	11	9	14	7	11	12	28	25	18	21	26	28	29	20	34	18	21	42	24	21	45	52	58	fdd
FE			1	1		1	4	3		5	5	5	8	9	14	17	17	10	13	19	32	44	35	32	53	29	26	41	25			FE
G	8	9	4	8	30	17	29	18	15	23	53	62	83	83	133	122	90	61	87	76	90	112	162	160	240	257	240	221	283	345	390	G
GA						2	2	9	4	12	5	3	2		1	1	1				1		1									GA
GB						1		1		4	2	3	1		3	1																GB
GC										1	2	1					1		3	2	3	4	1	2		1	3		1		4	GC
GD						1				1	4	1			2	2	1		4	3	5	8	18	13	14	8	16	7	1	2		GD
GE														1	1	1							6		2	7	6	10	3	3	2	GE
GF															4	4	3	3	2	4	2	1	6	19	10	12	7	18	9	2	8	GF
GG													1	2	2	5	2		1	1		3		3	4	2	1	1	2	9		GG
GH					1	1				1		1	1	2	2	1	3		1	3	3	2	6	5	2	7	1	4	3	5	3	GH
GI			1		1						1	1	2	2	1	1		1		2	3	3	3	1	1	1	2	3	5	6	4	GI
GJ	8	9	3	8	29	13	23	14	12	17	36	43	58	67	110	98	72	50	66	47	58	73	112	111	143	162	148	156	193	263	323	GJ
GK						3	3	2	1	3	5	3	7	7	9	11	5	7	9	16	18	22	30	23	50	58	44	35	42	49	45	GK
H		1	1	10	48	27	19	5	8	25	36	22	34	36	47	41	40	24	40	30	59	43	76	66	105	107	92	70	124	131	140	H
HA		1	1	7	31	15	10	2	3	14	17	10	3	17	11	9	5	1	3	4	12	7	12	6	8	3	2	14	8	1	1	HA
HB				3	17	12	9	3	5	11	19	12	31	19	36	32	35	23	37	26	47	36	64	60	97	107	89	68	110	123	139	HB
I		1	1	2	3	3	10	6	5	7	6	4	6	11	7	13	11	13	5	9	10	4	25	25	23	28	30	16	26	31	16	I
J	1	1		2	3	3	5	2	5	4	9	9	14	14	13	18	12	16	16	16	28	21	50	36	32	37	37	59	80	112	70	J

Ohio Business Incorporations by Special Acts, 1803–1851*

INDUSTRIAL CATEGORIES	1803	1804	1805	1806	1807	1808	1809	1810	1811	1812	1813	1814	1815	1816	1817	1818	1819	1820	1821	1822	1823	1824	1825	1826	INDUSTRIAL CATEGORIES
Total	2	0	0	0	0	2	3	1	1	2	1	3	1	18	18	3	2	2	0	1	0	2	3	8	Total
A																									A
AE																		2	1	1					AE
B																								1	B
BD									1			1				1									BD
bdb																1									bdb
BQ																								1	BQ
bqf																								1	bqf
BX									1																BX
C																									C
CA							2	1				2	1	5	12	1	1	1		1		2	3	5	CA
cam												2	1	1								1		1	cam
cap												1											1		cap
CC							2							4	12	1	1	1		1		1	3	4	CC
ccc								1						1										1	ccc
ccd														2	1						1		2	1	ccd
cce							2							1	11	1	1	1				1		2	cce
G	1					2	1			2	1			12	5	1	1							2	G
GA						2	1			2	1			12	5	1									GA
GI																	1							2	GI
GJ	1																								GJ
J	1													1	1										J

INDUSTRIAL CATEGORIES	1827	1828	1829	1830	1831	1832	1833	1834	1835	1836	1837	1838	1839	1840	1841	1842	1843	1844	1845	1846	1847	1848	1849	1850	1851	INDUSTRIAL CATEGORIES
Total	7	8	12	17	8	37	14	31	38	71	92	55	67	10	9	11	10	29	53	49	22	80	103	192	170	Total
A											1	3												1	1	A
AA																				1						AA
aaf																				1						aaf
AB												3												1		AB
AD											1															AD
ada											1															ada
AE																									1	AE
B			2	6	1	5	1	3	11	9	26	11	16	2		2	1	2	4	5	1	1	1		7	B
BA											4															BA
bae											1															bae
bag											3															bag
BB											1															BB
bbe											1															bbe
BD				1		2		1		3	6	1	7							1					BD
bda						2				1	1									1					bda
bdb				1				1																	bdb
bdc										2		5	1	7											bdc
bdg												1														bdg
BK													2						1							BK
BM										1												1			1	BM
bma										1												1			1	bma
bmh																						1				bmh
BQ				1	1	1		3	5	1	1	2	2						1			1				BQ
bqa								1																		bqa
bqe								1																		bqe
bqf				1	1	1			5	1	1	2	2						1			1				bqf
BR																				1						BR
brc																				1						brc
BT				1							1	3		1				1		1						BT
bta				1																						bta
btd												1														btd
bti												3		1				1		1						bti
BV			1									2	1													BV
bvc			1									2	1													bvc
BX			1	3		2	1		5	4	11	5	4	1		2	1	1	2	2	1				6	BX
C	6	8	7	9	4	29	11	13	22	55	55	38	47	8	9	8	3	22	42	38	19	73	94	176	137	C
CA	2	3		5	2	13	1	8	10	38	23	4	4	3	1	2	1	3	8	13	4	18	13	20	22	CA
caa					1	11		5	7	32	10	2	4	2		2		3		11	4	15	19		21	caa
cak		1		2	1	2	1	2	2		4	1		1						1		2	1			cak
cam	2	2		2				2		5	8	1					1									cam
cap										1	1											1	1		1	cap
caq				1				1												1		1				caq
CB																							1	1	3	CB
cbb																							1	1	3	cbb
CC	4	5	7	4	2	16	10	5	12	17	32	34	43	5	8	6	2	19	34	25	15	55	80	155	112	CC
ccb				1							1									2		1	2	1	1	ccb
ccc			1	1			2			3	1	1						1		2			1		1	ccc
ccd	3	2	2	1		6	2	1	4	5	6	9	5	1				2	2	4	1	12	4	3	5	ccd
cce	1	3	3	1		9	6	4	5	11	19	20	34	4	7	6	2	17	30	12	14	37	73	148	103	cce
ccf											1	1	1											1		ccf
ccg			1			1					4	4	3		1				7	1		3	1	1	2	ccg
F								1	1	1	1											1	1	1	8	F
FA								1	1	1	1											1	1	1	8	FA
faa								1	1	1	1											1	1	1	8	faa
G	1		3	2	3	3	2	14	4	5	8	2	4			1	6	5	7	5	2	5	8	14	17	G
GA			2		3	1	1	12	1			1					3	1		1		1	4	1		GA
GI	1		1	2		2	1	2	4	4	8		2						1	1		2	3	5	14	GI
GJ													2			1	2	4	5	4	1	2	1	8		GJ
GK																									1	GK
J										1	1	1														J

* Classification is based upon data cited in the Ohio 1803–51 section of App. 3.

OHIO BUSINESS INCORPORATIONS UNDER GENERAL LAWS, 1856–1930*

INDUSTRIAL CATEGORIES	1856	1857	1858	1859	1860	1861	1862	1863	1864	1865	1866	1867	1868	1869	1870	1871	1872	1873	1874	1875	1876	1877	1878	1879	1880	1881	1882	1883	1884	1885	1886	INDUSTRIAL CATEGORIES
Total	64	47	49	97	36	25	26	51	91	358	281	266	295	333	304	336	401	360	298	333	266	237	227	286	391	508	598	612	477	515	626	Total
A	6	7	3	1	5	9	2	4	36	245	106	25	28	47	32	25	56	35	35	30	17	6	13	24	34	29	42	30	29	38	72	A
AA														1			9	1						1	1		1			1		AA
aaa																																aaa
aab																												1			1	aab
aac											1	1																1		1		aac
aad			1								1	4	4	7	1	1	8	3	6	9	2	1	5	9	18	5	7	2	1	1		aad
aae																1	2	1	1						1	2	4		1			aae
aaf																	1			1	1			1	1					1		aaf
AB	4	1			2	1	1	3	4	6	13	9	9	19	13	10	16	7	11	11	5	1	8	11	10	8	16	15	16	10	14	AB
AC	1	1		1	1	7	1	1	29	217	77	4	4	1	2	1	2	2	2	1	1	1						2	7	21	48	AC
acb	1	1		1	1	7	1	1	29	217	77	4	4	1	2	1	2	2	2	1	1	1		1					7	21	48	acb
AD													3	3	4	10	9	6	4	4	5		4		2	1	2	2			1	AD
ada													3	3	4	9	8	6	4	1	4				2	1	2	2			1	ada
adb																1	1		1	1	1	2						1	2			adb
AE	1	5	2		2	1			3	22	14	7	12	16	14	9	19	16	9	4	4	2		3	3	11	11	7	4	5	8	AE
A/B											2	1					1	1								1	1	2	1	1		A/B
B	13	17	10	15	6	2	10	12	14	29	64	70	74	88	106	128	149	159	107	92	72	79	75	119	185	206	299	300	220	237	254	B
BA							1		1		2	2				9	2		5		3		3	11	2	7	9	19	15	22	24	BA
baa									1							1								2				3	2	1	3	baa
bab													1																1	1	1	bab
bac																1			1				1	2	2	2	2	3	1	1	1	bac
bad																			2	1	3			3	2	2	3	2	1			bad
bae							1					2			2	3	2	4	3	2	1		4	2	2	7	10	7	13	7		bae
baf											1				2	4		2	1			1		2	2	2	3	3	4		11	baf
bag											1								1						2	2	2	1				bag
bah																1		1			1			1	1	4	1	4	1	2	3	bah
bai																												1			1	bai
BB						1				2	2	1	2		1	2	6	1	2		1		2	1	4	6	9	7	8	7	7	BB
bba												1			1	1	1	1			1			1	2	4	5	3	4	7	4	bba
bbb						1										1			1						1		1	4	2			bbb
bbc				1						2	2	1	1	2	4			1		1											1	bbc
bbd																															2	bbd
bbe																	2			1		1			1		2	2	2	1	3	bbe
BC																		2	4	1	5			1	2		2	2	2	1	3	BC
BD		1				1	1		1		1		4	4	2	7	8	1	4	5	2		1	1	6	3	4	3	2	1	2	BD
bda																		1	1						1	1						bda
bdb					1	1			1		2	5	1	4	2	7	6	1	3	5	1				5	1					1	bdb
bde													2						1													bde
bdf																												1				bdf
bdg																									1	1						bdg
bdi		1															2							1	1	2	2	1	1	1	1	bdi
bdj																						1					2					bdj
BE													1								1	1		1		1		2	3		3	BE
bea																					1	1		1								bea
beb																													1			beb
bee																												2	1	1		bee
bef													1															1	1		3	bef
BF						1							2	3			5	4			1	1	1	1	2	6	4	7	5	5	6	BF
bfa						1							1								1				1						1	bfa
bfb													2				3	4					1		1	2	2	6	3	1	3	bfb
bfc											1		1				2					1		1	4	2	1	2	4	2	bfc
BG																	1								1	1	1	1	1			BG
bgb																	1								1	1	1	1				bgb
BH											3	2	2	7	2	5	10	9		1		1	1	2	4	9	7	6	12	7	BH
bha											1	1		4		4	2				1				3	5	3		3	1	bha
bhb											1	1		4	3	2	5	5			1			3	3	1	1	2	3	3	bhb
bhc											2		1		1		4	1		1		2	3	1	4	1	2	9	3	bhc
BI	1	2	1				1		2	2	6	4	6	4	4	6	11	16	12	12	7	3	2	7	9	6	19	21	14	12	14	BI
bia		1					1	1		2	4	2	1	1	1	4	7	5	8	3				4	3	5	5	8	5	4	10	bia
bib			1								2	1	1	1	3	1	6	8	4	3				1	6	4	2	3	4	4	2	bib
bic	1	1							1		2	2	4	1	1	3	6	8	6	1	4	2	2	6	5	10	11	7	6	4	3	bic
BJ	1		1		1		1			1	2	2	2	2	4	3	3	8	8	1	3	3	1	9	9	9	7	6	6	6	3	BJ
BK	1		1						2	1	6	4	5	2	4	10	18	12	13	10	12	8	7	16	18	20	29	19	18	32	26	BK
BM	1			1	1		3	2	2	1	5	6	2	4	3	1	3	6	5	3	5	8	7	16	17	19	27	18	14	14	17	BM
bma	1			1													2	2	1	1		1		1	2	2	6	4	3		2	bma
bmb				1					1		1	1					2	2	1		1			3	1					4	bmb
bmc											1			1	1		2	1	1			1			3	8	4	5			9	bmc
bme											1							1						1	3	3					bme
bmf																					1			1	1	6	4	5		1	bmf
bmh					1		2			1	1	1						1		1	3	2	1	3	1	2	3	1	4	5	6	1	bmh
bmi					1	1			1		1	1						1	1	3	2	1	2	2	3	1	2	3	5	bmi
BN		1		7							4	1				1	1	1	2		1	2	1	2	4	1	2	3	1	1	10	BN
bna		1									4					1	1	1	2		1	1	1	2	2	1	2	2	1	1	7	bna
bnb				7							1					1						1	1								3	bnb
BP		2	1						1		3	6	2	3	3	9	12	8	7	15	3	5	4	11	14	14	25	22	17	16	22	BP
bpa		1									2	4		1		1	4	4	2	3		1	1	3	2	2	7	10	8	7	8	bpa
bpb															1		1	1		1		1	4	2	2	4	2	2	1		5	bpb
bpc			1	1							1	1	1	1	1		4	4	4	2	1	1	1	4	5	6	4	1	1		5	bpc
bpd														1			1	1	1	1		1			1	1						bpd
bpe																	2		5	1	1	2		2	2	2	3	5	2	2	3	bpe
bpf											1		1	2	1		2	2	2					2	2	2	2	1	6	3	bpf
bpg				1							1						1	1	1					2	2	1	2	2	2	3	bpg
BQ	1		1		1		3	1	3	12	16	13	16	15	28	35	40	19	15	12	25	18	36	45	41	45	53	31	45	35	BQ
bqa							3	1	2	4		2	2	3	3	6	5	1		2		1	5	8	4	2	3		5	4	bqa
bqb										2					4		5	1		2	3		5	1		2	7	1	1		bqb
bqc															1					1											bqc
bqd											1		1	2	2	4	9	2	2	6	3	3	2	5	8	12	3	11	7	7	bqd
bqe		1								5	4	5	6	7	2	4	1	7	2	6	3	3	8	7	12	10	16	9	14	8	bqe

* Classification is based upon data cited in the Ohio 1856–1936 section of App. 3.

OHIO BUSINESS INCORPORATIONS UNDER GENERAL LAWS, 1856–1930 (cont.)

INDUSTRIAL CATEGORIES	1856	1857	1858	1859	1860	1861	1862	1863	1864	1865	1866	1867	1868	1869	1870	1871	1872	1873	1874	1875	1876	1877	1878	1879	1880	1881	1882	1883	1884	1885	1886	INDUSTRIAL CATEGORIES
bqf	1			1			1	2	1	1	3	11	6	6	3	15	18	17	13	7	5	17	8	19	19	17	18	23	9	16	12	bqf
bqg															2	2	1	1		1		3	1			1	2	2	7	2	3	bqg
BR												1	1	2	2	1		4	3	2	1	2		2	3	3		4	11	1 5	1 2	3 6	BR
bra																		1	3					1	1	1	4	7	1 1			bra
brc												1	1	2		2	1	3	2	2		1		2	3	1	7	6	4	2	6	brc
BS													1			1			2				1	1	2	3			2	2	10	BS
bsc																							1	1	1	1					2	bsc
bsd																			2				1	1	2				2	9	8	bsd
BT	1	2			2		1		2		4	9	6	13	8	20	13	22	18	17	16	11	7	12	18	30	27	48	33	41	30	BT
bta				1								1	6		1	2	1	4		3	2	2			4	5	1	6	6	13	5	bta
btb	1	1							2		1	2	5	1	5	11	4	7	4	3	3	1	2		2	9	5	11	6	7	9	btb
btc														1						1						1					2	btc
btd												1			2	3	3	1	1		5		1	1	4	3	2	2		1	3	btd
bte																		1		1		1				3	1	3	2	1		bte
btf									1	3		2		2	4	4	7		8	5	1	3	5	6	8	10	9		1	8	btf
btg																					1					1						btg
bth				1		1					1	1	3	2		1		2		1	2	2	2	4		2	4	6	1		bth
bti		1						2			1	1		1		4	3	1	4		3	2	1	5	13	4	6	1	3		bti
BV		1					2				1		4	2	5	5	15	6	3	1	1	4	5	7	17	20	27	18	10	11	6	BV
bva		1					1						4	1	4	3	10		1	1		1	3		9	6	7	5	3		2	bva
bvc															1								1	2	1	1	1			1	bvc
bve							1				1		1	1	1	5	6	2		2		3	1	5	14	11	20	9	4	7	3	bve
BW			1								1		1	4	3	1	5		2	2	4	6	4	5	5	8	16	13	9	9	5	BW
bwa													1	3	2	1		3				4	4		2	1	4	1	1	1	1	bwa
bwb			1								1	1	1	1	1		2		2	1	2	3	3	7	12	12	8	8	5		bwb
BX	7	8	5	5			1	3	7	9	13	13	13	23	25	15	7	5	6	3	4	3	1	4	12	14	10	8	29	18	BX
C	38	17	31	72	21	14	10	26	22	42	62	74	76	80	85	98	84	49	48	62	53	61	63	64	76	154	89	89	69	80	123	C
CA	7	3	4	26	6	3	6	8	13	21	27	27	46	61	74	84	49	28	52	35	46	42	45	48	102	71	47	35	31	64	CA
caa	7	2	3	7		3	5	2	8	10	14	17	29	30	48	58	56	30	18	27	25	36	33	32	34	84	44	37	20	20	32	caa
cab																										2					cab
cac			1	12	5			6	4	4	4	4	10	10	6	13	16	16	9	19	5	5	4	4	6	7	5	4	3	11	cac
cad																				1				1							cad
cae																								1							cae
caf																								1	1						caf
cah												2	1				2		3					4	6	11	1	4	2	5	cah
caj																	1			1					1		3	2	8	caj
cak								2	5	3	4	4	3	1	7	2	1		1	3	2	5		1	5	2	3	1	5	cak
cam															1															cam
can											1									1			2							can
cap								1	1	4	1	2			1	1	2			2	1	2	2	3	1	1	1	1	2	cap
caq		1		7	1		1		2				1	3	1					1	1						2	1	caq
CB			1					2	4	2		1	1		3	2	1	3	4	5	2	12	19	13	6	10	7	4	5	CB
cba													1		2	2	1	3	4	5	2	7	17	12	1	7	1	2	1	cba
cbb			1					2	4	2			1		2		1				1	5	1	1	5	1	1	2	1	cbb
cbd													1		1						1		1	2	5	1	1	2	cbd
CC	31	14	26	46	15	11	4	16	5	21	33	47	28	30	18	11	11	9	19	7	14	10	19	7	9	39	12	32	27	45	54	CC
cca																									21	2	17	14	8	13	cca
ccb	8	6	1	3	4	4		1		2	3	7	6	6	4	3	4	4	7	6	4	1	9	3	2	4	5	10	11	34	28	ccb
ccc	1				1		1	3			1			1		1		2		4	2	3	8	4	2		4	ccc
ccd	4			1	3	1		1	1		2	2	3	2	2	1	1			1	2	4					4	ccd
cce	17	8	25	42	7	6	4	14	3	16	28	38	19	22	12	5	6	4	11	1	9	2	5	1	2	1	1	2	3	cce
ccf	1																			2				1		1	ccf
ccg																1	1	1		1	1	2	1	1	2	5	ccg
D																							1	1	4	5	3	4	2	5	D
DA																									3	3	1	1	2	3	DA
DB																								1	1	1	1	2		DB
DC																								1	1	1	1		2	DC
E											1	5	5	5		2	4	3	4	12	29	12	4	3	8	10	16	14	18	17	30	E
EA																				1			1	1	2	6	2	4		EA
ED												2	1										1	1		2	2	1	3	2	ED
EE																										1	1	EE
EF											1															1	1	1	EF
EG																										1	EG
EH																									1	EH
EK																									1	1	EK
EM														1											2	2	2	3	8	EM
EN																1	1	1							1	1	2	EN
EP																			3					1	1	3	1	1	EP
EQ											3	4	4		2	3	2	3	11	26	12	2	2	5	5	4	3	4	8	12	EQ
F				1					4	5	6	8	10	9	6	20	10	29	32	34	36	27	24	22	24	32	43	60	44	47	F
FA									2	3	2	2	3	3	1	3	3	2	1	2	2	1		2	3	5	1	7	2	3	FA
faa									1														1	1	2	1	1	faa
fab									1															1		1	fab
fad																							1	4	fad
FB												2	2		4	3	5	4	2	2	1		3	1	3	5	6	10	FB
fba												2											1	1	2	5	1	fbb
fbb													2		4	3	5	4	2	2	1	3	2	5	5	9	fbb
FD									2	3	5	5	4	4	17	7	18	23	21	23	18	16	16	14	20	26	36	34	26	FD
fdc									1		3	3	4	2	5	1	6	10	1	6	4	8	5	5	fdc
fdd									2	3	5	5	3	4	14	4	15	19	19	21	17	11	13	14	22	28	29	21	fdd
FE				1					2	1	1								5	6	7	6	3	4	6	13	12	2	6	FE
G	3	2	3	8	3		2	6	13	28	15	53	91	85	64	89	66	90	71	95	57	41	35	47	60	63	94	115	65	65	79	G
GA				1							1	1	3	1	1		21	13	20	10	5	2	2	5	10	6	2	10	GA
GB												42	86	81	56	82	60	58	53	64	35	31	28	41	49	50	84	91	53	58	63	GB
GC																									1	2	1	GC
GG																									1		2	GG
GH			1																	1					1		1	GH
GI	3	1	2	4	3		2	5	13	26	11	10	1	2	5	4	2	5	2	6	8	3	4	3	4	3	2	6	1	4	GI
GJ		1		3				1		2	2	1		1	1	3	4	6	3	2	1	1	6	4	5	2	3	1	4	GJ
GK											1	6	1	1	6			2			6	1	1	1	GK
H											1	6	4	1	6		2	1		4	3	1		1	10	4	2	1	4	3	H
HA																				4					10	2	2	1	1	HA
HB											1	6	4	1	6		2	1		3	1		1	2		2	1	3	2	HB
I													1	1			2	1	2			8	2	1	2	2	10	7	9	7	I
J	4	4	2	1			2	3	6	10	25	26	10	20	7	1	4		6			2	1	2	5	6	5	22	6	J

INDUSTRIAL CATEGORIES	1887	1888	1889	1890	1891	1892	1893	1894	1895	1896	1897	1898	1899	1900	1901	1902	1903	1904	1905	1906	1907	1908	1909	1910	1911	1912	1913	1914	1915	1916	1917	INDUSTRIAL CATEGORIES
Total	832	661	725	768	834	854	713	835	872	763	714	701	1005	1102	1468	1459	1657	2086	2338	2397	2306	2146	2681	2275	2368	2328	2269	2374	2460	3098	3166	Total
A	163	49	44	51	55	51	37	62	70	94	66	37	116	118	114	149	186	209	193	145	152	241	353	168	137	117	114	265	134	175	360	A
AA	1				2	3	1	5			2		1	8	1	1	1	3	5	5	1	1	2	1	1	2	1		2	4	1	AA
aaa					1			3						6	1	1				1				1						2		aaa
aab																						1										aab
aac						3							1	2			1	2	3	4									2	1	1	aac
aad	1				1			2			2							1	1				1									aad
aae																							1		1					1		aae
aaf							1												1		1					2	1					aaf
AB	14	18	12	9	16	17	14	24	9	12	17	7	15	29	25	46	75	55	67	42	55	40	44	46	43	40	29	28	28	54	188	AB
AC	132	17	22	32	21	13	11	18	47	74	33	19	91	55	60	80	82	116	83	64	60	166	279	97	67	54	54	218	73	82	102	AC
aca																											1					aca
acb	132	17	22	32	21	13	11	18	47	74	33	19	91	55	60	80	82	116	83	64	60	166	279	97	67	54	53	218	73	82	102	acb
AD	9	4	4	7	8	7	7	6	7	5	5	5	1	7	8	6	9	5	11	6	7	10	7	6	6	8	12	10	13	11	33	AD
ada	7	4	2	7	6	7	6	5	5	5	4	1	1	4	6	4	7	4	11	4	6	8	4	4	5	6	7	6	8	5	24	ada
adb	2		2		2		1	1	2		1	4		3	2	2	2	1		2	1	2	3	2	1	2	5	4	5	6	9	adb
AE	7	10	6	3	8	11	4	9	7	3	9	6	8	19	20	16	19	30	27	28	29	24	21	18	20	13	18	9	18	24	36	AE
A/B	1				2								1		1			5	1		4	1				1				2		A/B
B	295	313	337	387	427	451	379	418	399	353	330	335	425	501	627	657	730	1018	1124	1108	1017	937	1062	936	1019	917	845	811	821	1021	936	B
BA	22	21	26	15	51	68	62	67	40	25	30	33	42	48	58	54	73	95	89	79	100	84	97	96	81	82	72	74	78	75	69	BA
baa	1		2	1	4	1	1	3	1	2	1	3	3	1	5	4	8	5	12	8	11	13	14	7	9	7	10	9	8	12	15	baa
bab			1		2	5	4	3	2	5	2	2		7	7	7	7	11	13	8	13	11	19	16	12	15	14	11	13	4	7	bab
bac	1	4	5		1	4	6	8	6	5	1	7	10	7	4	3	9	24	5	7	14	9	6	10	6	9	4	4	1	8	3	bac
bad		3	3		1	4	3	4	1				4	2	5	1	7	5	5	2	8	2	7	2	9	5	6	4	2	3	8	bad
bae	5	9	8	4	13	9	8	15	7	4	10	7	5	17	13	16	19	26	17	16	15	15	21	22	16	14	11	10	17	11	14	bae
baf	12	4	2	4	27	42	36	27	19	7	13	6	13	10	18	16	13	16	19	26	23	25	20	25	14	17	18	20	26	25	14	baf
bag	1							1				2	1					1	2	3	4		1	3	2	1	1			1	1	bag
bah	1	1	5	6	2	2	4	5	4	2	3	5	5	4	4	3	9	5	12	4	8	5	3	4	4	4	5	6	4	8	3	bah
bai	1				1	1		1				1	1		2	4	1	2	4	5	4	4	6	7	9	10	3	10	7	3	4	bai
BB	16	10	10	8	14	13	8	10	8	11	11	9	13	15	17	22	22	27	38	26	14	13	15	10	18	18	9	10	12	8	7	BB
bba	3	4	5	6	10	7	4	2	4	6	5	5	3	7	6	15	8	11	20	9	7			1	3	4	1	3	1		1	bba
bbb	12	5	2			3	2	1	1	2	1	2	3	3	3	4	6	5	7	7	3	4	4	5	6	5		1	1	3	2	bbb
bbc	1	1	1	1				2		2			1	3	1	1	1	4	3	2			1		2	1	1	1	1			bbc
bbd			2		2	2	2	2	3	1	3	1	6	2	5	2	5	7	6	7	2	9	6	4	4	6	6	4	4	3	3	bbd
bbe				1	2	1		3			2	1			2		2		2	1	2		4		3	2	1	1	5	2	1	bbe
BC	2	1	3	7	1	2	3	2	1	2	2	2	2	7	10	10	5	10	14	17	15	8	10	13	3	7	12	8	3	7	3	BC
BD	1	8	5	4	7	5	2	3	6	3	4	3	9	10	10	6	8	10	7	11	12	9	7	10	11	13	4	8	10	9	14	BD
bda			2	1	1										1			2		1	1	1					1			1	1	bda
bdb		2		1	1	2		1	3		2		2	1	1	3	2	4	2	2	2		2	2	1	1		1	1	1	6	bdb
bdd																													1			bdd
bde	1	2				2	1			1		1	2	3	2	1	1		2	5	3	2	4	3	5	7	1	4	2			bde
bdf																1			2		2	1	1	2	1				1			bdf
bdg				1	1						1		1	1	1	1	2	2		1	1	1			1	1					3	bdg
bdh														1			1			1		1			2	1			1	2	2	bdh
bdi		3	2	1	3	1	1	1		2	1	1	3	3	2		1		1		1	1		1		1	1	2		3	1	bdi
bdj		1	1		1			1	3			1	1	1	3		1	2		1	2	2		2	1	2	1	1	4	2	1	bdj
BE	1	4	2	2	5	4	3	8	5	7	5	7	11	12	18	24	27	33	36	41	38	39	31	37	38	36	56	35	46	45	23	BE
bea		3	1	1		2	2	4				1	2	5	5	7	3	5	15	6	1	6	1	7	4	7	7	4	10	6	5	bea
beb	1								1	1				2	1		5	6	3	5	12	7	6	7	7	5	6	4	9	5	2	beb
bec					1										1					1	2			1		1				1		bec
bed						1	1	1	2	2	1	1	2	1	2		3	2	1	6	3	2	1	6	5	3	3	2	2	4	1	bed
bee				1	1			1	1	1		3	1	2	3	3	4	6	2	6	7	8	5	6	3	4	6	2	6	3	2	bee
bef		1	1		3	1		2	1	3	4	2	6	2	6	14	12	14	15	17	13	16	18	10	19	16	34	23	19	26	13	bef
BF	7	2	10	8	12	12	11	16	9	10	13	8	14	17	24	24	14	24	21	16	20	16	14	12	18	16	10	6	8	15	9	BF
bfa	1		1			1	1	2	1		1	1		1	6	1	2	3	4	2	3	3	3	1	1		1		1	3	2	bfa
bfb	5	1	5	6	7	8	5	10	6	9	7	6	8	12	13	13	9	14	13	7	8	8	7	7	12	7	7	3	2	7	5	bfb
bfc	1	1	4	2	5	3	5	4	2	1	5	1	6	4	5	10	3	7	4	7	9	5	4	4	5	9	2	3	5	5	2	bfc
BG		2	1	2		4		3	4	1	5	5	4	10	7	2	6	9	16	13	9	9	11	15	15	16	20	22	32	46	35	BG
bga						2		1	2	1		1						2	5	3	6	2	3	6	5	7	11	13	23	25	13	bga
bgb		2	1	2		2		2	2		5	4	4	10	7	2	6	7	11	10	3	7	8	9	10	9	9	9	9	21	22	bgb
BH	7	9	18	17	25	13	16	10	9	15	10	10	13	22	34	24	41	46	59	62	48	54	33	37	34	27	21	22	10	19	7	BH
bha	1	1	6	5	4		4	3	1	2		2	1	7	8	4	5	7	13	8	11	14	8	8	7	3	3	7	1	6	2	bha
bhb	3	5	7	5	11	11	4	3	3	3	4	3	4	5	4	5	3	7	7	11	6	7	6	2	5	10	1	2	3	7	3	bhb
bhc	3	3	5	7	10	2	8	4	5	10	6	5	8	10	22	15	33	32	39	43	31	33	19	27	22	14	17	13	6	6	2	bhc
BI	17	19	18	27	21	34	22	21	20	20	11	11	21	21	35	46	43	45	47	35	53	41	45	37	42	42	35	34	29	33	13	BI
bia	10	11	13	18	12	12	11	9	10	15	5	6	10	8	17	25	23	21	23	12	22	18	25	20	18	19	15	21	19	17	8	bia
bib	3	6	2	7	4	2	8	6	5	2	3		3	4	5	8	5	15	11	9	14	13	11	3	8	10	8	4	4	4	2	bib
bic	4	2	3	2	5	20	3	6	5	3	3	5	8	9	13	13	15	9	13	14	17	10	9	14	16	13	12	9	6	12	3	bic
BJ	14	8	9	8	8	5	8	9	6	3	4	9	11	3	6	8	14	17	21	18	15	11	10	8	12	10	10	6	14	13	6	BJ
BK	24	26	18	40	36	42	44	41	49	39	35	39	37	48	50	56	66	78	84	88	83	72	96	68	92	78	61	67	59	74	73	BK
BM	16	28	14	21	25	27	32	24	33	27	29	26	42	42	52	52	59	67	82	83	67	72	77	69	82	73	72	89	77	94	63	BM
bma	3	6		5	2	4	7	3	6	3	2	1	2	6	12	5	9	7	10	12	11	16	13	5	18	10	17	14	10	8	7	bma
bmb	3	2	2	2	3	4	4	2	3	5	2	2	4	7	8	4	4	6	6	3	5	7	2	7	3	5	3	3	2		5	bmb
bmc	2	10	4	9	11	10	9	9	9	9	12	10	25	12	17	29	28	30	46	40	32	25	38	30	32	31	25	38	30	30	21	bmc
bme		1	1		2		3	2	3	1		3	2	2		1	4	6	4	3	1	2	2	2	3	4	3	3		3	1	bme
bmf	3	3	2			1	1		1		1	1			1			1	1									1			1	bmf
bmg								1																		1				1		bmg
bmh	4	2	3	3	3	4	4	5	6	7	8	6	7	9	8	7	7	11	10	16	14	12	12	14	11	9	12	14	18	19	11	bmh
bmi	1	4	2	2	4	4	4	2	5	2	4	3	2	6	6	6	7	6	5	9	4	10	10	11	15	13	12	16	17	33	17	bmi
BN	5	2	3	2	3	2	1	2	2	3	4		2	3	6	2	2	3	4	6	2	4	3	3	10	5	4	4	6	7	8	BN
bna	4	1	3	2	3	2				2	3		1	1	1		2	3	3	5	2	4	1	2	7	3	3	4	5	6	6	bna
bnb	1	1					1	2	2	1	1		1	2	5	2			1	1			2	1	3	2	1		1	1	2	bnb
BP	29	32	34	45	44	53	24	28	29	24	23	23	40	36	36	70	68	107	107	103	91	77	114	76	77	54	51	42	45	49	38	BP
bpa	8	5	13	22	26	26	9	10	9	8	6	7	18	13	8	32	15	32	28	32	27	22	31	20	19	11	9	8	11	13	11	bpa
bpb	1	6	2	7	5	8	1	7	4	7	6	8	6	7	10	11	12	12	9	9	12	4	8	6	7	5	4	5	4	2	6	bpb
bpc	11	13	11	5	7	6	5	3	5	2	3		7	8	5	7	5	14	13	15	7	8	15	7	13	5	14	6	4	13	6	bpc
bpd		1	1	1					1	1	1	1	1	2	1	1	1	2	1	3	3	2	2	1		1	1			1		bpd
bpe	1	3	1	3	2	3	1	4	6	2	3		2	2	3	7	12	22	20	18	18	18	22	13	17	13	11	7	8	7	10	bpe
bpf	5	2	4	4	1	5	2		1	1	2	1	2	1	3	7	12	6	12	11	14	16	13	7	10	8	5	6	4	3	2	bpf
bpg	3	2	2	3	3	5	6	4	3	3	2	6	4	3	6	5	11	19	24	15	10	7	23	22	11	11	7	10	14	10	3	bpg
BQ	51	44	49	49	48	39	38	53	49	40	37	36	45	71	68	67	70	112	130	130	116	84	107	101	105	99	84	74	67	111	100	BQ
bqa	7	3	6	2	11	4	1	5	8	6	4	2	8	8	6	8	6	2	5	5	12	8	9	2	4	4	5	4	2	6	3	bqa
bqb	2		1	1	5	1	2	2	2	2		2	2	2	2	3	1	2	4	8	3	6	4	5	3	4		6	1	6	3	bqb
bqc	1			1	2	3	3	3	1	1		1	1	1	4			4	1	2	1	1	1	2				1	1	2		bqc
bqd	6	11	6	9	3	6	6	9	6	7	7	7	5	7	11	7	13	11	25	24	14	15	18	19	31	16	19	16	15	19	12	bqd

Ohio Business Incorporations under General Laws, 1856–1930 (cont.)

Industrial Categories	1887	1888	1889	1890	1891	1892	1893	1894	1895	1896	1897	1898	1899	1900	1901	1902	1903	1904	1905	1906	1907	1908	1909	1910	1911	1912	1913	1914	1915	1916	1917	Industrial Categories
bqe	10	9	18	15	11	9	11	13	18	1	11	5	16	19	15	17	18	40	39	23	29	26	33	23	20	31	21	19	13	17	25	bqe
bqf	25	18	17	21	11	14	14	19	13	23	15	18	11	28	29	29	31	53	48	64	52	28	40	46	42	40	34	25	31	55	56	bqf
bqg		3	1		5	2	1	2	1			1	2	6	1	3	1		8	4	5		2	4	5	4	5	3	4	6	1	bqg
BR	10	8	6	11	7	5	10	4	8	7	13	6	9	16	18	19	17	24	32	32	30	24	42	29	34	33	45	38	25	43	38	BR
bra			1		1			1			2			1	1	1	1	2	1	1	2		1	1			1	3		3		bra
brb		1	1	2	2		2	1	4	1	3		3	1	1	2	4	1	7	4	2	1	9	4	5	4	9	5	2	1	2	brb
brc	10	7	4	9	4	5	8	2	4	6	8	6	6	14	16	16	12	21	24	27	26	23	32	24	29	29	35	30	23	39	36	brc
BS	1	4	7	8	10	8	9	16	12	11	11	6	12	6	21	13	18	28	39	29	28	27	35	30	36	28	18	29	39	33	51	BS
bsa																	1		1	4		1	2	5	1	3	1	1	5	11	12	bsa
bsb																									1							bsb
bsc	1			2	1		1	1	2				1		2	1	1	1	6		1	7	1		6	6		6	2	6	10	bsc
bsd		4	7	6	9	8	8	15	10	11	11	6	11	6	19	12	16	27	32	25	27	19	32	25	28	19	17	22	32	16	29	bsd
BT	29	38	49	52	45	50	34	36	39	37	24	41	41	33	63	59	79	110	122	125	126	113	117	114	104	108	101	91	98	135	167	BT
bta	4	5	8	7	3	8	5	3	6	7	2	9	3	7	6	8	18	12	16	19	19	23	19	21	12	18	8	10	6	14	18	bta
btb	12	12	10	12	9	10	5	7	6	4	7	14	10	9	18	10	15	16	30	29	37	24	23	19	15	20	24	16	26	40	47	btb
btc			4	4	2	2	2	1			2	3	8	3	8	4	5	5	8	11	3	5	9	6	7	5	12	11	10	21	45	btc
btd	2	4	4	6	5	5	4	6	5	6	3	3	3	5	7	10	14	11	10	4	14	4	15	14	19	13	12	11	11	9	7	btd
bte	2		4	1	3		2	2	2	1		2	4	2	1	5	5	6	15	7	6	9	9	9	4	4	2	2	4	3	5	bte
btf	2	12	7	8	6	7	3	2	6	5	1	3	2	1	9	7	7	14	12	12	2	8	8	4	6	10	9	9	7	8	13	btf
btg	2	3	3	2	6	8	2	6	3		2	1	3	1	2	3	4	14	13	19	12	18	12	8	7	12	11	7	6	8	4	btg
bth	2		2	4	2	2	2	2	6	3	1		3	1		3		3	8	5	10	5	9	7	8	12	9	10	8	2	5	bth
bti	3	2	7	8	9	8	9	7	5	11	6	6	5	4	12	9	11	29	10	19	23	17	13	26	26	14	14	15	20	30	23	bti
BU									1		1	1	1	6	13	6	8	15	25	30	22	26	40	51	46	38	44	26	49	69	84	BU
bua																													1	1	2	bua
bub									1		1	1	1	6	13	6	8	15	25	30	22	26	40	51	46	38	44	26	48	68	82	bub
BV	10	14	20	20	27	26	13	23	25	25	22	16	20	25	20	27	20	39	29	19	20	20	17	17	25	20	10	14	7	10	21	BV
bva	2	4	4	5	1	5	7	5	5	2	6	1	5	1	6	5	2	6	7	4	4	8	8	6	6	5	5	1	3	3	6	bva
bvb																				1	2		2	3	8	4	3	1	1	2	10	bvb
bvc		1	1					2	1			1	2		2			4	2	2	2	3	1	1		2	1	2		2	2	bvc
bvd			1	2	3	9	2	5	12	14	7	5	3	4	2	1			1			1	1		2			4	1		2	bvd
bve	8	9	14	13	23	11	4	11	7	8	9	9	10	18	8	20	18	29	19	12	12	8	5	7	9	8	1	6	2	3		bve
bvf						1				1				2	2	1										1					1	bvf
BW	18	16	19	25	20	21	14	27	29	22	18	30	21	25	49	31	38	71	62	96	48	70	89	51	90	64	54	52	52	70	61	BW
bwa	3		5	8	4	2	1	6	1	3	4	5	6	4	18	4	11	13	11	26	7	9	10	5	15	5	9	3	4	7	5	bwa
bwb	15	15	14	17	16	19	13	21	28	19	14	25	15	21	30	27	27	57	50	70	41	58	78	45	74	58	43	49	43	57	50	bwb
bwc		1													1			1	1			3	1	1	1	1	2		5	6	6	bwc
BX	15	17	16	16	18	18	25	15	15	21	18	14	15	25	12	35	32	48	60	49	60	64	52	52	46	50	52	60	55	56	46	BX
C	164	96	123	106	94	89	83	104	116	69	90	106	163	178	249	197	217	180	218	215	146	116	139	116	101	106	105	94	116	131	131	C
CA	77	48	67	67	58	61	67	48	71	40	46	42	78	83	161	104	108	94	103	111	75	50	76	63	55	71	72	48	60	94	104	CA
caa	44	22	28	35	17	25	26	15	25	13	13	10	17	15	41	25	31	16	10	15	13	2	8	4	7	3	3	3	5	4	4	caa
cac	20	12	18	15	24	20	22	22	28	14	18	17	44	37	99	54	57	30	42	51	25	13	19	18	9	12	9	6	8	2	1	cac
cad			1	1										1	2								1				1		6	2	5	cad
cae																					1	3	2	1				1			2	cae
caf	1			1		1				1								1	2			3	7	12	9	9	9	5	8	14	11	caf
cag																															4	cag
cah	2	5	6	3	5	5	5	5	5	2	3	6	5	9	6	13	15	24	31	20	21	15	28	14	17	32	41	18	19	34	58	cah
cai																		1						1	1						2	cai
caj	3	3	3	1	1						1		1			2								2		1		2			2	caj
cak	3	3	6	5	8	5	5	3	5	7	2	5	5	10	8	8	2	12	14	17	11	9	6	5	4	4	4	5	5	16	5	cak
cam															1			1	1	1	1											cam
can													1				1	3								1			1			can
cap	4	3	3	4	3	2	4	2	5		2		2	8	4	1	1	4	3	7	2	3	3	4	5	8	2	6	3	4	3	cap
caq			2	2		3	5	1	3	3	7	4	3	3		1	1	2			1	2	2	2	3	1	3	2	5	18	7	caq
CB	5	3	2	2	5	4	2	26	29	15	28	40	52	68	56	52	69	62	80	66	39	27	24	24	5	7	8	9	8	11	2	CB
cba		1					2	23	22	14	26	36	46	67	54	50	67	61	77	64	38	27	24	24	5	6	6	9	8	11	2	cba
cbb	3	1	2	1	2	2		1	1		2	2	3	1						1							2					cbb
cbd	2	1		1	3	2		2	6	1		2	3		2	2	2	1	3	1	1					1						cbd
CC	82	45	54	37	31	24	14	30	16	14	16	24	33	27	32	41	40	24	35	38	32	39	39	29	41	28	25	37	48	26	25	CC
cca	19	27	40	22	20	11	8	21	11	5	9	12	17	14	14	16	24	12	18	14	22	22	16	8	24	15	16	13	20	18	11	cca
ccb	44	13	9	9	4	8	3	4	4	5	5	8	11	5	2	12	13	5	4	11	6	13	9	13	6	8	5	22	14	5	9	ccb
ccc	11	4	3	3	2	2	2	2		2	1	2	3	2	4	4			3	2	3	2	5	7	5	1	2	2	3		3	ccc
ccd	2			1	2								1	1		1	1	2	3	1				1	1	1			2			ccd
cce			1	1	1		1								1												1					cce
ccf			1		1	1		1		1				3	4	2	1	1	2	1		1	1		2	2			9	1		ccf
ccg	6	1		1	1	2		2	1	1	1	2	1	2	7	6	1	4	5	9	1	1	8		3	1	1			2	2	ccg
D	8	3	5	9	10	24	13	13	9	8	17	10	19	10	19	18	17	17	15	21	25	21	31	31	31	35	27	14	27	45	44	D
DA	8	2	5	7	6	19	9	10	7	5	8	8	13	10	13	15	9	6	5	11	17	15	15	17	24	23	14	9	21	37	36	DA
DB		1			3	4	3	3	1	3	4	1	6		6	3	6	9	8	7	5	5	12	10		5	6	4	4	6	8	DB
DC				2	1	1	1		1		5	1					2	2	2	3	3	1	4	4	7	7	7	1	2	2		DC
E	46	32	41	37	55	53	74	73	79	79	41	60	77	72	118	101	117	191	237	286	312	289	364	341	349	388	437	425	497	620	663	E
EA	9	2	8	12	8	8	6	11	8	15	6	7	10	9	16	17	21	18	25	19	25	21	62	38	57	63	50	41	34	34	28	EA
EB																								1	4	1			1			EB
EC																							2			1				1		EC
ED	3	5	6	3	13	8	14	6	16	12	8	8	8	9	14	15	17	32	34	42	37	37	38	39	38	54	60	52	55	46	94	ED
EE	1		1		2	2	2	3	8	2	1	3	3	3	5	4	6	8	6	11	12	10	6	14	4	5	12	7	11	18	11	EE
EF			3	2	2	1	1	3	4	8	2	10	2	4	16	3	11	14	35	31	27	38	43	30	42	32	53	62	66	59	68	EF
EG		1	2	1		1	4		3	1		3	4	1	3	3	2	8	10	10	15	13	15	19	15	13	20	24	21	23	26	EG
EH				1	1	1	1		1		1	2	1	1	4	1	2	7	2	9	4	12	12	9	9	10	13	9	14	16	23	EH
EI												1		1		1		2		6	4	12	38	45	44	43	45	51	77	134	134	EI
EJ																											2	2	2	6	4	EJ
EK	5	5	3	2	6	8	4	5	15	4	1	2	7	4	13	16	13	16	17	26	23	12	20	21	15	19	19	18	10	12	14	EK
EM	3	5	5	3	3	5	5	8	7	11	6	7	11	7	8	8	8	14	15	23	37	24	24	25	23	31	33	35	43	44	46	EM
EN	4	2			2	2	6	1	1	3	3	1	1		1		1	1	1	4	3	6	6		4	6	6	11	7	9	32	EN
EP	12	8	11	9	11	13	24	26	12	15	8	18	18	24	20	17	18	45	47	45	62	62	72	76	77	92	113	102	118	171	129	EP
EQ	9	4	2	4	7	4	7	10	4	8	5	7	12	9	18	16	18	26	45	60	63	42	26	24	17	18	11	11	38	47	54	EQ
F	40	47	46	38	60	78	35	59	81	69	66	50	75	75	89	88	117	174	168	204	211	186	277	201	248	257	265	265	313	336	300	F
FA	5	7	4	3	11	18	5	10	10	12	6	7	16	13	20	18	27	38	40	45	37	34	53	43	38	53	53	54	62	74	69	FA
faa		6	2	1	3	9	3	2	3	8	2	2	3	5	8	3	9	11	18	13	16	13	14	18	3	14	21	19	24	28	25	faa
fab	3	1	2	1	5	5	1	7	2	3	2	2	11	7	10	14	14	23	17	22	14	17	24	22	26	19	19	18	19	27	22	fab
fac	1				1	1				1	1	1					1		1	2	1		2			1	1	3	1	3	3	fac
fad	1			1	2	3	1	1	5		1	2	2	1	2	1	3	4	4	8	6	4	13	3	9	19	12	14	18	16	19	fad
FB	8	9	5	6	7	5	5	7	9	5	7	9	12	2	12	11	12	20	19	18	17	13	35	24	32	40	37	37	51	33	29	FB
fba			1	1	3	1	1	3	3	2	1	2	4		3	4	3	4	3	3	4	2	10	2	6	17	15	10	16	9	10	fba
fbb	8	9	4	5	4	4	4	4	6	3	6	7	8	2	9	7	9	16	16	15	13	11	25	22	26	23	22	27	35	24	19	fbb
FC																		3	6	7	14	7	15	9	13	17	21	21	30	40	51	FC

INDUSTRIAL CATEGORIES	1887	1888	1889	1890	1891	1892	1893	1894	1895	1896	1897	1898	1899	1900	1901	1902	1903	1904	1905	1906	1907	1908	1909	1910	1911	1912	1913	1914	1915	1916	1917	INDUSTRIAL CATEGORIES
FD	24	30	31	26	35	44	20	34	46	37	43	24	30	35	41	39	49	71	69	100	106	96	114	75	129	110	127	107	145	142	114	FD
fda																					3	6	6	3	4	6	8	7	9	28	13	fda
fdb																					2	4	5	1	10	7	25	17	21	23	14	fdb
fdc	5	4	7	2	4	7	3	5	6	4	4	1	4	3	2	1	8	8	5	17	13	15	13	14	16	16	20	29	26	15	11	fdc
fdd	19	26	24	24	31	37	17	29	40	33	39	23	26	32	39	38	41	63	64	83	88	71	90	57	99	81	74	54	89	76	76	fdd
FE	3	1	6	3	7	11	5	8	16	15	10	10	17	25	16	20	29	42	34	34	37	36	60	50	36	37	27	46	25	47	37	FE
G	102	109	111	115	112	89	55	75	90	69	70	59	89	125	203	179	207	176	256	298	312	249	309	337	344	375	334	339	384	590	520	G
GA	9	6	18	26	25	24	15	11	12	9	12	18	21	41	56	42	67	51	54	62	68	37	27	28	29	18	22	32	29	40	19	GA
GB	80	99	84	77	75	52	31	27	37	20	21	20	21	18	20	23	13	10	9	12	20	14	19	15	16	13	10	15	23	27	14	GB
GC		1		1	2		1	1	3	1	1	1			1	2	4	2	2	3	7	4	3	2	2	2	1	6	8	10	11	GC
GD															1						1	1	1									GD
GF			1	1							1		1		1	2	7	4	2	1	3	7	10	3	2	5	7	4	6	18	15	GF
GG	1		2			2		3			1		1		3	2	3	2	10	8	4	7	6	4	10	10	8	6	2	8	7	GG
GH	1			1						1			2		1					1	2	1	2	1		4	2	2	5	3	6	GH
GI	4	1			2				3	2	2	2	3	1	8	9	12	6	10	19	19	20	13	21	24	33	12	14	12	19	9	GI
GJ	7	2	6	6	7	11	8	32	35	35	31	18	39	65	111	90	91	86	160	167	173	148	208	238	231	272	258	238	280	436	400	GJ
GK				3	1			1		1	1		1		1	9	10	15	9	25	15	10	20	25	30	18	14	22	19	29	39	GK
H	4	7	6	6	6	8	16	16	12	12	18	24	27	21	38	34	39	62	74	91	84	71	84	84	82	78	79	100	101	126	158	H
HA		1	1				2			1			1	1	5	3	2	2		1		1	1		2							HA
HB	4	6	5	6	6	8	14	16	12	11	18	24	26	20	33	31	37	60	74	90	84	70	83	84	80	78	79	100	101	126	158	HB
I	3	2	8	11	9	4	12	6	8	5	5	3	5	1	5	11	5	22	21	15	12	18	25	29	24	15	19	16	27	19	22	I
J	6	3	4	8	4	7	9	9	8	5	11	8	8	1	[illegible]	25	22	32	31	14	31	17	37	32	33	39	44	45	40	33	32	J

INDUSTRIAL CATEGORIES	1918	1919	1920	1921	1922	1923	1924	1925	1926	1927	1928	1929	1930	INDUSTRIAL CATEGORIES
Total	2151	4352	4643	3855	4233	4050	3640	4051	3893	3808	4151	4148	3872	Total
A	229	226	374	256	197	185	136	137	96	113	119	130	94	A
AA	2	2	4	1	1		1	1		1	2			AA
aaa			4				1							aaa
aab		1												aab
aac	1							1		1	2			aac
aad		1			1									aad
aae				1										aae
aaf	1													aaf
AB	128	64	118	87	75	87	53	42	41	37	34	26	23	AB
AC	66	136	223	143	102	84	71	76	42	57	66	81	56	AC
acb	66	136	223	143	102	84	71	76	42	57	66	81	56	acb
AD	9	13	11	10	6	2	4	7	7	6	7	11	8	AD
ada	7	8	8	9	4	2	4	4	6	5	5	8	8	ada
adb	2	5	3	1	2			3	1	1	2	3		adb
AE	24	11	18	15	13	12	7	11	6	12	10	12	7	AE
A/B		2	1											A/B
B	729	1536	1541	1226	1389	1145	948	1016	950	981	1044	988	816	B
BA	51	186	159	117	136	94	85	87	80	85	97	97	81	BA
baa	10	46	42	24	31	20	13	22	25	19	23	34	15	baa
bab	7	44	33	24	24	20	20	19	14	17	20	14	7	bab
bac	1	7	2	4	2		4	1	6	2	2	3	2	bac
bad	4	10	4	6	6	6	3	4	4	3		1	11	bad
bae	8	22	21	18	21	8	16	5	6	9	11	5	1	bae
baf	16	36	24	27	33	24	22	17	9	10	20	16	20	baf
bag	1		4	1	1			1						bag
bah	2	8	11	5	11	5	2	8	5	7	6	8	6	bah
bai	2	13	18	8	7	11	5	10	11	18	15	16	19	bai
BB	7	36	16	11	15	8	14	20	10	9	17	22	15	BB
bba			1		1									bba
bbb				1	1			1						bbb
bbc			1											bbc
bbd	4	22	9	7	7	7	10	18	10	5	14	14	11	bbd
bbe	3	14	5	3	6	1	4	1		4	3	8	4	bbe
BC	1	6	15	10	7	7	4	8	6	3	3	5	2	BC
BD	17	21	14	15	16	13	17	17	15	11	15	10	7	BD
bda	1	3		2	1	2		1	1	1				bda
bdb	2	2	1	1	3	2			1	1	1			bdb
bdc							1	1				1		bdc
bdd			1											bdd
bde	5	6	3	5	7	3	9	7	8	4	5	2	3	bde
bdf	1		1	1	1	1	2	2	2	1	4	3	2	bdf
bdg		2	1			1		2		1	2		1	bdg
bdh	1	4		1			1	1						bdh
bdi	3	1				2	2	1	2	1	3	2		bdi
bdj	4	3	7	5	4	2	2	2	1	2		2	1	bdj
BE	33	62	57	76	67	47	43	73	57	62	42	40	43	BE
bea	4	10	8	4	8	11	11	14	5	5	9	3	11	bea
beb	8	9	4	10	3	3	10	12	9	7	6	7	4	beb
bec		2	4	2	1		2	3	3	3	1	4	4	bec
bed	1	2	1	3	2	2	4	5	9	5	1	3	1	bed
bee	6	2	6	6	10	4	4	3	4	9		6	6	bee
bef	14	37	34	51	43	27	12	36	27	33	25	17	17	bef
BF	13	14	21	14	14	20	21	11	14	10	8	9	6	BF
bfa	1	1	3	2										bfa
bfb	7	4	7	6	7	13	16	7	5	7	6	6	4	bfb
bfc	5	9	11	6	7	7	5	4	9	3	2	3	2	bfc
BG	25	90	49	49	59	39	31	29	17	25	18	11	13	BG
bga	12	60	24	22	25	13	7	5	6	10	6	5	4	bga
bgb	13	30	25	27	34	26	24	24	11	15	12	6	9	bgb
BH	5	23	40	19	36	33	26	18	18	20	13	10	6	BH
bha	4	9	7	4	10	3	2	1	3	2	2	3	4	bha
bhb		5	5	2	8	4	4	3	7	6	5	5	1	bhb
bhc	1	9	28	13	18	26	20	14	8	12	6	2	1	bhc
BI	19	44	67	42	45	48	38	40	53	51	49	40	26	BI
bia	13	26	36	25	29	24	21	26	34	37	31	23	13	bia
bib	2	3	5	4	2	3	3	2	2	3	5	5	3	bib
bic	4	15	26	13	14	21	14	12	17	11	13	12	10	bic

INDUSTRIAL CATEGORIES	1918	1919	1920	1921	1922	1923	1924	1925	1926	1927	1928	1929	1930	INDUSTRIAL CATEGORIES
BJ	6	15	19	10	12	29	10	10	11	10	14	10	8	BJ
BK	56	67	96	64	117	95	89	70	79	90	84	84	65	BK
BM	57	136	133	114	100	104	96	94	73	94	100	85	91	BM
bma	6	20	23	23	20	21	18	23	11	18	13	8	12	bma
bmb	4	7	10	3	8	7	5	5	5	6	7	2	5	bmb
bmc	18	52	49	43	42	40	37	34	29	30	35	27	39	bmc
bme	1	4	5	1	7		3	1		2	3	3	2	bme
bmf											1	1		bmf
bmg			1		1	1				1		1	1	bmg
bmh	15	27	12	15	8	20	17	8	10	7	19	13	8	bmh
bmi	13	26	33	29	14	15	16	23	18	30	22	30	24	bmi
BN	10	14	17	16	16	17	11	20	11	9	10	14	11	BN
bna	7	13	14	14	12	12	11	17	10	8	8	12	8	bna
bnb	3	1	3	2	4	5		3	1	1	2	2	3	bnb
BP	38	69	64	55	70	57	40	48	44	40	49	41	27	BP
bpa	7	16	12	7	11	14	9	7	13	10	16	6	9	bpa
bpb	3	7	11	8	12	9	4	6	4	4	5	2	3	bpb
bpc	7	11	6	10	12	10	10	7	4	7	5	4	2	bpc
bpd			1		2		1	1	1					bpd
bpe	10	7	13	12	9	8	7	10	9	7	10	8	4	bpe
bpf	3	7	10	10	7	6	3	6	5		5	11	3	bpf
bpg	8	21	11	8	17	10	6	11	8	12	8	10	6	bpg
BQ	71	144	160	100	117	101	71	95	84	76	93	94	81	BQ
bqa	3	13	14	6	5	9	6	5	6	7	5	3	3	bqa
bqb		8	7	4	1	5		2	2	4	3	4	5	bqb
bqc		2	2	1	3			1			1	2	2	bqc
bqd	14	26	22	25	18	8	14	8	10	9	11	13	5	bqd
bqe	21	23	30	30	37	28	19	32	40	25	36	34	34	bqe
bqf	30	67	81	33	47	51	31	47	26	30	35	38	32	bqf
bqg	3	5	4	1	6		1			1	2			bqg
BR	35	61	106	53	61	63	40	42	44	39	59	46	37	BR
bra	2			2	1	1	1	2	1	3			1	bra
brb	1	4	9	6	11	11	6	6	4	6	8	6	3	brb
brc	32	57	97	45	49	51	33	34	39	30	51	40	33	brc
BS	21	56	58	76	117	58	62	85	59	59	56	70	39	BS
bsa	3	12	5	30	11	3	4	8	3	4	5	5	1	bsa
bsb				1	45	10	27	40	17	16	15	17	3	bsb
bsc		5	7	6	11	8	1	7	8	8	5	9	8	bsc
bsd	18	39	46	39	50	37	30	30	31	31	31	39	27	bsd
BT	134	190	169	151	127	100	84	82	117	117	103	93	90	BT
bta	15	16	18	15	16	11	8	10	11	9	21	10	9	bta
btb	26	54	41	31	24	27	14	21	30	29	17	18	18	btb
btc	34	29	28	10	10	7	4	6	13	6	9	15	10	btc
btd	7	10	14	17	9	10	10	8	1	7	8	5	3	btd
bte	5	6	8	6	5	5	8	2	4	13	5	3	4	bte
btf	18	23	11	15	7	6	3	4	9	4	5	6	5	btf
btg	2	6	6	7	10	8	3	8	3	5	7	5	6	btg
bth	1	7	4	16	11	7	12	2	12	13	8	4	5	bth
bti	26	39	39	34	35	19	22	21	34	31	23	27	30	bti
BU	29	108	104	83	79	78	45	48	44	30	42	32	19	BU
bua	1	3	1			1								bua
bub	28	105	103	83	79	77	45	48	44	30	42	32	19	bub
BV	12	11	13	5	7	7	4	6	7	15	20	33	14	BV
bva	3	3	5		3	1	2		1	3	1	2	4	bva
bvb	3	6	5	1	2	6	2	2	5	10	17	27	8	bvb
bvc	3	1	1					2	1	1	1	3	2	bvc
bvd	1	1			2			1						bvd
bve	1		1	4				1		1		1		bve
bvf	1		1								1			bvf
BW	41	109	86	76	108	76	65	70	63	75	89	87	69	BW
bwa	3	12	6	7	10	5	4	5	2	5	8	2	3	bwa
bwb	35	87	74	66	91	67	61	64	61	68	81	84	64	bwb
bwc	3	10	6	3	7	4		1		2		1	2	bwc
BX	48	74	78	70	63	51	52	43	44	51	63	55	66	BX
C	92	171	159	132	145	185	152	176	192	150	217	213	178	C
CA	71	125	113	84	109	149	107	139	143	113	180	180	141	CA
caa	2	1	1		6	4	6	3	4	1	3	1	1	caa
cac	2	3	1	1	2	3					3	4	5	cac

Ohio Business Incorporations under General Laws, 1856–1930 (concl.)

Industrial Categories	1918	1919	1920	1921	1922	1923	1924	1925	1926	1927	1928	1929	1930	Industrial Categories
cad	3	3	6	9	10	18	11	23	16	11	9	10	2	cad
cae	1	3	2	5	16	31	12	25	30	11	18	12	8	cae
caf	7	16	11	11	14	27	19	15	15	13	32	25	12	caf
cag	1	2	3		1	2	2	1	3	3	11	14	15	cag
cah	40	68	59	30	39	38	34	43	44	44	53	46	35	cah
cai		4	9	3	2	1	2	5	3	11	35	27	18	cai
caj						1						1	1	caj
cak	2	5	5	7	8	8	6	2	10	4	3	1	6	cak
can			3			1							2	can
cap	6	7	6	11	7	11	8	11	11	12	10	14	12	cap
caq	7	13	7	7	4	4	7	11	7	3	3	25	24	caq
CB	4	9	4	8	6	5	11	15	20	19	9	12	14	CB
cba	4	8	4	8	6	5	10	14	18	13	6	7	7	cba
cbc		1					1		2	6	3	5	7	cbc
cbd								1						cbd
CC	17	37	42	40	30	31	34	22	29	18	28	21	23	CC
cca	12	27	37	30	25	21	25	14	11	7	15	8	6	cca
ccb	2	6	3	4	2	4	5	6	7	5	8	5	14	ccb
ccc	2	3		2	1	2	1	1	4	3	4	5	2	ccc
ccd				3	1	1	1		5		1	1		ccd
ccf						1			1	2		1	1	ccf
ccg	1	1	2	1	1	2	2	1	1	1		1		ccg
D	49	75	70	86	60	71	67	54	50	36	50	52	58	D
DA	38	59	52	36	42	58	49	38	38	36	41	51	51	DA
DB	7	11	8	4	5	7	14	14	7		2	1	2	DB
DC	4	5	10	46	13	6	4	2	5		7		5	DC
E	477	783	885	776	823	811	742	927	985	888	1001	1048	1111	E
EA	17	42	43	35	40	28	30	55	73	51	72	71	61	EA
EB			1					1				1		EB
EC	1		3		1	1		1					1	EC
ED	63	136	184	97	82	88	62	95	85	100	97	100	121	ED
EE	13	21	31	31	32	35	29	26	39	24	30	41	48	EE
EF	48	68	50	81	83	86	88	113	89	105	99	110	124	EF
EG	13	20	17	23	33	34	25	28	49	46	39	50	44	EG
EH	20	31	20	27	30	21	50	52	58	46	79	73	77	EH
EI	104	201	194	180	197	163	158	214	217	185	223	196	183	EI
EJ	1	6	12	17	24	22	31	34	48	49	36	36	40	EJ
EK	10	19	24	21	24	39	29	22	16	17	24	14	21	EK

Industrial Categories	1918	1919	1920	1921	1922	1923	1924	1925	1926	1927	1928	1929	1930	Industrial Categories
EM	30	48	47	62	58	73	51	61	60	48	69	59	56	EM
EN	25	11	19	19	32	16	23	15	34	29	35	19	29	EN
EP	107	141	176	129	135	146	130	174	186	171	168	234	247	EP
EQ	25	39	64	54	52	59	36	36	31	17	30	44	59	EQ
F	183	423	408	379	409	362	393	419	437	471	463	455	506	F
FA	46	75	62	58	71	67	61	74	95	121	110	112	116	FA
faa	14	25	22	25	27	22	15	20	27	32	34	26	19	faa
fab	19	30	28	16	21	31	24	28	35	44	30	49	53	fab
fac		2	4	3	1	4		5	6	4	7	8	5	fac
fad	13	18	8	14	22	10	22	21	27	41	39	29	39	fad
FB	10	43	41	53	50	50	54	54	69	58	52	61	83	FB
fba	4	19	20	20	27	18	32	29	40	30	32	33	50	fba
fbb	6	24	21	33	23	32	22	25	29	28	20	28	33	fbb
FC	37	90	65	59	61	50	64	77	53	61	85	81	72	FC
FD	62	140	153	143	169	147	157	141	154	159	137	123	172	FD
fda	5	11	15	11	9	10	2	3	9	7	4	2	2	fda
fdb	10	14	6	1	3	9	11	8	1		3	2	3	fdb
fdc	8	27	25	30	43	25	20	19	37	54	44	38	43	fdc
fdd	39	88	107	101	114	103	124	111	107	98	86	81	124	fdd
FE	28	75	87	66	58	48	57	73	66	72	79	78	63	FE
G	285	911	932	744	987	1024	940	1058	888	836	909	928	844	G
GA	14	56	37	19	30	51	15	14	6	16	10	7	4	GA
GB	14	33	32	67	132	87	4	3	3	1	5	6	1	GB
GC	6	27	30	59	53	38	44	43	14	11	10	6	4	GC
GD		2		8	16	24	7	8	3	5	8	23	11	GD
GE		1	2	1	2	3	2	11	19	18	27	41	31	GE
GF	8	29	50	42	33	30	11	16	8	3	12	13	23	GF
GG	5	16	37	41	63	39	31	44	70	100	76	62	70	GG
GH	2	2	5	5	1	7	11	7	4	7	10	13	10	GH
GI	15	9	18	19	34	29	37	48	54	35	53	69	71	GI
GJ	198	675	626	409	547	667	725	816	672	612	656	627	580	GJ
GK	23	61	95	74	76	49	53	48	35	28	42	61	39	GK
H	67	146	156	159	164	174	176	186	238	250	251	252	176	H
HA						1							1	HA
HB	67	146	156	159	164	173	176	186	238	250	251	252	175	HB
I	16	30	51	28	19	37	36	28	34	42	54	46	50	I
J	24	49	66	69	40	56	50	50	23	41	43	36	39	J

Pennsylvania Business Incorporations under General Laws, 1888–1920*

Industrial Categories	'88	'89	'90	'91	'92	'93	'94	'95	'96	'97	'98	'99	'00	'01	'02	'03	'04
Total	477	717	667	572	760	604	578	573	530	540	484	687	854	1171	1530	1608	1345
A	52	74	76	51	69	49	50	39	41	36	23	51	104	104	135	167	117
AA	1	4	1		1				1	3		1	1	4	3	1	1
aaa	1	1	1														
aab																1	
aac		1			1									1	1		
aad		1							1	3		1					
aae														1			
aaf		1											1	2	2		1
AB	23	26	27	21	47	32	35	26	26	18	16	25	74	59	83	114	71
AC	20	36	31	12	7	4	4	1	7	4	2	7	9	15	15	21	21
aca										1						1	
acb	20	36	31	12	7	4	4	1	7	3	2	7	9	15	15	20	21
AD	5	8	15	16	10	10	4	11	6	10	4	16	15	22	23	22	19
ada	4	7	13	11	9	10	4	10	6	9	4	14	10	18	22	19	19
adb	1	1	2	5	1			1		1		2	5	4	1	3	
AE	3		2	2	4	3	7	1	1	1	1	2	5	4	11	9	5
B	187	243	255	288	324	285	261	280	268	265	253	376	399	525	637	645	559
BA	11	12	11	12	20	29	22	21	13	19	20	30	28	37	44	41	56
baa			1	2	1	1	1	2		4	1	2	2	10	5	6	7
bab		2		1	1	3	3	3	1	5	3		4	3	3	4	5
bac	2	1		2	4	1	1	1	2	2	1	3	6	1	6	9	14
bad		2	1			2	3	2	1					1	8	5	7
bae	4	2	3	2	6	4	3	5	4		1	9	2	5	5	5	9
baf	5	4	2	3	5	16	11	6	2	4	9	13	12	13	14	12	13
bag		1	2		1									1			
bah			2	2	1	1		2	1	2		2	2		2		1
bai					1	1			2	2	5	1		3	1		
BB	2	1	7	12	7	4	8	11	10	25	9	13	15	19	24	31	19
bba	1	1	7	11	7	2	8	10	8	22	7	11	14	13	13	17	9
bbb														5	6	9	7
bbc																	
bbd	1			1		2		1	2	3	2	2	1	1	4	4	1
bbe															1	1	2
BC	1		2	2	4	2		4	2	3	5	2	2	2	11	5	8
BD	17	10	19	16	16	14	11	16	12	16	19	25	28	40	56	57	42
bda	1			1	2		1		2	1		1				1	1
bdb	1		4	2	3	1	2		1		1	3	2	5	6	2	2
bdc	1		4	2			1	1	1	3	3	3	5	4	7	13	2
bdd							1										
bde	5	5	2		2	4	2	3	2	3	9	10	5	15	20	13	17
bdf			1	3				1	1			2	1	2		1	1
bdg	1		1	2	1	1		1	1	1	2			2	4	2	5
bdh						1		2	2	1			4	1	9	5	3
bdi		2		2	2	1			2	2	1		3	2	3	6	5
bdj	8	3	7	4	6	6	4	8		5	3	6	8	9	7	14	6
BE	2	3	5	3	5	2	1	1	2	9	2	5	6	6	14	8	8
bea	1	3	3		2	1				2	1	3	2	1	1	1	2
beb				1						2				1	1		
bec																	
bed										3						1	1
bee					2				1	1	1				2	2	1

Industrial Categories	'05	'06	'07	'08	'09	'10	'11	'12	'13	'14	'15	'16	'17	'18	'19	'20	Industrial Categories
Total	1469	1528	1611	1114	1517	1523	1658	1659	2095	1322	1366	1694	1958	1277	2297	2918	Total
A	103	115	96	68	92	85	72	104	116	97	102	124	453	237	158	310	A
AA	2	2	1			1		3	1	2		2			2		AA
aaa	1	1						1	1	1					2		aaa
aab		1	1														aab
aac								2				1					aac
aad	1																aad
aae												1					aae
aaf						1				1							aaf
AB	55	74	56	40	51	44	38	66	76	63	65	77	385	194	118	216	AB
AC	22	15	16	14	23	15	22	18	23	17	12	23	29	16	19	68	AC
aca																	aca
acb	22	15	16	14	23	15	22	18	23	17	12	23	29	16	19	68	acb
AD	19	20	19	10	15	22	11	14	14	11	20	19	18	16	17	15	AD
ada	19	20	18	9	11	19	10	11	13	9	19	19	15	15	17	13	ada
adb			1	1	4	3	1	3	1	2	1		3	1		2	adb
AE	5	4	4	4	3	3	1	3	2	4	5	3	21	11	2	11	AE
B	617	610	622	440	569	496	504	508	527	477	470	533	492	415	711	778	B
BA	52	32	31	38	37	42	36	51	49	49	44	45	48	34	106	99	BA
baa	6	6	3	5	5	4	7	11	7	9	13	10	9	8	36	27	baa
bab	7	7	6	6	7	8	7	8	5	4	5	4	9	1	11	14	bab
bac	10	2	2	3	1		4	2		3	1	5	1	2	1		bac
bad	6	6	8	8	4	7	2	3	5	5	1	2	3		3	5	bad
bae	11	5	3	4	6	5	4	9	11	3	3	7	4	7	12	15	bae
baf	6	4	5	9	11	9	7	15	17	16	16	11	16	12	27	23	baf
bag													1				bag
bah	1	1	2	2	3	5	4	1	1	5	3	4	4	3	7	11	bah
bai	5	1	2	1		4	1	2	3	4	2	2	1	1	9	4	bai
BB	23	27	30	15	10	17	21	16	12	16	7	11	11	8	18	16	BB
bba	14	15	13	6	4	10	7	9	4	6	4	3	1	3		2	bba
bbb	6	7	11	4	4	3	7	2	2	2		2	2	1	1	3	bbb
bbc									1								bbc
bbd	3	4	5	1	1	1	4	3	1	5	3	5	7	4	17	9	bbd
bbe		1	1	4	1	3	3	2	4	3		1	1			2	bbe
BC	19	7	6	4	5	4	8	10	9	3	6	6	8	7	8	13	BC
BD	46	55	70	28	81	53	62	44	64	43	43	66	52	75	127	92	BD
bda		1		2	2		1		2	1		5	1	1	1	2	bda
bdb	2	4	7	5	6	1	4	2	5	3	4	4	1	9	1	3	bdb
bdc	11	10	9	2	17	12	8	10	11	8	7	7	4		35	31	bdc
bdd			1														bdd
bde	16	15	25	12	27	19	20	11	17	13	14	20	33	34	48	29	bde
bdf	1	4	2	1	1	2	1	1			1					1	bdf
bdg	2	2	3		5	3	5	1	2	2	1	3	1		2	4	bdg
bdh	1	2	6		7	3	5	5	4	7	6	6	1	7	11	5	bdh
bdi	2	2	3	1	4	3	1		3	1	4	3	2	5	2	3	bdi
bdj	11	15	14	5	12	10	17	14	20	8	6	18	9	19	27	14	bdj
BE	10	14	25	16	20	18	20	31	25	24	25	39	23	24	29	39	BE
bea	2	2	5	4	4	2	3	2	1	6	4	13	3	3	3	14	bea
beb	2	5	11	3	4	6	9	9	10	7	10	12	6	7	9	7	beb
bec						1											bec
bed	1	1	1	1	2	1	1	2	2	3	1		1	1	2	1	bed
bee	2	1	2	2	2	4	3	2	2		3	1	2	3	4	1	bee

* Classification is based upon data cited in the Pennsylvania 1887–1921 section of App. 3.

INDUSTRIAL CATEGORIES	'88	'89	'90	'91	'92	'93	'94	'95	'96	'97	'98	'99	'00	'01	'02	'03	'04	'05	'06	'07	'08	'09	'10	'11	'12	'13	'14	'15	'16	'17	'18	'19	'20	INDUSTRIAL CATEGORIES
bef	1		2	2	1	1	1	1	1	1		2	4	4	10	4	4	3	5	6	6	8	4	4	16	10	8	7	13	11	10	11	16	bef
BF	7	10	6	11	14	10	8	3	9	7	10	7	10	15	14	12	23	14	13	18	14	14	15	10	14	20	6	19	8	8	5	17	24	BF
bfa	1	2	1	4	2	4	4	1	5	3	1	4	5	2	6	7	12	7	6	6	3	5	3		4	5		2	2	1	1	3	2	bfa
bfb	5	6	3	5	8	5	3		4	4	7	3	4	9	4	4	6	2	5	5	9	4	8	7	7	7	3	13	5	4	3	10	11	bfb
bfc	1	2	2	2	4	1	1	2			2		1	4	4	1	5	5	2	7	2	5	4	3	3	8	3	4	1	3	1	4	11	bfc
BG	1		1		1	1	3		1	1	1	1			1	2	1	3	3		2	3	3	4	2	5	4	5	6	3	3	10	5	BG
bga									1		1					1			1		1	3	1	1		3	3	4	1	1		5	1	bga
bgb	1		1		1	1	3			1		1			1	1	1	3	2		1		2	3	2	2	1	1	5	2	3	5	4	bgb
BH	10	21	11	10	12	7	11	11	8	10	15	11	11	27	39	33	29	39	40	27	23	11	24	20	22	23	14	22	7	9	9	11	28	BH
bha	6	1	2		2	1		2	1		1	1		6	9	9	5	13	16	10	7	3	6	10	8	12	5	2	2	4	4	4	6	bha
bhb		2	1	2	2	3	5	5	3	2	9	7	6	12	21	15	13	15	16	12	10	7	14	8	9	8	6	15	2	3	4	4	12	bhb
bhc	2	5	8	5	6	2	6	4	3	6	4	3	5	9	9	9	11	11	8	5	6	1	4	2	4	3	3	5	3	2	1	3	10	bhc
bhd	2	13		3	2	1			1	2	1														1									bhd
BI	2	7	4	10	16	18	11	10	16	6	9	12	18	18	19	33	34	26	26	24	16	33	22	16	14	26	17	12	19	21	11	23	24	BI
bia	1	6	2	6	6	11	2	7	7		4	5	11	9	7	10	14	14	13	9	4	16	11	9	8	14	10	4	8	13	5	8	11	bia
bib					3		1		1		2	1		2	5	4	1	2	5	2	2	7	4	2	3	3	2	4	3	2	2	2	1	bib
bic	1	1	2	4	7	7	8	3	8	6	3	6	7	7	7	19	19	10	8	13	10	10	7	5	3	9	5	4	8	6	4	13	12	bic
BJ	5	4	8	8	5	3	4	6	6	2	6	5	5	11	10	11	14	12	6	11	9	8	10	11	16	7	9	17	17	12	12	14	15	BJ
BK	10	23	23	26	25	19	23	20	24	26	13	23	40	24	42	55	46	44	51	49	34	43	31	40	41	42	45	36	39	33	25	38	50	BK
BM	13	10	16	18	27	23	13	16	18	19	23	35	17	39	45	53	26	36	41	32	39	45	45	29	29	33	29	43	36	35	20	55	59	BM
bma	4	4	2	2	4	5	2	1	2	7	3	5		3	4	6	3	4	9	6	3	4	5	7	7	4	3	8	3	4	3	2	6	bma
bmb	2	1	1	3	1	1		2	3		1	1	1	2	4	4	2	2	6	1	4	1	2	2		1	3	2	1		1	6	4	bmb
bmc	2	1	6	6	8	7	6	5	1	3	4	8	6	9	14	17	7	9	14	15	21	18	14	12	7	10	5	12	13	6	2	14	21	bmc
bme	1	1		4	2	1	1	1	3	1	3	3	1	3		2	1	2	1	1	1		2	1	1		2	3	1		3	3	1	bme
bmf			1						1									2	1									1		1		3	3	bmf
bmg								1																			1	1	1					bmg
bmh	3	2	4	3	12	9	2	6	4	7	8	16	6	18	17	18	11	11	5	5	4	14	12	7	6	12	9	12	6	12	6	12	7	bmh
bmi	1	1	2				2		4	1	4	2	3	4	6	6	2	6	5	4	6	8	10		8	6	6	4	11	12	5	15	17	bmi
BN	6	7	4	3	5	3	4	7	5	4	4	8	6	11	8	11	3	7	14	16	6	11	5	6	11	6	7	9	11	12	7	14	11	BN
bna	4	6	1		1	2	3	1	2	1	1		3	2	4			1	1	1	1		1	2	4	3	3	4	4	5	4	9	6	bna
bnb	2	1	3	3	4	1	1	6	3	3	3	8	3	9	4	11	3	6	13	15	5	11	4	4	7	3	4	5	7	7	3	5	5	bnb
BP	16	29	15	31	41	32	27	20	32	23	24	46	59	62	63	76	70	67	57	56	44	42	40	35	39	39	32	24	26	25	15	34	45	BP
bpa	5	14	9	15	14	15	11	7	16	5	6	10	24	25	29	29	23	17	24	14	11	10	14	13	16	16	10	9	9	11	8	14	11	bpa
bpb			1			1	2	1		1		3	2	1	2	2		1	1	2	1	1	1	1					1			1	1	bpb
bpc	7	12	4	8	18	10	12	7	9	8	12	18	19	21	12	19	21	16	13	10	8	8	10	4	8	11	13	8	4	6	1	2	6	bpc
bpd	1		1	3	1	1		2		4	2	8	5	4	6	3	2	2	4	2			1	2	2				1		3	1		bpd
bpe				2	1	1			3		1	2	5	1		8	6	15	7	14	13	5	3	5	7	2	2	1	1	1	3	3	6	bpe
bpf	1	2		1	4	3	2	2	2	3	3	3	2	7	7	9	11	6	5	10	7	13	10	7	3	9	5	6	2	4		8	14	bpf
bpg	2	1		2	3	1		1	2	2		2	2	3	7	6	7	10	3	4	4	5	1	3	3	1	2		8	3		5	7	bpg
BQ	38	53	59	60	57	40	37	42	35	31	30	60	52	69	85	59	51	74	60	68	43	59	51	54	44	46	59	41	48	40	42	45	61	BQ
bqa	5	3	2	5	10	6	7	10	7	13	8	15	10	16	17	11	7	7	6	3	3	8	5	8	7	4	10	5	12	8	7	5	10	bqa
bqb			1	1	1	1	2	1	5			1	1	2	2	4		5	2	5	3	3	1	4	2	2	6	2	4	2	1	4	4	bqb
bqc	1				1	1								1								1	1	1	2	1				1				bqc
bqd	5	3	2	5	1	4	5	4	3	3	1	3	6	6	7	5	6	9	4	10	6	8	4	9	12	5	9	4	5	3	8	3	9	bqd
bqe	5	5	7	10	12	4	8	9	11	8	7	11	12	14	7	11	18	14	18	13	15	17	15	15	10	10	14	14	7	8	8	10	6	bqe
bqf	18	11	16	11	17	15	12	16	8	5	12	26	19	23	48	24	17	28	22	31	15	18	23	13	11	23	19	12	20	17	8	19	29	bqf
bqg	4	31	31	28	15	9	3	2	1	2	2	4	4	7	4	4	3	11	8	6	1	4	2	4		1	1	4		1	10	4	3	bqg
BR	1	7	5	3	2	6	5	5	4	5	3	10	5	13	13	11	14	10	14	13	5	15	12	15	10	10	10	11	13	21	4	16	24	BR
bra		2		1	2							1		1		1		1			1	1											1	bra
brb														1	1			1	2	1		1	2	2	2	2		1	1			1		brb
brc	1	5	5	2		6	5	5	4	5	3	9	5	11	12	10	14	8	12	12	4	13	10	13	8	8	10	10	12	21	4	15	23	brc
BS		3	5	5	1	2		2	1	4	5	1	4	10	8	10	8	12	14	12	8	9	9	9	13	15	9	8	4	7	10	7	15	BS
bsa																						1											2	bsa
bsb																		1									1							bsb
bsc														1	1			1	2	1	1	4	3	4	4	4	2	2	1	1		1	1	bsc
bsd		3	5	5	1	2		2	1	4	5	1	4	9	7	10	8	10	12	11	7	4	6	5	9	11	6	6	3	6	10	6	12	bsd
BT	18	15	17	21	23	23	15	23	19	18	16	27	25	41	49	64	49	46	47	59	44	44	36	46	38	48	40	31	53	67	38	48	82	BT
bta	8	6	4	7	5	4	4	5	5	2	6	3	3	8	10	7	9	12	8	6	3	10	6	5	9	13	5	3	4	12	2	10	10	bta
btb	6	3	10	4	11	8	3	11	7	5	6	13	11	15	22	26	21	10	15	18	16	13	16	13	21	15	15	14	23	25	17	19	35	btb
btc		1			1		2		2	1			1	4	2	6	2	1	3	7	1	3		6	2	3		1	2	7	4	3	10	btc
btd	1			2	2	2	1		2	1	1	3	3	3	7	5	1	4	2	4	2		3	5	1	5	3	1	1	3	2	3	1	btd
bte				4			3			1		3		1		1		2	6		2	2	4	7	2	3	1	2	2	6	3	4	2	bte
btf	2	2		2	1	2		1		2			1	3	1	2	2	2	1	1	2	2		2			1	2	2	1	1	1	2	btf
btg		1	1	1	1	3		1				2	1		2	2	2		1	6	4	2	1	4	1	2	8		5	2		1		btg
bth	1	2				2		2	1		3					2	2	1	1	1	2	2	2			1	1	2	1	2		1	2	bth
bti			2	1	2	2	2	3	2	6		3	5	7	5	13	10	14	10	16	12	10	4	4	2	6	6	6	13	9	9	6	20	bti
BU									1	1		2	2	3	3	4	2	9	8	11	9	6	13	10	12	10	15	17	10	7	17	11	18	BU
bua																												1				1	3	bua
bub									1	1		2	2	3	3	4	2	9	8	11	9	6	13	10	12	10	15	16	10	7	17	10	15	bub
BV	4	5	6	13	11	6	8	11	9	3	7	7	4	10	8	13	11	9	10	12	6	9	9	12	8	5	4	7	4	6	5	6	2	BV
bva	2	1	1	3	3	2	4	2	2	1	1	2	1	4	5	3	2	4	5	4	1	4	1	8	6	3	1	3	1	3	2	4	1	bva
bvb																							1	1						1	1	1		bvb
bvc				2		1						2	1						1		1		2	2		1			1	2	2			bvc
bvd			1	3	3	1	2	6	6	2	4		1							1						1	2	1						bvd
bve	2	4	4	5	5	2	2	3			2	3	1	5	3	10	7	5	3	6	3	4	4		1		1	2	2				1	bve
bvf									1					1			2		1	1	1	1	1	1	1			1				1		bvf
BW	8	7	21	13	15	17	17	23	13	13	14	18	38	28	37	34	23	37	44	31	25	53	27	27	32	19	32	23	45	31	24	48	36	BW
bwa	2	2	13	4	7	8	11	8	3	4	7	10	26	15	10	16	6	9	19	17	6	23	6	11	5	5	7	3	9	3	4	8	5	bwa
bwb	6	5	8	9	8	9	6	15	10	9	7	8	11	13	27	18	17	28	24	14	18	30	19	16	26	14	25	19	33	28	19	34	26	bwb
bwc													1						1		1		2		1			1	3		1	6	5	bwc
BX	15	16	10	11	17	24	33	28	28	20	18	28	24	40	44	22	22	22	27	21	12	11	10	13	11	14	10	20	20	13	20	26	20	BX
C	89	167	150	97	173	137	123	152	121	123	118	142	198	258	265	249	201	256	184	177	134	224	303	437	444	770	95	157	215	164	70	123	151	C
CA	16	20	28	21	21	15	16	16	3	9	8	9	11	18	27	16	20	14	17	24	17	49	49	60	52	62	26	26	30	48	26	33	46	CA
caa																						9	14	12	15	20	5	3	9	4	1	1	2	caa
cab		1																	1															cab
cac	7	6	5	5	3	2	1	2											1			21	15	21	18	15	2	3	6	3	2	1	2	cac
cad		1	1	2	1								1	1	1	2	2		2		1	2	2			1		1		1				cad
cae														1			1			2		1	2	2		7	2	1		8	1	1		cae
caf															1					1	4	4	1		1	3	5	4	3	10		7	5	caf
cag																										1	1	1			3	1	2	cag
cah	3	5	5	1	3	2	6	3	1	3	6	1	2	7	10	9	10	4	11	12	7	5	5	14	8	8	6	5	3	10	11	12	22	cah
cai																																1	2	cai
caj		1	1	2	2			1												1				2	1	1						1		caj
cak		2	1	5	3	1	1	2	1	1		4	1	3	2	1	2	2		4		3	1		1		1	1	2	2		1		cak
cam																															1			cam

Pennsylvania Business Incorporations under General Laws, 1888–1920 (concl.)

INDUSTRIAL CATEGORIES	'88	'89	'90	'91	'92	'93	'94	'95	'96	'97	'98	'99	'00	'01	'02	'03	'04	'05	'06	'07	'08	'09	'10	'11	'12	'13	'14	'15	'16	'17	'18	'19	'20	INDUSTRIAL CATEGORIES
can	6	2	11	5	7	10	7	7	1		5	2		4	6		6	10	4	3	6	1	3	2		1	1		1		1		2	can
cap			4	1			1	1					1		1	1	1	1	1		2	1	3	4	2	1	1	3	5	5	1	5	7	cap
caq		2			2									2		1	1		2	3	5	4	4	4	4	3	3	2	2	4	6	2	2	caq
CB	5	5	1	1	1	1	4	13	21	22	14	20	21	22	20	21	14	20	38	35	33	33	36	29	16	18	21	5	8	1	2	5	1	CB
cba	2	2	1	1	1		4	7	12	13	6	6	6	12	9	16	7	10	10	7	14	11	11	7	5	3	5	4	2			1		cba
cbb	3	2						1							1										1				2					cbb
cbc																									1									cbc
cbd		1					5	9	9	8	14	15	10	10	5	7	10	28	28	19	22	25	22	11	14	15	1	1	6	1	1	4	1	cbd
CC	68	142	121	75	151	118	94	115	96	100	90	112	165	220	217	219	161	204	132	120	84	139	225	361	374	687	64	128	177	115	42	85	104	CC
cca	16	40	59	31	44	31	32	27	15	27	28	27	32	40	50	61	30	42	66	59	45	72	143	289	281	615	48	114	164	103	25	81	94	cca
ccb	4	15	11	6	11	4	9	10	24	19	11	21	13	8	25	33	14	39	24	19	11	17	40	33	31	24	9	3	5	4			6	ccb
ccc	33	61	42	28	74	63	41	52	35	37	31	50	101	151	87	90	97	85	22	27	16	30	25	23	13	16	5	3	5	4	9	1	6	ccc
ccd	8	17	5	3	15		5	16	4	4	7	5	11	8	7	9	3	9	7	3	2	1	3		3	1	1	1		1				ccd
cce	1	3	2		2	3	1	1	2		3	2		1	2	1	2			3	1			1										cce
ccf	3	5	2		2	6	5	3	1	4	9	6	6	7	15	5	10	13	6	7	6	6	4	5	9	7	1	1	1	2	5			ccf
ccg	3	1			3	2	1	6	15	6	2	3	1	4	32	19	7	16	9	23	4	13	10	11	36	24	1	1	1	2	2	3	4	ccg
D								1	15	13	14	13	23	28	31	37	37	23	23	45	40	40	41	27	48	29	32	28	34	67	42	81	108	D
DA								1	13	13	13	13	23	26	25	29	30	19	19	43	34	35	35	24	35	18	23	21	28	47	33	50	80	DA
DB														2		3	5	2	1	1	2		4	2	3	6	4	5	6	6	2	15	8	DB
DC							2				1				3	3	5	3	3	2	3	3	1	7	7	7	4	1	11	7	7	16	20	DC
E	1	1								1		1		34	105	125	125	140	169	181	143	168	159	202	181	202	197	207	256	305	204	426	533	E
EA														13	15	48	38	35	57	55	42	40	36	44	42	49	45	37	61	86	57	97	134	EA
EB																1								1	1	3			1				1	EB
EC																								2	2		1		1				1	EC
ED														1	6	6	11	16	19	11	18	14	12	19	19	14	25	19	23	26	16	39	38	ED
EE											1			2	2	6	3	2		7	3	1	3	8	10	16	5	4	7	6	4	21	21	EE
EF														4	7	3	12	7	15	12	11	13	14	19	19	17	16	29	32	21	41	58	EF
EG														3	3	5	10	12	11	6	13	8	14	9	10	5	9	10	7	10	11	18	EG
EH															2	3	3	2	3	5	6	4	1	4	4	3	9	7	3	6	2	4	6	EH
EI														3	3	2	8	16	17	10	21	41	35	16	31	31	44	60	77	38	119	137	EI
EJ																	1							1				1				1	1	EJ
EK														3	10	12	7	8	7	16	11	9	8	6	10	9	8	5	3	3	5	6	11	EK
EM												1		1	10	14	11	22	16	24	12	16	2	11	12	13	8	21	20	19	19	23	19	EM
EN														1	3	2			1				3	5	1	3	4	4	1			3	20	EN
EP														2	7	6	15	15	18	17	11	24	11	20	17	14	15	15	21	18	14	32	40	EP
EQ	1	1												4	40	16	13	10	7	10	6	17	20	14	19	18	24	25	17	25	18	28	29	EQ
F	4	6	9	7	9	8	11	7	6	13	6	8	13	29	55	49	53	72	85	109	70	119	111	100	78	117	106	106	101	101	78	143	168	F
FA	3	3	5	4	6	6	5	8	5	9	6	3	6	11	23	16	14	20	24	20	19	32	28	20	19	18	31	30	23	27	18	35	33	FA
faa	3	3	5	3	6	4	8	5	5	2	3	2		5	11	6	7	10	13	5	8	13	15	7	8	12	14	16	5	12	4	17	12	faa
fab				1		1			2				1	6	10	8	6	6	3	13	7	17	10	8	6	3	14	8	14	8	10	14	13	fab
fac									1				1		1				1	1	1				1	1	1		1	1	2	2	3	fac
fad														1	2	1	4	2	1	3		2	2	5	5	2	2	5	4	6	3	2	5	fad
fae																						1												fae
FB	1	1							1					1	4	8	2	12	5	10	9	13	19	11	9	13	12	12	13	4	5	6	18	FB
fba														1		4	2	2	3	3	1	2	6	4	5	4	6	6	1	2	2	2	9	fba
fbb	1	1							1						4			10	2	7	8	11	13	7	7	8	8	6	7	3	3	4	9	fbb
FC													1			2	1	1	2	3	2	5	12	8	6	10	12	13	25	26	19	43	35	FC
FD		1	4	3	3	3	2	1	1	2	1		5	8	18	12	25	27	41	55	26	47	38	47	33	61	43	38	25	29	25	36	57	FD
fda																					1	2	7	3	1	6	3	1		4	5	4	4	fda
fdb		1														2		4	5	1	3	1	7	9	14	7	12	7	4	7	4	5	5	fdb
fdc		1	3	3	3	3	2		1	2	1		5	2	8	8	7	3	6	11	6	10	10	8	11	17	5	8	4	8	4	8	5	fdc
fdd		1						1						6	10	4	18	24	35	42	15	30	20	33	18	36	23	13	13	9	10	19	43	fdd
FE		1					1	1		1		2	2	9	10	11	11	12	13	21	14	22	14	14	11	15	8	13	15	15	11	23	25	FE
G	141	221	169	124	178	121	127	92	76	79	60	88	108	177	248	284	188	194	249	293	156	229	268	248	212	246	239	232	333	281	159	546	747	G
GA	2	2	7	2	6									1			1		1			4	13	16	14	13	11	13	17	14	18	32	31	GA
GB	91	136	94	67	108	70	87	58	42	45	30	37	22	37	40	66	56	49	84	103	51	71	86	86	81	91	66	92	139	112	41	311	470	GB
GC	2	16	10	4	2	6	1	6	1		5		5	17	50	71	69	14	23	19	15	5	6	12	4	3	9	9	3	10	8	16	34	GC
GD																3	3							1			1	1		1		2	5	GD
GF														1		3						5		1	4	2	4	5	7	5	8	8	7	GF
GG																	1				2	3	1	3	11	8	9	4	11	8	9	9	14	GG
GH	5	6	4	2	2	6	2	1	2	2	2	1	1		3	3	1	3	4	2	6	3	2	2	1	1	2	1	1	2	7	1	1	GH
GI															3	1	2	2		12	6	10	15	14	9	9	9	14	12	6	7	18	19	GI
GJ	39	61	54	49	60	39	37	27	31	32	23	44	68	90	129	137	110	116	142	158	91	128	129	123	99	107	129	96	141	120	70	134	146	GJ
GK	2														1		2	1		1	1	2	2	2		4	4				2	16	19	GK
H	2	1	5	3	1	4	1		3		6		2	5	10	41	40	45	46	61	56	39	56	42	46	61	60	46	41	59	56	34	73	77	H
I		1	3	3	1	1			1		6	1	2	2	3	7	5	9	7	13	10	8	8	7	18	17	13	18	14	12	12	9	10	15	I
J	1		3			5		5	1		4	2	4	4	3	6	7	11	11	19	22	16	12	11	4	6	15	15	9	27	27	29	26	31	J

MANUFACTURING AND PUBLIC UTILITY INCORPORATIONS (monthly)*

A New Jersey, 1875–1907

Year		J	F	M	A	M	J	J	A	S	O	N	D
1875	Mfg.	2	0	0	0	1	3	5	2	5	2	3	4
	P.U.	0	3	0	1	0	4	0	0	0	1	1	1
1876	Mfg.	2	0	1	2	3	4	3	0	3	0	3	2
	P.U.	1	1	3	2	4	1	1	1	0	0	4	2
1877	Mfg.	9	2	0	0	4	3	3	3	2	3	3	3
	P.U.	0	0	0	1	0	2	0	2	2	1	1	1
1878	Mfg.	3	3	2	1	2	3	2	2	0	5	4	3
	P.U.	3	1	0	3	2	0	1	1	1	1	3	3
1879	Mfg.	2	3	1	4	3	5	1	3	4	2	7	7
	P.U.	1	1	1	2	2	4	2	1	0	2	2	1
1880	Mfg.	10	4	6	6	6	4	5	3	4	4	7	6
	P.U.	4	3	6	5	0	3	1	4	10	4	4	1
1881	Mfg.	11	13	18	13	9	11	17	14	21	20	8	17
	P.U.	5	3	8	3	4	7	5	1	6	12	4	3
1882	Mfg.	11	15	23	9	14	19	13	17	6	11	15	19
	P.U.	6	5	1	2	3	5	4	3	2	2	8	2
1883	Mfg.	11	10	14	15	15	15	11	13	10	10	8	14
	P.U.	4	5	3	4	8	2	1	2	1	8	5	5
1884	Mfg.	14	18	16	5	14	9	9	9	10	5	8	9
	P.U.	1	9	6	4	4	5	5	4	1	4	0	6
1885	Mfg.	12	8	15	9	8	11	7	9	15	18	5	21
	P.U.	1	2	3	5	1	4	7	2	5	5	5	4
1886	Mfg.	15	13	16	25	14	13	12	12	11	15	29	22
	P.U.	5	7	7	12	7	7	6	2	1	5	10	5
1887	Mfg.	16	16	16	27	23	20	10	18	20	13	26	26
	P.U.	7	5	2	6	6	7	6	2	2	4	4	4
1888	Mfg.	23	35	27	20	27	25	31	26	25	24	24	28
	P.U.	9	2	2	7	7	6	9	2	4	7	8	9
1889	Mfg.	41	31	37	30	36	20	25	27	22	22	41	33
	P.U	8	10	4	7	9	11	7	9	5	10	13	5
1890	Mfg.	37	41	48	38	38	59	55	30	36	51	41	59
	P.U.	9	8	9	14	8	6	4	4	5	6	8	7
1891	Mfg.	60	58	55	63	50	64	45	39	44	55	47	74
	P.U	3	8	10	5	5	4	9	4	6	12	12	13
1892	Mfg.	73	75	81	55	57	59	45	45	44	55	39	61
	P.U.	6	6	13	9	10	12	13	10	7	2	9	8
1893	Mfg.	64	62	60	56	41	43	35	24	31	31	35	40
	P.U.	17	12	12	5	11	9	4	7	3	2	6	5
1894	Mfg.	41	50	57	48	49	37	32	38	28	38	46	40
	P.U.	8	5	14	6	15	6	6	8	4	3	6	8
1895	Mfg.	49	36	40	43	35	35	42	33	35	55	60	52
	P.U.	9	5	12	17	8	7	11	9	6	7	6	6
1896	Mfg.	38	53	55	44	36	42	38	30	24	37	22	37
	P.U.	7	8	12	13	8	14	7	3	3	7	5	10
1897	Mfg.	55	50	55	37	46	37	32	41	47	54	40	57
	P.U.	10	5	7	5	10	8	13	14	7	9	10	10
1898	Mfg.	66	45	62	48	33	45	28	39	39	52	58	63
	P.U.	15	12	17	7	12	12	6	4	5	9	7	9
1899	Mfg.	71	52	82	85	121	113	93	97	93	83	94	109
	P.U.	13	22	28	21	32	22	14	12	9	13	17	21
1900	Mfg.	90	94	109	107	92	81	85	80	60	84	84	96
	P.U.	18	13	14	22	20	12	13	7	13	10	13	28
1901	Mfg.	119	120	141	128	125	111	87	72	61	72	96	99
	P.U.	14	13	28	26	18	24	21	12	16	18	17	14
1902	Mfg.	106	73	110	114	96	84	106	92	91	101	83	85
	P.U.	21	9	15	13	19	16	11	11	11	9	11	15
1903	Mfg.	144	117	117	103	85	85	81	52	51	60	58	66
	P.U.	13	21	14	22	10	11	11	7	7	6	8	5
1904	Mfg.	60	64	75	75	60	71	65	52	54	54	47	74
	P.U.	6	12	8	9	4	7	13	15	9	10	8	10
1905	Mfg.	82	53	73	65	96	65	67	55	63	47	39	38
	P.U.	12	7	13	16	3	12	7	11	15	10	9	21
1906	Mfg.	77	75	77	80	57	53	41	57	49	62	54	63
	P.U.	5	5	9	9	8	13	6	9	9	9	9	8
1907	Mfg.	73	57	65	67	55	51	61	48	43	52	44	42
	P.U.	9	12	12	6	7	8	6	8	6	3	3	2

B Ohio, 1875–1930

Year		J	F	M	A	M	J	J	A	S	O	N	D
1875	Mfg.	6	7	15	10		7	6	4	8	14	3	3
	P.U.	8	7	5	7	4	8	3	7	2	6	2	3
1876	Mfg.	12	8	9	5	6	4	3	4	8	2	4	7
	P.U.	3	6	9	7	4	4	3	1	3	1	5	7
1877	Mfg.	4	5	10	3	8	10	9	4	8	5	9	4
	P.U.	1	3	5	10	8	2	6	8	1	6	4	7
1878	Mfg.	8	7	7	5	4	7	5	8	5	8	8	3
	P.U.	9	4	4	4	12	4	2	4	3	7	4	6
1879	Mfg.	13	10	7	13	10	8	10	8	9	9	10	12
	P.U.	3	5	4	1	4	6	7	10	4	4	6	10
1880	Mfg.	16	24	16	16	10	18	11	12	10	15	10	27
	P.U.	10	9	7	9	5	5	2	5	4	6	9	5
1881	Mfg.	13	6	22	27	15	17	9	18	14	19	22	24
	P.U.	8	18	27	10	14	10	9	10	17	9	9	13
1882	Mfg.	33	27	27	31	23	28	22	16	19	24	26	23
	P.U.	10	13	10	6	3	9	6	6	6	4	11	5
1883	Mfg.	31	32	20	24	28	25	23	28	15	20	22	32
	P.U.	8	9	8	7	5	6	5	4	6	13	10	8
1884	Mfg.	19	25	23	22	16	14	21	12	12	23	14	19
	P.U.	6	10	5	10	4	6	6	7	1	5	3	6
1885	Mfg.	24	23	24	12	23	23	20	19	11	15	23	20
	P.U.	6	6	11	3	3	6	7	8	5	5	10	10
1886	Mfg.	21	22	16	18	24	22	21	15	21	24	15	35
	P.U.	10	18	13	8	8	12	8	9	9	8	12	8
1887	Mfg.	26	27	31	27	20	21	19	26	21	27	22	28
	P.U.	12	3	20	31	29	17	7	9	13	13	5	5
1888	Mfg.	40	31	29	22	37	20	22	22	22	15	22	31
	P.U.	8	6	9	5	9	7	9	8	8	10	7	10
1889	Mfg.	42	30	29	24	26	21	33	29	22	22	23	36
	P.U.	13	14	9	13	9	11	17	10	5	11	3	8
1890	Mfg.	38	35	33	25	35	27	23	25	35	37	31	43
	P.U.	4	11	17	9	14	9	7	15	3	4	7	6
1891	Mfg.	56	33	42	28	35	38	29	26	24	37	30	49
	P.U.	7	9	13	11	7	6	3	9	10	6	9	4
1892	Mfg.	43	44	48	41	40	29	19	44	28	33	37	45
	P.U.	6	9	5	13	9	4	6	8	7	6	10	6
1893	Mfg.	58	45	33	42	45	26	24	15	16	23	18	34
	P.U.	10	10	11	14	9	8	3	4	3	1	5	5
1894	Mfg.	35	33	57	31	40	38	32	31	29	29	30	33
	P.U.	6	2	13	9	13	8	9	6	9	9	8	12
1895	Mfg.	39	20	50	32	30	37	27	29	34	42	36	23
	P.U.	10	5	16	9	12	10	11	11	9	9	4	10
1896	Mfg.	36	46	37	27	43	37	25	19	16	12	22	33
	P.U.	8	9	14	5	5	7	6	1	0	6	3	5
1897	Mfg.	27	29	32	35	26	20	27	29	25	25	21	34
	P.U.	9	10	6	6	11	10	5	3	7	9	8	6
1898	Mfg.	35	30	45	29	25	27	18	28	19	30	20	29
	P.U.	7	10	11	7	9	7	5	9	7	10	12	12
1899	Mfg.	45	32	43	26	33	39	38	31	28	40	36	34
	P.U.	11	11	15	17	16	17	16	16	11	11	8	14
1900	Mfg.	53	51	53	39	43	38	31	23	36	37	43	54
	P.U.	15	22	19	14	13	15	9	13	13	14	15	16
1901	Mfg.	55	48	61	52	59	46	44	54	46	53	47	62
	P.U.	27	15	35	27	28	22	14	21	11	19	14	16
1902	Mfg.	78	63	68	53	54	48	47	60	48	43	39	56
	P.U.	27	15	18	22	16	15	17	15	5	18	13	16
1903	Mfg.	81	69	58	57	64	55	56	40	57	44	49	100
	P.U.	22	29	22	27	19	6	18	15	15	18	10	16
1904	Mfg.	106	112	103	80	90	61	81	63	70	90	73	89
	P.U.	17	10	23	15	22	16	12	11	17	13	11	13
1905	Mfg.	111	89	120	103	97	94	89	84	65	86	87	99
	P.U.	23	16	24	25	20	25	14	17	13	8	17	16
1906	Mfg.	117	126	102	102	109	81	74	70	68	88	90	81
	P.U.	26	15	20	20	27	17	8	16	21	16	14	15
1907	Mfg.	93	89	104	110	102	74	95	83	64	79	66	58
	P.U.	8	10	20	9	18	15	18	12	7	11	6	12
1908	Mfg.	77	83	91	83	81	64	66	72	67	83	72	98
	P.U.	9	7	14	13	12	9	12	8	6	7	7	12
1909	Mfg.	97	99	125	80	90	104	89	71	71	72	76	88
	P.U.	8	12	12	24	10	7	11	4	17	12	10	12
1910	Mfg.	91	100	95	89	82	81	64	61	58	75	64	76
	P.U.	10	12	13	11	10	12	7	4	7	8	12	10
1911	Mfg.	93	93	109	94	77	84	88	74	67	89	68	83
	P.U.	3	11	8	6	8	18	7	8	8	6	6	12
1912	Mfg.	96	69	91	81	72	65	87	72	64	68	75	77
	P.U.	14	6	12	19	9	11	10	4	5	7	3	6
1913	Mfg.	106	95	78	65	81	63	75	58	55	61	37	71
	P.U.	10	5	15	7	19	13	5	3	5	8	5	10
1914	Mfg.	88	80	95	70	89	55	67	45	60	55	47	60
	P.U.	13	4	16	7	4	7	8	5	4	10	10	6
1915	Mfg.	58	70	74	94	67	69	77	57	58	64	62	71
	P.U.	11	9	13	11	10	7	12	7	7	9	9	11
1916	Mfg.	78	87	115	82	104	73	66	64	77	72	96	107
	P.U.	15	7	18	14	11	11	8	9	5	11	10	12
1917	Mfg.	125	90	109	69	75	68	65	80	60	69	71	55
	P.U.	12	17	15	7	8	11	10	10	10	10	11	10
1918	Mfg.	88	70	64	83	62	49	56	64	44	36	37	76
	P.U.	10	12	10	9	4	4	11	4	6	7	7	8
1919	Mfg.	104	112	118	136	112	144	129	131	105	127	136	182
	P.U.	12	11	16	17	20	7	11	17	12	15	15	18
1920	Mfg.	177	165	177	146	153	133	107	84	114	113	79	93
	P.U.	9	8	22	11	19	11	15	16	8	17	12	11
1921	Mfg.	91	103	127	115	113	80	98	104	94	90	96	115
	P.U.	13	9	15	14	7	12	11	10	10	7	12	12
1922	Mfg.	134	128	153	107	157	116	82	87	95	98	84	148
	P.U.	14	12	14	21	11	13	5	12	13	12	6	12
1923	Mfg.	158	110	122	120	110	66	86	94	53	69	61	96
	P.U.	11	14	13	19	25	20	15	22	5	9	18	14
1924	Mfg.	95	92	92	87	76	66	70	65	85	67	54	99
	P.U.	20	16	13	16	11	7	15	10	7	12	10	15
1925	Mfg.	101	115	98	99	98	75	83	82	60	60	75	70
	P.U.	13	23	18	17	13	22	11	16	15	8	7	13
1926	Mfg.	74	77	97	85	89	93	87	76	47	85	64	76
	P.U.	22	13	19	14	13	19	16	13	15	12	19	17
1927	Mfg.	109	88	114	85	60	79	83	72	74	67	75	75
	P.U.	16	18	17	9	7	17	15	13	10	10	14	4
1928	Mfg.	112	82	107	87	83	91	74	81	84	69	74	100
	P.U.	6	23	24	13	20	21	9	19	21	20	20	21
1929	Mfg.	92	87	103	104	111	76	64	75	78	66	58	74
	P.U.	22	19	25	26	18	18	14	19	13	13	12	14
1930	Mfg.	78	77	79	82	74	60	47	65	67	67	57	63
	P.U.	20	18	10	16	19	14	14	14	14	13	10	16

*Compiled from data in the sources cited in the following sections of Appendix 3: New Jersey 1846–1918, Ohio 1855–1936, and Pennsylvania 1887–1921.

MANUFACTURING AND PUBLIC UTILITY INCORPORATIONS (monthly) (concl.)

C Pennsylvania, 1887–1920

Year		J	F	M	A	M	J	J	A	S	O	N	D
1887	Mfg.							13	12	9	12	12	13
	P.U.							10	12	6	11	4	9
1888	Mfg.	14	16	16	23	11	14	13	19	13	16	15	17
	P.U.	16	3	5	8	3	8	5	8	5	12	6	10
1889	Mfg.	20	10	20	19	22	18	28	19	16	15	26	30
	P.U.	15	12	20	13	12	13	22	13	21	4	9	13
1890	Mfg.	23	29	24	15	21	27	23	14	15	16	20	28
	P.U.	9	13	14	18	12	11	16	11	6	9	13	18
1891	Mfg.	13	28	32	20	16	32	19	28	17	19	28	36
	P.U.	6	8	12	5	10	7	5	5	11	10	11	7
1892	Mfg.	25	29	28	38	20	33	27	30	12	24	17	41
	P.U.	13	11	14	14	22	24	14	14	12	11	8	16
1893	Mfg.	29	30	34	30	34	25	21	17	10	14	20	21
	P.U.	18	12	7	15	16	14	10	13	8	6	10	8
1894	Mfg.	20	28	27	18	28	19	18	20	18	16	24	25
	P.U.	6	8	9	7	9	10	16	10	10	11	10	17
1895	Mfg.	20	27	31	24	21	22	27	23	21	24	18	22
	P.U.	11	13	14	16	12	15	16	15	9	8	5	18
1896	Mfg.	21	29	30	18	27	21	23	18	13	18	20	30
	P.U.	14	13	14	6	10	10	17	5	4	7	4	17
1897	Mfg.	19	16	24	33	25	23	20	14	19	20	27	25
	P.U.	15	13	10	11	8	9	7	14	8	11	6	11
1898	Mfg.	32	18	32	22	25	25	13	19	12	17	20	18
	P.U.	14	13	11	10	11	15	10	6	5	11	5	7
1899	Mfg.	32	15	27	26	39	44	40	33	23	33	31	33
	P.U.	14	8	8	14	9	20	17	5	15	12	10	10
1900	Mfg.	32	37	41	36	43	31	35	28	28	18	32	38
	P.U.	12	11	19	7	14	15	13	16	21	27	30	13
1901	Mfg.	35	33	52	39	38	50	46	44	36	40	47	65
	P.U.	12	15	9	22	18	26	37	30	22	18	29	20
1902	Mfg.	45	47	52	56	56	60	45	53	53	68	35	67
	P.U.	16	11	12	17	33	35	19	23	18	37	22	22
1903	Mfg.	60	48	81	57	72	49	63	30	46	47	33	59
	P.U.	16	29	23	48	18	27	14	9	9	24	13	19

Year		J	F	M	A	M	J	J	A	S	O	N	D
1904	Mfg.	38	56	63	38	47	48	51	51	44	27	33	63
	P.U.	6	8	15	6	31	18	22	22	14	20	12	27
1905	Mfg.	55	67	71	60	59	56	36	32	49	49	44	39
	P.U.	41	31	44	36	7	13	29	22	4	14	9	6
1906	Mfg.	68	47	62	52	47	65	20	51	56	53	4	43
	P.U.	14	4	16	22	31	27	12	14	18	17	4	5
1907	Mfg.	94	60	71	41	33	65	62	41	45	46	31	33
	P.U.	20	19	14	12	11	11	20	11	21	15	5	18
1908	Mfg.	39	31	39	38	36	38	36	32	36	40	34	41
	P.U.	2	12	10	16	16	5	13	4	12	10	17	17
1909	Mfg	41	50	52	47	52	54	38	39	53	39	49	55
	P.U.	20	4	13	17	10	26	34	24	28	17	11	20
1910	Mfg.	36	52	54	56	37	45	34	40	35	31	38	38
	P.U.	20	36	14	26	32	20	13	29	33	9	60	11
1911	Mfg.	42	47	55	46	38	43	36	49	35	22	38	43
	P.U.	26	27	46	64	53	55	31	38	25	26	29	17
1912	Mfg.	42	61	52	61	35	47	39	30	49	39	28	25
	P.U	18	21	31	40	73	59	43	25	33	22	60	19
1913	Mfg.	56	53	45	56	47	36	51	38	44	35	31	35
	P.U.	56	60	184	122	112	33	11	10	44	21	27	90
1914	Mfg.	42	41	59	38	43	53	43	29	38	33	27	31
	P.U.	2	3	4	6	5	10	21	3	8	20	9	4
1915	Mfg.	49	41	60	44	38	24	22	35	41	30	27	59
	P.U.	17	11	4	5	4	8	7	29	6	8	14	44
1916	Mfg.	51	58	50	54	51	46	37	28	40	43	31	44
	P.U.	12	16	7	1	36	35	16	12	36	9	11	24
1917	Mfg.	56	44	51	44	50	54	39	25	31	43	31	24
	P.U.	9	16	9	6	32	25	13	12	8	10	20	4
1918	Mfg.	43	43	34	34	43	32	36	20	39	32	21	38
	P.U.	5	4	10	3	13	10	4	2	6	6	2	5
1919	Mfg.	38	46	48	59	55	57	70	57	60	62	84	75
	P.U.	4	4	3	3	6	10	13	5	33	6	26	10
1920	Mfg.	94	83	70	83	72	71	48	57	56	36	57	51
	P.U.	24	4	9	5	9	24	24	8	10	10	14	10

APPENDIX 5

TWO TESTS

Capital Stock as an Index of the Size of a Corporation

The Charter as a Source of Information on Corporate Purposes

To test the reliability both of authorized capital stock as an indicator of the size of a company and of charters as a source of information on the purposes for which corporations have been chartered, samples of Pennsylvania incorporation data were drawn for 1889, 1902, and 1916 (see Ch. 6 and 7).

The 1889 incorporations used in this study were the first 225 in the list of incorporations in the Appendix to the Pennsylvania laws of 1889.[1] Since in this source charters are arranged for the most part chronologically, the companies selected for study were practically the first 225 chartered in 1889.[2]

The 225 companies of 1902 drawn for special study were taken from the *List of Charters of Corporations* for June 1, 1901, to May 31, 1903.[3] As the entries are arranged in proper chronological order, the companies drawn were the first 225 companies chartered in 1902, that is between January 1 and March 4.

The 1916 sample of 225 items was drawn from the *Alphabetical List of Charters of Corporations* for June 1, 1915 to May 31, 1917.[4] In this volume the incorporations are fairly well alphabetized except that building and loan associations, commercial banks, water companies, and natural gas, telephone, street railway, and railroad corporations are grouped at the end. Cooperatives, mergers, and foreign corporations that took out Pennsylvania charters were also at the end of the volume. As none of these three groups is large nor of any one industrial category, their position in the volume does not seriously affect the quality of the sample for these tests. Thus the first 225 items for 1916 selected for study included companies incorporated in every month of the year, but the sample does not include the particular groups first mentioned above which form distinct industrial classes.

Each company in each sample was looked up in a Bradstreet book of commercial ratings, published three years after the year of incorporation. For each company found in a Bradstreet volume, the type of business

in which the corporation was engaged and its "estimated pecuniary strength" were noted. This figure, apparently an estimate of the liquidation value of a concern's assets, was in the form of a range, for example, $5,000–10,000. When a single figure for estimated pecuniary strength was needed for the test, a simple arithmetic mean of the extremes given by the range was employed.[5] For most of the 1889 corporations under study the volume used did not give "estimated pecuniary strength," but did report "capital paid in". When estimated pecuniary strength was not given, the paid-in capital figure was used as an indicator of size. For banks, paid-in capital (or the combination of paid-in capital and surplus, when both were given) was always used as the indicator of actual size, since for such institutions estimated pecuniary strength was never given.

Not all companies included in each sample were found in the Bradstreet rating books; and for those found, information on both estimated pecuniary strength (or its substitute) and type of business was not always given. Of the 1889 group of 225 items, 46 were found in the Bradstreet volume.[6] Of these 46, information on paid-in capital was given for 36 and on type of business for 31.[7] That a small proportion of the total sample was found in the Bradstreet rating book is not surprising.[8] Many of the charters taken out were certainly never utilized; some companies that started would not have survived the three years between the date of incorporation and the date of publication of the rating book (see Ch. 2); and certain types of company were not likely to be—or at least do not seem to have been—included to any appreciable extent in the rating books. For example, among the 1889 companies identified in the 1892 Bradstreet's there were no building and loan associations, no real estate companies, and no concerns supplying water to the public; while in the sample of 225 companies there were 57 building and loan associations, 22 real estate companies, and 17 water companies.

Of the 225 companies in the 1902 group, 110 appeared in the Bradstreet rating book of 1905 (Vol. 151). Of these 110, statements of estimated pecuniary strength (or its substitute) were available on 98 com-

---

[1] These companies formed 31 percent of total incorporations of 1889; *Pennsylvania Laws, 1889*, pp. a95–a132.

[2] The 225th corporation selected was chartered on April 24, 1889. The disarrangement of chronology was such that seven companies incorporated earlier in April were excluded from the sample.

[3] These companies formed 15 percent of total incorporations of 1902; *List of Charters of Corporations enrolled in the office of the Secretary of the Commonwealth during the two years beginning June 1, 1901, and ending June 1, 1903* . . . (1903), pp. 51–65.

[4] These companies formed 13 percent of total incorporations of 1916; *Alphabetical List of Charters of Corporations enrolled in the Office of the Secretary of the Commonwealth During the Two Years Beginning June 1, 1915, and Ending May 31, 1917* (Harrisburg, 1917), pp. 3–36.

[5] For a few companies the estimated pecuniary strength was given in the following form: $1,000,000 and above. In the work described below the lower limit of such a range was used to represent the rating book's indication of wealth.

[6] *Bradstreet's Commercial Reports Embracing the Bankers, Merchants, Manufacturers, and Others, in the United States and the Dominion of Canada* (Bradstreet Company, September 1892), Vol. 99.

[7] The type of business was given for 6 more companies, but descriptions were too indefinite to permit classification.

[8] The proportions of the 1889, 1902, and 1916 samples found in Bradstreet's were 20, 49, and 44 percent, respectively.

panies and the type of business was clearly identifiable for 91.[9] As in the case of the 1889 sample, certain types of corporation were not found in the rating book though they were fairly numerous in the sample. For example, though the sample contained 5 building and loan associations, 11 real estate companies, and 13 water supply corporations, none was listed in Bradstreet's except one real estate company and it was given as a building contracting concern.

Of the 225 companies in the 1916 group, 99 were found in the 1919 Bradstreet's rating book (Vol. 207). Of these 99, information on estimated pecuniary strength (or its substitute) was given for 74 companies and clear-cut designations of business for 79.[10] Again certain types of company represented in the sample were apparently not included in the Bradstreet volume. None of the 21 real estate companies and none of the 24 electric light public utilities in the sample was found.

The simple coefficient of linear correlation showing the relation between authorized capital stock and estimated pecuniary strength (or its substitute) was calculated on ungrouped data for each of the three sets of corporations.

1889. The correlation coefficient for the 36 companies chartered in 1889 for which Bradstreet's reported estimated pecuniary strength (or its substitute) is +.81 with a standard error of .06.

Since in the study of incorporations a classification of companies on the basis of size is useful and since elsewhere three categories of size are used—companies with less than $100,000 authorized capital stock, companies with $100,000–1,000,000, and companies with $1,000,000 or more—another test of the relation between authorized capital stock and estimated pecuniary strength was made. Using for both authorized capital stock and estimated pecuniary strength the dollar ranges specified above, it was found that 83 per cent of the 36 companies on each of which there was a Bradstreet figure for estimated pecuniary strength fell into the same size group on the basis of both criteria. That is, a company that was small on the basis of its authorized capital stock (one that had less than $100,000) was in general small when judged by its estimated pecuniary strength (that is, had an estimated pecuniary strength of less than $100,000).

1902. The correlation coefficient for the 98 companies charted in 1902 is +.39 with a standard error of .09. If, however, 11 (approximately 12 percent of the total) are omitted, the coefficient becomes +.92 with a stand-

ard error of .02. Among these eleven are four large companies, which may well be eliminated because their values dominate the coefficient.[11] The other seven companies had very small authorized capital stock and fairly large estimated pecuniary strength figures.[12] Some were perhaps family or close corporations or—as were two of the seven—public utilities which might be expected to have a much larger pecuniary strength than capital stock account.

A second test, similar to that employed on the 1889 data, was also made. It was found that 81 percent of the 98 companies fell into the same size group—under $100,000, or $100,000–1,000,000, or $1,000,000 and over—whether authorized capital stock or estimated pecuniary strength was used as the indicator.

1916. The correlation coefficient for the 74 companies chartered in 1916 is +.47 with a standard error of .09. If, however, three companies (approximately 4 percent of the total) are omitted, the coefficient becomes +.67 with a standard error of .07.[13] The coefficient increases to +.84 with a standard error of .04, if 5 more companies are excluded.[14] Further dropping of small groups of companies would change the correlation coefficient relatively little.

The second test showed that 84 percent of the 74 companies fell into the same size group whether authorized

---

[9] The type of business was given for 15 other companies, but descriptions were too indefinite to permit classification.

[10] For 20 other companies the Bradstreet descriptions of business activity were inadequate for classification.

[11]

COMPANY	AUTHORIZED CAPITAL STOCK (THOUS. OF DOLLARS)	ESTIMATED PECUNIARY STRENGTH (THOUS. OF DOLLARS)
A	1,000	9,263
B	400	1,000
C	3,000	1,000 & over
D	1	1,000

[12]

COMPANY	AUTHORIZED CAPITAL STOCK (THOUS. OF DOLLARS)	ESTIMATED PECUNIARY STRENGTH (THOUS. OF DOLLARS)
A	1	275
B	10	750
C	10	350
D	1	350
E	5	450
F	1	350
G	1	750

[13]

COMPANY	AUTHORIZED CAPITAL STOCK (THOUS. OF DOLLARS)	ESTIMATED PECUNIARY STRENGTH (THOUS. OF DOLLARS)
A	5	275
B	250	63
C	75	450

[14]

COMPANY	AUTHORIZED CAPITAL STOCK (THOUS. OF DOLLARS)	ESTIMATED PECUNIARY STRENGTH (THOUS. OF DOLLARS)
A	150	350
B	150	350
C	60	175
D	10	125
E	5	175

capital stock or estimated pecuniary strength was used as the indicator.

When the above tests of the relation between authorized capital stock and the Bradstreet figures that give an idea of size are reviewed, it is clear that authorized capital stock may be used as a *rough* indicator of size, particularly when broad classes of authorized capital stock are utilized, as is the case in this study.

It must be remembered, however, that certain types of corporation were not worked into the tests. Since building and loan associations were almost always chartered with an authorized capital stock of $1,000,000 or more, they had to be treated as large companies; perhaps such treatment was correct, but it seems to overrate their size. Water supply companies, in contrast, had low authorized capital stock. The average capital stock for the 61 water supply companies chartered in 1889 was approximately $29,600, while the average for the 17 companies drawn in the sample was $19,700. The water supply companies chartered in 1902 were smaller. The average authorized capital stock for the 13 companies in the 1902 sample was $4,100, each of 9 having only $1,000. There were no water companies in the 1916 sample, and each of the 6 that were incorporated in that year was chartered with $5,000. Another group occasionally represented in the tests consisted of companies supplying electricity. As in the case of concerns supplying water, the electric light corporations were chartered with small authorized capital stock, and the companies of 1889 seem to have been on the whole larger than those of 1916. In the latter year it was customary to incorporate such business units with either $5,000 or $10,000.[15] Though most of these water and electric light companies were probably organized to supply services to small towns, it is likely that in many the authorized capital stock at incorporation suggests a smaller company than that launched. Concerning the other groups that either did not appear in Bradstreet's or appeared infrequently, no special comment is needed except that there is no reason to believe that authorized capital stock and estimated pecuniary strength (or some such indicator of size) would not have been, or were not, closely related. The conclusion, therefore, is that authorized capital stock is a fairly good indicator of the relative size of a company soon after its organization.

When the purposes of the corporations as determined from their charter abstracts were correlated with Brad-

street's designations of the businesses in which the companies were actually engaged three years after chartering, the results are interesting. For example, for 71 of the 91 companies chartered in 1902 found in Bradstreet's,[16] the industrial allocations made on the two bases were 'identical', that is, on the basis of both criteria the company was placed in the same group of Table 19. If Bradstreet's styled a corporation a "manfacturer of paints", it would have been placed in the category labeled 'bma' in Table 19. If the charter description had permitted merely an allocation to 'bmi', a chemical company of indeterminate type, the classifications would not have been identical. On the other hand, since there are no subdivisions for real estate companies in Table 19, an allocation of a corporation to group 'GJ'—a two-digit category—on both bases constituted identical classification.

In addition to the 71 companies chartered in 1902 that were classified identically, 9 others may be said to have been almost identical. Bradstreet's labeled them either trust or savings and trust companies; in the charter abstracts, however, they were designated title companies. In all probability, they were both title guarantee and trust companies. There does not seem to be any serious difference between the charter information and that contained in Bradstreet's. Consequently, it may be said that 80 of the 91 companies (88 percent), for which the type of business is clear-cut in Bradstreet's, were classified in the same way on the basis of both sources of information. In checking the 11 that were not classified in the same way when the two sources were used, it was found that the discrepancies in classification were not great. For example, a concern that Bradstreet's identified as a general store could not be classified more clearly by the charter abstract than as a corporation engaged in either wholesale or retail trade of uncertain character; a corporation that according to Bradstreet's was a department store was a retail store of unclassifiable type on the basis of the charter abstract; a wholesale confectionery in Bradstreet's was identified from the charter abstract as an unclassifiable manufacturer of food products. The similarity of results obtained by using the charter abstracts and the Bradstreet volumes is shown in Table 20.

The two industrial classifications of the 1889 and the 1916 companies made from the two sources yielded results parallel to those obtained for 1902. Of the 31 companies chartered in 1889 upon which the Bradstreet descriptions of type of business were clear-cut,[17] 21 were placed in the same industrial category on both bases.

---

[15] Each of 117 of the 164 companies organized in 1916 to supply electricity to the public, 71 percent, was chartered with an authorized capital stock of $5,000. In each of 36 others created in that year, 22 percent, the authorized capital stock was $10,000. Moreover, every electric light company in the 1916 sample had an authorized capital stock of either $5,000 or $10,000.

[16] For 15 companies of this year the Bradstreet descriptions of business were not clear.

[17] For 3 companies the Bradstreet business descriptions were too indefinite to admit of classification.

Four more companies may also be said to have been identically classified. According to Bradstreet's one was a title and trust company and another was a trust company; the charters stressed the title guarantee business of these concerns. Both were probably title guarantee and trust companies. The other two were electric light and power (or electric light, heat, and power) companies according to Bradstreet's, while the charters definitely described each as a company to supply electricity. If these four companies are viewed as classified in the same way on both bases, 25 of the 31 companies (81 percent) were placed in the same industrial group. Three of the 6 companies not identically classified received closely related industrial designations. One company, for example, was placed in "Manufacturing, Machinery (except electrical)", though it was not put into the same subgroup of this two-letter category. Similarly, two companies were classified as "Manufacturing, Iron and steel and their products", but were not put into the same subgroup. The remaining three companies identified clearly in Bradstreet's were manufacturing concerns and were so considered on the basis of charter descriptions, but the two sources of information on type of business led to different placements within the manufacturing group.

Of the 79 companies chartered in 1916 whose type of business was described adequately,[18] 59 were identically classified on both bases. Two more corporations were trust companies according to the rating book and title guarantee companies according to the charter purpose statements. If, as above, these companies are con-

[18] For 20 other companies the Bradstreet descriptions of business activity were inadequate for classification.

sidered to have been identically classified, then 77 percent of the companies with clear-cut Bradstreet statements of business activity were classified industrially in the same fashion on both bases.

The three tests indicate that the Pennsylvania abstracts of charter purpose statements reveal corporate objectives fairly accurately. The classification of three groups of companies—samples drawn for 1889, 1902, and 1916—resulted in 'identical' assignments to the categories of Table 19 in 81, 88, and 77 percent, respectively. In view of the detail of Table 19 the similarity between industrial determinations based upon charter abstracts and upon Bradstreet's descriptions of the business *three years after* incorporation is striking. Moreover, many companies, of which the purposes were almost certainly revealed by the charter abstracts, were not in Bradstreet's. Had they been, the percentages of agreement would have been much higher. For example, none of the 164 companies organized in 1916 to supply electricity to towns was found in the 1919 Bradstreet volume. It is hard to believe that had they been in the rating book they would have been listed as anything but power and light companies. Likewise, the 315 incorporations of 1889, 1902, and 1916 that on the basis of charter abstracts were classified as building and loan associations would almost certainly have been so designated had they been rated in Bradstreet's. The same sort of statement could be made about the real estate corporations, of which according to the charter descriptions there were 61 in 1889, 129 in 1902, and 141 in 1916. Other groups, such as printing and publishing, could also be cited, but further elaboration of the point seems superfluous.

APPENDIX 6

Total Incorporations

Used in

Constructing the Monthly Aggregate Index of Incorporations (Table 38)

and in

Analyzing Cyclical Movements

	UNADJUSTED FOR SEASONAL VARIATIONS												ADJUSTED FOR SEASONAL VARIATIONS												
	J	F	M	A	M	J	J	A	S	O	N	D	J	F	M	A	M	J	J	A	S	O	N	D	

Connecticut, Massachusetts, New Jersey, Ohio

	J	F	M	A	M	J	J	A	S	O	N	D	J	F	M	A	M	J	J	A	S	O	N	D	
1860	12	12	9	3	8	6	3	8	7	6	5	11	10	10	6	2	7	6	4	10	11	8	7	12	1860
1861	9	4	13	7	6	5	0	3	2	3	4	1	7	3	9	5	5	5	0	4	3	4	6	1	1861
1862	10	5	8	6	7	5	8	3	5	4	10	4	8	4	6	5	6	5	11	4	8	5	14	4	1862
1863	10	10	17	13	11	13	8	6	3	16	12	22	8	8	11	10	9	13	11	8	5	21	17	23	1863
1864	29	16	49	45	36	27	28	26	22	20	17	38	23	13	33	34	31	28	39	32	35	26	24	40	1864
1865	66	91	79	52	47	47	31	36	41	30	35	40	53	74	53	40	40	48	44	45	66	39	49	43	1865
1866	60	64	43	60	55	44	23	34	35	34	40	40	48	52	29	46	47	45	32	42	56	44	56	43	1866
1867	49	40	47	39	42	35	34	37	22	33	30	36	39	33	31	30	36	36	48	46	35	43	42	38	1867
1868	56	55	51	46	48	33	23	40	24	32	29	32	45	45	34	35	41	34	32	50	39	42	41	34	1868
1869	37	38	63	60	52	38	29	32	27	29	27	39	30	31	42	46	44	39	41	40	44	38	38	41	1869
1870	45	43	50	43	37	33	31	29	28	19	47	45	36	35	33	33	32	34	44	36	45	25	66	48	1870

Maine, Maryland, Massachusetts, New Jersey, Ohio

	J	F	M	A	M	J	J	A	S	O	N	D	J	F	M	A	M	J	J	A	S	O	N	D	
1870	53	50	68	51	48	40	38	35	38	26	59	54	42	41	45	39	41	41	54	44	61	34	83	57	1870
1871	63	52	61	54	72	48	46	48	35	61	44	54	61	48	51	47	60	47	51	51	44	72	53	55	1871
1872	45	78	63	73	67	56	59	52	45	38	55	43	44	72	52	63	55	55	65	55	56	45	66	43	1872

Maine, Maryland, Massachusetts, New Jersey, Ohio, Texas

	J	F	M	A	M	J	J	A	S	O	N	D	J	F	M	A	M	J	J	A	S	O	N	D	
1872	50	84	69	74	70	63	64	55	47	42	58	45	48	82	53	60	59	61	70	61	62	52	72	45	1872
1873	63	69	88	70	66	62	52	65	42	34	32	50	61	67	68	56	56	60	57	72	55	42	40	50	1873
1874	47	49	71	60	61	55	45	59	52	57	42	52	45	48	55	48	52	53	49	66	68	71	52	52	1874
1875	61	65	88	81	66	68	56	54	65	51	46	60	59	63	68	65	56	65	62	60	86	64	58	60	1875
1876	53	54	78	91	61	56	42	33	38	23	34	38	51	52	60	73	52	54	46	37	50	29	42	38	1876
1877	42	44	54	43	62	46	48	40	34	50	42	50	40	43	42	35	53	44	53	44	45	62	52	50	1877
1878	56	46	52	55	50	39	40	39	22	43	46	50	54	45	40	44	42	38	44	43	29	54	58	50	1878
1879	56	48	44	51	58	51	47	41	34	39	57	80	54	47	34	41	49	49	52	46	45	49	71	80	1879
1880	101	120	114	128	90	74	76	67	79	78	88	95	91	110	91	113	83	75	83	82	99	89	100	92	1880
1881	93	112	171	123	144	124	129	118	119	149	137	154	84	103	137	109	133	125	140	144	149	169	156	150	1881

Connecticut, Maine, Maryland, Massachusetts, New Jersey, Ohio, Texas

	J	F	M	A	M	J	J	A	S	O	N	D	J	F	M	A	M	J	J	A	S	O	N	D	
1881	104	118	184	133	152	130	134	121	121	154	146	161	94	108	147	118	141	131	146	148	151	175	166	156	1881
1882	143	137	165	146	148	159	120	129	108	131	133	139	129	126	132	129	137	180	130	157	135	149	151	135	1882
1883	139	154	164	155	161	164	128	132	114	138	121	150	125	141	131	137	149	166	139	161	142	157	138	146	1883
1884	157	163	173	164	137	129	120	91	90	92	71	116	141	150	138	145	127	130	130	111	112	105	81	113	1884
1885	135	122	134	108	110	205	114	102	105	117	99	140	122	112	107	96	102	207	124	124	131	133	113	136	1885
1886	154	165	164	158	142	145	147	99	113	136	175	186	139	151	131	140	131	146	160	121	141	155	199	181	1886
1887	200	182	241	265	233	199	149	159	154	185	174	167	180	167	193	235	216	201	162	194	192	210	198	162	1887
1888	215	204	232	188	225	179	156	157	172	149	161	209	194	187	186	166	208	181	170	191	215	169	183	203	1888

Connecticut, Maine, Maryland, Massachusetts, New Jersey, Ohio, Pennsylvania, Texas

	J	F	M	A	M	J	J	A	S	O	N	D	J	F	M	A	M	J	J	A	S	O	N	D	
1888	269	235	276	237	256	216	190	194	199	192	196	264	242	216	221	210	237	218	207	237	249	218	223	256	1888
1889	293	271	331	292	299	240	308	246	260	215	284	276	264	249	265	258	277	242	335	300	325	244	323	268	1889
1890	304	322	362	345	338	322	338	246	265	292	282	331	274	295	290	305	313	325	367	300	331	332	320	321	1890
1891	353	351	362	333	317	353	309	248	279	306	290	415	318	322	290	295	294	357	336	302	349	348	330	403	1891
1892	385	398	461	398	366	351	306	346	258	288	300	403	347	365	369	352	339	355	333	422	322	327	341	391	1892
1893	426	365	392	399	400	292	261	207	182	188	216	272	384	335	314	353	370	295	284	252	228	214	245	264	1893
1894	317	280	394	302	331	277	257	260	242	290	276	302	286	257	315	267	306	280	279	317	302	330	314	293	1894
1895	338	285	373	362	309	296	320	288	273	322	314	346	305	261	298	320	286	299	348	351	341	366	357	336	1895
1896	346	349	398	348	321	288	289	206	170	218	202	312	312	320	318	308	297	291	314	251	212	248	230	303	1896
1897	349	315	397	327	320	296	259	272	310	309	308	341	293	294	318	295	288	296	291	332	388	347	358	341	1897

Connecticut, Illinois, Maine, Maryland, Massachusetts, New Jersey, Ohio, Pennsylvania, Texas

	J	F	M	A	M	J	J	A	S	O	N	D	J	F	M	A	M	J	J	A	S	O	N	D	
1897	460	410	509	433	405	381	348	357	398	395	406	468	387	380	407	390	365	381	391	435	498	444	472	468	1897
1898	556	474	563	442	379	404	308	303	299	353	387	405	467	439	450	398	341	404	346	370	374	397	450	405	1898
1899	592	541	716	629	634	630	581	524	480	531	534	576	497	501	573	567	571	630	653	639	600	597	621	576	1899
1900	681	599	695	642	674	576	519	459	496	545	563	684	572	555	556	578	607	576	583	560	620	612	655	684	1900
1901	764	746	926	997	1060	832	741	703	575	674	668	792	642	691	741	898	955	832	833	857	719	757	777	792	1901
1902	919	855	954	885	955	798	820	703	696	844	732	868	772	792	763	797	860	798	921	857	870	948	851	868	1902
1903	1106	1017	1085	1006	936	867	778	649	723	778	698	928	929	942	868	906	843	867	874	791	904	874	812	928	1903
1904	965	929	1001	858	951	856	809	803	724	793	768	1020	811	860	801	773	857	856	909	979	905	891	893	1020	1904

	UNADJUSTED FOR SEASONAL VARIATIONS												ADJUSTED FOR SEASONAL VARIATIONS												
	J	F	M	A	M	J	J	A	S	O	N	D	J	F	M	A	M	J	J	A	S	O	N	D	
Connecticut, Florida, Illinois, Maine, Maryland, Massachusetts, New Jersey, Ohio, Pennsylvania, Texas, Virginia																									
1904	1021	979	1070	917	1007	919	867	859	780	856	834	1075	858	906	856	826	907	919	974	1048	975	962	970	1075	1904
1905	1245	1079	1274	1090	1207	1045	946	941	939	984	1009	1062	1092	990	1027	982	1128	1045	1017	1094	1092	1118	1173	1095	1905
1906	1382	1238	1481	1216	1314	1211	955	1050	973	1100	1080	1223	1212	1136	1194	1095	1228	1211	1027	1221	1131	1250	1256	1261	1906
1907	1498	1341	1514	1377	1308	1238	1196	973	902	955	740	793	1314	1230	1221	1241	1222	1238	1286	1131	1049	1085	860	818	1907
1908	980	976	1100	1066	966	973	938	863	904	921	884	1102	860	895	887	960	903	973	1009	1003	1051	1047	1028	1136	1908
1909	1270	1355	1533	1318	1225	1185	1170	978	1089	985	1096	1217	1114	1243	1236	1183	1145	1185	1258	1137	1266	1119	1274	1255	1909
1910	1259	1299	1302	1287	1200	1122	908	960	905	912	1023	1069	1104	1192	1050	1159	1121	1122	976	1116	1052	1036	1190	1102	1910
1911	1305	1214	1444	1211	1146	1151	990	1009	985	992	1004	1089	1145	1114	1165	1091	1071	1151	1065	1173	1145	1127	1167	1123	1911
1912	1318	1277	1414	1263	1218	1126	1207	1057	1039	1125	1038	1170	1156	1172	1140	1138	1138	1126	1298	1229	1208	1278	1207	1206	1912
1913	1425	1355	1462	1408	1316	1104	1075	979	1026	1071	884	1182	1250	1243	1179	1268	1230	1104	1156	1138	1193	1217	1028	1219	1913
1914	1219	1175	1442	1241	1169	1085	1071	815	833	858	809	890	1069	1078	1163	1118	1093	1085	1152	948	969	975	941	918	1914
1915	1162	1071	1305	1233	1180	1087	1084	1052	980	1040	1099	1352	1019	983	1052	1111	1103	1087	1166	1223	1140	1182	1278	1394	1915
1916	1332	1374	1586	1394	1399	1313	1150	1057	1202	1211	1221	1387	1168	1261	1279	1256	1307	1313	1237	1229	1398	1376	1420	1430	1916
1917	1676	1450	1742	1432	1396	1276	1230	1085	1001	1188	1105	953	1470	1330	1405	1290	1305	1276	1323	1261	1164	1350	1285	982	1917
Connecticut, Delaware, Florida, Maine, Maryland, Massachusetts, Ohio, Pennsylvania, Texas, Virginia																									
1916	1109	1182	1382	1196	1241	1181	1042	919	1043	1072	1049	1294	973	1084	1115	1077	1160	1181	1120	1069	1213	1218	1220	1334	1916
1917	1510	1311	1579	1338	1374	1241	1166	1044	994	1110	1107	873	1325	1203	1273	1205	1284	1241	1254	1214	1156	1261	1287	900	1917
1918	1026	985	1093	1032	1043	829	880	741	622	590	576	840	900	904	881	930	975	829	946	862	723	670	670	866	1918
1919	1253	1268	1455	1603	1596	1633	1755	1666	1636	1720	1733	2107	1099	1219	1233	1444	1492	1649	1950	1872	1902	1890	1992	2026	1919
Connecticut, Delaware, Maine, Maryland, Ohio, Virginia																									
1918	676	629	691	636	625	532	520	477	354	372	376	506	593	577	557	573	584	532	559	555	412	423	437	522	1918
1919	824	808	941	993	1010	1059	1117	1062	1037	1124	1089	1387	723	776	797	895	944	1070	1241	1193	1206	1235	1252	1334	1919
1920	1507	1333	1496	1387	1246	1180	1024	980	954	1006	914	950	1322	1282	1268	1250	1164	1192	1138	1101	1109	1105	1051	913	1920
1921	1018	959	1153	1072	997	926	823	891	834	823	856	947	893	922	977	966	932	935	914	1001	970	904	984	911	1921
1922	1054	1009	1155	1082	1215	1073	935	914	930	996	909	1135	925	970	979	975	1136	1084	1039	1027	1081	1095	1045	1091	1922
1923	1230	1104	1262	1248	1090	1007	933	922	737	833	900	1044	1079	1062	1069	1124	1019	1017	1037	1036	857	915	1034	1004	1923
1924	1099	1004	1088	1014	939	864	801	749	835	901	761	1080	964	965	922	914	878	873	890	842	971	990	875	1038	1924
1925	1154	1058	1141	1082	1084	1034	1009	982	912	968	886	1081	1012	1017	967	975	1013	1044	1121	1103	1060	1064	1018	1039	1925
Connecticut, Delaware, Maine, Maryland, New York, Ohio, Virginia																									
1924	3098	2768	3008	2831	2638	2296	2164	2025	2124	2297	2273	3162	2671	2714	2571	2646	2512	2273	2404	2328	2559	2444	2498	2928	1924
1925	3120	2813	3371	3077	3171	3140	2896	3001	2804	3225	2966	3510	2690	2758	2881	2876	3020	3109	3218	3449	3378	3431	3259	3250	1925
Connecticut, Delaware, Illinois, Maine, Maryland, New York, Ohio, Virginia																									
1925	3690	3321	3883	3600	3625	3559	3327	3400	3230	3704	3326	4020	3181	3256	3319	3364	3452	3524	3697	3908	3892	3940	3655	3722	1925
1926	4307	3590	4109	3739	3662	3803	3339	2988	2965	3366	3230	3717	3713	3520	3512	3494	3488	3765	3710	3434	3572	3581	3549	3442	1926
1927	4112	3585	4411	3966	3725	3718	3188	3197	3111	3354	3477	4016	3545	3515	3770	3707	3548	3681	3542	3675	3748	3568	3821	3719	1927
1928	4319	4070	4433	4018	4354	4096	3464	3392	3013	3855	3782	4145	3723	3990	3789	3755	4147	4055	3849	3899	3630	4101	4156	3838	1928
1929	4697	4189	4637	4513	4457	3870	3704	3756	3417	3694	3297	3382	4232	4148	4140	4140	4205	3757	3940	3996	3797	3848	3747	3523	1929
1930	3917	3664	3944	3862	3939	3588	3360	3031	3253	3443	3065	3441	3529	3628	3521	3543	3716	3483	3574	3224	3614	3586	3483	3584	1930
1931	3727	3451	4022	3866	3653	3693	3390	3202	2950	3359	3204	3531	3358	3417	3591	3547	3446	3585	3606	3406	3278	3499	3641	3678	1931
1932	3899	3475	3792	3642	3398	3675	3049	3449	3147	3075	2866	3109	3513	3441	3386	3341	3206	3568	3244	3669	3497	3203	3257	3239	1932
Delaware, Illinois, Maine, Maryland, New York, Ohio, Virginia																									
1931	3623	3359	3930	3780	3564	3613	3307	3127	2880	3290	3149	3420	3264	3326	3509	3468	3362	3508	3518	3327	3200	3427	3578	3563	1931
1932	3790	3383	3700	3552	3303	3592	2950	3357	3054	3007	2802	3011	3414	3350	3304	3259	3116	3487	3138	3571	3393	3132	3184	3136	1932
1933	3830	3255	3053	3117	3847	3392	2820	2814	2472	2636	2694	2861	3246	3356	2726	2969	3735	3392	2968	3059	2874	2746	2866	2778	1933
1934	3258	2445	2956	2769	2707	2505	2357	2330	2078	2475	2368	2362	2761	2521	2639	2637	2628	2505	2481	2533	2416	2578	2519	2293	1934
1935	2965	2528	2713	2702	2679	2495	2481	2388	2319	2645	2375	2661	2513	2606	2422	2573	2601	2495	2611	2596	2697	2755	2527	2583	1935
1936	3116	2596	2891	2656	2624	2675	2523	2243	2307	2479	2375	2856	2641	2676	2581	2530	2548	2675	2656	2438	2683	2582	2527	2773	1936
Delaware, Illinois, Maine, Maryland, New York, Virginia																									
1934	2996	2209	2648	2537	2434	2285	2141	2120	1876	2257	2180	2184	2539	2277	2364	2416	2363	2285	2254	2304	2181	2351	2319	2120	1934
1935	2730	2301	2486	2445	2439	2294	2268	2169	2088	2401	2167	2486	2314	2372	2220	2329	2368	2294	2387	2358	2428	2501	2305	2414	1935
1936	2781	2328	2618	2418	2394	2422	2295	2033	2119	2265	2194	2616	2357	2400	2337	2303	2324	2422	2416	2210	2464	2359	2334	2540	1936
1937	2773	2346	2730	2555	2259	2279	2053	1941	1787	1922	1946	2104	2350	2419	2437	2433	2193	2279	2161	2110	2078	2002	2070	2043	1937
1938	2288	1875	2213	2009	2040	1977	1889	1919	1711	1821	1880	2028	1939	1933	1976	1913	1981	1977	1988	2086	1990	1897	2000	1969	1938
1939	2317	1917	2342	2004	2315	1842	1817	1817	1558	1900	1942	2004	1964	1926	2091	1909	2248	1842	1912	1975	1812	1979	2066	1946	1939
Delaware, Illinois, Louisiana, Maine, New York, Virginia																									
1938	2301	1903	2199	2014	2026	1968	1869	1898	1706	1824	1869	2002	1950	1962	1963	1918	1967	1968	1967	2063	1984	1900	1988	1944	1938
1939	2327	1897	2324	1976	2316	1809	1815	1800	1547	1890	1927	1971	1972	1956	2075	1882	2249	1809	1911	1957	1799	1969	2050	1914	1939
1940	2475	2037	2089	2371	2210	1701	1805	1704	1619	1722	1567	1857	2097	2100	1865	2258	2146	1701	1900	1852	1883	1794	1667	1803	1940
1941	2173	1812	1964	1890	1824	1591	1694	1401	1399	1475	1292	1469	1842	1868	1754	1800	1771	1591	1783	1523	1627	1536	1374	1426	1941

Advertising (fba in Table 19 & App. 4), incorporations for, 69
Agriculture (I in Table 19 & App. 4)
   corporations: New Jersey, Ohio, & Pennsylvania, 59, 62
   incorporations for: Maryland, 14; New Jersey, 15, 59–62, 66; New York, 17; Ohio, 18–9, 59–62, 66; Pennsylvania, 59–62, 66
Air transportation (cai in Table 19 & App. 4), incorporations for, 72
Aircraft & parts manufacture (bvb in Table 19 & App. 4), incorporations for, 72
Alabama, constitutional provision concerning incorp., 11
Amplitude of fluctuations of incorporations
   explanation of variations in, 33, 34
   in number & capital stock, 34, 36–41
   variation with size of incorporation, 42–4, 49
   see also Seasonal variation
Amusements (FD in Table 19 & App. 4)
   incorporations for: Maryland, 14; New Jersey, 15, 66, 68–9; New York, 17; Ohio, 18–9, 66, 68–9; Pennsylvania, 68–9
Arizona
   constitutional provision concerning incorporation, 11
   dates of series, 2
   nonbusiness incorporations, 2n, 89–90, 90n
   period of inclusion in indexes, 34, 79, 81
   Reports of Corporation Commission, 96
   sources of data, 96
   total incorporations, 32, 96
Arkansas, constitutional provision concerning incorp., 11
Arrows on charts indicate turning points of business, 36
Auditoriums (fdc in Table 19 & App. 4), incorporations for, 69
Authorized capital stock
   'adjusted', 36–40, 79n
   and number of incorporations, 3, 36–41, 79n
   as indicator of
      nature of business, 1–2
      relative size, 6, 6n, 42, 42n
   average, in Ohio, 40
   index of, 34
   total, 37–40
   total and 'adjusted' contrasted, 36–40
   see also Amplitude, Colorado, Delaware, Florida, Illinois, Maryland, Massachusetts, New Jersey, Ohio, Pennsylvania, Texas, Virginia
Automobile & automobile equipment manufacture (BU & bub in Table 19 & App. 4), incorporations for, 67–8, 69
Automobile repair (FC in Table 19 & App. 4), incorporations for: New Jersey, Ohio, & Pennsylvania, 69

Bakery products manufacture (baa in Table 19 & App. 4), incorporations for, 69
Banking (GA in Table 19 & App. 4)
   incorporations for: episodes in, 24, 26, 27–8; Maryland, 14, 20, 26; New Jersey, 15, 20, 27, 69; New York, 17, 20, 26–8; Ohio, 18–20, 26, 29, 69; Pennsylvania, 24, 24n, 58–9, 69
BELLAMY, EDWARD, 31
Beverage manufacture (BB in Table 19 & App. 4), incorporations for, 67–8, 69
Big business
   effect on incorporations, 31, 50, 69, 72
   periods of, 49
BLANDI, J. G., 2, 12, 14, 112
BOER, A. E., 7n
Bradstreet's Book of Commercial Ratings, 42, 54–8, 172–5, 172n, 173n, 174n, 175n
Brick & tile manufacture (bpa in Table 19 & App. 4), incorporations for, 69
Bridges (ccd in Table 19 & App. 4)
   incorporations for: Maryland, 14, 26; New Jersey, 15, 27; New York, 17, 28; Ohio, 18, 19, 29
Building & loan associations (GB in Table 19 & App. 4)
   incorporations for: long waves in, 69, 71–2; Maryland, 14; New Jersey, 15, 66, 69, 71; New York, 17; Ohio, 10n, 18–9, 27, 29, 66, 69, 71–2; Pennsylvania, 66, 69, 71–2, 139–40
BURNS, ARTHUR F., 24n, 76n, 85n, 87
Business cycles
   and incorporations, 1, 3, 24, 31, 75–88
   chronology of ('reference dates'), 24n, 88

cyclical analysis, 84–8
   see also Episodes in chartering, Long cycles of incorporations, Timing
Business services (FB in Table 19 & App. 4), incorporations for: New Jersey, Ohio, & Pennsylvania, 69
Busses, city & suburban (cad in Table 19 & App. 4), incorporations for, 72
Busses, interstate & interurban (cae in Table 19 & App. 4), incorporations for, 72

California, constitutional provision concerning incorp., 11
Canals (cam in Table 19 & App. 4)
   incorporations for: in general, 26; Maryland, 14; New Jersey, 15; New York, 17; Ohio, 18–9, 29
Capital stock. *See* Authorized capital stock
Carriers, interstate motor freight (cag in Table 19 & App. 4), incorporations for, 72
Central Statistical Board, 53
Chemicals & allied products manufacture (BM in Table 19 & App. 4), incorporations for, 67–8
Coal mining (AB in Table 19 & App. 4)
   incorporations for: New Jersey, 67; Ohio, 66–7; Pennsylvania, 66–7
COLE, A. H., 1n
Colorado
   capital stock of incorporations, 37, 97–8
   constitutional provision concerning incorporation, 11
   dates of series, 2
   incorporations grouped by size, 43–4, 47, 96–7
   incorporations, industrial data, 44, 44n, 53n, 73
   period of inclusion in indexes, 34, 79, 81
   Reports of the Secretary of State, 73, 98
   sources of data, 98
   total incorporations, 32, 43, 96
   trend of incorporations, 47
Combinations and incorporations, 5
   see also Big business, 'Trusts'
Commercial & Financial Chronicle, 47, 49n, 72
Communications (CB in Table 19 & App. 4)
   incorporations for: long waves in, 68, 70, 72; Maryland, 14; New Jersey, 15, 68, 70; New York, 17; Ohio, 18–9, 68–70; Pennsylvania, 68, 70
Competition between states for corporate chartering, 1, 33
Confectionery manufacture (bab in Table 19 & App. 4), incorporations for, 69
Conformity, measures of, 87
Connecticut
   dates of series, 2, 12n
   no constitutional provision concerning incorporation, 11n
   nonbusiness incorporations, 89–90, 90n
   period of inclusion in indexes, 34, 79, 81
   sources of data, 99, 100
   total incorporations, 12–3, 32, 98–101
   trend of incorporations, 33
Consolidations & incorporations, 5
   see also Big business, 'Trusts'
Constitutional provisions & incorporation under general laws, 11, 12, 20, 31
   see also each state
Construction (H in Table 19 & App. 4)
   corporations: New Jersey, Ohio, & Pennsylvania, 59, 62
   incorporations for: long waves in, 3; Maryland, 14; New Jersey, 15, 59–62, 66; New York, 17; Ohio, 18–9, 59–62, 66; Pennsylvania, 59, 62, 66
Corporation Trust Co., 2, 35
Corporations
   abortive
      defined, 4, 4n, 5–6
      frequency, 5–7, 6n
      relation to size of enterprise, 6–7
   business, defined, 1–2
   existing: New Jersey, Ohio, & Pennsylvania, 59, 62
   see also Life of corporations
Cycles. *See* Business cycles, Long cycles
Cyclical patterns
   reference-cycle pattern of total incorporations, 87–8
   specific-cycle patterns of total incorporations, 85–7

Dairy products manufacture (baf in Table 19 & App. 4), incorporations for, 69
DAVIS, JOSEPH S., 2, 10, 16, 16n, 20, 20n, 112, 126
Delaware
 capital stock of incorporations, 36–7, 103–4
 constitutional provision concerning incorporation, 11
 dates of series, 2
 incorporations grouped by size, 43–4, 47, 49, 101–3
 List of Corporations, 104
 nonbusiness incorporations, 89–90, 90n
 period of inclusion in indexes, 34–5, 79, 81
 sources of data, 101, 104
 total incorporations, 32, 37, 43, 101
 trend of incorporations, 3, 31, 33, 49
 very large incorporations, 49
Depressions, effect on incorporations, 33, 42, 79, 88
 see also Timing
Dissolutions, voluntary, 6, 9, 9n
 see also Forfeitures of charters
Domestic & personal services (FA in Table 19 & App. 4), incorporations for: New Jersey, Ohio, & Pennsylvania, 68–9
Drug manufacture (bmc in Table 19 & App. 4), incorporations for, 69
Dun & Bradstreet, 5n
Dun's Review, 5n
Dun's Statistical Review, 35, 35n

Electric light & power industry (cca in Table 19 & App. 4), incorporations in, 69, 72, 74
Electric World, 74n
Electrical machinery manufacture (BS in Table 19 & App. 4), incorporations for, 67–8
Entrepreneur, activities reflected in incorporations, 1, 4, 5, 27–30, 31, 50, 88
Episodes in chartering
 banks, 24, 26–7
 hypothesis concerning, 27–30
 in general, 3, 33, 35, 72–4
 insurance, 24, 26–7
 mining, 24, 27
 petroleum industry, 33, 72
 railroads, 21, 24, 27
EVANS, G. H., JR., 1n, 27n

FALKNER, R. P., 34n
Ferries (can in Table 19 & App. 4)
 incorporations for: Maryland, 14; New Jersey, 15; New York, 17; Ohio, 18–9
Finance (G in Table 19 & App. 4)
 corporations: New Jersey, Ohio, & Pennsylvania, 59, 62
 incorporations for: Maryland, 14; New Jersey, 15, 59–62, 66, 69; New York, 17; Ohio, 18–9, 59–62, 66, 69; Pennsylvania, 59–62, 66, 69
 incorporations in 2-letter categories, 69
Florida
 capital stock of incorporations, 37, 106
 constitutional provision concerning incorporation, 11
 dates of series, 2
 incorporations grouped by size, 44, 47, 49, 105
 period of inclusion in indexes, 34, 79, 81
 Reports of Secretary of State, 106
 sources of data, 106
 total incorporations, 32, 104
 trend of incorporations, 47, 49
Food & kindred products manufacture (BA in Table 19 & App. 4), incorporations for, 67–8
Footwear manufacture (bfb in Table 19 & App. 4), incorporations for, 69
'Foreign' corporations, 5
Forfeitures of charters
 and number of incorporations, 6–7, 9
 and voluntary dissolutions, 9n
 classified by size of corporation, 6, 91–3
 see also Corporations, abortive
Furniture & finished lumber products manufacture (BI in Table 19 & App. 4), incorporations for, 67–8

Gas producing & distributing (acb & ccb in Table 19 & App. 4)
 incorporations for: in general, 26; Maryland, 14, 26; New Jersey, 15, 67; New York, 17; Ohio, 18–9, 66–7, 73; Pennsylvania, 67, 73, 139–40

General incorporation laws
 constitutional provisions necessitating, 11–2, 20, 31
 dominant after 1875, 10
 effect of, in Massachusetts, 75
 incorporations under
  Arizona, 32, 96
  Colorado, 32, 96–8
  Connecticut, 12, 32, 98–101
  Delaware, 32, 101–4
  Florida, 32, 104–6
  Illinois, 32, 107–10
  in general, 3, 10, 31
  Louisiana, 32, 110
  Maine, 12, 32, 111–2
  Maryland, 32, 113–9
  Massachusetts, 12, 32–3, 75, 119–25
  New Jersey, 12, 15, 20, 24n, 27, 32, 60–2, 64–5, 65n, 126–32, 156–9
  New York, 12, 16n, 17, 20, 28, 32, 132–3
  Ohio, 12, 19–20, 29, 32, 60–2, 64–5, 65n, 134–9, 161–6
  Pennsylvania, 32–3, 60–2, 64, 64n, 65–6, 139–43, 166–8
  Texas, 32, 144–9
  Virginia, 32, 149–51
Georgia, constitutional provision concerning incorporation, 11
Gold mining (aad in Table 19 & App. 4)
 incorporations for: Colorado, 73; New Jersey, 66
Golf courses, incorporations for, 50
Government policy, effect upon incorporations, 33
 see also Competition, 'Liberal' incorporation laws
Great Britain
 abortive English companies, 6n
 incorporations in, 35, 75–6
Growth, economic, and incorporations, 1, 72
Growth of incorporations. *See* Trend

Harvard University Committee on Economic Research, 76
Heating apparatus manufacture (bqe in Table 19 & App. 4), incorporations for, 69
HEILMAN, A. E., 7n
'High finance', periods of, 49
HOOD, JOHN, 12, 15, 16, 16n, 125
Hotels (faa in Table 19 & App. 4)
 incorporations for: Maryland, 14; New Jersey, 15, 66; New York, 17; Ohio, 18–9; rise in, 69
HUTCHINSON, A. R., 7n
HUTCHINSON, RUTH G., 7n

Idaho, constitutional provision concerning incorporation, 11
Illinois
 amplitude of fluctuations of incorporations, 33
 capital stock of incorporations, 36–7, 40, 108–9
 constitutional provision concerning incorporation, 11
 dates of series, 2
 incorporations grouped by size, 44, 47, 49, 107–8
 period of inclusion in indexes, 34, 35, 79, 81
 Reports of Secretary of State, 109
 sources of data, 109–10
 total incorporations, 32, 40, 44, 107, 109
 trend of incorporations, 47, 48
Indexes of incorporation
 annual aggregate, 33–5, 35n
 annual median, 33, 33n, 34–5, 35n
 capital stock, 34
 Corporation Trust Co., 35, 76
 in general, 3
 monthly aggregate, 33–4, 35n, 79–82, 84, 85n, 177–9
 monthly median, 35n, 79, 81–5
 New York Journal of Commerce and Commercial Bulletin, 34–5, 35n, 76
Indiana, constitutional provision concerning incorporation, 11
Individual proprietorship, prior to incorporation, 5
Industrial objectives of incorporations
 classification scheme, 51–3, 58
 criteria for determination of, 12, 16, 20, 50, 53
 difficulties in classifying, 50
 distribution by
  1-letter categories, 59–62, 66–7, 79, 169–70
  2-letter categories, 67–9
  3-letter categories, 69, 72
 full data for 3 states, 153–68
 general treatment, 3, 12–29, 50–74

Industrial objectives of incorporations—cont.
  number of categories used in classifying, 63–4
  rise of corporations in 3-letter categories, 69, 72
  see also Colorado, Maine, Maryland, 'New', New Jersey, New
    York, Ohio, Pennsylvania, Texas; & specific industries
Insurance (GI in Table 19 & App. 4)
  incorporations for: episodes in, 24, 26–8; Maryland, 14, 26;
    New Jersey, 15, 26; New York, 17, 26–8; Ohio, 18–9, 26, 29
Investment opportunities, reflected in incorporations, 1, 4, 5
Iowa, constitutional provision concerning incorporation, 11
Iron & steel & their products manufacture (BQ in Table 19 &
    App. 4), incorporations for, 67–8

JACKSON, CHARLES T., 24n

Kansas, constitutional provision concerning incorporation, 11
KEASBEY, E. Q., 132
Kentucky, constitutional provision concerning incorp., 11
KESSLER, W. C., 16n

LARCOM, R. C., 2, 101
Large incorporations
  and amplitude of fluctuations of incorporations, 3, 42–4, 49
  Colorado, 43–4, 44n, 47, 97
  defined, 42
  Delaware, 43, 47, 49, 102–3
  effect on total capital stock, 36–40
  Florida, 47, 49, 105
  Illinois, 47, 49, 108
  Maryland, 45, 47, 49, 116
  Massachusetts, 47, 49, 122–3
  New Jersey, 35n, 46–9, 129–30
  Ohio, 46–7, 49, 136–7
  Pennsylvania, 47, 49, 141–2
  percentage of total incorporations, 42, 44, 47, 49
  Texas, 47, 49, 146
  trend in, 47, 49
  trend in capital stock of, 34–5
  Virginia, 49, 150
Laundries (fab in Table 19 & App. 4), incorporations for, 69
Law, incorporations & changes in private corporate, 33, 75
  see also General incorporation laws, Special charter
'Liberal' incorporation laws, 5, 9, 31, 44, 49, 79
Life of corporations
  life table for Maryland corporations, 7–9
  method of stating length of life, 4n
  Virginia corporations, 9
Local factors, effect on incorporations, 33
Long cycles of incorporations
  dates for, prior to 1875, 10, 12, 31
  explanations for, 21, 27–30, 72
  in industry generally, 27
  see also Amplitude, Building & loan associations, Business
    cycles, Communications, Episodes in chartering, Manu-
    facturing, 'Other' public utilities, Public utilities, Rail-
    roads, Street railways, Transportation, Turnpikes
Louisiana
  constitutional provision concerning incorporation, 11
  dates of series, 2
  period of inclusion in indexes, 34, 79, 81
  source of data, 110
  total incorporations, 32, 110
Louisiana Business Review, 2, 110

MACGREGOR, D. H., 4, 6n, 42n, 44n, 76
Machinery, manufacture, incorporations for
  except electrical (BT in Table 19 & App. 4), 67–8
  general industrial (btb in Table 19 & App. 4), 69
  metal-working (btc in Table 19 & App. 4), 69
Maine
  Business Corporations, 110, 112
  constitutional provision concerning incorporation, 11
  dates of series, 2
  incorporations, industrial data, 24
  period of inclusion in indexes, 34, 35, 79, 81
  Public Documents, 24
  seasonal variation in incorporations, 87
  sources of data, 110, 112
  total incorporations, 10, 12–3, 32, 77, 110–2
  trend of incorporations, 31, 33

Manufacturing (B in Table 19 & App. 4)
  corporations: New Jersey, 59, 62, 169; Ohio, 59, 62, 169;
    Pennsylvania, 59, 62, 170
  incorporations & business cycles, 78–9
  incorporations for: in general, 20–1; Maryland, 14, 20, 23;
    New Jersey, 15, 20, 23, 59–62, 66–8, 78; New York, 17, 20,
    23; Ohio, 10n, 18–20, 23, 59–62, 66–8, 78; Pennsylvania,
    59–62, 66–8, 78
  incorporations in 2-letter categories, 67–8
  long cycles in incorporations for, 21, 21n, 28
MARSHALL, ALFRED, 75–6
Maryland
  abortive corporations, 5–7
  capital stock of incorporations, 37, 40, 117–8
  constitutional provision concerning incorporation, 11, 12
  corporation life table, 7–9
  corporations on forfeiture lists classified, 6–7, 91–3
  dates of series, 2
  forfeiture of corporate charters, 6, 6n, 7, 9
  incorporations & business cycles, 75
  incorporations & pre-incorporation data, 4–5
  incorporations grouped by size, 6, 44–5, 47, 49, 93, 114–6
  incorporations, industrial data, 12, 14, 20, 22–6
  period of inclusion in indexes, 34, 79, 81
  Reports of Bureau of Industrial Statistics, 75n, 119
  sources of data, 111, 119
  State Tax Commission, 4, 5, 6, 7, 9n
  tax assessment returns, 4–5, 6
  total incorporations, 12–3, 32, 45, 112–3
  trend of incorporations, 33, 47, 49
Massachusetts
  Abstracts of Returns of Corporations, 75n, 124–5
  capital stock of incorporations, 40, 123–4
  dates of series, 2
  incorporations & business cycles, 75
  incorporations & the 1903 law, 33
  incorporations grouped by size, 44, 47, 49, 120–3
  no constitutional provision concerning incorporation, 11
  period of inclusion in indexes, 34, 79, 81
  sources of data, 124–5
  total incorporations, 10, 12–3, 32, 119–20
  trend of incorporations, 47, 49
McGARRY, E. D., 7n
Medium-sized incorporations
  and amplitude of fluctuations of incorporations, 3, 42–4, 49
  Colorado, 43, 97
  defined, 42
  Delaware, 43, 47, 102
  Florida, 47, 105
  Illinois, 107–8
  Maryland, 45, 47, 115
  Massachusetts, 47, 121–2
  New Jersey, 46, 47, 128–9
  Ohio, 46, 136
  Pennsylvania, 141
  percentage of total incorporations, 42, 44, 47, 49
  Texas, 145–6
  trend for, 47, 49
  Virginia, 150
Merchants' Magazine and Commercial Review, 24
Michigan, constitutional provision concerning incorp., 11
MILLER, WILLIAM, 2, 20, 20n, 21, 21n, 24n, 139
Mining & quarrying (A in Table 19 & App. 4)
  corporations: New Jersey, Ohio, & Pennsylvania, 59, 62
  incorporations for: Colorado, 44, 44n, 73; episodes in, 24, 27;
    in general, 20; Maine, 24; Maryland, 14, 20, 26; New
    Jersey, 15, 20, 24, 27, 59–62, 66–7; New York, 17, 20;
    Ohio, 10n, 18–9, 20, 24, 27, 29, 59–62, 66–7; Pennsylvania,
    59–62, 66–7
  incorporations in 2-letter categories, 67
  see also Coal mining, Gas producing & distributing, Gold
    mining, Petroleum industry, Silver mining
Minnesota, constitutional provision concerning incorp., 11
Mississippi, constitutional provision concerning incorp., 11
Missouri, constitutional provision concerning incorporation, 11
MITCHELL, WESLEY C., 24n, 76n, 85n, 87
Montana, constitutional provision concerning incorp., 11
Mortality, corporate. *See* Life of corporations
Moving averages and elimination of seasonal variation, 36n, 76
Mutual companies, nonbusiness concerns, 2, 2n, 12, 16, 20, 20n

Name as criterion of nature of business, 2, 2n
Nebraska, constitutional provision concerning incorp., 11
Nevada, constitutional provision concerning incorporation, 11
'New'
  corporations, 5
  fields of corporate enterprise, 31, 63, 64–5
  firms generally, 5n
New Hampshire, no constitutional provision concerning incorporation, 11
New Jersey
  capital stock of incorporations, 37, 130–1
  constitutional provision concerning incorporation, 11
  corporations in, 59, 62
  Corporations of New Jersey, 49n, 132
  criteria for nonbusiness incorporations, 2n
  dates of series, 1–2
  general incorporation act, 24n
  incorporations grouped by size, 44, 46–7, 127–30
  incorporations, industrial data, 12, 12n, 15, 16, 20, 21n, 22–4, 24n, 25–7, 53, 59–73, 78–9, 154–9, 169
  period of inclusion in indexes, 34, 79, 81
  sources of data, 125–6, 132
  total incorporations, 10, 10n, 12–3, 32, 77, 125–7
  trend of incorporations, 47, 49
  very large incorporations, 48, 49
  see also Large incorporations
New Mexico, constitutional provision concerning incorp., 11
New York
  constitutional provision concerning incorporation, 11
  dates of series, 2
  general incorporation act, 20
  incorporations & business cycles, 75
  incorporations, industrial data, 16–7, 20, 23–8, 50
  period of inclusion in indexes, 34–5, 79, 81, 84
  press releases of Secretary of State, 7n, 50, 75, 76n, 133
  Report of the Department of State, 132, 133
  small incorporations, 7n
  sources of data, 132–3
  total incorporations, 12–3, 32, 132–3
  trend of incorporations, 3, 31, 33
New York Journal of Commerce and Commercial Bulletin, 34–5, 35n, 76
New York State Constitutional Convention Committee, 11n
NEWCOMER, MABEL, 7n
Nonbusiness incorporations
  and indexes of business incorporations, 35, 35n
  criteria for, 2, 2n, 16n
  see also Arizona, Connecticut, Delaware, Ohio
Nonpar shares, treatment of, 36
North Carolina, constitutional provision concerning incorp., 11
North Dakota, constitutional provision concerning incorp., 11

Objectives of incorporations. *See* Industrial objectives of incorporations
Ohio
  capital stock of incorporations, 37, 39–40, 137–8
  constitutional provision concerning incorporation, 11, 20
  corporations in, 59, 62
  dates of series, 1–2
  incorporations grouped by size, 44, 46–7, 49, 135–7
  incorporations, industrial data, 10n, 16, 18–20, 21n, 22–7, 29, 50, 53, 59–73, 78–9, 160–6, 169
  nonbusiness incorporations, 2n, 89–90, 90n
  period of inclusion in indexes, 34, 79, 81
  Reports of the Secretary of State, 16, 20n, 50n, 64, 64n, 133, 138
  seasonal variation in incorporations, 76
  sources of data, 133, 138–9
  total incorporations, 10, 12–3, 32, 39, 77, 133–5
  trend of incorporations, 33, 47, 49
Oklahoma, constitutional provision concerning incorp., 11
Oregon, constitutional provision concerning incorporation, 11
ORTON, EDWARD, 73n
'Other' public utilities (CC in Table 19 & App. 4)
  incorporations for: long waves in, 68, 71–2; Maryland, 14; New Jersey, 15, 68, 71; New York, 17; Ohio, 18–9, 68, 71; Pennsylvania, 68, 71–2
OXENFELDT, A. R., 5n, 6n

Paint manufacture (bma in Table 19 & App. 4), incorporations for, 69
Palgrave's Dictionary of Political Economy, 35
Partnership, prior to incorporation, 5

Peaks in business. *See* Business cycles, chronology of
Peaks in incorporations
  dates for ('specific cycles'), 85
  lead or lag at business peak, 3, 75–6, 79, 85, 87–8
  see also Business cycles, Long cycles, Timing
Pennsylvania
  amplitude of fluctuations of incorporations, 33
  capital stock of incorporations, 37, 142–3
  constitutional provision concerning incorporation, 11
  corporations in, 59, 62
  dates of series, 2
  'foreign' corporations, 5
  incorporation data tested, 54–8, 171–5
  incorporations & changes in the law, 33
  incorporations grouped by size, 44, 47, 49, 140–2
  incorporations, industrial data, 24, 24n, 53–74, 78–9, 139, 166–8, 170
  List of Charters, 50, 54n, 58, 73, 143, 172, 172n
  Messages of Governor, 74n
  period of inclusion in indexes, 34, 79, 81
  Public Service Commission, 74
  Reports of Banking Commissioner, 58
  Report of Water Supply Commissioners, 73
  sources of data, 139, 143
  total incorporations, 12–3, 32, 77, 139–40
  trend of incorporations, 47, 49
  Water Supply Commission, 73–4
  see also Tests
Petroleum production (AC in Table 19 & App. 4)
  incorporations for: New Jersey, 24, 67; Ohio, 24, 66–7; Pennsylvania, 67, 139–40; Texas, 33, 44, 72–3
Pre-incorporation history, 4–5
Printing, publishing, & allied industries (BK in Table 19 & App. 4), incorporations in, 67–8
Public interest, decline in incorporations tinged with, 20, 21, 21n
Public utilities (C in Table 19 & App. 4)
  corporations: New Jersey, Ohio, & Pennsylvania, 59, 62
  incorporations & business cycles, 78–9
  incorporations for: Maryland, 14, 20; New Jersey, 15, 20, 59–62, 66, 68, 78, 169; New York, 17, 20; Ohio, 18–20, 59–62, 66, 68, 78, 169; Pennsylvania, 59–62, 66, 68, 78, 170
  incorporations in 2-letter categories, 68
  long cycles in incorporations for, 3, 68
  see also 'Other' public utilities
Purposes of incorporation, industrial. *See* Industrial objectives

Quarrying. *See* Mining

Radio manufacture (bsb in Table 19 & App. 4), incorporations for, 72
Railroads (caa in Table 19 & App. 4)
  incorporations for: episodes in, 21, 24, 27–30; long waves in, 21, 24, 30, 72; Maryland, 14, 24–6; New Jersey, 15, 24, 24n, 25, 27; New York, 17, 24–5, 27–8; Ohio, 10n, 18–9, 24–5, 29, 72
Random movements. *See* Episodes in chartering
Real estate (GJ in Table 19 & App. 4)
  incorporations for: in general, 26; Maryland, 14, 26; New Jersey, 15, 27, 69; New York, 17; Ohio, 18–9, 29, 69; Pennsylvania, 69
'Reference dates'. *See* Business cycles, chronology of
Renewal of charter, treatment of, 2–3
Reorganization, treatment of, 2–3
Reports of the Constitutional Convention Committee, 11n
Review of Economic Statistics, 34, 34n
Rhode Island, no constitutional provision concerning incorporation, 11

SCHUMPETER, J. A., 1n
Seasonal variation
  computation of index of, 81
  in incorporations, 76, 80
  use of moving averages, 36n, 76
Service (F in Table 19 & App. 4)
  corporations: New Jersey, Ohio, & Pennsylvania, 59, 62
  incorporations for: Maryland, 14; New Jersey, 15, 59–62, 66, 68–9; New York, 17; Ohio, 18–9, 59–62, 66, 68–9; Pennsylvania, 59–62, 66, 68–9
  incorporations in 2-letter categories, 68–9

Silver mining (aad in Table 19 & App. 4)
   incorporations for: Colorado, 73; New Jersey, 66
Size, relative
   and New York incorporations, 7n
   and short-lived corporations, 6–7
   classification of incorporations by, 3, 6–7, 42–9
   criterion of, 42
   see also Amplitude, Colorado, Delaware, Florida, Illinois,
      Large incorporations, Maryland, Massachusetts, Me-
      dium-sized incorporations, New Jersey, Ohio, Pennsyl-
      vania, Small incorporations, Texas, Virginia
Skating rinks, incorporations for, 50
Small incorporations
   and amplitude of fluctuations of incorporations, 3, 33, 42–4,
      49
   and new fields of enterprise, 31
   Colorado, 43, 96–7
   defined, 42
   Delaware, 43–4, 47, 101–2
   Florida, 105
   Illinois, 107
   length of life, 7
   Maryland, 45, 47, 114
   Massachusetts, 120–1
   New Jersey, 46–7, 127–8
   Ohio, 46, 135
   Pennsylvania, 140–1
   percentage of total incorporations, 3, 33, 42, 44, 47, 49
   Texas, 144–5
   trend for, 47, 49
   Virginia, 149
South Carolina, constitutional provision concerning incorp., 11
South Dakota, constitutional provision concerning incorp., 11
Special charter, incorporation by
   in general, 3
   Maine, 12, 110–1
   Maryland, 12, 14, 20, 26, 112
   New Jersey, 12, 15, 20, 27, 64–5, 125–6, 154–6
   New York, 12, 17, 20, 28, 132
   Ohio, 12, 18, 20, 29, 64–5, 133, 160
   Pennsylvania, 12, 139
   period of, 10–30, 31
Statistical Abstract for the United Kingdom, 35
Statistical Abstract of the United States, 34
Statistics of Income, 59
Steamboats (cak in Table 19 & App. 4)
   incorporations for: in general, 26; Maryland, 14, 26; New
      Jersey, 15, 26; New York, 17, 28; Ohio, 18–9
Stock. *See* Authorized capital stock, Nonpar shares
STOKE, H. W., 132
Stone, clay, & glass products manufacture (BP in Table 19 &
   App. 4), incorporations for, 67–8
Stone, sand, & gravel quarrying (ada in Table 19 & App. 4),
   incorporations for, 69
Street railways (cac in Table 19 & App. 4), a wave of incor-
   porations for, 72
Survey of Current Business, 35, 35n

Tax assessment returns. *See* Maryland
Taxicabs (caf in Table 19 & App. 4), incorporations for, 72
Telegraphic communication (cbb in Table 19 & App. 4)
   incorporations for: in general, 26; Maryland, 14; New Jersey,
      15, 26; New York, 17; Ohio, 18–9
Tennessee, constitutional provision concerning incorp., 11
Termination of charter. *See* Dissolutions, Forfeitures of charters
Tests
   capital stock as index of corporate size, 42, 171–4
   of accuracy of industrial classification, 54–9, 174–5
Texas
   capital stock of incorporations, 37, 38, 147–8
   constitutional provision concerning incorporation, 11
   dates of series, 2
   incorporations grouped by size, 44, 47, 49, 144–6
   incorporations, industrial data, 33, 44, 53n, 72–3
   period of inclusion in indexes, 34, 79, 81
   Reports of the Secretary of State, 73, 148
   seasonal variation in incorporations, 76

   sources of data, 148
   total incorporations, 32, 38, 144
   trend of incorporations, 31, 47, 49
Textile-mill products manufacture (BD in Table 19 & App. 4),
   incorporations for, 67–8
THORP, WILLARD L., 24n
THORPE, FRANCIS NEWTON, 11n
Timing
   of incorporations & business cycles, 3, 75–6, 79, 85, 87–8
   of incorporations in different size groups, 44
   number of incorporations & authorized capital stock, 35–6
Trade (D & E in Table 19 & App. 4)
   corporations: New Jersey, Ohio, & Pennsylvania, 59, 62
   incorporations for: Maryland, 14; New Jersey, 15, 59–62, 66;
      New York, 17; Ohio, 18–9, 59–62, 66; Pennsylvania, 59–
      62, 64, 64n, 66
Transportation equipment (except automobiles) manufacture
   (BV in Table 19 & App. 4), incorporations for, 67–8
Transportation (CA in Table 19 & App. 4)
   incorporations for: long waves in, 68, 70, 72; Maryland, 14;
      New Jersey, 15, 68, 70; New York, 17; Ohio, 18–9, 68,
      70, 72; Pennsylvania, 68, 70
Trend in incorporations
   effect of war on, 31
   hypothesis concerning, 31
   in different industries, 66–9, 72
   in different size groups, 47, 49
   in general, 3, 21, 30–5
   see also Medium-sized incorporations, Large incorporations,
      Small incorporations
Troughs in business. *See* Business cycles, chronology of
Troughs in incorporations
   dates for ('specific cycles'), 85
   lead at business trough, 3, 76, 79, 85, 87–8
   see also Business cycles, Long cycles, Timing
Trucking & warehousing, local (cah in Table 19 & App. 4),
   incorporations for, 69, 72
'Trusts', incorporation of, 47–9, 50
Turning points in business. *See* Business cycles, chronology
   of
Turnpikes (cce in Table 19 & App. 4)
   incorporations for: in general, 21; long waves in, 21, 27–8;
      Maryland, 14, 22; New Jersey, 15, 21n, 22; New York,
      17, 21n, 22; Ohio, 18–20, 21n, 22; Pennsylvania, 21, 21n, 22
Twelfth Census of the United States, 42n

U. S. Census Office, on stock as index of corporate size, 42n
U. S. Office of Internal Revenue, 59
Utah, constitutional provision concerning incorporation, 11

VANDERBLUE, H. B., 2, 16, 16n
Vermont, constitutional provision concerning incorp., 11
Virginia
   capital stock of incorporations, 37, 150–1
   constitutional provision concerning incorporation, 11
   corporate dissolutions & surrenders of charters, 9
   dates of series, 2
   incorporations grouped by size, 44, 49, 149–50
   life of corporations, 9
   period of inclusion in indexes, 34, 79, 81
   Reports of Corporation Commission, 151
   sources of data, 151
   total incorporations, 32, 149
   trend in incorporations, 49

War, effect upon incorporations, 31, 33, 35, 64, 66, 72, 85n
Washington, constitutional provision concerning incorp., 11
Waterworks (ccc & water power of ccg in Table 19 & App. 4)
   incorporations for: in general, 26; Maryland, 14, 26; New Jer-
      sey, 15; New York, 17, 26, 28; Ohio, 18–9; Pennsylvania,
      72–4
West Virginia, constitutional provision concerning incorp., 11
WILLIAMS, ALBERT, JR., 73n
WILLOUGHBY, WOODBURY, 31n
Wisconsin, constitutional provision concerning incorp., 11
Wyoming, constitutional provision concerning incorp., 11